THE ANCIENT NEAR EAST

LAKE
ARAL

OXUS RIVER

ASIA

(AFGHANISTAN)

INDUS RIVER

ERSIA
(RAN)

•Persepolis

(PAKISTAN)

INDIA

N GULF

INDIA

AN

SERT

INDIAN OCEAN

Bernhard W. Anderson
Emeritus, Princeton Theological Seminary
Adjunct, Boston University

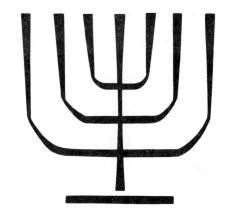

UNDERSTANDING THE OLD TESTAMENT

FOURTH EDITION

PRENTICE HALL, Englewood Cliffs, New Jersey 07632

Library of Congress Cataloging-in-Publication Data

Anderson, Bernhard W.
    Understanding the Old Testament.

    Bibliography: p. 652
    Includes index.
    1. Bible. O.T.—History of Biblical events.
2. Jews—History—to 70 A.D. I. Title.
BS1197.A63 1986   221.6   85-25733
ISBN 0-13-935925-7

Editorial supervision and interior design: Serena Hoffman
Cover design: Lundgren Graphics
Manufacturing buyer: Harry P. Baisley

Printed in the United States of America

20 19 18 17 16

ISBN 0-13-935925-7

90000

9 780139 359255

Prentice-Hall International (UK) Limited, *London*
Prentice-Hall of Australia Pty. Limited, *Sydney*
Prentice-Hall Canada Inc., *Toronto*
Prentice-Hall Hispanoamericana, S.A., *Mexico*
Prentice-Hall of India Private Limited, *New Delhi*
Prentice-Hall of Japan, Inc., *Tokyo*
Simon & Schuster Asia Pte. Ltd., *Singapore*
Editora Prentice-Hall do Brasil, Ltda., *Rio de Janeiro*

Contents

Part II
ISRAEL BECOMES LIKE THE NATIONS   211

11 The Rediscovery of Mosaic Torah 356

12 The Doom of the Nation 391

Part III
THE COVENANT COMMUNITY IS RENEWED   425

13 By the Waters of Babylon 427

14 The Dawn of a New Age 467

Illustrations and Aids

MAPS

A major source used in the preparation of maps has been *The Westminster Historical Atlas to the Bible*, Revised Edition, Copyright 1956 by W. L. Jenkins, The Westminster Press.

PHOTOGRAPHS

COLOR PLATES

CHRONOLOGICAL CHARTS

See also the Comprehensive Chronological Chart on pp. 646–651

KEY CHARTS AND TABLES

DEFINITIONS

Preface

Since this book first appeared almost three decades ago, a lot of water has gone under the bridge, and as someone has appropriately added, a lot of bridges have gone under the water. The whole field of biblical studies has been changing rapidly, owing to the explosion of knowledge, the use of new methods of study, and the reevaluation of past accomplishments. Pluralism of approach and interpretation characterizes this field, as is true of other areas of scholarly research. That this book has undergone three editions in the course of almost thirty years and now appears in a fourth seems to indicate that it provides an inviting path into the study and appreciation of the Hebrew Bible, often designated as the Old Testament.

From the first, the aim of this book has been to interweave the oft-separated elements of historical and archaeological research, literary criticism, and biblical theology by pursuing the story of ancient Israel from the time of its crucial beginnings in the Mosaic period to the flowering of its literature in the late period of biblical Judaism, the so-called Maccabean period. A study of the first paragraph of the book in all four editions will show that the theme of "the story of our life" has been a constant. Admittedly, in recent years there has been a strong tendency in biblical studies to shift exclusively to "story," while downplaying the closely related dimension of "history"—or to shift to studying books of the Bible in their final literary form, while underestimating the history of traditions with which scholars have been concerned in the past.

In the ongoing discussion, I have been—and still am—firmly convinced that the best way to understand the faith of ancient Israel is to use an approach that takes into account the interrelated dimensions of story and history, of history of traditions and final literary formulations. Hence, even though fresh nuances and necessary modifications have appeared in this presentation, the basic outline of the book has remained essentially the same in all four editions. The exposition begins with the formative event of the Exodus and its corollary, the Sinai covenant, and then traces Israel's life story through the procession of the years to the dawn of the Common Era, when Jews and Christians appropriated in differing ways the scriptural heritage of ancient Israel in the Talmud and New Testament, respectively.

This edition differs significantly from previous editions in several respects. For one thing, the chapters dealing with the period before David have been rewritten to take account of reevaluations of historical and archaeological data, particularly in the case of the history (story) of Israel's ancestors and the widely debated question of the Israelite occupation (conquest) of Canaan. Also, in this edition the emerging Israelite epic (that is, the J and E narratives) is treated not in the context of the national renaissance of the early Israelite monarchy, but in the context of the Tribal Confederacy, when an all-Israelite consciousness began to appear. To avoid misunderstanding, it should be emphasized that the epic *began* to emerge in the premonarchic period, although the storytelling was a long process that continued through the whole history of Pentateuchal traditions until the final canonical shaping by Priestly redactors in the time of Ezra. This mode of treatment, admittedly debatable, has the pedagogical advantage of avoiding refined source analysis at the introductory level and of concentrating on the Israelite story, which was always being contemporized as it was retold from generation to generation. Finally, in this edition the discussion conforms to current standards of inclusive language with respect to men and women, Jews and Christians, believers and seekers.

As in previous editions, I call the reader's attention to several basic matters:

1. At the beginning of each chapter, a footnote outlines appropriate readings in the Old Testament. This book is not a substitute for going directly to the biblical materials. On the contrary, the Bible, as someone has said, throws a lot of light on the commentaries!

2. The source footnotes should not be regarded as excess baggage. To be sure, they may be passed by, especially on first reading, but they serve important purposes. Not only do they provide necessary documentation, which may invite further study, but they also bear witness to the fact that biblical interpretation occurs in an ecumenical circle that includes Jewish, Protestant, and Catholic representatives. An introductory text of this kind must be presented in responsible relationship to a scholarly community, even though the author takes his own stand in that community. The bracketed numbers in the footnotes refer to the Selected Bibliography at the end of the book, where complete information is given. Notice that the bibliographical entries are arranged under general topics (for example, the section on Biblical Criticism [48–88]) and also under the various chapters of the book.

3. The biblical quotations are from various modern English translations, which are indicated by an appropriate abbreviation (for example, RSV. for Revised Standard Version). When no abbreviation is given, the translation is by the author. My colleagues and I advocate the policy of providing translations in nonsexist language, when appropriate; but I recognize that, in many cases, masculine language with respect to God must be retained if one is to be true to the language of the Hebrew text. To be sure, the holy God of the Bible transcends sexuality—a point that became clear in the encounter between Yahwism and Canaanite religion. But God's personal relationship with human beings, and particularly with the Israelite covenant community, is expressed in language that is sociologically and historically conditioned.

4. One of the most difficult problems in the study of the Old Testament is the dating of events, for here we deal with a long sweep of time when none of our modern calendars was in existence. For the sake of consistency, I have adopted the chronology given in John Bright, *A History of Israel* [91]. Also, to promote greater inclusiveness, I have used B.C.E. (Before the Common Era) and C.E. (Common Era) instead of the traditional Christian distinctions of B.C. and A.D.

A project of this magnitude is possible only because of the creative work of many persons who have influenced me, directly or indirectly. Time would fail me if I were to attempt to list all the people to whom I am indebted: my teachers, especially the late James Muilenburg; my colleagues in various colleges, universities, and theological schools; theologians with whom I have been in dialogue, like G. Ernest Wright, Will Herberg, and Abraham Joshua Heschel. I also want to express appreciation to many students, both at the undergraduate and graduate levels, whose feedback has contributed to my understanding of scripture.

In preparing this edition, I have been singularly fortunate in having the assistance of my colleague at the Boston University School of Theology, Dr. Kathe Pfisterer Darr. She reread the book at the initial stage and made various suggestions chapter by chapter, read critically every chapter as I rewrote it, and finally reviewed the whole manuscript at an early stage of printing. Indelibly imprinted upon the book in its final form is her salutary influence: her artistic and literary sensitivity, her insightful perception as a woman, and her creative scholarship.

Finally, my thanks go again to my publisher, Prentice-Hall, for the technical execution of this project, and especially to the religion editor, Emily Baker, and to my production editor, Serena Hoffman.

In a special category, I express thanks to my wife and family, to whom this book is dedicated. They have accompanied me patiently and lovingly, and in untold ways have assisted during the three decades of the history of this book.

We now approach the year 2000 and the new horizons that lie beyond—assuming that in the meanwhile human beings have not brought civilization on this planet to a tragic end in a nuclear holocaust. How far the history of this book will extend into the future is undeterminable; it is my hope, however, that this revision will enjoy a future of continuing usefulness.

Bernhard W. Anderson

INTRODUCTION

The Old Testament as the Story of a People

Memory is one of humanity's supreme endowments. Each of us acts today and hopes for tomorrow in the light of past experiences that have been woven into a life-story. When we want to know someone else, we ask that person to tell us something of the story of his or her life, for in this way personal identity is disclosed. To be a self is to have a personal history. This is what defines one's uniqueness.

In a larger sense this is true of human communities, especially those in which people are bound together primarily by shared experiences rather than natural factors like blood and soil. National self-consciousness finds expression in the remembrance of events that people have lived through and that have given them a sense of identity and destiny. If, for instance, a visitor from outer space were to drop down on American soil and ask why this country is a *United* States rather than a mixed multitude, citizens would probably try to explain what it means to be an American by narrating a history: the dramatic epic of the migration of the Pilgrims to the New World, the Revolutionary War and the Declaration of Independence, the Civil War, the conquest of the frontier, and the recent events that have thrust this nation into the center of the world arena. To be an American is to share a particular history, whose events are retold and relived from generation to generation. By the same token, this is true of other peoples, for instance those of Great Britain, Australia, Nigeria, or Korea.

Biblical readings: A good way to be introduced to Israel's life-story is to read some of the recitations found in the Book of Psalms, such as Psalms 78, 105, 106, 135, 136; also the psalm in Exod. 15:1–18.

1

THE SENSE OF TRADITION

The most distinctive feature of the Jewish people is their sense of tradition, a theme that was celebrated in the Broadway musical, *Fiddler on the Roof*. In many respects, the Jews have always been diverse—in theology, in culture, and even in racial characteristics. But Judaism is the religion of a people who have a unique memory that reaches back through a long chain of tradition to the stirring events of their Bible, events that formed them as a people with a sense of identity and vocation. Whenever the Passover is celebrated, whenever the Torah is read in the synagogue, whenever parents instruct their children in the tradition, this memory is kept alive. Indeed, if historical memory were erased, the Jewish community would soon dissolve.

Christians, too, have this sense of tradition. The Christian church is diverse culturally, socially, and to a considerable extent theologically; but it is also a distinctive community with a long memory that reaches back through the centuries to the crucial events of which the Bible is the record and witness. To be sure, Christian remembrance focuses especially on the coming of Jesus, the Christ—his life, death, and resurrection. In the Christian community, however, this crucial event is viewed as the climax of the historical drama set forth in Jewish scriptures (Luke 24:13–27, 44–47). The Christian faith may be expressed in many ways, but in the last analysis there is no substitute for retelling what Christians consider "the story of our life"—that is, the dramatic history to which the Old and New Testaments of the Christian Bible bear witness.[1]

Furthermore, the Moslem religion known as Islam, in which Mohammed (c. 570–632) is acclaimed as the founder and supreme prophet, traces its ancestry to Ishmael, the son of Abraham and Hagar (Gen. 21:9–21). Significantly, the three great monotheistic religions—Judaism, Christianity, and Islam—each claim Abraham as their common father and hence seek their roots at the source of biblical tradition.

The Hebrew Bible

"Old Testament" is a widely used designation for the Hebrew Bible, the scriptures of ancient Israel. Immediately we should recognize that the distinction between scriptures of the "Old Testament" and the "New Testament" is a Christian one, though based on a passage from the prophet Jeremiah (Jer. 31:31–34). The Christian Bible is one book in two parts. For the Jewish community,

---

[1] See H. Richard Niebuhr, *The Meaning of Revelation* [173], chap. 2.

Note: To keep footnote material as brief as possible, we have adopted the device of using numbers in brackets which refer to the bibliography at the end of the book, where full information is given.

however, there is only one Testament or "Covenant," namely the Hebrew Bible. Today the Jewish people refer to their scriptures as *Tanak,* an acronym made up of the initial consonants of the three major divisions of the Hebrew Bible: Torah ("Law"), Nebi'im ("Prophets"), and Kethubim ("Writings"). The Jewish Bible, which excludes the New Testament, is one book in three parts.

As shown by the accompanying chart, the Hebrew Bible is fundamentally the same as the Old Testament of the Christian Bible, although the arrangement differs. The Hebrew Bible may be understood according to the scheme of three concentric circles. The inner circle, the Torah, presents the basic story of the people and includes the laws which are to guide them in living. The next circle, the Prophets, is a critical commentary on the life of the people to whom the Torah is given. The outer circle, the Writings, a diverse and open-ended collection, broadens out from Israel's worship and festal celebration to wisdom reflections.[2]

On the other hand, the Christian Bible, after the first five books (Torah), displays a different order and, in some cases, a fuller content. These differences are accounted for, in part, by the fact that the early Christian church, a Greek-speaking community, read the scriptures of Israel in Greek, particularly in the Septuagint, a translation begun in Alexandria, Egypt, in the third century B.C.E. As can be seen from the chart, in this translation prophetic writings were placed last; moreover, it included a number of works which once enjoyed considerable favor in Jewish circles but did not find their way into the Hebrew Bible.

The use of this Greek translation in Christian worship has led to some disagreement over the number of books making up the Old Testament. Ever since the Reformation, Protestants have restricted the canon of the Old Testament to the number of books in the Hebrew Bible. The extra books, found in the Septuagint, have been relegated to a separate section of the Bible under the caption "Apocrypha" (meaning hidden or secret writings), with an explanatory note that they deserve to be read but are not on a par with the rest of the Scriptures. Most of these extra books, according to the official verdict of the Roman Catholic Church, deserve canonical recognition, even though there was a long period of uncertainty about their status.[3] Thus the Roman Catholic canon, when compared with the Protestant (and Jewish) canon, is seven books longer. Eastern Orthodox churches also recognize almost all of the extra books.

These differences, however, should not be overestimated. Despite the

---

[2] See the stimulating treatise by Walter Brueggemann, *The Creative Word: Canon as a Model for Biblical Education* [170].

[3] In Catholic usage "protocanonical" refers to the books whose place in the canon was never challenged, and "deuterocanonical" refers to those which were recognized only after a period of hesitation and debate. The criterion of canonicity which the Council of Trent (C.E. 1545–63) used was that of long use in the church, as evidenced by the presence of the books in the Latin Vulgate. See *The Jerome Biblical Commentary* [9], pp. 516–24, 536.

The Books of the Old Testament

	HEBREW BIBLE	CHRISTIAN BIBLE		
		Protestant		Roman Catholic[b] and Orthodox[c]
Torah	1. Bereshith ("In the beginning")[a] 2. Shemoth ("Names") 3. Wayiqra ("And he called") 4. Bemidbar ("In the wilderness") 5. Debarim ("Words")	1. Genesis 2. Exodus 3. Leviticus 4. Numbers 5. Deuteronomy	Pentateuch	1. Genesis 2. Exodus 3. Leviticus 4. Numbers 5. Deuteronomy
Nebi'im (Prophets) Former	6. Yehoshua 7. Shofetim ("Judges") 8. Shemuel 9. Melakim ("Kings")	6. Joshua 7. Judges 8. Ruth 9–10. I and II S. ąl 11–12. I and II Kii 13–14. I and II Chr.icles 15–16. Ezra and Nehemiah Apocryphal Apocryphal 17. Esther	Historical Books	6. Joshua 7. Judges 8. Ruth 9–10. I and II Samuel 11–12. I and II Kings 13–14. I and II Chron-icles 15–16. Ezra and Ne-hemiah 17. *Tobit* 18. *Judith* 19. Esther[d]
Latter	10. Yeshayahu 11. Yirmeyahu 12. Yehezqel 13. Tere Asar ("Twelve") Hoshea Yoel Amos Obadyahu Yonah Micah Nahum Habaqquq Zephanyah Haggai Zekaryahu Malaki	18. Job 19. Psalms 20. Proverbs 21. Ecclesiastes 22. Song of Solomon Apocryphal Apocryphal	Poetry and Wisdom	20. Job 21. Psalms 22. Proverbs 23. Ecclesiastes 24. Song of Solo-mon 25. *Wisdom of Solo-mon* 26. *Ecclesiasticus* (Wisdom of Ben Sirach)

problem of fixing the outer boundary of the Old Testament, it is clear that Jews, Protestants, and Catholics hold in common a body of sacred literature which is substantially the same.

This sacred library is in many respects very diverse. The Greek words *ta biblia*, "the books," from which our word "Bible" comes, aptly suggest the diversity of the literature. But the Old Testament is more than a mere collection of books under one cover. The various writings bear witness to the unique his-

The Books of the Old Testament (*cont.*)

	HEBREW BIBLE	CHRISTIAN BIBLE		
		Protestant		Roman Catholic[b] and Orthodox[c]
Kethubim (Writings)	14. Tehillim ("Praises") 15. Iyyob 16. Mishle ("Proverbs of")	23. Isaiah 24. Jeremiah 25. Lamentations Apocryphal		27. Isaiah 28. Jeremiah 29. Lamentations 30. *Baruch* includ-
	17. Ruth 18. Shir Hashirim ("Song of Songs")		*Prophetic Writings*	ing The Let- ter of Jeremiah" (R.C. only)
Festal Scrolls	19. Qoheleth ("Preacher") 20. Ekah ("How") Lamenta- tions) 21. Ester	26. Ezekiel 27. Daniel 28. Hosea 29. Joel 30. Amos		31. Ezekiel 32. Daniel[d] 33. Hosea 34. Joel 35. Amos
	22. Daniel 23. Ezra-Nehemyah 24. Dibre Hayamim ("Chronicles")[e]	31. Obadiah 32. Jonah 33. Micah 34. Nahum 35. Habakkuk 36. Zephaniah 37. Haggai 38. Zechariah 39. Malachi		36. Obadiah 37. Jonah 38. Micah 39. Nahum 40. Habakkuk 41. Zephaniah 42. Haggai 43. Zechariah 44. Malachi
		Apocryphal Apocryphal		45. *I Maccabees* 46. *II Maccabees*

[a]In the Hebrew Bible books are often titled by opening or key words.

[b]In this column deuterocanonical books are italicized. The spelling is that of the Common Bible rather than the Douay-Rheims Bible (1609/10) which was based on the Vulgate.

[c]Note that item 30 was not included in the Old Testament canon established for Orthodox churches at the Synod of Jerusalem in C.E. 1672.

[d]Two books of the Roman Catholic canon, Esther and Daniel, are larger than their counterparts in the Protestant and Jewish canons. This surplus material is included in the Protestant Apocrypha as Additions to Esther and Additions to Daniel (The Story of Susanna, The Song of the Three Children, and The Story of Bel and the Dragon). The Prayer of Manasseh, also found in the Apocrypha, is not included in the Roman Catholic canon.

[e]The number twenty-four is reached by counting as one book each of the following: I and II Samuel, I and II Kings, I and II Chronicles, the Twelve (minor prophets), and Ezra-Nehemiah.

torical experiences of a particular people, Israel, from the time of its beginning shortly after 2000 B.C.E. down to the period of the Maccabean Revolution, which broke out slightly more than a century and a half before the "Christian" or "Common" era. The Old Testament is the life-story of Israel, "the people of God." Judaism and Christianity may differ in their understanding of the outcome of this historical drama, but they agree on the unique character of the history with which the Old Testament deals.

DEFINITION: "ISRAEL"

Let us pause to think about an important term that will recur frequently in our study.

Today "Israel" is the name of a powerful state in the Middle East, one of the members of the United Nations. In the Old Testament, however, as we shall see more clearly as we go along, Israel cannot be reduced to nationhood. The term—once applied to a covenant people before they made the transition to a monarchic state—is more inclusive and, in the last analysis, transcends political, racial categories. In this larger, more inclusive sense, the apostle Paul spoke of the Christian community as being essentially related to, and indeed, part of Israel, the people of God (Gal. 3:7, 9, 14, 29; see especially Romans 9–11).

Since the term transcends politics and even ethnic divisions, it is appropriate in our introductory study of the literature that Jews and Christians have in common, to shift from the traditional calendar terminology, B.C. ("Before Christ") and A.D. ("In the Year of the Lord") to the inclusive calendar framework B.C.E. ("Before the Common Era") and C.E. ("Common Era").

Today we take for granted a calendar which has had a long and complicated history. It was Julius Caesar who introduced the "Julian" calendar, based on 365 days in the year with a leap year of 366 days every fourth year. This calendar marked time *anno urbis conditae*, "from the foundation of the city [of Rome]." By the time of the fall of the Roman empire, however, various methods of reckoning were used. In the year 525 of our era a learned monk, Dionysius Exiguus, proposed a chronology which made the year 1 the presumed date of the nativity of Jesus. But several centuries passed before there was anything like a standard calendar in the West. Even in the Middle Ages, several methods of calendar reckoning were in use.

The shift to B.C.E. and C.E. is in line with the universalism of the *Pax Romana* and the potential inclusiveness of the term "Israel."

THE STORY OF THE BIBLE

Leaving aside the prologue to this historical drama, which is given in the first eleven chapters of Genesis, the biblical history—reduced to its barest skeleton—may be summarized as follows:

GENESIS 12–50   Shortly after the turn of the second millennium B.C.E., Israel's ancestor, Abraham, migrated from Mesopotamia into the land of Canaan, otherwise known as Palestine. The "patriarchs," or ancestors of Israel, moved about in the hill country of Canaan, with Abraham, Isaac, and Jacob succeeding one another. Eventually, during a time of famine, Jacob's family migrated to Egypt.

EXODUS–DEUTERONOMY   After enjoying initial favor in Egypt, the descendants of Jacob were subjected to forced labor by Pharaoh. Under the leadership of Moses (about 1300 B.C.E.), however, and favored by an extraordinary series of events, they escaped into the desert of the Sinaitic Peninsula, where they were forged into a community with a single religious allegiance. Unable to enter Canaan from the south, they spent a long time (forty years) in the wilderness and eventually made a roundabout journey through Transjordan.

JOSHUA, JUDGES Under the leadership of Joshua, the Israelites crossed the Jordan from their base in Transjordan, and in a lightning military campaign overran the native population and claimed the land as their own. During this time (the period of the ''Judges''), they had to wage ceaseless wars of defense to maintain their hold on the ''promised land.''

I–II SAMUEL, I–II KINGS (I–II CHRONICLES) In time, enemy pressure became so intense that a monarchy was established. Under the great kings David and Solomon (1000–922 B.C.E.), Canaan became an Israelite empire which took its place proudly in the circle of nations. On the death of Solomon, however, the United Kingom split into the two kingdoms of north and south Israel (Ephraim and Judah). These kingdoms, by virtue of their strategic location in a buffer zone between Mesopotamia and Egypt, were drawn into the power struggle of the Near East. The Northern Kingdom fell under the aggression of Assyria (721 B.C.E.); the Southern Kingdom, after more than a century of vassalage to Assyria, fell victim to the Babylonians, who wrested world rule from Assyria. Jerusalem fell to the Babylonians in the year 587, and many of the people were carried away into Babylonian captivity.

EZRA, NEHEMIAH Then, under the benevolent rule of the next empire, Persia, the exiles were permitted to return to their homeland, where they rebuilt Jerusalem and the temple and resumed their way of life. The restoration took place chiefly under the leadership of Ezra and Nehemiah (about 450–400 B.C.E.).

I, II MACCABEES After more than two centuries of Persian rule, Palestine came within the orbit of Greek control as a result of the world conquest of Alexander the Great (332 B.C.E.). Alexander's policy of imposing Hellenistic cultural uniformity upon the world was continued by those who inherited his divided empire, especially by the Seleucid rulers of Syria. When this policy was forced upon the Jewish community by one Seleucid king, open revolution broke out under the leadership of the house of the Maccabees (168 B.C.E.). Literature of the Hebrew Bible suddenly breaks off at this point (the book of Daniel), though the story is continued in the apocryphal, or deuterocanonical, book of I Maccabees. The result was the achievement of a period of Jewish independence, which was finally eclipsed by the next world empire—Rome. The events heralded in the Christian collection of writings known as the New Testament transpired within the vast arena of the Roman Empire.

The Scroll of the Prophet Isaiah was found in Cave I at Qumran in 1947. In the left-hand column, to the left
of the black blot, the text (reading right to left) says: "A voice cries: 'In the wilderness prepare the way of
the Lord' " (Is. 40:3; cf. Mark 1:3). From such a scroll Jesus read in the Nazareth synagogue (Luke 4:16–30).
Notice the scribal corrections of the text, the sewing together of the parchment sheets, and the soiled
outer side of the scroll caused by handling. Until the discovery of this scroll, our oldest known manuscript
of the Hebrew Bible of any extent was no earlier than the ninth century C.E. The Qumran scroll dates from
the second century B.C.E.

From a secular viewpoint, this history is no more unusual than the courageous story of other small nations that have been caught in the whirlpool of
power politics. In this sense, Israel's history is a minor sideshow in the larger
history of the ancient Near East, and its culture is overshadowed by the more
brilliant cultures of antiquity. *But the Old Testament does not purport to be simply a
book of secular history or culture.* It is *sacred* history, to both Jews and Christians,
because in these historical experiences, as interpreted by faith, the ultimate
meaning of human life is disclosed. From Israel's standpoint, this history is not
just the ordinary story of wars, population movement, and cultural advance or
decline. Rather, the unique dimension of these historical experiences is the disclosure of God's activity in events, the working out of God's purpose in the
career of Israel. It is this faith that transfigures Israel's history and gives to the
Bible its peculiar claim to be sacred scripture. To put it in a nutshell, the Old
Testament is Israel's witness to its encounter with God.

For this reason, we cannot begin to understand the Old Testament so long as we regard it merely as great literature, interesting history, or the development of lofty ideas. The Old Testament presents the story of God's participation in the history of a particular people. All human history is the sphere of God's sovereignty, and nature too displays the Creator's handiwork; but God became particularly involved in the career of a comparatively obscure people, thereby initiating a historical drama that has changed human perspectives and has altered the course of human affairs.

The Crucial Event

When seeking to understand the meaning of our individual life stories, we do not actually begin with birth or infancy, even though one's written autobiography may start at that point. Rather, we view or re-view our early childhood in the light of later experiences that are impressed deeply on the memory. Analogously, Israel's life-story did not really begin with the time of Abraham or even the Creation, although the Old Testament in its present form starts there. Rather, Israel's history had its true beginning in a crucial historical experience that created a self-conscious historical community—an event so decisive that earlier happenings and subsequent experiences were seen in its light.

This decisive event—the great watershed of Israel's history—was the Exodus from Egypt. Even today the Jewish people understand their vocation and destiny in the light of this revealing event which made them a people and became their undying memory. Just as Christians remember and relive the sacrifice of Jesus Christ in the celebration of the Lord's Supper, so Jews recall and make contemporary the Exodus as they celebrate the Passover. This act of worship is not just a form of "archaism," a retreat from the present into the unrecoverable once-upon-a-time. Rather, believing Jews see themselves as participants in that experience; this event of the past enters into the present with deep meaning. According to the traditional interpretation of the Passover:

> In every generation one must look upon himself as if he personally had come forth from Egypt, in keeping with the Biblical command, "And thou shalt tell thy son in that day, saying, it is because of that which the Lord did to *me* when I went forth from Egypt." For it was not alone our fathers whom the Holy One, blessed be He, redeemed, but also us whom He redeemed with them, as it is said, "And *us* He brought out thence that He might lead *us* to, and give *us*, the land which He swore to our fathers."[4]

Down through the ages Israelites have reenacted this historic moment when God marvelously brought the people out of bondage. Indeed, the story of the deliverance of slaves from the yoke of Pharaoh, and their march through

---

[4] David and Tamar de Sola Pool, eds., *The Haggadah of the Passover* (New York: Bloch, 1953), p. 51. See Will Herberg, "Beyond Time and Eternity: Reflections on Passover and Easter," in *Christianity and Crisis*, IX (1949), 41–43; also in *Faith Enacted as History* [172], pp. 66–71.

the wilderness toward a promised land, has had a powerful appeal to the religious imagination, such as the time when pilgrims crossed the ocean to seek a new world, or more recently when oppressed groups have identified with the symbolism of the story.[5] This habit, however, of regarding the Exodus as a paradigm—as "a mould in which other stories of rescue from ruin may be cast"— goes back to the Old Testament itself, where the Exodus story forms the basic "pattern of deliverance" to which all other liberation motifs are accommodated.[6] The Exodus was regarded as the clue to who God is and how God acts to deliver the downtrodden and oppressed; more than that, it provided the model for how the people of God should seek justice in society as the only appropriate response to the liberation they had experienced (Micah 6:1–8).

This is the note that is struck again and again in the literature from the period before the fall of the nation in 587 B.C.E., the so-called pre-exilic period. It is interesting to notice that the prophets of this period do not even mention the migration of Abraham, as related in Genesis 12. Instead, they trace the historical beginning of the Israelite people to the time of the Exodus, when God acted on their behalf and laid upon them lasting obligations to God and fellow human beings. In the eighth century, Amos reminded his hearers that Israel was bound together as a "whole family" by God's act of deliverance from Egypt (Amos 3:1–2), and he rebuked the people for forgetting the great events in which their God became known to them (Amos 2:9–11). Hosea, his contemporary, traced Israel's "call" to that same event:

> When Israel was a child, I loved him,
> and out of Egypt I called my son.
> —HOSEA 11:1 (RSV)

Indeed, according to this prophet Israel's knowledge of God is based on the Exodus event:

> I am the Lord your God
>   from the land of Egypt;
> you know no God but me,
>   and besides me there is no savior.
> —HOSEA 13:4 (RSV)

About the time of the nation's fall, Ezekiel put the matter emphatically.

> Thus said the Lord God:
>   On the day that I chose Israel, I gave My oath to the stock of the House of Jacob;

---

[5] See James Hutchison Smylie, "On Jesus, Pharaohs, and the Chosen People: Martin Luther King as Biblical Interpreter and Humanist," *Interpretation*, 24 (1970), 74–91. Among Latin American liberation theologians, see, J. S. Croatto, *Exodus: A Hermeneutics of Freedom* [212]. In *Exodus and Revolution* (New York: Basic Books, 1984), Michael Walzer treats the Exodus as an ancient story of revolution that is "continuously reinvented."

[6] David Daube, *The Exodus Pattern in the Bible* (London: Faber and Faber, 1963), p. 11.

when I made Myself known to them in the land of Egypt, I gave my oath to them. When I said, "I the Lord am your God," that same day I swore to take them out of the land of Egypt into a land flowing with milk and honey, a land which I had sought out for them, the fairest of all lands.

—EZEKIEL 20:5–6 (TNK)

And in many of the Psalms, composed for use in worship, the liberation from Egyptian bondage provides the motive for the service of God and the basis for future welfare.

> Hear My people, and I will admonish you;
>   Israel, if you would but listen to Me!
> You shall have no foreign god,
>   you shall not bow to an alien god.
> I the Lord am your God
>   who brought you out of the land of Egypt;
>   open your mouth wide and I will fill it.
>   —PSALM 81:9–11 (TNK; RSV 81:8–10)

Other passages in the literature of the prophets and the Psalms stress the pivotal significance of the Exodus.[7] The theme still reverberates in literature composed late in the Old Testament period, such as Daniel (Dan. 9:15) or the Wisdom of Solomon (15:18–19:22).

The Heart of the Pentateuch

The same accent is found, though not so obviously, in the section of the Hebrew Bible that is regarded as most authoritative by Jewish tradition: the books of Genesis, Exodus, Leviticus, Numbers, and Deuteronomy. The Hebrew word for these five books is *Torah*, often translated inadequately as "Law," but better rendered as "Teaching"; that is, the divine guidance or direction which God gives the people in their historical pilgrimage. Scholars also refer to these books as the Pentateuch, a word based on a Greek term referring to five scrolls (*he pentateuchos biblos*, "the book of the five scrolls"); and frequently the first six books of the Old Testament (Pentateuch plus Joshua) are considered as a unit called the Hexateuch.

As it now stands, the Pentateuch begins with an extended prologue to the story of the Exodus: the account of primeval beginnings (Gen. 1–11) and the stories of the Israelite "patriarchs" or ancestors (Gen. 12–50). Actually, when we begin with Genesis and read to Exodus, we are reading the story backward, as it were, for the period before Moses was remembered and interpreted in the light of events that brought Israel into existence in the Mosaic period, just as Americans view Columbus's voyage and the landing of the Pilgrims in the light of the decisive historical events of the Revolutionary War. In a later time of theological reflection, Israel could trace the beginning of its history back beyond

---

[7] See Amos 9:7; Hosea 2:14–15; 12:13; 13:4; Micah 6:4; Jeremiah 2:2–7; 31:32; Psalms 66:6; 78:18–53; 136:10–11.

the Exodus to the first Hebrew, Abraham, and could portray its "call" (election) in the story of Abraham's migration into the Land of Promise (Gen. 11:31–12:9). Actually, however, the call of Israel was based on the event of the Exodus, the "root experience" that was enshrined in the memory of the people.[8] Properly, the book of Genesis must be regarded as a prologue to the time when the curtain rises on the scene of the oppression of Hebrews in Egypt at the beginning of the book of Exodus.

We should not be surprised to discover, then, that in the earliest period of Israel, long before the tradition was composed in the form of a written epic, the Exodus story was celebrated in poetry and song. An excellent example is the ancient poem found in Exodus 15:1–18, the "Song of the Sea," which displays the influence of Canaanite style and mythology.[9] The poet extols "the glorious deeds" of the God of Israel who liberated a fugitive people from Pharaoh's army and guided them into the land of Canaan. Here we find ourselves on the ground of the primary confession of Israel, which was elaborated in later epic narrative and poetry (e.g., Pss. 77; 114).

The centrality of the Exodus in Israelite epic tradition is evident in a liturgy found in the book of Deuteronomy, a book which received its present form after the fall of Jerusalem in 587 B.C.E. The liturgy is couched in relatively late "Deuteronomic" style, yet the content, in the judgment of some scholars, may be much older. The passage is a confession of faith which the worshiper is to make when presenting the first fruits of the harvest at the sanctuary:

> My ancestor was a wandering Aramean who descended to Egypt. There he sojourned with a small band and there he grew to be a great, powerful and populous nation. But the Egyptians maltreated us, humiliated us, and imposed upon us heavy servitude. Then we cried to Yahweh, the God of our ancestors; and Yahweh heard our cry and saw our affliction, our trouble and our oppression. Yahweh caused us to go out of Egypt with a strong hand and an outstretched arm, with great terror, with signs and wonders, and brought us to this place and gave us this land, a land flowing with milk and honey.
>
> —DEUTERONOMY 26:5–9; see also 6:20–23

This "historical credo," as it has been called,[10] is not a private prayer but is a confession of faith that is to be made in connection with an act of worship. The

---

[8] On Israel's "root experiences," see Emil Fackenheim, *God's Presence* [213].

[9] See Frank M. Cross, "The Song of the Sea and Canaanite Myth," *Canaanite Myth and Hebrew Epic* [112], pp. 112–44; also Patrick D. Miller, Jr., *The Divine Warrior in Early Israel* [215].

[10] This is the view of Gerhard von Rad, who has isolated examples of "the short historical credo" (Deut. 6:20–25; 26:5–10; Josh. 24:2–13) which constitute the thematic nucleus out of which the epic tradition evolved. See his study of "The Form-Critical Problem of the Hexateuch" [181], pp. 1–27, which is summarized in the introduction to his commentary on Genesis [271], pp. 13–24. The antiquity of this creedal statement has been questioned by some scholars, e.g., Leonhardt Rost, *Das kleine Credo und andere Studien zum Alten Testament* (Heidelberg: Quelle & Meyer, 1905), pp. 11–25; J. P. Hyatt, "Were There an Ancient Historical Credo in Israel and an Independent Sinai Tradition?" in *Translating and Understanding the Old Testament* [159], pp. 152–170.

worshiper identifies with the story that the community tells, as evidenced by the plural pronouns ("The Egyptians maltreated *us; We* cried to Yahweh . . . and Yahweh heard *our* cry," etc.) Even more important for our immediate purpose is the content of the confession. Only a brief reference is made to the ancestral period: one of the patriarchs, Jacob, is called "a wandering Aramean." The confession dwells primarily on the liberating events of the time of the Exodus and concludes with a grateful acknowledgment that the God who delivered a people from bondage also led them into "a land flowing with milk and honey." [See the content of the Song of the Sea, Exod. 15:1–18, referred to above.] It is not too much to say that the Old Testament as a whole is a symphonic exposition of these major themes that were enunciated at the beginning, when Israel entered upon the historical stage as a people.

Blaise Pascal, a famous French writer of the seventeenth century, once observed that the God of the Bible is "the God of Abraham, Isaac, and Jacob," not the God of the philosophers and the sages. This is true in the sense that biblical faith, to the bewilderment of many philosophers, is fundamentally historical in character. It is concerned with events, social relationships, and concrete situations, not abstract values and ideas existing in a timeless realm. The God of Israel is known in history—a particular history—through socially conditioned relations with Abraham, Isaac, and Jacob—and we may add, with Sarah and Hagar, Rebekah, Rachel, and Leah. The attempt to reason away the essential historical content of biblical faith, says a modern Jewish interpreter, is like paraphrasing poetry: "Something called an 'idea content' remains, but everything that gave power and significance to the original is gone."[11]

It is important to realize, however, that the history of God's dealings with the ancestors of Israel is understood in the light of the crucial, revealing event of the Exodus. As a psalmist testified:

Yahweh achieves righteousness,
  and justice for all who are oppressed.
To Moses Yahweh made known his ways,
  his deeds to the Israelite people.
                    —PSALM 103:6–7

Throughout the generations, Israel's God, invoked by the cultic name Yahweh (a matter to which we shall return in the next chapter), was praised as the Holy One who brought a band of slaves out of Egypt, formed them into a people, and gave them a future (Exod. 20:1). The Exodus, therefore, is the central moment in Israel's history. Here was Israel's true beginning, the time of its creation as a people. Here began the purposive movement of events that made it possible later to see all history and nature embraced within the divine design. So deeply

[11] Will Herberg, "Biblical Faith as Heilgeschichte: The Meaning of Redemptive History in Human Existence," in *Faith Enacted as History* [172], pp. 32–42.

was the Exodus etched upon Israel's memory that the maturing faith of the people was essentially a reliving and reinterpretation of this historic event.

A Look Ahead

Accordingly, we shall begin our exploration of the Old Testament with the Exodus. It will be helpful, however, to view this event in the context of the history and culture of the ancient Near East during the second millennium B.C.E. and to consider events of the ancestral period which, at least in retrospect, were regarded as preparatory to the Mosaic period. Therefore, in the next chapter we shall consider the prologue to the Exodus: the story of Israel's descent into Egypt and the oppression under the pharaohs. Then in successive chapters we shall take up the deliverance from Egypt and the making of the covenant, the conquest of Canaan, the rise of the monarchy, and the nation's involvement in the vortex of the world struggle. In other words, the outline of our book is based on Israel's historical career. No other approach, we believe, does justice to the historical character of Israel's faith.

This approach demands that in each chapter we must keep before us several things at once. Literary criticism is necessary, for the traditions dealing with a certain episode of biblical history often come from later times or have been reworked by editors. Also, we must consider Israel's relation to the political, sociological, and cultural situation in the ancient world. This will make it necessary to look beyond the biblical text to other historical sources and to heed the important contributions of archaeology. And, of course, we must never lose sight of our central task: the exposition of Israel's faith. Many books on the Old Testament treat these three elements—literary development, historical study, and theology—separately. We shall attempt to weave them together in fugue-like fashion as the story of God's dealings with Israel unfolds chapter by chapter.

Our attention will focus on the community of Israel, known as ''the people of God.'' Individualism, in the modern sense of the word, has no place in the mainstream of Israel's faith. To study isolated personalities like Moses, or to deal with abstract ideas like ''the idea of God,'' is to miss the point of the Old Testament. Personalities and ideas must be considered in relation to the corporate experiences of Israel in the drama of its history.

Our task, then, is to try to understand the biblical message in its dynamic context of culture, politics, and geography. We shall seek to enter into the concrete life situations out of which the various writings have come, and to understand what the writers were saying to their times. Toward this end, a series of maps has been provided to help the reader become familiar with the biblical setting. Pictures and chronological charts have been included to show how Israel's sacred history is bound up with the international affairs of the ancient Near East.

One final word: If we are really to enter sympathetically and imaginatively into this community and to relive its sacred history, there is no substitute for reading the Bible itself. The purpose of the present book is to aid in the understanding of the Bible—not to urge the mastery of another book about the Bible. The literal meaning of "understand" is "stand under." Through the reading of selected Bible passages, which are listed at the beginning of each chapter, it is hoped that readers will "stand under the Bible," so that the light it sheds upon the meaning of human life may fall directly upon them.

Note: Unless you are one of the rare persons who can read the Old Testament in the original Hebrew, it is advisable to consult more than one English translation, preferably selected from the following:

The Revised Standard Version (RSV)†
The New English Bible (NEB)
The Jerusalem Bible (JB)
TANAKH: Translation of the Jewish Publication Society (TNK)*
The New American Bible (NAB)
The New International Version (NIV)

† The scripture quotations marked RSV contained in this text are from *The Revised Standard Version of the Bible.* Copyright © 1946, 1952, 1971 by the Division of Christian Education of the National Conference of the Churches of Christ in the U.S.A. Used by permission. All rights reserved.

*TANAKH is an acronymn based on the initial letters of the three parts of the Hebrew Bible: Torah (Teaching), Nebi'im (Prophets), and Kethubim (Writings).

PART I

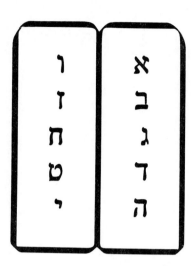

If you will obey my voice
and keep my covenant,
you shall be my own possession
among all peoples;
for all the earth is mine.
—EXODUS 19:5

THE CREATION
OF A PEOPLE

CHAPTER 1

The Beginnings of Israel

A stirring historical drama unfolds in the book of Exodus. The protagonist is Yahweh, the God of Israel, who intervenes in behalf of a helpless band of slaves. The plot, developed through a succession of suspense-filled episodes, is God's contest against Pharaoh, the mightiest emperor of the day. The denouement comes when, in the nick of time, Israel's pursuers are swallowed up in the waters of the Red Sea. The leading theme of the drama is the action and triumph of Israel's God.

Viewing the Exodus story as a historical drama rather than as a colorless, factual report will help us enter more imaginatively and sympathetically into its spirit. Drama emphasizes involvement; it pictures life in contemporaneous terms; it purports to tell *our* story in the actions that unfold. It was in these terms that the Israelites retold and relived the Exodus story down through the generations. Some think that Exodus 1–15 reflects an old Passover narrative that was recited annually in connection with the feast celebrating the deliverance of Israel from Egypt.[1] This view should not be taken to mean that the whole story was invented as a "cult legend"[2] to explain the feast, for as we shall see, the

---

Biblical readings: In this and the following two chapters, our attention will focus on the story of the Exodus and Sinai Covenant, found in Exodus 1–24 and 32–34. At this point it is essential for the reader to become familiar with the prologue to these events as related in Genesis 12–50.

[1] This is the view of Johannes Pedersen, *Israel* [117], III–IV, 384–415, 728–737. This view is accepted with considerable modification by Martin Noth, *Pentateuchal Traditions* [70], pp. 65–71.

[2] For a criticism of excessive emphasis on the cult, see G. E. Wright, "Cult and History," *Interpretation*, 16 (1962), 3–20.

narrative, like a historical novel, is based upon real historical experiences. Nevertheless, it was in the cult, or worshiping community, that the story was remembered and retold. In other words, these narratives are written in the confessional language of worship, not in dispassionate prose. The purpose of the story is to communicate the meaning of the story or history that the worshiping community shares and celebrates.

DEFINITION: "STORY, HISTORY"

There is a very fine line between "story" and "history." In fact, in some modern languages one word covers both, for instance, the German *Geschichte* or the French *histoire*. Check the dictionary for the ancestry of the English word "story" and its relation to "history."[3]

The biblical story is not history, if "history" means a detached report of events. But neither is the biblical history story, if "story" means a tale spun out of the imagination. We are dealing with a history-like story, or a story-like history, and there is no razor sharp enough to make an absolute separation between these dimensions of the biblical narrative. This should be kept in mind throughout this study, especially in the chapters that deal with the origins of Israel. (See further, James Barr, "Story and History in Biblical Theology" [175].)

THE NATURE OF THE TRADITION

It is proper to begin by reading the story—its prologue (Gen. 12–50) and its main body (Exod. 1–15)—as a totality, allowing the text to make its own first impact. This initial textual encounter, with its so-called "first naiveté," may be the beginning of an exploration that enables us to reread the text later, after critical study and reflection, with what has been called a "second naiveté," that is, a postcritical understanding.[4] Just as the analysis of a Beethoven symphony may lead to deeper musical enjoyment when the work is performed, so criticism may lead to rereading and rehearing the biblical narrative with enhanced appreciation. The point needs to be emphasized, however, that the beginning and end of the study of Scripture is the canonical text that we have received.

After the initial encounter with the biblical story, we discover that various literary problems arise as our attention turns to the parts and the details. In the modern period since the Renaissance and Reformation, many students, pondering the Pentateuch carefully, have become aware of repetitions, stylistic peculiarities, and inconsistencies that can hardly be accounted for on the

---

[3] On the ambiguity of the words "history" and "historical," see Will Herberg, "Five Meanings of the Word 'Historical,' " in *Faith Enacted as History* [172], pp. 132–137.

[4] The critical rereading of Scripture is discussed in "Tradition and Scripture in the Community of Faith," by B. W. Anderson, *Journal of Biblical Literature*, 100 (1981), 5–21; see especially p. 16.

assumption of a single, human author. The history of Pentateuchal criticism actually goes back at least to the medieval Jewish scholar Ibn Ezra (twelfth century C.E.), who brooded over certain passages which seemed to imply a date later than Moses, the traditional author of the Pentateuch (the so-called "Five Books of Moses"). Ibn Ezra suspected, for instance, that the statement in Genesis 12:6 ("At that time the Canaanites were in the land") implies a time after Moses when the Israelites were actually in the land and the native Canaanites had ceased to be a separate people. Earlier rabbis, writing in the Talmud, questioned whether Moses really wrote the account of his own death and burial (Deut. 34:5–12), and suggested that perhaps Moses' epitaph was written by Joshua, his successor.

One of the clearest evidences of diversity, at least in our way of thinking, is the occurrence of the same material in different versions. We find this phenomenon right at the beginning of the Bible, where the opening account of creation (Gen. 1:1–2:3) is paralleled by another creation story, written in a different literary style and with a different sequence of events (Gen. 2:4b–25). In the Abraham cycle (Gen. 12–25) there are two accounts of God's covenant with Abra(ha)m,[5] one found in Genesis 15 and the other in Genesis 17. Moreover, we discover that on two different occasions the patriarch told a "white lie" which almost got his wife into sexual trouble with a foreign king (Gen. 12:10–17 and 20:1–18). It seems hard to believe that Abraham learned nothing from the first experience; moreover, the same story is told about Abraham's son, Isaac (26:6–11). Turning to the Exodus story, we find two names for one sacred mountain (Sinai, Horeb) and two versions of the Ten Commandments (Exod. 20 and Deut. 5). In addition, there are two versions of the call of Moses and the appointment of Aaron, one taking place in the land of Midian (Exod. 3:1–4:17) and the other in Egypt (Exod. 6:2–7:7). In the first account, this theme is dealt with in a vivid literary style which depicts Moses' encounter with God in the wilderness and the question-and-answer dialogue that ensued. In the subsequent passage, on the other hand, this episode is recapitulated in a different literary style and theological perspective and gives more emphasis to the role of Aaron in the story (compare 4:14–17 and 7:1–6). And as we shall see, these two versions also differ on when the cultic name, Yahweh, was introduced. The question is, then, how are we to account for these—and other—irregularities, discrepancies, and repetitions?

Before proposing a possible answer to this question, let us proceed inductively by noticing three major types of material in the Pentateuch. A cursory glance through Deuteronomy (the book that contains a second version of the Ten Commandments) shows that it presents exhortations by Moses in an impassioned "sermonic" style. This "Deuteronomic" style, which is not found to any great extent elsewhere in the Pentateuch, is distinguished by long, verbose sentences, characteristic words and phrases, and urgent appeals to be faithful to the covenant with Yahweh. Deuteronomy 30:15–20 is a good example.

---

[5] The name *Abraham* is a dialectical variant of *Abram*, the more original form. See Gen. 17:1–8 for a harmonizing explanation of the survival of the two names in the tradition.

Turning to the remaining four books of the Pentateuch, we find large sections that are dominated by priestly interests such as genealogies, institutions (e.g. sabbath, circumcision, sacrifice), and other cultic matters. Material of this sort is concentrated in the last part of Exodus (chaps. 25–40, minus chaps. 32–34), the book of Leviticus, and much of the book of Numbers. But it is also found in the book of Genesis, for instance, in the first creation story (Gen. 1:1–2:3) and in the second account of the covenant with Abraham (Gen. 17). Indeed, Priestly material provides the encompassing framework for the final form of the Pentateuch, or more exactly the Tetrateuch (first four books), for as we have seen, Deuteronomy seems to stand by itself in the Pentateuch. This Priestly work is marked by a finely wrought literary style, a special vocabulary of words and phrases, and a distinctive theological point of view. Compare the style of the second account of the call of Moses with that of the first (see above).

After we take away Deuteronomy and Priestly sections, there is still material to be accounted for. What is left appears to be the remains of an Old Epic narrative that was presented in the lively style of storytellers, who had their distinctive vocabulary and human interests. We may get a feeling for this epic tradition by reading, for instance, the paradise story (Gen. 2:4b–3:24), the story of the testing of Abraham (Gen. 22:1–19), or the story of Moses at the burning bush (Exod. 3:1–4:17).

The dominant theory held by Jewish, Protestant, and Catholic scholars is that the Pentateuch is a composite work in which various major literary strands have been artistically combined during the course of transmission through the generations. According to this hypothesis, which rests on the critical labors of more than two centuries of intensive study, several traditions coexisted in ancient Israelite society and were eventually blended together to form the Pentateuch, the five scrolls of the Torah. In our previous brief examination of the types of material in the Pentateuch, we have identified these traditions in a preliminary way: the Deuteronomic, Priestly, and Old Epic traditions. The widely accepted "source" hypothesis, which now enjoys a kind of classical status, further differentiates the Old Epic tradition into parallel northern (Ephraimitic) and Southern (Judean) versions, reflecting the division of United Israel after David's time. In addition, it maintains that the literary traditions reflect historical stages in the development of the Pentateuch.

According to this view, these strands of tradition were woven together in various stages until the Pentateuch reached its present and final form about 400 B.C.E., the time when, under the leadership of Ezra, the Torah became the constitutional basis of the restored community of Israel.[6]

Keep in mind that this is a hypothesis which attempts to account for the observed diversity in the Pentateuch, and like any hypothesis, this one is con-

---

[6] We shall consider these traditions and their combination at later points in our study. See Chapter 5 for "The Formation of the Israelite Epic," Chapter 7 for discussion of the Yahwist, and Chapter 9 for the Elohist. D is considered in Chapter 11 and the Priestly Work is taken up in Chapter 13. For brief introductions to Pentateuchal criticism, see N. C. Habel, *Literary Criticism of the Old Testament* [62]; also E. A. Speiser, *Genesis* [273], pp. xxii–xxvii; *Jerome Biblical Commentary* [9], pp. 1–6.

The Source Hypothesis

			Oral Period c. 1200–1000 B.C.E.
Old Epic {	J	A Judean source, presumably written during the United Monarchy, which prefers to use the divine name Yahweh (sometimes spelled Jahweh).	c. 950
	E	An Ephraimitic or North Israelite source which favors the use of the divine name Elohim ("God").	c. 850
Deuteronomic Tradition	D	A tradition, best represented in the book of Deuteronomy, which reflects the literary style and theology prevalent at the time of Josiah's reform (621 B.C.E.).	c. 650 and later
Priestly Work	P	A literary corpus, marked by the style and cultic interests of the priestly circle of Jerusalem, which became prominent in the period after the fall of Jerusalem in 587 B.C.E.	c. 550 and later

stantly being subjected to testing in scholarly study and debate. One vulnerable point is found in the Old Epic tradition, specifically the division of this material into two strands, the Yahwist [J] and the Elohist [E], and the dating of each. Some scholars maintain that the hypothesis, stated this way, puts too much emphasis on "documents" or "sources" and fails to do justice to the dynamic of the oral tradition that preceded, and even accompanied, writing.[7] Others question whether the Old Epic tradition has to be divided into separate "Yahwist" and "Elohist" versions; we may be dealing with a single tradition that has been enriched or supplemented in the course of transmission. In the face of differing scholarly opinions, the proper response is not to throw up one's hands in despair. Rather, we should realize that the Torah (Pentateuch) is a very subtle and complex body of literature that challenges the exercise of all the "heart, soul and strength" (Deut. 6:5) if one is to enter into its meaning.[8]

At this point we shall not go further into this kind of biblical criticism or other approaches. For our immediate purpose, it is sufficient to say that "source criticism," in its own way, points up the enduring importance of the Exodus story in the life of the Israelite community. The various inconsistencies, repetitions, and stylistic differences reflect the ways in which the story was retold, reworked, and reinterpreted in different historical periods and life situations. In this literary "mosaic," the fundamental tone of the Mosaic tradition has been preserved and blended with the overtones of meaning experienced by the com-

---

[7] This is the view of the so-called Scandinavian school; see Bibliography [Nos. 72–74].

[8] The various listings in the Bibliography under "Biblical Criticism" [Nos. 48–88] are intended to help the student who is ready to go further into this matter. Note especially the work of Hermann Gunkel (1862–1932), who pioneered in the study of the preliterary (oral) tradition, by studying the genres of oral tradition and the history of their transmission in various stages of composition.

munity throughout the generations. The final text of the Torah preserves both the original themes of Mosaic tradition and the subsequent variations on them.

THE ORAL TRADITION

Even if we assume, with a host of scholars of past generations, that the Pentateuch is composed of several literary traditions, this kind of analysis is, at best, only a provisional starting point for understanding the dynamic of the Torah tradition. The likelihood is that behind the earliest *written* stages of the Exodus story, which may well date from the period of the Israelite monarchy, there was a long period during which the tradition was handed down *orally* by poets and storytellers; and even after it was given written form in court or priestly circles, the oral tradition persisted among the people. It is difficult for us to understand this, for ever since the Renaissance our culture has placed a great premium upon the printed book. Therefore, when we hear about the "book" of Exodus, we are apt to think of an author who sat down in a study to write for a reading public after having consulted sources available in a library. This situation, however, did not prevail in antiquity, when only a few could read and write, and the tradition was often passed on through oral performance on ceremonial or informal occasions.

The literature of the Pentateuch in its written form surely reflects a long history of oral recitation. There are analogies for the role of oral tradition, for instance, in the recitation of generations of family history among bedouins,[9] or the "singer of tales" in Slavic society.[10] Indeed, it is no exaggeration to say that the early period of Israel's life—that is, the centuries before David (c. 1000)— was a creative time when the essential story of Israel was rehearsed and elaborated with contributions from the experiences and traditions of the various tribes. Undoubtedly many of the irregularities and diversities that scholars have tried to explain by literary analysis are vestiges of the period when the tradition was transmitted in song and story, by word of mouth.

It is probable, then, that during the early oral period the main outlines of the later Pentateuch were beginning to take shape, as skilled narrators recreated the tradition they had received and improvised on it in fresh ways. The great themes of the Israelite story, reinterpreted, expanded, and handed down to posterity, were

1.   The promise to the ancestors
2.   The liberation of Israel from Egyptian bondage

---

[9] For a good discussion of the relation between literary sources and preliteray oral tradition, see Roland de Vaux, *History* [92]. K. A. Kitchen, *The Bible in Its World* [96], pp. 66–68, gives interesting examples from the second millennium of the reliable transmission of traditions across several centuries.

[10] See the illuminating work by Albert B. Lord, *The Singer of Tales* [260], in which Homeric literature (*The Odyssey* and *The Illiad*) is studied in the light of the performance of oral singers of Yugloslavia.

3.   The manifestation of God (theophany) at Sinai and the giving of the law
4.   The providential guidance in the wilderness
5.   The inheritance of the promised land

In the early oral period these themes were already being blended into a great historical epic, long before they took shape in written form.[11]

Thus the Pentateuch is the end result of a long and dynamic process of tradition, from the time when the Israelite story was shaped orally and enriched with specific narrative contributions from the various tribes, on to the time when it was given literary formulation in various circles during the monarchy, and finally to the time when these literary strands were brought together by the Priestly Writer into the canonical Pentateuch which we have received. Sometimes the literary traditions stand out clearly, as in the case of the Priestly and Old Epic versions of creation. But very often these traditions cannot be disentangled, especially in the Exodus story, not just because the final editing was so skillful, but because each of the circles of storytellers drew upon a common fund of oral tradition. The following diagram presents a broad outline of the history which lies behind the Pentateuch in its final form.

The Narrator's Point of View

Two problems have already arisen in our study of the biblical story: (1) there are irregularities and even dissonances in the narrative that suggest diverse literary traditions; (2) the literary traditions are several centuries removed from the time of the Exodus, and this period is bridged primarily by oral transmission. But there is a third problem. The Exodus story, both in its original oral form and its written version, does not pretend to be objective history. It is obviously an interpretive account of events which, viewed from another standpoint, could very well be presented in quite a different manner. In this story, unlike the usual historical narration that we are familiar with today, God appears on the historical stage as the main actor. Indeed, for the believing and worshiping community, this is a "good story" and even a "God-story"—the original meaning of the Anglo-Saxon word "god-spel" (or gospel).

The fact that this story is told to confess faith in God does not necessarily discredit its historical value, even though at some points it may appear fanciful to the modern mind. Historians today usually recognize that there is no uninterpreted history. History is not a series of naked facts arranged in chronological order like beads on a string. It is absurd to suppose that an event is a kind of

---

[11] This is the position of Martin Noth, a leading advocate of the traditio-historical method, which attempts to trace the process by which units (genres) of oral tradition evolved into the literature of the Pentateuch. See his basic work, *A History of Pentateuchal Traditions* and the introductory essay which places this approach in the context of twentieth century biblical criticism [70]. A succinct discussion of this method is found in Walter E. Rast, *Tradition History and the Old Testament* [71]. The implications of this approach are elaborated in Douglas Knight, *Tradition and Theology in the Old Testament* [138].

History of Pentateuchal Traditions

	B.C.E.		
Ancestral Period (Abraham and after)	c. 1800–1300		Beginning of oral tradition
Mosaic Period	c. 1300–1250		
The Israelite Confederacy (Joshua and Judges)	c. 1250–1000		Israelite story shaped orally
Period of the Monarchy (David to fall of nation)	1000–587		Beginning of written Pentateuchal tradition
Period of Exile and Restoration (to Ezra)	587–400		Completion of Pentateuchal tradition (canon)

This diagram shows the length of the oral tradition before it was reduced in various stages (J, E, D, P) to written form. The broken lines indicate that even during the period of writing down the Israelite story, the tradition continued in oral form. Some scholars maintain that the whole process, from beginning to final canonization in the time of Ezra, was oral. See Ivan Engnell, *A Rigid Scrutiny* [72], pp. 50–67. A judicious evaluation is given by R. E. Clements, "Pentateuchal Problems," in *Tradition and Interpretation* [153], pp. 66–124.

"thing in itself" which can be recovered after all interpretation is stripped away. An event is a meaningful happening in the experience of a people. And history is the narration of these experienced events—events so memorable that they are preserved in oral tradition and eventually written down in records. Obviously historians do not report everything, as though they had at hand a movie camera which objectively recorded all that was done or a tape recorder that took down all that was said. Historical narrative is inevitably selective and interpretive. Historians recount only the events that to them, or to the community they represent, are meaningful or history-making. Sometimes the meaning of historical events is expressed in legends, in which the events are embellished with popular imagination, as they may have been in the case of the legends of King Arthur and the Knights of the Round Table.

Some events have a public meaning which can be discerned by anyone in the vicinity of the occurrence. Let us take an illustration from American history. The Civil War was a political struggle to preserve the unity of the nation at a time when slavery was a divisive issue. Of course, historians differ in their assessments of the historical data and the place of the event in the whole context of American history. Even today there may be different nuances of interpretation, depending on whether the historian comes from the South or the North, or whether the history was written by someone outside the American scene. But as a political event, the war has a public meaning. It can be appreciated by any people who have struggled to preserve national unity or to overcome the cleavages of race or class.

In his Second Inaugural Address, however, Abraham Lincoln perceived another dimension of meaning in the conflict: the judgment of God upon the involvement of both North and South in the inhumanity of slavery. To him the war was not just a political event with a public meaning, but an event fraught with divine meaning when viewed in the perspective of religious faith. His famous address raises important questions that ought to be faced by the historical interpreter. Did God's judgment really find expression in the tragedy of the Civil War? Is the historical view too narrow if we fail to see God at work in human affairs? Is history not just the narration of human deeds, but of the activity of God as well?

When we deal with the Exodus, the question of the meaning of a crucial event is put in the sharpest form. From one standpoint, the Exodus was merely a political event: the liberation of a band of slaves from Pharaoh's yoke. This was its public meaning. So viewed, it can be described externally or objectively and compared with similar political events in the lives of other peoples. But to the biblical narrators, who spoke out of a community of faith, the Exodus was pregnant with divine meaning. What happened was not just the escape of fugitives from slavery, but God's liberation of oppressed slaves and God's creation of a people out of chaos. The Exodus was a ''root experience'' that disclosed the saving power of the God who is holy, who completely transcends the human world.[12] It was the sign of God's historical presence, of God's intervention in an apparently hopeless human situation. Therefore, the Exodus story is indeed a *godspel* (''God-story''). It deals with history in a different dimension, or, some would say, ''on a higher plane,'' from ordinary history.[13]

But to speak of history ''on a higher plane'' may be misleading. It may suggest that the biblical story belongs in some Olympian realm far removed from the ordinary affairs of human life, or that the story may be treated merely as the poetry of faith, that has no direct connection with prosaic historical facts. This would be a grave misunderstanding of biblical history. To be sure, as we have already recognized, the narrative has been embellished imaginatively to communicate the astounding wonder and the revelatory power of the event; but *it is in the concrete affairs and relationships of people that God becomes known as saving presence and ethical demand.* No external historical study can demonstrate that the Exodus was an event of divine liberation; but to Israel this ''political'' event was the medium through which God's presence and purpose were disclosed. God's revelation did not come like a bolt out of the blue. It came *through* concrete events and crises and *to persons* who perceived in these shared experiences a divine dimension of meaning of which the general public was unaware.

Thus the story of Israel's beginnings does not belong to a completely different sphere from that with which the historian can deal. The Old Testament reflects a concreteness and actuality which have to be taken into account if we are to do justice to the narrative of God's dealings with Israel, ''the people of God.'' So before examining the Exodus story more closely, we shall consider

[12] Emil L. Fackenheim, in *God's Presence in History* [213], regards Exodus and Sinai as ''root experiences'' of Jewish tradition. In his view, these ''epoch-making events'' have three dimensions: (1) they are decisive past events; (2) they have a public, historical character; and (3) they are reenacted in the community of faith as a present reality.

[13] Johannes Pedersen expresses this view in his discussion of the Passover legend, *Israel*, III–IV [117], 719–737.

what bearing the archaeological exploration of the ancient Near East has upon our understanding of the biblical narrative. Archaeology can help us to place the period of Israel's ancestors and the Exodus itself in a broad cultural horizon and a meaningful historical context.

THE PROLOGUE TO THE EXODUS

The account found in the opening chapters of the book of Exodus is linked closely with the history and religion of the ancestral period—that is, the period covered by chapters 12 through 50 of the book of Genesis. This continuity is indicated by a reference to events that transpired after the death of Joseph, one of the twelve sons of Jacob (Exod. 1:8), and by the vivid story of the theophany, or manifestation of God, in the episode of the "burning bush." There we read that Moses was addressed in these words: "I am the God of your father, the God of Abraham, the God of Isaac, and the God of Jacob" (3:6). These narratives, at least in their present form, presuppose that the speaker is the same God who appeared to the ancestors of Israel, and that the period of the ancestors is the prologue to the liberating event of the Exodus.

What can be said about the historical antecedents of the Exodus? This is an extraordinarily difficult question to answer—for two reasons. First, as we have just seen, the story of the beginnings of Israel has come to us through a long process of oral and written tradition and has been shaped to confess faith in God. This is clearly the case with the narratives about the prehistory of Israel in Genesis 12–50 which belong to the Old Epic tradition. Not only is the prior saving purpose of the God of the Exodus traced back into the whole course of previous ancestral history, but also the conception of the unity of *Israel, the people of God*, is pushed back into the times of Abraham, Isaac, and Jacob, that is, to a time well before the period of the "Judges" (c. 1200–1000) when Israel as a tribal confederacy came into existence (see Chapter 6). This pushing of a pan-Israelite consciousness back into the period of the ancestors results in an over-simplified picture, something like a historian tracing the conception of the *United States* back into the period before the Revolutionary War when, as a matter of historical fact, there was no sense of overall national unity. This view of Israel's prehistory may make sense as a confession of faith, but is it a theological construction? Considering the difficulty of this question, it should not be surprising to hear that some scholars are skeptical about the historical reliability of the biblical traditions concerning the pre-Mosaic period. In their view, the scriptural portrayal of the ancestral period is story, but not history in the usual sense of the word.[14]

[14] This skeptical view, espoused in the nineteenth century by Julius Wellhausen (*Prolegomena to the History of Israel*, 1878), has been revived especially by two scholars: T. L. Thompson, *The Historicity of the Patriarchal Narratives* [191] and J. Van Seters, *Abraham in History and Tradition* [192]. For critical rejoinders, see *inter alia* K. A. Kitchen, *The Bible in Its World* [96], chap. 4; J. T. Luke, *Journal for the Study of the Old Testament* 4 (1977), 35–47; H. Cazelles, *Vetus Testamentum* 28 (1978), 241–255; Nahum Sarna, *Biblical Archaeology Review* 3 (1977), 5–9.

Secondly, the only source for our knowledge of the ancestors of Israel is the biblical story/history itself, written in a time far removed from the events described. It would be a great boon if archaeology could provide external sources of knowledge, but so far, as a leading historian of Israel says, "it is impossible to relate any person or event in Gen. chs. 12–50 to any person or event otherwise known, thereby establishing a synchronism."[15] However, pause for a moment to reflect. We really should not expect archaeology to prove that the biblical story is true just as written. Archaeology aims to be a scientific discipline, and as such it is not in the service of any special interest. It brackets out all philosophical or theological perspectives and deals with the evidence presented on the field. Moreover, archaeology is still in its youth; up to this point it has provided only the most general and circumstantial information that bears upon the ancestral period.[16]

Despite these difficulties, however, it is likely that the narratives in Genesis reflect to some degree the life and times of Palestine in the early second millennium B.C.E., that is, the period which archaeologists designate as the Middle Bronze age, extending from the twentieth century to the sixteenth century (c. 2050–1550). The "history" of Abraham, Isaac, and Jacob found in Genesis 12–35 seems to preserve the memory of clan movements and social relationships which later were understood as a preparation for the decisive event of the Exodus and the formation of the people Israel.[17]

To consider the prologue to the Exodus, we must turn our attention to the area known as the Fertile Crescent. As the accompanying map shows, this title is applied to the fertile arc of land that skirts the Arabian desert, reaching from the Persian Gulf up through the alluvial plain of the Tigris and Euphrates Rivers, curving around through Syria and Palestine, and continuing toward the Nile in Egypt. As the cradle of ancient civilization, the Fertile Crescent had been a scene of human activity for centuries before the appearance of the first Hebrews.

The ancestral history begins in "Ur of the Chaldeans" in the southernmost part of Mesopotamia. To be sure, there is some textual uncertainty about this, for the Greek translation (Septuagint) of the third century B.C.E. speaks only of "the land of the Chaldeans" at Genesis 11:28. Some are inclined to follow this reading, for other biblical passages indicate that the ancestral home was located in Haran in northwest Mesopotamia. However, the original location at Ur is firmly fixed in the Hebrew Bible, not only in Genesis 11:31 (credited to Priestly tradition) but also in 11:18 and 15:7 (Old Epic tradition). So it is best to follow the more difficult reading given in the Hebrew text—difficult because it has Terah, the father of Abra(ha)m, move his family from Ur near the Persian Gulf

---

[15] John Bright, *History* [91], 83.

[16] On the task and limitations of archaeology, see William G. Dever, in *Israelite and Judean History* [93], pp. 71–79; previously, R. de Vaux, "On the Right and Wrong Uses of Archaeology," *Near Eastern Archaeology* [108] 64–80; G. E. Wright, "What Archaeology Can and Cannot Do," *Biblical Archaeologist* 34 (1971), 70–76.

[17] Leading historians who advocate this position are Roland de Vaux [92] and John Bright [91].

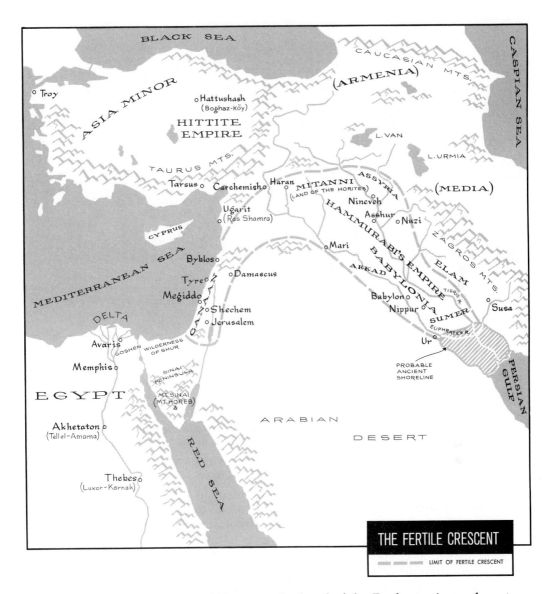

THE FERTILE CRESCENT

▬▬▬ ▬▬▬ ▬▬▬ LIMIT OF FERTILE CRESCENT

all the way to the city of Haran on the bend of the Euphrates in northwestern Mesopotamia, some 600 miles away.[18] From there, Abraham migrated into Canaan (the earlier name of Palestine). Stopping first at Shechem (Gen. 12:9), a great Canaanite commercial center, he moved down through the central hill country and eventually settled in southern Canaan, near Hebron. Abraham was succeeded by his son Isaac, and Isaac by his son Jacob, whose twelve sons carried the names of the twelve tribes of Israel.

[18] See de Vaux, *History* [92], pp. 187–191.

The Royal Standard of Ur, *a brightly colored mosaic panel found during excavation of the royal cemetery of Ur. This side of the panel portrays a victory celebration. In the top row the king (larger figure), surrounded by attendants, sits facing six distinguished guests, possibly military commanders, who join in the feasting with upraised cups. To the right stands a lyrist and a black-haired woman, apparently a singer. The middle and lower rows show food, animals, and other spoils of war being brought to the king.*

These ancestors are described as living peacefully on the fringes of the native Canaanite population, although they maintained contact with relatives back in Haran and secured wives from that source rather than mixing freely with the Canaanites (Gen. 24 and 29). Their social organization was not that of a political government (a state or nation), but rather that of a clan or extended family with a chieftain at the head. In this family story various troubles developed, such as the quarrel between Isaac's twin sons, Jacob and Esau, and the rivalry between Jacob and his Aramean father-in-law, Laban. These troubles came to a climax in the dissension that broke out in the circle of Jacob's twelve sons. Jealous of Joseph, his brothers conspired to send him off to Egypt. There Joseph rose to the position of prime minister of Egypt, the most influential post next to that of Pharaoh himself. Then, in a time of famine, the family of Jacob migrated to Egypt, where they settled in the Delta area near Pharaoh's capital and received the bounty of Joseph's wise administration. The book of Exodus takes up the story at this point, stating that Hebrew fortunes changed when a new Egyptian king, who ''did not know Joseph,'' came to power.

POPULATION UNREST IN THE FERTILE CRESCENT

Considerable light has been thrown on Israel's ancestral period by the study of international developments in the Fertile Crescent that marked the transition from the Early Bronze to the Middle Bronze ages, to speak in archaeological

DEFINITION: "SEMITE"

The terms Semite and Semitic, used in previous paragraphs, need to be clarified. Today they are often used loosely to refer to the Jewish people, but this is an unwarranted reduction. In the modern world the Semitic family also includes peoples who live in Turkey, Lebanon, Syria, Iraq, Jordan, Israel, Arabia, and North Africa. Thus the term "Semite" is ethnic—certainly not racial. Originally it was used to refer to Shem, one of the three sons of Noah (Gen. 9:18). In the table of peoples found in Genesis 10, Noah's descendants are broadly classified according to language groups and geographical areas, the Japhethites belonging to a northern area (southern Europe, Asia Minor), the Shemites being situated in the center (Fertile Crescent and its fringes), and the Hamites being located to the south (northern Africa). Curiously, in this table the Canaanites are linked with Ham, even though they are Semitic.

In scholarly discussion today, the word Semitic is used more precisely to refer to ancient peoples who spoke related languages which are subdivided into general geographical groupings: East Semitic (Akkadian, that is Babylonian and Assyrian), Northwest Semitic (including Phoenician/Canaanite, Aramaic, Hebrew), and Southern Semitic (including Arabic and Ethiopic).

---

terms. Ur, Abraham's ancestral city at the southern end of the Euphrates River, has been excavated by archaeologists, and its remains bear eloquent witness to its ancient glory. Other archaeological discoveries, especially in northern Mesopotamia around Haran, have helped us to become better acquainted with the early ancestral period. Let us take a brief look at the situation in Mesopotamia as it may be seen by the "dawn's early light" of history. Particularly, we shall consider a number of peoples that were on the move: Amorites, Hurrians, 'Apiru, and Arameans.

The Coming of the Amorites

During the third millennium (3000–2000 B.C.E.) the alluvial plain of the Tigris and Euphrates was the scene of a struggle between two centers of power, Sumer in the south and Akkad in the north (see map on p. 29). For a good part of the time, the Sumerians were able to establish a brilliant civilization in Mesopotamia (c. 2850–2360), based on a loosely organized system of city-states. On the whole, this was a relatively prosperous and secure period when agriculture, urban life, industry, and the arts flourished.

Then in the twenty-fourth century this cultural treasure came under the control of a Semitic people known as the Akkadians. Their dynamic leader was Sargon I of Akkad, who has been called the first empire builder of history. The Akkadian empire lasted for almost two centuries (c. 2360–2180), reaching its zenith with the spectacular accomplishments of Sargon's grandson, Naram-Sin. It was in this period that the city of Ebla, a rival to Akkad located in northern Syria, rose to commercial and military power and finally was destroyed, apparently by Naram-Sin. Interestingly, excavations at the site of this ancient city have uncovered a cache of some 15,000 tablets which, reportedly, include stories

The Victory Stele of Naram-Sin *(twenty-third century* B.C.E.*), the grandson of Sargon I. With his soldiers, the Akkadian king triumphantly ascends a mountain whose peak almost touches the stars, while his victims, the mountain-dwelling Lullubians, fall beneath his feet or plunge headlong from the cliffs.*

of creation and flood, personal names known also in Israel's patriarchal traditions (e.g. Abram, Ishmael, Israel), and place names familiar in biblical tradition, for instance Nahur (cf. "the city of Nahor" in Gen. 11:24–26) and other names such as Hazor, Megiddo, Jerusalem, Lachish, Gaza. The Ebla evidence is too

Some of the Approximately 15,000 Tablets Belonging to Ebla's Archives, discovered by Italian archaeologists at Tel Mardikh in 1975. The business documents were apparently stored on shelves above, which crumbled away. The tablets, however, were found in place, still lined up in rows, as they had been arranged on the shelves.

early to throw direct light on the ancestral period, but it helps us to understand its linguistic and cultural background.[19]

Let us return to our story. Once again the political pendulum swung, owing to a barbarian invasion from the Zagros mountains that brought an end to Akkadian rule. The Sumerians returned to power at the end of the millennium under the so-called Third Dynasty of Ur (c. 2060–1950 B.C.E.). Ur-nammu, the founder of the dynasty, made Ur a thriving commercial center and adorned the city with an impressive ziggurat, or tiered temple-tower, the remains of which can still be seen (see pictures, pp. 166–167). Even more significant was Ur-Nammu's promulgation of a code of law, the oldest one discovered to date, which

---

[19] The royal palace of Ebla and its library of documents was discovered in 1974–75, and the publication and interpretation of these materials will go on for some time. See the account by one of the Italian archaeologists, Paolo Matthiae, *Ebla: An Empire Rediscovered*, trans. Christopher Holme (Garden City, N.Y.: Doubleday, 1980). For a brief introduction see, e.g., K. A. Kitchen, "Ebla—Queen of Ancient Syria," *The Bible in Its World* [96], chap. 3.

influenced subsequent jurisprudence in the ancient Near East.[20] But the Sumerian revival was brief. The Ur III regime was brought to an end in a devastating attack by Elamites, who stormed down from their mountainous homeland (modern Iran) into the coveted Mesopotamian plain. The next two centuries witnessed the struggle of various petty states to move into the power vacuum. In the south, the major contestants were the cities of Isin and Larsa; in the north the major center was first Asshur (Assyria) on the upper Tigris River, then Mari on the middle Euphrates, and later Babylon. By this time Ebla was out of the political picture.

In the period of confusion following the downfall of the Kingdom of Ur (Ur III) about 2000 B.C.E., a seminomadic horde of Semites flooded the country from the Arabian desert, the cradle of all Semitic peoples, including the earlier Akkadians. With amazing political energy, they overran all of Mesopotamia, establishing dynasties in practically every major city. Because their major center of power came to be in the northwest (Upper Mesopotamia and Syria), where they spoke dialects of Northwest Semitic, they were known as *Amurru* (Amorites), an Akkadian term meaning "Westerners."

For a time the city of Mari, near the border between modern Syria and Iraq, was the focal point of Amorite rule, but eventually the leadership shifted to the city of Babylon, where Amorites established the First Babylonian Dynasty, whose greatest king was Hammurabi (c. 1728–1686). By the middle of the eighteenth century B.C.E., these Westerners had extended their influence from Mesopotamia down through Syria and Palestine, where they came to be the dominant element of the Canaanite population.

A vivid picture of the so-called "Mari Age" (c. 1750–1697), when Mari held the political ascendancy, was provided by the excavation of the site of that ancient city during the years immediately before and after World War II. Archaeologists uncovered the remains of a once-magnificent palace, consisting of about three hundred rooms and covering several acres. Of greatest interest to the reader of the Bible, however, was the discovery of about twenty-five thousand clay tablets on which business and administrative matters were written. Many of these documents represent diplomatic correspondence between the Amorite king of Mari, Zimri-Lim, and officials in surrounding states, some of them with king Hammurabi of Babylon.

Hammurabi conquered Mari in 1697 B.C.E. Hence the Mari documents, written in the preceding golden age of the city's existence, illuminate the cultural backgrounds of the early ancestral period. It is striking that they mention biblical names like Ishmael and possibly Levi, that Benjamin appears as the name of a warlike band of tribes, and that Peleg, Serug, and Nahor—names in Abraham's genealogy (Gen. 11:10–16)—are given as the names of towns in the neigh-

---

[20] See James B. Pritchard, ed., *Ancient Near Eastern Texts: Relating to the Old Testament*, 3rd ed. with supplement, pp. 523–525. Copyright © 1969 by Princeton University Press. Scattered quotes in this text are reprinted with the permission of Princeton University Press.

The Stele of Hammurabi *is a monolith nearly eight feet tall, inscribed with a code of laws. The relief at the top depicts Hammurabi, King of Babylon, standing before the sun god Shamash, who extends a rod and ring, symbols of royal authority to the worshiping king.*

borhood of Haran. Further, the phenomenon of prophecy, which loomed large in Israelite society, was known at Mari, a matter to which we shall return later (Chapter 8).

In the judgment of some historians, Abraham's migration into Canaan as portrayed in Genesis 12:1-6 was connected in some way with the Amorite infiltration into Mesopotomia and Syria.[21] In this view, Abraham lived during the eighteenth century B.C.E. and may have been a contemporary of the Amorite king, Hammurabi. Haran, Abraham's home town (if not his birthplace), was an Amorite settlement in this period. The Amorite personal names, such as Benjamin (*Binu-yamina*), Jacob (*Ya'qub-el*), and Abram (*Abamram*), may not refer to the biblical characters themselves, but they certainly point to a common Semitic

---

[21] The leading proponent of the Amorite hypothesis is Roland de Vaux; see his *History* [92], chap. 7. The view is also forcefully advocated by John Bright in his *History* [91], chap. 2 and is cautiously supported by William G. Dever. *Israelite and Judean History* [93], pp. 70–120.

background.[22] Earlier we noticed that the common Semitic background of personal and town names can be traced back to Ebla, which flourished in the Sumerian period.

It is possible that the ancestors of Israel brought with them from their Amorite homeland some of the traditions that were later transformed and incorporated into the religious epic now found in the biblical primeval history (Gen. 1–11): stories of the Creation, the Garden of Eden, the Flood, and the Tower of Babel. From the time of the First Dynasty of Babylonia comes the creation story known as *Enuma elish*, as well as the flood story preserved in the Gilgamesh Epic.[23] Both stories show formal similarities to the biblical accounts, although—as we shall see later (Chapter 7)—there is a world of difference between them. Furthermore, the prototype of the biblical "Tower of Babel" (Gen. 11:1–9) is the ziggurat, or tiered temple-tower of the city of Babylon, one of the famed wonders of the age of Hammurabi (compare the Ur ziggurat, pp. 166–167). This tower was known as Etemenanki, "The House of the Terrace-platform of Heaven and Earth."

Finally, the Hebrews may have come to know Mesopotamian law in their Amorite homeland, although it is more likely that they were later influenced by the famous Code of Hammurabi through the Canaanites among whom they settled. A copy of the code can be seen today in the Louvre Museum, inscribed on a huge black stele beneath a relief of Hammurabi, who is portrayed standing before Shamash, the sun god, who controlled cosmic order and justice. This code, which incorporated elements from previous codes (including that of Ur-Nammu), attempted to improve and standardize the administration of justice. One of the most brilliant achievements of the empire created by Hammurabi, it set the basic pattern of jurisprudence for centuries to come. As we shall see, Israelite law, known as the Covenant Code, has been influenced by it both in style and, to some degree, in content (Chapter 3).

The Hurrian Movement

Into the political vacuum caused by the downfall of the Sumerian dynasty of Ur came another wave of population known as Hurrians, a name possibly related to the Horites, or even the Hivites, of the Old Testament. Even before the turn of the second millennium, this non-Semitic people started to push down from the Caucasian mountains of Armenia into the plain of the Tigris and Euphrates. Unlike the Amorites, they came not as military conquerors, but in a steady, ever-increasing stream of infiltration. At first they settled in northern Mesopotamia, around Mari and Haran, but by the time of Hammurabi they had

---

[22] The Amorite background of Abraham is stressed by E. A. Speiser in his Genesis commentary [273], pp. xxxvii–lii.

[23] See J. B. Pritchard, *Ancient Near Eastern Texts* [1], pp. 60–99 and 501–507.

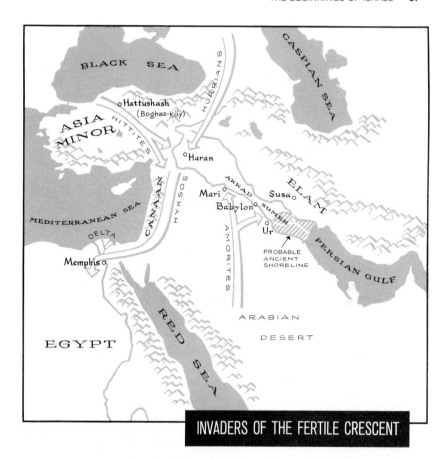

BLACK SEA

CASPIAN SEA

HURRIANS

ASIA MINOR

HITTITES

oHattushash
(Boghaz-köy)

oHaran

ELAM

AKKAD

Mari o   Susa o

Babylon o   SUMER

MEDITERRANEAN SEA

CANAAN

SOSKYII

AMORITES

DELTA

o Ur

Memphis o

PROBABLE
ANCIENT
SHORELINE

PERSIAN GULF

EGYPT

RED SEA

ARABIAN

DESERT

INVADERS OF THE FERTILE CRESCENT

spread through the entire country. By the fifteenth century their political power
had become so great that they constituted the majority of the population in a
new state in Upper Mesopotamia known as Mitanni. Adept in the use of new
instruments of war, such as the composite bow, they frequently came into conflict with Egyptian armies who at the time advanced on numerous occasions
into Canaan, Syria, and Upper Mesopotamia. Indeed, Hurrians migrated into
Canaan in such numbers that Egyptians, from the time of the Eighteenth Dynasty, referred to the area as Hurru (Hurrian) land. Almost nothing was known
of the Hurrians before 1919 C.E., when thousands of clay tablets dating from the
time of the Mitannian kingdom (c. 1500–1370 B.C.E.) were discovered at the Hurrian city of Nuzi, located some distance east of the Tigris River.[24]

[24] See F. W. Bush, "Hurrians," in *Supplement to the Interpreter's Dictionary* [26], pp. 423–424
and the literature cited there. On the reevaluation of alleged parallels between social customs and
family law of Nuzi and the period of Israel's ancestors, see the useful summary by George Ramsey,
The Quest [99], chap. 2, especially 29–33.

The Hittites

Even before the rise of the Hurrian kingdom of Mitanni, another political power encroached upon the Fertile Crescent. Beyond the western mountains, in the region of present-day Turkey, a people known as Hittites established a vigorous nation.[25] From time to time they ventured from their mountain-locked homeland in Anatolia or Asia Minor to expand into Mesopotamia, Syria, and Palestine, and eventually they vied with Egypt for the control of the Fertile Crescent. In the heart of their rugged land, atop an impressive height, they built their lofty capital of Hattushash, and not far away they carved upon the walls of a rock-sanctuary scenes of their major deities and of lesser gods marching in procession (see pictures, p. 99). Not too long ago the Hittites were little more than a name. But the excavation in 1907 of the Hittite capital, now called Boghazköy, has uncovered evidence of the former glory of the Hittite empire, manifest

A God Embracing a Hittite King, a sculpture in rock at the sanctuary of Yazilikaya, near the ancient Hittite capital. The god, wearing a pointed cap and shoes with upturned toes, holds his left arm protectively around the king, who wears a long robe and holds a curved staff. Above the king's head is a cartouche giving his name as Tudhaliyas (thirteenth century B.C.E.).

[25] Although the Hittite state was formed in the seventeenth century B.C.E., the real expansion came later. The first Hittite empire was created in the sixteenth century (1600–1500). Hittite power was temporarily eclipsed by the rise of the state of Mitanni (1500–1370). See O. R. Gurney, *The Hittites* [1961].

not only in massive fortifications and impressive structures, but also in a whole library of literature, including a code of laws and treaties with other peoples. The biblical tradition that Abraham purchased his burial cave from some Hittites (Gen. 23) suggests that their influence extended south as far as Canaan.

The 'Apiru

We see, then, that the ancestral period was a time of unrest, when many peoples were mingling together in the Fertile Crescent. Canaan was, indeed, "the land of the Canaanites, the Hittites, the Amorites, the Perizzites, the Hivites, and the Jebusites" (Exod. 3:17).

Particularly interesting are the numerous references in the documents of the second millennium to 'Apiru or Habiru, a comparatively inconspicuous people scattered through Asia Minor, Mesopotamia, Syria, Canaan, and Egypt.[26] The term does not refer primarily to a racial or ethnic group, although apparently many Semites were involved. Rather, it refers to a social stratum of people who lacked citizenship in the established nations of the Near East. The 'Apiru were "wanderers" or "outsiders" who lived a rootless existence on the fringes of society. Like modern gypsies or migrant workers, many of them moved from place to place with their families and possessions. Sometimes they formed themselves into guerilla bands, attacking caravans or making nuisance raids on villages. Sometimes they hired themselves out as mercenary soldiers or were forced into slave labor on public projects. It was not unheard of for one of them to rise to a position of leadership in an established nation.

There seems to be some connection—though this is a hotly debated matter—between the word *'Apiru* and the biblical word "Hebrew" (*'ibri*), a term found almost exclusively in biblical materials dealing with the period before David. Whatever the connection, there is general agreement that the mention of *'Apiru* in Mesopotamian and Egyptian texts of the second millennium does not refer specifically to those Hebrews who were relatives of Abraham and who eventually understood themselves to be "Israelites" (*Benê Yisrael*).[27] Rather, the biblical Hebrews belonged to the larger floating class of rootless people to whom more established groups applied the descriptive term 'Apiru.

This picture agrees with the description of Abraham, the traditional ancestor of those Hebrews who became Israelites (Gen. 14:13). He is regarded as a "sojourner" (*ger*) in the midst of the established peoples of Canaan. With his family and his flocks, he moved through the sparsely settled hill country of Canaan, wandering from place to place to find seasonal pasture, until eventually

---

[26] A fundamental study of this question is that of Moshe Greenberg. *The Hab/piru* [185]. For a more recent discussion see R. de Vaux, *History* [92] pp. 105–112, 209–216.

[27] Although the ancestry of Abraham is traced to *'Eber* (Gen. 10:21–24), which is linguistically equivalent to Habiru/'Apiru, the word "Hebrew" usually occurs in early traditions where foreigners speak of Israelites or Israelites identify themselves to foreigners. The term is not an apt expression of Israelite self-understanding.

he pitched his tent at Mamre, near the place where Hebron was later established. The same picture is given of his son and grandson, Isaac and Jacob. Like true 'Apiru, the patriarchs tended to shun the settled life of cities and, with few exceptions (e.g., 33:10; 26:12), did not sink their roots long enough in one place to own land or to farm the soil. Indeed, so shallow were the roots of these Hebrews in Canaan that, during a time of great famine, Jacob migrated with his family into Egypt. Their mode of life must have been quite similar to that of seminomads portrayed on the wall of the tomb of Beni-Hasan in Egypt (see picture, pp. 174–175). The impressive painting, which dates back to a time before Abraham (nineteenth century B.C.E.), shows a family entering Egypt on foot, clad in garments of many colors, with their children and goods carried on donkeys.

The Appearance of the Arameans

There is still one more people who should be mentioned, though admittedly their appearance in Israel's ancestral history is a bit puzzling. As we read the biblical story, we hear again and again about the land of Aram (modern Syria) and the people of Aram, the Arameans. We read that Abraham sent his servant to the ancestral home, located in Aram Naharaim ("Aram of the Two Rivers"), or Mesopotamia (Gen. 24:10). Elsewhere, especially in the Jacob cycle, we hear about Paddan Aram ("The Plain of Aram"), the country to which Isaac sent his son Jacob to find a wife (Gen. 28:2. 5–7). Laban, Jacob's father-in-law, is repeatedly called "the Aramean" (e.g., Gen. 25:20, 28:5). The difficulty is, however, that Aram did not appear on the political scene until the twelfth century B.C.E., the time when the people of Israel, after the Exodus from Egypt, were settling in the land of Canaan. It seems that the ancestral history embraces two widely separated movements: the Amorite infiltration that occurred in the wake of the downfall of the Ur regime (c. 2000), and the appearance of the Arameans following the collapse of the Hittite and Egyptian empires (c. 1200). How are we to understand the relation between the "Amorite" Abraham and the "Aramean" Jacob?

Some scholars cut the Gordion knot by saying that the whole ancestral tradition is late and has historical value only for the time when it was composed. The link between Israel's ancestors and the Arameans, it is argued, is much stronger than the link with the Amorites; hence, the tradition in Genesis has to be removed from the Middle Bronze period to the Early Iron age, which began about 1200 B.C.E. This extreme view would place the ancestors of Israel after the time of Moses (early thirteenth century, as we shall see presently).[28]

---

[28] So Siegfried Hermann, *History* [94], pp. 41–55, who maintains that the table of peoples in Genesis 10 supports this conclusion, and W. Malcolm Clark in *Israelite and Judean History* [93], pp. 142–148. Others go to greater extremes, dating the composition of the story in the time of the monarchy, as does T. L. Thompson [191] or later in the case of J. van Seters [192].

If the ancestral period is in any sense a historical prologue to the Exodus, this view is obviously unsatisfactory. A constructive solution to the Aramean problem may be reached by keeping two things in mind. First, in the patriarchal history the narrator refers to the ancestral period by using later terminology, just as today we usually speak of the ancient setting of the Fertile Crescent as the "Near East" or the "Middle East," language which presupposes a modern vantage point. Some historians argue forcefully that the "Arameans" referred to are a later phase of an early Amorite ("proto-Aramean") stock, referred to in various extra-biblical texts, and that hence "there was a continuity between the Amorites of the patriarchal age and the Arameans of the eleventh and tenth century B.C."[29] After all, the incursion of the Amorites into the Fertile Crescent was not a one-shot affair but a complex rhythm of migrations, wave upon wave, over a long period of time. The biblical narrator's portrayal of a back-and-forth movement from Haran to Canaan, for the purpose of keeping in touch with Mesopotamian relatives, apparently reflects the ethnic continuity from Amorites to Arameans. Quite properly, then, Israelites remembered Jacob as "a wandering Aramean" in their confession of faith (Deut, 26:5).

This discussion points up another important matter. The story of the ancestors of Israel was related from the vantage point of the time of the Israelite tribal confederacy (c. 1200–1000 B.C.E.), when Aram and the other peoples referred to were political powers (e.g. Moab and Ammon in the Abraham/Lot narrative, and Edom in the Jacob/Esau story). Thus the story of the ancestors was contemporized by being told and retold as "the story of our life." Accordingly, we shall return to the story of Israel's ancestors later when we consider the formation of the Israelite epic during the period of the tribal confederacy, the two centuries before David (Chapter 5).

THE GOD OF ISRAEL'S ANCESTORS

So far we have seen that there is reason to believe that the story of Israel's ancestors found in Genesis 12–50, although understood in the light of later experiences, reflects in some degree the cultural background of the second millennium B.C.E., roughly the centuries after Hammurabi sketched above. Several kinds of evidence make this conclusion credible. First, in this period parents gave their children names also found in Israel's ancestral tradition, such as Abraham (found in Ebla documents and Mari archives) or Benjamin and Jacob, which also occur in extra-biblical texts. Second, the social customs and legal usages found in Israel's ancestral tradition are much more in harmony with Mesopotamian practice during the second millennium than with Israel's social

---

[29] Roland de Vaux adduces texts to show that Arameans (or "Ahlamu") were referred to in the fourteenth century B.C.E., and possibly earlier. See his *History* [92], pp. 200–209; quotation, p. 209.

life during the monarchy. For instance, Mesopotamian law codes specified the rights of inheritance for children born to a man who had more than one wife (compare the situation of Jacob in relation to his two wives, Leah and Rachel, as well as the handmaids, Bilhah and Zilpah); and ancient jurisprudence under certain circumstances protected the inheritance rights of a child born to a "slave wife" (which perhaps helps us to understand Abraham's reluctance to cast away his son Ishmael born to Hagar (Gen. 21:10–11).[30] But there is also a third and more cogent kind of evidence. The religion of Israel's ancestors—the worship of "the God of the fathers"—authentically belongs to the period that preceded Moses. Of course, it is hard to tell exactly what the religion of Israel's ancestors was, because, as we have already seen, the traditions of Genesis have been revised in the light of the Exodus and the Sinai covenant. Still, many statements in the book of Genesis, when considered against the background of the culture of the Fertile Crescent, help us to understand the probable character of religious beliefs before Moses.

Let us jump ahead of where we are for just a moment. Joshua 24 describes a great assembly at Shechem at which Joshua summoned the people to renew their allegiance to the God whose power and purpose were manifested in the Exodus and the guidance into the land of Canaan. Specifically, the people were challenged to "put away the gods which your ancestors served beyond the River [Euphrates] and in Egypt" (Josh. 24:14b; see also verse 2). This passage indicates that Israel's ancestors had been under the influence of the religious views that prevailed throughout the Fertile Crescent, from Mesopotamia to Egypt. Accordingly, the Exodus was not just a flight from political oppression but was, so to speak, an "exodus" or departure from the religions of the ancient world or, to say the same thing differently, from the myths that expressed the relationship between the social order and the divine order of reality. Moses had led the people in this kind of exodus, even as Abraham earlier had followed a divine command to depart from Mesopotamian culture. And at Shechem the invitation was given to a later generation to join those who exit from the old and enter into the new.

Joshua's challenge to the people is illumined by studies in the field of the history of religions, especially works dealing with mythical symbolism.[31] These studies help us to understand that the issue was not simply "the service of other gods" (polytheism) versus the service of the one God revealed in the event of the Exodus, although this was clearly involved. Rather, the choice was between two different views of reality, one expressed in the myths of Mesopotamia, Canaan, and Egypt, and the other in the Israelite story or *mythos* which Joshua recited to the people (Josh. 24:2–13).

One of the main concerns of the mythology of ancient Mesopotamia was

---

[30] See K. A. Kitchen, *The Bible in Its World* [96], pp. 68–71, who judiciously places the evidence from Nuzi and Mari in a broader Mesopotamian context.

[31] See the bibliographical entries under "Ancient Religion" [120–127].

to provide assurance that human society is integrated into the divine order of the cosmos. The empire in its spatial organization was regarded as a reflection of the order of the cosmic sphere, where the supreme god presided over the heavenly council in a somewhat "democratic" fashion. Yet the heavenly order, like the earthly sphere, was threatened by the powers of chaos evidenced in violence, social change, and the cyclical recurrence of winter. Religion, however, provided the hope for salvation. For at the *omphalos* (navel or sacral center) on which the temple was founded—the place where heaven and earth meet and divine power flows into society—the social order was periodically renewed through the recitation of myth and the performance of a ritual drama. This happened especially during the New Year festival, when the king, serving as the representative of the victorious deity Marduk, reenacted the annual victory of the powers of creation over the powers of chaos.[32]

Egyptian culture also was based on the view that the divine order was reflected in the order of society. Pharaoh was regarded as the "image" or representative of the creator-God, through whom the divine *Maat* (order, justice, truth) was mediated to society. The Egyptian style of attunement of society with the divine order produced a static and stable civilization that survived without essential change, despite a succession of dynasties, for more than two thousand years. This view, in contrast to the more democratic view of the heavenly council in Mesopotamia, endowed Pharaoh with absolute authority.

Against this background, the phenomenon of Israel represented a distinct break in the culture of the ancient Near East. As one political philosopher says, in Israel there appeared "a new type of man on the world-political scene," typified by Moses and, before him, by Abraham.[33] Although we do not know all the factors involved in Abraham's decision to leave his country and kindred in Haran, his venture of faith, as described in Genesis 12:1–7, must have been prompted by a new religious vision which required a renunciation of the cults of Mesopotamia.

When the Hebrew wanderers left Mesopotamia, they brought with them their own religious beliefs and practices, including the worship of their chief God, Shaddai (Gen. 17:1; 23:3; 35:11, 43:14; 48:3), perhaps of Amorite origin. Because this divine name means "The Mountain One"—that is, the exalted deity who dwells on the cosmic mountain—it was natural for the religion of the ancestors to find points of contact with the worship of El, the supreme father-god of the Canaanite pantheon. In pre-Israelitic times, El was worshiped at particular sanctuaries in Canaan under compound epithets: El Bethel ("God of Bethel") at Luz (Gen. 31:12; 35:7; cf. 28:19); El Elyon ("God Most High") at

---

[32] It would be rewarding to make a comparison of the view presupposed in the Babylonian creation myth, *Enuma elish,* and that of the creation story found in Genesis 1:1–2:3. See B. W. Anderson, *Creation versus Chaos* [128], especially chap. 1, and *Creation in the Old Testament* [129], especially the essay by Hermann Gunkel, chap. 1.

[33] Eric Voegelin, *Israel and Revelation* [146], p. 22. Voegelin discusses Israel's "exodus from cosmological civilization" and the breakthrough into divine transcendence.

Jerusalem (Gen. 14:18–20); El Olam ("Everlasting God") at Beer-sheba (Gen. 21:33); El Roi ("God of Seeing") at a sacred place in the southern wilderness (Gen. 16:13). Because the ancestral religion had something in common with Canaanite religion, Israel's ancestors could identify their God with El in his various manifestations and thus could use the epithet El Shaddai.[34] But in spite of affinities with native religion, the worship of "the God of the fathers" also displayed some major differences which in the course of time became profoundly significant.

One of these distinctive traits seems to be implicit in the usage of the name Shaddai in the book of Genesis, where it is associated with a covenant relationship between God and the ancestors. In Genesis 15:7–21 a curious incident is described. Abraham cut some animals in two, placing half of the carcasses over against the other half. Then after the sun had set and an eerie darkness had fallen over the place, "a smoking fire pot and a flaming torch"—representing the presence of the deity—passed between the pieces. The account, though overlaid with later theological interpretation, preserves a very ancient ritual of covenant-making in which the deity makes a binding commitment, sealed by the power of a curse, to fulfill a promise. If we may appeal to the Mari texts which mention the sealing of treaties (covenants) by killing an ass (a practice that is echoed in Jer. 34:18–19), this strange narrative seems to mean that the covenant partner, by passing through the bloody corridor, submits to the curse of becoming like the divided animals if the covenant obligation is ever violated. In any case, the story points up one of the main characteristics of the religion of Israel's ancestors: the practice of entering into a personal relationship or "covenant" with the deity. So we are told that Abraham entered into relationship with the God known as the "Shield" of Abraham (Gen. 15:1), Isaac with "the Fear [possibly "the Kinsman"] of Isaac" (Gen. 31:42, 53), and Jacob with "the Mighty One of Jacob" (Gen. 49:24). In each case, the family God entered into a personal relationship with the patriarch and made demands and promises. Therefore the deity was designated by the name of the person who received the revelation: the God of Abraham, the God of Isaac, or the God of Jacob. In the early tradition, the deity was associated with a particular patriarch ("the god of your father"; Gen. 26:24; 28:13), though later the three family cults were combined into one, under the formula "the God of the fathers."[35]

Also, the religion of Israel's ancestors was characterized by a strong clan or family solidarity. Even the names borne by individuals suggest the close personal relationship between the clan and the deity who was regarded as "father," "brother," or patron of the "family." So, for instance, the name Ab-ram, which contains the element "father" (*'ab*) means "The (Divine) Father is exalted."

---

[34] See de Vaux, *Ancient Israel* [113], pp. 289–94, for discussion of the veneration of the supreme God, El, at the sanctuaries of Shechem, Bethel, Mamre, and Beer-sheba. See also essays 2 and 3 in Frank M. Cross, *Canaanite Myth and Hebrew Epic* [112], 13–75.

[35] See H. G. May, "The God of My Father—A Study in Patriarchal Religion," *Journal of Bible and Religion*, IX (1941), 155–58, 200.

Considering the vivid awareness of the deity's involvement with the patriarchal family, as reflected in names of this type, it is proper to say that "the God was the unseen head of the house; its members, the members of his family."[36]

Furthermore, this religion found expression in faith in the God who makes promises and guides into the future like a Shepherd who leads his flock (see the Shepherd's Psalm, Ps. 23). Jacob, for instance, prays to the God "before whom my fathers Abraham and Issac walked, the God who has led [Hebrew: "shepherded"] me all my life long to this day, the angel who has redeemed me from all evil" (Gen. 48:15–16). This "nomadic faith," as Martin Buber described it, has a different accent from that of the religions of sedentary peoples of the Fertile Crescent, in which the cult was bound to sacred places. In Canaan a sanctuary like the one at Bethel was regarded as the very "gate of heaven" (Gen. 28:17) where the deity became manifest in a special way. The book of Genesis portrays Israel's ancestors visiting these ancient Canaanite places (Shechem, Bethel, Beer-sheba); but these visits are included in the itinerary of their wandering from place to place. For "the God of the fathers" is not bound to a place. The guiding God uproots Abraham from his homeland and leads him into new places and along new paths, ever holding before him and his descendants the promises of land and posterity. And the same is true of Isaac and Jacob. In the traditions of Genesis, the ancestors are described as wanderers and adventurers who, in response to a divine summons, make a pilgrimage into the unknown and the uncertain—toward a land that their God would give them in due time. They venture forth in faith, trusting that their family life is in the hand of their mobile God, who leads them into the future, toward the realization of the divine promises.[37] As we have already noticed, the story of Abraham's migration from Mesopotamia, in response to God's call, is colored by later theological reflection. Yet, taking this into account, some dim apprehension of divine guidance of a people's historical pilgrimage must have provided the background of the account in the book of Exodus which relates that Moses, in the dark period of the oppression of Abraham's descendants in Egypt, was addressed by "the God of your fathers, the God of Abraham, the God of Isaac, and the God of Jacob" (Exod. 3:6, 15).

THE DESCENT INTO EGYPT

In the latter part of the book of Genesis, we find the story of Joseph's rise to power in Egypt and the friendly reception of the family of Jacob into the Delta area during a time of famine. Egyptian history during the second millennium

[36] John Bright, *History* [91], p. 99, gives illustrations of names compounded with "father" ('*ab*), "brother" ('*aḥ*), and "kindred people" ('*amm*). He points out that names of this type were frequent among the Amorite population.

[37] See Jürgen Moltmann, *Theology of Hope,* trans. James W. Leitch (New York: Harper & Row, 1967), chap. 2, where the difference between divine epiphany in a place and divine guidance toward the future is highlighted.

provided examples of Asiatics who were given government positions. In fact, in the fourteenth century, Pharaoh Akhnaton promoted a certain Semite named Tutu to a high position, which entitled him to act as the representative of the crown in certain areas, such as the inspection of public works. The murals on the walls of his tomb in El Amarna portray scenes that are reminiscent of the elevation of Joseph (Gen. 41:41–43). Pharaoh gave him a gold chain and caused him to ride in his chariot, while the people prostrated themselves before him and acclaimed him. In an inscription, Tutu says that he was "the superior voice in the whole country" and that, among his duties, he received foreign delegations and conveyed their words to the palace.[38] In the light of this, there is nothing particularly incredible in the story of Joseph's elevation to political leadership and the reception of the family of Jacob into Egypt.

Admittedly, the biblical story about Jacob and Joseph contains elements of folklore, such as the motif of the false accusation of adultery with Potiphar's wife after Joseph had in reality rejected her sexual advances—a motif found also in the Egyptian "Story of Two Brothers" (c. 1225).[39] Although dependent upon oral tradition, the Joseph story seems to have been given its present form in the period of Solomon, when relations with Egypt were close, a fact that helps to account for the Egyptian color of the narrative, including the mention of Egyptian names, titles, dream interpretation, embalming, and so forth. When taken by itself, the story is a great piece of literature, whose creative artistry captures the interest of modern novelists like Thomas Mann; and when read in its present context, where it serves as a transition from the ancestral period to the Mosaic age, it is governed by an overarching theological purpose (see Chapter 5). Nevertheless, the Joseph story is not pure fiction; it is a historical novel which belongs within the setting of the second millennium B.C.E..

The Hyksos Invasion

Earlier, we considered two great waves—the Amorite invasion and the Hurrian movement—which surged into the Fertile Crescent shortly after the turn of the second millennium B.C.E. In the wake of these and other political disturbances came another tidal wave, known as the Hyksos movement, which swept down through Syria and Palestine into Egypt. The Hyksos—or "rulers of foreign countries," as the Egyptian word means—were a motley array of peoples. Many of them seem to have been Semites, but some were Hittites and Hurrians. Unlike the earlier Hurrian movement from the Caucasian highlands, this wave of Asiatics was bent on conquest. Specializing in a swift and powerful military weapon, the horse-drawn chariot, they invaded Egypt at a time of political weakness and overthrew the native rulers. The date of their invasion of Egypt is placed at

---

[38] Cited by de Vaux, *History* [92], p. 284; the murals are reproduced and discussed by N. de G. Davies, *The Rock Tombs of El Amarna*, VI (London; 1908), 7–15, 27; plates xi–xx.

[39] See J. B. Pritchard, *Ancient Near Eastern Texts* [1], pp. 23–25.

about 1720 B.C.E. The Egyptian historian Manetho (about 275 B.C.E.) recalled with horror the Hyksos invasion in the reign of Tutimaeus, probably a ruler of the Thirteenth Dynasty:

> In his reign, for what cause I know not, a blast of God smote us; and unexpectedly, from the regions of the East, invaders of obscure race marched in confidence of victory against our land. By main force they easily seized it without striking a blow; and having overpowered the rulers of the land, they then burned our cities ruthlessly, razed to the ground the temples of the gods, and treated all the natives with a cruel hostility.[40]

Manetho also reports that one of the Hyksos was made king in Memphis and that he rebuilt the powerful stronghold of Avaris (Tanis) in the Delta area.

During the seventeenth century, the Hyksos dominated Egypt. The rulers of the Fifteenth and Sixteenth Dynasties, who were all Hyksos, established a powerful empire that included Palestine and Syria. Excavations have shown that during this period Shechem was a Hyksos fortress, equipped with the characteristic ramparts which the Hyksos introduced to protect a city from attack by horse-drawn chariots.[41] Shortly after 1600, however, an Egyptian revolution broke out. At about 1550 B.C.E., Ahmose I, the founder of the brilliant Eighteenth Dynasty, overthrew the hated foreign regime. The city of Avaris was captured, the routed Hyksos were pursued into Palestine, and cities like Shechem were overthrown. Thus began an Egyptian revival which, especially under the Napoleon-like Pharaoh Thutmose III (c. 1490–1436), resulted in the extension of Egypt's sway throughout Palestine and Syria.

The account of the Hebrew descent into Egypt accords well with circumstances in Egypt. It is quite credible that the pressure of famine forced Jacob's family to settle in "the land of Goshen," the fertile area in the eastern part of the Nile Delta. Seminomads in Palestine, a land that depended on seasonal rainfall, would naturally turn their eyes in time of drought toward Egypt, where the periodic overflow of the Nile irrigated the land. We know from Egyptian records that it was the practice of Egyptian officials to allow hunger-stricken people from Palestine and the Sinaitic peninsula to enter the Delta frontier. One Egyptian frontier official in about 1350 B.C.E., sent word to Pharaoh that some nomads "who knew not how they should live, have come begging a home in the domain of Pharaoh . . . after the manner of your father's fathers since the beginning."[42]

It is tempting to connect the Hyksos movement into Egypt with the biblical story of the descent of Jacob and his family into Egypt. One small but significant detail prompts some scholars to entertain this possibility. According to the biblical narratives, the Hebrew settlement in the Goshen area or the Wadi Tumilat

---

[40] *Manetho,* trans. Helen Waddell, pp. 79–81; see Josephus, *Against Apion,* I, 14 (75–76).

[41] Consult G. Ernest Wright, *Shechem* [251], chap. 5.

[42] See *The Westminster Historical Atlas* [34], 29; also J. B. Pritchard, *The Ancient Near East in Pictures* [2], pp. 14–20.

(called "the land of Rameses" in Gen. 47:11) was near Pharaoh's court (Gen. 45:10; 46:28 ff.). Before the Hyksos period the Egyptian capital had been at Thebes, but the Hyksos built their capital, Avaris, in the Delta or Goshen area. When Ahmose expelled the Hyksos, Avaris was destroyed and the capital was moved back to Thebes. Thus the location of Pharaoh's capital, as presupposed by the Joseph story, suggests that the Hebrew settlement in Egypt took place during the Hyksos period. It takes little imagination to go beyond this and suppose that the pharaoh who favored Joseph was one of the Hyksos kings, perhaps a Semite like himself and therefore hospitable to other Semites. The only trouble is that there is no clear evidence to support the view, attractive and plausible though it may be.[43] Neither in the Joseph story nor in the early chapters of Exodus is any monarch explicitly named; and, though our historical knowledge of the Hyksos regime in Egypt is poor, nothing known in Egyptian records now available suggests the figure of Joseph as prime minister under Pharaoh. Because the biblical account depicts a peaceful migration into Egypt, the Hebrew settlement in the Delta area could not have been a part of the Hyksos movement, for the Hyksos came as conquerors. But there may have been some connection between the two events. The patriarchal migration may well have occurred on the fringe of the Hyksos population movement. The ancestors of Israel may have entered Egypt in several migrations, beginning with the early period of Hyksos domination. Undoubtedly the biblical tradition, for the sake of presenting a vivid, straightforward story, has telescoped events that took place over a long period of time, and has simplified issues that were actually very complex.

THE OPPRESSION IN EGYPT

Now we are ready to return to the first chapter of the book of Exodus. There we are told that after Joseph's death the family of Jacob lost favor in Egypt, owing to a change of administration. "Now there arose a new king over Egypt, who did not know Joseph" (Exod. 1:8). As a result, the Hebrews were reduced to the status of state slaves and were put to work building the store cities of Pithom and Rameses in the Delta.

[43] This view is defended by G. Ernest Wright in *Biblical Archaeology* [110], pp. 54–58. There are, of course, other possibilities for reconstructing the historical background of the patriarchs. Some historians, such as C. H. Gordon in *Introduction to Old Testament Times* (Ventnor, N.J.: Ventnor Publishers, 1953), pp. 75, 102–4, place the ancestors in the period after the expulsion of the Hyksos (i.e., after 1500 B.C.E.), specifically during the disturbances of the Amarna Age (see pp. 126–128) and the establishment of such small states as Aram, Edom, Moab, and Ammon. This would account for the absence of reference to the Egyptian domination of Canaan in the book of Genesis; but the view hardly does justice to the Amorite connections of Abraham. Other historians modify this view by connecting Abraham with the period of Hammurabi and associating Jacob with the Amarna period of the fifteenth-fourteenth centuries. So, for instance, H. H. Rowley, *From Joseph to Joshua* [190], chap. 3, who specifically connects Joseph with the time of the Amarna king Akhnaton (1364–1347 B.C.E.). But, as Rowley admits, this requires a radical separation of Abraham (and Isaac) from Jacob and Joseph. For an updated discussion, see George Ramsey, *The Quest* [99], chap. 3.

The Pharaoh of the Oppression

Unfortunately, the biblical account does not identify the pharaoh who introduced the change of political policy that resulted in the oppression of Semites in the Delta region. Some historians believe that the account at the beginning of the book of Exodus points back to the beginning of the Eighteenth Dynasty,

Rameses II was Pharaoh of the Exodus. This granite statue shows him wearing the distinctive royal helmet and holding the symbolic scepter. The small figure at his side is his wife. (See also the colossal statues of Rameses, Color Plate 2.)

when Ahmose I expelled the Hyksos and, as a symbol of his new nationalism, moved his capital to the city of Thebes, where it had been before the Hyksos took over. According to this view, not all the Semites were driven out when the ruling class was expelled. Many Semites—and particularly the relatives of Jacob—survived Ahmose's purge and remained in the Delta. There they fell victim to the oppressive policies that accompanied the Egyptian revival during the Eighteenth and Nineteenth Dynasties. During this period—the fifteenth through the thirteenth centuries—the pharaohs needed cheap labor for their ambitious projects. According to Egyptian documents, they conscripted the service of 'Apiru (Habiru)—a term which, as we have seen, is not necessarily limited to the particular Hebrews with whom we are concerned. The difficulty with this view is that it necessitates quite a gap of time between Exodus 1:8 (Ahmose, the "king who did not know Joseph") and the narrative beginning in Exodus 1:9 which tells about slave labor at Pithom and Rameses, fortified cities that were rebuilt around the turn of the thirteenth century, as we shall see presently. This view has some slim support from the statement in Exodus 12:40 that "the time that the people of Israel dwelt in Egypt was four hundred and thirty years." If this statement refers to the total time the Hebrews lived on the Delta area and not just to the years of oppression,[44] and if the date of the Exodus is reckoned to be about 1290 B.C.E., it brings us back to approximately the time of the Hyksos invasion (1290 + 430 = 1720 B.C.E.). The situation of Egypt may have been something like this:

Period of favor: c. 1720–1552	HYKSOS RULE *XV to XVI [XVII]* *Dynasties*	Capital at Avaris
Period of disfavor: c. 1552–1306	EGYPTIAN REVIVAL *XVIII Dynasty*	Capital moved to Thebes

Period of the Exodus:
  Seti I (c. 1305–1290)
  Rameses II (c. 1290–1224)
  (Pharaoh of the Exodus)
	EGYPTIAN REVIVAL
	XIX Dynasty
		Capital at
		Avaris

Period of the Conquest: Merneptah (c. 1224–1211)		

Since all of this is quite uncertain, it is understandable that historians at present are reserved about associating the descent of the family of Jacob into

---

[44] However, Exodus 12:40 can be interpreted to refer only to the years of oppression, as in Genesis 15:13. The Greek version of the Old Testament (Septuagint) complicates the matter by saying, in Exodus 12:40, that the Israelites lived in Egypt *and in the land of Canaan* 430 years. In other words, the figure covers the whole period from the call of Abraham to the Exodus (see also Gal. 3:17). None of these figures can be taken with mathematical exactness, but must be weighed against archaeological and biblical evidence. On the figure given in I Kings 6:1, see G. E. Wright, *Biblical Archaeology* [110], pp. 83–84.

Egypt with the Hyksos invasion and therefore seeing in Ahmose I the new king who was unfavorable to Joseph. The situation becomes much clearer, however, when we come to the period of the Nineteenth Dynasty, which began toward the end of the fourteenth century B.C.E. The account at the beginning of the book of Exodus seems to presuppose this period when, once again, the Egyptian court was moved from Thebes to the Delta frontier in order that the pharaohs might be in a better position to regain their Asiatic empire which had slipped out of control during the so-called Amarna period (see pp. 126–128). Seti I (c. 1305–1290), the first strong king of the Nineteenth Dynasty, began the reconstruction of the old Hyksos capital, Avaris. The project was continued by his son Rameses II (c. 1290–1224), who renamed the capital Pi-Rameses, the "House of Rameses." Also, building work was carried on at Pr-Itm (Pithom), west of Lake Timsah in the very region where Joseph's brothers had settled.[45] These cities are specifically mentioned in Exodus 1:11, where we are told that Hebrew slaves were employed in their construction. Furthermore, according to Egyptian documents, these pharaohs used 'Apiru in public projects.

In short, despite the problem of relating Joseph to a particular pharaoh, the background of the opening chapters of Exodus seems to be the situation in Egypt under the Nineteenth Dynasty, specifically under the oppressive regimes of Seti I and Rameses II. Although it is impossible to pinpoint a definite date, many scholars believe that the Exodus took place early in the reign of Rameses II, whose mummy is on display at the Cairo Museum—that is, c. 1280 B.C.E. or shortly afterward.[46] The next pharaoh, Merneptah (c. 1224–1211), bragged about victory over Israel in Canaan about 1220, and this report indicates that at that time the people were already present, though not settled, in the land (see pp. 130–131).

From all that has been said, it is clear that the biblical narratives reflect the sober realities of the political situation. But these realities were interpreted through the eyes of Israelite faith. Many other peoples, and many other 'Apiru, were involved in the disturbed political situation of the Fertile Crescent during the latter half of the second millennium. But only the Hebrews who stood in the circle of Moses experienced the depth of historical meaning that led to the remembering and eventually the writing down of these historical traditions. Historical investigation can help us to understand that the biblical story was intimately tied up with the political and social developments of the time. But it takes religious imagination to go beyond the externals to the inner meaning of the events that Israel proclaimed in the exalted language of worship. In the last

[45] According to K. A. Kitchen, *The Bible in Its World* [96], pp. 76–77, this site is located not at Tanis, as some have thought, but at Tell el-Dab'a. For geographical and topographical evidence for this identification, he refers to M. Bietak, *Tell el-Dab'a II* (1975).

[46] This is the position of the American scholar, W. F. Albright, which has gained wide acceptance. See his historical summary, *The Biblical Period* [90] pp. 6–13. John J. Bimson, *Redating the Exodus and Conquest* (JSOT Supplement Series 2, 1978) attempts, without success, to revive the older theory of a fifteenth-century date.

analysis, the significance of the Exodus is determined not by its date but by its place in the unfolding of the divine purpose in human affairs. We must now turn attention directly to Moses and the drama of liberation in which he had a decisive role as leader and interpreter.

Chronological Chart 1

	B.C.E.	EGYPT	PALESTINE AND SYRIA	MESOPOTAMIA (AND ASIA MINOR)
(Middle Bronze Age)	2000 to 1900	XII Dynasty	Egyptian Control	Third Dynasty of Ur (c. 2060–1950) Hurrian Movement Amorite Invasion
	1900 to 1800	XII Dynasty		First Babylonian Dynasty (c. 1830–1530)
	1800 to 1700	Hyksos Invasion (c. 1720)	Abraham	The Mari Age Hammurabi (c. 1728–1686)
	1700 to 1600	Hyksos Rule (XV to XVI Dynasties) XVII (Theban) Dynasty	Hyksos Control Descent of Jacob family into Egypt	Decline of Babylonia
(Late Bronze Age)	1600 to 1500	XVIII Dynasty: Ahmose (c. 1552–1527) Expulsion of Hyksos	Egyptian Control	Old Hittite Empire (c. 1600–1500)
	1500 to 1400	Thutmose III (c. 1490–1436)		Kingdom of Mitanni (c. 1500–1370)
	1400 to 1300	Amenhotep III (c. 1403–1364) Amenhotep IV or Akhnaton (c. 1364–1347)	Amarna Age (c. 1400–1350) Egyptian Weakness	New Hittite Empire (c. 1375–1200) Rise of Assyria (c. 1356–1197)
	1300 to 1200	XIX Dynasty: Seti I (c. 1305–1290) Rameses II (c. 1290–1224) Merneptah (c. 1224–1211)	Egyptian Revival (The Exodus, c. 1280) Israelite Conquest (c. 1250–1200) Merneptah's Victory (c. 1220)	Assyrian Dominance

Note: The date of Hammurabi is still uncertain. Some scholars put him in the nineteenth century—that is, the early Amorite period. Others argue for a date in the seventeenth century—the period of Babylonian decline. The former suggestion would not affect our basic outline.

CHAPTER 2

Liberation from Bondage

In their fundamental confession of faith, the Israelite people affirmed that the God whom they worshiped "heard our voice, and saw our affliction, our toil, and our oppression" and, in a never-to-be-forgotten demonstration of grace, "brought us out of Egypt with a mighty hand and an outstretched arm, with great terror, with signs and wonders" (Deut. 26:5–9; see 6:21–25). Israel understood its history as originating in a marvelous liberation from distress and oppression. A dispirited band of slaves, bound together only by their common plight, would never have become a people—a covenant community with a sense of historical vocation—had God not acted on their behalf when they were helpless and hopeless. The verbs of the narrative sweep to a climax: God heard, God saw, God rescued.

In this chapter and the next one we turn our attention to the narratives of the book of Exodus which elaborate the theme of the Exodus and its sequel, the covenant at Sinai. Let us consider, first of all, the story that is recounted in Exodus 1–15. Before raising critical questions about this material, it would be well to read through the chapters as you would read a drama. For, despite inconsistencies and repetitions inherited from the stage of oral tradition and from the literary composition of the tradition in various circles, it is quite clear that these chapters in their present form constitute a dramatic unity. The major elements of the story are:

Biblical readings: The section of the biblical narrative treated in this chapter is Exodus 1–15.

1.   The oppression of Jacob's descendants in Egypt (chap. 1).
2.   The rise of Moses: his infancy, early life in Egypt and Midian, and his call and commission (chaps. 2:1–7:7).
3.   The contest with Pharaoh (chaps. 7:8–10:29), culminating in the final plague of the death of the first-born and the celebration of the Passover (Exod. 11:1–13:16).
4.   The flight from Egypt and the victory at the Sea (chaps. 13:17–14:31).
5.   A concluding hymn of triumph in two versions: The Song of the Sea (chaps. 15:1–18) and the Song of Miriam (chaps. 15:19–21).

Consider the plot of this drama. We have here a contest between two opposing powers: on the one side is "the God of the Hebrews" who is represented by Moses and his assistant, Aaron; on the other is stubborn Pharaoh with his crafty magicians and all the imperial power and glory of Egypt. Notice that Moses' God does not enter into conflict with the gods of Egypt (they are mentioned only in 12:12) but with Pharaoh, who presumptuously supposes that he is determining the issues of history. This is not the arrogance of an ordinary mortal, however, for according to Egyptian religion Pharaoh was the embodiment of deity, and therefore he was believed to possess superhuman wisdom and absolute power.[1] It was the time, you will remember, when Rameses II had shifted his political center to the Delta area in order to be in a better position to control Egypt's Asiatic empire, which had slipped out of control during the Amarna period. (See Chapter 1, pp. 49–52) The construction work at Pithom and Rameses, in which 'Apiru were employed as state slaves, was part of his grandiose political ambition.

The narrative is written from the presupposition that the God who speaks and works through Moses is fully in control, for the whole earth belongs to Yahweh (Exod. 9:29). Nevertheless, the story is told in such a way as to create dramatic suspense. At the outset the initial moves are made by Pharaoh, who acts to crush the spirit of the Hebrews by imposing hard labor upon them and, in an act of desperation and genocide, commands that all newborn male infants of the Hebrews be killed. Even at this point, however, the king's sovereignty is implicitly threatened, for by a strange turn of events the infant Moses—the future leader of the people—is rescued from the Nile by the Egyptian princess and is taken to the palace to be brought up right under Pharaoh's nose! Later on, this Moses, having been nurtured with Egyptian culture and empowered by a divine commission, challenges Pharaoh in the name of "the God of the fathers." In a series of episodes the narrator heightens the dramatic suspense. Each visit to Pharaoh accentuates the crisis; each plague increases the gravity of the situation in Egypt. Finally, Pharaoh's stubborn hold on the Hebrews is relaxed. In a moment of weakness, he permits them to leave, only to change his mind and send his warriors in hot pursuit. The denouement is reached when the

---

[1] Egyptian kings were regarded as the divine sons of the supreme god of Egypt, the sun-god Re or Amon. A typical letter to Pharaoh begins: "To my king, my lord, my sun-god" (see, for instance, Amarna Letter No. 288, in Pritchard, *Ancient Near Eastern Texts* [1], p. 488).

Israelites, trapped between the Egyptian forces and the watery expanse ahead of them, are marvelously delivered as the waters of the Sea close in upon their pursuers. Here is a story filled with powerful dramatic qualities that have stirred the imagination down through the centuries.

THE ROLE OF MOSES

The Exodus story is not a heroic epic told to celebrate the accomplishment of Moses as the liberator of his people. The narrator's major purpose is to glorify the God of Israel, the "Divine Warrior" whose strong hand and outstretched arm won the victory over formidable adversaries, Pharaoh and his hosts. Nevertheless, in this story Moses plays an essential role. It was through Moses, the political leader, that the people were brought out of the land of Egypt; and it was through Moses, the mediator between God and the people, that the meaning of the crisis and the miraculous deliverance from it was declared. While brooding over the fate of the people during his exile, Moses' understanding was illumined by an experience that took place in a lonely mountain spot in the Sinaitic wilderness. On the strength of this experience, he returned to Egypt, where he rallied his countrymen and announced the meaning of the events that were taking place. Let us turn, then, to the narratives dealing with Moses in Exodus 2–4.

Moses' Background

All that we know about Moses is contained in the biblical narratives. Even this knowledge is limited by the fact that the narrators were not interested in Moses' biography. Although the narrative portrays a historical figure of imposing stature, it focuses not so much on Moses' personality as on the God who prepares and summons him to be the agent in the accomplishment of the divine purpose.[2]

The tradition of Exodus 2 that Moses was brought up and trained in Egyptian circles is probably authentic, although it is colored with elements of folklore. The story of the baby in the basket of bulrushes (Exod. 2:1–10), for example, is reminiscent of a similar legend about Sargon of Akkad (c. 2300 B.C.E.), to whom we referred in the previous chapter (p. 31). In an inscription, Sargon says that his mother gave birth to him in secret, placed him in a basket of rushes sealed with bitumen, and cast the basket adrift on the river. Akki, the drawer of water, lifted him out of the water and reared him as his son. So from humble beginnings Sargon rose to be the mighty king of the city of Agade, from which the Akkadians took their name.[3] Moreover, the motif of the adoption of the infant

---

[2] In this connection Gerhard von Rad's little study, *Moses* [218], is illuminating.

[3] See Pritchard, *Ancient Near Eastern Texts* [1], p. 119.

Slaves Making Bricks *for Pharaoh are shown in a tomb painting from the period of the Eighteenth Dynasty. The clay is moistened by water drawn from the pool (left), kneaded with the aid of small hoes, and carried in baskets to the brickmakers, who shape it in rectangular moulds. After the bricks are laid out to dry in the sun (just right of the pool), they are carried away. Notice the two dark-skinned taskmasters who oversee the work. These scenes illumine the story of how the Hebrews made "bricks without straw" during their oppression in Egypt.*

Moses by Pharaoh's daughter (Exod. 1:7–10) is strikingly paralleled in an ancient Mesopotamian legal text, which stipulates that a foundling be turned over to a nurse who is to receive wages for suckling the child; then, after a three-year period of guardianship, he shall be adopted and shall receive an education as a scribe.[4] Clearly, the tradition of Moses' humble birth and his upbringing in Pharaoh's court has been influenced by various elements that appealed to popular imagination. Yet Moses' name is an authentic indication of his Egyptian nurture, which is after all one of the main points of the story. To be sure, the Israelite storyteller, by a play on words, tries to derive the name Moses (Hebrew: *Mosheh*) from a Hebrew verb meaning "to draw out" (*mashah*), and even says the Egyptian princess knew enough Hebrew to explain the name in this manner (2:10). But this is an example of the popular explanation of names on the basis of assonance, or the similarity of sound, as though we were to explain the name Abel by the English verb "to be able." Actually *Mosheh* is the Hebrew form of an Egyptian verb (*mose*) meaning "is born" and frequently appears in such theophorous (referring to a deity) names as Tuth-mose (i.e., "the god Toth is born"), Ptah-mose, or Ra-meses. Royal children born on the anniversary of a particular deity were named in this fashion; and sometimes pharaohs of the Nineteenth Dynasty were referred to in the shortened form *Mose*, without the name of the deity.[5] Other members of Moses' tribe, the tribe of Levi (Exod. 2:1), also had Egyptian names, for instance Merari and Phinehas (6:16, 25). Possibly the name Aaron is Egyptian too.

[4] See Brevard S. Childs, "The Birth of Moses," *Journal of Biblical Literature*, 84 (1965), 109–22; *The Book of Exodus* [210], on Exod. 2–4.

[5] See R. de Vaux, *History* [92], p. 329. D. M. Beegle, *Moses* [206], pp. 53–55.

Despite his nurture in Pharaoh's court, Moses continued to have a strong feeling of identification with his Hebrew kin, as is shown vividly by the story of his impulsive action on seeing an Egyptian taskmaster beating a Hebrew slave (Exod. 2:11–15). The rumor of his act of murder spread quickly and, fearing the

---

DEFINITION: "HEBREW"

Let us stop to think about the meaning of the word "Hebrew," which has been used several times in the above paragraphs. Today the term is often used to refer to the Jewish people or to their classical language, Hebrew, but it once had a much wider meaning.

In the Old Testament the term appears most frequently in the Joseph story (e.g. Gen. 39:17; 40:15; 41:12), the Exodus story (e.g. Exod. 1:16; 2:7; 3:18; 5:3; 7:16), and the story of the Philistine wars (e.g. I Sam. 4:6; 13:19; 14:11). The word is generally used by outsiders in speaking of the Israelites or by Israelites when speaking to outsiders. It does not express the sense of communal solidarity implied by the word "Israel," for there were Hebrews who were not members of the Israelite community.

Abraham is called a Hebrew for the first and only time in a peculiar tradition found in Genesis 14 about Abraham's wars with the kings of the east (Gen. 14:13). According to biblical tradition, Abraham the Hebrew ('*ibri*) was a descendant of Eber ('*eber*). In the genealogy found in Genesis 10:26–30, however, Eber was also the ancestor of other peoples. Arabs, Arameans, Moabites, Ammonites, and Edomites could trace their ancestry to him. Moreover, as we have already seen, there are numerous references to Habiru/'Apiru in the documents of the second millennium B.C.E. (e.g., the Amarna Letters) as a floating class of the population.

All of this suggests that the term "Hebrew" originally was more inclusive than it is in biblical texts, which refer specifically to those Hebrews who were slaves in Egypt and who eventually became the community known as Israel. Later on, when these social realities were forgotten, the term was restricted to the biblical Hebrews, the Jewish people, as in the Jonah story (Jon. 1:9). The Apostle Paul insisted that he was "a Hebrew born of Hebrews" (Phil. 3:2).

wrath of Pharaoh (probably Seti I, who began the imperial projects in the Delta), he fled for his life, not to return until there was a change of administration—that is, at the beginning of the reign of Ramses II (see Exod. 2:23; 4:18–20). He took refuge in "the land of Midian," an area of the Sinaitic Peninsula controlled by certain Midianite shepherds.[6] There, after showing kindness to some women at a well, he was given hospitality in the tent of "the priest of Midian" and eventually married one of his daughters, Zipporah (2:15–22). Various traditions have survived about the name of Moses' father-in-law. Sometimes he is called Jethro (Exod. 3:1; 18:1), sometimes Hobab (Judg. 4:11), and apparently Reuel (Exod. 2:18; cf. Num. 2:14), though perhaps the latter was the head of the clan and the father of Jethro. In any case, Moses' connection with the Midianites is undoubtedly authentic.

The Burning Bush

It was while tending the flocks of his father-in-law in the wilderness that Moses stumbled upon "the mountain of God." The story of Moses' encounter with "the God of the fathers" in that sacred place and the mighty struggle that his God-given task precipitated within him is one of the masterpieces of the Pentateuch (Exod. 3:4–17). It should be read with imagination and empathy, as one would read a piece of poetry, for it communicates a dimension of meaning that cannot be confined within the limits of precise prose. When the narrative is read critically, various irregularities become evident: for instance, Moses' father-in-law is here named Jethro, not Reuel or Hobab; the sacred mountain is explicitly called Horeb, not Sinai;[7] and, as we shall see presently, there is some alternation in the usage of the names for the deity. In the past many scholars attempted to account for these and other disparities by the theory that separate literary traditions have been woven together,[8] although increasingly it is recognized that the narrative bears the marks of oral tradition that preceded literary composition. In any case, the story comes to us in its final form as a superb example of narrative art.

Once the story is read poetically, some of the modern reader's problems—like the miracle of the bush that burned without being consumed—are minimized or fade into insignificance. Here we are dealing with a genre of narrative

---

[6] Geographers usually locate Midian in Arabia, to the southeast of the Gulf of Aqabah (see map, p. 77). However, because of their roving way of life and their special interest in copper resources, the Midianites extended their power into the southern part of the Sinaitic Peninsula. See *Wesminister Historical Atlas* [34], p. 38.

[7] Perhaps the narrator intends to make a veiled allusion to the alternate name of the mountain, Sinai, for the word for "bush" (s^e*neh*) may be understood as a word-play on *Sinai*.

[8] See the supplement to Martin Noth's *Pentateuchal Traditions* [70], pp. 261–76, where the results of source analysis are displayed in an analytical outline of the Pentateuch.

that portrays the divine calling and commission of a prophetic figure. The story shares some features with the account of Jeremiah's call and commission (Jer. 1:4–14), such as expostulation with God, the assurance of the divine presence, and the "sign" (the almond rod and the boiling pot). Since the story deals with an inner event, namely, a person's vocation or calling from God, attempts to rationalize the burning bush and thereby explain away the sense of wonder are beside the point. Whatever Moses saw with the naked eye, it became a sign that he was in the presence of the Holy. The wilderness spot was transfigured into a sacred place, a sanctuary where sandals must be removed. The response to this divine manifestation is described tersely (Exod. 3:6): "Moses hid his face, for he was afraid to look at 'Elohim [deity]."

The experience of the holy, which both fascinates and repels, is a well-known phenomenon in the history of religions.[9] In this instance, however, the holy is not a numinous, suprarational mystery or *mysterium tremendum*, but is identified with the God of Abraham, Isaac, and Jacob. In this theological context, holiness is divine power which breaks into the human world in order to upset the oppressive regime of Pharaoh and to deliver helpless, hopeless slaves.

Notice how the narrator quickly shifts attention from Moses' seeing the bush that did not burn up to his hearing the God who speaks to him in the historical hour. The manner of God's speaking provides clear evidence that the problem of the Hebrew slaves in Egypt lay heavily upon Moses' heart. It must be remembered that Moses had run away from Egypt after an indignant outburst of anger which resulted in the murder of a slavedriver. God's word to Moses, spoken with historical accent, announces what God is going to do. Several verbs are employed to describe the divine intention: "I *have seen* the affliction of my people . . . and *have heard* their cry . . . I *know* their sufferings, and *have come down to deliver them* . . ." (Exod. 3:7–8). In contrast to the God of the philosophers, Plato and Aristotle, the God of Moses is not aloof from the human scene and apathetic about human suffering; rather, the "God of pathos," as Abraham Heschel observes, is sensitive to the human condition and participates in human history with saving power.[10] The presence of the holy God is known not only in word but also in deed, not only in promise but also in action which accomplishes the divine purpose. In this narrative we come to the very heart of Israel's historical faith.

Moses' encounter with God sharpened his sense of individuality and made him acutely conscious of the demands of the historical situation. In the "I and thou" dialogue, Moses was given a task and was summoned to take part with God in the historical drama: "Come, I will send you to Pharaoh . . ." (Exod. 3:16). With sensitive religious insight, the narrator describes Moses' uneasiness

[9] See Rudolf Otto's classical work, *The Idea of the Holy* [125].

[10] See the illuminating discussion of "the pathos of God," including the "passion" of wrath and mercy, judgment and compassion, by Abraham Joshua Heschel in *The Prophets* [315], chaps. 12–14.

about the call and the various protests he offered in an attempt to stay on the comfortable sidelines of history.

THE DISCLOSURE OF GOD'S NAME

One of Moses' protests was that if he were to go to the Hebrews in Egypt and tell them about his experience at Sinai, he would have to know God's name (Exod. 3:13). In antiquity this was a vital question, not just because it was popularly believed that there were many gods, but because the character or identity of a god (or person) was expressed in the name. This way of thinking may seem somewhat strange. We use names as convenient labels to distinguish one thing from another, one person from another. So we are apt to say with Shakespeare's Juliet, "What's in a name?" (*Romeo and Juliet*, Act II, scene ii). Surely, we think, Moses could have used any current label (Shaddai, El, Baal, Re, etc.) and the meaning of his report would have not been affected substantially. Moreover, in some Oriental religions in the world today (e.g., Hinduism) the very notion of the name of God makes no sense, for the Ineffable cannot be defined or limited by distinguishing It from something else in the realm of sense experience. In the thought of ancient Israel, however, as in some societies which still exist, it was believed that the name was filled with power and vitality.[11] At the human level, the name represented the innermost self or identify of a person. Consequently, the naming of a child was a significant event; and when a person, as in the case of Jacob (Gen. 32:27–28), went through a transforming experience, he or she was given a new name. If one wanted to know somebody personally, it was necessary to know that person's name. Analogously, it was exceedingly important to know the name of God (think of Jacob's nocturnal wrestle again, Gen. 32:27, 29) if one were to establish personal relationship with God and, above all, to "call upon the name of Yahweh" in worship (see Ps. 116:12–14).

It is natural to suppose, at first glance, that Moses' question about God's name was a concession to the polytheism of the ancient world. In an environment where many divine powers were present, some known and some unknown, people naturally would want to know which god had chosen to show favor on them or which god they may have offended.[12] However, the narrative in Exodus 3 rises above the naive level of popular belief. Clearly the narrator wants us to know that it was the very same God who spoke of old to the ancestors who in this new situation confronted Moses and announced the divine plan to intervene in behalf of Hebrew slaves. Moses' question, then, amounted to an attempt to know the mystery of the divine self, that is, the identity of God. It was tantamount to saying, "Who are you?"

---

[11] See the discussion of "Name" by Johannes Pedersen in *Israel* [117], 1–11, 245–59. For a similar conception in African society, see E. B. Idowu, *Olódùmarè: God in Yoruba Belief* (London: Longmans, Green and Co., 1962), chap. 4.

[12] See the ancient Sumerian "Prayer to Every God" (Pritchard, *Ancient Near Eastern Texts* [1], pp. 391–92) in which a supplicant, not knowing what god he has offended and why he is suffering, addresses any god and all gods, whether known or unknown.

DEFINITION: "JEHOVAH," "THE LORD"

The personal divine name YHWH, cryptically referred to in the above passage, has had an interesting history. In the Old Testament period the Hebrew language was written only with consonants; vowels were not added until the Common Era, when Hebrew was no longer a living language. On the basis of Greek texts, which of course use both vowels and consonants, it is believed that the original pronunciation of the name was *Yahweh*. Notice the shortened form of the divine name in the exclamation, "Halleluyah"—"Praise Yah."

However, because of its holy character, the name Yahweh was withdrawn from ordinary speech during the period of the Second Temple (c. 500 B.C.E. and later) and the substitute Hebrew word— actually a title not a personal name—Adonai, or (The) Lord, was used, as is still the practice in synagogues. Scholars who translated the Hebrew Bible into Greek (the Septuagint) in the third century B.C.E. adopted this synagogue convention and rendered YHWH as (*ho*) *kurios*, "(The) Lord." From this Greek translation the practice was carried over into the New Testament.

The word Jehovah is an artificial form that arose from the erroneous combination of the consonants YHWH with the vowels of Adonai—written under or over the Hebrew consonants to indicate that the substitute is to be pronounced. This hybrid form is often held to be the invention of Peter Galatin, confessor of Pope Leo X, in a publication dated 1518 C.E., but in actuality it can be traced back to a work by a certain Raymond Martin in 1270 (see *Jewish Encyclopedia,* VII [1904], 88).

Jewish reverence for the Name has influenced numerous modern translations which, like the Septuagint translators, follow the ancient synagogue practice and substitute Adonai, which translates as "El Señor" in Spanish, "Der Herr" in German, "The Lord" in English, and so on. In this book, however, we shall go back to the presumed original form, Yahweh (as is done also in the Jerusalem Bible).

The Great I AM

At this point we come to one of the most cryptic passages in the Old Testament. Let us look at the repetitious account, in which there are no less than three introductions to God's answer to Moses' question.

3:13 Moses said to *'Elohim* [God],
   "All right, when I go to the Israelites and tell that the God of their ancestors has sent me to them, they will ask me, "What is his name?" and what am I going to say to them?"
14a   *'Elohim* replied to Moses,
   'ehyeh 'asher 'ehyeh
   ["I am who I am" or "I will be who I will be"]
14b   And he [*'Elohim*] said,
   'ehyeh ["I Am"] has sent me to you.
15a   Again *'Elohim* said to Moses,
   "Thus you shall say to the Israelites,
   YHWH [RSV: "the Lord"; NEB: "Jehovah"], the God of your ancestors, the God of Abraham, the God of Isaac, and the God of Jacob has sent me to you."

15   This is my name for all time, and this is how I am to be designated for generations to come.

Notice that the direct answer to Moses' query about how he should answer the "Israelites" in Egypt (verse 13) comes at the conclusion of this passage (verse 15). In the intervening verse 14, with its separate sections (a and b), the tradition connects the consonantal form YHWH, the special name for the God of Israel, with the Hebrew verb translated I AM (or, I Will Be). In Hebrew I AM (*'ehyeh*) is the first person singular of the verb *h-y-h* or, in its older spelling, *h-w-h* (to be); YHWH is the third person singular of the same verb, "He is" or "He will be." The first person form is used in verse 14 because God, when speaking personally, says "I am" rather than "He is."

Even in English translation the threefold repetition in verses 14 and 15 seems a bit awkward: "*'Elohim* said," "And he said," "*'Elohim* again said." Because the repetition is excessive, it may be that originally Moses' question in verse 13 was followed by the clear answer in verse 15: the personal name of "the God of the fathers" is Yahweh. If this is true, we may conjecture that at some point in the history of the tradition the story was expanded with the explanation of the divine name given in verse 14.[13] In any case, it is noteworthy that this is the only place in the whole Old Testament where there is a clear attempt to explain the name on the basis of the verb "to be." And much ink has flowed in the scholarly attempt to explain the explanation! Let us consider briefly three of the main interpretations that are current today.

According to one view, it is necessary to go behind the present reading (vocalization) of the consonants that was handed down in Jewish tradition and finally spelled out by rabbinical scholars known as the Masoretes around 700 C.E. Originally, it is maintained, the divine name YHWH was based on a causative form of the verb "to be," namely, "He causes to be, creates" (*yahweh*). This interpretation demands no change in the Hebrew consonants of the verbs in verse 14 and only a slight change in the vowels which were written in later (*'ahyeh* instead of *'ehyeh*). Moreover, it has the virtue of explaining the divine name as it was in all probability originally pronounced—that is, Yahweh. Thus the enigmatic expression is said to emphasize God's creative activity: "I cause to be what I cause to be," or, "I create what I create"; in other words, natural phenomena and historical events have their origin in the will of the God who is Creator and Lord.[14]

Another interpretation is based on the present reading of the text, that is, the simple form of the verb which is translated "I am." This is the case with the Greek translation (Septuagint), which renders, "I am the One who is" (*ego*

---

[13] This view is held by Martin Noth, *Exodus* [217], p. 30 and R. de Vaux, *History* [92], p. 350.

[14] This view was championed by the late W. F. Albright, *From the Stone Age to Christianity* [111] pp. 258–61, and is upheld by some of his students: D. N. Freedman, "The Name of the God of Moses," *Journal of Biblical Literature*, 79 (1960), 151–56; D. M. Beegle, *Moses* [206], pp. 69–73; and Frank M. Cross, "Yahweh and the God of the Patriarchs" [183], who gives the theory a new twist by regarding Yahweh as a cult name of the high God El.

eimi ho ōn). To this interpretation the objection may be raised that it introduces a philosophical notion of God's *eternal being* that seems alien to the Israelite way of thinking. The ancient Greeks, who struggled philosophically with the problem of the changing and the Changeless, would have favored the view that God's being is not essentially affected by the flux and flow of time. But in Israel, on the other hand, there was concern about God's historical activity and the movement of God's purpose toward a temporal goal—not about the divine being or essence within the Godhead. This is a point worth considering. Yet if the verb "to be" is understood in a dynamic sense (often it means "happen," as in the phrase, "it came to pass") and if the declaration in verse 14 is read in its narrative context, it is possible to find here an emphasis upon the divine *will*: Yahweh's zealous activity and exclusive claim of sovereignty. As one interpreter puts it, Yahweh is "the only one who exists for Israel." Unlike the gods of Egypt and Canaan, who were involved in the cyclical phenomena of the natural world, Yahweh is the holy and transcendent God, whose sovereign will is manifest in a succession of events that moves toward a goal.[15]

A third view, one that is favored by probability, is also based on the present reading of the text, although the simple form of the verb is translated in the future tense ("I will be"). According to this interpretation, the declaration in verse 14 must be understood in the immediate context, where the God of the ancestors promises to be with and to go with Moses: "I will be with you" (Exod. 3:12); "I will be with your mouth" (4:12, 15) or "I will be your God" (6:7). Thus the divine name signifies God, whose being is turned toward the people, who is present in their midst as deliverer, guide, and judge, and who is accessible in worship. Yet in giving the divine name (self) and, so to speak, being at the disposal of the people, Yahweh retains the divine freedom that eludes human control: "I will be gracious to whom I will be gracious, and will show mercy upon whom I will show mercy" (33:19). As a commandment of the Decalog states (Exod. 20:7), Yahweh's name cannot be taken in vain—that is, used for human purposes. Perhaps the enigmatic words in 3:14 suggest God's reticence about giving the divine name.[16] Moses had inquired into the mystery of the divine nature (the name), but his request was answered somewhat evasively, lest the people, by knowing the name, would try to hold God under (magical) control (see Gen. 32:29 and Judg. 13:27–28) and make God "their God" in a possessive sense.[17] The God who speaks to Moses is the Lord, not the servant of the people. Hence the question, "Who is God?" would be answered in future events that would display the meaning of divine grace and divine demand, preeminently in the Exodus (Exod. 20:2).

[15] This is the view of R. de Vaux, "The Revelation of the Divine Name YHWH," in *Proclamation and Presence* [158], pp. 48–75, reprinted with some changes in *History* [92], pp. 349–357.

[16] Johannes Pedersen remarks (*Israel* [117], I–II, p. 252): "If one is to enter into relation with somebody, he must know his name, and if he knows it then he may use it and exercise influence over him."

[17] This view is expressed by Martin Buber, *Moses* [207], pp. 51–55, and has been restated by Gerhard von Rad in his *Moses* [218], pp. 18–28.

The Origin of the Yahweh Cult

Moses was to say to Pharaoh: "Yahweh, the God of the Hebrews, has met with us" (Exod. 3:18). Even though it is difficult to explain the word Yahweh on the basis of verses 13 and 14, we can at least ask this question: Where did this name come from? How does it happen that Yahweh, rather than some other name, is the personal name of "the God of Israel"?

Careful reading of the narrative in Exodus 3 discloses that two terms for deity are used alternately. At times the general term translated "God" (Hebrew: *Elohim*) is used (3:1; 4, 11, 12, 13); sometimes the special Hebrew word Yahweh is found (3:2, 4, 7, 15). This is one of the evidences that led many scholars to conclude that the narrative represents a blending of traditions so closely that they can hardly be separated.[18] As a matter of fact, study of the Pentateuch received a great impetus from the discovery, in the eighteenth century, of this alternation in the use of divine names in the book of Genesis. The narrative of Creation (Gen. 1:1–2:3), for instance, consistently uses the name Elohim; and the story of the Garden of Eden (Gen. 2:4b–3:24) uses Yahweh (in combination with Elohim). The same alternation is found in the rest of Genesis. This criterion, along with the evidence of differences in style, theological idiom, and the presence of repetitions and inconsistencies, led to the hypothesis that various "sources" are woven together in the Pentateuch.

The alternation in the usage of divine names seems to be based on two views of the time when the name Yahweh was introduced. According to one Old Epic tradition in the book of Genesis, the worship of Yahweh reached back into the period before the Flood, to the generation of Enosh, the grandson of Adam:

> At that time it became customary to call upon the name of Yahweh.
> —GENESIS 4:26b

Accordingly, this tradition portrays Yahweh appearing to Israel's ancestors beginning with Abraham (Gen. 12:7). On the other hand, some traditions tend to refrain from using the name Yahweh in the period covered by the book of Genesis, insisting that the name is associated primarily with the special revelation to Moses. In the alternative account of Moses' call, given in Priestly tradition (P), the matter is put emphatically:

> And God ['*Elohim*] said to Moses, "I am Yahweh. I appeared to Abraham, to Isaac, and to Jacob, as God Almighty ['*El Shaddai*], but by my name Yahweh I did not make myself known to them."
> —EXODUS 6:2–3; *cf.* GENESIS 17:1

---

[18] On the basis of source analysis Exod. 3:1–8 belongs to J, with the exception of the second half of verse 4, which suddenly introduces the word "God" (*'Elohim*), and verse 6. The section 3:9–15, which begins with a duplication of the statement that *'Elohim* has heard the people's cry (compare verse 7 [J]) belongs to E. For the source analysis see the supplement to Noth's *Pentateuchal Traditions* [70], p. 267.

Apparently the passage in Exodus 3:13–15, in which Moses asks for the name of "the God of the fathers," reflects an ancient oral tradition in which the name Yahweh was unknown up to that time.[19] Some have argued that the passage does not say that Moses received a new name for God but only a new explanation of the name which had been known previously during the ancestral period. But the words of verse 15, "This is my name for all time, and this is how I am to be designated for generations to come," seem to indicate that a new name was introduced in the circle of Moses. And, as we have said, the statement made in the second version of Moses' call (Exod. 6:3) leaves no room for doubt.

Here, then, we have two distinct traditions. According to one, God was known and worshiped as Yahweh from the earliest times; according to the other, the cultic name was introduced in the period of Moses. Which of these is right?

One stream of tradition (usually identified as the Yahwist epic, or J) underscores the *theological* conviction that Yahweh, the God of Israel, is actually the Sovereign of all history and creation; therefore the worship of Yahweh is traced back to the remote beginnings, with the result that the Israelite story is placed in an ecumenical perspective. Various efforts have been made to show that this tradition is also *historically* correct in the sense that the name Yahweh was actually in use in the pre-Mosaic period, perhaps among the Amorites or in patriarchal clans, although the results are inconclusive at present.[20] The other streams of tradition (E and P) seem to be truer to the actual situation when they suggest that the name became commonly accepted during and after the time of Moses. It is worth noting that parents began giving their children names compounded with an abbreviated form of the name Yahweh (such as Joshua, which means "Yahweh is salvation") after the time of Moses, whereas in the pre-Mosaic period names of this type are lacking in the biblical traditions. This evidence suggests that the name Yahweh gained currency in the time of the Exodus. Indeed, according to one hypothesis, Yahweh was formerly the mountain god of the Kenites, a clan of the Midianites, and Moses was initiated into the Yahweh cult through his marriage to the daughter of Jethro, "the priest of Midian." While Moses was tending Jethro's flocks in Midianite territory, he received a commission from Yahweh at Horeb (Exod. 3:5). The supposition is that Yahweh was worshiped by the Kenites and that the mountain was a Midianite holy place. Moses went back to Egypt and acquainted his kin with the new deity, whom they had not known previously, and rallied them to return with him to the mountain and worship him there.[21]

---

[19] Literary critics generally assign this passage to the E or Elohistic tradition, which at this point echoes ancient oral tradition more definitely than the parallel J or Yahwistic tradition, in which Yahweh is identified as "the God of the fathers." See Brevard Childs, *Exodus* [210], pp. 64–70.

[20] See especially Frank M. Cross, "Yahweh and the God of the Patriarchs" [183]; see also Bright, *History* [91], pp. 151–152, and R. de Vaux, *History* [92], pp. 338 ff.

[21] The Kenite hypothesis is usually associated with the name of Karl Budde; see his *The Religion of Israel to the Exile* (New York: G. P. Putnam's Sons, 1899), chap. 1. For a recent defense of the hypothesis, see H. H. Rowley, *From Joseph to Joshua* [190], p. 149; for a vigorous criticism, see T. J. Meek, *Hebrew Origins* [97], chap. 3; also Martin Buber, *The Prophetic Faith* [311], pp. 24–30.

The honest truth is that we do not know for sure the source from which Moses received the name Yahweh. But the significant point here is not where the name came from, or even what its literal meaning was. Rather, the important point is what the name stood for in the worship of Israel from the time of Moses on. Even if the name originated among the Amorites, patriarchal clans, Midianites, or some other people, we must recognize that *Yahweh* meant something radically different in the experience of the Hebrews who followed Moses out of Egypt. And granting that the name literally meant something that we can no longer recover with certainty, still it was filled with a new meaning in the time of the Exodus. The Israelites knew and worshiped God as the One who had heard their cry of oppression, who had graciously intervened on their behalf, who had led them toward a future full of promise. In itself, the word Yahweh can be only a name, either empty of meaning or symbolic of many meanings. But in Israel's experience, as interpreted by Moses, it had just one meaning: ''I am Yahweh your God, who brought you out of the land of Egypt, out of the house of bondage'' (Exod. 20:2). To worship Yahweh was to remember that revealing event, to accept its demand, and to live in its promise.

THE CONTEST WITH PHARAOH

It should not be forgotten, after this discussion of the disclosure of the divine name, that the central theme of the story in Exodus 3 and 4 is Yahweh's commission to Moses: ''Come now, I will send you to Pharaoh that you may bring forth my people, the Israelites, out of Egypt'' (Exod. 3:10). Like the prophets who followed him, Moses is portrayed as one who was *sent* to deliver a message in the name of Yahweh, the Sender. The role of the messenger (prophet) is clear in a key passage in the Exodus story:

> ''You shall say to Pharaoh:
>   'This is what Yahweh says:
>   'Israel is my first-born son.
>   I tell you to let my son go that he may serve [worship] me.
>   If you refuse to let him go,
>   then I am going to slay your first-born son!''
> —EXODUS 4:22–23

In view of Moses' role as spokesman of Yahweh and the messenger form of a passage like this, it was appropriate for Hosea to say, years later, that

> By a prophet Yahweh brought up Israel out of Egypt,
>   and by a prophet Israel was protected.
> —HOSEA 12:13

In the above passage (Exod 4:22–23) the narrator anticipates the final round in the power struggle between Yahweh and Pharaoh. The passage is introduced

*The **Temple of Karnak** has 134 of these massive pillars in its Hypostyle Hall. On the north wall of this temple, built by Rameses II in the thirteenth century B.C.E., appears the Karnak List, which refers to Shishak's invasion of Palestine (c. 918 B.C.E.).*

by the statement that even when Moses performs the "wonders" which Yahweh has put in his power, they will have no effect because Yahweh will "harden" Pharaoh's heart. Although Pharaoh (Rameses II) was pursuing his own ambitions, from the standpoint of the narrator Yahweh was completely in control; indeed, everything was foreknown and foreordained! No attempt is made to resolve the paradox of human freedom and divine sovereignty. Repeatedly it is said that Yahweh hardened Pharaoh's heart, but at the same time it is asserted that Pharaoh hardened his own heart—that is, his obstinacy was the expression of his own will (8:15, 32, 9:34). The narrator's central purpose was to tell the story in such a way as to glorify the God of Israel. Pharaoh was given a lot of rope, as we would say, but he could not run beyond the bounds of Yahweh's sovereign control (cf. Romans 9:17). Indeed, the purpose of the story of the contest with the stubborn Pharaoh is didactic—that is, to teach future generations of Israel how Yahweh "made a toy" of the Egyptians by performing "signs" among them, "so that you may know that I am Yahweh" (Exod. 10:2; see also Deut. 6:20–25).

The Plagues against Egypt

According to the story, the first audience with Pharaoh was a complete failure (Exod. 5:1–6:1). The petition for a leave of absence so that the slaves could celebrate a feast for Yahweh in the wilderness was regarded as an alibi (which it probably was). Pharaoh is represented as saying that he did not know a god named Yahweh, and that he had no intention of letting his slaves go (5:2). Orders were given for the workload to be increased; the slaves not only had to produce the same quota of bricks each day, but they also had to scout around and find the straw that was used as binding material.

The sequel is the story of the ten plagues which Yahweh inflicted upon Egypt to break the will of Pharaoh (Exod. 7:8–11:10).[22] The modern reader has many difficulties with the Exodus story at this point. One question inevitably comes to mind: How could all this have happened? Credulity is strained by the repeated claim that none of the plagues touched Israel in the land of Goshen, for Yahweh "made a distinction" between the Hebrews and the Egyptians (8:23) with the result that not even a dog growled against the people of Israel (11:7–8). Before considering the whole question of miracle, a few things should be said about the nature of the story.

Remember what has already been said about the motive for remembering and writing down these traditions. The Israelites did not have our kind of historical curiosity. These narratives do not purport to be an objective, photographic report of exactly what took place, devoid of all bias and interpretation. Rather, they testify to events as Israel experienced them, as they were interpreted within the community of faith. The supreme event to which the narratives bear witness, the liberating action of God on behalf of slaves in bondage, belongs to a dimension of history with which modern historians often are unwilling or unable to deal. The happenings could have been interpreted differently by others who stood outside the community of faith and who viewed them from a different stance or perspective. But for Israel the events were interpreted as the acts of Yahweh.

But having said all this, we need not jump to the conclusion that the whole account belongs to the realm of pure fancy or fiction. The action of God takes place within concrete situations and actual crises. Therefore, the biblical account must be taken seriously, although critically. The wisest course lies between a naive, unquestioning acceptance of the record just as it stands, and an equally dogmatic, wholesale rejection of the tradition as having no credibility. One scholar asserts that "none of these plagues, except the last, contains anything

---

[22] The material in Exod. 6:2–7:7 is a recapitulation of the story of Moses' commission and the appointment of Aaron in a priestly version (P). It summarizes what was narrated in the Old Epic tradition (JE) in 3:1–6:1.

strange or abnormal; all are events which may naturally take place at the end of the inundation of the Nile.''[23] This may be going too far, however, and it still leaves a major question unanswered: How do the events ''which naturally take place at the end of the inundation of the Nile'' come to signify the redemptive action of God?

The Nature of the Tradition

Several things should be kept in mind when dealing with this dramatic story. Even if it is granted that the story reflects natural phenomena which were known in Egypt, such as the blood-red Nile caused by red soil carried at flood season, scourges of frogs and grasshoppers, or the desert wind (sirocco) which blackens the sky with sand, it is quite clear that many elements of popular folklore are present. A good illustration is the serpent rod. According to one passage, Moses cast his rod on the ground, and it became a serpent (Exod 4:2-5). In another passage, Aaron did the same thing with the same result (Exod 7:8-13). But neither action is treated as extraordinary, for the magicians of Egypt, who specialized in serpent magic, are said to have accomplished as much by their secret arts. ''For every man cast down his rods, and they became serpents'' (Exod. 7:12). These and similar features of the account have a meaningful place in the story when read as a dramatic whole, but taken by themselves they are relics of the folklore of Egypt and Palestine.

    Again, the story in its written form is separated by several centuries from the time of Israel's sojourn in Egypt. Granting that the oral tradition of Israel has authentically preserved the recollection of historical events in the Mosaic period, we still have to take account of the irregularities, repetitions, and differences of interpretation which arose in the history of transmission and are now evident in the story in its written form. It is generally agreed that the account of the plagues (chaps. 7-12) received its final form at the hands of the Priestly Writer (P) who incorporated the Old Epic tradition (J) into the overall narrative framework which contained additional material preserved in the circle of priests. As the chart on p. 70 shows, there are a few differences in the way the story was transmitted. The Old Epic tradition, which is followed essentially in Psalm 78, recounts eight plagues, and in the completed Priestly edition the number is expanded to ten, as in Psalm 105.[24]

---

[23] W. O. E. Oesterley and T. H. Robinson, *History of Israel* (Oxford: Clarendon, 1932), I, 85. See also J. L. Mihelic and G. E. Wright, ''Plagues in Exodus'' (*Interpreter's Dictionary* [25], III, 822-24, who maintain that there is a natural basis for the first nine plagues, even though the tradition has been heightened in liturgical usage. Similarly, Greta Hort, ''The Plagues of Egypt,'' *Zeitschrift für die alttestamentliche Wissenschaft*, 69 (1956), 84-103; 70 (1958), 48-59, who maintains that the plagues correspond to a chain reaction of natural events during the seven-month period from August to March; this view is followed by D. M. Beegle, *Moses* [206], pp. 97-118.

[24] The number is seven if the plague of darkness (sandstorm) is attributed to E with many literary critics. J. L. Mihelic and G. E. Wright demonstrate that Psalm 78 in its rehearsal of the Exodus events follows the seven-plague tradition of J, and that Psalm 105 is based on the completed P account of ten plagues. See *Interpreter's Dictionary* [25], III, 822-23.

The Plagues against Egypt

OLD EPIC TRADITION		COMPLETED PRIESTLY VERSION	
Old Epic Account (J)	*Psalm 78:43–51*	*Old Epic + P Supplements*	*Psalm 105:27–36*
1. Water to blood 7:14–18, 20 (from "in the sight of") –21 (to "from the Nile"), 23–24	1. Rivers to blood verse 44	1. Water to blood 7:19–20 (to "Yahweh commanded"), 21 (from "and there was blood") –22	1. Darkness verse 28
2. Frogs 7:25; 8:1–4, 8–15	2. Flies verse 45a	2. Frogs 8:5–7	2. Waters to blood verse 29a
———————	3. Frogs verse 45b	3. Gnats 8:16–19	3. Dead fish verse 29b
3. Flies 8:20–32	4. Locusts verse 46	4. See J (flies)	4. Frogs verse 30
4. Cattle plague 9:1–7	5. Hail (and frost) verse 47	5. See J (cattle plague)	5. Flies verse 31a
		6. Boils on humans and beasts 9:8–12	6. Gnats verse 31b
———————	———————		
5. Hail 9:13–35	6. Cattle plague verse 48a	7. See J (hail)	7. Hail verse 32a
6. Locusts 10:1–20	7. Lightning verse 48b	8. See J (locusts)	8. Lightning verse 32b
7. Darkness 10:21–29	———————	9. See J (darkness)	9. Locusts verses 34–35
8. Death of first-born 11:1–8	8. Death of first-born verse 51	10. Death of first-born 11:9–10	10. Death of first-born verse 36

This chart shows variations in the tradition about the plagues. The final version (P), has two extra plagues: gnats, and boils on humans and cattle (Nos. 3 and 5 in the third column); but these may be duplications of flies and cattle plague in the older tradition (Nos. 3 and 4 in column 1).

Some source critics find Elohistic (E) elements in the plagues of water to blood and the plague of hail (which stress Moses' rod); also E elements in the locust plague; and the plague of darkness (10:21–23, 27) is attributed to E. For this refined literary analysis, see S. R. Driver, *Introduction* [38], pp. 24–29. Martin Noth (*Exodus* [217], pp. 67–84) persuasively insists that only two literary strata, J and P, are present here.

Differences in content and in literary style become evident when these traditions are studied closely. For one thing, in the Old Epic tradition Moses is the chief actor in Pharaoh's presence, while Aaron, if he is mentioned at all, stands by silently. In the final Priestly version of the story, however, Aaron—the great ancestor of the Jerusalem priests—always accompanies Moses and acts as his priestly spokesman in negotiations with Pharaoh. This view of the relation between Moses and Aaron is set forth in the Priestly passage dealing with the appointment of Aaron (6:28–7:7) and in the introduction to the plagues (7:8–13). It is noteworthy, too, that in the Old Epic tradition the plagues are described with more restraint than in the Priestly version. For instance, the Old Epic account of the locust plague affirms that an east wind brought a cloud of locusts and, with a shift of wind, they were driven into the Red Sea. Farmers in Egypt and other parts of the world have often witnessed such a plague. Here the miracle is not the natural event itself but the fact that Moses predicted it and that it came at a particular time and with a particular meaning. The Priestly version, however, shows a tendency to heighten the miracles by putting greater stress on the wonder-working power of the rod. Furthermore, in the Priestly version Moses is overshadowed by the priestly figure, Aaron. Yahweh commands Moses: "Say to Aaron, 'Stretch out your rod . . . ' ' "; and Aaron wields the rod with the most marvelous results (see, for instance, 8:16–19).

The History of the Tradition

The main importance of literary criticism of this kind is that, as we have noted in another connection (pp. 19–22), it enables us to understand that the story in its present form is the end product of a long history of transmission, reaching back into the oral stage when the story was told and retold with variation and improvisation. Indeed, it is quite likely that the original nucleus of the account was an ancient Israelite story told to interpret the celebration of the Passover. Even before the period of Moses shepherds observed this nomadic festival in the springtime at the first full moon just before setting out for summer pastures. During the nocturnal celebration it was customary for families to sacrifice a young animal and eat the meat in their tents, along with unleavened bread and desert herbs. The original purpose, still echoed faintly in the Old Epic tradition (Exod. 12:21–39), was to secure the welfare and fertility of the flocks when the baby lambs and goats were being born, and to drive away evil spirits, thought to be especially active at such a time. Accordingly, the blood of the sacrificed animal was smeared on the entrance to the tents to ward off the Destroyer (specifically mentioned in 12:23) who attacked people and animals. This primitive meaning, however, was superseded by a new understanding of the rite. As the story was retold in the light of the Exodus, the custom of shepherds leaving for summer pastures was reinterpreted to refer to Hebrews departing for a new land. Yahweh became the "Destroyer" who spared the blood-marked Hebrew dwellings when "passing over" them, so that no scourge would destroy them (12:13 [P]).[25] In the course of time, in the judgment of some scholars, nine other plagues were added as a dramatic introduction to the great plague of death (an epidemic?) which struck Egypt.[26] Moreover, when the Israelites settled in Ca-

[25] The original meaning of the word translated "Passover" (Hebrew, *Pésach*, Greek, *Pascha*; see our adjective "Paschal") is lost. In Hebrew the verbal form means "limp" (cf. I Kgs. 18:21, which refers to some kind of a skipping or limping dance). In Exod. 12:13, 23, 27 the verb means "to skip by, spare."

[26] This is essentially the view of Martin Noth, *Pentateuchal Traditions* [70], pp. 65–71. See also Dennis J. McCarthy, "Plagues and the Sea of Reeds," *Journal of Biblical Literature*, 85 (1966), 137–58, who maintains, though differing from Noth in some ways, that the plagues developed in the history of the tradition to enhance the core of the story.

naan, the nomadic Passover rite came to be connected with the Feast of Un-leavened Bread, an agricultural festival celebrated at the barley harvest.[27]

The fact that the story of the plagues has had a long history is evident when one examines the literary features of the whole account. The story of the first nine plagues (Exod. 7:14–10:29) seems to be a literary unity, carefully wrought by the Priestly redactors who incorporated the Old Epic tradition into the final work. This story is governed by an overall scheme, with a clear beginning and a definite finish, and makes use of formulas that are characteristic of this section.[28]

Furthermore, the story of nine plagues seems to presuppose the view that the Exodus was a secret flight, not an expulsion. The narrative comes to a conclusion at the end of the ninth plague, when Pharaoh, firm in his refusal, tells Moses to get out and never see his face again (Exod. 10:27–29). According to one tradition, there is some evidence that the Hebrews, having failed in their negotiations, slipped away without Pharaoh's knowledge (14:5a). On the other hand, the material in chapters 11 through 13 does not seem to depend on previous plagues but stands apart somewhat independently, as suggested by the introductory statement that Moses and the people enjoyed great esteem among the Egyptians and even among members of the royal court (11:2–3). Clearly, the story of the tenth plague presupposes the view that the Exodus was an expulsion.[29] After this grievous blow, Pharaoh "drove out" the Hebrews, and the Egyptians were so glad to get rid of them that they gave them whatever they asked for, including jewelry and clothing (12:31–36)! Moreover, the tenth plague is closely tied in with the celebration of the Passover. Right in the midst of the tense crisis—between the announcement of Yahweh's intention (11:1–10) and the falling of the plague (12:29–32)—the narrator pauses to introduce the ancient feast, as the following outline shows:

Egyptian Plagues and Hebrew Exodus

	Epic Tradition	Priestly Expansion
Announcement of plague	11:1–8	11:9–10
Institution of Passover	12:21–23(24–27a)	12:1–20,28
Occurrence of plague	12:29–36	
THE EXODUS	12:37–39	12:40–42
Passover legislation	(13:1–16)	12:43–51

(The two passages in parentheses are akin to Deuteronomic style)

[27] On the origin and significance of both feasts, see R. de Vaux, *Ancient Israel* [113], pp. 484–93.

[28] The literary unity of the story of the nine plagues is stressed both by scholars who follow source analysis (e.g., R. de Vaux, *History* [92], pp. 359–370, D. M. Beegle, *Moses* [206], chap. 5), and those who do not, e.g., Umberto Cassuto, *Exodus* [209], pp. 92–135.

[29] Roland de Vaux maintains that both the "exodus-flight" and the "exodus-expulsion" traditions are historically important, for they indicate that there were two different exoduses of Hebrews, one group taking a northern route, the other a southern. See his *History* [92], pp. 370–376.

In summary, the Exodus story as we have received it is the end result of a long history of tradition, in the course of which it was reinterpreted and embellished by various circles of narrators. From the earliest period, as we have seen, the story was rehearsed at the celebration of the Passover. It was in this cultic setting that the event of Israel's liberation from Pharaoh's yoke was remembered and elaborated. And eventually, after centuries of transmission, the Priestly Writers brought the traditional story to the final, written version of the dramatic contest with Pharaoh which moves dynamically toward the denouement of Yahweh's decisive victory.

Signs and Wonders

In the preceding discussion we have been speaking about the "plagues" against Egypt. It is noteworthy, however, that this word appears rarely in the Exodus story (notably Exod. 9:14; 11:1; cf. 8:2). Usually in the Exodus narratives the so-called plagues are described as "signs" and "wonders." Likewise, in the recitations found in Psalms 78 and 105, as well as in creedal summaries (Deut. 26:5–9), this language is used. This raises the question of miracle, which we can only touch on here.

In the Bible, the meaning of miracle differs from our conception of miracle as a disruption of natural law.[30] As a matter of fact, the biblical writers had no conception of "nature" or the "cosmos" as an independent, self-operating realm, governed by its own laws. Rather, they believed that God who created the universe is constantly involved—sustaining and maintaining it. Hence, there are regularities on which people can count—"seedtime and harvest, cold and heat, summer and winter, day and night" (Gen. 8:22)—for God has made a covenant with the creation, an ecological covenant which embraces humans, animals, birds, and the earth itself (Gen. 9:10–17). Because God is constantly active, God's will may be discernible even in a "natural" event, like the coming of the spring rains or the birth of a child. There is biblical truth behind Gilbert Chesteron's whimsical remark that the sun does not rise by natural law, but because God says: "Get up and do it again!"

In addition to these regularities of the world, however, there are extraordinary events that show God's power to intervene, and are therefore special "signs." These signs were not proofs given to convince people once and for all that God is sovereign, however. The narratives of the Exodus show that their meaning was not self-evident to those who witnessed them. Whom did they really convince? We are told that the first two plagues (water to blood, the scourge of frogs) left Pharaoh unmoved because his magicians were able to per-

---

[30] Martin Buber, in *Moses* [207], p. 76, observes: "Miracle is not something 'supernatural' or 'superhistorical,' but an incident, an event which can be fully included in the objective, scientific nexus of nature and history; the vital meaning of which, however, for the person to whom it occurs, destroys the security of the whole nexus of knowledge for him, and explodes the fixity of the fields of experience named 'Nature' and 'History.' "

form the same feats (Exod. 7:22, 8:7). Beyond that point, the Egyptian sorcerers could not go. Nevertheless, although Pharaoh was impressed by subsequent miracles, he was not so completely convinced that he was willing to let the slaves go. Furthermore, the Israelites, though they had witnessed the signs performed by Moses, did not believe him ''because of their broken spirit and cruel bondage'' (6:9). Even after their successful escape across the Sea they murmured in disbelief and longed for the fleshpots of Egypt. So a miracle, in the biblical sense, is an indication of God's purposive activity, but never a final proof. Evidence is given of God's presence and redemptive purpose, but in an ambiguous way that demands faith and trust.

DEFINITION: ''SIGNS AND WONDERS''

A ''sign'' may be defined as a visible evidence of the presence and purpose of God. The use of the word does not conform to our distinction between ''natural'' and ''supernatural.'' In the Exodus story everything that happens is a potential sign. It might be an ordinary event such as the coming of a plague of locusts, or some phenomenon connected with the overflow of the Nile. (Elsewhere the word ''sign'' is applied to the rainbow, the heavenly bodies, the birth of a child, or a seeming coincidence in the day's affairs.) Or it may be an extraordinary event, a sensational wonder like the death of the firstborn in Egypt. (Other examples of this type are the restoring to health of a leprous hand, the turning of water into blood, the retreat of the sun's shadow on a dial.)

This approach to the subject by no means answers all our questions, but it may lead us to ask the questions in a new way. Basic to Israel's faith is the conviction that God is not aloof from the world of daily affairs or bound by an iron chain of cause-and-effect sequences. The Israelites had a sense of the immediacy of God's presence. They believed that any event—ordinary or extraordinary—could be a sign that God was in their midst. To them an event was *wonder*-ful, or *sign*-ificant, not because it abrogated a natural law, but because it testified to God's presence and activity in their midst. (See further ''Signs and Wonders,'' *Interpreter's Dictionary IV* [25], 348–351.)

Every reader of the Bible has to make up his or her own mind about the historical nucleus which lies at the heart of the tradition that has been elaborated and colored by Israel's faith over a period of generations. Some miracles are more central to the Exodus story, more native to the Mosaic period, than others. Other aspects of the story are an artistic and imaginative expression of the conviction that Yahweh was active in history, delivering slaves from servitude and calling them to be the people of God. Because the whole account is interpretive, it is very difficult to separate sharply the central elements of the tradition from later accretions. Nevertheless, Israel's ancient faith undoubtedly was based on the experience of actual events which facilitated the escape of slaves from Egypt, events in which they perceived in moments of faith the work of God. The clearest historical evidence for this is found in the account of the crossing of the Sea. No event was fixed more firmly in Israel's memory.

THE VICTORY AT THE SEA

In the narrative of the book of Exodus, the crossing of the Sea is the climactic moment in a series of events springing from the last plague, the death of the firstborn of the Egyptians. As we have noticed already, the primitive meaning of the ancient nomadic Passover festival was superseded by a radically new understanding, which is now preserved in all levels of the tradition, to the seventh-century book of Deuteronomy (Deut. 16:1–3). As a result of Moses' prophetic interpretation of the Exodus, it became a time to remember that in the darkest hour Yahweh broke Pharaoh's yoke and graciously delivered the people of Israel.

> When your children ask you, "What does this rite mean to you?" you shall respond,
> "It is the *Pesach* ("Passover") sacrifice to Yahweh, for he passed over [*pasaḥ*] the houses of the Israelites in Egypt when he struck the Egyptians, but spared our dwellings."
>
> —EXODUS 12:26–27

The Festival of Unleavened Bread (Mazzoth), which is now closely associated with the Passover, is traced back to the time when the people left Egypt in a hurry and did not have time for their dough to be leavened (12:34, 39). As in the Passover Seder (service) today, ancient Israelites explained this custom to their children by saying: "It is because of what Yahweh did *for me* when I came out of Egypt" (13:8; see the Passover Haggadah cited on p. 9).

The Route of the Flight

The people set out from Egypt in haste. According to the statement in Exodus 12:37, there were "six hundred thousand men on foot" (see also Num. 11:21)— that is, men of military age twenty years and older. If we count in addition women, children, teenagers, and old men, this would bring the total to over two million people! One historian has estimated that a column of this size, marching in single file, would have extended at least all the way from Egypt to Sinai and back. This picture of a mass exodus is a later exaggeration, perhaps based on census figures from a much later time, for it does not square with the information in Exodus 1:15–20 that two midwives were sufficient to serve the whole Hebrew colony. Clearly, the Delta area could not have accommodated so many Hebrews and their animals, and the wilderness of southern Canaan could not have supported them. Undoubtedly, the band of slaves was comparatively small. The record is correct, however, in stating that they were a motley group: not only the family of Jacob but a "mixed multitude" (12:38) representing 'Apiru of other origins. Indeed, it is historically inaccurate to speak of these peoples as "Israelites" at this stage, although the narrative does so repeatedly. Only later, as they shared the experiences of the desert and remembered a common history, were they forged into a *community*, the people Israel.

You will remember that a repeated demand that Moses made to Pharaoh, according to the story of the nine plagues, was that the Hebrews be allowed to make a three-day journey into the wilderness to sacrifice to Yahweh (Exod. 5:3; 7:16, 26, etc.). Not even Pharaoh's concession that the Hebrews could make their sacrifice in the land of Goshen (8:25) or on the Egyptian border (8:28) was acceptable. This suggests that originally the destination of the flight was the sacred mountain where Moses had his experience (see 3:12)—not the land of Canaan. Only later did these fugitives look longingly toward the goal which the narrator now has in view: the occupation of Canaan. This is another indication that the story is told from the perspective of later experience.

One passage declares that the very route of escape was providential, for "when Pharaoh let the people go, God did not guide them by the way of the land of the Philistines, although that was close" (Exod. 13:17). We find here more evidence that the story is told from the standpoint of a later period, for strictly speaking the expression "the way of the land of the Philistines" is anachronistic, that is, it reflects later usage. The Philistines did not occupy that area until shortly after 1200 B.C.E., almost a century after the time of Moses. The route referred to in this fashion was the main highway leading from Egypt along the Mediterranean coastland. Because this major commercial and military route was heavily fortified with Egyptian outposts, the Hebrews would not have had a chance on that road. Before they could face such military hazards, the people needed to be bound together by the experiences of the desert. So instead of a shortcut, the strategy called for a roundabout journey. "God led the people round about by way of the wilderness . . . " (13:18). In other words, they left "the land of Rameses" (Goshen), where they had been working, and struck out into the wilderness that today borders the Suez Canal, touching first at points called Succoth and Etham (13:20).

The present biblical texts do not give a clear picture of their route of escape. There is some evidence of at least an initial move along a northern route toward Baal-saphon on Lake Sirbonis, a lagoon which lies on the Mediterranean side of the coastal highway. On the whole, however, evidence seems to favor a southern route, at least in the case of those Hebrews who arrived at Sinai.[31] Notice that according to the statement in Exodus 13:18, the fugitive Hebrews took "the way of the wilderness" which led in the direction of *Yam Suph* (which is often translated as "Red Sea").

As the map clearly shows, this route could not have taken them to the Red Sea, unless we are to suppose that the Egyptian army chased the Hebrews many

---

[31] This complex question is discussed in J. L. Mihelic's article, "Red Sea," in *Interpreter's Dictionary*, IV [25], 19–21; G. Ernest Wright, *Biblical Archaeology* [110], 60–67; D. M. Beegle, *Moses* [206], 145–58. As noted in a previous connection, de Vaux advocates a double exodus, one group taking the northern (Lake Sirbonis) route and cutting over to Kadesh, the other taking a southern route and going directly to Sinai. See his *History* [92], pp. 370–381.

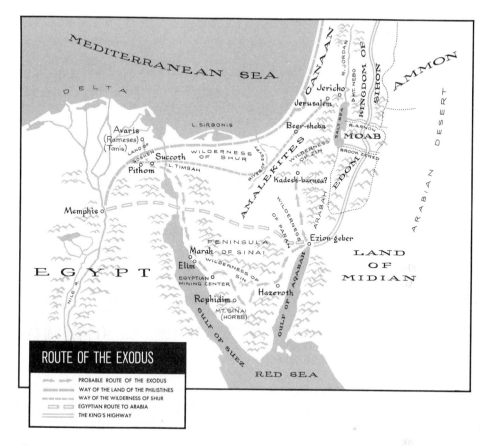

miles to a point opposite the tip of the Sinaitic Peninsula. It is true that in some biblical passages *Yam Suph* has a wide meaning which could apply to the Gulf of Suez (Num. 33:10–11) or the Gulf of Aqabah (I Kings 9:26), the two arms of water which extend out of the Red Sea. The words were understood in this wider sense when the Greek translation of the Old Testament (Septuagint) was made in the third century B.C.E., and this understanding has been passed on to us through the Latin Vulgate. Today historians believe that *Yam Suph*, when used in contexts dealing with the Exodus, should be translated "Reed Sea" or "Papyrus Lake." In Hebrew *yam* means "sea" (e.g., the Mediterranean Sea) or an inland body of water (e.g., the Sea of Galilee); and *suph* means "reed, papyrus," the reference being to the reeds that grow around the body of water. The designation was probably given to some marshy lake at the northern extension of the Gulf of Suez, around the area of Lake Manzaleh (perhaps Lake Timsah). The route of the escaping Hebrews took them into this area. Although we cannot be certain about the exact location of the crossing, there is no need to make the story more difficult than it actually is by supposing that they somehow negotiated the Gulf of Suez where, as a matter of fact, reeds do not grow.

It is worth noting that the account of the miraculous crossing in Exodus 14 speaks only of the sea (*yam*), though the parallel poetic account in Exodus 15 speaks specifically of *Yam Suph*.

The narrative expresses the conviction that God was guiding the people on their journey. As their leader, Yahweh "went before them." One passage from the Old Epic tradition expresses this by saying that "Yahweh went before them by day in a pillar of cloud to lead them along the way, and by night in a pillar of fire to give them light" (Exod. 13:21f.). It has been proposed that this language reflects the ancient practice of carrying a burning brazier at the head of a marching army or caravan to indicate the line of march.[32] This suggestion agrees with the description of how the signal, seen by day as a cloud and by night as a flame, moved about as the leader at the head of the caravan changed course; but it does not explain every mention of the pillar (e.g., 14:19b–20). It may be that the fire and cloud reflect a meteorological phenomenon, such as the electrical rainstorm that often accompanied the hot desert wind (sirocco); if so, the tradition has been enhanced with poetic imagery used in the ancient world to portray the divine appearance (theophany) in cloud, fire, lightning, and rain,[33] especially the storm phenomena of the northern mountains (see Ps. 18:8–16). The narrative affirms that Yahweh was with the people, liberating them from their past bondage and guiding them toward their destination at Sinai.

A Path Through the Waters

Realizing that the fugitives were heading toward the frontier, and supposing that they would be "entangled in the land" and "shut in" by the wilderness (Exod. 14:3), Pharaoh sent his charioteers in hot pursuit. The suspense of the drama now reaches its greatest intensity. Trapped between the barrier of the Sea on one side and the Egyptian forces on the other, the panic-striken people were on the verge of revolting against Moses and going back to their miserable life in the Delta; "for it would have been better for us to serve the Egyptians than to die in the wilderness" (14:11–12). The murmuring of the people (a frequent theme in the wilderness narratives) contrasts sharply with the indomitable faith of Moses, who believed that the Divine Warrior was fighting for the people (14:13–14). Even though it was, according to human perception, a "no-exit" situation, the divine imperative was: "Tell the people of Israel to go forward!"

The ensuing account of the miraculous opening of a path through the waters (Exod. 14:15–31) belongs to the poetry of Israel's faith. The event constitutes, in the language of Emil Fackenheim, a "root experience" which to the

---

[32] See, for instance, U. Cassuto, *Exodus* [209], p. 158; D. Beegle, *Moses* [206], p. 149.

[33] Thomas W. Mann, in "The Pillar of Cloud in the Reed Sea Narrative," *Journal of Biblical Literature* 90 (1971), 15–30, draws attention to poetic parallels in Canaanite literature. See further by the same author, *Divine Presence and Guidance in Israelite Traditions: The Typology of Exaltation* (Baltimore: Johns Hopkins University Press, 1977), especially chap. 5, "The Reed Sea and Sinai."

present day is celebrated in the Passover Service as the sign of "a saving Presence" in history.[34] Even historians who are skeptical about many of the ancient Mosaic traditions admit that at this point we strike "the bedrock of an historical occurrence," an event "so unique and extraordinary that it came to constitute the essence of the primary Israelite confession and was regarded as the real beginning of Israel's history and the act of God fundamental for Israel."[35] Undoubtedly, the story of the Event at the Sea is not pure fiction; it rests upon something that actually happened, something that aroused ecstatic jubilation and became the undying memory of the people. Yet it is almost impossible to penetrate behind the faith language of the account and to deal with the inevitable question of the modern reader: What really happened at the Reed Sea?

One way to consider this question is to analyze the levels of tradition in the prose narrative of Exodus 14. It is generally recognized that the account in its present form comes from the Priestly Writing (P). As the chart (p. 80) on the traditions in Exodus 14 shows, the Priestly Writing provided the basic narrative pattern of divine command and divine execution and enriched the narrative by drawing upon the Old Epic tradition. After separating the materials which display Priestly language and interests, the remaining material portrays a crossing that was faciliated by wind and tide.

> Yahweh drove back the sea with a strong easterly wind all night, and he made dry land of the sea . . .
> In the morning watch, Yahweh looked down on the army of the Egyptians from the pillar of fire and of cloud, and threw the army into confusion. He so clogged their chariot wheels that they could scarcely make headway. "Let us flee from the Israelites," the Egyptians cried. "Yahweh is fighting for them against the Egyptians!"
>
> —EXODUS 14:21b, 24–25 (JB)

Such an occurrence, as reported by the Old Epic tradition, is not impossible in the marshy area of Lake Menzalah; in fact, it has been witnessed at other times. The miracle was that it happened at a particular time and with a particular meaning. To Israel it was not a freak of nature, but a sign of the saving presence of Yahweh in their midst, who used a power of the natural world (the wind) to accomplish a saving purpose.

If this was the substance of the old tradition, it has been expanded in the course of retelling with other materials, mainly from the Priestly circle (P), in order to heighten the wonder of the event. According to the expanded version, Moses held out his wonder-working rod and the waters of the sea were divided, allowing the people to pass over on dry ground while the waters stood up like walls on both sides of the passageway (verses 21a, 22). When the Egyptians

---

[34] Emil Fackenheim, *God's Presence in History* [213], pp. 8ff.
[35] Martin Noth, *Pentateuchal Traditions* [70], p. 50).

The Traditions in Exodus 14

Basic Priestly Narrative	Enrichments from Epic Tradition

A. The Egyptian Pursuit
  1. *Command:* verses 1–4
   (Note characteristic language:
   "harden the heart," "get glory,"
   "know that I am Yahweh.")	

	⟵————————— Verses 5–7: Pharaoh's Change of Mind
2. *Execution:* verses 8–9	
	⟵————————— Verses 10–14: Israel's Murmuring

B. The Splitting of the Sea
  1. *Command:* verses 15–18
   (Compare language with verses
   1–4; note the motif of the rod
   used to divide [literally, "split"]
   the sea.)	

	⟵————————— Verses 19–20: The Pillar of Cloud (Compare Exod. 13:21–22)
2. *Execution:* verse 21a, ⟵————	Verse 21b ("And Yahweh drove the sea back . . . made the sea dry land")

the rest of the verse
   ("and the waters were divided"), and 22–23
   (Note the "rod," "dividing"
   ["splitting"] the waters, and
   the "walls" of waters.)	

	⟵————————— Verses 24–25: Egyptian Panic

C. The Return of the Waters
  1. *Command:* verse 26
  2. *Execution:* verse 27a, ⟵————
	Verse 27a (from "the sea returned") to
	   the end of verse 27b

and verses 28–29
   (Note again the rod [outstretched
   hand], and the walling of the
   waters.)	

	⟵————————— Verses 30–31: Yahweh's Victory and Israel's Response

attempted to pursue the fugitives into the sea bed, Moses stretched out his rod again and they were overwhelmed by the waters (verses 23, 26–28). However, "the people of Israel walked on dry ground through the sea, the waters being a wall to them on the right hand and on their left hand" (verse 29).

The main value of this kind of analysis is that it shows how the story has undergone a long history, from the early oral period, when it was told and retold by skilled narrators, to the final stage of its literary formulation by the Priestly Writer. Yet at no time in the history of the tradition was the purpose of the narrators to give a straightforward account which would satisfy modern historical curiosity. Their intention was to glorify the God whose saving presence was marvelously manifested in an unforgettable historical experience.

A Holy Event

The narrative comes to a climax when it tells how Miriam, the sister of Moses and Aaron, took a tambourine and, while all the Israelite women followed her with music and dancing, sang an ecstatic hymn of praise to Yahweh:

> Sing to Yahweh!
>   for he is powerfully ascendant.
> Horse and charioteer
>   he has hurled into the sea.
> —EXODUS 15:21

This couplet is one of the oldest pieces of poetry in the Old Testament, and in all probability it originated during the very event it celebrates. It is an eyewitness testimony to the meaning of the event. The occurrence was experienced at the time as a "wonder"—an event that signified the redemptive activity of God on behalf of the people. It was, as the Jewish philosopher Martin Buber puts it, a "holy event" which was, for those who participated in it, "transparent," permitting "a glimpse of the sphere in which a sole power, not restricted by any other, [was] at work." To be sure, the event occurred in the context of "the objective, scientific nexus of nature and history," as we have observed in our discussion of the "high wind" theory; but the wonder of the event cannot be eliminated by any causal explanation. "The great turning-points in religious history," Buber observes, "are based on the fact that again and ever again an individual and a group attached to him wonder and keep on wondering: at a natural phenomenon, at a historical event, or at both together; always at something which intervenes fatefully in the life of this individual or this group."[36]

Israel's capacity "to wonder and keep on wondering" is evident in various passages in the Old Testament where the miracle at the Sea is rehearsed in such a way as to bring out its rich overtones of meaning. One of these passages is the Song of the Sea (Exod. 15:1–18). Here the Song of Miriam, now transposed into the first person ("I will sing . . ."; compare Exod. 15:21) becomes the opening refrain of an ancient poem which celebrates the events reported in the dramatic prose of Exodus 14. This poem probably comes from the period before David, as is evident from its affinities with ancient Canaanite poetic style and imagery. Given its antiquity, the poem is particularly significant because it expresses the transcendent and wonderful dimension of the event at the Sea by drawing upon Canaanite mythical views. Indeed, the poem seems to reflect a Canaanite mythic pattern: the conflict of the Divine Warrior with adversaries,

---

[36] Martin Buber, *Moses* [207], pp. 75–77. This passage is quoted and discussed by Emil Fackenheim, *God's Presence in History* [213], pp. 11–14.

the building of a temple for the triumphant deity on the sacred mountain, and the celebration of the god's everlasting kingship.[37] Yahweh, the victorious Divine Warrior (15:2; cf. 14:13–14), is supreme in the Heavenly Council of the gods:

> Who is like you in the heavenly council, Yahweh?
>> Who is like you, majestic in holiness?
>> You who are awesome in deeds, who does wonders?
> You stretched out your right hand,
>> Earth swallowed them.
>>> —EXODUS 15:11–12

The poet then describes a further demonstration of divine power: the guidance of the people to Canaan, depicted as the mythical mountain of the gods (15:17).

> In your faithfulness you led the people that you redeemed,
>> You led them in your power to your holy abode.
>>> —EXODUS 15:13

Panic overwhelmed the rulers of Canaan, says the poet,

> While your people passed over, Yahweh,
>> while your people passed over whom you have created.
>>> —EXODUS 15:16b (Frank Cross translation)

In this poetic portrayal the event is more than a deed of liberation. It is the event of the creation of a people. Here we find the beginning of the tendency to communicate the wonder of the event by enhancing the historical account with mythical elements. In the poem Yahweh's adversaries are Pharaoh and his armies, and the Sea is a passive element under Yahweh's control. But later on in the history of the Reed Sea tradition the Sea came to represent the mythical powers of chaos which Yahweh conquers in order to demonstrate kingship over Israel and the world. According to this reinterpretation, Yahweh's victory was not over pharaonic powers of flesh and blood but over *Sea*, the mythical symbol of the chaos and evil that threaten the creation (Psalms 74:12–17; 77:16–20; 114; Hab. 3). In other words, the victory at the Sea came to be understood as a victory over the Sea.[38]

In view of the overwhelming significance of the Exodus in the biblical narratives, it may seem strange, at first glance, that the Egyptian records, so far as they are known, make no reference to Moses and the escape of the Hebrew fugitives from Pharaoh's power. We are reminded again that archaeology and

---

[37] See Frank M. Cross, "The Song of the Sea and Canaanite Myth" [112], pp. 112–44; also his chapter, "The Divine Warrior" [112], pp. 91–111, and Patrick Miller, *The Divine Warrior in Early Israel* [215], pp. 74–128.

[38] On the use of mythical imagery to elaborate the Exodus tradition, see further B. W. Anderson, *Creation versus Chaos* [128], pp. 93–109, and some of the essays in *Creation in the Old Testament* [129].

the study of ancient history give, at best, only circumstantial evidence to support the credibility of the Israelite record. But the Egyptian silence is not really so strange. For one thing, the Delta residence of Rameses II, with its imposing stone temples and splendid royal palace, has vanished. Its archives—if they ever contained records of Hebrew slaves and their rebel leader Moses—are also gone, "irrevocably lost."[39] But, even more important, we would hardly expect the escape of a band of runaway slaves to figure in Egyptian annals, when far more dramatic things were happening. This border incident, which caused scarcely a ripple in Egyptian affairs, was not a memorable, history-making event from the standpoint of Egyptian historians. In their perspective, the decisive events were the wars and cultural achievements of the pharaohs of the Nineteenth Dynasty. But to the Israelites who participated in this event and who passed on the story to their children and children's children, this was the most important event of the time. It was in the light of the meaning of this event that they described what was going on in Egypt. And in its light they understood the subsequent events of their history, as well as their prehistory in the ancestral period.

[39] This point is emphasized by K. A. Kitchen [96], pp. 76–77, in his discussion of the capital city of Pi-Ramesse, identified as Tell el-Dab'a (with M. Bietak, *Tell el-Dab'a II*, 1975).

CHAPTER 3

Covenant in the Wilderness

Deeply etched upon Israelite tradition is the memory that the people of Israel had their origin in the wilderness. Those who followed Moses in the flight from Egypt were, as we have seen, a variegated company, a "mixed multitude" as we are told specifically (Exod. 12:38), who were held together primarily by their common desire to be free from slavery. Clearly, they lacked the consciousness of identity, the commitment to a common way of life, and the shared history which constitute a *people*—that is, a historical community. In the wilderness of the Sinaitic Peninsula, however, this motley band began to be "the people of Yahweh," to use the expression which frequently recurs in the Old Testament (e.g., Judg. 5:11, 13) and which influenced the later conception of church and synagogue.[1] Prophets harked back to the time when Yahweh "found Israel" like "grapes in the wilderness" (Hos. 9:10), when Israel "followed" Yahweh in the wilderness with all the devotion of her youth (Jer. 2:2–3). And by the same token, they declared that in the time of Israel's new beginning Yahweh would lead Israel back to the wilderness and there, away from the allurements of city culture, would "speak to her heart" (Hos. 2:14–15). The Torah tradition also testifies that it was in the wilderness that God spoke to Moses and that the

Biblical readings: Primarily Exodus 19–24 and 32–34. A biblical commentary on the whole story, Exodus and Sinai Covenant, is given in the book of Deuteronomy; see especially chaps. 5–28.

[1] Cf. Acts 7:38, "The church in the wilderness." In the Septuagint *ekklesia* and *synagogé* are used to translate Hebrew words which refer to Israel as "the people of God [Yahweh]."

people, submitting to the demand and promise of that Voice, became Yahweh's special people.

GUIDANCE IN THE WILDERNESS

As we have seen in the last chapter, when the Hebrews turned their backs on the land of Egypt, they took the road leading into the wilderness. According to the narratives found in Exodus 15:22–19:2, they set out for the Wilderness of Sinai, for Moses had been sent to bring the people to the mountain rendezvous so that they might find their freedom in serving (worshiping) God there (see Exod. 3:12). It was a difficult journey, fraught with many hardships and uncertainties. Freedom in the desert, in the judgment of many of the pilgrims, was a poor substitute for slavery in Egypt, and on many an occasion they longed for the "fleshpots of Egypt" (16:3). Food and water were scarce. And, as though the inhospitable natural environment were not enough, there were hostile desert tribes who roamed the area and resented the intrusion of the fugitives. It is a tribute to the realism of the narrators that they present life as it surely must have been under such precarious circumstances. In these stories the wilderness is not portrayed according to some "nomadic ideal." To be sure, Israel experienced grace in the wilderness, but it was also a time of grumbling, revolutionary discontent, internal strife, rebellion against Moses, and above all, lack of faith. Despite all that had happened, including the marvelous crossing of the Reed Sea, the people complained, "Is Yahweh among us or not?" (17:7).

Signs of Yahweh's Aid

In various ways the narratives emphasize the positive theme of Yahweh's guidance and gracious aid in the wilderness in response to the people's petitions in times of need or emergency. First of all, daily sustenance—the elemental necessities of food and water—was provided. Here, again, we encounter the issue of miracle—that is, the signs of God's presence in ordinary or extraordinary events (see above, pp. 73–74). Two illustrations are the stories about the manna and the quail (see Exod. 16:1–36). Both are familiar phenomena of the Sinaitic wilderness. Manna is a sweet, sticky substance produced by a number of insects that suck the tender twigs of tamarisk bushes in the desert region. This "honeydew excretion" falls to the ground where, in the hot desert air, the drops quickly evaporate, leaving a solid residue. During the day the sweet grains are carried off by ants, but overnight they accumulate and early risers can gather the substance for food. The Hebrews were evidently unfamiliar with this desert food. Thus the word is explained on the basis of the question, *man hu'*, which in Hebrew means, "What is it?" (Exod. 16:15), a question that receives from Moses the answer: It is "the bread which Yahweh has given you to eat" (cf. John 6:31). In the Arabic world *man* is still the name for these plant insects, and their honeydew, which is regarded as a great delicacy, is called *man essimma* or "manna from heaven,"[2] As for the quails (16:13; compare Num. 11:31–34), flocks of them migrate over this region in the spring, and, when exhausted, are easily caught. Some modern readers might say that these occurrences showed how "lucky" the Hebrews were. In Israel's faith, however, these were signs of Yahweh's daily guidance, although they were never proofs that removed the possibility of doubt.

Moreover, the tradition affirms that divine guidance was given in the fierce struggle for survival against hostile desert tribes. Chief among these were the Amalekites, who claimed the desert oases in the Negeb, the southern wilderness of Canaan. The battle against the Amalekites (17:8–16) made a deep impression on the memory of the Hebrews and was the beginning of a long and bitter feud (see I Sam. 15; Deut. 25:17–19). The story, which comes from the Old Epic tradition and which gives us our first glimpse of Joshua, shows fanciful features like the magic power of Moses' rod. But the fierce battle, in which "Joshua mowed down Amalek and his people with the edge of the sword" (to cite the vivid RSV translation), undoubtedly rests on an actual experience and was another event that sharpened the historical awareness of Israel's faith. Out of this conception of "holy war," to which we shall return subsequently, came the later prophetic demand for faith in Yahweh who alone gives the victory—a demand that found expression preeminently in the prophet Isaiah (see Isa. 7:7–9).

Murmurings in the Wilderness

Along with this positive theme of Yahweh's gracious answer to the people's petition in times of need is a negative theme: the wilderness sojourn was the time when the people persistently murmured against Yahweh and against the servant of Yahweh, Moses. If the period of the wilderness was, according to the interpretation given in an important passage in Deuteronomy, a time when the people were "tested" to see if they lived in complete and daily dependence upon Yahweh's providing mercy (Deut. 8:3, quoted in part in Matt. 4:4), it was also a time when the people put Yahweh to the test, demanding proof that Yahweh was really present. Not even the manna was satisfactory to the "rabble," for they remembered the better diet they had in Egypt, including fish, cucumbers, melons, onions, and garlic (Num. 11:4–6). In the stories dealing with the wilderness, Israel's grumbling happens time after time, and even seems to increase in intensity, as can be seen from the following passages:

Israel's Murmurings in the Wilderness

Exod. 15:22–26	Brackish water at Marah
Exod. 16:2–3	Longing for the fleshpots of Egypt

---

[2] F. S. Bodenheimer, "The Manna of Sinai," in *The Biblical Archaeologist*, X (1947), 2–6; reprinted in *The Biblical Archaeologist Reader*, I [101], 26–80.

Exod. 17:2–7	Water complaint at Massah and Meribah
Num. 11:4–6	Complaint about manna
Num. 12:1–2	Criticism of Moses for marrying a Cushite wife
Num. 14:2–3	Complaint against the leadership of Moses and Aaron
Num. 16:12–14	Accusation made by Dathan and Abiram
Num. 20:2–13	Complaint about wilderness life
Num. 21:4–5	Impatience during the march through Transjordan

It is probable that this murmuring theme has been accentuated in some circles as the story was handed down from generation to generation.[3] Nevertheless, the tradition undoubtedly preserves the memory of real struggles that took place in the wilderness. Even though things happened which Moses interpreted as "signs" of divine guidance and aid, it was difficult for the people to believe in Yahweh as they moved from the relative security of life in Egypt to the awesome uncertainty of life in the wilderness. When you stop to think of it, it is striking that Israel's story-tellers have been so candid about the wavering faith, or even the complete lack of faith, which characterized the people at the beginning of their historical pilgrimage. Moreover, even Moses came under this judgment, according to Israelite interpreters, with the result that he was not permitted to enter the Promised Land. Where else in the ancient world— or in the modern world, for that matter—has a people had the courage to say that its origin was characterized by weakness, if not failure? This is another reminder that Israel tells its history not from the standpoint of human achievement, but in the consciousness of God's searching judgment.

The Arrival at Sinai (Horeb)

Despite enemy attack, lack of food and water, and the murmurings of the people, the indomitable Moses led the pilgrims on until at last they staggered into the oasis of Sinai. Here they had an opportunity to reflect upon the experiences that had brought them together. Here they came to understand in a deeper way the nature of the community into which they had been called. The peculiar nature of this community is expressed in the covenant relationship between Yahweh and the people, and the laws and institutions by which this relationship was to be expressed. In Israel's traditions, the scene of the establishment of the Mosaic covenant was located at "the mountain of God" (Exod. 24:13; see also 3:1), called Horeb in some circles and Sinai in others.[4]

Unfortunately, the location of the sacred mountain cannot be determined

---

[3] This point has been emphasized by George W. Coats in *Rebellion in the Wilderness* [223]. Relying on Ps. 78, he believes that the murmuring tradition was a polemic of Jerusalem priests against the northern kingdom of Israel. See further Brevard Childs, *Exodus* [210], pp. 254–264.

[4] The name Sinai appears in Old Epic (J) and Priestly (P) traditions, while the name Horeb was favored in northern circles represented by the Elohist stratum (E) and Deuteronomy (D). A northern (Ephraimitic) tradition portrays Elijah making a pilgrimage to "Horeb, the mountain of God" (I Kings 19:4–8).

with certainty. Because the narrative associates Yahweh's manifestation with a
volcanic eruption that shook the mountain and enveloped it in smoke (Exod.
19:18), some have proposed a site in northern Arabia, to the east of the Gulf of
Aqabah, where there is evidence of volcanic activity in historical times. But this
language, which is found elsewhere in connection with theophanies (e.g., Judg.
5:5; Ps. 97:2–5; Mic. 1:3–4), in all probability is only a poetic portrayal of the
awesomeness of Yahweh's appearance. Others suggest a location in the vicinity
of Kadesh-barnea, the desert oasis where the Israelites encamped for a considerable time; but this does not square with statements indicating that the mountain was quite a distance from this oasis (eleven days' march, according to Deut.
1:2). A third possibility, which is quite attractive, is Jebel Musa (Arabic for
"Mountain of Moses") in the southern part of the Sinaitic Peninsula, an impressive mountain which rises about 7,500 feet above sea level and overlooks a
plain where the Israelites may have camped. We know that this remote site in
the forbidding wilderness was visited by Christian pilgrims in the fourth century
C.E.. And the custom of making pilgrimages to the site may go back to a much
earlier time. As early as the ninth century B.C.E., Elijah the prophet left Beer-
sheba and journeyed "forty days and forty nights" (an expression meaning "a
long time") into the wilderness until he came to "Horeb, the mountain of God"
(I Kings 19:8). Some strong arguments can be adduced in favor of identifying
the "mountain of God" with Jebel Musa, the traditional Mount Sinai. For one
thing, it was within relatively easy reach of the fugitives from the Delta, who

Mount Sinai, *the traditional "Mount of Moses," is located in the mountainous tip of the Sinaitic Peninsula.*

perhaps followed the old Egyptian route to the copper and turquoise mines at Serabit el-Khadim in the southern Sinaitic Peninsula. Moreover, it is approximately eleven days' march from Kadesh (Deut. 1:2); in fact, in 1906 a caravan of the École Biblique in Jersusalem took exactly that amount of time to cover the distance.[5] Yet after all has been said, the plain truth is that we cannot be absolutely certain about this identification. Those who handed on the traditions were not interested primarily in geography but in the covenant that was made in the wilderness after the Exodus from Egypt. For throughout the subsequent generations it became increasingly clear that the covenant was the basis of Israel's existence as a people.

DEFINITION: "COVENANT"

From this point on, the word "covenant" will appear frequently. Today the term refers to "a binding and solemn agreement" made by two or more parties which involves mutual responsibilities, as for instance, a marriage covenant, an agreement among members of a religious body, or a treaty between sovereign political powers.

In the judgment of some scholars, the Hebrew word *běrîth*, translated "covenant," may be derived from an Akkadian (Babylonian) word *birîtu*, meaning "fetter, bond." Be that as it may, in the Old Testament the word is used to describe a binding relationship that is based on commitment, that carries with it promises and obligations, and that has the quality of constancy or durability. The friendship between Jonathan and David was based on a covenant (I Sam. 18:3), and there are various examples of covenants between heads of families or socio-political groups, such as Jacob and Laban (Gen. 31:44–50), the conquering Israelites and the Gibeonites (Josh. 9:3–27), or David and the elders of Israel (II Sam. 5:3). Often there is specific mention of a solemn oath which gives force to the covenant (Gen. 26:28; cf. 31:49–50), and sometimes the word "oath" may be used instead of "covenant" (Josh. 9:20).

As we shall see, there are different theological understandings of the covenant between God and Israel, depending on whether the accent falls on God's being bound to Israel unconditionally, or on Israel's being bound to God conditionally. Both are covenants of divine grace which entail human responsibility, but in the latter case the conditionality stems from Israel's success or failure in meeting its obligations. See further George E. Mendenhall, "Covenant," *Interpreter's Dictionary* I [25], 714–723.

The Sinai Narratives

Before we turn to the covenant itself, let us take a look at the material which, in the present arrangement of the Pentateuch, is connected with the sojourn at Sinai. In the sequence of the narrative, the Israelites arrive at Sinai in Exodus

---

[5] R. de Vaux alludes to this in connection with his judicious discussion of the location of Sinai, *History* [92], 426–439. Identification of the sacred mountain with Jebel Musa is also defended by G. E. Wright, *Biblical Archaeology* [110], 64; *Westminster Historical Atlas* [34], 38–39; Y. Aharoni in B. Rothenberg, *God's Wilderness*, trans. Joseph Witriol (London: Thames and Hudson, 1961), p. 170; *Macmillan Bible Atlas* [31], map 48.

19:1; they do not break camp until Numbers 10:11. All the intervening material has its setting at Sinai. In other words, the central portions of the Pentateuch— the last half of the book of Exodus, all the book of Leviticus, and the first ten chapters of the book of Numbers—deal with incidents and laws associated with Israel's encampment at Sinai. Notice too that this large block of material (Exod. 19 to Num. 10:10) is inserted right into the heart of another body of narratives dealing with Israel's experiences in the wilderness, as can be seen from the following outline.

A. Israel in the wilderness   Exodus 15:22–17:16[6]
  [Israel at Sinai: Exodus 19:1 to Numbers 10:10]
B. Israel in the wilderness   Numbers 10:11 to 20:22

Note: In the Hebrew Bible the title for the book of Numbers
  is "In [the] Wilderness" (B^emidbar).

It is striking that some of the stories of the B section of the above outline seem to be located in the same general area (Kadesh) as those of the A section. We shall return to this matter later, when we take up the question of whether the Sinai covenant tradition is separate from the Exodus-Conquest tradition.

Much of the material in this long Sinai section belongs to the relatively late Priestly tradition (P), as evidenced by the priestly interest in various cultic matters, including the tabernacle, sacred objects (especially the Ark), ordination to the priesthood, and various kinds of sacrifices. All of the book of Leviticus is Priestly material, as are the first ten chapters of Numbers, with the exception of the last few verses (Num. 10:29–36). Of the Sinai material in Exodus, a good proportion belongs to Priestly tradition: chapters 25 through 31, and chapters 35 through 40. So by a process of reduction, most of the rest belongs to the Old Epic tradition—that is, the so-called J and E sources which have been woven together in such a way that it is not easy to separate them. (Deuteronomic material [D] is not present in any significant degree in the Pentateuch until the book of Deuteronomy.) After taking away the Priestly sections, the residue of Old Epic tradition is chapters 19 through 24, and 32 through 34, roughly speaking.[7]

In isolating the Priestly material we do not mean to imply that it has no historical value. Although the Priestly Work (P) was finally written down only in the period after the fall of the nation in 587 B.C.E., it actually preserves many ancient recollections. In dealing with biblical literature it is axiomatic that the *date of a writing is no sure index of the age of the traditions it records*. This principle also holds for the Old Epic (J and E) tradition. Although presumably written down in the period of the monarchy (that is, after David, c. 1000 B.C.E.), it not

---

[6] Exodus 18 is apparently out of order, for it locates Jethro's visit to Moses at "the mountain of God" (verse 5), whereas the Israelites reached the mountain in Exodus 19:1–2, according to the present arrangement.

[7] For a source analysis of materials dealing with Sinai, see the supplement to Noth's *Pentateuchal Traditions* [70], pp. 270–273.

only reflects the interests of the day, but also preserves material from earlier periods. Some of this Old Epic material in the book of Exodus goes back to the time of Moses; some of it reflects Israel's life in the agricultural situation of Canaan—that is, the time of Joshua and later. Hence, in later chapters, when it is appropriate, we shall have occasion to refer to some of the Sinai material, for instance the agricultural laws preserved in the Old Epic tradition (Exod. 20:23–33:23) or the institutions of the Priestly Work (see Chapters 4 and 13).

THE COVENANT AT SINAI

The story related in Exodus 1–24 deals with two series of episodes. The first is the deliverance from Egypt and its sequel, the guidance through the wilderness; the second is Yahweh's revelation at Sinai, the giving of the Law, and the making of the covenant. In the story as it has come down to us, these two series are inseparably related. The first is the preparation for the second (see Exod. 3:12), and the second is based theologically on the first.

The "Eagles' Wings" Passage

The essential connection between these two aspects of Israelite tradition—Exodus and Sinai—is stressed in a small unit found at the beginning of Exodus 19, immediately after the notice in verses 1–2a (derived from the Priestly [P] itinerary) that Israel arrived at Sinai about three months after leaving Egypt. According to this passage (Exod. 19:3b–6), which serves as a transitional link, Yahweh had been carrying the people, just as a mother eagle lifts her young, toward this mountain spot for a special purpose. Notice the rhythmic style and balanced unity:

> Thus you shall say to the house of Jacob,
>   and tell the Israelites:
>
>> "You have observed what I did to Egypt,
>>   and how I carried you on eagles' wings,
>>   bringing you unto me here.
>
>> Now, then, if you will only hear my voice,
>>   and keep my covenant,
>>   You shall be to me [*lî*] a special possession among all peoples,
>>   for [*kî*] to me [*lî*] the whole earth belongs;
>> and you shall be to me [*lî*] a kingdom of priests,
>>   and a holy nation."
>
> These are the words you shall speak to the Israelites.
>   EXODUS 19:3b–6

If you look at this passage carefully, you will probably agree with literary critics who maintain that it stands by itself, having a beginning formula ("Thus you shall say . . . ") and a rounded-off conclusion ("These are the words which you shall speak . . . "").[8] Notice too the prevailing parallelism of the structure in which the thought of one line is echoed and balanced in the next one, and the climactic use of "for" (Hebrew: *kî*), which provides the theological basis for the choosing of Israel. Also, the Hebrew text displays assonances and the emphatic use of certain recurring words (e.g. *lî*, "to me"). The carefully chiseled form and rhythmic style of this independent unit suggest that before it was placed in its present literary setting it may have been shaped by catechetical usage, perhaps in connection with services of covenant renewal. In any case, the restrained and simple style of the passage sets forth a mature theological reflection on the meaning of Israel's special calling (election). This calling is grounded on the event of the Exodus, which manifested God's action in delivering Israel from Egyptian bondage ("you have seen what I did"). But Yahweh's initiative evoked a response from the people. It placed them in a situation of decision, summoned them to a task within the divine purpose. What Moses had experienced earlier at Sinai—the call to take his part in Yahweh's historical plan—was experienced by all the people at the same sacred mountain, and with far-reaching implications for the future. Whether in fact these people would be the people of Yahweh depended upon a condition: "if you will only obey my voice and keep my covenant." Then they would be Yahweh's personal "possession" (the Hebrew word means "personal property"), the community that belongs to Yahweh in a special sense and whose vocation is to order its entire life according to Yahweh's sovereign demands. Here we find a characteristic of Israel's faith that will engage our attention later on: the strange combination of the universal and the particular. Yahweh's sovereignty knows no boundaries, for "all the earth is mine" (Exod. 19:5b). But from many peoples Yahweh singles out one people, not for privilege but for a task. They are to be "a kingdom of priests"—that is, a community separated from the world and consecrated to the service of God (cf. I Peter 2:5, 9).[9]

After this theological introduction, the narrative describes the divine appearance (theophany) on Sinai, which was accompanied by the giving of the laws that were to be binding upon the covenant people (Exod. 19:9–20:20). Some scholars argue, on the basis of this passage, that Sinai was once a volcanic mountain or that the theophany was accompanied by a violent thunderstorm (see verses 16–19). As we have seen, however, it is more likely that the traditional storm imagery of "earthquake, wind, and fire" (cf. I Kings 19:11–13) is used to describe the awesome divine holiness and the majesty of God's coming

---

[8] See James Muilenburg, "The Form and Structure of the Covenantal Formulations," *Vetus Testamentum*, 9 (1959), 347–65. Martin Buber discusses the theological significance of this passage in *Moses* [207], pp. 101–9.

[9] The expression translated "kingdom of priests" is not altogether clear. It may express Israel's uniqueness—that is, its separation from the profane and its peculiar belonging to God; so William L. Moran, in *The Bible in Current Catholic Thought*, ed. J. L. McKenzie (New York: Herder and Herder, 1962), pp. 7–20. Or it may mean that Israel is "a kingdom set apart like a priesthood" for a special service; so R. B. Y. Scott in *Oudtestamentische Studien*, VIII, ed. P. A. H. de Boer (Leiden: Brill, 1950), 213–19. The verse seems to affirm that Israel's priestly role is to minister on behalf of the nations before Yahweh (cf. Gen. 12:3).

to visit the people. It is significant that Israel adopted religious metaphors not from the quiet rhythms and beauties of nature, but from the violent storm that shakes the earth, overwhelming people with an awareness of the transcendence and holiness of God and a sense of the frailty and precariousness of human life (see Isa. 2:12–22; Ps. 29).

The Ratification of the Covenant

The Old Epic tradition portrays the ceremony of the making of the covenant in the important twenty-fourth chapter of Exodus, in which two ancient strands of tradition are blended together. According to one version (Exod. 24:1–2, 9–11), the covenant is made effective in a sacred meal on top of the mountain. The participants in this "summit meeting" are the "distinguished ones" or representatives of Israel who, in addition to Moses, include the priestly Aaron and his two eldest sons (cf. Exod. 6:23), and seventy elders. The unusual statement that "they beheld God, and ate and drank" suggests that during the covenant meal the presence of the holy God was so real that, like the prophet Isaiah later, they envisioned the heavenly king, enthroned in cosmic majesty (24:10; cf. Isa. 6:1–3); and yet, despite the warning that no human being could see God and live (Exod. 33:20; cf. Isa. 6:5), divine holiness caused them no harm. In its own way, the story deals with a fundamental theme of Israelite tradition: the presence of the transcendent God in the human world.

According to the other tradition found in Exodus 24:3–8, the whole assembly of Israel takes part in a covenant ceremony at the foot of the mountain. In this case the covenant is made effective by a sacrifice. Moses builds an altar and sets up twelve pillars to represent the people according to the twelve tribes. Animals are sacrificed, and half the blood is dashed against the altar as a symbol of Yahweh's participation in the rite. The other half is put in basins, and Moses, acting as covenant mediator, reads to the people "the book of the covenant." When they pledge themselves to accept and obey Yahweh's demands, Moses dashes the blood upon the people, saying, "Behold the blood of the covenant which Yahweh has made with you in accordance with all these words."

As we see, these two traditions differ in regard to the ceremonial means of concluding the covenant. Sharing a common meal was one way to seal a covenant, as we know from the contract that Jacob and Laban made (see Gen. 31:46 and especially verse 54). Moreover, the practice of making a covenant by a sacrifice was well known in ancient society. In the Mari tablets, referred to earlier (see p. 34), a treaty or covenant alliance was consummated in the sacred rite of "killing the ass" (compare Gen. 15:7–21 and especially Jer. 34:18–19). Not exactly the same practice is described in Exodus 24, but we do find there the ancient belief that sacrificial blood has the sacramental power to bring together two parties in covenant. The belief in the efficacy of blood figures prominently in the theology of sacrifice in the Old Testament, and is further refined in the covenant theology of the New Testament, as can be seen from such a passage as I Corinthians 11:25.

However, even more important than the different views of the covenant ceremony are the divergent understandings of the covenant itself which each tradition presupposes. In one, the people are involved only through their representatives; in the other, the people take part directly. In one no stipulations seem to be imposed as part of the covenant-making ceremony; in the other the covenant rite includes the reading of requirements in which the big "If" of Exod. 19:5 reverberates: "If you will obey my voice and keep my covenant. . . . "[10] Both of these covenant conceptions were deeply rooted in Israel's history. And because both were important for a full understanding of Yahweh's relationship with the people, they are dovetailed together in Exodus 24.

Although the Old Epic tradition included ceremonies for sealing the covenant and, at least in some passages, emphasized that the keeping of laws was the conditional basis for the continuance of the covenant relationship, these features were played down when the traditional materials were incorporated into the Priestly Work to form the Torah (Pentateuch) in its final form. Priestly traditionists had no doubt about the validity of the Sinai covenant, and therefore they included the Old Epic material found in Exodus 19–24 *in toto*. But they subsumed the Sinai covenant under the theology of the "everlasting covenant" (*bĕrîth ôlām*)—that is, a covenant which God establishes *in perpetuity*, regardless of human performance. In the Priestly scheme, the ecumenical covenant with Noah (Gen. 9:1–17) and the special covenant with Abraham (Gen. 17) belong to this type of "everlasting covenant." Given this theological assumption, it was appropriate for the Priestly Writer to embrace the Sinai covenant within the "everlasting covenant" that El Shaddai (Yahweh) had made with Abraham and his descendents (Gen. 17:7–8) and even to regard the Sinaitic covenant itself as a "perpetual covenant" (*bĕrîth 'ôlām*), the sign of which is the sabbath (Exod. 31:12–17). Accordingly, the deliverance of the people from Egyptian bondage is based on Yahweh's "remembrance" of the covenant with Abraham, Isaac, and Jacob (Exod. 2:24; 6:2–8 [P]); and the establishment of the cult at Sinai (chaps. 25–31, 25–40) is the fulfillment of Yahweh's pledge to be God to the people (Gen. 17:7) and to "tabernacle" in their midst (Exod. 29:45–46). Later on we shall return to this Priestly theological perspective (Chapter 13). Here it is important to notice that, by contrast, the Old Epic tradition, as evidenced particularly in Exodus 19:3b–6 and 24:3–8, insists that the covenant contains a *conditional* element which the people must take with the utmost seriousness. Some of Israel's prophets, as we shall see later, stood on the platform of the Mosaic covenant of the Old Epic tradition, announcing the people's failure to obey Yahweh's voice and threatening them with divine judgment for their breaking of the cov-

---

[10] Source critics usually assign the mountaintop ceremony (Exod. 24:1–2, 9–11) to the Yahwist Epic (J) and point out that in this tradition the covenant law is not introduced until 34:10–28. The ceremony at the base of the mountain (24:3–8), which may have included the Decalogue (Exod. 20:1–17), is often assigned to the Elohist (E). See Murray L. Newman, *The People of the Covenant* [231]. He maintains that the two covenant traditions, with their different theological emphases, originated at Kadesh in two different, but related, groups.

enant. These two understandings of the covenant—the conditional and the un-conditional—stood in tension within one another throughout the history of Israel's traditions.

COVENANT AND LAW

According to the Old Epic tradition, then, the making of the covenant included the announcement of the convenant stipulations. The story of the covenant ceremony in Exodus 24:3–8 is introduced this way:

> Moses came and told the people all the words [d*barim*] of Yahweh, and all the ordinances [*mishpatim*]. Then all the people, answering with one voice, said: "All the words [d*barim*] that Yahweh has spoken we will do."
>
> —EXODUS 24:3

Clearly, this passage refers to the Ten Commandments (or "Ten Words"), which have been introduced previously in the narrative (20:1–17), and which are specifically designated as "words" (d*barim*) at the opening (20:1). But the covenant ceremony, according to the passage cited above, was also preceded by the reading of the "ordinances" (*mishpatim*). This seems rather strange, because the people responded by saying that they would obey the "words"; and it is the "words" which figure in the following service from beginning to end (see verses 4, 7, 8). It seems, then, that an editor, wishing to insert the "ordinances" found in Exodus 21–23 (the so-called Covenant Code), has slipped in the loosely hanging phrase "and all the ordinances" at the end of the sentence. Originally, however, the "book [or document] of the covenant," which Moses read to the people (24:7), probably contained the Ten Commandments.[11]

The editorial procedure, which we have just discussed, gives a clue that other law collections from later times and circles have been inserted into the story of Israel's sojourn at Sinai. By placing subsequent laws in the context of the Sinai revelation, later editors emphasized the contemporaneity of the covenant for other generations, a point that is made in Deuteronomy 5:2–3:

> Yahweh, our God, made a covenant with us in Horeb. Not with our ancestors did Yahweh make this covenant, but with us, we who are here, all of us who are alive today.

In addition, editors wanted to show that later covenant laws also stand under the umbrella of Mosaic authority. It is generally recognized that a number of separate bodies of law have gravitated to Mount Sinai, as the following table shows:

---

[11] The civil and religious laws in Exodus 20–23 are often called "The Covenant Code" on the basis of the phrase in 24:7, "The Book of the Covenant." But this is inaccurate. It may be, however, that these laws were promulgated in later covenant services, a point to which we shall return in the next chapter.

Bodies of Legal Material in the Pentateuch

At Sinai:	
1. The Decalogue	Exod. 20:1–17 (repeated in Deut. 5:6–21)
2. Civil and religious laws, often called the "Covenant Code"	Exod. 20:22–23:33
3. A set of ritual laws, often thought to be another decalogue	Exod. 34:10–26
4. Priestly legislation:	
Cultic instructions	Exod. 25–31 (executed in Exod. 35–40)
Priestly laws	Lev. 1–18, 27
The Holiness Code	Lev. 19–26
Priestly supplements	Num. 1–10
After Sinai:	
1. Priestly supplements	Num. 28–31, 33–36
2. Deuteronomic Code	Deut. 12–26
3. Laws sanctioned by a curse	Deut. 27

Thus the Pentateuch in its present form, with its great diversity, shows how successive generations continued to respond to Yahweh's covenant demand in the changing circumstances of their history. The Priestly legislation found in Exodus 25–31, as we have said, bears the stamp of later times. The Covenant Code, for the most part, betrays the interests of an agricultural rather than a wilderness environment, as we shall see in the next chapter. And the group of ritual laws in Exodus 34:10–26 reflects a Canaanite background for the most part. So, by a process of reduction, not much is left that may have come from the time of Moses.

Does all this mean that no laws were transmitted from the Mosaic period, but only an undefined sense of absolute responsibility to the will of God that had to be spelled out in detail later on? Some scholars have answered this question in the affirmative. But on the basis of studies of the form and content of laws in the Pentateuch, it can be affirmed that the Jewish tradition which traces the covenant law—particularly the Decalogue—back to Moses is fundamentally authentic.

Absolute Law and Case Law

Two general types of law are found in the Pentateuch: conditional (or case) law, and absolute (or apodictic) law.[12] Conditional law has a characteristic pattern: if *this* happens, then *that* will be the legal consequence. And the case can be

---

[12] This form critical distinction was made by Albrecht Alt in his important study of "The Origins of Israelite Law," first printed in German in 1934 and now available in *Essays on Old Testament History and Religion* [151], pp. 101–71. Subsequent studies have modified his thesis by tracing apodictic law to ancient clan circles and by drawing attention to the presence of this type of law in other ancient law codes. See the studies on the Ten Commandments by J. J. Stamm and M. E. Andrew [234], Brevard Childs, *Exodus* [210], pp. 385–439, and Walter Harrelson, *The Ten Commandments and Human Rights* [224].

more carefully defined to include various subconditions, as would be evident in modern law books. This type of law is found in ancient law codes, such as the Code of Hammurabi, and it is found repeatedly in the legislation of the so-called Covenant Code, mentioned above, and the legal corpus found in Deuteronomy 12–26. Absolute law, on the other hand, has no "ifs" or "buts" about it. It is unconditional; it is stated in sharp, terse language. The difference between the two types of law may be seen at a glance by comparing the casuistry of the law about buying a Hebrew slave (Exod. 21:2–6) with the staccato command: "Whoever curses his father or his mother shall be put to death" (Exod. 21:17). Absolute law seems to be more characteristically Israelite and expresses the unconditional demands of the covenant. In all probability, law of this type goes back to the wilderness period. It is noteworthy that the Decalogue, unlike the "ordinances" of the casuistic type in Exodus 21–23, does not necessarily presuppose an agricultural society.[13]

In the light of this analysis, there is reason to believe that the Ten Commandments in Exodus 20:1–17 come from Moses. In Hebrew they are called "the Ten Words." Several of the commandments are expressed in two or three words; and others, though they are much longer in their present form, undoubtedly have been expanded in the process of being handed on. It is probable that originally all Ten Commandments were terse, absolute demands of the apodictic type mentioned above. Here is one possible reconstruction of the original Decalogue:[14]

> God spoke all these words: I am Yahweh your God, who brought you forth out of the land of Egypt, out of the house of slaves.

1. You shall have no other gods before me.
2. You shall not make for me any graven images or any likeness.
3. You shall not invoke the Name of Yahweh your God in vain.
4. Remember the Sabbath day to keep it holy.
5. Honor your father and your mother.
6. You shall not commit murder.
7. You shall not commit adultery.
8. You shall not steal.
9. You shall not bear false witness against your neighbor.
10. You shall not covet your neighbor's house.

[13] Compare, for instance, the laws dealing with an ox (Exod. 21:28–36) and those dealing with damage done to a vineyard or grain field (22:5–6). It should be noticed that the Covenant Code also contains a few sharply stated, unqualified laws of the apodictic type, e.g., 21:15, 16, 17. Usually these laws, however, are not cast in the "thou shalt" form of the Decalogue, but in Hebrew begin with a participial word (meaning, the one who does something) and conclude with strengthened verbal forms which demand the death penalty absolutely.

[14] See James Muilenburg. "The History of the Religion of Israel," *Interpreter's Bible*, I [16], 303. Roman Catholics, Eastern Orthodox, and Protestants (Lutheran and Reformed) differ on the way the Ten Commandments are to be numbered. See D. M. Beegle (*Moses* [206]), where these differences are tabulated (p. 217) and the meaning of the commandments is discussed (pp. 218–34).

With the exception of commandments 4 and 5, the Decalogue is a series of prohibitions, each beginning with a verb in the second person singular, indicating that each member of the covenant community is addressed. This should not be taken to mean that the Mosaic commandments, with their predominant "don't do this" or "don't do that," advocated the negative attitude which some people have associated with biblical religion. Actually, the intention was just the opposite. The Decalogue merely stakes out general limitations which are defined by the covenant relationship; but within these limitations there is wide latitude for freedom of action or for interpretation of obligation to God and to one's fellow human beings. Indeed, the purpose of the case laws was to try to spell out the implications of the apodictic commandments in the changing and complex situations of Israel's life. Eventually the commandments were reduced to two and stated in positive form—namely, "You shall love Yahweh your God with all your heart, and with all your soul ["being"], and with all your strength" and "You shall love your neighbor as yourself" (Deut. 6:5; Lev. 19:18b; see Mark 12:28–31). But even when the commandments are stated in positive form, the people have to decide, within the context of the community and its traditions, what the absolute law means in specific situations.

Treaty and Covenant

The Law, then, was intended to be the social expression of the covenant bond. The term "covenant" (Hebrew *běrîth*) was often used for a political treaty, as is still the practice today. For instance, we are told that Solomon negotiated with Hiram, king of Tyre, to supply timber for the building of the temple and that "the two of them made a treaty" (literally, "cut a covenant"; I Kings 5:26b). The concept of "covenant" was drawn from the field of politics and used as a model for expressing God's relationship with Israel. Needless to say, the parties in this covenant (God and Israel) are not equal in rank; hence it is Yahweh who "cuts" the covenant.

New light has been thrown on the relationship between covenant and law by a study of international treaties of the late second millennium B.C.E., found chiefly in Hittite archives.[15] On the basis of an analysis of the form and content of these treaties, scholars distinguish two types of covenants: parity and suzerainty. A parity covenant is reciprocal—that is, both parties, being equal in rank, bind themselves to each other by bilateral obligations. The suzerainty covenant, on the other hand, is more unilateral, for it is made between a suzerain, a great king, and his vassal, the head of a subordinate state. To his vassal, the suzerain "gives" a covenant, and within the covenant the vassal finds protec-

---

[15] See the basic work by George E. Mendenhall, *Law and Covenant in the Ancient Near East* [229] and also his more recent article on "Covenant" in *Interpreter's Dictionary* [25]; and Klaus Baltzer, *The Covenant Formulary* [221]. A good general introduction to the subject is Delbert Hillers, *Covenant* [225].

A Procession of Hittite Gods carved in bas-relief on the walls of the rock sanctuary at Yazilikaya. This picture shows three deities out of a line of twelve, each of whom wears a pointed cap and shoes with upturned toes and holds a sickle-sword in his right hand. It was thought that the whole Hittite pantheon—"the thousand gods of Hatti"—were present in the holy place. Hittite treaties (covenants) were placed under the protection of the gods.

A Rock Sanctuary built by the Hittites at Yazilikaya ("Inscribed Rock"), about two miles east of the great mountain fortress of Hattushash, the former Hittite capital (see Color Plate 3). The sanctuary, a monument to Hittite state religion of the thirteenth century B.C.E., lies in a natural circle of rocks which is entered through a narrow gorge.

tion and security. As the subordinate party, the vassal is under obligation to obey the commands issued by the suzerain, for the suzerain's words are spoken with the majesty and authority of the covenant author. To make a covenant in no way infringes upon the sovereignty of the great king. And yet the covenant is not just an assertion of power over an inferior, as though the vassal were forced into obedience. The most striking aspect of the suzerainty covenant is the great attention given to the king's deeds of benevolence on behalf of the vassal, deeds which evoke a response of grateful obedience.

The suzerainty treaty form contains six characteristic features:[16]

---

[16] For an example of the suzerainty treaty, see the "Treaty between Mursilis and Duppi-Tessub of Amurru" in Pritchard, *Ancient Near Eastern Texts* [1], pp. 203–5. No. 4, which is missing in this example, is not always present in the treaty form. Other examples, biblical and extrabiblical, of this treaty form are given in J. Arthur Thompson, *The Ancient Near Eastern Treaties and the Old Testament* (London: Tyndale Press, 1964).

1. *Preamble.* Here the great king of the Hittite realm gives his name and the titles of his imperial sovereignty; for instance, "Thus speaks the Sun, Mursil, the Great King, the king of the country of Hatti, the favorite of the god Teshup, the son of . . . "

2. *Historical prologue.* The suzerain then proceeds to rehearse antecedents to the treaty, especially the deeds of benevolence performed on behalf of the vassal. Thus the vassal's motive for obligation is gratitude.

3. *Stipulations imposed on the vassal.* The most important requirement is that the vassal must take a loyalty oath, pledging not to recognize the sovereignty of other powers and vowing to come to the aid of the king in time of war.

4. *Attention to the treaty document.* This clause requires that copies of the treaty be preserved in the temples of both countries, and that it is to be read publicly in the vassal state once a year.

5. *Witnesses to the treaty.* Although the gods of both countries are invoked as witnesses, precedence is given to the Hittite gods. Moreover, included among the witnesses are natural powers such as heaven and earth, winds and clouds, mountains and rivers.

6. *Sanctions.* Blessings will result from obedience to the treaty, but curses will fall upon the vassal if he is unfaithful. The king offers protection within the terms of the treaty, but the threat of judgment, even total destruction, falls upon a vassal-state that violates the treaty.

The correlation between this treaty form and the Mosaic covenant in Exodus 19–24 is so striking at points that some scholars have concluded that it must have provided the model in terms of which Israel portrayed the relationship which Yahweh had initiated with the people. Indeed, in the context of the Old Epic narrative in Exodus 20–24, some of these elements are present. The preamble seems to be present in God's self-identification ("I am Yahweh, your God," Exod. 20:1), and the historical prologue may be found in the affirmation that Yahweh delivered the people from Egyptian bondage (20:2; cf. 19:4). Furthermore, the decalogue of Exodus 20 provided the stipulations, which Moses wrote in a document called "the book of the covenant" and read in the hearing of the people (24:4a, 7). The other elements of the suzerainty treaty form (Nos. 4–6) are not present in the Old Epic tradition, although, of course, we should not expect the witness clause, at least in the same form, because Yahweh does not recognize other "gods." Moreover, as critics of this hypothesis have pointed out, the Sinai narratives have elements which are not found in the Hittite treaty, especially the theophany to the people and the ceremony of the sealing of the covenant.

It is conceivable that Moses became acquainted with this treaty form in Egypt, which had a long history of dealing with the Hittites, and that he used it to interpret the meaning of Yahweh's initiative in freeing the people.[17] But this political analogy would not have been particularly meaningful to wanderers in the wilderness. The suzerainty treaties belonged to a world of settled peoples.

---

[17] John Bright argues, *History* [91], pp. 149–57, that the "overlord" (Hittite) covenant type was known to the founders of Israel. See also D. M. Beegle, *Moses* [206], pp. 204–213.

They defined political relations between Hittite kings and subordinate states in Asia Minor and northern Syria. Because these dealings between sovereign states were far removed from the realities of life in the wilderness, it is likely that this way of thinking had its greatest influence later on, when the Israelites had settled in Canaan and had begun to adjust to the political realities of the ancient world.[18] We shall have occasion to return to this matter, then, in the next chapter when we consider Israel's occupation of Canaan.

These studies have made one thing clear: the Mosaic covenant was in no sense a parity contract in which both parties were equal and mutually dependent. It was a relationship between unequals, between God and human beings; and the holiness and majesty of God are portrayed in the account of the awesome thunder and lightning before which the people stood back in fear. The covenant was *given* by God; the relationship was conferred upon the people by their Sovereign. Yahweh was not legally bound to Israel, in this way of thinking. In freedom Yahweh initiated the relationship and, as later prophets like Hosea and Jeremiah said, Yahweh was free to terminate it, with the result that Israel would no longer be "the people of God" (Hos. 1:8). On the other hand, Israel was bound to Yahweh, their Liberator, who had performed "mighty acts" on their behalf. Therefore Israel's pledge of obedience, as expressed in the covenant ceremony ("All the words that Yahweh has spoken we will do"), was predicated on gratitude for Yahweh's marvelous goodness, in response to Yahweh's gracious initiative. Israel, in short, was beholden to Yahweh. Salvation was the basis for obligation.

Such was the character of the relationship between God and people, Sovereign and servant, according to the Mosaic covenant tradition. It is significant that the unconditional obligations set forth in the Ten Commandments are prefaced with a brief historical prologue: "I am Yahweh your God, who brought you out of the land of Egypt, out of the house of bondage" (Exod. 20:2). Thus the Law was preceded by Israel's gospel—the "good news" of what God had done.

Exodus and Covenant

Some historians have raised the question of whether the sequence of "gospel and law"—that is, Exodus and Sinai covenant—resulted from *editorial arrangement* of the traditions, perhaps under the influence of the suzerainty treaty form, or whether the connection was rooted in the people's *historical memory* that Sinai really did come after the Exodus in the experience of those who departed from Egypt under Moses' leadership. On first consideration, there is some reason for supposing that the former is the case: the connection is purely formal. We have already noticed (p. 90) that the large block of Sinai material seems to be inserted

---

[18] Discussions of this subject are summarized in Dennis J. McCarthy, *Old Testament Covenant* [228]. See also R. de Vaux, *History* [92], pp. 439–452.

into, and to interrupt, a sequence of narratives dealing with Israel's experiences in the wilderness, especially at the oasis of Kadesh located about fifty miles south of Beer-sheba. This has led some to argue that the fugitives from Egypt went directly to the oasis, and that the Sinai sojourn pertains to another group.[19] Moreover, in typical Israelite confessions of faith, which some hold to be early in their thematic content, mention of the Sinai covenant is conspicuously absent (Deut. 26:5–9; 6:20–25; Josh. 24:2–13). These epitomes of the sacred history concentrate on the beginnings of the ancestral history, the deliverance from Egyptian oppression, and the entrance into the Promised Land. The silence regarding the Sinai covenant has been interpreted to mean that originally the Exodus-Conquest story and the Sinai story were separate traditions, based on events once experienced by different groups and commemorated on separate cultic occasions. When these groups came together into the larger Israelite community, they pooled their traditions into a unified epic and eventually, through the creative artistry of the author known as the Yahwist (J), the Sinai covenant material was neatly inserted into the heart of the expanded sacred history.[20]

But arguments from silence are notoriously fragile. Advocates of the suzerainty treaty hypothesis are right in calling attention to the essential connection between the Exodus and the Sinai law, as indicated in the Ten Commandments (see Exod. 20:2; also in the "Eagles' Wings" passage, 19:4, 5). The Sinai covenant is not mentioned in some of the confessional summaries and in early poetry like the Song of the Sea (Exod. 15:1–18) for the simple reason that it was not one of Yahweh's mighty acts, but rather Israel's *response* to that action,[21] just as the Eucharist (Lord's Supper) is not included in the Christian confession because it is the occasion for responding in gratitude to God's gracious action in Christ.[22] Even these creedal summaries show that the latter analogy is a good one. Indeed, Joshua's rehearsal of the sacred history is part of a service which

[19] The strict separation of these materials has been challenged by R. de Vaux, *History* [92], pp. 401–419, who argues that there were actually two exoduses. One group (an "exodus-expulsion") took a northern route along the coast and then veered to Kadesh. Slightly later, under Moses another group (an "exodus-flight") took a southern route which led first to Sinai, then to Kadesh.

[20] This view is set forth by Gerhard von Rad in his essay on the form-critical problem of the Hexateuch [181]; see also his commentary on *Genesis* [271], pp. 13–24. Martin Noth accepts von Rad's position in general, but instead of stressing the literary work of the Yahwist (J), he maintains that the unification of the two separate themes, Sinai and Exodus, took place in the previous oral period and thus belonged to the *Grundlage* or basic epic which underlies the literary sources. See his *Pentateuchal Traditions* [70], pp. 46–51, 59–62; *History* [98], pp. 126–37.

[21] This point has been emphasized by Artur Weiser, *The Old Testament* [47], pp. 83–99, and has been further strengthened by Herbert H. Huffmon in "The Exodus, Sinai and the Credo" [226]. Walter Beyerlin also gives strong arguments for the common origin of the Sinai and Exodus traditions in his study of the Sinaitic traditions [222].

See also J. P. Hyatt, "Were There an Ancient Historical Credo in Israel and an Independent Sinai Tradition?" in *Translating and Understanding the Old Testament* [159], 152–70. Hyatt, along with a number of scholars, questions the antiquity of the creedal confession isolated by G. von Rad and doubts that it is a full expression of Israel's faith. E. W. Nicholson, *Exodus and Sinai* [216], also argues for a historical connection between the events.

[22] The comparison is made by John Bright, *Early Israel* [176], p. 105.

included the making of a covenant and the reading of the law (Josh. 24:25–28); and the historical recitation in Deuteronomy 6:20–25 is explicitly intended to be a response to the question about the meaning of God's giving the law to Israel. In short, there seems to be good reason to affirm that the sequence of Exodus and Sinai is historically correct: the Sinai covenant actually took place *after* the Exodus in the experience of a single group of Hebrews. In the light of Moses' prophetic interpretation, the people accepted the obligations of the covenant in gratitude for what Yahweh had already done in their behalf.

Of course, when we move back through the chain of tradition to the beginnings of Israel, we find ourselves in a misty area where uncertainties abound. Nevertheless, the whole tradition clearly has its source in "root experiences": "the saving experience" (Exodus) and "the commanding experience" (Sinai).[23] From the very first, divine grace and divine demand, gospel and law, or—in Jewish terms—*haggadah* (narrative) and *halakah* (commandment) were inseparably connected in Israel's experience.

THE BREAKING OF THE COVENANT

So far in this chapter we have focused our attention on the Sinai narratives in Exodus 19–24. The Old Epic tradition found in these chapters continues in chapters 32–34 after an interlude of Priestly material.[24] This section begins with the dramatic episode of the making of the Golden Calf and culminates with a reissuing of the commandments and a reaffirmation of Yahweh's covenant with Israel.

The story of the Golden Calf provides a good example of how the Mosaic traditions were reinterpreted in new situations of Israel's history. There are striking similarities between this story and the account in I Kings 12:25–33, which reflects a political situation after the death of Solomon, when the United Kingdom was split into north Israel (Ephraim) and south Israel (Judah). The account tells how Jeroboam I (ca. 922–901 B.C.E.), the first king of northern Israel, set up golden bulls at two shrines, Dan and Bethel, in order to consolidate his kingdom politically. Indeed, the king's announcement "Behold your gods, O Israel, who brought you up out of the land of Egypt" (I Kings. 12:18) is the same as that of Aaron in the Golden Calf story (Exod. 32:4)! The narrator, whose loyalty was to the southern kingdom, clearly wanted to condemn Jeroboam's innovation by likening it to the apostasy that Moses once condemned. Some scholars have even gone to the extreme of saying that the story of the Golden Calf itself was created *ad hoc* as a polemic against the northern king, "who made Israel to sin."[25]

---

[23] See Emil Fackenheim, *God's Presence in History* [213], chap. 1.

[24] That chapters 25–31 come from Priestly tradition (P) is evident from the different style and the concern for cultic matters such as the tabernacle, the Ark, priestly ordination, etc. The instructions given in these chapters are carried out in chapters 35–40, which involves considerable repetition of content.

[25] This view is championed by Martin Noth, *Pentateuchal Traditions* [70], pp. 141–45. See also his commentary on *Exodus* [217], p. 246.

An Israelite Bronze Bull, dating from the period of the Judges (c. 1200 B.C.E.). Found on a "high place" or cultic site in the hills of Samaria, this figurine (7 inches long, 5 inches high), symbolizing power and fertility, apparently was associated with the worship of Yahweh as well as Baal (cf. Judg. 6:25)

It is likely, however, that the story in Exodus 32 rests upon a tradition much older than Jeroboam I and indicates that some ancient circles believed that the bull could legitimately be used to symbolize the supremacy of Yahweh.[26]

In any case, the revised story, which deserves to be read for its own sake, now serves an important function in the larger Pentateuchal narrative. We have seen that a recurrent theme in the wilderness stories is the impatient murmuring of the people. Here they are restive because of Moses' long absence on the mountaintop, where, as the story says, Yahweh had been speaking with him. Supposing that some accident had happened to Moses, they ask Aaron (who had good clerical standing) to make them "gods ['elohim] who shall go before us."[27] Like many religious people, ancient and modern, they wanted a God who was near at hand, not far off (cf. Jer. 23:23–24). And above all they wanted a

[26] See Frank M. Cross, "Yahweh and El" [112], 73–75, who argues that in northern circles the Bull was a symbol of the high god 'El, with whom Yahweh was identified. Bethel, he points out, was an old sanctuary where "Bull 'El" was worshiped (not Baal, the god of fertility, also portrayed as standing on a young bull); Jeroboam's policy was to reestablish the old sanctuary of Bethel, with its 'El worship, as a rival to the Jerusalem sanctuary.

[27] The narrator's bias is indicated by the assumption that polytheism was involved; thus the word 'elohim, which may mean either "God" or "gods" in Hebrew, is construed with plural verbs in verses 1 and 4. But the story speaks of only one calf-symbol, and the feast is explicitly called "a feast to Yahweh" in verse 5. The same bias is reflected in I Kings 12:28 where 'elohim probably should be translated "God" rather than "gods."

God whose presence was compatible with contemporary culture—in this case, Canaanite culture with its emphasis upon sexual vitality and fertility. The ensuing "feast to Yahweh" was in good Canaanite style, with sacrifices, eating and drinking, dancing, and perhaps sexual orgies (verses 5-6). The story goes that when Moses, coming down the mountain, saw the wild spectacle he was overcome with anger and smashed the tablets on which the Decalogue was written, thereby dramatizing that the covenant had been broken.

This sets the stage for the narratives that follow (chapters 33 and 34). For a time it seemed that all hope for the future was lost; for how could Yahweh accompany such a sinful people without divine holiness becoming a consuming fire? Yet Moses, the covenant mediator, interceded for the people and received the assurance that Yahweh's name (character, identity) is holy love, which includes both judgment and forgiveness. Yahweh acts in divine freedom:

> "I will be gracious unto whom I will be gracious,
>   and I will be compassionate to whom I will have compassion."
> EXODUS 33:19

Forgiveness is not cheap and easy, but discloses the new opportunity which only God can give, and therefore evokes awe and wonder (cf. Ps. 130:4). In this context there appears for the first time a great confession of faith, centering in the "name" of God, which is echoed in various parts of the Old Testament:

> Then Yahweh passed by before him [Moses] and proclaimed:
>   YAHWEH, YAHWEH!
>   God who is compassionate and gracious,
>   slow to anger and full of loyalty [*hesed*] and faithfulness,
>   extending *hesed* to thousands,
>   forgiving iniquity, rebellion, and sin;
>   but who will definitely not exempt from punishment,
>   visiting the sins of the parents upon the children,
>   and to children's children to the third and fourth generation.
> EXODUS 34:6-7

These narratives in Exodus 32-34 are marked by a sober realism. They show that Israel could not claim to be *better* than other nations, either morally or religiously, for the people displayed the same weakness and strength that are found in the life of any people. If there was any difference, it lay in the extraordinary experience that had formed them into a community and the destiny to which they were called in the service of God. Moses is represented as saying: "Is it not in thy going with us, so that we are distinct, I and thy people, from all other people that are upon the face of the earth?" (Exod. 33:16). It was with the conviction that Yahweh, their Leader, was going before them that the people faced the future. Above all, here we find the dawning recognition of something that later prophets announced: the covenant that is broken by human folly and rebellion can be renewed only on the basis of divine forgiveness (see Jer. 31:34b), which goes beyond what may be expected and opens a new way into the future.

In this context we find another tradition about the making of the covenant (Exod. 34:10–28), which parallels the one we have discussed previously. Here there are virtually no resemblances to the suzerainty treaty form. Instead of a historical prologue, the covenant is introduced by the promise of marvels which Yahweh will accomplish in the *future* (verses 10–11). Moses' impulsive destruction of the first tables of stone on which the Decalogue was inscribed provides the occasion for a new edition, symbolizing the renewal of the covenant. But strangely, although the second set of tables was to contain "the words that were on the first tables" which Moses broke (34:1), the laws found in 34:11–26 display few points of contact with the first decalogue (notably verses 14 and 17, which prohibit the worship of other gods and the making of molten images). And though it is indicated at the end of verse 28 that the new edition was a decalogue ("ten words"), it is very difficult to find exactly ten commandments here. These laws are sometimes referred to as the "ritual decalogue," owing to concentration on cultic matters such as the seasonal festivals or the prohibition against the Canaanite practice of boiling a young goat in its mother's milk. For the most part these laws presuppose the later situation of Israel's settlement in Canaan, when agricultural festivals were adopted and some Canaanite practices were repudiated. The narrative scheme, which includes Moses' breaking of the first tables, has made it possible for this separate set of laws to be included here.

THE MOSAIC FAITH

Looking back over the last two chapters, let us summarize the main aspects of the Mosaic faith. First, as the preface to the Ten Commandments indicates, Yahweh is preeminently the God whose liberating power was revealed in a historical-political event, the Exodus—an event so crucial that it became the undying memory of the people. To be sure, Israel was not alone in witnessing to divine activity in history; other ancient peoples believed that their gods were active in upholding the political and cosmic order as well as insuring the beneficent movements of nature.[28] But no other nation of antiquity, as far as we know, took divine activity in history to be central in the self-understanding of a people and its understanding of God's relation to them, as expressed in celebrations of worship and in the writing of historical narratives. The passion of this conviction was later expressed by Hosea, who declared that Yahweh is Israel's God "from the land of Egypt" and that besides Yahweh the people "know" no other deity (Hos. 13:4–5). Not that Yahweh's power was limited to

---

[28] See Bertil Albrektson, *History and the Gods* [194], who argues that testimonies to divine activity in history were not peculiar to ancient Israel. However, Albrektson admits, at the conclusion of his study, that "the idea of divine acts in history," in Israel on the one hand and in Mesopotamia on the other, "may well have occupied a different place in the different patterns of beliefs" (p. 115).

the arena of history. Yahweh's theophany could be described in the thunder and lightning bursting over Sinai; Yahweh could command the wind to drive back the waters of the Reed Sea; Yahweh could bring plagues to remind even the most hard-hearted that "the earth belongs to Yahweh" (Exod. 9:29; cf. Ps. 24:1); Yahweh graciously supplied the people with food and water in the wilderness. But Yahweh was no natural power: a sun-god, a storm-god, or a god of nature's mysterious fertility. Rather, Israel affirmed that Yahweh could use the powers of nature to achieve a historical purpose: to challenge the mighty empire of Pharaoh, to liberate a people from the bondage of slavery, and to open a path through the wilderness into the future. The Mosaic faith has a special penchant for historical events, precisely because it rests upon "root experiences" that bear witness to the God who transcends both nature and history. Accordingly, Israel's traditions include various historical writings, as we shall see more clearly later on, which review history from the standpoint of this basic theological perspective.

Secondly, Israel believed that in a series of extraordinary events, centering in the crossing of the Reed Sea, Yahweh had taken the initiative to establish a close relationship with a people. The narratives never suggest that the distance between God and people was removed. Even Moses, through whose mediation Yahweh spoke to the people, was warned that he could not see Yahweh's "face" (or "presence"), "for a human being may not see me and live" (Exod. 33:20). The narrator goes on to relate that Moses, hidden in a cave, was enabled to catch a glimpse only of Yahweh's "back" (33:17-23; compare I Kings 19:9-12)— a figurative way of saying that even in the experience of the divine presence God remains hidden (cf. Isa. 45:15). But Israel believed that the holy God who is "far off" (transcendent) is also "near" (immanent)—indeed, that God had taken the initiative to enter into relationship with a people and thus to become, in a special sense, "the God of Israel." The tradition testifies that Israel's relation to Yahweh was not that of a slave who serves God by performing menial tasks, but that of a "first-born son" (4:22-23) who has been graciously redeemed and given an inheritance. Gratitude for divine liberation was the primary motive for Israel's response of faith. And that faith was expressed in obeying the laws of the covenant and in facing the future in the confidence that Yahweh would be with, and go with, the people. The covenant relationship—"coexistence with God" as Abraham Joshua Heschel puts it[29]—was the basis of the Israelite community.

Finally, for Israel there was to be only one God—Yahweh. The first command of the Mosaic Decalogue says categorically: "You shall have no other gods before [or besides] me." If the First Commandment implies that other gods exist, they were not to claim Israel's allegiance, and they paled into insignificance

---

[29] The main aspects of Heschel's important book, *God in Search of Man: A Philosophy of Judaism* (New York: Farrar, Straus and Giroux, 1955) are presented and discussed by the author in "Coexistence with God: Heschel's exposition of Biblical Theology," in *Abraham Joshua Heschel: Exploring His Life and Thought*, ed. John C. Merkle (New York: Macmillan, 1985).

before the glory of Yahweh. As we have seen, the contest in the Exodus drama is between Yahweh and Pharaoh—not between Yahweh and the gods of Egypt. Yahweh alone controls the events of history and the powers of nature. Moreover, in Israel's faith Yahweh is not part of a pantheon, even though the idea of the Heavenly Council, composed of the "sons of God" (heavenly beings), could be used to portray Yahweh's cosmic majesty (see Exod. 15:11). Another evidence of Israel's protest against polytheism is found in the fact that Yahweh is never represented as having a consort, a female counterpart, as was true in the case of all the major deities of the ancient Near East. Indeed, the whole conception of the mother-goddess, which played an important role in ancient religions, was repudiated, although there are numerous passages in the Old Testament which employ feminine imagery for God (Isa. 42:14–15; 66:13). Some may object that this sounds too much like male chauvinism elevated to the theological level. Israel's intention, however, was to challenge the sexual model for understanding the divine-human relationship and to insist on the primacy of historical-political models like the liberation from oppression and the covenant (treaty).

The second commandment of the Decalogue goes a step further by saying that Yahweh is not to be worshiped in the form of any image or likeness. This was a revolutionary view in a world in which it was believed that the divine presence was concretely represented in an image, whether an image in human form (the statue of a god or goddess) or in animal form (a bull, lion, etc). Ancient people believed that the mystery of divinity burst forth all around them in many forms: natural, animal, or human. Without some concrete representation of deity—that is, a cult image—they could not have found divine meaning in life. Yet in spite of this human need, Israel affirmed from the Mosaic period on that Yahweh is the Incomparable One who cannot be likened to "anything that is in heaven above, or that is in the earth beneath, or that is in the water under the earth" (Exod. 20:4)—in other words, in the whole realm of creation, pictorially conceived.[30] This intolerance of images, inherited from the Mosaic period, received its supreme expression in later prophecy (see especially Isa. 40:18–26). The only exception to this iconoclasm is the view found in Priestly tradition that 'adam (human being), consisting of "male and female," is created in the image of God, to represent God's sovereign rule on the earth (Gen. 1:26–28).

The question is often raised as to whether Mosaic religion was monotheistic—that is, whether it affirmed belief in only one God. It is doubtful whether the question should be put in this way, because it assumes a degree of intellectual sophistication that is alien to Israel's ancient faith. Instead of raising the abstract question as to whether or not other gods existed, Israel heard the command that it was forbidden for other gods to lay claim on its allegiance. The commandment does not say, "There are no other gods," but "*You* shall have

[30] Apropos of this, see Gerhard von Rad, "Some Aspects of the Old Testament World View," in *The Problem of the Hexateuch and other Essays* [166], p. 147.

no other gods.''[31] The covenant ceremony itself was an invitation to decision: to serve Yahweh or not. There is not the slightest hint that the people were generously allowed to straddle the fence: to serve Yahweh *and* some other god of their preference. It was either/or. Yahweh made a complete, absolute claim upon Israel's devotion. Hence the earliest way of expressing Israel's sense of divine sovereignty was in terms of Yahweh's ''jealousy.'' Yahweh's name is Jealous, we are told (Exod. 34:14). This is a figurative expression of the truth of the First Commandment: Yahweh makes an unconditional demand upon the loyalty of the people. As we shall see in subsequent chapters, this religious demand was put to the test when the Israelites settled down in Canaan and faced the temptation of serving other loyalties (see 34:11–16).

A stream, as we say, never rises higher than its source. This proverb may be applied to the source of Israel's faith in the Mosaic period. In subsequent periods the stream was widened, its channel was deepened, its flow was interrupted by many cataracts. But Israel's greatest moments of worship and prophetic insight were regarded as a return to the source: the Exodus and the covenant of Sinai.

---

[31] See Martin Buber, *The Prophetic Faith* [311], pp. 19–23.

CHAPTER 4

The Promised Land

The struggle for land has always been one of the most powerful drives in national history. This is obviously true, for instance, in the case of the United States. In story and song, Americans rehearse the stirring epic of immigrants who landed on the Atlantic seaboard and, at the cost of great hardship and often fierce warfare, pushed the frontier to the shores of the Pacific. The tragic side of the story, of course, is that the native Indians, who had developed their own culture on the land, were disposessed and almost exterminated. Nevertheless, in times of thanksgiving Americans affirm their belief that, despite the sordid aspects of injustice and violence, the hand of God was guiding the "pilgrim feet"—to echo the words of the patriotic song "America, the Beautiful"— "whose stern, impassioned stress, a thoroughfare for freedom beat, across the wilderness."

From earliest times the Fertile Crescent was the scene of a fierce struggle for land. As we have seen, this coveted area periodically was invaded by peoples from Arabia, Asia Minor, the Caucasian highlands, or Egypt—peoples who sought a strip of the good earth to call their own or who fought to expand their territory, at the expense of others. Palestine was, by virtue of its geographical location, inevitably drawn into the incessant conflict. This little country was the

Biblical readings: The reader should turn to the account of Israel's sojourn in the wilderness and the march through Transjordan, found in Numbers 11 through 14, and 18 through 24 plus chap. 32 (Old Epic narratives in the main). Also the narrative of the conquest in Joshua 1–12 and the account of the Shechem assembly in Joshua 24.

place where small nations rudely and brutally fought for living space, and where big nations fought their wars of empire.

Into this dynamic arena came the Hebrews. Like other 'Apiru in the ancient world, they were at first a landless people. They belonged to the floating population, the unsettled elements of society. But these wanderers were seeking a land, in order that they might participate fully in society and fulfill their historical destiny. Their struggle to obtain land entailed much suffering and bloodshed, and the slaughter of many Canaanite natives. But it was their firm conviction that Yahweh, their God, was with them in the rough-and-tumble of the conflict, leading them victoriously into the land.

A LAND FLOWING WITH MILK AND HONEY

In the faith of ancient Israel "the guidance out of Egypt" was inseparably connected with "the guidance into the arable land."[1] This is evident from a passage in the book of Deuteronomy which deals with religious instruction of the younger generation.[2] "When your child asks" about the motive for obeying the commandments, the answer is to be given in terms of a recitation of events which happened "for us"—that is, the whole community—past, present and future:

> Once we were Pharaoh's slaves in Egypt,
>   and Yahweh brought us out from Egypt with a mighty hand.
> Before our very eyes Yahweh displayed great and ominous signs
>   and wonders against Pharaoh and all his court.
> Us he brought out from there so that he might bring us in, to give
>   us the land which he promised by oath to our ancestors.
>
> —DEUT. 6:21–23

The same inseparable sequence of events ("Yahweh brought us out . . . in order that he might bring us in") is found in another liturgical recitation (Deut. 26:5–9), to which we have referred before (see p. 12). When offering the first fruits of the harvest at the pilgrimage festival (Feast of Weeks or Pentecost), the worshiper is to confess gratefully that "Yahweh brought us out of Egypt with a mighty hand and an oustretched arm" and that "Yahweh brought us to this place, and gave us this land, a land flowing with milk and honey." Anyone who has been in Palestine, and has been impressed with the abundance of rocks on every hand, may wonder at the extravagant description of the "land flowing with milk and honey." According to the ancient view, milk and honey in abundance were blessings of Paradise. To wanderers who were used to life in the barren wilderness, Canaan was a veritable paradise (see Deut. 8:7–10). It was

---

[1] See Martin Noth, who, in *Pentateuchal Traditions* [70], pp. 51–54, rightly stresses that "the constitution of a 'free' Israel on its own soil" was implicit in the primary theme of the Exodus.

[2] In this connection, see Walter Brueggemann, *The Land* [237], pp. 14–39.

therefore with deep gratitude that they affirmed: "Yahweh brought us to this place."

Since the liturgy in Deuteronomy 26:5–9 was connected with a harvest festival, it is clear that it dates from a time well after Israel had settled in Canaan and had made the transition to agriculture. Some scholars believe that the promise of land had been an aspect of "the faith of the fathers"—that is, the religion of the ancestors (see above, pp. 41–45). It is quite true that the Pentateuch in its present form gives great emphasis to this theme in the stories of the ancestors. According to Genesis 12:7, at Shechem Yahweh said to Abram, "To your descendants I will give this land." This promise was reaffirmed to Isaac and Jacob, and was renewed in the time of Moses. Hence Canaan is known as "the Promised Land." We must keep in mind, however, that these traditions were written down after the occupation of Canaan was an accomplished fact. Whatever the promise of the land meant in the period of Israel's ancestors, it was understood more clearly later on, when the traditions were recast in the light of Yahweh's revelation in the event of the Exodus.

It is significant that this liturgy—which has been called by von Rad "the Hexateuch in miniature"—comes to a climax with the affirmation about Yahweh's gift of the land. This is understood to be the high point in the rehearsal of Israel's sacred history. As such, it is given great prominence in the Pentateuch and especially in the book of Joshua (Hexateuch), which deals with the conquest of Canaan. True, this theme is colored by Israelite nationalism, which accounts in part for its important place in the narrative. But it is noteworthy that even the great prophets, who vigorously attacked Israel's proud nationalism, did not surrender the conviction that the gift of the land was the supreme sign of Yahweh's benevolence toward the people. The prophet Amos, who was anything but a chauvinistic nationalist, appealed to the sacred tradition of what Yahweh had done for Israel:

> It was I [Yahweh] who brought you up from the land of Egypt,
> I who led you in the wilderness forty years,
>   to take possession of the land of the Amorites.
> —AMOS 2:10 (NEB)

Similar statements about Yahweh's gift of the land are found in other prophets, such as Hosea (chap. 2) and Jeremiah (2:7; 3:19). And the book of Deuteronomy, which is a sermon about life in the Promised Land, describes the land of Canaan as Israel's "inheritance," received from Yahweh.

Considering the terrible suffering involved in the conquest of Canaan, especially for the defeated people, it is difficult for most of us to understand the Israelite conviction that God was actually taking part in the struggle. Yahweh is portrayed as a God of holy war who ruthlessly demands the ḥérem—the sacrificial destruction of Israel's enemies. The book of Joshua bristles with theological difficulties, many of which were removed or refined by Israel's prophetic movement, as we shall see. On the other hand, Israel's faith is not founded upon a conception of God who is aloof from the human struggle. Rather it rests upon a response to the God who is active within the social struggle, guiding and shaping the course of human affairs according to divine purpose. In Israel's experience the conquest of Canaan did not happen by accident of circumstance or by the assertion of superior human power. It occurred within the providence of God. Therefore, the land was not a possession to boast about, but a gift to be received with humility and gratitude (Josh. 24:13).

With this preparation, let us turn our attention to the narratives that deal with Israel's sojourn in the wilderness, its designs to invade Canaan, and the long circuit through the countries of Transjordan. In general terms, this period of Israel's history is covered by the books of Numbers (from 10:11 on), Deuteronomy, and Joshua. Fortunately, it is not necessary to read through all this material at this stage of our study. A great deal of Priestly material (P) is found in the latter half of the book of Numbers, and possibly the last part of the book of Joshua, and we shall defer treatment of it to a later chapter (see Chapter 13). Moreover, the book of Deuteronomy, which purports to be a sermon given by Moses on the eve of the invasion of Canaan, belongs to the Deuteronomic (D) tradition, which was written down in the period just before and after the fall of the nation in 587 B.C.E., and will be considered later on (Chapter 11). We are left, then, with the Old Epic tradition of the book of Numbers (found mainly in chaps. 11–14, 20–24, and 32), and the story of the conquest in the book of Joshua (chaps. 1–12).

FORTY YEARS OF WANDERING

According to the tradition, Israel spent forty years wandering in the wilderness south of Beer-sheba. We must not take this figure as being mathematically exact. The number forty is often a stylized expression for a full generation and sometimes it means only "a long time," as in the statement that Elijah journeyed into the wilderness forty days and forty nights (I Kings 19:8), or the tradition that Jesus fasted in the wilderness for the same period of time (Mk. 1:13). Nevertheless, here the statement is probably approximately right. We are told that none of the adults who left Egypt were permitted to enter into Canaan; all of them died during the sojourn in the wilderness (Num. 14:26–35; 26:63–65). It was a new generation, under the leadership of Joshua, that was privileged to set eyes on Canaan.

The Sojourn at Kadesh

The narratives of the Pentateuch in their present form concentrate on the sojourn at Mount Sinai. As we have seen, the Israelites arrive at Sinai in Exodus 19:1 and break camp (ten months and nineteen days later) in Numbers 10:11.

The Oasis of 'Ain El-Qudeirat which, in the judgment of some scholars, is the location of Kadesh-barnea, where the Israelites settled for a long time during their wilderness sojourn. The spring pictured here is one of three in the area, all of which the Israelites may have used.

All the intervening material deals with the laws and institutions—given at Sinai—by which the covenant people are to live. The Israelites undoubtedly spent the greater part of their wilderness sojourn at a desert place called Kadesh or Kadesh-barnea (Num. 13:26; 20:1, 16; Deut. 1:46). The site is identified with the oasis, watered by three springs, in the barren Negeb about fifty miles south of Beer-sheba (see picture).[3] Some of the traditions about episodes in the wilderness, as we have already noticed (p. 90), have their original setting at Kadesh, which was said to be eleven days' journey from Sinai (Deut. 1:2) and located on the edge of territory controlled by Edom. This seems to be true of some of the wilderness material placed before Sinai (that is, Exod. 15:23–18:27),[4] but it is clearly true of much of the post-Sinai material found in Numbers 11–20 which comes basically from the Old Epic tradition—with the exception of chapters 15, 17, 18, and 19, which come entirely from Priestly tradition.

The sojourn at Kadesh undoubtedly had a profound influence upon the people who later came to be known as Israel. Unfortunately, however, it is difficult to determine what groups were there, where they all came from, and how long the Moses party stayed. Some historians have emphasized the importance of the Kadesh sojourn by arguing that Kadesh, not Sinai, was the original des-

---

[3] See Y. Aharoni, "Kadesh-Barnea and Mount Sinai," in B. Rothenberg, *God's Wilderness*, trans. Joseph Witriol (London: Thames and Hudson, 1961), 117–40.

[4] Note that Exod. 15:23–27 relates a murmuring experience at Massah and Meribah, presumably two of the springs of the Kadesh area. The incident is paralleled in Num. 20:2–13, where the location is clearly Kadesh (or Meribath-Kadesh, Deut. 33:5). Some maintain that all the material in Exod. 15:23–18:27 belongs to Kadesh, but this is doubtful.

tination of the Hebrews who fled from Egypt, and that it was at this oasis that their basic community life, administration of law, and style of worship were established. This hypothesis is supported by appeal to a historical summary found in Judges 11:16–18, which jumps from the Exodus to Kadesh in one sentence without any reference to a stop at Sinai. This argument from silence, however, is a slender reed on which to lean. The same telescoped summary is found in Numbers 20:14–16, where Moses sends a message to the king of Edom. In this case, as in the case of Jephthah's later message to the king of Ammon (Judg. 11:12–28), it was appropriate to mention only those matters which were politically relevant without going into the whole story. We may be sure that the historical situation was much more complex than can be gathered from a first glance at the biblical account, which intends to magnify the revelation at Sinai and to emphasize Moses' leadership in the journey. Yet there is sufficient reason to believe that the Hebrews who fled from Egypt followed a southern route which took them first to Sinai and then to Kadesh. When they arrived at the oasis, they must have come into contact with other Hebrews, perhaps some who had come down from Palestine earlier or who had departed from Egypt under other circumstances.[5]

In Numbers 11–20 we find a renewal of the theme that, in spite of the providence of Yahweh, the people continued to murmur and, on occasion, to rebel against the leadership of Moses. The desert fare of manna was not good enough for them, for they remembered too well their highly seasoned diet in Egypt (Num. 11:4–6). Dissension broke out in Moses' own tribe, the tribe of Levi, over his leadership. The revolt was instigated by his own brother and sister, Aaron and Miriam (Num. 12). It was renewed on a larger scale by a certain Korah, who stirred up factional strife among the Levites, and also by Dathan and Abiram, who aroused other tribesmen against Moses (Num. 16). Not too much is known about the years of Israel's sojourn at Kadesh and its vicinity, but the tradition affords vivid glimpses of how the people were forged together into greater unity and solidarity through bitter struggle and suffering.[6]

It is apparent, then, that the "rabble" (Num. 11:4) under Moses' leadership did not become a stable, unified community overnight. A powerful centripetal force, the liberating action of Yahweh, had pulled them toward the center of a common covenant allegiance. But there were also powerful centrifugal forces that pulled away from that center: human factors such as tribal rivalry, power struggles for leadership, hunger and thirst, and the human incapacity for faith. At the oasis of Kadesh-barnea these two forces came into sharp conflict. Hu-

---

[5] For further discussion of the historical problem, see H. H. Rowley, *From Joseph to Joshua* [190], pp. 106–64, who advocates two invasions; R. de Vaux, *History* [92], pp. 419–425, who advocates two exoduses; Martin Noth, *Pentateuchal Traditions* [70], pp. 51–54; 71ff. and *History* [98], 68–84, who argues that the tradition preserved by the central Palestinian tribes has crowded out other traditions of the occupation of the land; Murray Newman, *People of the Covenant* [231], pp. 72–101, who in his own way argues for two invasions.

[6] On "controversy at Kadesh" see Murray L. Newman, *The People of the Covenant* [231], chap. 3. The murmuring narratives are discussed by George Coats, *Rebellion in the Wilderness* [223].

manly speaking, there is every reason to expect that the covenant bond would have dissolved in the disruptive tensions of the wilderness. But as Israel looked back on the desert experience in the perspective of the covenant faith, it became clear—much clearer, no doubt, than in the wilderness days—that through these trials Yahweh was uniting and disciplining the people for the historical task that lay ahead of them. A later discourse forcefully affirms this truth:

> You must remember the entire journey that Yahweh, your God, caused you to take during these forty years in the wilderness in order to make you feel humble, to test you so as to know what is in your heart—whether you would keep his commandments or not. Yahweh humbled you and let you get hungry, giving you manna to eat which you did not know and your ancestors had not known, in order to make you realize that it is not by bread alone that a human being lives, but rather it is by every utterance of the mouth of Yahweh that a person lives.
>
> —DEUT. 8:2–3

The Holy One in the Midst of Israel

According to ancient tradition, Yahweh's presence in the midst of the people was signified by two sacred objects. One was the Tent of Meeting, first mentioned in connection with the sojourn at Sinai (Exod. 33:7–11) and later in connection with Kadesh and the wilderness (Num. 11:16–17, 24–26; 12:1–8; see Deut. 31:14–15). The Priestly (P) tradition also gives an elaborate description of this tent or "tabernacle" in Exodus 26–27 and 35–38. Not all of the Priestly description fits the ancient wilderness situation; a great deal of it reflects later theological and cultic development. However, the Priestly account undoubtedly preserves authentic reminiscences of the ancient desert sanctuary, which must have been something like the red leather tent-shrines known among ancient Semites.[7] We are told that Moses pitched the Tent outside the camp and that he used to go there to encounter Yahweh, who would descend from heaven in a pillar of cloud to the door of the tent and speak with him "face to face, as a man speaks to his friend" (Exod. 33:11). The Tent was the place of "meeting" with Yahweh, where an oracle could be sought or where Yahweh's word could be proclaimed to assembled Israel. Those who had difficult problems would go out to the Tent and Moses would bring their petitions before Yahweh. In this way, we may imagine, the covenant law was expounded and expanded.

The other sacred object was the Ark of the Covenant, which the Priestly Writing describes in Exodus 25:10–22 and 37:1–9, probably in reliance upon ancient tradition. Originally, the Ark seems to have been a portable throne on which, it was believed, Yahweh was invisibly enthroned. As we observed in the previous chapter, Mosaic religion strictly vetoed the worship of Yahweh in the form of a visible image. In this respect, the religion of Israel differed radically

---

[7] See Frank M. Cross, Jr., "The Tabernacle," in *The Biblical Archaeologist*, X (1947), 45–68. Reprinted in *The Biblical Archaeologist Reader*, I [101], 201–28.

from the religions of other ancient peoples, who represented the deity's presence by setting up the image of a god or goddess in a temple or by bearing the image of the deity in festival processions. Nevertheless, it was firmly believed that the holy God of Israel was invisibly present in the midst of the people. In times of wandering or of battle Yahweh went before them in person as their leader, enthroned upon the Ark. One of the oldest fragments of the Pentateuch is the "Song of the Ark":

> As the ark set out, Moses would say:
>   "Arise, Yahweh, may your enemies be scattered
>   and those who hate you run for their lives before you!"
>
> And as it came to rest, he would say,
>   "Come back, Yahweh,
>   to the thronging hosts of Israel!"
>   —NUMBERS 10:35-36 (JB)

This song is found in a narrative context which states that "the Ark of the Covenant of Yahweh" went before the people when they set out from Sinai, suggesting that the construction of the Ark at one time must have been related in the Old Epic tradition. Indeed, according to a tradition found in Deuteronomy (10:3–5), Moses constructed an ark of acacia wood at Sinai and put in it the tables on which the Decalogue was inscribed.[8]

Strikingly, nowhere does the Old Epic tradition indicate explicitly that the Ark was placed inside the Tent shrine. Silence on this matter has led some interpreters to conclude that originally these cultic objects were independent, each being the focal point of a particular theological understanding and each being identified with a separate group of people. According to this attractive view, the Tent represented a theology of "manifestation" (the transcendent God from time to time appears to Moses and the people); the Ark stood for a theology of "presence" (Yahweh is present in the midst of the people). The Tent, supposedly the shrine of a southern group (especially the tribe of Judah), and the Ark, allegedly identified with a northern group (the Joseph tribes that Joshua led into Canaan), went their separate ways until they were eventually united in the history of the traditions, as can be seen in the Priestly Writing which affirms that Moses put the Ark inside the Tabernacle at Sinai (Exod. 20:2–3, 21; see also 25:22; Num. 7:89).[9] In view of the scanty evidence from the Epic tradition, however, we cannot be certain about this. In the early monarchy the Ark was stationed in a "tent" (II Sam. 7:2; see also 6:17), and this may indicate that David

---

[8] The Old Epic tradition about the construction of the Ark has apparently been replaced by the fuller treatment found in Priestly tradition (Exod. 25:10–22).

[9] This is the view of Gerhard von Rad, *Old Testament Theology*, Vol. 1 [142], 234–41. Murray Newman, in *The People of the Covenant* [231], pp. 55–71, maintains that two different covenant theologies were associated with the Tent and the Ark respectively and traces the separation of these cultic shrines to a major controversy at Kadesh.

conservatively maintained a cultic arrangement that goes back at least to the former Tribal Confederacy (cf. Ps. 78:60).[10]

In any case, during the sojourn in the wilderness, especially at Sinai and Kadesh, the people undoubtedly borrowed patterns of worship and community organization from others. Sacred objects like the Tent and the Ark were found among other peoples of antiquity. Under Moses' interpretation, however, they came to express the distinctive faith of Israel. Yahweh was worshiped as the transcendent God who dwells in heaven and who, without any limitation upon divine sovereignty, is present immanently in the midst of the people. Furthermore, it is striking that Jethro, a Midianite, proposed a scheme of administration of law in order to ease Moses' responsibilities as leader (Exod. 18:13–27). This story also indicates Israel's indebtedness to its neighbors.

A Foolhardy Attack on Canaan

Eventually, the hardships of the desert and the lack of living space compelled the Hebrews to look elsewhere for a home. A group of spies was sent out from the Kadesh base to survey the hill country of Canaan in the vicinity of Hebron, which lay directly north (Num. 13 and 14). This reconnaissance force brought back the report that the land was fertile, indeed that it was "a land flowing with milk and honey." However, the scouts also reported that the land was strongly fortified and that the inhabitants were of such great stature that "we seemed to ourselves like grasshoppers, and so we seemed to them" (Num. 13:32–33). A sharp division of opinion arose over whether the people should try to enter Canaan from the south. Two of the spies, Joshua and Caleb, were in favor of making the attack in spite of the odds against them, but the majority of the people were so discouraged that they proposed finding a leader to guide them back to Egypt, which, in contrast to their condition in the wilderness, seemed like "a land flowing with milk and honey" (see Num. 16:13). Finally, believing that an adventurous attack was preferable to wandering for a lifetime in the wilderness, they decided to make the attempt. The foolhardy move lacked divine sanction, for the Ark of the Covenant and Moses remained at Kadesh. The result was what might be expected. The Hebrews were decisively repulsed by the Amalekites of the Negeb and by the Canaanites of the hill country in the vicinity of Hormah, a few miles east of Beer-sheba (Num. 14:39–45). Another account of the battle of Hormah, though misplaced and perhaps relating to another situation (see Judg. 1:16–17), is found in Numbers 21:1–3. When the king of Arad, a Canaanite city in the Negeb, heard that the invaders were attempting to move north into Canaan, he sent out an army to intercept them, but this time the tables were turned. The account of the decisive victory of the Hebrews pro-

---

[10] Frank M. Cross, in "Ideologies of Kingship in the Era of the Empire" [112], states emphatically: "The Ark had always been associated with a tent shrine, wherever it wandered, wherever the central sanctuary was established" (p. 242).

vides a name explanation for the city Hormah ("Destruction," based on the Hebrew word for the sacrificial ban, *ḥerem*).

Because the Hebrews were too weak to break past the fortresses guarding the southern approach to Canaan, they had to seek another way to escape from the wilderness. There was only one other route: a long circuit through the country of Transjordan.

DETOUR VIA TRANSJORDAN

The rest of the book of Numbers deals with the advance of the Hebrews through "the other side of the Jordan" (Num. 32:19) in order to penetrate Canaan from the east. This route, too, was beset with many hazards, for Transjordan was occupied by settled peoples who resented the appearance of a band of armed intruders. A glance at the map (p. 133) will reveal the tactical problems that these Hebrews had to face. Just south of the Dead Sea, and directly opposite Kadesh-barnea, was Edom, traditionally related to Israel through Esau, the twin brother of Jacob (Gen. 36). Just above Edom lay Moab, with the river Arnon as its northern frontier and the brook Zered as its southern limit. Above Moab, on the edge of the Arabian desert, was Ammon. According to biblical tradition, both Moab and Ammon were distant relatives of Israel through Lot, the nephew of Abraham (Gen. 19:30–38). To the west of Ammon was situated the Amorite kingdom ruled by King Sihon, bounded by the river Arnon to the south and by the river Jabbok to the north. Still farther north lay the land of King Og, known as Bashan.

Whether these countries at this time were nations with flourishing populations is open to question. The archaeological evidence, which is incomplete, seems to indicate that Moab and Edom did not achieve national unity until a later period.[11] However, since both peoples are mentioned as adversaries of the people of Yahweh in early Hebrew poetry (Song of the Sea, Exod. 15:15), and appear in Egyptian texts from the thirteenth century B.C.E.,[12] we may assume that other 'Apiru groups were in the process of establishing themselves in the area at the time when those Hebrews who came to be known as Israel were seeking a homeland.

Disputes over Thoroughfare

Let us follow the biblical story further. According to Numbers 20:14–21, Moses sent messengers from Kadesh to the king of Edom, asking for permission to travel on the King's Highway. This ancient route, which is still followed by the modern road in that area, is the highway link between Syria and Ezion-geber,

[11] See Hayes and Miller, *History* [93], pp. 258–59.
[12] Ibid., pp. 250–251.

The King's Highway *seen from the air as it runs north to cross the Brook Zered. The Israelites attempted to use this ancient caravan road during their detour via Transjordan (Num. 20:17). Paved by the Romans, the road has remained visible in its outline through the centuries. The rectangular structure beside it is the ruin of an ancient guardpost.*

the seaport town which was located on the Gulf of Aqabah. From Ezion-geber, the road ran north through Moab, then through the Amorite land of King Sihon, skirting the border of the kingdom of Ammon, and on up through the territory of King Og (Bashan) to Damascus, the capital of Aram or Syria. In spite of Moses' promise that the Hebrews would stay on the highway, turning neither to the right nor to the left, the suspicious Edomite king refused to grant them passage. So they traveled along the western border of Edom, turning east at the boundary brook Zered, in order to skirt Moab.

As the Hebrews approached the territory of the Amorite kingdom of Sihon, Moses again sent messengers asking for permission to use the King's Highway. The king not only refused but also sent an army to crush the invaders (Num. 21:21–32). The result was the first major military victory that Israel ever achieved. So decisively did the Hebrews defeat the Amorites that they took possession of the whole kingdom. The taste of victory spurred them to move farther north, where they met and defeated the king of Bashan, a gigantic man named Og, whose main claim to fame was his unusually large and sturdy bed (Num. 21:33-35; Deut. 3:1-11). Thus they came into possession of a large strip of land in Transjordan, including the lands of Sihon and Og. The Hebrews were now encamped in "the plains of Moab" (Num. 22:1)—that is, the Moabite lowlands just across the Jordan River opposite Jericho. The stage was set for a bold thrust into Canaan from the east.

The Oracles of Balaam

At this point the narrator has placed the story of Balaam, a Babylonian diviner who was summoned by the king of Moab to pronounce a potent curse against the victorious Israelites (Num. 22-24). The story has elements of popular humor and fancy—as in the incident of Balaam's ass, which is described as speaking up in protest because of his master's irate treatment of a "dumb" beast. The "talking ass" is not the main feature of the story, however. Rather, it is what Balaam said as a prophetic spokesman of God. In ancient times it was believed that words spoken as a curse or as a blessing had power to achieve the desired result. A familiar illustration is the case of Jacob, who, to the great distress of his brother Esau, stole the deathbed blessing of their father, Isaac (Gen. 27). Because of this belief in the power of the spoken word, Balaam was invited to stand on a hilltop where the Israelites could be seen, and say, with a force greater than any show of military power, "Let them be damned." But the tradition affirms that a foreign diviner like Balaam had to obey the dictate of Israel's God, even though King Balak promised him a good fee and great honor:

> How can I curse whom God does not curse,
>   and how can I damn whom Yahweh does not damn?
> For from the top of the rocks I see them,
>   from the hills I observe them—
> behold, a people living apart,
>   not counting themselves among the nations.
> Who can count the dust of Jacob?
>   or number the mass of Israel?
>   —NUMBERS 23:8-10

According to this ancient view, Israel was not a nation, but a unique people set apart by Yahweh, who had delivered them from Egypt (cf. Deut. 7:6). Hence no magic or divination could avert the blessing that Yahweh chose to bestow upon them. The oracles of Balaam, which in their original poetic form may date back to the thirteenth or twelfth century B.C.E., express the lusty faith of the victorious Israelites. These oracles find a later echo in an Aramaic inscription from a Palestinian site, Deir 'Alla, dating about 700 B.C.E., which throws light on the role of a prophetic intermediary ("seer of the gods").[13]

---

[13] See Robert Wilson, *Prophecy* [328], p. 132. The text is published and discussed in J. Hoftijzer and G. van der Kooij, *Aramaic Texts from Deir 'Allah* (Leiden: E. J. Brill, 1976).

A more refined expression of Israel's covenant faith is given in Deuter-onomy, the last book of the Pentateuch, which we notice only in passing (see Chapter 11).[14] The book is cast in the form of a farewell address given by Moses in the plains of Moab just before the Israelites crossed over the Jordan to storm the land of Canaan. Moses is rehearsing the stirring events of Israel's history—the Exodus, the making of the covenant, the wandering in the wilderness, the victories in Transjordan—in order to exhort the people to remember gratefully all that Yahweh has done for them and to be faithful to the covenant obligations amid the temptations of Canaan. In its present form, the address comes from a time centuries later than Moses. But it shows how this "sacred history" was kept alive in Israel's memory through the generations and was reflected upon with deepening insight.

THE INVASION OF CANAAN

The book of Deuteronomy ends with an account of the death of Moses and the elevation of Joshua to be his successor (Deut. 34). In this abrupt manner the Torah or Pentateuch breaks off. It is quite obvious, however, that the story is not intended to end at this point, for the climax, toward which the narratives of the Pentateuch point, lies in the future: the fulfillment of the promise that Israel will be given an inheritance in the land of Canaan. Moses' death on Mount Nebo, in full sight of the Promised Land, occurs just when the Israelites are poised for the attack.

The story is resumed in the book of Joshua. This is the first book in the second major division of the Hebrew Bible, known as the Prophets. As can be seen from the accompanying chart, the canon of the Prophets is subdivided into two sections, each of which has four scrolls. The first is known as the Former Prophets; the second is known as the Latter Prophets. In the rest of this chapter we shall consider the first book of the Former Prophets, Joshua.

At first glance it may seem strange that the book of Joshua, which is largely historical narrative, should be considered as "prophecy." The major reason is that all the books of the Former Prophets are governed by a prophetic interpre-tation of Israel's history which was profoundly influenced by the great prophets of the eighth and seventh centuries. This theology of history was championed by a Deuteronomistic historian who reworked Israel's traditions in the period shortly before and just after the fall of the nation in 587 B.C.E. The characteristic style and viewpoint of the Deuteronomistic historian, which are well illustrated in the sermonic material in the opening chapters of Deuteronomy, pervade the books of the Former Prophets. Since Deuteronomic (D) material is not found to any significant degree in the first four books of the Old Testament, Genesis through Numbers, it is proper to regard all the material found in Deuteronomy

---

[14] The rest of the book of Numbers, with few exceptions, comes from the Priestly tradition, and deals largely with ritual matters.

The Law and the Prophets*

TORAH	NEBI'IM	
Genesis	Former Prophets:	
Exodus	Joshua	
Leviticus	Judges	
Numbers	I-II Samuel	
Deuteronomy	I-II Kings	
	Latter Prophets:	
	Isaiah	
	Jeremiah	
	Ezekiel	
	The Twelve:	
	Hosea, Joel, Amos, Obadiah, Jonah, Micah, Nahum, Habakkuk, Zephaniah, Haggai, Zechariah, Malachi	

*For a complete table of the arrangement of books in the Hebrew Bible see the chart on pp. 4–5.

through I-II Kings as a comprehensive Deuteronomistic history which begins with the Mosaic period and interprets the events of Israel's history to the time of the fall of the nation.[15]

The Land of Canaan

The first verses of the book of Joshua (1:1–9) are written in the style and from the theological perspective of the Deuteronomic writer. Yahweh is represented as summoning Joshua to lead Israel across the Jordan into the Promised Land, a land extending from the southern wilderness to the high Lebanon ranges to the north—and even beyond to the river Euphrates (see Gen. 15:18). Joshua is told that this segment of the Fertile Crescent will be Israel's on one condition: that the "book of the law" (the Deuteronomic Law) must be obeyed and studied diligently (Josh. 1:7–9). This is the key to success. Here we find the Deuteronomic formula for success and failure: obedience to Yahweh's commands will be rewarded with victory and prosperity; disobedience will bring the divine judgment of suffering and failure. This rather neat doctrine of reward and punishment, which may have arisen out of ceremonies of covenant renewal when the formulas of divine blessings and curses were solemnly recited (see pp. 98–101), runs through the whole Deuteronomistic History.

It stands to reason that whatever success the Israelites had in the invasion of Canaan depended upon other factors besides their faithful obedience to the covenant law, important though that was. Israel's success was facilitated by the

---

[15] This view has been advanced by Martin Noth in *The Deuteronomistic History* [246] and is now widely accepted. This history work is discussed further in Chapter 6 (see Definition, p. 183) and Chapter 11.

historical situation in the whole Fertile Crescent: the lay of the land, the culture of Canaan, the political relation of this strategic corridor to the foci of political power in Egypt and Mesopotamia. It may be that in another time and under different circumstances, the occupation of the land would have been no more successful than had been the earlier attempt to storm Canaan from the south. Now, however, the time was right for a bold venture, and Israel had been prepared and disciplined for it by years of experience in the wilderness. This is not to deny Israel's doctrine of providence, the conviction that "Yahweh your God is with you wherever you go" (Josh. 1:9). Rather, we must view the doctrine of God's providential guidance of Israel in a wider perspective, such as archaeology and ancient history provide, if we are fully to appreciate its significance. So, before considering the narrative of the conquest in Joshua 2–12, let us look for a moment at the situation in Canaan.

The Lay of the Land

First, we need a general idea of the geography of Canaan, or Palestine (the later name).[16] The most striking topographical feature, as can be seen by looking at the map inside the back cover of this book, is the central backbone of hill country lying between the deep cleft of the Jordan and the coastland of the Mediterranean. The hill country is cut, in the area of Mount Carmel, by a valley known as Jezreel (or Esdraelon),[17] which gives access to the Jordan Valley. In ancient times, the main military and commercial highway from Egypt to Mesopotamia ran along the coast, then turned into the Valley of Jezreel and veered northward to Damascus. Important fortified cities were located along this route—notably Megiddo, which guarded the pass leading from the southern coastal plain into the Valley of Jezreel. Many decisive battles, ancient and modern, have been fought for the control of this strategic pass (see picture, p. 197) and for the fertile valley.

As we have seen, the advancing Hebrews finally stationed themselves in "the plains of Moab"—that is, Moab's lowland territory down in the Jordan Valley. This valley is part of a deep geological rift that starts with the Kara Su valley in modern Turkey, runs down through the Beka Valley between the Lebanon and anti-Lebanon ranges, extends through the Dead Sea, the deepest place on the earth's surface (1285 feet below sea level), and follows the Arabah valley toward Egypt, eventually reaching Victoria Falls in southern Zambia. In this great rift lies the Jordan River. Fed by springs at the base of Mount Hermon, it winds in a serpentine course to the Sea of Galilee and eventually pours into the Salt Sea (Dead Sea), whose heavy saturation of salt forbids marine life or

---

[16] See the brief treatment in the *Westminster Historical Atlas* [34], pp. 17–20, or H. L. Grollenberg, *Atlas of the Bible* [29], pp. 11–16. Also, Denis Baly, *The Geography of the Bible* [30].

[17] In Greek the name Jezreel was corrupted to Esdraelon—a term used to designate the western part of the valley.

surrounding vegetation. In between Mount Hermon and the Dead Sea, however, the Jordan Valley is lush with vegetation, but the temperature in the summer is terribly hot. It is understandable, then, that the invaders looked with envious eyes toward the highlands of Canaan, beyond the west bank of the Jordan.

This Canaanite hill country may be divided into three areas. To the north, beyond the valley of Jezreel, lie the mountains of Galilee; below this is the central hill country of Ephraim (Samaria), whose major center in antiquity was Shechem, situated in the pass between Mount Gerizim and Mount Ebal (see picture, p. 260). Still further south—though separated by no natural frontier—is the hill country of Judah which, not far beyond Beer-sheba, fades into the southern wilderness (the Negeb). This strip of central hill country, from Mount Hermon to the Judean wilderness, was the scene of the Israelite struggle.

The broken terrain of Canaan was not well-suited for the establishment of a strong, centralized government, such as was achieved in the plain of Mesopotamia or the valley of the Nile. In the period of the Israelite occupation, Canaan was divided into a number of autonomous city-states—that is, political centers that embraced a fortified city and a number of satellite cities or villages. Since the best farming land was located on the coastal plain and in the valleys of Jezreel and the Jordan, most of the major Canaanite cities were concentrated in these areas. In addition, cities located on the plains could be defended by chariots and other heavy military equipment. The central hill country was more suited to a pastoral economy and was vulnerable to attack by guerrilla bands.

The political importance of Canaan lay in the fact that it was a strategic corridor between Egypt and Mesopotamia. The possession of this corridor was indispensable for any nation that sought to extend its control through the Fertile Crescent. Ever since about 2000 B.C.E., Canaan had been either nominally or actually under Egyptian suzerainty. But Egyptian control of Canaan fluctuated with the changing fortunes of Egypt's internal political affairs. We saw earlier (Chapter 1) that in the latter part of the eighteenth century a flood of Hyksos swept into Egypt and seized control. The expulsion of the Hyksos by Ahmose I, however, renewed Egypt's determination to regain control of its Asiatic empire.

The pharaohs of the early Eighteenth Dynasty (1570–1310 B.C.E.) carried out extensive military campaigns in Canaan and Syria. Egyptian outposts in Canaan were strengthened, such as the one at Beth-shan in the upper Jordan Valley (see picture on p. 221). Egyptian inspectors saw that local Canaanite rulers paid tribute and supplied laborers to work on Egyptian projects. Troops supported the Egyptian officials as they policed and exploited the country under the authority of Pharaoh.

At this time the only military power strong enough to challenge Egyptian imperialism was the kingdom of Mitanni (see above, pp. 36–37), which dominated northern Mesopotamia. But the two powers, each fearing the increasing threat of the Hittites of Anatolia (Asia Minor), eventually entered into a peace

Thutmose III the Warrior, *as portrayed in a vivid action scene on the walls of the temple of the god Amon at Karnak. The king (c. 1490–1436 B.C.E.) grasps a batch of captives by their hair as they kneel and raise their hands in a plea for mercy. His right arm, upraised to smite, is missing. To the right a goddess leads a group of conquered chieftains with a rope. Below the king's feet are rows of prisoners of war. The partially destroyed figure in the upper right hand corner is the god Amon.*

treaty during the reign of Thutmose IV (c. 1412–1403 B.C.E.). Thus Egypt was free to consolidate its position in Canaan, Phoenicia, and Syria.

The Amarna Age

Toward the end of the Eighteenth Dynasty, however, Egyptian control over Canaan weakened considerably, especially during the reign of Pharaoh Amenhotep IV, in the fourteenth century B.C.E. Archaeologists have excavated the library of his Egyptian capital, modern Tell el-Amarna, and have found many documents that shed light on Egyptian foreign affairs in Canaan during the turbulent fourteenth century, the so-called Amarna Age.[18] Unlike his predecessors of the Eighteenth Dynasty, this king was far less interested in pursuing an aggressive

---

[18] The Amarna Age covers the reigns of Amenhotep III (c. 1403–1364 B.C.E.) and Amenhotep IV (c. 1364–1347 B.C.E.). See the chronological chart on p. 52.

foreign policy than in effecting a religious revolution in Egypt with the introduction of a kind of monotheism based on the worship of the sun disc, the Aton. To demonstrate his break with the established priesthood of the high god Amon, he changed his name to Akhnaton (meaning ''The Splendor of Aton''); and he moved from Thebes and built a new capital which he called Akhetaton (''Horizon of Aton''), near modern Tell el-Amarna. Owing to his preoccupation with domestic affairs, the situation in Canaan got completely out of hand.

Pharaoh Akhnaton and his wife, Nefertiti, offering a libation to the sun god Aton, represented by the solar disc. Each of the rays streaming from the sun ends in a hand opened caressingly, and the two hands just above the faces of the royal pair hold a hieroglyph meaning "life."

In Akhnaton's archives was found the correspondence from a number of Canaanite kings, which gives a vivid picture of the disorder.[19] Apparently these city-state rulers were taking advantage of Egyptian weakness to advance their own political purposes, though they protested their loyalty to the Egyptian crown. The Egyptian officials were so corrupt that they only contributed further to the confusion and intrigue. The correspondence from a certain 'Abdu-Heba, Egyptian ruler of Jerusalem, mentions 'Apiru raids that were having a devastating effect on Egyptian control in Canaan.[20] He complains that he is not to blame for the loss of Egyptian land, for "like a ship in the midst of the sea" he is surrounded by opposition on every hand. The situation, he says, is one of anarchy, and "now the 'Apiru capture the cities of the king." In desperation, he begs: "Let the king take care of his land!" Even a garrison of fifty men to guard the land would help considerably, he pleads.

Some have supposed that the Amarna letters refer to the events described in the book of Joshua, but this is hardly the case. As we have seen (pp. 39-40), the term 'Apiru had a broad meaning, including people of all sorts who had no standing in the established order of society. In the Amarna period these restless, rootless elements had gained sufficiently in numbers and strength to function as a revolutionary force. There is no need, then, to equate the 'Apiru raids of the Amarna period with the Israelite conquest. It is quite likely, however, that some of the 'Apiru who entrenched themselves in the hill country and took control of a large area of central Canaan were relatives of—or at least sympathizers with—the followers of Joshua, who entered the country more than a century later. The Amarna letters refer to a certain Lab'ayu, Canaanite ruler of Shechem, who is bitterly accused of turning over his land to the 'Apiru.[21] As we shall see later, it was precisely in the Shechem area that Joshua met with no resistance and where he seems to have made a covenant alliance with Hebrew relatives and others who had not been in Egypt.

Egypt's New Bid for Power

The Amarna Age of Egyptian weakness in Canaan soon came to an end. After the death of Akhnaton, all traces of his monotheistic "heresy" were removed, and Egypt began to restore order and prosperity within its borders. But, in the shifting fortunes of world politics, the respite was brief. The Hittites, against whom the Egyptians and the Mitannians had formed a treaty of mutual protection, rose to world power under the leadership of the great king Shuppiluliuma (c. 1375-1335 B.C.E.). This new development occurred at approximately the time when there was an enormous revival of Egyptian power under the

---

[19] The texts are found in Pritchard, *Ancient Near Eastern Texts* [1], pp. 483-90. See E. F. Campbell, "The Amarna Letters and the Amarna Period," *Biblical Archaeologist,* XXIII (1960), 2-22; T. O. Lambdin, "Tell el-Amarna," *Interpreter's Dictionary* IV [25], 529-33.

[20] See Pritchard, Ibid., letters 286-290, pp. 487-89.

[21] Pritchard, letter 289, p. 489.

pharaohs of the Nineteenth Dynasty, especially Seti I and Rameses II, whom we have already met in connection with the Exodus. Owing to the disruptive attacks of the 'Apiru and the intrigue of Canaanite rulers, Hittite imperialism extended into Syria, Phoenicia, and even into Canaan itself. Seti I carried out military expeditions as far north as Syria, but the military showdown between the two powers came in the fifth year of the reign of Rameses II (1290–1224). The Egyptian army, under the personal command of Rameses, was ambushed and severely mauled by the forces of the Hittite king Muwatallis (c. 1306–1282) in the vicinity of Kadesh on the Orontes River in Syria. With pharaonic modesty, Rameses claimed that by personal valor he saved his army from the trap and even won a whopping victory, the report of which he published and illustrated on the walls of temples along the Nile, including the famous temple at Abu Simbel (see Color Plate 2).[22] The military stalemate was finally ended by a peace treaty between Rameses II and the next Hittite king, Hattusilis (c. 1275–1250), copies of which have been discovered in both countries. Throughout the rest of Rameses' long rule the Hittite boundary remained north of Mount Lebanon, and Canaan was under the hegemony of Egypt.

At the death of Rameses, weakness set in once again—and this time it was chronic. Rameses' son Merneptah (c. 1224–1211) lacked both the youth and the ability to control the Egyptian empire, which was being menaced by a threat far more serious than the Hittites. Beginning around the time of the Amarna period there was a great surge of population in the area of the Aegean Sea, the arm of the Mediterranean that reaches up between Greece and Anatolia (Turkey). Some of these homeless people swept into Asia Minor, where they brought the old Hittite empire to an end. Others overran the island of Crete, eclipsing the Minoan civilization, and moved on to Greece where they merged with the indigenous population. Still others sailed to and took control of Cyprus, then moved on to the mainland of Syria-Palestine, where they conquered important cities, including Ugarit (Ras Shamra), about which more will be said later (Chapter 6). Another wave pounded against Egypt, some coming by sea and others by land. These "Peoples of the Sea," as they are called in Egyptian documents, included an assortment of names, one of which was the Peleset (Philistines)—the people from whom Canaan later received the name "Palestine." Merneptah was able to hold back the flood during his brief reign; but pressure increased, especially during the reign of his successor Ramses III (c. 1183–1152). On the walls of Rameses III's temple of Medinet Habu at Thebes, the pharaoh described the threat of the confederation: "They laid their hands upon the lands as far as the circuit of the earth, their hearts confident and trusting: 'Our plans will succeed!' "[23] Ramses III checked the confederation's attempt to penetrate Egypt, thrusting the Philistines back into their beachhead on the coast of Canaan. This effort exhausted Egyptian power, and in the succeeding centuries Egypt never regained its former glory.

[22] See Pritchard, *Ancient Near Eastern Texts* [1], pp. 255–58.
[23] Ibid., pp. 262–63.

The Stele of Merneptah contains the earliest mention of "Israel" outside the Bible. Under the winged sun disc stands the god Amon in double representation. The king is also shown twice, standing before the god with a sickle-sword in one hand and a scepter in the other. Behind him stands the goddess Mut (extreme left) and the falcon headed god Horus (extreme right).

It is against this background of political turmoil and social upheaval that we must understand the biblical account of the invasion under Joshua, which apparently began about 1250 B.C.E. The powerful pharaoh Rameses II was on the throne (see Color Plate 2), but already his hold on Canaan was beginning to slip owing to preoccupation with the Hittite power to the north. Egypt found it increasingly difficult to cope with the volatile situation in Palestine. The invading Hebrews, according to the biblical account, moved into the central hill country, avoiding contact with Canaanite strongholds and Egyptian outposts on the plains. At one point, however, Merneptah found it necessary to act. In about the year 1220 he set up a victory stele in which he claims to have quelled unrest in the lands of Syria and Palestine. The inscription, actually a hymn of triumph over Libya as well as Asiatic peoples, contains these poetic lines:[24]

> Israel is laid waste, his seed is not.
> Hurru is become a widow for Egypt.

This is a highly significant text, for it contains the earliest reference to Israel outside the Bible. The text locates Israel in Palestine, but speaks only of a people. The translator notes that ''the word 'Israel' is the only one of the names in this context which is written with the determinative of people rather than land. Thus we should seem to have the Children of Israel in or near Palestine, but not yet as a settled people.''[25]

Obviously the military claim was exaggerated. Whatever happened in the encounter between Israelite and Egyptian forces, the Old Testament passes over the incident in discreet silence. And Merneptah could not give further attention to the matter, for his energies were diverted by the greater problem of resisting other invaders, the Sea Peoples, who threatened his country in great numbers. Thus the stage was set providentially for Israel to inherit the Promised Land.

ISRAEL'S CONQUEST OF CANAAN: THE DEUTERONOMISTIC VIEW

The first section of the book of Joshua (Josh. 1–12) sets forth the dramatic story of the Israelite conquest of Canaan. The reader is told how the whole land fell into the hand of Joshua in three swift, decisive military campaigns.

The first campaign gave the Israelites a firm foothold on the western side of the Jordan River, which was dammed back at Adam (modern ed-Damiyeh), presumably by one of the landslides that occur now and then in the geological fault followed by the river. (It is reported, by the way, that in 1267 C.E., and again in 1927, a slide caused by an earthquake dammed the river for a time.)[26] After crossing the dry river bed with the Ark in the lead, the people encamped at Gilgal (Josh. 3–5). From this base in the Jordan Valley they laid seige to Jericho, which fell at the sound of trumpets in the morning (Josh. 6). Spurred by the taste of victory, a military force ascended to the West Bank where they captured Ai by subterfuge (7:1–8:29). (Nothing is said about the conquest of nearby

---

[24] Pritchard, *Ancient Near Eastern Texts* [1], 376–78. The Egyptians referred to Palestine as Hurru—i.e., the land of the Hurrians (see above, p. 37).

[25] *Ibid.*, p. 378, n. 18.

[26] Nelson Glueck, *The River Jordan* (New York: McGraw-Hill, 1968) p. 118.

Bethel; cf. Judg. 1:22–26). Apparently the Israelites found no resistance in the central hill country, so they moved north as far as Shechem, where Joshua built an altar on a mountain overlooking the city (8:30–35).

In a second campaign the victorious Israelites penetrated into the southern hill country. Near the fortress of Jerusalem, which they seem to have bypassed temporarily, the Israelites were tricked into making a treaty with four federated cities, chief of which was Gibeon (Josh. 9). Because of their covenant (treaty) with Israel, the Gibeonites were threatened with reprisals from a coalition of Canaanite kings led by Adonizedek, king of Jerusalem; but the Israelites moved swiftly to their defense. According to a quotation from a lost book of Israelite poetry, the Book of Jashar (see also 2 Sam. 1:18), Joshua wished that the sun would stand still over Gibeon and that the moon would pause over the Valley of Aijalon so that his soldiers might have enough time to finish the battle decisively (Josh. 10:12–13a),

> "Sun, stand still over Gibeon,
>   and moon, you also, over the Vale of Aijalon!"
>   —JOSHUA 10:12b (JB)

Other poets, ancient and modern, have also expressed the wish that time would stop, or even turn back in its flight. However, the narrator who quoted from the old poetic collection apparently took the poetry literally (see 10:13–14)—as have many interpreters of Scripture—and commented that the sun and moon actually stopped in their course (or in scientific terms, that the earth ceased to rotate for almost a whole day). The purpose of the quotation and commentary is to testify that Yahweh, the Divine Warrior who commands the host of heaven, was fighting for Israel (10:14: cf. Judg. 5:20).

From this victory the Israelites moved on to further conquests in the south that included the city-states of Libnah, Lachish, Eglon, Hebron, and Debir (Kiriath-sepher), bypassing some heavily fortified towns like Gezer and Beth-shemesh (Josh. 10:16–43). In the case of Gezer, it should be noted, the biblical account (Josh. 10:33) does not state that the city was destroyed, but only that forces from the city attempted to intercept the Israelites and were defeated (see 16:10).

Finally, in a third campaign the Israelite forces won significant victories in the northern hill country, above the Valley of Jezreel in the area known as Galilee (cf. Isa. 9:1). Here Joshua was victorious over a coalition of northern kings (Josh. 11:1–9); but above all he won a decisive victory at the fortified city of Hazor, which was destroyed and burned (11:10–5).

According to this account, Joshua, the leader of united Israel, masterminded an effective strategy from a military base at Gilgal and, in three lightning campaigns into the center (chaps. 7–9), the south (chap. 10), and the north (chap. 11), took complete possession of Canaan in a short time. At least three fortified cities (Jericho, Ai, Hazor) were burned to the ground. Resisting Canaanites were destroyed with the edge of the sword; all obstacles were swept away in the

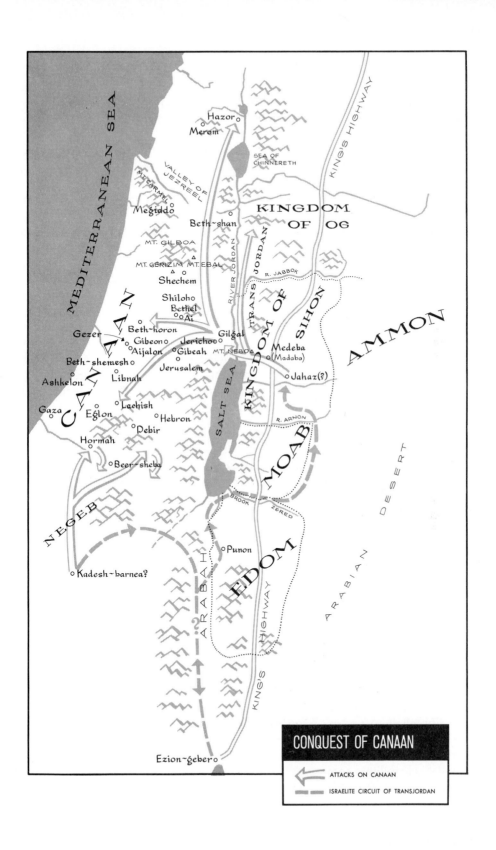

MEDITERRANEAN SEA

Hazor
Merom

SEA OF
CHINNERETH

VALLEY OF
JEZREEL

MT. CARMEL

Megiddo

Beth-shan

KINGDOM
OF OG

KING'S HIGHWAY

MT. GILBOA

MT. GERIZIM   MT. EBAL

Shechem

RIVER JORDAN

TRANS-JORDAN

R. JABBOK

Shiloho
Bethel
Ai

Gezer   Beth-horon
Gibeon   Jericho
Aijalon   Gibeah
Gilgal
MT. NEBO

KINGDOM OF SIHON

AMMON

Beth-shemesh

Medeba
(Madaba)

Ashkelon
Libnah

Jerusalem

Jahaz(?)

CANAAN

Gaza   Eglon
Hormah

Lachish
Hebron
Debir

SALT SEA

R. ARNON

Beer-sheba

MOAB

DESERT

NEGEB

BROOK ZERED

Punon

KADESH~BARNEA?

ARABAH (?)

EDOM

KING'S HIGHWAY

ARABIAN

ARABIAN

Ezion-geber

CONQUEST OF CANAAN

ATTACKS ON CANAAN

ISRAELITE CIRCUIT OF TRANSJORDAN

inexorable advance of Israelite forces. The "whole land" was given to the invaders in a holy war "because Yahweh, the God of Israel, fought for Israel" (10:42). The thoroughness of the conquest is indicated in the summary found at the conclusion of the account (11:16–23).

This, then, is the view of the Deuteronomistic historian, whose characteristic style and theological viewpoint dominate the story in Joshua 1–12 and Joshua's farewell address in Joshua 23. Undoubtedly this historian used older traditions: tribal stories, cultic legends, and perhaps material from the Old Epic tradition found in Genesis, Exodus, and Numbers. The historian picked up on the theme of the promise of the land to Israel's ancestors, and the Mosaic tradition of the obligations to the covenant, and then showed how all of this came to marvelous fulfillment in the time of Joshua. But apparently this writer was carried away with religious enthusiasm. As a result, the historical realities of the invasion of Canaan are made to appear much simpler than they actually were. Even this historian realized that Joshua did not make a clean sweep of the land, for the aging Joshua is told that "there remains yet very much land to be possessed" (Josh. 13:1–7). In his farewell address Joshua exhorted the Israelites not to join "the remnant of these nations left here among you" or else "Yahweh your God will not continue to drive out these nations before you" (Josh. 23:12–13). Apparently there was much work to be done before the Israelites could claim, as the Deuteronomistic historian does in a climactic moment, that "the land had rest from war" (Josh. 11:23).

AN ALTERNATIVE VIEW OF THE CONQUEST IN JOSHUA AND JUDGES 1

A more complex picture begins to appear as we compare the Deuteronomistic view of the conquest with statements found elsewhere in the book of Joshua and especially in the first chapter of the book of Judges. In Joshua 10:36–37 it is stated that Joshua destroyed the city of Hebron, but in Judges 1:10 the city is said to have been taken by the tribe of Judah. And in Joshua 10:38–39 Joshua is reported to have taken the city of Debir (or Kiriath-sepher) while in Joshua 15:13–19 and Judges 1:11–15 the credit is given to a Calebite named Othniel. Furthermore, the book of Joshua mentions a number of cities from which the Israelites were unable to expel the Canaanites, including Jerusalem (15:63), Gezer (16:10), Beth-shean, Taanach, and Megiddo (17:11–13).

A completely different picture of the invasion is given in the first chapter of the book of Judges. Despite the victory announcement made in the book of Joshua, this chapter states that the first question asked after Joshua's death was: "Who shall go up first for us against the Canaanites, to fight against them?" (Judg. 1:1). What follows is another version of events which seems to oppose the view that the land was conquered by Israelite forces acting in unison under the single military command of Joshua. Here we find a fragmentary, and at times puzzling, account of independent tribal actions. Strangely, it is claimed that the tribe of Judah captured and burned Jerusalem (Judges 1:8; but compare verse 21!), although we know on other grounds that this fortress was not captured until David (2 Sam. 5:6–7). The capture of Hebron and Debir, associated with Caleb and Othniel (as in Josh. 10:36–37), was accomplished under the leadership of Judah and Simeon (Judg. 1:9–20). And Bethel, the city near Ai that was not mentioned in connection with Joshua's first military campaign, was conquered by the house of Joseph (1:22–26). In general, this account stresses the incompleteness of the occupation of the land (see 1:19, 21, 27–29).

In the past, critical historians have agreed almost unanimously that these scattered statements in Judges 1 are fragments of an older more reliable Epic tradition (J) which presents a view different from that of the Deuteronomistic historian. According to this tradition, the Israelite occupation of Canaan was a complex process that occurred over a long period of time. Tribes acted independently or in groups under widely separated circumstances. Some came from the south via Arad and Hormah; others entered from the east by way of the Plains of Moab; still others settled in the land during the ancestral period. Later on, when the tribes were unified into the covenant community of Israel, the various tribal traditions were combined in the narrative of an all-Israelite conquest under Joshua.

Evidence from Archaeology

Before going further with this discussion, let us see what light archaeological investigation sheds. Here, again, it must be said that archaeology does not attempt to prove or disprove the biblical record. It is, at best, a science that describes what is found and infers from the data hypotheses that are tested in scholarly debate.[27]

Speaking in archaeological terms, we are concerned with the transition from the Late Bronze (LB) period (c. 1550–1200 B.C.E.) to the Early Iron (Iron I) period (c. 1200–900). When considering the Amarna Age, we saw that these centuries (the fourteenth and thirteenth) were marked by political upheaval and social turmoil, owing in great part to the aggression of the Sea Peoples and the feverish Egyptian attempt to hold on to its Asiatic empire. The ferment was increased by major technological advances: the use of iron instead of bronze for tools and weapons, the use of waterproof plaster-lined cisterns to improve the storage of rain water (making it possible for people to move into areas away from springs and streams), and the use of terracing to cultivate the the sides of hills.

With regard to the situation in Canaan (Palestine), the picture provided by archaeology is blurred, at least if we examine the data with a biblical interest. On the one hand, there is clear evidence that some fortified cities were violently destroyed, as indicated by layers of ash. This is true, for instance, with regard

[27] Discussions of the complex archaeological evidence are given by J. Maxwell Miller in Hayes and Miller, *History* [93], pp. 252–79, and Philip J. King, "The Contribution of Archaeology to Biblical Studies," *Catholic Biblical Quarterly*, 45 (1983), 1–16.

The Mound of Jericho shows this deep cut made by archaeologists at the site of the oldest city of Palestine. The upper edge of an excavated stone tower runs across the base of the photo. Dating back to about 7000 B.C.E., this circular structure was part of the city's defense system in the Stone Age. One level of occupation was built upon another through the centuries until the city came into the possession of Israel, though the story of Joshua's conquest is archaeologically enigmatic. In the background is the traditional Mount of Temptation.

to Bethel in the central hill country (a city which Joshua did not take), Lachish in the south, and Hazor in the north (a city that Joshua is said to have burned).[28] On the other hand, some fortified cities that Joshua took, according to the biblical account, were not destroyed in this period. Jericho, it is said, was burned to the ground (Josh. 6:24); but archaeological investigation has shown that the wall which supposedly ''came tumbling down'' in Joshua's time actually dates back to the third millennium B.C.E. and was destroyed in the middle of the sixteenth century, perhaps in connection with expulsion of the Hyksos from Egypt. In the time of Joshua, according to archaeological evidence, the mound of Jer-

---

[28] See Yigael Yadin, *Hazor* [252].

icho was in ruins and was not reoccupied for a considerable time.[29] Also Ai, which Joshua is said to have burned (Josh. 8:19–20), was at the time a heap of ruins. Indeed, archaeologists say that there was a gap in occupation from about 2400–1200 B.C.E. (Early Bronze to Iron I), and even the Iron Age settlement was just a small, unfortified village.[30] And the Late Bronze archaeological evidence from Gibeon is negligible, although the city apparently gained importance during the twelfth century.[31]

THE NATURE OF THE ISRAELITE OCCUPATION

Given the literary difficulties with the book of Joshua and the tantalizing ambiguity of the archaeological evidence, it is not surprising that scholars have come to different conclusions about the Israelite "conquest." In general, three views or "models" claim attention: (a) gradual infiltration; (b) military invasion; and (c) peasant revolution.

(a) According to the first view, the actual history was a *Landnahme* or Settlement that took place over several generations and was not completed until the time of David. Initially, there was no military assault on the land, but only a gradual, nomadic infiltration. Pastoral nomads from the desert to the east and south of Canaan moved into the sparsely settled hill country in search of pasture for their flocks and cattle. As a rule, they lived on good terms with the Canaanites, and even intermarried with them. There were occasional clashes but no serious conflicts until the eleventh century (the time of the Judges), when the expanding Israelites moved beyond the hills into the fertile plains where strong Canaanite cities were located.

In this view, then, the story of Joshua's swift conquest is a product of the religious imagination of the Deuteronomistic historian who sought to stress Yahweh's mighty power. When studied critically, Joshua 1–12 proves to be a chain of etiological stories intended to explain such things as the existence of "the Ai" (which in Hebrew means "the ruins") or the subordinate status of the Gibeonites ("hewers of wood and drawers of water," Josh. 9:17). Indeed, it has been questioned whether Joshua was really the successor of Moses. Originally Joshua was only a local Emphraimite tribal hero whose fame grew as his people, "the house of Joseph," gained prominence. Eventually the folk tales were embellished and exaggerated until at last Joshua became the hero of united Israel, upon whom the mantle of Moses fell.[32]

---

[29] Kathleen M. Kenyon, *Digging up Jericho* [241]; also "Jericho," in D. Winton Thomas, *Archaeology and O. T. Study* [109], 164–75.

[30] J. A. Callaway, "New Evidence on the Conquest of 'Ai'," *Journal of Biblical Literature* 87 (1968), 312–20.

[31] J. B. Pritchard, "Archaeology and the Future of Biblical Studies," *The Bible in Modern Scholarship* [161], 313–324.

[32] See especially Albrecht Alt, "The Settlement of the Israelites in Palestine," *Essays* [151], 133–69. The view is championed by Alt's student, Martin Noth, in his various writings, including *Pentateuchal Traditions* [70], pp. 71–74 and *History* [98], pp. 68–84. This view is also maintained by Manfred Weippert, *Settlement* [249].

This view has attractive features, but it suffers from serious weaknesses. For one thing, it has become increasingly clear that there is no basis for the notion that Israelites were pastoral nomads who came in from the desert. Rather, these Hebrews were agriculturalists, accustomed to a village way of life.[33] Moreover, archaeological evidence for the violent destruction of Canaanite cities in the thirteenth century is disregarded or thought to have no bearing on the biblical account. And, of course, the tradition that was deeply imprinted on Israel's memory, namely, that Yahweh brought the people out of Egypt and led them victoriously into Canaan (Josh. 24:5–13; Amos 2:9–10; etc.), is considered to be a purely "confessional" claim.

(b) At the opposite extreme is the view of scholars who take seriously the biblical tradition that Israelites made a "forced entry" into Canaan. Those who entertain this view admit that Joshua 1–12 presents a glorified account. The purpose of the Deuteronomistic historian was not to give a colorless, factual report, but to proclaim to the Israelite community the dramatic story of the victory of Yahweh, the Divine Warrior. Hence the writer telescoped the account of the invasion by attributing feats to the military commander Joshua which were actually carried out by others, or he magnified the story by reporting modest gains as whopping victories, as is still done in modern war summaries. Nevertheless, in spite of signs of telescoping and exaggeration, there is good evidence for the central claim of the book of Joshua, that in the thirteenth century the war-like Israelites, probably spearheaded by the Joseph tribes and the tribe of Benjamin, were victorious in wresting a good part of the central hill country from the Canaanites. In biblical tradition the Joseph tribes (Manasseh and Ephraim) and the tribe of Benjamin were linked closely together, for Joseph and Benjamin were Jacob's two sons by his favorite wife, Rachel (Gen. 30:22–24; 35:16–20). Significantly, Joshua was an Ephraimite.

This view of military conquest claims some support from archaeological excavations. As we have seen, there is archaeological evidence for violent destruction of some Canaanite cities in the late thirteenth century. Cities attacked by Joshua, notably Lachish and Hazor, actually did fall in that period. Other cities—Bethel, Debir, Eglon—also suffered violent destruction at that time. Presumably some cities taken by Joshua in the thirteenth century had to be retaken later, which may account for the fragmentary reports in the first chapter of Judges. Contrary to a common assumption, however, Judges 1 is not a single document, a remnant of "the lost J [Old Epic] account of the conquest," but an anthology of material from differing dates and circumstances."[34]

---

[33] The notion of Israelite pastoral nomadism has been severely criticized by Norman Gottwald, *The Tribes of Yahweh* [240], pp. 435–463; see also Marvin Chaney, "Ancient Palestinian Peasant Movements and the Formation of Premonarchic Israel," in *Palestine in Transition* [239], 41–44.

[34] W. F. Albright's view of the conquest has been defended and elaborated by G. Ernest Wright, "The Literary and Historical Problem of Joshua 10 and Judges 1," *Journal of Near Eastern Studies*, V (1946), 105–114; see also his *Biblical Archaeology* [110] for further discussion. Some others who maintain this view are Paul W. Lapp, "The Conquest of Palestine in the Light of Archaeology," Concordia *Theological Monthly*, 38 (1967), 283–300; A. Malamat, "Origins and Formative Period," in *The History of the Jewish People*, ed. H. H. Ben-Sasson (London/Cambridge: Weidenfeld and Harvard University Press, 1976), 1–87, who discusses the biblical account from the standpoint of military

Those who hold to this view are embarrassed by the archaeological evidence that two cities allegedly burned to the ground by Joshua, Jericho and Ai, were actually unfortified at the time. A British excavation, conducted during 1930–36, set the date of the violent destruction of the city, apparently by earthquake, at about 1385 B.C.E., which suggested a tempting connection with the activity of the 'Apiru invaders described in the Amarna letters. Later exploration of the site, however, disclosed that virtually nothing from the thirteenth century remains. In contrast to the cultic account in Joshua 6, "the Jericho of Joshua's day may have been little more than a fort."[35] As for Ai, "the ruin," it is surmised that Joshua's conquest of that place perhaps was confused with nearby Bethel, which actually was destroyed in the same period (see Josh. 12:16; Judg. 1:22–26). This conjecture has the merit of explaining the strange fact that the Canaanite city of Bethel, which lay directly on Joshua's path, is not mentioned elsewhere in the account of his first military campaign.

(c) According to a third view, the conquest was not so much an invasion from the outside as it was an uprising inside the land of Canaan, inspired by faith in Yahweh, the liberating God of the Exodus. The social revolution actually began in Transjordan, where the Israelites joined with restive elements to overthrow the kingdoms of Sihon and Og. Migrating Israelites then carried the revolution to the west bank of the Jordan where they joined with discontented elements of the population who were eager to overthrow the city-state system maintained under Egyptian hegemony. There must have been many people of the 'Apiru type (recall our discussion of the revolutionary activity of 'Apiru in the Amarna Age, p. 128), dispossessed elements with no security in Canaanite society and resentful of the injustices imposed upon them. They would have sympathized with the newcomers under the leadership of Joshua and in their own way abetted the sociopolitical upheaval. So regarded, the conquest was really not a military conquest but a "peasant's revolt against the network of interlocking Canaanite city-states." The conflict was essentially between the villages, where the peasants were subject to taxation, and the cities, where the Canaanite kinglets were in power.[36]

This intriguing view has increasingly gained attention, for it illumines some aspects of the biblical account. It helps us to understand why there was no resistance in some areas, for instance in central Canaan around Shechem; apparently, friendly elements were there. It may explain why some cities fell to Israel without any reported military attack, why there is no archaeological evidence for the destruction of some cities claimed by the revolutionaries, and why some

---

feasibility; W. G. Dever, *Archaeology and Biblical Studies: Retrospect and Prospect* (Evanston: Seabury-Western, 1974).

[35] G. E. Wright, *Biblical Archaeology* [110], p. 79. For the excavator's account, see Kathleen Kenyon, *Archaeology in the Holy Land* [105], pp. 209–212.

[36] This view was advanced by George E. Mendenhall, "The Hebrew Conquest of Palestine," *Biblical Archaeologist* 25 (1962), 66–87; reprinted with slight revision in *The Biblical Archaeologist Reader* [100]. The view has been adopted and championed by Norman K. Gottwald in *The Tribes of Yahweh* [240], who understands the revolution in Marxist terms as a class struggle between peasants and their feudal overlords in the Canaanite city-states.

Canaanite elements (e.g. the Gibeonites) hastened to join the Israelite cause. Even the story of Rahab, the prostitute, who harbored the spies sent to Jericho by Joshua (Josh. 2), may suggest collusion between "outside agitators" and restive elements of the Canaanite population against the royal power structure.[37]

Nevertheless, this view has its difficulties too.[38] There is no *explicit* indication of a peasant's revolt in any of the levels of biblical tradition in the books of Joshua and Judges. Furthermore, the hypothesis does not do justice to the reality of entrenched political power, for human history shows that an establishment (in this case, the Canaanite city-state system) does not surrender its hold without violence and military action. This view also downplays the evidence for the violent destruction of cities in the Canaanite hill country during the late thirteenth century, to say nothing of discounting the biblical account of a military invasion under Joshua.

The Wars of Yahweh

These three models of the "conquest"—gradual infiltration, military invasion, and peasant revolution—show that the Israelite occupation of Canaan was far more complex than one would gather from an initial reading of the biblical account. One eminent historian, John Bright, maintains that all three models have to be taken into account. "The conquest was to some degree," he says, "an 'inside job'!" Large numbers of Hebrews were already long settled in Palestine, and these joined with the Hebrews coming from the desert. Their joining struck the spark that ignited Palestine, and out of the revolution emerged the tribal confederacy known as Israel. Yet " . . . it was not simply a matter of local uprisings, . . . " he continues; "there were military operations on a larger scale as well." Indeed, the revolution was "a bloody and brutal business," just as the Bible portrays it. There was a decisive campaign by Joshua in the thirteenth century which smashed into the hill country and "broke the back" of Canaanite resistance. Some cities were burned to the ground, others were bypassed and neutralized. It may be that Merneptah, who claimed to have defeated "Israel," found it necessary to intervene on behalf of Canaanite overlords in the latter part of the thirteenth century. The conquest, however, was not a *blitzkrieg*, a quick victory, but rather "a seesaw struggle that went on for years."[39]

It should be noticed that the Israelites were successful mainly in the hill country, where they could use their fairly simple methods of warfare and could take full advantage of the broken terrain. Even in the rather one-sided picture given by the Deuteronomistic historian there is no claim that the Israelites at-

---

[37] See Marvin Chaney, "Ancient Palestinian Peasant Movements," in *Palestine in Transition* [239], 68–69.

[38] See, for example, Alan J. Hauser, "Israel's Conquest of Palestine: A Peasants' Rebellion?" and the ensuing responses from other participants in the symposium (Thomas L. Thompson, George E. Mendenhall, Norman K. Gottwald) in *Journal for the Study of the Old Testament*, 7 (1978), 2–52.

[39] John Bright, *History* [91], pp. 140–143. See further the discussion in G. W. Ramsey, *The Quest* [99], chap. 4.

tacked the major Canaanite strongholds and Egyptian outposts located along the coastal plain and in the Valley of Jezreel. The reason for honest silence on this matter is undoubtedly given in the following statement:

> Yahweh was with Judah and he took possession of the hill country, but he could not dispossess the inhabitants of the plain because they had iron chariots.
>
> —JUDGES 1:19

Against the weapons of the Iron Age, Israel was about as effective as Indians with bows and arrows facing the white men's guns. Consequently, the major Israelite assault upon the hill country in the thirteenth century had to be followed up by continued struggle for possession of the land after Joshua's death. As we have seen, in more restrained moments the Deuteronomistic historian recognized that there was much to be done in the way of mopping up remaining centers of Canaanite resistance (Josh. 13), although this side of the picture is not presented as fully as it should be. After the initial assault, continued military action was necessary, sometimes carried out by individual tribes in local areas. Moreover, the conquest of the Canaanites was facilitated by treaty, intermarriage, and the absorption of city-states into the Israelite confederacy, about which we shall have more to say presently.

DEFINITION: "HOLY WAR"

The view of holy war expressed in the biblical traditions of the conquest of Canaan should not be confused with modern notions of religiously sanctioned warfare or even with the fanaticism of Islamic *jihad* (holy war). Moreover, biblical holy wars were quite different from the kind of warfare introduced by David and Solomon, which was characterized by military conscription, a professional corps of officers, a standing army, and pitched battles with mechanized equipment.

Holy war in the tribal period was a kind of guerrilla warfare based on voluntary response to a summons in the name of the deity, the Divine Warrior, to whom the tribes owed allegiance. It was not just defensive, as some have maintained, but was often offensive warfare. According to Joshua 1–12 and Judges 1, a relatively small band of warriors could be successful through the use of scare tactics, ambush, surprise maneuvers, feigned flight, and so on. Religiously speaking, it is God who gives the victory; the triumph is not won by sheer military force (Josh. 24:12b: "It was not by your sword or by your bow"). On this point, see further Millard C. Lind, *Yahweh is a Warrior* [243].

One of the practices of holy war, both in ancient Israel and among other peoples, was that of *ḥerem* or sacrificial ban, that is, the dedication of persons, booty, or cities to God. The story of the capture of Jericho and the sequel involving Achan (Josh. 6–7) is a good illustration. When something is devoted to God it becomes holy and belongs only to God, having been withdrawn from common use. The *ḥerem* was practiced only in the case of resisting cities, according to the biblical account (e.g. Hormah, Num. 21:1–3; the kings Sihon and Og, Josh. 2:10; Jericho, 6:17; Ai, 8:24–29; some southern cities, Josh. 10:28–43). In Deut. 20:16–18 it is said that the Israelites were to utterly destroy the Canaanite cities, saving alive nothing that breathed, but this is an overstatement. As we have seen, Israel's conquest of the land did not involve the wholesale extermination of the Canaanite population. See further discussion of holy war in connection with Deborah (pp. 196–198) and Saul (pp. 217–218).

Undoubtedly historians will be discussing the Israelite conquest for years to come. Whatever the nature of the conquest, deeply ingrained in Israel's memory was the conviction that these victories were not achieved by mere military power or strategy. Rather, Israel was fighting "the wars of Yahweh." In those stirring events the Israelites recognized the active presence and guidance of Yahweh, who had delivered oppressed slaves from bondage and in a marvelous way had led them into a land where they could fulfill their historic role. It was their faith in the God who actively took part in the historical struggle that unified them and inspired them with tremendous zeal. Against these invaders from the desert, the Canaanites, split up into city-states, divided by the hills and valleys, and lacking a dynamic religious faith, were unable to stand.

THE FORMATION OF THE TRIBAL CONFEDERACY

We turn now to the important incident related in the last chapter of Joshua. We have noticed that the Deuteronomistic portion of the book of Joshua is confined to chapters 1–12 and the concluding address found in chapter 23. The intervening material (Josh. 13–22) consists for the most part of ancient lists of tribal borders and towns, which need not concern us here. Chapter 24, however, is one of the most important chapters in the Old Testament. After Joshua's farewell address in chapter 23, this chapter seems to stand by itself and may well relate an incident that happened earlier in Joshua's career. In the judgment of some literary critics, much of the narrative is based on an old literary stratum (E) which runs through the Pentateuch into the book of Joshua; but in substance it seems to date back to an ancient period when the tradition circulated orally.

The Assembly at Shechem

The subject of Joshua 24 is a great convocation at Shechem, a city located near Joseph's grave (Josh. 24:32) and Jacob's well (John 4:6). From at least the beginning of the second millennium B.C.E., it was a great Canaanite city-state, strategically located in the narrow pass between Mount Gerizim and Mount Ebal. From this vantage point it commanded the major highways that necessarily ran between the two mountains. Excavations at the site (the modern village of Balatah, near Nablus) have uncovered the impressive remains of the ancient city.[40] The discovery of a type of rampart known to be typical of the Hyksos indicates that for a while it was a strong fortress of the Hyksos empire. Evidence of violent destruction in the middle of the second millennium suggests that the city was retaken by the Egyptians when Ahmose I expelled the Hyksos from Egypt and carried his conquests into Palestine. In the fourteenth century, as we know from

[40] The American archaeological expedition, which had its first campaign in the summer of 1956, was under the archaeological direction of G. Ernest Wright. See his book, *Shechem* [251].

the Amarna letters, it was lost to Egypt as a result of Lab'ayu's treaty with 'Apiru. So the city was the scene of decisive political struggles long before Joshua arrived.

Not only was Shechem an important fortress, but also it was a religious center. In the acropolis was built a large temple, called the temple of Baal Berith ("Lord of the Covenant"; see Judg. 9:4). Today the visitor to the ruins can see the foundations of this ancient temple—one of the largest pre-Roman temples that archaeologists have ever discovered in Palestine—and can visualize how impressive the shrine must have been in ancient times. According to the story, Joshua gathered the people "before God" at the city of Shechem (Josh. 24:1).

In the presence of the assembled Israelite tribes and their leaders, Joshua rehearsed Israel's "sacred history," beginning with the ancestral period and dwelling especially on the events of the Exodus and the conquests in Transjordan and the Canaanite hill country (Josh. 24:2–13). On the basis of this confessional summary, Joshua then challenged the people to decide either to serve Yahweh in sincerity and faithfulness, or to serve the gods their ancestors served beyond the River (Euphrates) and the gods of the Amorites (Canaanites). With the warning ringing in their ears that Yahweh is a jealous God, a holy God who would not tolerate the worship of "strange gods," the people affirmed their

The Temple of Baal-Berith (or El-berith), first built by Canaanites during the Hyksos period (c. 1650 B.C.E.) and, in a later phase, standing when the city peacefully passed into the control of Israel and became the first center of the Tribal Confederacy. During excavations in 1960 and 1962, the sacred pillar was restored to its original position in front of the temple, and a retaining wall was built around the reconstructed temple courtyard.

decision to serve Yahweh, who had brought them out of Egypt and guided them into Canaan. Accordingly, Joshua demanded that they put away the foreign gods. The ceremony concluded with the making of a covenant, the giving of law, and the erection of a memorial stone beneath a sacred tree.

It is quite clear that Joshua was not officiating at a covenant ceremony that brought Yahweh and Israel together for the first time. Israel did not become in *this* moment "the people of Yahweh," nor did Yahweh only then become "the God of Israel." This was not the initiation of the covenant relationship, but a reaffirmation of the sacred covenant that was made at Sinai. To be sure, Joshua's rehearsal of the events of Israel's past makes no reference to the Sinai covenant, but this was hardly appropriate since, as we have previously seen (pp. 101–103), the Sinai covenant was not one of Yahweh's mighty acts but rather the response to those deeds. It was appropriate that this covenant renewal took place in the new land of Canaan where the people, in the flush of victory, were tempted to violate their covenant obligation and adopt the religious practices of Canaan. Joshua's challenge was put with the urgency that was later voiced by the prophets: *Today* you must decide! Yahweh demands exclusive devotion from the people. In the answer of the people, "We will serve Yahweh, for he is our God," we hear a reaffirmation of the Mosaic belief that for Israel there can be only one God.

New Converts to the Mosaic Faith

There was probably more to this ceremony than a renewal of the covenant allegiance by those who had taken part in the wilderness wanderings. It is significant that the ceremony took place at Shechem. One of the strange things about the story of the conquest of the hill country is the complete silence about any activity in the area around Shechem. The fact that Shechem was not attacked and, moreover, that it was the scene of the tribal convocation, suggests that the people of this vicinity were friendly to the invaders, either through kinship or alliance. We have already seen (pp. 126–128) that in the Amarna Age 'Apiru were active in the vicinity of Shechem and entered into a treaty with the Canaanite ruler of the city. It has been suggested that before Joshua's time there existed at Shechem an alliance of six tribes, based on a covenant allegiance and the common worship of 'El (the name of the chief Canaanite deity). Old traditions relate that Jacob purchased land near Shechem where he erected an altar to "'El, the God of Israel" (Gen. 33:18–20) and that Hebrew tribes very early attempted to enter into cordial relations with this Canaanite city-state (Gen. 34).

There are faint recollections, then, that some of Israel's ancestors—broadly speaking, the Leah tribes[41]—settled in Canaan at a comparatively early date and did not take part in the Exodus or the experiences of the wilderness. If the invaders under Joshua—that is, the Rachel tribes of Joseph and Benjamin—found

[41] For Jacob's six sons by Leah, see Gen. 29:31–35; 30:14–20. The duality of the Leah tribes and the Rachel tribes undoubtedly reflects the historical relationships of the tribes in the early period.

friends or relatives already settled in central Canaan, we can understand why it was unnecessary for them to conquer this region. Supposing all this to be true, then Joshua 24 describes not just the renewal of the Mosaic covenant but its extension to embrace other Hebrews who had not been involved in it before. To them, Joshua's words would have had special force: "Choose ye this day!" If they were to choose the service of Yahweh, they had to put away all foreign gods, whether retained from the period of the ancestors or adopted from the Canaanites in whose midst they had been living.

But why did Joshua rehearse to these new converts to the covenant community the stirring events of the Exodus and the wilderness sojourn—events in which neither they nor their immediate ancestors had participated? How could they say, "This is *our* life-story too"? This is not so strange after all, for the only way outsiders can be initiated into a historical community is to share its memories and to participate fully in its life. In the United States, for instance, the stirring story of the Revolutionary War does not belong merely to the Thirteen Colonies or the descendants of the first colonists. Other states, joining the Union, appropriated those memories as their own. Moreover, many of us are children of immigrants who arrived on the American scene fairly late, but we too may thrill to the rehearsal of the epic of early American history and affirm that this is *our* story. Similarly, to become an Israelite was to appropriate the whole sacred past. It was not just a matter of blood relation, for even Canaanites were absorbed into Israel in the early period—as were the Gibeonites, for example. Fundamentally, it was a matter of being identified with the whole drama of Israel's history, and of being willing to acknowledge the God of the covenant and to accept the obligations of membership in the covenant community.

The name for this covenant community was Israel. We have already seen that the term 'Apiru had a broad meaning during the second millennium. Not all Hebrews were Israelites. The Israelites included only those Hebrews, whether they went down into Egypt or settled in Palestine before Joshua's time, who were bound into a covenant alliance. In other words, Israel is basically a "folk" or people (Hebrew: 'am)—not, in the first instance, a racial group or a nation.[42] The Old Testament shows how the general term "Hebrews" was eventually superseded by "Israelites" as the proper designation of the particular people whose life-story we have been following. The term "Israel," as we have noticed, was used on Merneptah's stele (see pp. 130–131) and it gained currency especially during the period of the conquest and the era of the judges.

The Twelve-Tribe Confederacy

One of the striking features of "Israel" was its organization into twelve tribes. In the book of Genesis this structure is read back into the ancestral period, for the sake of unifying the traditions and making them relevant for the whole peo-

---

[42] See E. A. Speiser, " 'People' and 'Nation' of Israel," *Journal of Biblical Literature*, 79 (1960), 157–63. Speiser points out that ancient Israelite tradition speaks of "the people of Yahweh," but not "the nation of Yahweh."

ple. Thus the patriarch Jacob is renamed Israel after a crucial experience (Gen. 32:28), and he is regarded as the father of twelve sons, each one the leader of a tribe (Gen. 29:16–30:24; 35:16–20). In the two centuries before David (c. 1200 to 1000 B.C.E.) when the Israelite tradition was being formed and transmitted orally, the pattern of twelve was so sacred that if one tribe dropped out, a way was found to fill its place. So, for example, when Levi lost tribal standing, "the house of Joseph" was split into the two tribes of Manasseh and Ephraim (Gen. 48).

It is important to notice that the number twelve, signifying the totality of Israel, was stressed on cultic occasions when the people assembled before Yahweh. During the ceremony of the sealing of the covenant at the foot of Mount Sinai, Moses set up "twelve pillars, according to the twelve tribes of Israel" (Exod. 24:4). Likewise, when the people crossed over the Jordan River from their base in the plains of Moab, which was a kind of reenactment of the crossing of the Reed Sea, twelve stones were set up in the sanctuary at Gilgal near Jericho, to symbolize "the number of the tribes of the people of Israel" (Josh. 4:3, 8, 20).[43] These traditions show that the pattern of twelve belonged fundamentally to Israel's self-understanding as a worshiping community, bound in covenant to the God who had delivered the people from Egyptian bondage.

This twelve-tribe structure was also found among some of Israel's neighbors. For instance, the Ishmaelites were organized into twelve tribes with a tribal prince at the head of each (Gen. 25:12–16), and the Edomites seem to have had a similar tribal system (Gen. 36:10–14). Some historians have turned to a more distant scene to find an analogy. The Israelite tribal federation has been likened to the sacral leagues of ancient Greece and Italy, to which the Greeks applied the term "amphictyony." In the amphictyony, a fixed number of tribes—six or, as in the case of the League of Delphi, twelve—were loosely bound together on the basis of a common religious obligation. There was a central sanctuary which the tribes cared for in turn. At this religious center regular festivals were held, and the basic laws that were binding upon all the tribes were administered. The bond that held these tribes together was primarily religious, in contrast to the political basis of a city-state or a nation. In times of military emergency, however, the tribes united to face the common foe, and the federation brought about some degree of unity in language, customs, and political interests.

Admittedly, this is a remote analogy from a later time and a different cultural setting, and we must be cautious about drawing parallels.[44] Nevertheless,

---

[43] According to another version (Josh. 4:5–7, 9), twelve stones were set up in the bed of the Jordan.

[44] This view was set forth by Martin Noth in his study of the scheme of the twelve Israelite tribes: *Das System der zwölf Stäame Israels* [287]; see also his *History* [98], pp. 85–108. The view has been accepted, with reservations, by some scholars including John Bright, *History* [91], pp. 162–163. Strong dissenting reactions have been given by various scholars, e.g. Harry M. Orlinsky, "The Tribal System of Israel and Related Groups in the Period of the Judges," *Oriens Antiquus*, I (1962), 11–20; G. W. Anderson "Israel: 'Amphyctyony' . . . " in *Translating and Understanding the Old Testament* [159], 135–151; Roland de Vaux, *History* [92], pp. 695–749. The latter finds analogies in the twelve-tribe federations among Arabs.

an organization something like this seems to have been instituted at Shechem and to have prevailed during the period of the judges, as we shall see. The tribes of Israel were bound together in a covenant alliance that allowed for considerable autonomy on the part of the twelve participants. Primarily it was a theocratic community, as indicated by the word Israel, which perhaps should be translated: "may God rule." Shechem seems to have been the center of the confederacy for a while, but later on the central sanctuary was located at Shiloh, where the Ark was kept and where the tribes assembled for religious festivals. Above all, the tribal covenant was based on a rehearsal of the great events in which Yahweh had acted in behalf of the people. In this respect it rested on the same basis as the Mosaic covenant.

The Covenant Service

It is striking that the covenant renewal service, as described in Joshua 24, contains features that were characteristic of the suzerainty treaty form which we have considered previously (pp. 98–101). The parallel becomes almost exact if one associates with this ceremony other passages, especially Joshua 8:30–35 and Deuteronomy 27, which describe ritual acts that took place at Shechem, located in the valley between Mount Gerizim and Mount Ebal. Notice the following elements of the cultic service when the representatives of the tribes "presented themselves before God," probably in the presence of the Ark (see Josh. 8:33).

1.   The covenant service is introduced by a preamble in which the covenant-maker speaks: "Thus says Yahweh, the God of Israel" (Josh. 24:2a).
2.   Next comes a long "historical prologue," cast in the I-Thou style characteristic of suzerainty treaties, in which Yahweh recalls prior relations to the "vassal" (24:2b–13). Here the emphasis falls upon Yahweh's benevolent deeds on behalf of Israel (chiefly the deliverance from Egypt) which should evoke a response of gratitude and obligation.
3.   The following section (24:14–24) deals with the fundamental stipulation of the covenant: the people are to place their complete trust in their Suzerain in remembrance of what had been done for them: Yahweh's guidance out of Egypt through the wilderness, and into the land (verses 16–18). Specifically this means that the people are to have no relations with other divine suzerains (i.e., "serve other gods"), for Yahweh is a "jealous God" who will not tolerate covenant unfaithfulness (verses 19–21). Accordingly, the people must renounce other gods, whether those their ancestors worshiped in Mesopotamia or those of the Canaanites (Amorites), and pledge themselves to "serve" Yahweh alone (verses 22–24).
4.   Joshua wrote the covenant stipulations in "the book of the law of God," after publicly proclaiming "statutes and ordinances" (24:25–26). It may be deduced, perhaps, that the covenant document was deposited in "the sanctuary of Yahweh," which was located outside the Canaanite city of Shechem at a sacred oak (see Gen. 12:6, "the Oak of Moreh"; 35:4). According to Deuteronomic tradition, the covenant law (Decalogue) was kept in the Ark (Deut. 10:5).
5.   Instead of the invocation of various gods as witnesses, which is ruled out, of course, by Mosaic theology, the people themselves are called as "witnesses against them-

selves'' that they have chosen to serve Yahweh (24:22). Moreover, there is another strange ''witness'': the large stone or pillar which Joshua erected in the sanctuary of Yahweh:

> Joshua said to all the people:
> ''Look! This stone will be a witness against us, for it has heard all the words that Yahweh has said to us. So it will be a witness against you in case you deny your God.''
>
> —JOSHUA 24:27

6.   According to other passages which seem related to Joshua 24, the Shechem ritual also included the sanctions of divine blessing and curse. In Joshua 8:30–35 we find that Joshua wrote on stones a copy of the covenant law and, after the Ark had been solemnly carried by the priests, ''he read all the words of the law, the blessing and the curse.''

The ''law'' referred to undoubtedly includes the absolute or apodictic law which, as we saw in the last chapter, was associated with the Mosaic covenant. This type of law is illustrated in the twelve curses found in Deuteronomy 27:11–26. Here are some examples:

> Cursed be the person who makes a graven or molten image.
> Cursed be the one who dishonors his father or his mother.
> Cursed be the one who removes his neighbor's landmark.
> Cursed be the one who slays his neighbor in secret.

These laws are formulated in the short, categorical manner that we have noticed in the Ten Commandments. The law is made absolutely binding by being put in the form of a curse that expresses Yahweh's unqualified disapproval of a particular act. The twelve curses are very old. They must go back at least to the time of the Israelite tribal confederacy. According to the above passage in Deuteronomy, they were recited in connection with a ritual ceremony that took place at Shechem, when the tribes arranged themselves half on Mount Gerizim and half on Mount Ebal.

It is clear from this analysis that the suzerainty treaty form, derived from the sphere of international politics, profoundly influenced Israel's understanding of its covenant relationship with Yahweh, especially during the period of the occupation of Canaan. It is tempting to go a step further and conclude that the assembly at Shechem provided the pattern for other tribal gatherings at the central sanctuary when the people heard again the great story of Yahweh's redemptive deeds, when they listened to the solemn recitation of the obligations that were binding upon them, and when they pledged themselves anew to Yahweh's covenant. Support for this view, which is widely held, comes from a passage in Deuteronomy 31:9–13 which stipulates that a gathering for public reading of the law is to take place every seventh year in the autumn (New Year) at the Feast of Booths. Such a covenant renewal service was actually held in the time of Ezra, after the people had returned from Babylonian exile (Neh. 8). Since the Feast of Booths was a yearly festival, it may be that the sabbatical scheme was a later modification of the practice of holding a covenant renewal ceremony annually.[45] If so, the Shechem assembly provided a cultic precedent for periodic gatherings of the people during the period of the Tribal Confederacy and even later during the period of the monarchy, a matter to which we shall return in subsequent chapters.

The Covenant Law

We are told that when Joshua made a covenant with the people at Shechem he also "made statutes [Hebrew: *hoq*] and ordinances [*mishpaṭ*] for them" (Josh. 24:25). "Statute" refers to the apodictic covenant law, exemplified by the twelve curses (Deut. 27:15–26) or the Decalogue. "Ordinance," however, refers to the case law which, as we have seen previously (pp. 96–98), spells out what the law means under certain conditions or circumstances. Since the so-called Covenant Code (Exod. 20:22–23:33) includes both types, though the "ordinances" (*mishpaṭim*) predominate, and since this code concludes with the promise of Yahweh's blessing and protection, it is tempting to believe that this was the law that Joshua promulgated at Shechem.[46] In any event, the Covenent Code presupposes the agricultural mode of life which Israel adopted during the period of the Tribal Confederacy.

Israel's law was covenant law. It was not "secular" law, or even civil law in a narrow sense. Indeed, Israel did not recognize any separation between the secular and religious realms. The whole of life was to be lived under Yahweh's demand, within the covenant. This sense of total accountability before God led to an expansion of law as new situations were faced, such as the new adjustment to the agricultural life of Canaan. Israel borrowed laws from the culture of the Fertile Crescent and transformed them according to its needs and religious concerns. Undoubtedly this legal development was accelerated during the period of the Tribal Confederacy. It has been suggested that covenant renewal festivals provided the occasion for arbitrating disputes between, or even within, the tribes.

Many of the "ordinances" (i.e., the *mishpaṭ* case laws) in the so-called Covenant Code (Exod. 20:22–23:33) are similar in form, and to a great degree in content, to the law codes of the Babylonians, Hurrians, and Assyrians. The same

---

[45] This view was set forth by the Scandinavian scholar Sigmund Mowinckel in his work *Le Décalogue* (Paris: Libraire Felix Alcan, 1927) and has been adopted with various modifications by other scholars including G. von Rad, *The Problem of the Hexateuch* [166], pp. 20–26; G. Ernest Wright, commentary on Deuteronomy in *Interpreter's Bible*, II [16], p. 326; and Artur Weiser, *The Psalms* [456], pp. 23–35. The view is criticized by R. de Vaux, *History* [92], pp. 405–408.

[46] This view is advocated by various scholars, including R. de Vaux, *Ancient Israel* [113], pp. 221–22.

is true of the code of Deuteronomy (12–26). Here is one example of the affinity between Old Testament legislation and the Code of Hammurabi:[47]

Code of Hammurabi Par. 120	*Covenant Code* Exod. 22:7–9 (RSV)
If a seignoir deposited his grain in a[nother] seignoir's house for storage and a loss has then occurred at the granary or the owner of the house opened the storage-room and took grain or he has denied completely [the receipt of] the grain which was stored in his house, the owner of the grain shall set forth the particulars in the presence of God and the owner of the house shall give to the owner of the grain double the grain that he took.	If a man delivers to his neighbor money or goods to keep, and it is stolen out of the man's house, then, if the thief is found, he shall pay double. If the thief is not found, the owner of the house shall come near to God, to show whether or not he has put his hand to his neighbor's goods. For every breach of trust, whether it is for ox, for ass, for sheep, for clothing, or for any kind of lost thing, of which one says, "This is it," the case of both parties shall come before God; he whom God shall condemn shall pay double to his neighbor.

Of course, the Old Testament law was not copied from the Code of Hammurabi; the latter code presupposes an aristocratic class system that did not prevail in Israel. Moreover, Israel never could accept the view that the state is the custodian of law; according to Israel's covenant faith, even kings were subject to the law, which had its ultimate source at Sinai (see Deut. 17:18–20). But the similarity of form and even of some of the details indicates that Israel borrowed from a fund of legal tradition that was known throughout the Fertile Crescent. Both laws are casuistic—that is, they begin with "if" and precisely define the case that is to be adjudicated. This conditional law contrasts with the unconditional law that was characteristic of the Israelite covenant.

Nevertheless, there are vast differences between Israelite law and other Near Eastern codes even when there is evidence of borrowing.[48] Israel's law is characterized by a humane spirit, a high ethical emphasis, and a pervading religious fervor which make it unique. This is because all the law of Israel, regardless of its source, is set within the "I" and "thou" of the covenant relationship. As the tribes gathered at their common sanctuary to rehearse the stirring events of their past and to hear the absolute requirements of Yahweh, the covenant was reaffirmed again and again. A passage in Deuteronomy says, "Yahweh made not this covenant with our ancestors, but with us who are here alive this day" (Deut. 5:3). This is not exaggerated language. In each great covenant-renewal ceremony, like the one described in Joshua 24, the covenant was made contemporaneous. The Deuteronomic passage preserves an echo of the spirit that animated the Tribal Confederacy and infused the expanding laws of the community.

[47] Pritchard, *Ancient Near Eastern Texts* [1], p. 171.

[48] On the nature of Israelite law, see Martin Noth, "The Laws in the Pentateuch" [165]; also Paul D. Hanson, "The Theological Significance of Contradiction within the Book of the Covenant," in *Canon and Authority* [156], 110–131.

CHAPTER 5

The Formation of an All-Israelite Epic

The convocation at Shechem, which we considered at the end of the previous chapter, was a momentous occasion. According to the narrative in Joshua 24, it was an all-Israelite affair, for Joshua is said to have convened "all the tribes of Israel," represented by their leaders, to present themselves "before God" at the sacred shrine. Joshua's address, too, had an all-Israelite appeal, for in the biblical text the pronouns (you, your) are in the plural: "Your ancestors formerly lived beyond the Euphrates" (Josh. 24:2); Yahweh "fetched your ancestor Abraham . . . and led him through all the land of Canaan" (24:3); later Yahweh "escorted your ancestors out of Egypt, and you came to the sea" (24:6); eventually Yahweh "brought you to the land of the Amorites" (24:8) and "you crossed the Jordan" (24:11). In short, the people heard from Joshua "the story of *our* life."

On the basis of our previous study it should be evident that this pan-Israelite story is oversimplified. Not all of the Israelite tribes had gone through all the stirring experiences that Joshua related. One group had experienced the events of the Exodus; some Hebrews must have entered Canaan from the south, while others entered via Transjordan; and undoubtedly there were "Israelites" who were already in the land, living among the Canaanites. Indeed, even in the ancestral period there seems to have been a proto-Israelite alliance in the region of Shechem organized around the worship of "El [God], the God of

Biblical readings: For readings, see the outlines of the primeval history (p. 159), the ancestral history (pp. 168–169), and the people's history, pp. 178–179.

151

Israel" (Gen. 33:18–20). In view of the complex historical situation, then, we may best understand Joshua's address as an invitation to various tribes, who did not belong to the core group, to identify with Yahweh, the liberating God of the Exodus. Conversion to Yahwism, which required discarding previous religious loyalties and having a single covenant commitment, would result in political unity and social solidarity. The Israelite tribal confederacy, consisting ideally of twelve tribes, came into being when the people pledged their allegiance to Yahweh and when Joshua, after pointing out the fateful implications of the decision, made a covenant with the people (Josh. 24:25).

Before we go on with Israel's life-story during the time of the tribal confederacy (the period of the Judges), it is appropriate to pause for a bit to consider the emerging all-Israelite epic which provided the basic outline of the Pentateuch that we have received. When the various tribes entered the confederacy, they not only identified with the "core story" of the exodus from Egypt and the guidance into the land, but they also brought with them their own traditions. The pooling of narrative resources, begun in this period, gradually resulted in an expansion and enrichment of the all-Israelite epic, as the story was told and retold throughout the generations. The people confessed that Yahweh who delivered slaves from bondage and made them a community is also the God of the ancestors. More than that, theirs is the God who in primeval times created the earth and all its creatures, and whose purpose guided the unfolding drama of all peoples who dwell on earth.

In the past it has been customary to say that the formation of Israel's national epic was a product of the literary awakening that occurred during the period of the United Kingdom. Stimulated by the stirring events of the times of David and Solomon, an unknown author known as "the Yahwist" (J)[1] composed a masterful prose epic that creatively interpreted Israel's covenant faith to express the new sense of national unity. As in the case of the period of Queen Elizabeth I of England, the political and cultural achievements of the time furnished the impulse for the creation of a classical literature. Later on, when the Davidic monarchy broke in two, another version of the epic, the Elohist (E), was composed (c. 850 B.C.E.) to express the interests and perspective of the northern kingdom, Ephraim. These two traditions (J and E) constitute overlapping and often inseparable versions of what we have referred to from time to time as the Old Epic tradition.[2]

It is undoubtedly true that the formation of the all-Israelite epic was profoundly affected by the political and social realities of the monarchy: the rise of the Davidic empire (c. 1000 B.C.E.), the split into two kingdoms (c. 922), the fall of the northern kingdom of Ephraim (721), and the demise of the southern king-

---

[1] This anonymous author is so designated because his writing employs the divine name Yahweh (spelled by German scholars with an initial "J": Jahweh) when dealing with the time before Moses, while the "Elohist" who wrote the E epic preferred Elohim. See above, pp. 21–22, 64–66.

[2] Gerhard von Rad, in his essay on "The Form-critical Problem of the Hexateuch," stresses the creative accomplishment of "the Yahwist" (*Essays* [166], 1–78). See further Peter Ellis, *The Yahwist* [265].

dom of Judah (587). Even a small matter like the echoes of the cultic reforms of Jeroboam I, the first king of Ephraim, in the story of the Golden Calf (see above, pp. 103–104) shows that the story was retold in the context of life during the monarchy. Nevertheless, parallel versions of the Israelite epic that circulated during the monarchy (Yahwist, Elohist) clearly rest upon a common, basic tradition. There is good reason to believe that in the period of the tribal confederacy this all-Israelite epic *began* to be shaped orally, perhaps largely in poetic form, as the tribes came to a new awareness of their unity and solidarity in covenant with Yahweh.[3] In the process of storytelling over a period of many generations, the basic narrative outline was further expanded and elaborated, and was eventually written down as the completed Torah.

FROM TRADITION TO LITERATURE

The period from Moses to David was the period *par excellence* of the oral tradition. To say this does not mean that, beginning with David, the oral tradition was superseded by a literary period, for unfortunately the matter is not that simple. Even after David's time, many of Israel's religious traditions—stories, hymns, and prophetic oracles—were handed down orally, with the result that there was a fruitful interplay between the written and the remembered word.[4]

The art of writing, of course, was known in Israel quite early. From the second millennium B.C.E. have come a number of literary works, among them the Canaanite Ras Shamra literature of the fourteenth century (see pp. 186–189). And future archaeological discoveries may show that writing was employed more widely in ancient Israel than the few allusions in the Old Testament seem to indicate (see Exod. 17:24; 24:4; Josh. 24:25). In any case, there are references to written sources that are no longer extant, and quotations are made from them. One of these is "The Book of the Wars of Yahweh," mentioned in Numbers 21:14. Another is "The Book of Jashar," from which quotations are made in Joshua 10:13 (the command for the sun to stand still), II Samuel 1:18 (David's dirge over Saul and Jonathan), and possibly I Kings 8:13 (Solomon's ritual of dedication).[5]

In general, however, the period before the monarchy was a preliterary one, in the sense that the poems, proverbs, and stories were inscribed primarily on the human memory. Writing played a fairly insignificant role, and was confined for the most part to business and practical affairs.

[3] In his *Pentateuchal Traditions* [70], Martin Noth maintains that literary sources (J, E) point back to, and are dependent on, a common *Grundlage* (G), that is, an all-Israelite epic tradition.

[4] Some Scandinavian scholars stress the persistence of oral tradition throughout the period of the monarchy and the flowering of literature after the fall of the nation in the sixth century B.C.E. A major champion of the Scandinavian school was Ivan Engnell; see his book, *A Rigid Scrutiny* [73]. See also Eduard Nielsen, *Oral Tradition* [74].

[5] In the Septuagint, the Greek translation of the Old Testament, this ancient ritual is said to have come from "The Book of Songs," which by a slight misreading of the Hebrew could have been "The Book of Jashar."

Yet we are not left in the dark about this early period just because we have no written documents. Our bias in favor of the greater reliability of writing contrasts with the practice of ancient people who "learned by heart" the traditions that were meaningful to them and trained the human memory to be extraordinarily retentive. The Homeric poems were transmitted orally for generations; Jewish rabbis committed to memory the traditions of the Mishnah centuries before any of them were written down; the materials of the Christian Gospels circulated orally before taking the form of written literature; and today there are Arabs who can recite the whole Koran without faltering, and Brahmins who know the whole Rig Veda by heart. Similarly, in the period before David the great religious traditions of Israel were preserved and shaped in the human memory, and no doubt were recited publicly by poets and singers at the great religious festivals or at other social gatherings.[6]

Forms of the Oral Tradition

In recent years, a great advance has been made in the study of the history of the oral tradition. On the basis of this study, we can isolate the small "memory units" and understand their characteristic type or genre. In each case, the unit of tradition came out of a living situation—that is, it was associated with some act or event, just as Americans remember the story of Paul Revere's midnight ride in connection with the Revolutionary War. An excellent example is the Song of Miriam (see p. 81), which was a spontaneous outcry of praise after a great victory.

Here we can give only a brief summary of the preliterary tradition, although it is discussed in detail in critical introductions to the Old Testament. There were various kinds of poetic units: songs to accompany work (the Song of the Well, Num. 21:17–18), songs of taunting victory (the Song of Deborah, Judg. 5), hymns of praise (Song of Miriam, Exod. 15:21), songs of lament (David's dirge over Saul and Jonathan, II Sam. 1:19–27). There were poetic sayings (aphorisms) of various kinds: the saying that was used when the Ark was carried (Num. 10:35–36), the saying about the shedding of human blood (Gen. 9:6), Lamech's saying about blood-revenge (Gen. 4:23–24), the proverb about Saul among the prophets (I Sam. 10:12), and Samson's riddle (Judg. 14:14, 18). There were all kinds of narratives: stories about creation and primeval history, about a place, a custom, a tribal hero, a cultic practice, or about the idiosyncrasy of a people. Sometimes stories were told to explain the origin of something (etiologies), sometimes for the purpose of entertainment, sometimes to express the moods and feelings evoked by daily affairs. Thus the oral tradition was marked by a diversity as rich as life itself.

The popular genres are very important in understanding the historical life of Israel during the age of song and legend. Often it is assumed that when

---

[6] An analogy perhaps is the "Singer of Tales" discussed by Albert Lord [260]; see above, p. 23.

something is "legendary," such as, for example, the legends of King Arthur, it has virtually no historical authenticity. What is legendary is opposed to what is historical—that is, according to our view, exact straightforward history. Now, it is quite true that legend (saga) lacks the precise accuracy demanded by a twentieth-century historian. In our sophisticated age no historian would think of writing history in the form of the narrative of the Flood, or the story of Jacob's dream at Bethel, or the Joseph cycle. But in a deeper sense these ancient popular genres tell us something about history that is sometimes ignored by the modern historian who is concerned only with giving a dispassionate report of wars, daily events, relations between nations, and so on. Saga is able to communicate to us out of the past *history as experienced*, the internal meaning of events and happenings. And if the deepest dimension of life's meaning is the relation of human beings to God, saga and poetry are exceedingly important ways of telling history.[7] (Recall what was said earlier about "history" and "story." See Definition, p. 19).

The Formation of an Israelite Epic

Some of the units of the oral tradition were non-Israelite in origin and probably were associated with Canaanite shrines that the Israelites took over. For instance, it is widely held that the story of Abraham's sacrifice of Isaac (Gen. 22) and the story of Jacob's dream at Bethel (Gen. 28) were pre-Israelitic, Canaanite cult legends that had completely different meanings in their original versions. These independent units of tradition were not just borrowed. Rather, they were *appropriated*, for Israel made them its own by baptizing them into the Yahweh faith.

The oral tradition did not take shape overnight. It was a gradual process that took place over many years. Undoubtedly the major catalyst was the Yahweh faith itself as confessed within the Tribal Confederacy. In Chapter 4, we noticed that the Confederacy was established at Shechem, deep in the heart of territory that had long been under the domination of Canaanite culture. There it would have been natural for Israel to inherit from Canaanites various types of tradition: agricultural laws, cult legends, stories about primeval history, etiologies, tribal tales, and so on. But what Israel borrowed it transformed and made the vehicle for expressing its covenant faith. For the Hebrews came into Canaan with their own native tradition, with the memory of the incidents in which Yahweh had delivered the people from Egyptian bondage and had graciously led them through the barren wilderness. Faith in Yahweh demanded that the pop-

---

[7] In this connection the fundamental study is *The Legends of Genesis* [257] by Hermann Gunkel, which is the preface to his monumental commentary on the book of Genesis. Because the English word "legend" has come to mean a fanciful story, it is perhaps better—as W. F. Albright points out in his introduction to this reprinted work—to use the old Norse word "saga," which refers to "a prose or more rarely a poetic narrative of historical origin or coloring." For a helpful discussion of the relation of saga to history, see Martin Buber's essay, "Saga and History" in *The Writings of Martin Buber* [see under 207].

ular traditions be changed to give expression to the deep experiences of Israel's history. Even the slightest change in an old story, one as minor as the addition of "Yahweh," was enough to bring about a complete change in its meaning.

Thus in the period before the monarchy the oral tradition was not just a formless mass, haphazardly thrown together. The story of Yahweh's dealings with Israel, later to assume elaborate form in the great historical narratives of the Hebrew Bible, was beginning to take shape. The tribes were weaving the units of tradition into cycles of stories, stamped with their peculiar interests and experiences. Moreover, it is probable that the annual ceremony of covenant renewal initiated at Shechem, and then performed at the confederate sanctuary of Shiloh, was an occasion for the recitation of laws and narratives that were binding upon all Israel. The early nucleus of Israelite themes celebrated in early story and song (e.g. Exod. 15:1–18), was being expanded into a great Israelite epic that included the career of the ancestors, the deliverance from Egypt, the wandering in the wilderness, the giving of the Law at Sinai, and the conquest of Canaan. Israel's traditions, shaped by liturgical usage at the central sanctuary, had reached a fairly unified *oral* form even before the rise of the monarchy.

THE SCOPE OF THE OLD EPIC NARRATIVE

With this background, let us consider the scope of the Old Epic narrative that began to develop during the period of the tribal confederacy—a period which in the view of some interpreters was the heyday of Israel, "the people of Yahweh."

One of the first things that strikes the reader's attention is that the Mosaic tradition (Exodus, Sinai, Wilderness, Entry into the Land) is placed in a comprehensive narrative context: the unfolding drama of Yahweh's historical purpose from the Creation to the occupation of Canaan, and even beyond into an open-ended future. The drama has three movements or "acts," which follow in succession and lead toward a climax. The basic structure is three types of "story" or "history."

A. *The Primeval History* (Gen. 2–11).[8] This history, which has its own structure and integrity, moves from creation toward chaos (the Flood) and the new beginning after the Flood. This history is ecumenical in that it includes all humankind.

B. *The Ancestral History* (Gen. 12–50). This history, which also has its own structure and dynamic, portrays Israel's prehistory, as represented in the family stories of the "founding" fathers and mothers. The Joseph story (Gen. 37–50), which has its own integrity, is now incorporated into this family history.

C. *The People's History* (Exod. 1 to the opening of the book of Joshua). This large block of narrative constitutes the Mosaic tradition, which extends from the oppression in Egypt to the entrance into the land of Canaan.

[8] Reference to the first chapter of Genesis is omitted here because, by general agreement, the story found in Gen. 1:1–2:3 comes from the Priestly work, which will be considered in Chapter 13.

The question is: How should we understand the interrelation of these three "histories" or "stories" which together make up the all-Israelite epic narrative?

It should be noticed, first of all, that each history has its own special character. The primeval history (A) deals with fundamental experiences of human beings: guilt and punishment, broken human relations, ambition for power, the search for security, the powers of chaos that threaten the ordered world.[9] There is no mention of Israel, the people of Yahweh, and for the most part the stories presuppose a Mesopotamian setting (Gen. 10:21). The ancestral history (B) is essentially a family history. With the exception of Genesis 14, the ancestors of Israel are not involved in politics but move quietly and peacefully on the fringes of Canaanite society. The people's history or the Mosaic tradition (C), however, plunges immediately into the political sphere as it portrays how enslaved Hebrews, victims of the imperial policies of the Egyptian govenment, were liberated from bondage and took part in the struggle to possess the land of Canaan.

Secondly, these three histories are presented from the standpoint of faith in Yahweh, the God worshiped by Israel. Earlier we found that the introduction of the sacred Name occurred in connection with the "root experiences" of Mosaic tradition—Exodus and Sinai (see above, pp. 60–66). It is significant, however, that in the ancestral history it is Yahweh who initiates Abraham's migration and who gives promises to each of the patriarchs. Furthermore, in the primeval history it is Yahweh who is creator of the world and director of human history. Indeed, the Old Epic narrative traces the worship of Yahweh to Seth, the grandson of Adam and Eve: "At that time people began to invoke the name of Yahweh" (Gen. 4:26b). There is a sense in which the whole epic narrative, in its three component sections, should be read backward, as it were, looking through the prism of the crucial historical experiences that had brought the community of Israel into being in the Mosaic period. For Yahweh's self-revelation in the Mosaic period cast new light upon the ancestral period, with the result that it became a period of anticipation—a movement toward the inheritance of the Promised Land and Israel's full participation in the divine plan that embraces all nations. That revealing light also fell upon the stories of primeval history; stories that deal with the potential glory and actual tragedy of human history and which prepare for the turning point in the unfolding drama: the call of Abraham.

The Gradual Elaboration of the Israelite Story

It is quite probable, then, that during the period of the Tribal Confederacy the Israelite epic, which centered in Exodus and Sinai, began to be expanded by extending the outline back to the beginning of human history and by filling in the outline with materials that once circulated independently. The storytellers reinterpreted the past in such a way that it could speak to their own situation.

---

[9] This "mythical" dimension of the primeval history is stressed by Claus Westermann in his essay, "Biblical Reflections on Creator-Creation," in *Creation in the Old Testament* [129], 90–101.

Even the primeval history, which transcends Israel's history, is adorned now and then with contemporary touches, for instance, in the story of Noah's drunkenness (Gen. 9:18–27), which reflects Canaan's subjugation to Israel. The ancestral history was also retold so as to make Jacob the eponym for "Israel" (Gen. 32:28) and the father of the twelve sons of the tribal confederacy. And, as we noticed when considering the historical background of the Exodus (above, pp. 27–41), the ancestral history mentions peoples who were neighbors or rivals of Israel in the period of the Confederacy: Arameans (Gen. 25:20; 28:5), Edomites (Gen. 32:3; cf. chap. 36), Moabites and Ammonites (Gen. 19:30–38), Philistines (Gen. 21:32; 26:1, 14), and so on.

It is impossible to draw a sharp line between the all-Israelite epic that emerged in the period of oral tradition and the literary formulations that were composed during the monarchy and even afterward. In later periods, as we have seen, other story-tellers took up anew the task of reinterpreting the sacred heritage for their own times. Perhaps much credit should be given to the literary creativity and theological sensitivity of the so-called "Yahwist" (J), who retold the story in the conviction that Yahweh's promises to Abraham were being fulfilled in the time of David and Solomon. Later on, in the judgment of many literary critics, another version of the Israelite epic, that of the Elohist (E), was produced, reflecting the interests of the Northern Kingdom. Still later, around the time of the fall of Jerusalem in 587 B.C.E., the Deuteronomistic historian wrote a great historical work based on the core of the book of Deuteronomy (D), in which attention focused on Yahweh's deliverance of the people from Egypt and the making of the covenant at Sinai. Later yet, during the period of the exile (c. 587–538), Priestly Writers (P) issued a comprehensive history of God's covenants, beginning with the Creation (Gen. 1:1–2:3) and incorporating the old Israelite epic (see Chapter 13). Thus the Pentateuch in its final form is the end result of a long process of transmission, as the story was told and retold through the generations. But none of these versions departs from the *basic* outline of the ancient Israelite epic, which received fixed, and even normative, form during the period of the tribal confederacy.

OVERVIEW OF ISRAEL'S EPIC NARRATIVE

Let us turn directly to the Old Epic narrative, reviewing the three "histories" that compose the whole. Some of this ground we have covered briefly in other contexts, when we were concerned with historical matters. Our concern now is to see how the whole narrative, despite its diversity, coheres as an all-Israelite epic, the purpose of which is to confess faith in Yahweh, the God whose purpose is traceable in a historical drama that extends from creation to the entry into the Promised Land. At this stage of study, we shall not attempt to separate out southern (J) and northern (E) versions of the epic tradition which may have been latent in tribal groupings within the confederacy from the first and which, in any event, surfaced during the period of the monarchy. Neither shall we attempt to distinguish between traditions present in the earliest stages of growth and those that were the products of a somewhat later time. It is sufficient to notice that we are dealing with an *evolving* story.

A. THE PRIMEVAL HISTORY

Since the dramatic power of the Old Epic tradition can be discerned in the way units of tradition have been joined together into a comprehensive story, it is important to read the episodes of the epic in sequence. At points it is difficult to separate the epic narrative from the surrounding Priestly (P) material in which it is embedded. On the whole, however, the Old Epic narrative stands out sharply enough for us to read it as a continuous narrative. Let us consider some of the main episodes in this dramatic account.[10]

The Story of Human Beginnings

The Garden of Eden	Gen.	2:4b–3:24
Cain and Abel		4:1–16
Cain and his descendants		4:17–26
Promiscuity of the Sons of God		6:1–4
The Flood (J and P blended in 6:5–8:22)		
Noah's favor with Yahweh		6:5–8
Into the Ark		7:1–5, 7–10, 12, 16b
The Flood comes		7:17a, 22–23
The Flood abates		8:2b, 3a, 6–12, 13b
Conclusion		8:20–22
Noah's culture of the vine		9:18–27
Noah's descendants		10:8–19, 21, 25–30
The Tower of Babel		11:1–9
The ancestry of Abram (Abraham)		11:28–30

For a long time it was held that the primeval history was placed before the ancestral history and the Exodus story by the so-called "Yahwist" (J), who wanted to view the call of Israel in the context of Yahweh's universal purpose and to subordinate creation to a history of salvation.[11] It now appears, however,

---

[10] In this outline and those that follow it is recognized that the Old Israelite Epic comes basically from the Yahwist (J), though no effort is made to separate sharply northern (E) and southern (J) versions of the epic tradition or to distinguish between early traditions and later elaborations. For a more refined analysis the student is directed to the Supplement to Martin Noth's *Pentateuchal Traditions* [70] or the appendix to Walter Harrelson's *Interpreting the Old Testament* [42].

[11] Gerhard von Rad advocated this view in various writings, including his commentary on Genesis [271], pp. 13–31; but he later came to believe with other scholars that the primeval history belonged to the Israelite epic before the Yahwist (J). See Dennis J. McCarthy, " 'Creation' Motifs in Ancient Hebrew Poetry," *Creation in the Old Testament* [129], p. 76 and the literature cited there.

that the primeval history belonged to Israel's basic narrative even in the period of oral tradition. The motifs of creation, paradise, the flood, and the deliverance of humankind from total destruction were expressed in various forms in the myths and legends of the ancient Near East. Indeed, an ancient Sumerian list of rulers makes a sharp distinction between the period "before the flood" and the period "after the flood" (see Gen. 10:1).[12] Israelite narrators, then, appropriated the ancient view of a "Golden Age" at the beginning of history, although transforming it into a time when violence (sin) began to increase on the face of the earth.

There is a striking parallel between the biblical Flood Story and the famous Gilgamesh Epic, which relates how Gilgamesh, a legendary king who once ruled in Sumerian times, tried to find out the secret of immortality from the hero of the flood, Utnapishtim. In Tablet XI, Utnapishtim vividly relates the story of how the gods capriciously decided to destroy humankind in a great flood. However, Ea, the god of wisdom, took it upon himself to advise Utnapishtim to build a large boat and take aboard the seed of all living things. Then the flood came with such destructive fury that "the gods cowered like dogs" and crouched against the walls of heaven, weeping about their decision to destroy humanity. The storm finally subsided on the seventh day, with the boat grounded on the top of Mount Nisir. Seven days later Utnapishtim sent forth a dove, a swallow, and—because these birds found no resting place—a raven. Then he offered a sacrifice of such sweet savor on the mountaintop that "the gods crowded like flies" around it.[13] The similarity of this ancient story to the biblical account shows that Israelite story-tellers borrowed freely from the reservoir of popular tradition, although transforming the material in accordance with their Yahwistic theological perspective.

The stories concerning primeval history, then, are not factual accounts of the sort that the modern historian or scientist demands. These stories are "historical" only in the sense that they plumb the depth of history's meaning and evince those fundamental experiences that have been common to human beings from the very dawn of history. The manner of presentation is poetic or pictorial, for the narrator is dealing with a subject that eludes the modern historian's investigation—namely, the ultimate source of the human drama in the initiative and purpose of God. Above all, the narrative is written in the conviction that Israel's root experiences, Exodus and Sinai, provide the clue to the meaning of all human history, right back to the beginning.

The Paradise Story

This is evident in the story of Paradise (Gen. 2:4b–3:24). Taken by itself, the story is filled with images—like the Tree of Life and the cunning serpent—which

---

[12] "The Sumerian King List," Pritchard, *Ancient Near Eastern Texts* [1], p. 265.
[13] See Pritchard, *Ancient Near Eastern Texts* [1], 93–97.

are found in ancient folklore. Indeed, the story evidently once circulated as the story-teller's answer to several questions: Why are man and woman attracted to each other? Why does social propriety demand the wearing of clothes? Why must there be the pain of childbirth and the misery of hard work? Why do people usually hate snakes? These, and other questions, were answered in the story that bears even yet the marks of an ancient popular tradition. But in the Israelite epic the story deals with the deeper question of why man and woman, God's creatures, refuse to acknowledge the sovereignty of their Creator, with the result that history is a tragic story of banishment from the life for which they were intended.

Read in the larger epic context, the story of "Paradise Lost" reflects the covenant faith of Israel.[14] Israel is the people whom Yahweh "created" (Exod. 15:16b), and therefore is totally dependent upon the divine grace and goodness manifested in its history. Israel is also portrayed as a rebellious people, bent upon flouting the goodness of Yahweh in order to pursue the devices and desires of its own heart. In this covenant perspective, to worship Yahweh is to experience divine holiness as redemptive concern and ethical demand. Yahweh is the merciful and faithful God, but the God who will not tolerate the people's attempt to substitute something or someone else as the supreme object of devotion. This was the meaning of Yahweh's dealings with Israel in its history; and the Paradise Story portrays this to be the meaning of all human history. For this story does not focus attention on Israel or even the Semites in a wider sense, but on "people" or "humanity," which is the meaning of the Hebrew word *'adam*.

In the Priestly story of creation in Genesis 1 it is affirmed that God made *'adam* (humanity) in "the image of God," and it is further said that God created *them* "male and female," an expression that indicates equality of role. In the Paradise Story, however, the creation of *'adam* takes place in two stages (Gen. 2:7 and 2:21–22), indicating that human creation is not complete until man and woman stand in partnership with each other.[15]

The two stories of creation supplement one another in interest, even though they differ from each other in many respects. The Old Epic narrative is not concerned primarily with cosmic creation—the creation of heaven and earth—which is the subject of the Priestly creation story, but with the creation of human beings and their earthly environment. The story of *'adam*, in the inclusive sense, is down to earth and existential. Human being is made from the soil (*'ădāmā*, a play on the word *'ādām*) and returns to the soil at death (Gen. 2:7 and 3:19b). Human being is a special creature of Yahweh God, whose breath ("spirit") animates the dust, making it become a "living *nefesh*"—a living being or, as we might say, a psychosomatic self. (The Greek dualism of a perishable body and

---

[14] In this connection, see Michael Fishbane, "The 'Eden' Motif/The Landscape of Spatial Renewal," in *Text and Texture* [82], 111–120.

[15] See the exquisite treatment of the Paradise story, "A Love Story Gone Awry," by Phyllis Trible, *God and the Rhetoric of Sexuality* [145], chap. 4.

a deathless "soul" is alien to the Hebraic view.) Human being is related to the animals who are also "living being" (2:19); but human being also has the power to give the animals their names and thus transcends the animal plane. A three-dimensional being, *'adam* exists in relationship to the natural environment, in relation to another human being, and in relationship to God. This is humanity's God-given freedom. To this free human being God can speak—giving a task ("to till and keep the garden") and a summons to decision ("You may freely eat of every tree of the garden, but . . . "). According to this pictorial presentation, human life is a dialogue between "I and thou"—in relation with God, in partnership with fellow human beings, and in the context of nature.[16] The story portrays life, not only as it was in the beginning, but also as it is now.

Here we cannot trace all of the nuances of the Paradise story.[17] Suffice it to say that the story goes on to portray the rebellion of human beings against divine authority and their determination to assert independence by grasping for the fruit of the forbidden tree. Sin, according to this story, is an act of the will in revolt against God. It is occasioned by ambition to overstep human status as a creature, who is dependent on God, and to become "like God" or perhaps "like the gods," the divine beings in Yahweh's heavenly court (Gen. 3:5; note the "us" in 3:22). It is the refusal to "let God be God" and the determination to do as one pleases, as though God's commands were not to be taken seriously. The story tells us that this human act of defiance brings in its train a sense of guilt ("They knew that they were naked," 3:7; cf. 2:25), the futile effort to hide from the inescapable God (cf. Ps. 139), the attempt to rationalize the act by shifting the blame to someone or something else, the misery of painful birth and of work that becomes drudgery, and finally the banishment from the primeval beauty and harmony of God's garden.

In this story we find a theme similar to that of the Greek tragedies: human pride (*hybris*) prompts human beings in Promethean fashion to assert themselves against Fate (*moira*), with the result that retribution (*nemesis*) comes upon them for a presumptuous deed. However, there is a profound difference between the Greek and the Hebraic view. In Genesis, human beings do not revolt against a blind, impersonal fate but against the will of the holy God who chooses to be involved in their history, and whose personal relation with the man and the woman is portrayed in delightful anthropomorphic language. (Notice the vivid portrayal of Yahweh God "walking in the garden in the cool of the day.") *'Adam* is an earthling who is related to the ground, the *'ădāmā*, but also a creature who is made for relationship with the Creator. This is who *'adam*, both man and woman, is. Therefore, revolt against Yahweh is also an act of violence against

---

[16] See the work of the Jewish philosopher, Martin Buber, entitled *I and Thou* (Edinburgh: T. & T. Clark, 1937).

[17] See the treatments of Gen. 2–3 in commentaries, e.g., by Gerhard von Rad [271], Nahum Sarna [272], and Walter Brueggemann [266]; also Michael Fishbane's essay on "Genesis 2:4b–11:32/ The Primeval Cycle" in *Text and Texture* [82], 17–39.

human nature—a revolt that evokes the judgment of God and a sense of human contrition. The punishment is that henceforth human beings must live in suffering and anxiety, with the prospect of death hanging overhead like a Sword of Damocles.

The Story of Cain and Abel

In the Israelitic epic narrative, banishment from the Garden of Eden is the beginning of a course of history in which 'adam is an agriculturalist, a "tiller of the 'ădāmā (ground)." The next episode, the story of Cain and Abel (Gen. 4:1–16), reflects a characteristic conflict of agricultural society: the animosity between the village farmer and the shepherd. We are told that Yahweh showed favor to the pastoral Abel, who sacrificed the firstlings of his flock, rather than to the farmer, Cain, who offered "the fruit of the ground ('ădāmā)." The story has some rough edges, as evidenced by the problem (which many readers have spotted) that Cain would have had difficulty finding a wife if he were actually the son of the first human couple. The story, which perhaps once circulated independently, now functions in the narrative context to illustrate how things began to go wrong in consequence of the rebellion in the Garden. Just as in David's court history (II Sam. 9–20) the father's sin had consequences that spread through the family, so in this case family life was spoiled by the parents' presumptuous action. Cain was also susceptible to an evil impulse—to sin, which couched at the door like a predatory animal, waiting for an opportunity to spring upon its prey (Gen. 4:6–7). The break-up of the community for which Yahweh had created human beings is evident in Cain's irresponsible question: "Am I my brother's keeper?" Again we hear that the ground ('ădāmā), polluted by murder, is accursed, for from it Abel's blood cries out to Yahweh for retribution (4:11; cf. 3:17–19).

It is ironic that, according to the narrative, the first city was built by Cain— a murderer (Gen. 4:17). Human culture got off to a bad start! The story-teller, of course, was not blind to progress in technology and the arts. One of Cain's descendants was Jubal, the ancestor of musicians; and another was Tubal-cain, a forger of metals—the metals that played such an important part in the culture of the second millennium (4:21–22). But cultural advance was accompanied by violence, lust, and unbridled passion—a chain reaction of evil that proceeded from bad to worse. The last straw, according to the epic scheme, was the violence perpetrated by heavenly beings ("the sons of God") who espied beautiful human maidens and had intercourse with them (6:1–4). This archaic story, which taken by itself defies understanding, was held up as final evidence that "the evil of humankind was great in the earth and that the whole tendency of the thoughts of the human heart was only evil all the time" (6:5). Yahweh is described as the God of pathos, who was "sorry," "grieved to the heart" about human failure and who resolved to make a new beginning.

The Great Flood

The Mesopotamian plain, subject to the annual innundation of the Tigris and Euphrates rivers, had been the scene of floods from time immemorial, as evidenced by various flood stories, including the famous Gilgamesh epic. In the Israelite epic narrative, however, the Great Flood was not just a natural event. The narrator used the ancient popular tradition as a vehicle to express a fundamental conviction of Israel's faith: the inescapable judgment of God in human affairs.

When one compares the biblical story with the Gilgamesh Epic, great differences leap to attention. To be sure, this account too has naive anthropomorphic touches, like the statement that Yahweh shut the door of the Ark (Gen. 7:16b), or that Yahweh smelled the pleasing fragrance of Noah's sacrifice (9:21). But these details, inherited from the popular tradition, do not obscure the central view that Yahweh, the sole God (in contrast to Babylonia's many gods), acts in human affairs in a meaningful and consistent way (in contrast to the caprice of the Babylonian deities).

Moreover, the narrative indicates that Yahweh's judgment is imbued with tender mercy. This has already been evident in the story of Eden, where Yahweh's judgment upon the human couple is followed by clothing them in skin garments (Gen. 3:21), and in the story of Cain, where Yahweh's wrath is mitigated by putting a protecting mark on Cain's forehead (3:15). Similarly, in the Flood story Yahweh's judgment upon an earth corrupted by human violence is not the last word, for Noah finds favor in Yahweh's sight. The narrator says that Yahweh took the initiative in instructing Noah on how to make a boat (an ark) and commanding him to take aboard his family and "families" of animals and birds. The ark, tossing helplessly on the rising flood waters, is a sign of Yahweh's intention to deliver a remnant with which to make a new beginning in history. The story concludes with the statement that even though "the imagination of the human heart is evil from youth," Yahweh would never again curse the earth with such a heavy calamity. The new beginning is based not on human possibilities but on Yahweh's grace. Henceforth the regularities of nature— "seedtime and harvest, cold and heat, summer and winter, day and night"— would continue uninterrupted as signs of God's covenant faithfulness (8:20–22).

The Temptations of Culture

But the divine judgment did not check the evil impulses of the human heart. In fact, human culture—especially the culture of the Fertile Crescent—was infected by evil. This is the point of the two episodes that followed the Flood: the story of Noah's drunkenness (Gen. 9:18–27) and the story of the construction of the Tower of Babel (11:1–9).

Noah, we are told, was the first successful tiller of the soil. He planted a vineyard—the chief symbol of Canaanite agriculture; and from the fruit of the

vine he made a potent wine. Drinking the wine put him into a drunken, de-
bauched condition, which led to what was regarded as a sexual abomination on
the part of one of his sons, Ham, the father of Canaan. The point of Noah's
indignation—contrary to the people who try to find support here for racial prejudice—is not that Noah placed a curse on Ham, the father of black-skinned
peoples, thereby degrading them to a position of inferiority. Rather, the passage
is a pointed attack on agricultural *Canaan* (represented as a person), with its
wine-drinking, sexual abandon. As we shall see later (Chapter 6), this culture,
unlike the wilderness situation from which Israel came, was obsessed with the
problem of controlling the fertility of the soil. In the time of Noah, so the story
implies, the curse on the ground was removed (see Gen. 5:29; also 3:17–19) and
Noah himself was successful as a farmer.[18] But Noah was unprepared for this
potent taste of Canaanite agriculture. When he saw that he was overcome by
the new powers of culture available to him, he pronounced a terrible curse on
Canaan.

After the Flood, we are told, the earth was peopled by the descendants of
Noah's three sons, Shem, Ham, and Japheth, who are regarded as the ancestors
of all the ancient nations and social groupings. This brings us to the conclusion
of the sketch of primeval history: the story of the Tower of Babel. Before this
tradition was incorporated into the epic scheme, it had circulated independently
as a story explaining the origin of diverse peoples and languages. The independence of this unit can be detected by comparing it with the table of Noah's
descendants (Gen. 10), in which the diversity of humankind is already presupposed. The narrator has placed the old story here, despite the inconsistent beginning (''Once the whole earth had one language and few words''), as an
appropriate climax to the primeval history and, at the same time, a transition
to the next major section of the epic narrative.

The scene is laid in Babylonia (Shinar), where nomads, wandering in the
east, found a plain and decided to establish a settled way of life—the culture
for which Babylon was to become famous. Urged by the ambition to achieve
political security and fearing social diffusion and diversity, they decided to build
a city and a tower. The tower is a reference to the Ziggurat, or terraced temple-
tower, the most famous of which was the one known as Etemenanki in Babylon.[19] As the story stands now, the episode is the climactic evidence of the
self-assertion which prompted people to revolt against Yahweh—to resist the
Creator's will for social diversity and to achieve a name, that is, to gain fame
for themselves. As in the case of the Flood, Yahweh again visited the earth with

---

[18] The statement, ''Noah was the first tiller of the soil'' (Gen. 9:20) apparently means that
Noah was the first to try farming successfully, in contrast to Cain, who, when tilling the soil, was
unsuccessful owing to the curse upon the ground (4:11–12).

[19] The Greek historian, Herodotus, gives some interesting comments on the ziggurat (*Persian
Wars*, I, 181–82). See the discussion by R. de Vaux, *Ancient Israel* [113], pp. 281–82. The ziggurat, as
he points out, was actually an artificial mountain with a huge stairway so that, ascending and de-
scending, worshipers and the god could meet.

The Ancient Ziggurat of Ur *as it may be seen today in reconstructed form. The upper terraces of this temple tower, which resembled the structure at Babylon (Gen. 11:1-9), have been destroyed. The Akkadian word "ziggurat" means "pinnacle" or "mountaintop." Believing that deities revealed themselves on mountains, dwellers in the plain constructed an artificial mountain with a sanctuary at the top.*

judgment and terminated the building project by frustrating their desire for unity—even a unity against God. By means of a Hebrew pun, the word Babel is understood to mean "confusion" (compare English "babble"), for Yahweh confused their languages so that they could not understand one another, and dispersed them in various language groups over the face of the earth.[20]

Primeval history, then, had a sad outcome, for humanity failed to find true wholeness—life in communion with God and in community with fellow human beings. From Cain to the Tower of Babel the human tragedy increased, despite advances in the arts and the sciences. History was urged on by an "evil impulse" that polluted God's creation, leaving human beings estranged from their Creator and at odds with one another. Taken by itself, the story would be extremely pessimistic. But the primeval history is now part of the larger Israelite epic. In this narrative context, it serves as a prologue to what follows: the call of Abraham and his venture of faith.

[20] For further discussion see "Unity and Diversity in God's Creation: A Study of the Babel Story," by Bernhard W. Anderson, *Currents in Theology and Mission* V, 2 (1978), 69–81; a shorter version appears in *Concilium*, No. 121 (1977), 89–97.

An Artist's Reconstruction *of the ziggurat of Ur, based on the restoration suggested by archaeologists who excavated the site between 1922 and 1934. At the top of the artificial mountain constructed with brick stands the temple of Nanna, the moon god who was worshiped at Ur.*

B. THE ANCESTRAL HISTORY

Passing from Genesis 11 to Genesis 12, we leave the nebulous realm of primeval history and enter the historical arena of the second millennium B.C.E. The form of historical narration in the ancestral history (Gen. 12–50) is saga, just as in the primeval history. There is, however, an important difference. The sagas of the ancestral period, as we saw in Chapter 1, are related in some degree to what was going on in the Fertile Crescent at that time. Historians can at least make the effort to establish some correlation between the ancestral history and the history of the ancient Near East. But none of the episodes of the primeval history is anchored to anything with which a modern historian could deal. An exception perhaps is the Table of Nations in Genesis 10 which, in the judgment of some historians, reflects circumstances in the late second millennium.[21] By and large, however, the primeval history is ''historical'' only in the broad sense that it portrays concretely the tensions and conflicts of human existence, and gives an interpretation of human history, in all its glory and tragedy, as the drama of God's dealings with humankind.

[21] See Siegfried Herrmann, *A History of Israel* [94], pp. 41–55.

Admittedly, in stating the matter this way, we are reading the story as modern persons. Undoubtedly the ancient Israelite narrator, and the people to whom the epic narrative was related, would have sensed a dramatic continuity in the progression from Genesis 11 to Genesis 12. The primeval history portrays the human situation in universal terms: human beings who should live in harmony, security, and mutual welfare—everything connoted by the Hebrew word *shalom* ("peace")—but who as a matter of historical fact are broken, divided, and scattered over the face of the earth in confusion and strife. This "history" provides the dramatic prologue to what is central in the ensuing parts of the epic narrative: the particular identity and special vocation of Israel in Yahweh's history-long and world-embracing purpose.

As the following outline shows, the family history of the ancestors of Israel concentrates mainly on Abraham, Jacob, and Joseph. Isaac is relegated to a rather minor role, overshadowed on the one side by Abraham and, on the other, by Jacob. Joseph is treated as the main figure in the story of Jacob's twelve sons. Nevertheless, the epic narrative is governed by the schematic sequence that appears at the outset of the Exodus story: Abraham, Isaac, and Jacob. It should be added that, despite the patriarchal character of ancient society, women play an important role in the story. This is particularly true of Sarah (or Sarai) who, together with her husband Abraham (Abram), made the venture into the land of Canaan (Gen. 11:31; 12:5).

The Family History of Israel's Ancestors*

The Abraham Cycle	
The promise to Abraham	Gen. 12:1–4a
Abraham and Sarah in Egypt	12:10–13:1
Abraham separates from Lot	13:2–18
[Abraham's victory: 14:1–24]	[special source]
Yahweh's covenant with Abraham	15:1–21
Ishmael, son of Abraham and Hagar	16:1–14
A son promised to Abraham and Sarah	18:1–16
The Fate of Sodom and Gomorrah	
Abraham's expostulation with God	18:17–33
Lot's deliverance from the holocaust	19:1–28
The birth of Moab and Ammon	19:30–38
Abraham and Sarah in Gerar	20:1–18
Isaac and Ishmael	21:1–21
Abraham's dispute with Abimelech	21:22–34
Abraham's near sacrifice of Isaac	22:1–19

*In this outline no attempt is made to separate putative J (Yahwist) and E (Elohist) elements of the Old Epic tradition or to identify editorial (Priestly) connective tissue. For a refined literary analysis, see the appendix in Martin Noth, *Pentateuchal Traditions* [70], pp. 263–67.

The Promise to Abraham

The key to the interpretation of the ancestral history is given in a divine address that is found at the outset. Out of the descendants of those who were dispersed from the abortive enterprise at Babel, Yahweh singled out one man and opened a new horizon before him.

> Yahweh said to Abram:
>   Betake yourself from your land, your kindred, and your
>   father's house to the land that I will show you.
>   I will make you a great nation; I will bless you
>   and magnify your name so that you will be a blessing.
>   Those who bless you I will bless,
>   and those who curse you I will curse.
>   By you all the families of the earth will bless themselves.
>   —GENESIS 12:1–3

To possess a land, to become a great nation, to be a blessing to the peoples of the earth—this threefold divine promise runs like a golden thread through the woven tapestry of the ancestral epic. These three elements of land, posterity and blessing apparently belonged to ancient patriarchal religion, as we saw earlier (above, pp. 41–45), but they are now highlighted and formalized, as evident in the divine addresses that punctuate the narrative.

Yahweh's Promissory Addresses

To Abraham:

In Haran before the migration	Gen. 12:1–3
In Shechem, the heartland of Canaan	12:7
In Canaan after separation from Lot	13:14–17
In Canaan (perhaps at Hebron)	15:4–5 (13–16)
In Hebron before the holocaust of Sodom	18:17–19
To Isaac in Gerar	26:2–5
To Jacob at Bethel	28:13–15
[quoted in the Joseph story: 48:1–4]	

Seen in this perspective, the migration of Abraham initiated a new kind of history: the history of Yahweh's promises which will bring benefits to Israel and to other peoples too. Thus from the beginning of the primeval history the narrative scope constantly narrows down until it concentrates upon the solitary figure of Abraham, the ancestor of the people chosen for a special task in Yahweh's historical purpose.[22] Coming almost immediately after the story of the Tower of Babel, which presents a dark picture of human pride and ambition,

---

[22] In the Priestly [P] scheme, the writer displays through genealogies the same movement from the universal to the particular: Creation-Adam-Noah-Shem (father of the Semites)-Terah and Abraham.

the story of the call of Abraham is like a burst of light that illumines the whole landscape. In contrast to the ambitious builders at Babel who aspired to make a name for themselves, it was promised that Yahweh would make Abraham's name great (Gen. 12:2; cf. 11:4). Israel's greatness would lie, not in its ambitions or achievements, but in the God who is active in its history to overcome the confusion, disharmony, and violence sketched in lurid colors in the universal primeval history.

DEFINITION: "BLESSING"

One of the dimensions of the promise to Abraham is that of blessing which somehow includes other peoples.

Blessing is the impartation of well-being ("peace") which is especially efficacious when given by a person who has superior prestige or power, such as an elder to a child, a king to a subject, or a priest to a suppliant. It is the opposite of a curse, which has negative effects. There are still societies today that revere the power of the word, when spoken in blessing (affirmation) or in curse (censure).

Originally a forceful word, spoken in blessing or curse, was supposed to go into effect immediately. This helps us to understand the importance attached to deathbed blessings (as in the case of Isaac and Jacob) or to imprecations against enemies (Balaam's refusal to curse Israel in the Balaam oracles). This dynamic understanding of the blessing and the curse prevailed in the period of Israel's ancestors. In the present revision of the ancestral history, however, a major change has taken place: the blessing is postponed to the future, beyond the lifetime of the original recipients, and hence becomes a *promise*. The postponement of the promise means that the whole ancestral period becomes an interim between promise and fulfillment, with the resulting tensions and anxieties of faith. When the interim seems unbearably extended, people raise cries of lament ("How long, O Yahweh?" "My God, why have you forsaken me?"), as in some of the Psalms (e.g. Pss. 13; 22).

One of the aspects of the promise of blessing is somewhat ambiguous, owing to the question of how to understand the Hebrew verbs (in a passive sense, "be blessed," or in a reflexive sense, "bless themselves"). Here we cannot go into the grammatical problem as it appears from time to time (Gen. 12:3; 18:18; 22:18; 26:4; 28:14). Probably the meaning intended is that other peoples will "bless themselves" in the sense that they invoke the name of the God of Abraham, or that they say to one another: "May we be as blessed as the people of Abraham." In any case, in the history of interpretation the promise was taken to mean that God would bless the nations *through*, that is, by means of Israel's role and witness. This view, found in the Greek (Septuagint) translation and in the Wisdom of Ben Sira (44:21), is adopted in the New Testament (Acts 3:25; Gal. 3:8). See further Claus Westermann, *Blessing* [cited under 148].

In working out the theme of the promise, the narrator—and this fact warrants repetition—wove together stories that once had a completely different meaning. What the ancestors were like in their oldest dress is difficult to say, in view of the complete reworking of the traditions over a period of generations. The evidence suggests that Abraham was once connected with the sanctuary of Mamre, near Hebron; Isaac, with the shrine of Beer-sheba; and Jacob, with the "house of God" (*beth 'El*) at Bethel. Each of these places was an old Canaanite shrine that had been taken over by the Israelites, and some of the stories about these three figures may have been Canaanite in origin. In any case, we are not dealing with biographies, but with stories in which Israel personified its history. The personification is clear in the case of Jacob and Esau, who represent Israel and Edom, respectively (Gen. 25:22–26). But it is also true with respect to Abraham. He too is more than individual; he is typical of the people of God who venture into the future in faith (Heb. 11:8–10).

During the period of the tribal confederacy, these miscellaneous traditions were being harmonized into the story of a single family bound together by the father-son-grandson sequence: Abraham, Isaac, and Jacob (cf. Exod. 3:6). The retrospective view of these stories is clearly indicated in Genesis 15:13–16, where we find references to the duration of the oppression in Egypt and to the Exodus. Thus, in retrospect, the ancestral period began to have a unity that did not actually exist in that time. This is what we would have if some modern historian were to project the unity of a United States, personified in "Uncle Sam," back to the heterogeneous peoples who settled in the land before 1776. No longer are the ancestral stories mere cult legends or tales of tribal heroes: they now pertain to the whole of Israel. For from Abraham's seed, in direct succession through Isaac and Jacob, sprang the twelve tribes of Israel. Moreover, the religion of the ancestors is no longer the worship of gods other than Yahweh (check Josh. 24:14 again!): El Olam at Beer-sheba (21:33), Baal Berith or El Berith at Shechem (see Judg. 8:33; 9:4, 46), or El Bethel at Bethel (Gen. 35:7). It is now the worship of Yahweh, the God of Israel who is also the God of Abraham, Isaac, and Jacob, and indeed the creator and ruler of human history. In the present form of the narrative, it is Yahweh who appears to each of the ancestors and renews the promise given to Abraham, a promise that has universal implications.

The Trials of Faith

In the narrator's perspective, then, the ancestors of Israel were wanderers toward a goal that Yahweh had set before them. Their history was a pilgrim movement from promise toward fulfillment, not an aimless meandering on the fringes of Canaan. Yet, according to the storyteller, it was not easy for them to live by the promise, for again and again they found themselves in situations in which the divine promise seemed incredible. At such times their trust in Yahweh was put to a severe test, and they reached the edge of despair. As we shall see, each element of the promise—land, posterity, blessing—was almost taken away. In episode after episode the narrator builds up a dramatic suspense, only to resolve the tension by showing how Yahweh intervened at the critical moment, just when everything seemed lost, and renewed the promise. Let us see how this theme is worked out, as we pay particular attention to the divine addresses listed above.

ABRAHAM We read that Abraham, after migrating from Mesopotamia, came to Shechem in the heart of Canaanite country. There, at a sacred oak, Yahweh appeared to Abraham and reaffirmed the promise to give the land to his descendants (*Divine Address*, Gen. 12:7). But after a while Abraham was driven by famine to Egypt, where, to save his life, he ingratiated himself with Pharaoh by an act of deceit involving his wife Sarah. True, his hunger was severe, and it seemed expedient to take things into his own hands rather than to trust Yahweh's providence. But Abraham's act was tantamount to surrendering the promise, even though it brought him great material advantage, for with Sarah (the ancestress of Israel) in Pharaoh's harem the Israel of the future could not come into being. Then, just in the nick of time, Yahweh saved the day, and Abraham, despite his rash deed, was sent away from Egypt a rich man (12:10–13:2). He returned to Bethel and "called upon the name of Yahweh," as he had done there before his Egyptian adventure.

The next moment of suspense came when strife between the herdsmen of Abraham and those of Lot made it necessary for the two relatives to part and go their respective ways. Lot, the ancestor of Moab and Ammon (see Gen. 19:30–38), was given the freedom to choose where to go, and the future of Israel hung in the balance of his decision. Providentially, Lot chose, not the Land of the Promise, but the area of the Jordan Valley, whose wicked cities—Sodom and Gomorrah—Yahweh later destroyed by volcanic fire and brimstone (13:3–13). Once again Yahweh renewed the promise to Abraham (*Divine Address*, 13:14–17).

But there was still a major obstacle barring the door to the future: Abraham had no son. It was incredible that the promise could be fulfilled when Abraham's sole heir was Eliezer, his household slave. Again Yahweh renewed the promise that Abraham would have a great progeny (*Divine Address*, Gen. 15:4–5) and that he (through his family) would inherit the land. This time the promise was sealed with a covenant (Gen. 15:7–21). The covenant ceremony is very archaic—an indication of the antiquity of the legend material used by the narrator (see p. 44). In its present context, however, Yahweh's covenant with Abraham is an anticipation of the covenant of Sinai.

ISAAC Yet it was still incredible that the promise could be fulfilled, for Sarah was barren. Faith needed more evidence. So this time Sarah took things in her hands, urging Abraham to have a child by her Egyptian maid, Hagar, only to regret her nagging and later to force the maid out of the house. Suspense is heightened when Hagar, at a well in the wilderness, received from Yahweh the promise that she would bear a son to Abraham and that Ishmael (regarded by Muslims as the ancestor of the Arabs) would grow to be a formidable bedouin— "a wild ass of a man." But Ishmael, who was conceived in a moment of failure

of faith in Yahweh, could not be the child of the promise, even though Yahweh was deeply concerned for Hagar and her non-Israelite child (Gen. 16). Later, Yahweh appeared to Abraham at the sanctuary near Hebron (by the sacred oak of Mamre; see 13:18) and announced that a son would be born to him. Sarah, who was eavesdropping on the conversation, laughed heartily to herself, knowing that she had reached the age when this was physically impossible. She failed to believe that with Yahweh all things are possible (18:1–16). The incident of Sarah's laughter is one example of the many puns in the epic narrative, for in Hebrew "she laughs" is *titzḥaq*, and "Isaac" is *yitzḥaq*. The laughter arises because of the ludicrous disproportion between the divine promise and the zero possiblity of the human situation.

The birth of Isaac, the son of Abraham's and Sarah's old age, is reported briefly in Genesis 21:1–2, after the story about the destruction of the cities of the Jordan Valley, Sodom and Gomorrah (18:17–19:38). In the preface to the story of the holocaust (see 19:24–25), we hear again the theme that "Abraham shall become a great and mighty nation, and all the nations of the earth shall bless themselves by him" (*Divine Address*, 18:17–19). Because Abraham was drawn into a special relationship with Yahweh, it was proper to take him into confidence about impending developments. In this context appears one of the most powerful passages in Scripture (18:22–33): Abraham's expostulation with God about the indiscriminate destruction of righteous people along with the wicked.

The story of the testing of Abraham (Gen. 22:1–14) betrays evidence that it once circulated independently, perhaps as a legend to explain the name of a sacred place and to justify the commutation of child sacrifice. Whatever its original meaning, however, it now functions in the history of the promise. According to the moving story Abraham was commanded by God to sacrifice his only son whom he loved dearly—the child of the promise who was the one link with the future. The reader follows this "Knight of faith" (S. Kierkegaard) along the lonely path that obedience constrained him to tread, and sees him undergo the supreme trial of faith as he prepares to slay Isaac and thereby to sacrifice the future of the people of God on the altar. But once again God intervened, just when the knife was upraised, and his eye was directed to a ram caught in

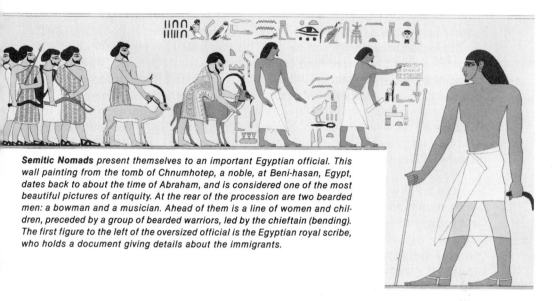

Semitic Nomads *present themselves to an important Egyptian official. This wall painting from the tomb of Chnumhotep, a noble, at Beni-hasan, Egypt, dates back to about the time of Abraham, and is considered one of the most beautiful pictures of antiquity. At the rear of the procession are two bearded men: a bowman and a musician. Ahead of them is a line of women and children, preceded by a group of bearded warriors, led by the chieftain (bending). The first figure to the left of the oversized official is the Egyptian royal scribe, who holds a document giving details about the immigrants.*

a thicket which he offered as a sacrifice instead. And once again the promise was renewed (*Divine Address*, 22:15–18).[23]

In the story of the selection of a wife for Isaac (Gen. 24), the author again has created dramatic suspense. Isaac could not marry a local Canaanite woman, for that would contaminate the line of Abraham and bring the promise to naught. So Abraham's servant was sent to the ancestral homeland in Mesopotamia (Haran) with express instructions to have the prospective wife brought back to the Promised Land. Would Abraham's servant find the right maiden? Would Rebekah decide to come to Isaac's country? The story leaves no doubt that Yahweh was guiding the servant's journey, despite the uncertainty in the servant's mind. Nothing happened by chance: Yahweh meant it to turn out just as it did.

JACOB   Then the drama is acted out all over again, this time with the spotlight on Jacob. (Not much is said about Isaac, who seems to be little more than a replica of his father; see Genesis 26 and the *Divine Address*, verses 2–5.) Rebekah, like Sarah, was barren, and would not have presented Isaac with a son had it not been for Yahweh's intervention. But a new complication arose that almost abolished the promise. Rebekah conceived two sons: Esau, the father of the Edomites, and Jacob, the ancestor of Israel. Already in the womb they were struggling together, as these nations did in real life. Esau won the first round,

[23] See Søren Kierkegaard's exposition of Abraham's "leap of faith" in *Fear and Trembling* (Garden City, N.Y.: Doubleday, 1954); also Erich Auerbach's discussion of Gen. 22 in *Mimesis: The Representation of Reality in Western Literature*, trans. by William Trask (Garden Ctiy, N.Y.: Doubleday, 1957), pp. 5–20.

because he was born first, and therefore had a right to be his father's heir (25:21–26). But Jacob shrewdly tricked his twin brother out of his birthright (25:27–34), and later tricked him out of their father's final blessing (Gen. 27). To appreciate the point of the latter story, it should be remembered that, according to the ancient belief, words spoken in blessing (or curse) were efficacious. They had the power to produce the intended result.[24] And, like an arrow in flight, they could not be retracted. So Jacob, having received his father's blessing, was destined to gain preeminence over Esau (Edom), as Israel later did, especially in the time of David.

In spite of Jacob's victory, however, everything seemed hopelessly lost. For what good was the blessing to him if, because of Esau's hostility, he had to flee to Haran, an exile from the land on which the promise was to be fulfilled? Jacob's flight to Haran gives the narrator a chance to introduce a cycle of legends that had originally circulated independently—legends dealing with the entertaining adventures of Jacob in the territory of Laban, the ancestor of Syria (Aram). The narrator, however, has built this cycle into his literary architecture, suspending it "like a bridge supported from within by two pillars."[25] Over on one side, the bridge is secured to the story of Jacob's dream at Bethel (Gen. 28:10–19); on the other, it is anchored to the story of his wrestle with an Assailant at the river Jabbok (32:22–32). In the first story, Yahweh meets Jacob in the time of his despair, appearing in a dream and renewing the threefold promise given to Abraham: to give to Israel the land; to make Israel a great and numerous people; and through Israel to bestow blessings upon all the families of the earth (*Divine Address*, 28:13–15). Assured that Yahweh was going with him and would bring him back to the Promised Land, Jacob journeyed to his kin in Haran. There, through the providence of Yahweh, not to mention his own shady dealings, Jacob came into the possession of great wealth: two wives (Leah and Rachel), two concubines, eleven sons, numerous servants, and the best portion of Laban's flocks (Gen. 29:31). With this wealth he managed to escape from the clutches of his wily Aramean relative and prepared to win over Esau by a lavish display of gifts (32:1–21).

Then we come to the other main pillar of the narrator's bridge spanning the Jacob-Laban stories. Formerly, Yahweh had appeared to Jacob in a noctural dream in the time of his despair; now Yahweh came in the form of a nocturnal visitor in the time of his prosperity, when it seemed that all he had to do was buy his way into the Promised Land by winning Esau's favor. With this angel (which, in the earliest form of the story, was perhaps a night demon) Jacob wrestled until daybreak. Jacob finally received the angel's blessing, but he went away limping from the wound of the combat. Soon he was reunited with Esau and thus gained access to the Promised Land (Gen. 33).

[24] See the discussion of Balaam's oracles, p. 121; also the Definition of "blessing," above p. 171.

[25] The figure of speech comes from Gerhard von Rad's commentary on Genesis [271], p. 39, whose interpretation we are following at this point.

*The Near East as seen from the Gemini II spacecraft while cir-
cling the earth in 1966. In the center of the picture is the Sinaitic
Peninsula; below this is the Gulf of Suez and above is the Gulf
of Aqabah. Extending north from the Gulf of Aqabah is the valley
of the Dead Sea and further north still is the Sea of Galilee. The
Jordan valley, which runs between these two bodies of water,
provides the eastern boundary of the Holy Land, and the Mediterranean Sea (upper left) forms the western boundary.*

PLATE 1

Rameses II's rock temple at Abu Simbel as seen shortly before being cut into huge blocks and reassembled on higher ground above the lake formed by the dam south of Aswan. Above: Two of the four colossi of the pharaoh which guard the entrance. Below: A view from the smaller queen's temple toward the king's temple, which—from entrance pylon to the innermost holy of holies—was hewn from solid rock.

The Hittite capital of Hattushash lay on the ridge (right) that slopes down to the modern city of Boghaz-köy; the rugged terrain enhanced its defenses.

The Lion Gate at Hattushash stands in the Hittite capital's ruins.

Excavated ruins of the fortified upper part (acropolis) of the Hittite capital.

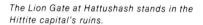

In the background the magnificent Mosque of Omar, a Byzantine
structure built over the sacred rock which was once the site of
Solomon's temple. Some maintain that the Holy of Holies, the
most sacred part of the temple, was once located on bedrock
beneath the cupola seen in the foreground.

PLATE 4

JOSEPH From this point the narrator moves quickly to the Joseph cycle (Gen. 37–50). We have already noticed (see pp. 45–48) that the Joseph story reflects to some degree the historical conditions of the second millennium, when it was not unheard of for a Semite to rise to power in the Egyptian court. In its present form, however, the Joseph story is embellished with various popular motifs. It has been suggested, for instance, that the account of Potiphar's wife attempting to seduce Joseph (Gen. 39:7–20) was influenced by the Egyptian "Story of Two Brothers," in which the same motif appears.[26] Whatever the source of the motifs, they have been blended into a short story in which scene follows scene in the artistic development of a single plot that discloses the hidden realization of God's purpose in human affairs. This view is magnificently expressed in Joseph's magnanimous words to his brothers:

> As for you, you meant evil against me; but God meant it for good, to bring it about that many people should be kept alive, as they are today.
> —GENESIS 50:20 (RSV)

This verse (see also 45:5–7) encapsulates the theme of the Joseph story. Human affairs are not governed by the evil designs of human beings, or by the economic stresses that forced Jacob to migrate to Egypt, but by the overruling providence of God, who works for the good in all things.

When the Joseph story, which once circulated independently, was incorporated into the ancestral history, the theme of God's hidden providence was linked with the theme of the divine promise in its threefold dimension: posterity, land, and blessing. It is not surprising, then, that here and there the narrator has added touches which suggest the function of the story in the larger epic context, as in Jacob's recollection of Yahweh's promissory address to him at Luz, that is, Bethel (Gen. 48:3–4), or in Joseph's reference, just before his death, to the promise made to the ancestors (50:24). Indeed, in its present dramatic context the Joseph story seems to hint that the promise made to Abraham, the promise that through Israel the nations would bless themselves, was moving toward fulfillment. For Joseph, elevated to the position of prime minister of Egypt, saved the land from famine and brought security and prosperity to the country.[27]

C. THE PEOPLE'S HISTORY

From the Joseph story the epic narrative moves on through the books of Exodus and Numbers—the story of Israel's life that we have considered in earlier chap-

---

[26] See Pritchard, *Ancient Near Eastern Texts* [1], pp. 23–25. The Egyptian seduction story tells of a man's refusal to lie with the wife of his older brother, the wife's false accusation to her husband, and the husband's attempt to destroy his brother for the alleged deed.

[27] See David J. A. Clines, *The Theme of the Pentateuch* [264], who shows that the three-fold promise to the ancestors is carried to partial fulfillment in the completed Israelite epic, the Pentateuch.

ters—toward the goal: Israel's occupation of the Promised Land. At the outset of the Mosaic tradition, the promise seemed to be eclipsed, for the descendants of Abraham and Sarah were reduced to the level of slaves—pawns in Pharaoh's game of power, who had no future and no hope. But Yahweh, who is identified as "the God of Abraham, Isaac, Jacob," remembered the promise to the ancestors and intervened, assuring Moses at the burning bush that the people were on the verge of being liberated and brought into a land flowing with milk and honey (Exod. 3:7-8). The following outline shows how the crucial events of Exodus and Sinai, the experiences in the wilderness, and the circuit via Transjordan toward the land of Canaan have been combined to form a dramatic narrative. As the story had opened with the birth of Moses, so it concludes with his death.

The Mosaic Tradition*

The Exodus Story

Oppression in Egypt	Exod. 1:8-22
The rise of Moses	2:1-22
Moses' call and commission	3:1-4:17
Moses' return to Egypt	4:18-31
Encounter with Pharaoh	5:1-6:1
Plagues against Egypt (combined with P)	7:8-11:10
The first Passover	12:21-28
Final plague and departure from Egypt	12:29-39
Route of the flight	13:17-22
Victory at the Sea (combined with P)	14:1-31
Song of the Sea	15:1-18 (19)
Song of Miriam	15:20-21

Beginning of Wilderness Wandering

First stations	15:22-27
Quails and manna (combined with P)	16:1-36
Water from the rock	17:1-7
Victory over the Amalekites	17:8-16
Visit of Moses' father-in-law, Jethro	18:1-27

The Sinai Covenant

Theophany at Sinai	19:1-25
The Decalogue	20:1-17
Theophany	20:18-21
The Covenant Code	20:22-23:33
Making of the Covenant	24:1-11

*Here again no attempt is made to separate Yahwistic and Elohistic (J and E) variations on the epic narrative or to distinguish between early and later stages of tradition. It should be noted that in this area the Priestly Writer (P) has shown greater interest in particular stories, as shown by the fact that Old Epic and Priestly narratives are blended together. For more refined analysis, see the appendix to Martin Noth, *Pentateuchal Traditions* [70], pp. 267-71, 273-76.

The Sinai Covenant (cont.)

Breaking of the Covenant: Golden Calf	31:1–35
Covenant renewal	33:1–34:28
Moses' transfiguration	34:29–35

Sojourn in the Wilderness (Kadesh)

Israel on the march	Num. 10:29–36
Murmuring in the wilderness	11:1–35
Miriam's punishment	12:1–16
Reconnaissance (combined with P)	13:1–33
Murmuring (combined with P)	14:1–38
Abortive attack on southern Canaan	14:39–45
Revolts against Moses (combined with P)	16:1–50

Circuit via Transjordan

Departure from Kadesh	20:14–22
Battle of Hormah	21:1–3
The bronze serpent	21:4–9
Itinerary	21:10–10
Victory over Sihon and Og	21:21–35
Balak and Balaam	21:1–40
The Balaam oracles	22:41–24:25
Apostasy in Moab	25:1–5
Allotment of land in Transjordan	32:1–42
Moses' death	Deut. 34:1–6

Previously we have observed that the narrator, even when dealing with the ancestral period which is in some degree related to the history of the ancient Near East, is concerned primarily with a deeper dimension of history than the events that we usually think of as historical. And this is also true of the story that extends from the Exodus to the occupation of Canaan. The narrator portrays the shared history of a people, one that has its setting in the ancient world about which we are coming to know more and more. The story of Israel's life, however, has two important dimensions. On the one hand, it was a history with Yahweh—a history that was set in movement toward the future by Yahweh's promise that opened new horizons of faith. It was a God-story, in the sense that Yahweh was an active participant and therefore the One whose judgment and grace had to be reckoned with in daily affairs and in political events. On the other hand, it was a story of a people who were invited to take part with Yahweh in the unfolding story.

Hence the stories of the ancestral history are mirrors that reflect the interior struggles of people of faith: perplexity about the hiddenness of God's ways, the temptation to trust more in human devices than in God's providence, and the alternation of faith and unbelief. This is also the case with the people's history

Chronological Chart 2

	B.C.E.	EGYPT	PALESTINE (AND SYRIA)	MESOPOTAMIA
(Iron Age)		XX Dynasty (c. 1185–1069)	Period of the Judges (c. 1200–1020)	Collapse of Hittite Empire
	1200 to 1100	Sea Peoples defeated by Rameses III (c. 1175) Egyptian decline	Philistines settle in Canaan Battle of Megiddo (c. 1125)	Assyrian decline
	1100 to 1000	XXI Dynasty (c. 1069–935) Egyptian decline	Philistine ascendancy Fall of Shiloh (c. 1050) Samuel and Saul (c. 1020–1000)	Brief Assyrian revival Tiglath-pileser I (c. 1116–1078)

that extends from the book of Exodus to the end of the Pentateuch. We find here not only the recital of the crucial events that formed Israel as a people (Exodus and Sinai), but also portrayals of the realities of human experience: the breaking of the covenant and its renewal in divine forgiveness, the murmurings in the wilderness that express the people's lament in the seeming absence of God, the trials of faith when people are up against great adversity. There is something very realistic, and even "honest to God" about these stories, which later generations have appropriated as "types" of the life of faith (e.g. I Cor. 10:6–12). Yet through the ups and downs of experiences runs the unshakable conviction, which governs the whole Israelite epic like a symphonic theme, that Yahweh's promise does not fail. Yahweh is faithful, not capricious. Events are linked in Yahweh's purpose, even when this is hard for human beings to perceive. And so the drama moves on toward the climax: the inheritance of the Promised Land and Israel's rise to the status of a great *goy* ("nation"; see Gen. 12:2; Exod. 19:6).

In succeeding chapters we shall consider the transformation of Israel from "the people of Yahweh" (*'am Yahweh*; see Judg. 5:11b), bound together by family ties and religious allegiance, to the "nation" of Israel with a political form of life like the surrounding nations.[28]

---

[28] In the period before David, Israel was basically regarded as *'am Yahweh* (people of Yahweh), not *goy Yahweh* (nation of Yahweh). See E. A. Speiser, " 'People' and 'Nation' of Israel," *Journal of Biblical Literature*, 79 (1960), 157–63.

CHAPTER 6

The Struggle between Faith and Culture

The turbulent scenes portrayed in the book of Judges show that life within the Israelite confederacy was a continuing struggle during the period between the death of Joshua and the rise of the monarchy under Saul. Those were "the days when the judges ruled" (Ruth 1:1)—the twelfth and eleventh centuries B.C.E. Having won a foothold on the soil of Canaan, Israel faced the problem of adjusting to the agricultural ways of the land and taking its place among the nations. In the days of the judges the Tribal Confederacy, straining under conflict with forces both without and within, found itself put to the severest test.

In part, the struggle was for Israel's physical survival. Although the decisive phase of the occupation took place in the thirteenth century, the contest for Canaan went on relentlessly for many years afterward. The Israelite offensive was continued by means of war, treaty, and the gradual absorption of the Canaanites into the Israelite alliance. But at a deeper level an even more important conflict was being fought on the soil of Canaan: a conflict of religious loyalties. In modern language, an ideological struggle was being waged, not just a military one. And it was as true then as it is now that final victory goes to the side that wins the allegiance of people's hearts.

Biblical readings: The book of Judges, at least 2:6–16:31, and the narratives in I Samuel 1–12. The theological commentary on the meaning of the settlement in Canaan, found in the book of Deuteronomy, is relevant here, but will be treated at length in Chapter 11.

TEMPTATIONS OF CANAANITE CULTURE

In the long course of the centuries, many victorious nations have been molded by the superior cultures that they vanquished. In ancient Mesopotamia, for example, the brilliant Sumerian culture was overcome by the aggressive Semitic Akkadians, who, under the leadership of Sargon, established the first empire in history. But the Akkadians were profoundly influenced by Sumerian culture. Centuries later, Rome vanquished the Greeks and established a political order, the famous Pax Romana, which probably has not been surpassed by any world empire. But Rome also was dependent upon the glorious legacy of Greek culture. During the Israelite occupation of Canaan, the stage was set for a similar development. Archaeological excavation in Palestine has shown that Israelite life was crude in comparison to the highly sophisticated, aristocratic culture of Canaan. Would the victor again be overcome by the vanquished?

Coming out of a desert background, Israel reacted strongly against the culture of the Fertile Crescent. Echoes of the antipathy for this culture are found in some of the Old Epic traditions preserved in Genesis 2–11. In its earliest form, the story of the Tower of Babel expressed scorn for the proud culture of the Fertile Crescent, which was symbolized by the famed temple-tower (ziggurat) of Babylon (Gen. 11:1–9). According to another narrative, the first city was built by a murderer, Cain, who was incensed that his agricultural offering of the "fruit of the ground" was not as acceptable to Yahweh as his shepherd brother's gift of the firstlings of the flock (Gen. 4:1–17). Noah, we are told, was the first man to till the soil and plant a vineyard—the characteristic agriculture of Canaan; but his activity led to a revolting spectacle of drunkenness and nakedness, and Canaan, the son of Ham, was cursed with a threefold curse (Gen. 9:18–27). This deep-seated reaction against Canaanite culture persisted in some Israelite circles long after the time of the conquest (see Jer. 35).

A negative attitude toward Canaanite culture was offset by the opposite extreme, which became increasingly popular in the period of the settlement in Canaan—namely, the wholesale adoption of Canaanite ways. This was a great temptation because, contrary to some of the exaggerated claims of the book of Joshua, the Canaanites were not exterminated or even reduced to insignificance by Israelite military victories. Although the Canaanite population may have been diminished a bit, the Israelites nevertheless had to settle down in their midst. Moreover, we must remember that the Tribal Confederacy had been formed at Shechem in the very heart of Canaanite culture, and it embraced new converts who previously had been worshiping the "strange gods" of the pre-Mosaic period. The very diversity of the Israelite confederacy undoubtedly made a relapse from the stern demands of the Mosaic faith unavoidable.

Hence the sermonic warnings of Moses in the book of Deuteronomy, although they were actually written many years later, appropriately emphasize the great dangers and temptations of life in Canaan. Israel's transition from the status of pastoral Hebrews to the sedentary existence of farmers in the Fertile Crescent had fateful and far-reaching implications. Previously, Yahweh had been the God of the wanderers, but now Israel's relationship was to the soil, which had to be tilled. The human problem increasingly came to center around relation to nature: the need of rainfall for crops, the dependence upon the rotation of the seasons, and the concern for fertility which pervaded the Fertile Crescent. In the past Yahweh's "strong hand and outstretched arm" proved to be effective in history; the new question was whether Yahweh could win out in the rivalry with the gods who controlled the cycles of nature upon which farmers depended for their existence.

The Deuteronomistic Interpretation

Our major source for studying the transitional twelfth and eleventh centuries is the book of Judges, the second book in the Deuteronomistic History. Not all the present book of Judges belongs to the Deuteronomistic edition. The preface (Judg. 1:1–2:5), which has been mentioned in connection with the "conquest" (see pp. 134–135), and the appendix (Judg. 17–21) contain extremely valuable information about the period. These passages, however, stand outside the Deuteronomistic framework which embraces the material found in Judges 2:6–16:31.

The Deuteronomists' "theology of history" is found in capsule form in their introduction to the period of the Judges (Judg. 2:6–3:6). After a recapitulation of the conclusion of the book of Joshua (compare Josh. 24:28–31 and Judg. 2:6–9), the narrative describes the new situation that prevailed after the death of Joshua. During Joshua's lifetime, we are told, the people remained faithful to Yahweh, for they lived under the creative power of "the saving experience" (Exodus) and "the commanding experience" (Sinai). But "there arose another generation after them, who did not know Yahweh or the work which he had done for Israel" (Judg. 2:10). Faith in Yahweh was not belief in a body of knowledge that could be transferred, like a bank account, from parents to children. To *know* Yahweh, in the proper sense of the Hebrew verb (*yada‘*), means to acknowledge Yahweh personally, to be in covenant relation with Yahweh. The faith of parents does not necessarily become the faith of their children, as we well know. Each generation must either renew or repudiate the covenant in its own way.

DEFINITION: "DEUTERONOMIC, DEUTERONOMISTIC"

The subtle distinction between the two adjectives "Deuteronomic" and "Deuteronomistic" will become clearer in the course of our study. "Deuteronomic" refers to the material found in the core of the book of Deuteronomy (Deut. 5–28). "Deuteronomistic" refers to the writings, influenced by the Deuteronomic torah, that comprise the so-called Deuteronomistic History that extends from Joshua through II Kings (to be discussed in Chapter 11; see Definition, p. 359). The Former Prophets, to use the canonical rubric, which include the historical books of Joshua and Judges, have been subjected to Deuteronomistic editing.

According to the Deuteronomistic historian, the history of the period followed a neat pattern. Israel's ups and downs illustrated the basic theological conviction of this school of thought: obedience to Yahweh's torah leads to welfare and peace; disobedience results in hardship and defeat. This lesson of history is illustrated graphically in the rhythm of events:

1. The people of Israel did what was evil by forsaking Yahweh, who brought them out of Egypt, and by turning to serve the gods of the surrounding peoples.
2. Therefore Yahweh's anger was kindled against them, and they were delivered into the power of their enemies, who oppressed them.
3. In their affliction, the people cried out in penitence. So Yahweh, moved to pity, raised up a judge who delivered them from their enemies. Throughout the lifetime of the judge, the land enjoyed rest.
4. However, when the judge died the people fell back into idolatry. Therefore the anger of Yahweh was kindled against Israel, and Yahweh sold them again into the hands of their plunderers.

This is the scheme that is outlined in Judges 2:6–3:6. Usually the Deuteronomistic summary is found at the beginning and end of the stories of the major judges, as in the cases of Othniel, Ehud, Deborah (and Barak), Gideon (also called Jerubbaal), Jephthah, and Samson. The account of Othniel (Jud. 3:7–11) is an excellent illustration. These stories, which were drawn from ancient tribal traditions, have been incorporated loosely into the Deuteronomistic framework, somewhat as an old picture is put into a new frame. As a result, the events of the period are interpreted as following a rhythm of rebellion and return.

This pattern is too neat and schematic to do justice to the complexity of events in the period of the judges. But it does contain much truth. History seems to show that the downfall of a people often begins not with external military pressure, but with internal moral and spiritual degeneration. The Deuteronomistic historian attempted to emphasize the central truth that Israel's vitality and solidarity lay in a united, exclusive loyalty to Yahweh. When this covenant faith was strong, Israel was in a better position to cope with the inrush of foreign ideas and armies. But when this ethically demanding faith was weakened by the syncretistic religion of the Fertile Crescent, Israel was an easy prey to its enemies. In that ancient period, the most divisive and destructive threat that Israel faced was the Canaanite religion. Undoubtedly Israel would have been lost in the cultural melting pot of the Fertile Crescent had it not been for the military crises which providentially rallied the Israelites to the standard of the Mosaic faith and renewed their loyalty to the God of the covenant.

Religion and Agriculture

To appreciate the nature of the struggle of the period of the judges, we must know something about the religion of Canaan, which in the Old Testatment is described as the worship of the Baals and Ashtarts (Judg. 2:13; 10:6; I Sam. 7:4;

12:10). The title "Baal" means "lord" or "owner," and designates the male deity who owns the land and controls its fertility. His female partner is known as "Baalath," "lady," although in the cases cited above her personal name is Ashtart. It was believed that these fertility powers were connected with particular localities or towns, in which case one could speak of many Baals and Ashtarts, as numerous as the cities of the land (see Jer. 2:28). But it was also possible to regard these local powers as manifestations of the great "Lord" and "Lady" who dwell in the heavens, in which case worshipers could address Baal and Ashtart in the singular as cosmic deities.

Modern farmers, despite their training in the science of agriculture, some-

*The **"Baal of the Lightning"** was found in a sanctuary at Ras Shamra, Syria. Apparently treading upon mountains, the god—lord of storm and fertility—wields a club in his right hand and with his left hand holds a lance, the upper part of which may symbolize lightning. On his helmet are the horns of the bull, the cult animal which represents the power of fertility. Notice the poetic use of this imagery in Numbers 24:8.*

times marvel at the strange powers of fertility that work in the soil (even yet called "Mother Earth") to bring about a fruitful harvest. In those moments they are linked with their ancient predecessors—people of the soil who from time immemorial have marveled at the astonishing mystery of nature without which there could be no agriculture. In the Fertile Crescent, where the whole culture was dependent upon the fruitfulness of the soil, this mystery was viewed in a religious way. The land, it was believed, is the sphere of divine powers. The Baal of a region is the "lord" or "owner" of the land; its fertility is dependent upon sexual relations between him and his consort. When the rains came and the earth and water mingled, the mysterious powers of fertility stirred again. New life was resurrected after the barrenness of winter. This astonishing revival of nature, people believed, was due to sexual intercourse between Baal and his partner, Baalath.

Furthermore, farmers were not mere spectators of the sacred marriage. It was believed that by ritually enacting the drama of Baal it was possible to assist—through magical power—the fertility powers to reach their consummation, and thereby to insure the welfare and prosperity of the land. The cooperation with the powers of fertility involved the dramatization in the temples of the story of Baal's loves and wars. Besides the rehearsal of this mythology, a prominent feature of the Canaanite cult was sacred prostitution (see Deut. 23:18). In the act of temple prostitution the man identified himself with Baal, the woman with Ashtart. It was believed that human pairs, by imitating the action of Baal and his partner, could bring the divine pair together in fertilizing union.

Enough has been said to indicate that Canaanite religion was highly erotic. But this eroticism was not just the expression of a desire for pleasure through sex (as it so often is in modern culture). Rather, it was believed that the whole natural sphere, to which the existence of the farmer was intimately bound, was governed by the vitalities of sex—the powers of the masculine and the feminine. Through sexual ceremonies farmers could swing into the rhythms of the agricultural world and even keep those rhythms going through the techniques of religious magic. The kind of magic in question is often called sympathetic or imitative magic. It rests on the assumption that when persons imitate the action of the gods, a power is released to bring that action about (For example: the "rainmaker" who, by pouring water from a tree and thereby imitating rain, induces the gods to end a drought.)

The Ras Shamra Epic

The pattern of Baal religion found in Canaan was of one piece with the myth and ritual which, in varying forms, was spread throughout the whole Fertile Crescent.[1] In Babylonia, for example, the Tammuz cult dramatized the relations between the god Tammuz and the goddess Ishtar. In Egypt the Isis cult was based on the worship of the god Osiris (Horus) and his female counterpart Isis

---

[1] See especially H. and H. A. Frankfort et al., *The Intellectual Adventure* [122].

The Mother-Goddess *known as "the queen of wild beasts": this ivory representation (from the fourteenth century B.C.E.) was found in a tomb near Ras Shamra. Two goats stand on their hind legs, apparently reaching for the stalks of grain she holds in her hands.*

(Hathor). And, as we have seen, in Canaan the Baal cult dramatized the relations between the storm god Baal and his consort, known as Anath or Ashtart (the Canaanite equivalent of Ishtar). The basic similarity of these religions encouraged a great deal of borrowing back and forth, for they appealed to a common concern about the relation of human beings to their natural and cosmic environment.

We can get a clear picture of Canaanite religion from the Ras Shamra tablets, first discovered in 1929 at Ras Shamra on the coast of northern Syria, the

---

² See Pritchard, *Ancient Near Eastern Texts* [1], pp. 129–55. A brief summary is given by W. F. Albright, "The Old Testament World," *Interpreter's Bible* I [16], 133–271. See also G. R. Driver, *Canaanite Myths and Legends* [282]; John Gray, *The Legacy of Canaan* [283].

site of the ancient Canaanite city of Ugarit.[2] These mythological texts date from about 1400 B.C.E.—that is, from the Amarna Age. Just as the Amarna letters (see above, pp. 126–128) give a picture of the political conditions in Canaan before the Israelite occupation, so the Ras Shamra texts give firsthand information about the religious situation. In many respects this was a highly developed, sophisticated religion, far ahead of the belief in local fertility spirits which scholars once thought the religion of the Baals and the Ashtarts to have been. At the head of the Canaanite pantheon was the high god, El, "the King, Father of Years," whose consort was Asherah. Next in rank was the great storm-god, Baal, the god of rain and fertility, who, like his father, takes the form of a bull, the animal of strength and fertility. His consort-sister is the warrior goddess Anath, known for violent sexual passion and sadistic brutality. She is described as rejoicing at her destruction of people from "the rising of the sun" to "the shore of the sea."

> Beneath her were heads like balls,
>   Above her were hands like locusts.
> She plunged her knees into the blood of warriors,
>   Her thighs into the blood of youths.[3]

It is difficult to piece together the fragments of the Baal epic into their original dramatic sequence. Apparently the drama opens with an account of Baal's rise to preeminence as a result of his victorious conflict with the primordial water dragon, who was known as Prince Sea and Judge River. We next hear of Baal's preparations to build a temple with the assistance of his sister, the maiden Anath. Evidently these plans are interrupted by the action of Mot ("Death"), the god of summer drought, who kills Baal and carries him down to the underworld. When the gods hear that "the lord of the earth" has perished, they mourn deeply; but Anath is seized by a great passion for Baal and searches for him.

> Like the longing [heart] of a wild cow for her calf,
> Like the longing of a wild ewe for her lamb,
>   So was the longing of Anath for Baal.[4]

When she finally finds him in the possession of Mot, a furious struggle ensues. Mot is killed, Baal is resurrected and put on his throne, and the lovers are reunited. There is great rejoicing in heaven.

> In a dream, O Kindly One, God of Mercy [?],
> In a vision, Creator of Creatures,
> The heavens rained oil,
> The dry valleys flowed with honey;

---

[3] Quoted from W. F. Albright, *Yahweh and the Gods of Canaan* [276], p. 130f.
[4] Ibid., p. 132.

So I know
That Triumphant Baal lives,
That the Prince, Lord of Earth, is alive![5]

These lines show the connection between Baal's resurrection and the revival of fertility. Indeed, the myth of Baal's death and resurrection represents the conflict waged in nature as the seasons come and go. Baal personifies the fertilizing powers of springtime; Mot personifies the destructive powers that bring death to vegetation and life. There is a rhythm in nature: springtime and summer, fertility and drought, life and death. According to the ancient view, the farmer's life is caught up in this alternation. Existence is a precarious dependence upon the powers of nature. It was believed that religion provided a way to control these powers and thereby to insure the fruitfulness of the soil. By reenacting the mythological drama of Baal's death and resurrection in the temple, so it was believed, a magical power was released that would guarantee fertility and well-being. And through myth and ritual the worshipers were related to what was believed to be divine.

Attempts at Compromise

Here, then, was a practical religion for farmers. In Canaan, Baal was recognized as the lord of the earth: the owner of the land, the giver of rain, the source of the grain, wine, and oil. People believed that the agricultural harvest would not be plentiful unless the fertility powers were worshiped according to the ways of Canaan. To have ignored the Baal rites in those days would have seemed as impractical as for a modern farmer to ignore science in the cultivation of the land.

In addition, it must be remembered that the Baal religion was part and parcel of the whole city-state system of Canaan which, under Egyptian hegemony, attempted to maintain order and security in the land. In a sociological sense, Baalism functioned to give legitimacy to the existing social structure, with its power centers in Canaanite cities, and at the same time to pacify farmers in the countryside who lived close to the soil and who had to yield taxes to the city-state kings.[6]

Given these conditions in agricultural Canaan, it is not surprising that many Israelites turned to the gods of the land. People did not mean to turn away from Yahweh, the God of the Exodus and the Sinai covenant. They would serve Yahweh and Baal side by side, like modern people who keep religion and science in separate compartments, or they would identify Yahweh and Baal, like those

---

[5] Translated by W. F. Albright, *Interpreter's Bible*, I [16], 261.

[6] The sociological dimension of the struggle between ''Yahweh'' and Baal was stressed by George E. Mendenhall, ''The Hebrew Conquest of Palestine'' [244], also *The Tenth Generation* [163], pp. 174–197; and this has been treated in depth by Norman Gottwald, *The Tribes of Yahweh* [240], see especially Part IX.

today for whom "God" is the symbol for the values of civil religion. In any case, it was not felt that the two religions were contradictory or mutually exclusive. Indeed, there was a strong tendency for the two faiths to coalesce in popular worship. As we know from archaeology, in the outlying regions of Israel people had in their possession figurines, small statuettes of the goddess of fertility, Ashtart. Elements of ritual and mythology were taken over from Canaanite religion and incorporated into the worship of Yahweh. Former Canaanite sanctuaries, like Bethel, Shechem, and perhaps Gilgal, were rededicated to Yahweh, and the Canaanite agricultural calendar was adopted for the timing of the pilgrimage festivals (Exod. 34:22–23). Parents began naming their children after Baal, apparently with no thought of abandoning Yahweh. One of the judges, Gideon, was also named Jerub-baal, which means "let Baal contend," or perhaps "may Baal multiply." Saul and David, both ardent devotees of Yahweh, gave Baal names to their children.[7] As late as the eighth century, Israelites—according to the prophet Hosea—actually addressed Yahweh as "Baal," and by worshiping Yahweh according to the rituals of Baal sought the blessings of fertility (Hos. 2). At the popular level this syncretism—that is, the fusion of different religious forms and views—went on to some degree from the time Israel first set foot on Canaanite soil.

As we have noticed, this syncretism was going on constantly in the commingling cultures of the Fertile Crescent, for the religions of the area had a great deal in common. But Israel's faith was based on the novel belief in a *jealous* God who would tolerate no rivals. According to the terms of the covenant, Israel was to have "no other gods before Yahweh." Yahweh's lordship over the people was absolute, extending into every sphere of life. Therefore, to believe that Yahweh was lord in one sphere (history) and Baal in another (fertilization of the soil) was a fundamental violation of the meaning of the covenant. Later, prophets saw clearly the basic conflict between the two faiths and threw down the challenge: Yahweh versus Baal. Joshua's appeal, voiced at Shechem, echoed through the years. "Choose this day whom you will serve!" There could be no compromise, for Yahweh claimed to be the sovereign of the whole of life and to receive the devotion of the whole heart.

Religion and Sex

It has been well said that "only as a religion has to meet the challenge of its opposite does it discover its own nature and potential strength."[8] Despite popular attempts to blend Canaanite religion and the Mosaic faith, the two were basically incompatible, like oil and water. Since both understood the relation of

---

[7] Two of Saul's children were called Mephi*baal* (Mephibosheth) and Ish*baal*. Jonathan had a son named Meri*baal* (Meribosheth). The word *bosheth* (Hebrew: "shame") was later substituted by an editor horrified at the presence of "baal" in the names. See II Sam. 21:8; 4:4; 9:6; I Chron. 8:34. One of David's daughters was named Beeliada (I Chron. 14:7).

[8] H. Wheeler Robinson in *A Companion to the Bible*, ed. T. W. Manson (Edinburgh: T. & T. Clark, 1939), p. 293.

human beings to the deity in radically different terms, they found expression in diametrically different world outlooks.[9] The opposition expressed in the phrase "Yahweh versus Baal" comes to focus in the meaning of sex.

In Canaanite religion, sex was elevated to the realm of the divine. The divine powers, it was believed, were disclosed in the sphere of nature—that is, in the mystery of fertility. The gods were sexual in nature and were worshiped in sexual rites. The erotic relations of god and goddess were hidden within the ever-recurring cycle of the death and renewal of fertility, represented mythologically by the annual death and resurrection of Baal. But this cycle of fertility, according to the ancient view, did not take place by itself through natural law. Rather, the purpose of religion was to preserve and enhance the fertility upon which people were dependent for their existence. It sought to control the gods in the interest of human well-being. And since this religion aimed to maintain the harmony and rhythm of the natural order, it was a serviceable tool for the aristocracy who wished to maintain the social *status quo* against disruptive changes. Baalism catered to the desire for security in the precarious environment of the Fertile Crescent.

In the perspective of Israel's faith, on the other hand, the power of the divine was disclosed in nonrecurring historical events, primarily the Exodus, which were perceived to be signs of God's liberation of the people from bondage and God's creation of a covenant community. The revelatory power of these events, as interpreted by prophets like Moses, was sensed by other clans and tribes who had not participated originally in the crucial historical experiences. "The symbolization of historical events," one scholar observes, "was possible because each group which entered the covenant community could and did see the analogy between bondage and Exodus and their own experience."[10] This analogy was perceived again and again in the period of the Judges when the Israelites suffered new forms of oppression (cf. Judg. 6:9).

In the course of time the encounter with Baal religion brought about an enrichment of Israel's faith, as we shall see, especially when considering the prophet Hosea.[11] However, in the formative period the encounter prompted interpreters of the covenant to point up the uniqueness of Yahweh in contrast to Baal. Unlike Baal, Yahweh has no consort, no female counterpart.[12] As the

---

[9] An excellent analysis of the religion of "archaic man" is found in the writings of Mircea Eliade, especially *Cosmos and History* [120], and *The Sacred and the Profane* [121]. In the preface to the former he writes (p. vii): "The chief difference between the man of the archaic and traditional societies and the man of the modern societies with their strong imprint of Judaeo-Christianity lies in the fact that the former feels himself indissolubly connected with the Cosmos and the cosmic rhythms, whereas the latter insists that he is connected only with History."

[10] George E. Mendenhall, "The Hebrew Conquest of Palestine," [244], p. 74.

[11] This "crisis due to the conquest" is discussed by Gerhard von Rad, *Theology*, I [142], 15–35, who points out that in the course of the struggle between Yahweh and Baal the Israelite faith adopted new forms of expression and "came more than ever before into its own."

[12] The Hebrew language, in fact, has no special word for "goddess." In the fifth century a Jewish colony in Elephantine, Egypt, did apparently believe that Yahweh had a partner, Anath. This interpretation, however, is challenged by W. F. Albright, *From the Stone Age* [111], pp. 286–87.

Nude Female Figurines,
emblems of the goddess of
fertility. The one with the high
headdress was found at
Megiddo, in a level which
dates to the general period
2000–1200 B.C.E. *The one with*
the head missing was found at
Beth-shan, in a level dating to
the fourteenth century B.C.E.

holy God, who transcends the human world, Yahweh is beyond sexuality. To be sure, in concession to the limitations of grammar and to ancient patriarchal society, Yahweh is spoken of in masculine terms; but this literary convention should not blind us to the fact that God-language includes feminine, as well as masculine, dimensions.[13] Moreover, Yahweh, like Baal, is lord of fertility; but Yahweh is not a fertility god subject to the death and resurrection of the natural world. Yahweh is "the Living God" whose vitality is disclosed in the social arena, where human lives touch one another, where injustices oppress and yearnings for deliverance are felt, where people are called to make decisions that alter the course of the future. Finally, the ethical demands of the covenant preclude worshiping Yahweh in licentious sexual rites (sacred prostitution) or in religious rituals that attempt to guarantee fertility of soil and womb. While Baal religion taught worshipers to *control* the gods, Israel's faith stressed *serving* God in gratitude for benevolent deeds and in fidelity to the demands of the covenant. Yahweh could not be coerced by magic. Yahweh could be trusted or betrayed, obeyed or disobeyed, but in all things the divine will is free and supreme.

With their desert background, Israel's more discerning leaders sensed the

[13] See especially Phyllis Trible, "God" in Supplement to the *Interpreter's Dictionary of the Bible* [26] and *God and the Rhetoric of Sexuality* [145].

fundamental opposition between the stern demands of Yahweh and the erotic religion of Canaan. Was the meaning of people's life in Canaan disclosed in relation to divine powers within nature, or in relation to the Lord of history? This fundamental question was not answered overnight. In Canaanite religion Israel's faith met the challenge of its opposite, but it took many generations for the true strength and uniqueness of the Mosaic faith to be seen. The victory, when it finally was won, shook the religious foundations of agriculture in Canaan and gave farmers a new understanding of their vocation.[14]

The first phase of the conflict was waged during the period of the judges. Israel's initial response to the new environment of Canaan was to turn to the Baal cult for agricultural success. Although obsessed with the problems of fertility, Israel could not forget the demands of history, for its existence was threatened by enemies on all sides. As the Deuteronomistic historian points out, in times of crisis, when Israel was oppressed by foes, the people turned with renewed zeal to the worship of Yahweh, the God of the covenant. Let us examine briefly the history of Israel during this period. (See Chronological Chart 2, p. 180.)

LEADERS IN CRISIS

Israel's invasion of Canaan and expansion in the hill country were made possible, as we have seen, by the lack of political interference by any strong power from Egypt or Mesopotamia. There is, significantly, no reference in the book of Judges to Egyptian intervention. After the death of Pharaoh Merneptah in about 1211 B.C.E., Egypt lost control of its Asiatic empire and, with the exception of a brief revival under Rameses III (c. 1183–1152), lapsed into confusion and political impotence. The Hittites, who had been fought to a standstill by the Egyptians, soon disappeared as a world power as a result of population disturbances in the Aegean at the beginning of the twelfth century. In Mesopotamia, Assyria was beginning to rise to power (about 1250), but as yet it posed no threat to Canaan. Thus Israel's political rivals were confined to Canaan and its immediate vicinity: the new nations in Transjordan, raiders from the Arabian desert, the Canaanite city-states, and the new arrivals known as the Philistines.

The stories in the book of Judges that picture the local conflicts and tribal jealousies of the period are unquestionably derived from very old sources. The Deuteronomistic editors have touched up some of the narratives by adding introductory and concluding formulas. But for some reason the narrative of Abimelech and the accounts of the so-called minor judges (Judg. 10:1–5 and 12:8–15) were not altered at all. Similarly, chapters 17–21 show no traces of Deuteronomistic editing, and were evidently added to the Deuteronomistic edition of

---

[14] This point is made forcefully by Martin Buber, *The Prophetic Faith* [311], pp. 70–76. It will become clearer in our later discussion of prophets such as Elijah and Hosea in Chapters 8 and 9.

Judges (2:6–16:31) by someone else. Thus when the Deuteronomistic "framework" is removed, we have at our disposal ancient and reliable traditions concerning the period which began with the death of Joshua (c. 1200 B.C.E.).

When we read these stories by themselves, we gain a clear impression of how loosely organized the Israelite tribes were. The present book of Judges relates how twelve judges, in successive reigns amounting to 410 years, held sway over all Israel. But this is an oversimplification. Actually, tribal leaders arose from time to time in certain trouble-spots in order to relieve the pressure on a specific area. For instance, Ehud was a member of the tribe of Benjamin. Sometimes these leaders were able to appeal to other tribes for support, but by and large their leadership was local in character and was confined to emergency situations.

Nevertheless, there was a sense of participating in a community that transcended the boundaries of any particular tribe. The twelve-tribe confederacy, whose beginnings we have already considered (see above, pp. 142–147), provided a common basis of worship and social responsibility. Not only did the tribes gather at the common confederate sanctuary of Shiloh for annual religious festivals, as we learn from Judges 21:19 (see also I Sam. 1:3; 2:19),[15] but in times of emergency they were also summoned to concerted action in the name of the God of the covenant. A vivid example of such action is given in the story of the Gibeah outrage, related in Judges 19–21. In this "text of terrors" we read that a Levite, incensed at the rape-murder of his concubine by some Benjaminites, cut up her corpse into twelve pieces and sent the parts throughout "all the territory of Israel."[16] The act of dividing the body into twelve parts (see also I Sam. 11:7) indicates, of course, the twelve-part structure of the Israelite confederacy. The tribal response to this symbolic act was quick and decisive, indicating that the tribes were bound together by a common sense of law and decency, even when one of the tribes was an offender:

> And all who saw it said, "Such a thing has never happened or been seen from the day that the people of Israel came up out of the land of Egypt until this day; consider it, take counsel, and speak."
>
> —JUDGES 19:30 (RSV)

So, we are told, all the men of Israel gathered together in the "assembly of the people of God" and resolved to take punitive action, "united as one person."

---

[15] After the central sanctuary was moved from Shechem, apparently Bethel was the confederate center for a time (Judg. 20:26–27) and then Shiloh was selected. During this period Gilgal, near Jericho, was probably visited by pilgrims who celebrated there the crossing of the Jordan and the entrance into the promised land. This suggestion has been advanced by H. J. Kraus, "Gilgal: Ein Beitrag zur Kultusgeschichte Israels," in *Vetus Testamentum*, I (1951), 181–99. See also his *Worship in Israel*, [443], pp. 152–65.

[16] See the powerful treatment of this story, from a feminist point of view, by Phyllis Trible, *Texts of Terror* [cited under No. 145], chap. 3.

The Role of the Judge

Within this framework of the Tribal Confederacy we must understand the role of Israel's judges. The Hebrew word *shofeṭ* is not an exact equivalent of our word "judge," which is restricted to legal functions. In ancient Semitic thought, the role of leadership involved procuring the right of the people either by taking military action or by judging legal disputes. The word *shofeṭ* is close in meaning to "ruler," as we see in this passage from Isaiah 33:22:

> Yahweh is our judge (*shofeṭ*), Yahweh is our ruler,
> Yahweh is our king; he will save us.

Hence the statement that so-and-so "judged Israel" must be taken in a wider sense than the English translation implies. While being primarily a military champion or "deliverer" (Judg. 2:16), the judge did play a part in internal arbitration, as in the cases of the judge Deborah (Judg. 4:4–5) and the last judge, Samuel (I Sam. 7:15–17). The authority of a judge extended beyond the locale of a particular tribe, and was recognized in the territory of the Tribal Confederacy. It is possible that when the tribes convened at the central sanctuary for convenant-renewal festivals, the judge presided as "covenant mediator."[17]

Unlike the dynastic office of the king, which was passed on from father to son, the office of the judge was nonhereditary and rested upon a special endowment of Yahweh's spirit. For this reason the judges have been called "charismatic leaders"—that is, leaders qualified to head the Tribal Confederacy by virtue of the divine *charisma*, or spiritual power, which possessed them. So we read, for instance, that "the spirit of Yahweh took possession of Gideon" or literally "clothed itself with Gideon," empowering him with an authority that was recognized not only in his own clan but also in surrounding tribes (Judg. 6:34–35). More vivid examples are found in the legendary Samson stories, where we read that "the spirit of Yahweh came upon him mightily," empowering him to accomplish superhuman feats (see 14:6). Deborah, too, was a charismatic leader who summoned the tribes of Israel to military action against the Canaanites in the name of Yahweh (Judg. 4–5). Presumably, charismatic success in battle or extraordinary physical prowess encouraged people from the various tribes to consult the judge in cases of legal dispute also. In this way, Israel's covenant law (see above, pp. 149–150) was applied to specific cases and was expanded.

Since the judges did not follow one another in chronological succession, contrary to the impression created by the Deuteronomistic historian, it is diffi-

---

[17] Martin Noth, in "Das Amt des 'Richters Israels'" (*Festschrift A. Bertholet* [Tübingen: J. C. B. Mohr, 1950], 404–17), maintains that the so-called "minor judges" mentioned in Judg. 10:1–5 and 12:7–15 were actually legal administrators selected by the Confederacy. But this theory presupposes the dubious view that the book of Judges tells about two different kinds of leaders, whereas the tradition indicates that the two functions—legal and military—were combined in one person.

cult to outline the sequence of events between the death of Joshua and the time of Saul, the first king of Israel. However, we do have in these stories vivid vignettes of conditions and crises during the twelfth and eleventh centuries B.C.E. We shall deal with them in terms of areas of pressure upon the Israelite Confederacy.

The Battle of Megiddo

The Israelites, as we have seen, had managed to entrench themselves in the central hill country but could not dispossess the Canaanites on the plains. The most strategic area under Canaanite control was the Valley of Jezreel, through which the main commercial route ran from Egypt to Mesopotamia. Guarding the pass into the valley was the Canaanite fortress of Megiddo, the scene of many decisive battles and, according to religious imagination, the scene of the final battle of Armageddon. (Ar-mageddon, referred to in the New Testament at Rev. 16:16, literally means "hill of Megiddo.") So long as the Canaanites were in control of this commercial lifeline, they could throttle Israel's economic life. This was the situation, we are told, during the days of the judge Shamgar (Judg. 3:31):

> In the days of Shamgar, son of Anath,
>   in the days of Jael, caravans ceased
>   and travellers kept to the byways.
>   —JUDGES 5:6 (RSV)

Spurred into action by Deborah and under the command of Barak, the Israelite forces met General Sisera's Canaanite army in the vicinity of the fortified city of Taanach (Judg. 5:19), which provides a commanding view of Megiddo and the whole plain. Apparently only half of the tribes of the Israelite confederacy responded to the summons of Deborah, a charismatic leader. Victory was theirs that day, thanks to a terrific rainstorm that caused the river Kishon, which flows through the plain of Jezreel, to overflow its banks, with the result that the Canaanite charioteers were helplessly trapped in clay.

The account of this battle is given in two versions: a poetic version, the Song of Deborah, in Judges 5; and a prose version in Judges 4, which differs somewhat in details. By general agreement, the Song of Deborah is a firsthand, authentic historical witness. It is one of the oldest passages of poetry in the Old Testament, written by one who stood very near the event, perhaps by a participant. Archaeological work at Megiddo has produced evidence for dating the battle and the song that celebrates the event in the latter part of the twelfth century B.C.E., approximately 1125 B.C.E.[18]

---

[18] W. F. Albright, who argues for this date, points out that the poetry of the Song of Deborah has striking affinities with Canaanite style known from the Ras Shamra literature. See his article "The Song of Deborah in the Light of Archaeology," *Bulletin of the American School of Oriental Research*, LXII (1936), 26–31.

The Pass of Megiddo *as viewed looking to the southwest. Through this pass ran the main coastal highway from the plain of Jezreel to Gaza and the Egyptian frontier. Many battles, ancient and modern, have been fought in this strategic area which in antiquity was guarded by the heavily fortified city of Megiddo.*

The meaning of the victory is far more effectively communicated in the poem than in the later prose version. Even in English translation readers are made vividly aware of the spirit of the battle. We sense the quickened pulse beat that responds to the summons to participate in the historic crisis. We are carried along with the "galloping rhythm" toward the climax of victory. We feel the fiercely victorious passion of Jael the Kenite (see Judg. 4:11), and by contrast the bitter pathos of Sisera's mother looking for a son who would never return. The poem deals with history as it was lived, not with history as reported by a detached observer.

To the author of the poem, the event was overwhelming because of its religious meaning. The storm that defeated the Canaanites is seen to be the sign of Yahweh's active presence as the leader and champion of the people. According to the poet's passionate faith, no array of human forces can stand against Yahweh, the Divine Warrior, who comes to the aid of Israel in the fury of a thunderstorm. Even the stars—conceived as Yahweh's heavenly army (host)—join in the battle:

> From heaven fought the stars,
> from their courses they fought against Sisera.
> —JUDGES 5:20 (RSV)

Hence the song begins and ends with an exclamation of praise. In the experience of the poet, it was Yahweh's participation in the battle that made the event historic and momentous.

The poem forcefully expresses the cardinal conviction of the Mosaic faith: Yahweh is the "God of Israel" (verses 3, 5) and Israel is "the people of Yahweh" (verses 11, 13). Although there is no specific reference to the covenant, this close relationship between God and people is the basis of the whole poem. Yahweh is praised as the Leader of the people, who comes in an earthshaking storm from Sinai through the region of Edom southeast of the Dead Sea (verses 4–5). The people are exhorted to rehearse "the triumphs [literally, "righteous deeds] of Yahweh" (verse 11)—the "mighty acts" by which the divine *Shopheṭ* (Champion of Justice) defends the justice of the oppressed. And since Yahweh is pictured as going forth at the head of the people, the tribes are summoned to decision—to rally for "holy war."[19] Those tribes who did not answer the summons, who "came not to the help of Yahweh against the mighty" (verse 23), are censured in the strongest terms, for they are not acting as "the people of Yahweh." Here we see that the basis of the Israelite community was not just political expedience or family ties, but voluntary dedication to Yahweh, the exclusive Suzerain of the Tribal Confederacy. To the true Israel belong only those clans or tribes who choose to serve Yahweh with their full measure of devotion. They are Yahweh's friends (or, as the Hebrew says, "those who love" Yahweh) who, at the conclusion of the poem, receive a benediction (verse 31). There is no clearer witness to the historical vigor of Israel's faith than the Song of Deborah.

Foes from Other Directions

Israel's decisive victory over Sisera's army marked the end of any united Canaanite resistance against Israel. However, troubles came to Israel from other directions. The newly established kingdoms of Transjordan looked with jealous eyes on Israel's holdings both in Transjordan itself and in Canaan. Moab, under the leadership of a king named Eglon, invaded Israelite territory and took "the city of palms," Jericho (see the mosaic map on Color Plate 8). The tide was turned by a deliverer named Ehud, who delivered "a message from God" to Eglon in a left-handed manner with a dagger (Judg. 3:12–30). Later, Israel suffered a series of attacks from the Ammonites, both in Transjordan and in the Canaanite hill country. This threat was met effectively by Jephthah (10:6–12:7), although at a terrible personal cost. The moving story of Jephthah's sacrifice of his daughter (11:29–40) in fulfillment of his religious vow, is one of the most tragic texts of Scripture.[20]

---

[19] On holy war (see Definition, p. 141), see especially Gerhard von Rad, *Holy War in Ancient Israel*, trans. by E. W. Conrad and M. Lattke (Sheffield: JSOT Press, forthcoming). Note the introduction by E. W. Conrad; and see further R. de Vaux, *Ancient Israel* [113], pp. 258–267.

[20] See Phyllis Trible, *Texts of Terror* [cited under 145], chap. 4.

Even more serious, however, was a series of devastating attacks by Midianite raiders who came in from the Arabian desert on camels. The use of the camel was something new in military tactics. The wild tribesmen of Arabia had learned how to use fleets of camels for traveling long distances to make surprise attacks on settled villages. So effective were the raids of these camel-riding nomads that the Israelites had to leave their villages and take to mountain caves:

> For they [the Midianites] would come up with their cattle and their tents, coming like locusts for number; both they and their camels could not be counted; so that they wasted the land as they came in.
>
> —JUDGES 6:5 (RSV)

In the face of these raids, the Israelites could not carry on their farming, and were in danger of losing everything they had gained in Canaan. In this dire emergency the day was saved by a judge named Gideon, otherwise known as Jerubbaal (Judg. 6–8). Gideon's military leadership was based on his charismatic zeal for Yahweh—zeal directed against those, even of his own family, who had turned to Baal. Although Gideon's father, Joash, had a Yahweh name (including the element *Yah* [Yo]), he erected a Baal altar with a fertility tree, an Asherah, beside it. Gideon destroyed the Baal cult objects and built an altar to Yahweh instead, much to the displeasure of the citizens of Ophrah (Judg. 6:25–32). This story is important because it shows how deeply Canaanite rites and conceptions had infiltrated, and because it shows how Israel's strength in time of crisis was connected with a revival of a vigorous faith in Yahweh, the God of the covenant. To the surprise of Gideon, and perhaps to the dismay of any person who wants to stand on his or her own feet, the narrator insists that the victory belongs to Yahweh *alone*, who permits a task force of only 300 warriors for the huge offensive.[21]

Throughout the twelfth and eleventh centuries, the threat to Israel was increased by the pressure of newcomers known as Philistines. As we have seen, the Philistines were one of a number of "sea peoples" who poured out of the Aegean onto the eastern shores of the Mediterranean (see above, pp. 129–131). Shortly after 1200 B.C.E., they swarmed into Canaan by sea and by land, and established a beachhead on the coastal plain. They came during a great transitional epoch which in archaeological terms marked the beginning of the Iron Age (1200–600 B.C.E.). Their natural aggressiveness was augmented by their skill in making instruments and weapons of iron, a trade in which they achieved a virtual monopoly. From their restricted base on the coast, the Philistines began to move inland, sweeping away Canaanite resistance and coming into contact with the already entrenched and victorious Israelites. In fact, the Philistines came close to making Canaan a Philistine empire.

---

[21] It is interesting to compare the biblical story with a modern interpretation: *Gideon, A New Play* (New York: Random House, 1962), by Paddy Chayefsky.

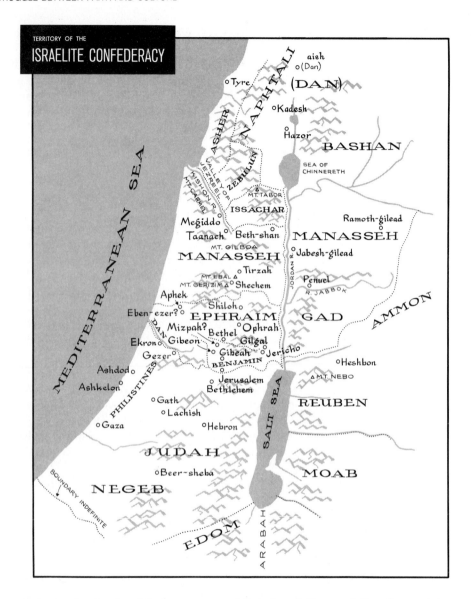

TERRITORY OF THE
ISRAELITE CONFEDERACY

Early in the book of Judges we read briefly of the exploits of a certain Shamgar, who slew six hundred Philistines with an oxgoad (Judg. 3:31). This must have occurred fairly early in the Philistine occupation, for Shamgar is referred to in the Song of Deborah (5:6). Elsewhere we hear of the Philistines only in passing, until we come to the Samson cycle at the very end of the Deuteronomistic edition of Judges (chaps. 13–16). It is unnecessary to go into the details of these lusty stories, which have as their theme the discomfiture of the Philistines by an Israelite Tarzan whose fatal weakness was women. The Samson

---

DEFINITION: "PALESTINE"

One of the great ironies of history is that the name later given to Israel's land, Palestine, is derived from the name of Israel's archenemies, the Philistines. It was the Greek historian Herodotus, sometimes called "the father of history," who in the fifth century B.C.E. designated the country south of Phoenicia as "Philistine Syria" (I, 105; II, 104). The Greek term *Palaistina* ultimately came into English through Latin *Palestina*.

The older name for the land, Canaan, is found in the Amarna Letters and other documents going back to at least the fifteenth century B.C.E. and may be Hurrian in origin. According to one theory, the name meant "red purple," a dye produced on the eastern coast of the Mediterranean. The Greek name of the country, *Phoinike* (Phoenicia), also seems to refer to this crimson color (*phoinix*).

---

stories are more legendary than any other material preserved in the book of Judges. Although Samson is regarded as a judge, he is unlike the other judges in that he was not a military leader. These stories deal with the marvelous exploits of an individual and are more designed to tickle the fancy than to record history.[22] Viewed theologically, the story of Samson's tragic demise portrays what happens to a person filled with *charisma* who disregards the guidance of Yahweh in a time of crisis to pursue personal whims of the moment.

The Samson tales, however, do give us a valuable picture of the relations between Israelites and Philistines, probably at the beginning of the eleventh century. We see that the Philistines had consolidated their position on the coast and were strong enough to worry the Israelites up in the hill country into spinning yarns that poked fun at their uncircumcised neighbors. But there were no pitched battles, and we find no expressions of despair over Philistine ascendancy. At the most, these stories reflect border incidents that were not sufficiently grievous to disrupt commercial relations between the two peoples. By the end of the eleventh century all this was to change, for the Philistines soon were to be in control of all the arteries leading into the Israelite hill country. As things turned out, this was the first stage in an all-out Philistine offensive that had only one objective: the total destruction, once and for all, of the Israelite Confederacy.

THE DECLINE OF THE CONFEDERACY

As political pressure mounted, it became increasingly apparent that the Israelite Confederacy was an ineffective organization for coping with the troubled situation in Canaan. Even in a time of great peril, as we have already noticed, only half the tribes responded to Deborah's charismatic summons and helped to hurl back Canaanite aggression under Sisera. The Israelite tribes were bound to-

---

[22] For an "esthetic" study of the Samson story, see James L. Crenshaw, *Samson* [80].

gether, not by a centralized government, but only by a common devotion to Yahweh, the God of the covenant, and by common religious and legal responsibilities. The Confederacy by its very nature encouraged a high degree of tribal independence. Yahweh alone was the ruler of the Israelite tribes. The divine rule was made known through charismatic judges and through the High Priest who attended the central sanctuary, like Eli at the shrine of Shiloh (I Sam. 1–4). Only when religious festivals were held at the confederate shrine, or when a dire emergency arose—such as the Gibeah outrage—did the tribes come together in concert ''as one person.'' This form of organization, at least for a time, spared Israel from the political despotism of the Near East. Moreover, in times of political crisis it threw the people back upon Yahweh, the God of the covenant, with the consequent renewal of Israel's distinctive historical faith. For all its merit, however, the Tribal Confederacy was vulnerable to the political forces of the time, as the Philistine menace made clear.

The Shechem Experiment

The first abortive experiment to establish a centralized government was carried out at Shechem, the very place where the Tribal Confederacy had been estab-

Prisoners of Rameses III are shown bound and tied together by a rope around the neck in this relief carved on the wall of a temple at Medinet Habu, near Thebes (Luxor). The structure was erected to celebrate Rameses' victory in repelling the Sea Peoples, one of whom was the Philistines. The figure wearing the feathered helmet (fourth from left) is one of the Sea Peoples, perhaps a Philistine. The others are Libyan (with pointed beard and side-lock), Syrian (wearing a kilt), Hittite (beardless and wearing a long garment), and on the far right another unfortunate captive from Syria.

lished in the time of Joshua. Although the name of Abimelech is connected with this incident, some precedent had been established for it previously in Ophrah, a city located in the hill country north of Jerusalem. The charismatic leadership of Gideon (Jerubbaal) had proved effective against the nomadic raids that had all but ruined Israel. Because of his success in the Midianite crisis, and doubtless also because of the increasing political tension caused by the Philistine menace, the Israelites offered to crown him king. ''Rule over us,'' they said, ''you and your son and your grandson also'' (Judg. 8:22). In other words, they proposed to change the basis of his authority from that of nonhereditary, charismatic judgeship to that of a hereditary monarchy modeled after the kingdoms of Transjordan, notably Moab and Ammon.[23] Gideon firmly replied: ''I will not rule over you, and my son will not rule over you; Yahweh will rule over you.'' His answer was consistent with the foundations of the Israelite theocracy. Yahweh alone was Israel's king, and it was presumptuous for any person to usurp the divine throne.

Now, besides the many wives of his harem, Gideon also had a concubine in the city of Shechem who bore him a son named Abimelech. Abimelech's career is recounted in Judges 9. After Gideon's death, so we are told, Abimelech went to his mother's kinsfolk in Shechem. Pointing out that he was a relative of the Shechemites, he persuaded them that he was entitled to rule over them as king. With money furnished him from the treasury of the Baal-berith (''Lord of the Covenant'') temple, he hired rascals as his followers and forthwith liquidated his seventy brothers, with the exception of the youngest, Jotham. With these rivals out of the way, the citizens of Shechem crowned him king, possibly near a sacred pillar that can be seen even today in the ruins of the acropolis known as Beth-millo (9:6; see the picture on p. 143).

But this incident did not go without rebuke. Standing on Mount Gerizim which overlooks Shechem, Jotham told the famous fable of the trees. Seeking for a king to rule over them, the trees asked the olive, the fig, and the vine in turn, and finally had to settle for the bramble, which still grows abundantly in the area (Judg. 9:7–15). The implication was that Abimelech's rule, like the inflammable bramble, would be a tinderbox for the fires of revolution. In this pointed attack upon Abimelech's kingdom, Jotham was expressing the attitude toward monarchy that prevailed in the conservative circles of the Israelite Confederacy. Abimelech's main support right from the first had come from the priesthood of the Baal-berith temple, who advocated a Canaanite form of government that ran counter to the Israelite theocratic ideal.

For three years (Judg. 9:22), Abimelech was able to impose his rule over a considerable territory, with Shechem as the chief city of his kingdom. True to Jotham's prediction, however, revolution broke out in Shechem. By means of a strategem of ambush, Abimelech successfully stormed the city and destroyed it, probably about 1100 B.C.E. (9:45). The revolution must have spread into other

---

[23] According to the list in Gen. 36:31–39, the kingship of Edom was dynastic; apparently the petty kings of the Canaanite city-states did not establish a hereditary line.

parts of his kingdom, for he met death while attacking a fortified tower in the city of Thebez, on the road from Shechem to Beth-shan. According to tradition, the credit for ending Abimelech's city-state kingdom goes to a certain woman, who from the top of the tower tossed an upper millstone upon the crown of his head, crushing his skull (9:53–54). Although the Shechem experiment in monarchy failed, it was a fateful shadow of things to come. The days of the Tribal Confederacy were coming to an end. A stronger form of government was needed.

The Fall of Shiloh

At this point we must turn from the book of Judges to the first twelve chapters of the book of I Samuel. In I Samuel 12, Samuel, the last judge of Israel, is giving his farewell address to Israel. Here the Deuteronomistic historian concludes his survey of the period of the judges. We shall not attempt to survey all the material in these twelve chapters, but shall refer only to those matters that bear on the collapse of the Tribal Confederacy during the period of Philistine aggression.

Chapters 1 to 3 of I Samuel deal with events at Shiloh, the central sanctuary of the Confederacy, to which it was customary for Israelites to make a pilgrimage each year (1:3, 7, 21) for the purpose of offering a sacrifice to Yahweh. There Eli, the High Priest, was "ministering to Yahweh," and the boy Samuel was ministering under Eli. In this troubled period, apparently it was hoped that the tribes would be united around the priestly rule of Eli and his sons, who were custodians of the Ark and the sacred oracle. Thus an alternative to monarchy was a hierocracy—that is, the hereditary rule of priests at the confederate sanctuary.

The next section (I Sam. 4:1–7:2) deals with the fortunes of the Ark of the Covenant, which was kept at Shiloh. The Philistines and the Israelites were at war, and the battle was going against Israel. After a serious reversal, the elders of Israel suggested that the Ark be brought out to the battlefield, as had often been done in the past (see the Song of the Ark, Num. 10:35–36), in order that Yahweh "may come among us and save us from the power of our enemies" (I Sam. 4:3). So the Ark was taken from Shiloh, accompanied by Eli's two sons. Its presence in the Israelite camp caused the raising of a mighty shout "so that the earth resounded." The Philistines were almost panic-stricken when they realized that—in their pagan language—"the gods have come into the camp." Nevertheless, they braced themselves to face the worst. Doubtless to their surprise, they decisively defeated Israel, and the Ark was then taken into Philistine territory as a trophy of war.

From this point on in the account of I Samuel, there is no more reference to Shiloh, the Israelite sanctuary. Why this strange silence? In a "story-telling psalm," it is said that Yahweh forsook "the tent" at Shiloh and delivered "his glory" (the Ark) into captivity (Ps. 78:60–64). Moreover, toward the end of the monarchy, when people of the Southern Kingdom were putting great confidence in the Temple of Jerusalem, Jeremiah reminded them of what had happened to Shiloh (Jer. 7:12–14; see 26:6, 9):

> Just go to my shrine that was in Shiloh, where I [Yahweh] once caused my name
> to dwell, and see what I did to it on account of the wickedness of my people Israel.
> —JEREMIAH 7:12

Archaeological evidence seems to suggest that Shiloh was destroyed in a great catastrophe, probably by the Philistines when they invaded the hill country of Palestine.[24] This would have occurred at the battle of Ebenezer, when the Ark was taken into captivity. In any case, Shiloh disappeared from Israel's history.

Quite obviously, Israel was in a desperate plight. A devastating blow had been struck at the very foundation of the Israelite Confederacy. The central sanctuary of Shiloh had been burned to the ground. The Ark of the Covenant, the ancient symbol of Yahweh's protecting and guiding presence in the midst of the people, had been seized by enemies. The Philistines were well on their way toward making Canaan a Philistine empire. The shock and despair that these events created among devout Israelites find expression in the stories that cluster around the fate of the Ark. When the High Priest Eli heard the shocking report of the outcome of the battle of Ebenezer, he keeled over, broke his neck, and died, apparently of a heart attack. His daughter-in-law, who gave birth to a son in the fateful hour of Israel's defeat, named the child Ichabod, an unhappy name which testified that "the glory has departed from Israel" (I Sam. 4:12–22)—that is, the Ark, the seat of Yahweh's presence, had gone into exile.

Why the Philistines failed to take full advantage of their military opportunity, when the mastery of Palestine was almost in their grasp, is something of a mystery. There may have been internal weaknesses in the Philistine alliance of city-states—that is, the Pentapolis comprising Gaza, Ashdod, Ashkelon, Gath and Ekron (see Josh. 13:3). But the one factor with which they could not reckon was the Yahweh faith, which, as we have seen in the case of previous disasters, showed an amazing resilience and vitality in times of political crisis. Yahweh's control of history was not bound up with any form of political organization, not even the Israelite confederacy. Therefore political defeat was not Yahweh's defeat, even though in times of despair this may have been the popular sentiment. Yahweh had the power to discipline the people with political disaster, as well as to bless them with victory. In terms of Israel's prophetic faith, political crisis was an occasion for the people to search their hearts penitently and to renew their allegiance to the God of the covenant. Such a religious renewal took place in the dark hour of the Philistine ascendancy.

---

[24] The archaeological evidence is uncertain, but it is likely that there was destruction by the Philistines. See *Biblical Archaeology Review* I (1975), 3ff.

THE LAST JUDGE OF ISRAEL

The person who was instrumental in this religious renewal was the prophet-judge Samuel, unquestionably the greatest spiritual leader of Israel since the time of Moses. His career marked the transition from the old type of charismatic leadership to the new prophetic leadership which, from this time on, played an outstanding role in Israel's life. Under his spiritual guidance, Israel made the shift from the politically inadequate Tribal Confederacy to the more stable government of the monarchy.

Samuel's leadership is portrayed in two types of tradition, which can be traced rather easily in I Samuel 1–12. In both, Samuel is described as playing an important role in Israel's fateful decision to establish a monarchy. One tradition, which was apparently the first to be written down, is found in I Samuel 9:1–10:16 and in I Samuel 11. Here we find the engaging story of how Saul, "a handsome young man" who "stood head and shoulders above any of the people," set out to search for his father's lost asses and found a kingdom. The story goes that Saul was on the verge of giving up the search for his father's livestock when, at the suggestion of his servant, he decided to obtain some clairvoyant advice from the seer, Samuel—in return, of course, for the necessary fee. It turned out that Samuel was more than a local seer. He was also the recognized priestly authority in the city who officiated at a sacrificial rite on a "high place," that is, a shrine; and, more than that, he was a prophet who, in the name of the God of Israel, could appoint a king. Seeing in Saul the man who could save Israel from the power of the Philistines and other enemies, Samuel took the initiative and secretly anointed Saul as "prince" over the people.

According to this tradition—let us, for convenience, call it the Saul Tradition—Saul was not publicly acclaimed king until after he had shown his victorious leadership in the battle described in I Samuel 11. This conflict was not with the Philistines, but with the Ammonites, who were expanding in Transjordan and were taking advantage of Israel's preoccupation with the Philistine menace. The men of Jabesh-gilead, finding themselves overwhelmed by Ammonite forces, asked for a treaty, only to receive the contemptuous reply from the Ammonite king that he would not make a treaty unless the right eye of every Israelite were gouged out. The men of Jabesh sent an appeal for help throughout all the territory of Israel. Saul happened to be coming from the field behind some oxen when he heard the report about the Ammonite ultimatum. Suddenly the divine charisma, "the spirit of God," came mightily upon him in a manner reminiscent of the ancient judges. What the spirit impelled him to do is exceedingly significant:

> He took a yoke of oxen and cut them in pieces which he sent by messengers throughout the territory of Israel with these words: 'If anyone will not march with Saul, this shall be done with his oxen!' At this, a dread of Yahweh fell on the people and they marched out as one man."
>
> —I SAMUEL 11:7 (JB)

Like the severing of a corpse into twelve pieces (see p. 194), this was a symbolic summons to the whole Israelite confederacy to engage in concerted action in the name of Yahweh. Inspired by Saul's charismatic leadership, the Confederacy brought about the decisive defeat of the Ammonites. As a result, the Israelite militia offered the crown to Saul. Unlike Gideon, he accepted, and was crowned in Gilgal "before Yahweh."[25]

The Request for a King

The other tradition—which for the sake of convenience we shall call the Samuel Tradition—is found in I Samuel 7:3–8:22, also 10:17–27, and chapter 12. Here the picture of Samuel is somewhat different. Samuel is not called a seer, but a judge—the last and the greatest judge of Israel. Undoubtedly his judgeship involved settling legal disputes, for which purpose he made an annual circuit of the shrines of Bethel, Gilgal, and Mizpah (7:15–17). But his judgeship also led to triumph against the Philistines, although he is said to have accomplished this not by military leadership but by prayer and sacrificial rite (7:5–14). Even more noteworthy, however, is the different way in which this source deals with the establishment of the monarchy. In the Saul Tradition, we find nothing about divine disapproval of the anointing of a king; indeed, Samuel, as Yahweh's prophetic spokesman, took the initiative in selecting Saul. But in the Samuel Tradition, the idea of the monarchy was displeasing to Samuel and, by the same token, to Yahweh. Samuel had tried to adapt judgeship to the political situation by changing it from a charismatic office to a hereditary one; hence he appointed his own sons as judges. But they did not have the same stature as their father. So we read:

> Then all the elders of Israel gathered together and came to Samuel at Ramah. They said to him, "Look, you are old, and your sons do not follow in your footsteps. Now appoint for us a king to rule us [literally, "to judge us"] like all the nations."
>
> —I SAMUEL 8:4–5

The Israelites were trying to set up a stable political government by imitating the nations around them. This attempt, however, was interpreted to be a rejection of Yahweh himself:

> Yahweh said to Samuel: "Listen to the voice of the people in all they say to you; for they have not rejected you, but *me they have rejected from being king over them*."
>
> —I SAMUEL 8:7

So Samuel sought to dissuade the people from their plan by warning them of what would happen if they had a king: by centralizing power, he would limit

---

[25] Verses 12–14, which speak of a "renewing" of the kingdom, are an editorial addition to harmonize the story with the account in 10:17–27, which comes from the second source. Similarly, the words "and Samuel" in 11:7 are an attempt to harmonize the two accounts.

their freedom and subject them to despotic tyranny. Nevertheless, the people insisted, and Samuel grudgingly consented to go along with them. I Samuel 10:17–27 reports Samuel's selection of Saul by lot from all the tribes of Israel. According to the Samuel Tradition, Saul was acclaimed king at the city of Mizpah (not Gilgal, as in the other tradition). Chapter 12 gives Samuel's valedictory speech as the last judge of Israel.

Probably the Samuel Tradition was written at a later date than the Saul Tradition. It bears the marks of Deuteronomistic revision, as can be seen from a passage like I Samuel 7:3–4, which reminds one of Deuteronomistic language found in the book of Judges. It has fanciful features, like the notion that the Philistines were subdued by a thunderstorm which came in answer to Samuel's prayer. Quite obviously, the portrayal of Samuel and the attitude toward the monarchy found in the two Traditions cannot be readily harmonized. However, we must not jump to the conclusion that the Saul Tradition, just because it is earlier and more restrained, is the only one that has historical value. Again we must underline this important axiom of biblical study: *The date at which a tradition is written down does not necessarily indicate the date at which the tradition originated.* Certainly the Samuel Tradition was not created by the Deuteronomistic historian, even though it was revised to fit into the Deuteronomistic History. The Deuteronomist was working with an older tradition that goes back at many points to the time of Samuel. We do not know exactly what Samuel's role was. The view that he was only a ''local seer,'' which is usually based on the Saul Tradition, has been grossly exaggerated. There is no absolute reason why he could not have been the last in the succession of Israel's judges, as the Samuel Tradition portrays him.

Moreover, what we know about the Israelite Confederacy makes the attitude toward the monarchy expressed in the Samuel Tradition seem authentic. Gideon had refused the crown for precisely the same reason Samuel opposed the kingship—namely, that Yahweh alone was Israel's king. Jotham's parable of the trees also expressed the distaste for centralized power that was felt by the Israelite Confederacy. Not everyone in Israel felt this strongly, however, as we saw in Abimelech's experiment with monarchy at Shechem. The Saul Tradition comes from the modernistic wing, and probably emerged from Saul's tribe, Benjamin, where he was glorified as a tribal and national hero. The Samuel Tradition, on the other hand, shows the persistence of the more conservative belief of the Israelite Confederacy.

Israel and the State

In the early part of this chapter, we saw that the struggle between Israel's faith and Canaanite culture found expression in the temptation to compromise with Canaanite naturalism, the worship of the fertility gods of the farmer's world. Now we see that the struggle was waged on a second front, that of nationalism. At the time, the cultural situation seemed to demand that Israel should become "like the nations," if it were to be saved from destruction. Yet this step, although expedient, threatened to undermine the distinctive character of the Israelite community. From the earliest times Israel was bound together, not by human factors such as race, economics, or politics, but by its relationship to Yahweh, the God of the covenant community. Israel was not a nation (*goy*) but a *people* ('*am*)—distinguished from the nations. The Tribal Confederacy, as we have seen, allowed for some political solidarity, especially in times of emergency, but fundamentally the basis of the organization was a religious covenant. In view of this history, the elders' request for a king was a shocking thing, for it threatened to destroy the true identity of Israel as the "people of God." In becoming like the nations, Israel would be a powerful state and thus no different from any other nation.

So in I Samuel the establishment of the Israelite monarchy is viewed in an ambivalent light. The Samuel Tradition is not just a reflection of the later unhappy experiences of the monarchy, but represents the early criticism made by representatives of the Tribal Confederacy. According to them, the Israelite state was not founded with divine blessing. Rather, it was allowed as a grudging concession, just as a parent lets children have their way in order that they may learn their folly from experience. And even in the Saul Tradition, where the monarchy is welcomed, it is not regarded as a divine kingdom descended from heaven to earth, like a Babylonian dynasty, but as a providential development in history occasioned by the Philistine menace.

In one sense, the establishment of the monarchy *was* providential, as the Saul Tradition emphasizes. In retrospect, one can say that events which brought about the collapse of the Confederacy and the rise of the Israelite state were not completely devoid of divine purpose. God's revelation is relevant to the whole of human life—to economics, politics, and every sphere of human activity. If God would speak to the nations through Israel, then Israel must undergo the experience of being a nation in order that it might both appreciate the wealth of nationhood and attack the idolatrous power of nationalism.[26]

Nevertheless, Israel could not, with an easy conscience, become a nation like the surrounding nations, for the religious faith of the Confederacy survived its collapse and found new expression in Israel's prophetic movement. Israel was not allowed to identify a human kingdom with the kingdom of God, for Yahweh alone was king. Sometimes great Israelite kings like David and Solomon, in their consuming ambition to make Israel great in the eyes of the world, forgot this truth, with the result that prophets arose to remind the people in the spirit of Samuel that Israel's calling was not to be "like the nations" but to be the people of the covenant. This conviction was underscored, as we shall see, by the prophetic criticism of the state and the announcement that the Israelite

---

[26] This discussion is indebted to an essay by the German scholar Walter Eichrodt, *Israel in der Weissagung des Alten Testaments* (Zürich: Gotthelf-Verlag, 1951), *Israel in the Prophecy of the Old Testament*, to give an English translation of the German title. See also E. A. Speiser, " 'People' and 'Nation' of Israel," *Journal of Biblical Literature*, 79 (1960), 157–63.

nation must fall in order that Israel might be reborn. And the conviction has found expression in modern forms of political thought which stress that the state cannot be given absolute devotion, as in totalitarianism, for God alone is king. God is the judge of every social order and the champion of minorities whose rights are crushed by those who arrogate to themselves absolute power.

It must be admitted, however, that the ambivalent attitude toward the monarchy, which finds expression in the combined Saul and Samuel Traditions, was rooted in Israel's actual historical experiences. The early account seems to have been written before Israel had succumbed to the dangers and temptations of becoming a kingdom after the model of its neighbors. It reflects the vigor and vitality of a new beginning, unspoiled by mistakes of the past or the corruptions of political power. Therefore, the monarchy is portrayed as a new possibility, received from the gracious hand of God in response to the people's petition, just as Moses was sent—according to the Exodus tradition (Exod. 3)—in answer to the people's cry of affliction. So the early tradition regards the anointing of Saul as Yahweh's saving action to send a deliverer.

> He shall save my people from the hand of the Philistines; for I have seen the affliction of my people, because their cry has come to me.
>
> —I SAMUEL 9:16b (RSV)

On the other hand, the later tradition looks back to the anointing of Saul through the disillusioning experiences which Israel had during the period of the monarchy. Like a "prophecy after the event," this account portrays the dire consequences that follow from Israel's decision to have a king like other nations. And these unhappy experiences added up to the conclusion, at least in the judgment of some prophetic interpreters, that this was a step taken in defiance of Yahweh's will. Just before the fall of the Northern Kingdom in 721 B.C.E., the prophet Hosea condemned the institution of the monarchy, seeing in it a rejection of Yahweh as king (Hos. 8:4; 9:15; 10:3, 9). When the Southern Kingdom fell almost a century and a half later (587 B.C.E.), it was clear to discerning interpreters that Israel's history as a kingdom had ended in failure. Because the traditions about the founding of the monarchy were shaped near the end of the monarchy, the negative judgment upon Israel's attempt to be a kingdom "like the nations" almost drowns out the other, more positive view.[27] Thus Israel's eventual failure as a nation, which we shall study in Part II, casts its lengthening shadow back across the pages of its history.

---

[27] This point is brought out effectively by Gerhard von Rad, *Theology*, I [142], 324–27.

PART II

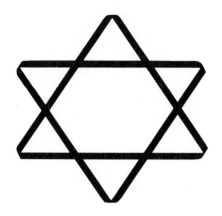

*A star shall come forth
out of Jacob, and a scepter
shall rise out of Israel.*
—NUMBERS 24:17

ISRAEL BECOMES
LIKE THE NATIONS

CHAPTER 7

The Throne
of David

In the twelfth century B.C.E. forces were set in motion that profoundly affected the whole Fertile Crescent and that inevitably left a deep impression upon the life and faith of Israel. In archaeological terms, this was the beginning of the Iron Age. The shift from the use of bronze to iron had important economic and political repercussions, somewhat like the changes brought about by the harnessing of nuclear energy in our own time.

The Philistines, who came into Canaan around the beginning of the Iron Age, capitalized on the new mode of life. They held control over smelting the new metal and guarded their monopoly so effectively that they were able to keep other small nations, like Israel, at their economic mercy. A picture of their stranglehold is given in I Samuel 13:19–22, where we learn that the Hebrews had no smiths who could make swords and spears, and that farmers had to go down to Philistine country to sharpen their agricultural implements. So long as the Philistines were powerful enough to throttle Israel's economic and political life, Israel had no future. The destruction of Shiloh and the ignominious capture of the Ark were vivid reminders of that fact.

Philistine aggression, as we have seen in the preceding chapter, gave the final blow to the old Tribal Confederacy. But this blow served as a stimulus for Israel to rally under a new form of political-religious unity: *the monarchy*. This

Biblical readings: This chapter covers the narratives found in I Samuel 13–31, all of II Samuel, I Kings 1–11. The account is paralleled in the Chronicler's History (I Chron. 10–II Chron. 9), which will be discussed more fully in Chapter 15.

happened under the leadership of the first kings of Israel: Saul, David, and Solomon. Under these kings, especially David, the long story of the occupation of Canaan came to an end. Israel established a miniature empire that extended from Mesopotamia to Egypt. Once the Philistine stranglehold had been broken, the way was opened for a period of economic boom and political fortune that enabled Israel to take its place proudly among the nations of the Fertile Crescent. For Israel, the Iron Age proved to be a Golden Age.

A TIME OF INTERNATIONAL FAVOR

As with Israel's earlier invasion of Canaan, so now its expansion was favored by the political situation in the Fertile Crescent. No nation to the north was strong enough to interfere. The Babylonians had fallen into political weakness after the demise of the Hammurabi regime and did not interfere in Canaan for more than a thousand years. The Hurrians, who founded the great kingdom of Mitanni (c. 1500–1370 B.C.E.) in northern Mesopotamia, were conquered in the fourteenth century by the Assyrians—a nation whose star was destined to rise later on the political horizon. The Hittites, who sought to expand from their base in Asia Minor throughout the Fertile Crescent, were finally overwhelmed by the population upheaval in the Aegean world at about 1200 B.C.E. With the Hurrians and the Hittites out of the way, Assyria was free to expand, but after the reign of Tiglath-pileser I (c. 1116–1078) it sank into obscurity until the ninth century, the time of the prophet Elijah.

Israel, then, was safe from the north, and the situation in Egypt was just as favorable. Although Canaan nominally was under the political control of Egypt during the Late Bronze Age (1500–1200 B.C.E.), Egypt's control vanished during the Twentieth Dynasty, especially after about 1150. During the reign of Solomon there was a brief revival under Shishak I (935–914), but after this Egypt was to remain politically impotent for more than three centuries.

It is against this favorable international background that we must read the account of how Israel attained national unity and extended its political control throughout Palestine and Syria. The account is stirringly presented in the books of Samuel and the first eleven chapters of I Kings. This material, it will be recalled, belongs to the great Deuteronomistic History. Within the Deuteronomistic framework, the historian has included materials that represent different circles of tradition and that show varying degrees of historical reliability. In discussing the account of the establishment of the kingdom (I Sam. 1–12), we have already noticed two types of narrative: a pro-monarchic tradition, and a theocratic tradition (see pp. 206–208). Attempts have been made to trace these two types of tradition throughout the rest of the books of Samuel, but after the conclusion of the Samuel story, the division becomes much less clearcut. Some material is undoubtedly legendary (for instance, the story of David and Goliath in I Sam. 17), and some shows a political or theological bias (e.g., the story of

Nathan forbidding David to build a temple, II Sam. 7). Allowing for legendary and theological embellishments, however, the narratives on the whole are so vivid and unimpeachable in their historical authenticity that they must have come from a time close to the events described. This trustworthiness is especially evident in the Court History of David found in II Samuel 9–20 and I Kings 1–2. This "succession narrative," regarded by scholars as one of the best examples of Hebraic prose in the Old Testament, evidently was composed during the reign of David. One authority praises the "early source of Samuel," especially the Court History, as "the outstanding prose writing and historical masterpiece of the Old Testament." Convinced that its account is so vivid and accurate that it must have been written by an eyewitness, he looks for the author among the persons associated with David's court. He acclaims this author as "the 'father of history' in a much truer sense than Herodotus half a millennium later," and points to the national renaissance under David as providing the conditions for this literary achievement.[1] By contrast, the history found in Chronicles is so thoroughly dominated by theological bias that the historical picture is blurred, even though some of the traditions preserved in this late work are valuable.[2]

ISRAEL'S RUSTIC KING

The account of Saul's reign in I Samuel 13–31 is the tragic story of a heroic leader who lived in the transitional period between the collapse of the old Tribal Confederacy and the birth of a new order. The psychic weaknesses that marked Saul's personality were only aggravated by the fateful historical situation in which he was destined to be Israel's first king. The tragedy of his career revolves around his alienation from two persons: Samuel, who represented the old order, and David, who represented the new. Samuel, as we have seen, is portrayed as the last representative of the old Confederacy, which gradually collapsed under the pressure of political necessity. David represents the youth and vigor of the new national order within which Israel was to find a new unity and was to search for a new formulation of its historic faith. Saul himself belonged more to the old period than to the new age that was coming with historical inevitability. But Saul's rejection by Samuel put him outside the sanctions and supports of the old regime; and David's popularity was a constant reminder that Saul could not enter the new. Caught between these two worlds, Saul's life became the arena on which was waged an intense psychic conflict—a conflict that eventually destroyed him.

---

[1] R. H. Pfeiffer, *Introduction to the Old Testament*, rev. ed. (New York: Harper & Row, 1949), pp. 356–59. Gerhard von Rad reaffirms this view by saying that the "realism" and "secularity" of the Succession Document represent a new kind of historiography, "without parallel in the ancient East" (*Theology*, I [142], 312–17).

[2] The Chronicler's History, comprising Ezra, Nehemiah, and I–II Chronicles, was composed in the post-exilic period and reflects the priestly theological interests of Judaism. See Chapter 15.

It would be interesting if we had a historical narrative written in a circle sympathetic to Saul—for instance, an account written by a member of Saul's own tribe of Benjamin. But the narratives of I Samuel are now dominated by the bias of historians of the southern kingdom of Judah, and Saul is put in an unfavorable light in order to enhance the prestige of David, who founded the dynasty of Judah. We must remember that all the traditions of the monarchy were preserved in and edited by Jerusalem circles, which were sympathetic toward David. From a different point of view, perhaps Saul would emerge as a heroic figure who, like Hamlet, was the victim of baffling, uncontrollable circumstances and the dark depths of his own sensitive and passionate nature. The narratives testify that Saul was capable of inspiring great devotion from his followers, even after Samuel deserted him. And Saul's military successes, though limited and finally eclipsed by the dismal defeat at Mount Gilboa, must have had considerable effect, especially in wresting from the Philistines their monopoly in iron smelting and thereby paving the way for the economic developments in the reigns of David and Solomon. His victories over Israel's enemies were impressive (I Sam. 14:48), and under his rule unity and harmony came to the tribes of Israel. Much can be said to Saul's credit![3]

Saul's Charismatic Leadership

One of the clearest points of contact between Saul and the old Tribal Confederacy was his possession of the divine charisma, the "spirit of Yahweh," which, as we have seen, endowed the judges with the authority of leadership. Throughout the territory of the Confederacy, Saul was acknowledged as leader not because of his heredity or a *coup d'état*, but because the spirit of Yahweh had rushed upon him and had enabled him to act as a deliverer in the Ammonite crisis, when the city of Jabesh-gilead was threatened (I Sam. 11:6–7). Recognizing that he was charismatic, the people of Israel made him king after this military success in the hope that he would deliver them from the Philistine oppression. Saul was more like one of the ancient judges than were the kings who succeeded him. In fact, the oldest source (I Sam. 9:16; 10:1) carefully avoids calling him a king (*melek*), but describes him instead as a "prince" or "leader" (*nagîd*). In contrast to David and Solomon, Saul made no attempt to transform the tribal structure of Israel into a centralized state. He levied no taxes, made no military conscription, had no hierarchy of court officials and no harem. His only army was a band of volunteers whom he recruited from his supporters (I Sam. 13:2; 14:52). Excavations at Saul's fortress of Gibeah have confirmed the biblical picture of the "rustic simplicity" of his court.[4] No Oriental despot, he perpetuated the tribal democracy of the earlier period, and claimed authority among the tribes

---

[3] See Robert Browning's poem, "Saul."

[4] Gibeah was excavated in 1922–23 under the direction of W. F. Albright; see his references in *The Biblical Period* [90], 24. Re-excavation of the site in 1964 under the direction of Paul Lapp largely confirmed Albright's results; see his report in *The Biblical Archaeologist* XXVIII, (1965), pp. 2–10.

only because of the divine charisma. Since his authority was charismatic, it is understandable that he became very melancholy when it seemed that the "spirit" had departed from him, owing to the rejection by Samuel and the popular acclaim that attended David's military exploits.

Reading the vivid story of Saul's reign at Gibeah, we sense that, for all his weakness, he was a man of sincere, passionate faith in Yahweh. According to one interpretation, in his early career Saul broke with the orthodox Mosaic faith and leaned toward the worship of Baal, the nature god of Canaan. The evidence for this interpretation is that while Saul's first son was given a Yahweh name, Jonathan (meaning "Yahweh [Yo] gave"), his later children were given Baal names—for instance, Ishbaal (meaning "man of Baal"). Moreover, Saul ruthlessly slaughtered the priests of the Eli family who had been the guardians of the central sanctuary at Shiloh (I Sam. 22). This interpretation, of course, would help to explain why Samuel came to repudiate the leader he had anointed. But it is doubtful whether the acts mentioned above give solid support to the view that Saul was a modernist or a heretic. Despite his impulsive actions, he evidently intended to serve Yahweh with his whole heart.

In contrast to Samuel, Saul was not gifted with profound insight into the meaning of Israel's faith. The chapters of Saul's tumultuous life portray life-situations in which persons were called to act in faith, to trust when the odds were desperate, and to decide and accept the consequences. Here is a story that belongs in Israel's scripture not because of its edifying ideas, but because of its clear, uncensored description of the human situation. Later prophets understood the covenant faith more profoundly. But Saul was no prophet, even though he came under prophetic influence on occasion—to the great surprise of acquaintances, whose incredulous question, "Is Saul also among the prophets?" has become proverbial (I Sam. 10:10–11; 19:18–24). He was a soldier who had to face a state of military emergency throughout his reign, for "there was hard fighting against the Philistines all the days of Saul." His task was to "fight Yahweh's battles," which, to the popular mind, were the same as the battles of Israel.

Through the narratives breathes an intensity that springs from the conviction that Yahweh was actively engaged in the conflict. Believing this, Saul was not deterred by Israel's pitiful lack of armor, by the number of discouraged Israelites who deserted when the going was rough, or by the handful of recruits who constituted his army. What mattered that the odds were against him when, as Jonathan put it just before setting out on a daring exploit at Michmash, "Nothing can hinder Yahweh from saving by many or by few" (I Sam. 14:6)! And when the tide of battle turned against Israel, Saul was humble enough to suspect that something had been done to incur Yahweh's displeasure. As a military strategist, he had a very limited view of the divine purpose in history, but he must be given credit for coming to realize through bitter experience that it was Yahweh who was in supreme command, shaping the course of events and demanding the zealous devotion of the people.

A Holy War

Saul's devotion to Yahweh was put to the test in an incident related in I Samuel 15, the battle with the Amalekites. In the judgment of many scholars, this chapter comes from a literary tradition related to the one we have earlier designated as the Samuel Tradition (see pp. 207–208). But although it may have arisen in circles different from the sources of some of the other narratives found in the Saul story, it is surely based on an authentic historical memory. The Amalekites, who lived in the Negeb to the south of Beer-sheba, were ancient enemies of Israel. Their all-out effort to destroy Israel during the wilderness march still rankled in Israel's memory (Exod. 17:8–16). Possibly the old animosity was reawakened by some immediate provocation, such as recent Amalekite raids upon southern settlements at a time when Israel was preoccupied with the Philistine problem. In any event, through the prophet Samuel, Saul was given the divine command to destroy them utterly—man, woman, child, cattle, and goods.

According to modern ethical standards, this act of total extermination was a barbarous thing (although it was scarcely less refined than modern warfare!). But instead of making a value judgment from our standpoint, let us try to understand the act within the religious perspective of ancient Israel. According to the story, the initiative was taken by Yahweh, who commanded Israel to punish Amalek for its ancient atrocity. In other words, this was not to be an ordinary "secular" war, but a "holy" war. It was to be a religious action.

To understand holy war, we must recall the period of the Tribal Confederacy, for instance, the discussion in connection with the Song of Deborah (pp. 196–198; also see Definition, Chapter 4, p. 141). In previous chapters we have seen that the covenant bond imposed certain obligations upon the participating tribes, one of which was to respond to Yahweh's summons given through a charismatic leader in time of battle. The response to the call was a test of loyalty to the God of the covenant, of rallying in faith to Yahweh's "going before" the people. The people would "offer themselves willingly" (Judg. 5:2, 9), and would consecrate themselves by submitting to certain disciplines such as abstinence from sexual intercourse (I Sam. 21:4–5; II Sam. 11:11). In such times they engaged in holy activity, for, it was believed, Yahweh was in their midst as their military leader. As in the case of Gideon (p. 199), the number of fighters and their weapon-power were inconsequential. The strategy of holy war was not so much to fight pitched battles as to frighten the enemy with the "terror of God" so that they would flee in panic and confusion.

In a holy war, the spoil was to be *ḥérem*—that is, devoted to Yahweh as a holocaust or sacrifice. Since the spoil belonged exclusively to Yahweh, it was regarded as a great sin for anyone to take anything, regardless of personal motive. The story of Achan, who stole some precious things from the spoil of Jericho with disastrous results for himself and his family, is an excellent illustration (Josh. 7). To take anything from Yahweh's sacrifice was regarded as "breaking faith" (Josh. 7:1); it was an offense against Yahweh's holiness.

With the collapse of the Tribal Confederacy, the old conception of holy war soon disappeared.[5] When the Israelite state emerged, charismatic leaders were superseded by hereditary kings who, after the manner of surrounding nations, fought wars with chariots and infantry and without a qualm took all the booty they could. But in Saul's day the old standard was still in effect. Saul was a charismatic leader who was commanded to destroy the Amalekites completely— that is, to put them under the sacrifical ban (*ḥérem*). So decisively did he defeat them that they vanished from the historical scene shortly afterwards.[6]

In terms of this old fashioned standard we must understand Saul's action in taking part of the spoil. According to the ancient view, his offense was that he used his own judgment in deciding how far to go in obeying the stipulations of holy war. To us, the sparing of Agag appears humane, and the taking of the best of the livestock seems practical wisdom; but in the ancient view these all belonged to Yahweh—they were holy. Saul's defect was his refusal to give complete obedience to Yahweh, as obedience was understood in holy war. It was an act of disloyalty that polluted the whole Israelite community. Not even Saul's explanation that Agag and the spoil were brought back to be sacrificed to Yahweh would satisfy Samuel, the spokesman of the old Confederacy, who is represented as saying:

> Behold, to obey is better than sacrifice,
> And to hearken than the fat of rams.
> —I SAMUEL 15:22b (RSV)

Because Saul had "rejected the word of Yahweh," said the prophet, Yahweh had rejected him as king over Israel. With fierce devotion to Yahweh, the enraged Samuel finished performing the sacrificial ban; he "hewed Agag in pieces before Yahweh in Gilgal" (I Sam. 15:33b).

A Rejected Man

This story marks the turning point in the cycle of stories dealing with Saul, although quite clearly it is colored by a bias in favor of David, the "neighbor" who was better than he (I Sam. 15:28). Not even Saul's confession of sin and plea for pardon could deliver him from the consequence of his deed, which, like a nemesis, pursued him in the days ahead. Just because he was so passionate in his devotion to Yahweh, the prophetic word of rejection preyed upon his mind and drove him to the edge of insanity. Outwardly he enjoyed some measure of popularity and success for a while, but inwardly his life was dis-

---

[5] The conception, however, was revived later by the writer of Deuteronomy (for instance, Deut. 7:1–2; 20:1–21:14). See Gerhard von Rad, *Studies in Deuteronomy* [367], pp. 45–49. The Deuteronomic rules for conducting a holy war were followed in the Maccabean Revolt and accepted by the Essene sect of Jews at Qumran (see pp. 635–636).

[6] The last reference to action by the Amalekites is their raid on a Philistine outpost, which was avenged by David (I Sam. 30).

tracted and maddened by his consciousness of being rejected. To him there were two developments that pointed clearly to his estrangement from Yahweh.

One was the decisive break with Samuel, the last representative of the Tribal Confederacy. A more sympathetic view of Saul would portray his impulsive acts, which led to the final rupture with Samuel, in a better light. Saul was a man of action who did not consider the religious implications of his acts, especially in times of emergency. He summoned the priest Ahijah to obtain a divine oracle, but evidently he abruptly terminated the investigation when the military situation indicated that there was no time to wait for Yahweh to give an answer (I Sam. 14:18–23). When his hungry soldiers slaughtered cattle and began to eat meat with the blood—that is, without the proper ritual procedure—Saul himself built an altar for sacrifice (I Sam. 14:31–35). These actions may show only Saul's impulsiveness, rather than his determination to take things into his own hands. But, together with the Amalekite episode, they were convincing evidence to Samuel that Saul was out to defy the Israelite theocracy, the "rule of God." Thus the break between prophet and king occurred, "and Samuel did not see Saul again until the day of his death" (I Sam. 15:35). To Saul, the absence of Yahweh's prophet was the absence of Yahweh. He was a man cast off by God, shut up within the loneliness of his own tumultuous being.

The other development that pointed to Saul's estrangement from Yahweh was the rise of David's star on the horizon. From Saul's point of view, David must have appeared as a threat to his very existence, even a greater threat than the Philistine menace. Denied the security of Yahweh's acceptance, Saul's instability was only aggravated by David's personal charm, gallantry, and success. It must have seemed that David had only one aim from the very first: to gain the throne for himself (see I Sam. 18:8). How else could one explain David's ability to ingratiate himself with the people, his cunning attempt to marry into the royal family, his friendship with Jonathan, and his support from the priests of Nob? The more Saul brooded over David's actions, the surer he was that David was a pretender to the throne. Haunted by his dark moods and inflamed by insane jealousy and rage, he suspected the loyalty of his best friends (I. Sam. 22:6–8) and was obsessed by one determination: to hunt David down and kill him.

This was more than a personal rift between two men of heroic stature. What really happened was that the divine charisma, the spirit that endowed the old Israelite leaders with authority and strength, had departed from Saul. This is the judgment given by the narrator in I Samuel 16:14, and this sorry fact must have tortured Saul's mind more than anything else. Everywhere, David met with success. Saul's plots to humiliate him were all turned to David's advantage. When Saul returned from his battles, the women met him with music and song; but his armor-bearer, David, received the greater praise:

Saul has slain his thousands,
but David his tens of thousands!
—I SAMUEL 18:7

This was more than Saul could stand. More and more it became apparent that David was the man of charisma. Indeed, one passage states that when Samuel anointed David, "the spirit of Yahweh came mightily upon David from that day forward" (I Sam. 16:13). His actions were evidence that Yahweh's favor was upon him. Ironically, Saul was still a man of charisma, but it was "an evil spirit from Yahweh" that tormented him until he was beside himself. Today, Saul would be regarded as a fit subject for a study in abnormal psychology. In antiquity, however, it was believed that unusual psychic behavior, such as David's feigned insanity in the Philistine court (I Sam. 21:12–15), was a sign that the divine spirit had invaded the center of one's being and had taken control. According to this view, the line separating the spiritual leader from the disordered mind is a very fine one indeed.[7]

Saul's desperate efforts to find himself again and to recover his kingly prestige proved futile. He suspected conspiracy against him on every hand, as evidenced by his wild command to massacre the priests of Nob, eighty-five in number, who showed kindness to David (I Sam. 22:9–19). Frustrated in his efforts to track down the fugitive David, he at last found himself confronted with a concerted Philistine drive into the plain of Jezreel. The Israelite armies were gathered by Mount Gilboa, on the southern flank of the pass that led to the Philistine fort, Beth-shan. Panic-stricken at the sight of the large army concentrated in the valley below, Saul made one last effort to inquire of Yahweh; but no answer came by any of the usual channels—either through the sacred lot (Urim and Thummim), dreams, or prophetic oracles (I Sam. 28:5–6). Even though he had banned mediums from the land, Saul made a clandestine visit to a necromancer at En-dor, hoping to hear a word from Yahweh through Samuel's ghost, which was summoned from the underworld. This story (I Sam. 28:8–25), one of the most vivid in the Bible, gives a moving portrayal of the tragedy of Saul's last hours. Having heard from Samuel the crushing prophecy of doom, he went out into the dismal night—and to the defeat and suicide of Mount Gilboa. We can hardly read the story without being moved by its pathos and by the greatness of its tragic hero. In his magnificent elegy, once contained in an old collection of Israelite poetry called the Book of Jashar, David paid immortal tribute to Saul, the fallen leader of Israel, and to his friend Jonathan, whose love for David surpassed the love between man and woman (II Sam. 1:19–27):

> How are the mighty fallen,
>   and the weapons of war perished!
>   —II SAMUEL 1:27 (RSV)

[7] It is interesting to note that prophets were sometimes called "madmen" (II Kings 9:11). Moreover, the Hebrew word used in I Samuel 18:10 to describe one of Saul's fits literally means to prophesy under the influence of the divine spirit (the Revised Standard Version translates "rave"). See further Simon B. Parker, "Possession, Trance, and Prophecy in Pre-Exilic Israel," *Vetus Testamentum* 28 (1978), 271–285.

DAVID, ARCHITECT OF THE ISRAELITE STATE

The Philistine victory at the battle of Mount Gilboa was decisive. The Israelite armies were dispersed in leaderless rout and Saul's decapitated body was impaled on the walls of the Philistine fortress of Beth-shan. The victors now controlled the valley route leading from the Mediterranean Sea to the Jordan Valley, and the complete conquest of Israelite territory was within easy reach. Why the Philistines did not follow up their victory by wiping out all pockets of resistance immediately is not altogether clear. One reason, certainly, was the rise of David, one of the greatest military commanders and statesmen of history. With amazing swiftness he reorganized the Israelite army, dealt a death blow to Philistine power, and established a dynasty that was destined to last for more than four hundred years.

The story of David's early career is interwoven with the fateful events of Saul's reign (I Sam. 13–31). Here we can only allude to the fascinating course of events: David's rise from the obscurity of a shepherd's life, his appearance as a harp player in the king's court, his victory over the giant Goliath, his gallant exploits among the Philistines, his adventures as the ''Robin Hood'' leader of a band of outlaws, and his elevation to the rank of king of Israel. The story, as we have already mentioned, was written to glorify the man whose personal charm and charismatic success had made him a great popular idol. It has cap-

The Imposing Mound of Beth-shan, *on the edge of the Plain of Jezreel, where it guarded the route inland from the coast to Damascus. Once a strategic outpost of the Egyptian empire, Beth-shan came to be a Philistine fortress and later came into possession of the Israelites.*

tured the imagination of people in every generation, including our own.[8] Indeed, posterity hailed David as the greatest of Israel's rulers—"a man after God's own heart." He was both the architect of the nation and the royal champion of Israel's faith.

This high estimation is all the more remarkable when we consider the true-to-life picture of David that is presented in the narratives. To be sure, the book of Chronicles, written some centuries later, touches up the portrait in order to make David's better traits stand out (I Chron. 11–29); but the account in the books of Samuel and Kings, especially the Court History or "Succession Narrative" in II Samuel 9–20 and I Kings 1–2, presents a series of candid snapshots of David in real life. He stands before us not as an idealized saint in a stained-glass window, but as a flesh-and-blood figure of extraordinary winsomeness and charm.

There are, of course, notable inconsistencies in the account. For instance, there are two accounts of how David was introduced into Saul's court. According to one (I Sam. 16:14–23), he was brought in as a musician to cheer the depressed king; according to the other (I Sam. 17:1–18:5), he first won the king's attention when he vanquished Goliath.[9] Moreover, in II Samuel 21:19 the slaying of Goliath is attributed to a certain Elhanan from Bethlehem, a detail that casts doubt on the story of David the giant-killer.[10] But taking into account these legendary stories that gathered around a great national hero (compare the stories about George Washington), we are given on the whole an authentic, if somewhat romanticized, account of David's rise from the sheepfolds to the royal throne.

The death of Samuel and Saul marked the passing of an era. With David, a new way of life began that was revolutionary when compared with the simplicities of the old Tribal Confederacy. Under Saul's charismatic rule the tribes were held together in the loose union of the Confederacy, and it is a tribute to his leadership that there were no signs of tribal rebellion during his lifetime. Despite military reverses and his preoccupation with David's maneuvers, Saul was able to preserve the unity of Israel and the affection of his countrymen. But with David we see the transition from charismatic leadership to a centralization of power in the crown. From a tribal league, Israel was transformed into a miniature empire modeled after the surrounding nations. David's problem was to maintain the tribal unity of the old Confederacy under the new nation-state.

David's Rise to Power

The methods used by David suggest that he was a shrewd politician who stopped at nothing to achieve his political ambitions. At the time of Saul's death,

---

[8] See, for instance, the novel by Joseph Heller, *God Knows* (New York: Alfred A. Knopf, 1984).

[9] Notice that in I Sam. 17:55–58 Saul questions David about his identity, which apparently indicates that he had not known of him before. Compare 16:17–22.

[10] This discrepancy is smoothed over in I Chron. 20:5 where it is stated that Elhanan killed the brother of Goliath, Lahmi, and not Goliath himself.

David was an exile in Philistia. His first task was to put himself in a strategic position from which his political scheme—to set himself up as ruler over the tribes of Israel—could be achieved. Fortunately, he had already prepared the way for readmission to his native tribe of Judah, from one of whose cities (Bethlehem) he had come. During his outlaw period, both in the Wilderness of Judah and in the service of Philistia, he had ingratiated himself with the Judeans by protecting landholders from robbers and by dividing with the elders of Judah the spoil taken from raids on their enemies (I Sam. 23:1–5; 25:2 ff.; 27:8–12; 30:26–31). It is not too surprising, then, that shortly after Saul's death David was anointed king at Hebron, where he reigned for over seven years, evidently as a kind of Philistine vassal.

During this period, however, David had his eye on the whole territory of Israel. The northern tribes still owed allegiance to Saul's weak son, Ishbaal,[11] who was only a stooge of his army general, Abner. David's Judean forces were under the command of his able general, Joab. Apparently the conflict between the house of David and the house of Saul was touched off by a curious incident that occurred by the pool of Gibeon, uncovered by archaeologists in 1956–57.[12] The two army commanders, facing each other from opposite sides of the pool, agreed to a test of strength. Twelve young men would represent each side in a kind of gladiatorial contest. But the ordeal settled nothing, for the champions only killed each other off, with the result that general fighting broke out between the armies (II Sam. 2:12–17). From this time on there was fighting off and on, with David's power growing stronger and stronger. The political struggle between David and the house of Saul came to an end when Abner, stinging under a deserved rebuke from Ishbaal, offered to deliver the remnant of Saul's kingdom to David. Part of the deal was for David to receive Michal, Saul's daughter and David's first wife. Michal's tearful parting from her own husband is described with great pathos (II Sam. 3:12–16). Governed chiefly by cold political calculation, David sought to establish a claim upon Saul's throne by taking Michal into his harem. Saul's male descendants were either liquidated in typical despotic style or put under careful custody (II Sam. 21:1–14). At the age of thirty-seven, David had become the unchallenged ruler of all Israel.

During David's reign at Hebron, the Philistines had not interfered with him. Probably they regarded him as their vassal and were content for Israel to be divided by civil war between the house of Saul and the house of David. But when David's power increased with the union of all the Israelite tribes, the Philistines felt that it was time to act (II Sam. 5:17). Not much is said about the Philistine wars, but one of David's greatest accomplishments was breaking the Philistines' control over Canaan once and for all and shutting them up in the coastal plain (see II Sam. 5:17–25; 21:15–22). Moreover, he waged successful

---

[11] In the biblical text he is called Ishbosheth. Editors have substituted *bosheth* (Hebrew, "shame") for Baal, the despised name of the Canaanite deity.

[12] See James B. Pritchard, *Gibeon: Where the Sun Stood Still* (Princeton, N.J.: Princeton University Press, 1962), pp. 64–72.

The Pool of Gibeon *was the scene of a gladiatorial contest, according to II Sam. 2:13. First excavated in the summer of 1956, Gibeon was one of four federated cities that entered into alliance with Joshua during his invasion of southern Canaan, and came to be an important Israelite city by the time of the early monarchy.*

wars against Moab, Ammon, Edom, Amalek, and Aram (Syria), and he concluded a treaty with the Phoenician king, Hiram of Tyre. So he became recognized as the ruler of an empire that stretched from the Lebanon mountains to the very borders of Egypt, from the Mediterranean Sea to the Desert of Arabia. The narrator, seeing the hand of God in these dazzling achievements, comments: ''David became greater and greater, for Yahweh, the God of hosts, was with him'' (II Sam. 5:10). Never before or after the time of David did Israel exceed this zenith of political power.

Consolidating the Nation

But David was more than a brilliant military commander. Desiring a greater centralization of power in the throne, he took several important and fateful steps to limit the independence of the confederate tribes. One of his most brilliant maneuvers was the capture of the old fortress of Jerusalem despite the boast of its occupants, the Jebusites, that it was an impregnable stronghold. Apparently David's men penetrated the stronghold by ascending a water shaft (II Sam. 5:8) that had been cut through rock, from the Gihon spring outside the walls to the

THE THRONE OF DAVID

interior of the old city, called Ophel. Consider what David's feat must have meant at a time when northern tribes had gathered around the house of Saul and southern tribes had sworn allegiance to David in Hebron. Bypassed by the forces of Israel at the time of the occupation of Canaan, Jerusalem had never been incorporated into the tribal territory of Israel. David made his bid for power by capitalizing on the sectional feeling of the southern tribes; but since his political ambitions also included the northern tribes, he wisely sought a place for his capital that was neither "northern" nor "southern." By selecting the neutral site of Jerusalem, right on the boundary of the northern and southern tribes, he revealed his intention of elevating his throne above all tribal claims and jealousies. His action has been compared with the selection of Washington, D.C., as the federal capital on territory independent of the states.

Jerusalem was known as "the city of David" (I Sam. 5:9). In his capital David gathered around him a group of courtiers who derived their position and support from the crown. This organization represented a great change from the days of the Confederacy when leadership was based on a person's status in a tribe or on the divine charisma. The administration of law, which previously had been vested in the tribal elders who "sat at the gate," or in the judges of the Confederacy, was taken over by the king himself, although we may infer that he delegated much of this responsibility to judges whom he appointed to office (see II Sam. 14:4–17; 15:1–6). Other royal officials are mentioned (II Sam. 8:15–18). In the cases of two of these officials—the Recorder and the Secretary—scholars have detected the influence of the governmental organization of Egypt. Thus Israel was rapidly becoming "like the nations," with a special class known as "servants of the king" who exercised power over Israel's social life.

It was not enough, however, to supervise the kingdom in this manner. If he was to capture the allegiance of all Israel, David also needed to establish his throne on the religious sanctions and Mosaic traditions of the Tribal Confederacy. He had to demonstrate that his political innovations would not sweep away Israel's sacred heritage, but bring it to glorious fulfillment. So one of his shrewdest acts was to rescue the Ark of the Covenant from the place of oblivion in which it had rested since the fall of the confederate sanctuary of Shiloh and to bring it to Jerusalem with great pomp and ceremony—on which occasion he performed a religious dance, virtually in the nude, much to the disgust of his wife (II Sam. 6). With the Ark stationed in a "tent" in Jerusalem, the city of David also became "Zion, City of God," for Yahweh's presence once again "tabernacled" in the midst of Israel. Moreover, the priests of the house of Eli (of whom Abiathar was the chief) who had survived Saul's bloody purge at Nob were brought to Jerusalem and attached to the royal court. In this way too David sought to encircle his crown with the religious halo of the past. Thus the religious center of Israel was shifted from the confederate sanctuary of Shiloh to the royal shrine in Jerusalem to which the people made pilgrimages for worship. Some of the Psalms (e.g., Ps. 24:7–10 and 132:6–10) apparently reflect a "Zion festival" in which the bearing of the Ark through the gates of Jerusalem, with

Jerusalem from the South *with the hill called Ophel, the site of David's city, highlighted in the center foreground. Behind the walls can be seen the Dome of the Rock, a mosque built over the site of Solomon's Temple. Ophel slopes off to the deep Valley of Kidron, on the right of which is the modern village of Silwan.*

Yahweh the "king of glory" invisibly enthroned upon it, was periodically reenacted. (On the Zion festival, see further Chapter 16, pp. 560–566).

David's innovations marked the beginning of a "royal theology" which challenged the anti-monarchic conservatism represented by leaders like Samuel. According to the royal view, Yahweh had made a special covenant with David, promising to establish David's throne securely through all generations (II Sam. 7). It came to be believed that Yahweh would certainly be in favor of any king who was a descendant of David.

David's ambitions soared ever higher. Already, it seems, he had placed the Ark of the Covenant within the Tent of Meeting (see II Sam. 7:2), thus joining together the two major cultic objects inherited from Mosaic times (see above, pp. 116–118). According to a tradition preserved in II Samuel 24:18–25, he purchased from a citizen named Araunah a threshing floor north of his palace upon which to build an altar to Yahweh. This was only the beginning of David's aspirations. He wanted to replace the old Tent with a splendid royal temple patterned after the temples of other nations. However, the conservative religious tradition of the Confederacy was voiced by the prophet Nathan, who argued that Yahweh had not dwelt in a "house" since the time of the Exodus but had been "moving about in a tent" (II Sam. 7:6). So David wisely conceded to the prophet that this was going too far—at least for the time being. He contented himself with building a tent-shrine (*mishkan*), perhaps along the lines of the "tabernacle" described in the book of Exodus (Exod. 25–31 and 35–40).[13] And he reorganized Israel's religion in other spheres, especially music. According to the Chronicler (I Chron. 25), David organized the musicians into guilds. Since David was a reputed musician (see Amos 6:5), this is not incredible.

David took other measures to control and modify the independence of the Tribal Confederacy. Against the advice of his counselors, he insisted on taking a census of all Israel, an ambitious project that took over nine months to complete. Evidently the census findings were to be the basis for military conscription, taxation, or forced labor. In this way David served notice to all citizens that they owed their primary allegiance to the king, not to their tribal unit. The plan backfired, however. The bitter popular resentment against numbering Israel's fighting forces is expressed in the story of a plague, interpreted as a sign of Yahweh's wrath against the king in the face of which he repented (II Sam. 24).[14] He also inaugurated the policy of forcing his subjects into work camps (II Sam. 20:24), a despotic practice which, under Solomon, became a hated symbol of tyranny.

David's Troubles

It is not surprising, then, that David's initial popularity began to wane. The people became more and more restive under the yoke of centralized power, and longed for the independence they had enjoyed before Israel became a state. Outwardly, the Israelite state was brilliant in its achievements, the envy of the nations round about, as we learn later from the story of the Queen of Sheba's visit to Solomon (I Kings 10:1-10). Throughout the Fertile Crescent, David's name was renowned. The city of Jerusalem, whose royal buildings were designed and constructed by the best artisans of Phoenicia, was a monument to the skill and diplomacy of David. Into David's kingdom poured the commerical wealth of the Near East. As a result, social life underwent profound changes, and Israel's faith was exposed to a more cosmopolitan atmosphere. New con-

---

[13] The confederate sanctuary at Shiloh must have been a tent (as in Ps. 78:60), not a temple (cf. I Sam. 1:7, 9). In his essay on "Temples and High Places in Biblical Times" (Jerusalem, 1981), Frank Cross maintains that the tabernacle portrayed in Priestly portions of the book of Exodus (Exod. 25-31, 35-40) reflects the tent shrine constructed by David. The building of a "house" or temple for Yahweh, in his view, was exclusively Solomon's project.

[14] The Chronicler attributed the temptation to number Israel to Satan rather than to David's imperial ambitions (I Chron. 21:1).

ceptions of property were introduced as commercial entrepreneurs, protected by the military power of the king, exploited the opportunities of trade. But all was not well. Even in David's reign were heard the volcanic rumblings that eventually, at the death of Solomon, broke forth with pent-up fury. Absalom, David's son, instigated a revolution in Judah that almost cost David his crown. And among the northern tribes a certain Sheba sounded the call to revolution:

> We have no share in David,
>   no inheritance in the son of Jesse.
> Every one to his tents, O Israel!
> —II SAMUEL 20:1

David proved equal to these crises, but they foreshadowed future trouble.

The story of David's domestic troubles is recorded in the Court History found in II Samuel 9–20 and I Kings 1–2.[15] Here we have a firsthand historical writing, so vivid and reliable that it must have come from one who was a contemporary of David and probably a member of his court. We are given a glimpse into the intrigues of David's own family. Only from this biographical angle do we learn about the character of David's administration. Unlike the Chronicler's portrait of David, the Court History portrays the king in his strength and his weakness. No attempt is made to depict him as either better or worse than he actually was, or to suppress or distort the facts in the interests of theological bias.

Nevertheless, the Court History is dominated by a religious theme that makes the David story one of the greatest biographical tragedies ever written. The key to the story is the encounter between David and the prophet Nathan, as recorded in II Samuel 12. The background of the incident is the Bathsheba affair, which understandably has captured the interest of the Hollywood movie industry. David desired Bathsheba. What was to prevent him, the most powerful man in the land, from satisfying his lust? Accordingly he took her, only to find out later that she had become pregnant. David then brought Bathsheba's husband, Uriah the Hittite, home from battle so that it would appear to everyone that Uriah was the father of the child who was conceived. But Uriah was a faithful warrior who refused to break the rules of purity that applied to a sanctified soldier during holy war (II Sam. 11:11). David entertained Uriah until he was drunk, hoping to weaken his will. When this attempt failed, he contrived Uriah's murder in a manner that would put himself beyond suspicion. It seemed to be a perfect crime; "but," says the record, "the thing that David had done displeased Yahweh." Then follows one of the most dramatic encounters recorded in Scripture. The prophet Nathan appeared before David as the spokesman of Yahweh, and got the king to condemn himself by his infuriated reaction to the parable of the poor man's pet ewe lamb that was stolen to provide meat for a

---

[15] The basic study of the Court History (or Succession Narrative) is Leonhard Rost, *Succession to the Throne* [308]. Gerhard von Rad builds upon this study in his excellent discussion of "Israel's Anointed" in his *Theology*, I [142], especially pp. 306–18.

rich man's table. Nathan's exclamation, "You are the man!" struck home like a dagger to David's guilty heart. With true remorse and penitence, he confessed, "I have sinned against Yahweh"; but not even his penitence could free him from the fateful consequences of his actions.

In the rest of the Court History we see how this incident set off a chain reaction of troubles as David's lust and murder, like a demonic spirit, corrupted his own sons. One episode followed swiftly upon another. Amnon forced his virgin half-sister, and Absalom in revenge assassinated Amnon. Estranged from his father, Absalom fomented a revolution and to the great sorrow of David was murdered by Joab as he dangled from a tree with his head caught in its limbs. There is no more poignant passage in the whole Old Testament than the description of the king's anguished response to the news about his rebellious son:

> And the king was deeply moved, and went up to the chamber over the gate, and wept; and as he went, he said, "O my son Absalom, my son, my son Absalom! Would I had died instead of you, O Absalom, my son, my son."
>
> —II SAMUEL 18:33 (RSV)

And at the very end of David's days his sons were engaged in intrigue and treachery over the succession to the throne. So Yahweh's word through Nathan came to dreadful fulfillment: "Behold, I will raise up evil against you out of your own house." Although still surrounded by the glories and wealth of the state he had created, the old man David described in I Kings 1–2 was a pathetic, broken-hearted, effete figure who, in vain, sought to warm himself at the dead embers of his former passions (I Kings 1:1–4). In Solomon, born of the fateful marriage with Bathsheba, the nemesis continued until the United Kingdom was split in two.

It is a testimony to the realism of the Israelite faith that tragedy like this could be written. Because the David story ascends the heights of human aspiration and plumbs the depths of human anguish, it has outlived the practical circumstances from which it came. In one sense, David was a victim of his own greatness, of an indomitable will that urged him to scale the tempting heights of power. Yet, in spite of his drive for success and national glory, he was never lacking in the magnanimity and charm that endeared him to friend and enemy alike. In a deeper sense, however, David was involved in the conflict with the God he sought to serve, the God with whose covenant law he had to reckon in the practical affairs of daily life. This, at any rate, is the testimony of the narrator who tells David's life-story. It is significant that tradition has ascribed to David the authorship of the great penitential psalm, Psalm 51, which is described as "a psalm of David, when Nathan the prophet came to him after he had gone to Bathsheba,"[16] If David was serious in his conviction that Yahweh, enthroned on the Ark, had entered triumphantly into the capital of the kingdom (see Ps. 24:7–10), he had to be ready to hear the word of Yahweh spoken by a

---

[16] Some psalms may have been composed by David, but it is generally agreed that he was not the author of the whole Psalter. (See further Chapter 16.)

prophet, the word that brought David's power under judgment. Faith in Yahweh's kingly rule prevented Israel from following the ancient Near Eastern practice of making the royal power absolute and—as in Egypt—of deifying the king.

The Ideal King

In time, David's weaknesses were forgotten and his greatness was extolled, just as tradition has idealized such figures of American history as Washington, Lincoln, and Lee. Israel's historians believed that David, more than any other king, typified the ideal combination of power and goodness. He was remembered as "Yahweh's servant," the God-fearing king who "executed justice and righteousness unto all his people" (II Sam. 8:15).

According to an important passage which we have touched on previously (II Sam. 7), the special relationship between Yahweh and David was extended to the whole dynasty of David. David asked the prophet Nathan for divine approval of his plan to build Yahweh a house of cedar, a temple comparable in glory to his own palace. But Yahweh refused David's request, promising instead to make David a "house" (a dynasty) and to establish the throne of his kingdom *forever*, in perpetuity (verses 11b–13). The Davidic king, according to Nathan's oracle, would be elected to the special relationship of Son of God (verse 14a; see Ps. 2:7). Furthermore, Yahweh promised that, although chastening divine judgment would fall upon individual kings for their failures in office, Yahweh's *ḥesed* or covenant loyalty would not be withdrawn from the Davidic house (verses 14b–16). Although II Samuel 7 is colored by the language and interests of the Deuteronomistic historian, undoubtedly the core of the chapter—especially the unit in verses 11b–16, which has its own formal introduction and conclusion—preserves a tradition of royal covenant theology which goes back to the early Jerusalem court.

> Yahweh announces to you that Yahweh will make a "house" for you:
>
> When your days are completed and you rest with your ancestors,
>   I will raise up after you your offspring, who will
>   issue from your body, and I will stabilize his kingdom.
>
> He shall build a "house" for my name,
>   and I will establish his royal throne in perpetuity.
> I will be Father to him, and he will be Son to me.
>
> When he does wrong, I will chasten him with the rod
>   of human punishment,
>   and with the stripes of human justice,
> but my loyalty [*ḥesed*] I will not withdraw from him,
>   as I did in the case of Saul, whom I removed before you.
>
> Before me your house and your kingdom will stand secure
>   perpetually,
>   your throne will be established in perpetuity.
>   —II SAMUEL 7:11b–16

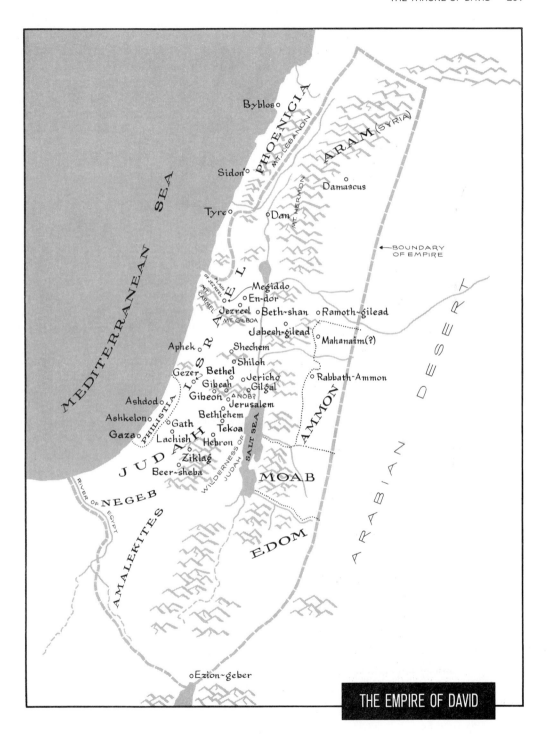

MEDITERRANEAN SEA

Byblos o

PHOENICIA

MT. LEBANON

ARAM (SYRIA)

Sidon o

Damascus o

Tyre o

Dan o

MT. HERMON

← BOUNDARY OF EMPIRE

PLAIN OF JEZREEL

MT. CARMEL

Megiddo

En-dor

Jezreel o Beth-shan o   Ramoth-gilead o

MT. GILBOA

Jabesh-gilead o

ISRAEL

Mahanaim (?) o

Aphek o   Shechem o

Shiloh o

Gezer o Bethel o

Jericho o   Gilgal o   Rabbath-Ammon o

Gibeah o

Gibeon o o NOB?

Ashdod o   Jerusalem o

Ashkelon o   Bethlehem o

PHILISTIA

Gath o   Tekoa o

AMMON

Gaza o   Lachish o Hebron o

Ziklag o

JUDAH

SALT SEA

WILDERNESS OF JUDAH

Beer-sheba o

MOAB

RIVER OF EGYPT

NEGEB

AMALEKITES

ARABIAN DESERT

EDOM

o Ezion-geber

THE EMPIRE OF DAVID

This theological circle believed that Yahweh made a solemn oath to David *unconditionally*, thereby assuring a social stability that could not be disturbed by the excesses of human freedom or the civil revolution that often erupted at the death or assassination of a king. This view of Yahweh's everlasting covenant (*berîth 'ôlām*) is brought out in II Samuel 23:1-7, the so-called "Last Words of David"—a passage which is so old in both style and content that it was either composed by David himself or by one of his court circle.[17] David says:

> Indeed, my house stands firm before God (*'El*);
>> for he has made a perpetual covenant (*berîth 'ôlām*) with me,
>> its terms duly stipulated and secured.
>
> —II SAMUEL 23:5

Earlier we noticed that the Mosaic covenant was influenced by the form of the suzerainty treaty (see pp. 98-101, 147-149). The Davidic covenant model was also influenced by Canaanite and other Near Eastern conceptions, in this case the institutions of kingship and temple. In the ancient world the king was regarded as a sacral person, the representative or "son" of God through whom the blessings of the divine order were mediated to society. And the temple was regarded as founded at the center or "navel" of the world, the meeting place of heaven and earth where creation is annually renewed in the mythical victory over the powers of chaos. Thus the king was a temple-builder, and the temple was a royal sanctuary where the king performed a cultic role. However, in the Davidic covenant model these views were modified by the announcement that at a definite stage in Israel's history Yahweh designated the Davidic king to be "the Anointed One" (messiah) and the temple of Zion to be the divine meeting place (see Psalm 132). Monarchy was not traced back to primordial times, "when kingship was lowered from heaven," as in the ancient Sumerian king list,[18] but it began providentially in the time of Saul and David. And the temple of Jerusalem was not a sacred center from time immemorial; it became Yahweh's dwelling place in the time of Solomon.[19] Therefore a Judean interpreter in Psalm 78 declares that Yahweh had done something new in the time of David. The Mosaic covenant, which he identifies with the northern tribes, had ended in failure

---

[17] Gerhard von Rad, *Theology*, I [142], 310-14, maintains that the motif of the "everlasting covenant" found in the "Last Words of David" is actually very ancient and prepares the way for II Sam. 7. On this matter, see especially Frank M. Cross, "The Ideologies of Kingship in the Era of the Empire" [112], 219-65. He argues that at first the Davidic covenant was "a covenant granted by divine initiative and conditional upon divinely imposed stipulations" and therefore was in line with the conditional (suzerainty) covenant of the Tribal Confederation. Under Solomon's "Canaanizing despotism," however, it evolved into the unconditional covenant that became "the standard Judean ideology." Other scholars maintain that David himself, relying on older covenant conceptions associated with Hebron, advocated an unconditional covenant. See Murray Newman, *The People of the Covenant* [231], chaps. 5 and 6; Ronald Clements, *Abraham and David* [293].

[18]Pritchard, *Ancient Near Eastern Texts* [1], p. 265. On the theology of kingship in the ancient Near East, see Aubrey Johnson, *Sacral Kingship in Ancient Israel* [442].

[19]For a discussion of the new "Zion theology," see Bennie C. Ollenburger, *Zion, The City of the Great King* [352]; Jon D. Levenson, *Sinai and Zion* [140], pp. 89-194.

owing to the people's rebellious betrayal of their Suzerain. According to this southern (Davidic) view, Yahweh rejected the northern history of failure and made a new beginning by choosing Mount Zion to be the central sanctuary (verses 67–69) and by elevating "David his servant," from a shepherd of flocks to be the shepherd of the people Israel (verses 70–72).

DEFINITION: "MESSIAH"

The familiar term "messiah" (Hebrew *mashiah*, Greek *christos*, English Christ), literally means "Anointed," reflecting the ancient practice of anointing, and thereby consecrating, a person for a particular office, such as prophet (I Kings 19:16; cf. Isa. 61:1), priest (Exod. 28:41; 29:7), or king (Judg. 9:15 in Jotham's fable).

Anointment of a person to be a monarch was an important moment in the coronation ceremony, sometimes carried out by a prophet (I Sam. 10:1; I Kings 19:16), and at other times by priests (I Kings 1:39; II Kings 11:12). The anointment made the monarch a "sacred" person *ex officio*, that is, the royal office conferred upon him a special relationship with God. This explains why David, who had an opportunity to kill Saul at one point, refused to stretch his hand against him, "seeing that he is Yahweh's anointed [*mashiah*]" (I Sam. 24:6, 10).

In the Old Testament the term messiah, or *mashiah*, when used in royal contexts, always refers to the reigning king, who was regarded as ruling as God's representative in the earthly kingdom. In later literature, beyond the boundaries of the Old Testament, the term took on the meaning of the king *par excellence* who would come in God's future to establish God's kingdom on earth. It is in this sense that the corresponding Greek term, "the Christ" (*ho christos*), is used in the New Testament (e.g. Mark 8:29).

The bitter political experiences of Israel after David's death gave rise to the hope that a Messiah ("Anointed One") would come, who would be of David's lineage, who would reunite the tribes of Israel, and who would restore Jerusalem to a position of prestige among the nations (see Isa. 9 and 11). In times of national calamity people prayed ardently to God to remember the covenant with David and to restore the kingdom of Israel. Psalm 89, for instance, is a poignant petition to God to look upon the distress of the people and, in divine mercy and power, to fulfill the promise once made to David by the prophet Nathan. When everything seemed lost, the people looked back to the glorious rule of David as the foreshadowing pattern of God's future kingdom on earth. Indeed, the whole conception of the kingdom of God, which plays such a large part in the Old and New Testaments, is profoundly influenced by the new impetus given to theological reflection by Israel's having become a nation under David. Just as Israel's covenant faith found new expression within the Tribal Confederacy, so it found new expression again within the radically different conditions of the monarchy. Hence the theological importance of the kingdom, the city of David, the Davidic dynasty, the Temple, and the covenant with David increased.

We must emphasize, however, that this fateful step in Israel's pilgrimage was resisted by the conservatives, who feared that the transition from confederacy to monarchy would corrupt the people of Yahweh by making Israel "like the nations." This prophetic reaction is voiced by Nathan in II Samuel 7:1–7, and is probably an authentic tradition even though the chapter, in its present form, comes from a late literary source which is concerned primarily with the continuance of the Judean, Davidic dynasty. David succeeded in transferring the traditions of the Confederacy to Jerusalem: the Ark, the Tabernacle, the priesthood. But in this change something happened to the character of "Israel," to the structure of the community. No longer was Israel, the people of God, bound together on the basis of *covenant allegiance* to Yahweh at the central sanctuary; Israel was now bound together *politically*, on the basis of a contract between king and people (II Sam. 5:3). As citizens of the state, the people of Israel owed allegiance to a king who could take a census, exact forced labor, and require submission to his power. Throughout the history of the monarchy there was a deep-seated conflict between these two conceptions of "Israel." As Israel became a state modeled after other Near Eastern monarchies, more and more it lost its distinctive character and faced the danger of being swallowed up in the power struggle and cultural stream of the ancient world.

SOLOMON IN ALL HIS GLORY

The familiar words of Jesus, "Even Solomon in all his glory was not arrayed like one of these," referring to the natural beauty of the lilies of the field (Matt. 6:29), show how the name of Solomon came to be the symbol of the wealth and glory of empire. No other king of Israel, not even David himself, ascended a higher pinnacle of worldly splendor. Solomon's vast building program, his fabulous wealth and large harem, his far-flung commercial enterprises, his up-to-date military program, his patronage of wisdom and the arts, all were admired with open-eyed wonder by his subjects and by visitors from afar like the Queen of Sheba.

An octogenarian of the time who had spent his or her early life amid the rustic simplicities of the last days of the judges must have marveled at the swift changes that had taken place during one lifetime. In the brief span of fifty or sixty years, Israel had risen from political obscurity to the rank of a small empire that could command the political attention and economic envy of nations roundabout. Much of the credit was due, as we have seen, to the leadership of David. Although Solomon, unlike his father, was not a military man, by political shrewdness and international diplomacy he was able to execute and stabilize the policies that David had initiated. To be sure, before his death the empire established by David had begun to slip out of control as a result of the revolt of Edom and Syria (I Kings 11:15–25); but during most of his reign peace prevailed.

Solomon's achievements were favored by the political situation of his day. Egypt continued to be politically feeble; Assyria was not to be a threat for almost a century; and other small nations were either kept in military subjugation or bound to Israel by commercial treaty. The outstanding figure on the political horizon was Hiram I, King of Tyre, under whose leadership the Phoenicians (one of the Canaanite peoples) established a vast colonial empire throughout the Mediterranean world. David had entered into alliance with Hiram; and Solomon, because he had military control of the land highways, could easily continue the policy of cooperation. Thus the stage was set for a period of dazzling material prosperity.

The Historian's Slant

The Court History of David concludes in I Kings 1–2 with an account of the intrigues that brought Solomon to power, rather than Adonijah, his half-brother, who was first in the line of succession. Solomon's claim to leadership was not based on charisma, as had been the case with Saul and even with David, but solely on his birth and the political influence of his supporters. By removing from the picture any possible contender to the throne, "the kingdom was established in the hand of Solomon" (I Kings 2:46). This was the royal road to power that kings of the ancient world frequently traveled, and in this respect Israel had indeed become "like the nations." Henceforth Israel's charismatic leadership was to be vested in a special class of people known as prophets (see Chapter 8). Later on, people wistfully looked to the messianic age of the future when the "spirit of Yahweh" would rest once again upon the king, as it had upon David (see Isa. 11:1–2).

The Davidic Court History ends abruptly at the conclusion of I Kings 2, and we must depend upon the material in chapters 3–11 for our knowledge of Solomon's reign. Evidently this historical information was extracted from a royal document no longer extant, one which is referred to in I Kings 11:41 as "the book of the acts of Solomon." In its present form, however, the account betrays the viewpoint of the Deuteronomistic History (see Chapter 11, and Definition, p. 183). Often the language is in the same style and shows the same thought as Deuteronomistic sections of Joshua, Judges, and Samuel, especially II Samuel 7 (see, for instance, I Kings 3:3–14; 5:3–5; 6:11–13; 8:14–61; 9:1–9; 11:1–13). The Deuteronomistic historians who composed this comprehensive history wanted to emphasize their central theological teachings; hence, they extracted from the royal annals whatever served their purpose and added interpretive passages.

The convictions of the Deuteronomists stand out rather clearly. For one thing, these historians adhered to the view that the true worship of Yahweh must be centralized in the Temple of Jerusalem, not in the outlying "high places." As a result, they glossed over or neglected many of Solomon's acts, and concentrated attention on the building of the Temple. Moreover, they wrote with the conviction that the Davidic line was the only legitimate one, for Yahweh had promised David that he would build him a "house" (I Sam. 7). So the editors did not hesitate to touch up the portrait of Solomon, the famous temple-builder. They apologized for Solomon by saying that at first he had to worship in "high places" because no temple had yet been built (I Kings 3:1ff.). But in the same breath it was stated that "Solomon loved Yahweh, walking in the statutes of David, his father," although this judgment is later qualified (I Kings 11:4–6). In later narratives of the books of Kings the historians affirmed that Yahweh was gracious to the kings of the Davidic dynasty "for David's sake." And finally, they looked back wistfully to the time before the sinful secession of the northern tribes when the people were united and strong. With a nostalgia for the glorious past, they remembered the time when Solomon ruled over all the kingdoms from the Euphrates River to the very border of Egypt, doubtless comparing that ideal situation with the unhappy state of affairs at the time of writing. Right in the midst of a passage that describes an oppressive policy of Solomon, we read: "Judah and Israel were as many as the sand by the sea; they ate and drank and were happy" (I Kings 4:20–21)! With some exaggeration, the boast is made that "Solomon excelled all the kings of the earth in riches and wisdom."

But this is a view of Solomon's reign seen through rose-colored glasses. As a matter of fact, the portraits of David and Solomon—father and son—present a study in contrasts. David came to the throne the hard way—up from the shepherd's field and the warrior's rough life. His greatness was that he never rose so high as to be cut off from the common soil and from the traditions of the Tribal Confederacy that had nourished him in his youth. Solomon, on the other hand, was "born to the purple," and never knew anything but the sheltered, extravagant life of a king's palace. From first to last he ruled with absolute power, caring little about the sanctities and social institutions of the former Confederacy. The legendary story in I Kings 3:3–15 describes him at the outset of his career as choosing God's gift of an understanding heart to judge (that is, to rule) his people, rather than riches and honor. But the actual facts of his administration show that he lacked the common touch that would have turned this pious dream into reality. Ambitious and selfish by nature, his lavish court in Jerusalem was a hall of mirrors that reflected the glory and reputation of the great king of Israel. The law in Deuteronomy 17:14–20, which specifies that an Israelite king shall not rule autonomously but shall be guided by the Torah of Yahweh, must have been composed with Solomon in mind.

A Program of Building and Expansion

Thanks to the favorable international situation, Solomon was able to concentrate on an ambitious twenty-year building program. Because the historians regarded the building of the Temple as the most important enterprise in this program, they gave a proportionately large amount of space to a description of its erection, design, and furnishings (I Kings 5–7). It was located on a ridge above (north of) the site of the old city, on ground that David had purchased for an altar (II Sam. 24:18–25)—probably the very spot marked by the sacred rock which today is enclosed by the Mosque of Omar, otherwise known as the Dome of the Rock.[20] (See Color Plate 4.) Compared with a modern cathedral, it was modest in size (about 90 × 30 × 45 feet), but for its time it was a great architectural achievement. It was appropriately consecrated as the central sanctuary by bringing the Ark of the Covenant from Zion, David's old city, and by an elaborate ceremony in which Solomon himself officiated, even to the offering of a magnificent prayer which is cast in the Deuteronomistic language of a much later time (I Kings 8:22–53)![21] The Ark, however, was one of the few points of contact with Israel's Mosaic heritage. By contrast, the Temple—designed by Phoenician (that is, Canaanite) architects—represented the invasion of Canaanite culture right into the center of Israel's life and worship.[22] Conservative Israelites who cherished the ancestral faith must have been shocked by Solomon's bold imitation of foreign ways. It took some years for the Temple, which was essentially a state sanctuary, to become the focus of Israelite affection, as in many of the Psalms (e.g. Pss. 120–134). Indeed, in the history of Israelite worship as many as a dozen Israelite temples were in use at different times.[23]

Actually, the building of the Jerusalem temple was overshadowed by other phases of Solomon's building program. Seven years were spent building the Temple, but thirteen years were devoted to the construction of his palace complex, consisting of government buildings, the king's house (about 150 × 75 × 45 feet), and the house of his Egyptian queen. Moreover, outside Jerusalem Solomon built "chariot cities" and other fortifications at Gezer, Megiddo, Hazor, and elsewhere (I Kings 9:15–19). A large fleet of horse-drawn chariots enabled him to protect his land and to control the trade routes over which wealth poured into his kingdom from Phoenicia, Egypt, Arabia, and other parts of the world (I Kings 4:26; 9:10; 10:26). Solomon's traders purchased chariots from Egypt and ranged far up into Cilicia (Kue), located in old Hittite country, to import horses. Solomon was, indeed, such a clever "horse dealer" that his agents exported horses and chariots to other nations at a handsome profit (I Kings 10:28–29).

---

[20] For a discussion of the location, see R. de Vaux, *Ancient Israel* [113], pp. 318–19.

[21] To the Deuteronomistic school of theologians, the idea of Yahweh dwelling in a temple was too limiting (I Kings 8:27). They overcame this difficulty by saying that Yahweh, who is transcendent and cannot be contained in even the highest heavens, causes the divine "name" (Yahweh's *alter ego*) to dwell in the temple (verses 28ff.).

[22] On the Canaanite architecture of the Temple see G. E. Wright, "Solomon's Temple Resurrected," *The Biblical Archaeologist*, IV (1941), 17–31; W. F. Albright, *Archaeology and the Religion of Israel* [111], pp. 142–55. De Vaux (*Ancient Israel* [113], pp. 312–30) discusses fully the structure, furnishings, history, and theology of the Jerusalem Temple.

[23] See Menahem Haran, *Temples and Temple Services* [397], chap. II. He observes (pp. 37f.) that uncertainty surrounds the identification of a structure at Arad, a site southeast of Beer-sheba, as a temple. It has been claimed that this temple, the only Israelite temple brought to light by archaeology, was built in the tenth century and enlarged in the ninth. See Yohanan Aharoni, "The Israelite Sanctuary at Arad," *New Directions in Biblical Archaeology* [103], 25–39.

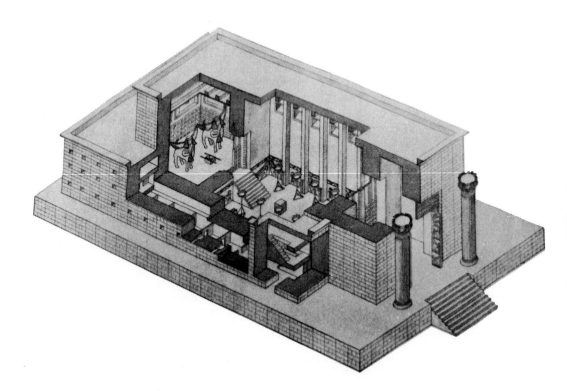

An excellent example of Solomon's far-flung commercial enterprises was his construction of a "fleet of ships" at Ezion-geber on the Gulf of Aqabah, an arm of water extending northward from the Red Sea (I Kings 9:26–28; 10:22). In cooperation with Hiram, King of Tyre, these ships were navigated to distant ports, thus giving Solomon what Palestine lacked most of all: a seaport. The Phoenicians, a seafaring people who were ancestors of the later Carthaginians, had already been exploiting the commercial opportunities of the Mediterranean world. Solomon's league with Hiram brought wealth into Palestine through Phoenician ports (see I Kings 10:22) and enabled him to take advantage of Phoenician maritime skill in exploiting the area of the Red Sea and Indian Ocean.

The building of the seaport at Ezion-geber was in itself a major political achievement.[24] It may be that the real purpose of the Queen of Sheba's long trip from southern Arabia to visit Solomon (I Kings 10:1–13) was to negotiate a commercial treaty with the king, who was cutting into the prosperous camel-caravan trade of Arabia. If that was her aim, when she "told him all that was on her mind" the conversation must have come around to economic relations between the two countries. Evidently her diplomacy was not in vain, for "King Solomon gave to the Queen of Sheba all that she desired" (I Kings 10:1–13). It is interesting to note that the rulers of Ethiopia traditionally have claimed direct descent from Solomon through the Queen of Sheba.

[24] Ezion-geber (Tell el-Kheleifeh) was excavated under the direction of Nelson Glueck in 1938–40. See his book, *The Other Side of the Jordan* (New Haven: American Schools of Oriental Research, 1940), chaps. 3 and 4. Glueck has retracted his earlier interpretation of the ruins as a copper refinery. See his discussion in *The Biblical Archaeologist*, XXVIII (1965), 70–87.

Solomon's Temple (upper left): a reconstruction showing the two massive, free-standing pillars flanking the ornamental east door. The Temple was originally built according to Phoenician architectural patterns. In front of the Temple was a courtyard, within which was placed the altar of burnt offering.

The interior of the Temple (lower left): a cutaway drawing by Edward S. Winters. (Since the drawing is isometric, the perspective is slightly distorted.)

The congregation worshiped in the court outside, near the high altar of sacrifice. Like other temples of the Syro-Phoenician region, this one was divided into three parts: the Ulam (vestibule), the Hekal (sanctuary), and the Debir (cella or inner shrine).

The priest first ascended the ten steps of the Temple, passed through the huge cypress doors guarded by two elaborately adorned bronze pillars, known as Jachin and Boaz, and entered the vestibule. He then passed through another pair of cypress doors into the main sanctuary, about 60 feet long, which contained the sacred furniture: the seven-branched golden candlesticks, the table of showbread, and a small altar. This huge room, 45 feet high, was paneled with cedar and floored with cypress. Its flat roof was supported by huge cedar beams, and the room itself was dimly lit by latticed windows on either side, just below the ceiling. On the wall panels were carvings of palm trees, flowers, chain work, and cherubim.

Just beyond the small cedar altar, which was situated in the center of the main sanctuary and decorated with gold leaf, another series of stairs led up to a raised room, a perfect cube 30 feet square, access to which was gained through a small double door. This was the Holy of Holies. It was lined with cedar and, having no windows, was pitch dark. In it were the two large cherubim, made of olive wood decorated with gold leaf, standing about 15 feet high. Beneath their outstretched wings stook the Ark of the Covenant, which was regarded as Yahweh's throne. (The above description is based on an article by G. E. Wright, "Solomon's Temple Resurrected," in The Biblical Archaeologist, IV [1941]. See also Roland de Vaux, Ancient Israel [113], Part IV, chap. 3).

Rumblings of Discontent

Had anyone withdrawn from this brilliant spectacle, however, he or she would have heard the rumblings of an approaching storm. Like the great pharaohs of Egypt, Solomon carried out his program of expansion by means of harsh measures of exploitation. To pay for his tremendous overhead, he divided his kingdom into twelve tax districts, each with an officer in charge (I Kings 4:7–19). One of the duties of these governors was to see that the royal larder was amply provided (I Kings 4:22–28). Historians have argued convincingly that the real purpose behind this administrative reorganization was to centralize power in the crown by replacing the old tribal system with twelve fiscal districts, under the supervision of royal appointees—two of them sons-in-law of Solomon.[25] The boundaries of about half the tribal territories were deliberately changed. No move could have been better designed to destroy the last remnants of tribal independence. In this respect, Solomon abandoned the administrative policy of his father, David, who respected the tribal divisions and the tribal representatives.

Equally oppressive was Solomon's program of forced labor. Although much of the slave labor for his building projects was drawn from conquered peoples, Solomon also brought the lash down heavily upon his own people. We are told that some 30,000 Israelites were conscripted and sent off to the labor camps in Lebanon one month out of every three (I Kings 5:13–18). It has been estimated that this number would be comparable to a draft of 5,000,000 Americans during the mid-40's! They felled the great cedars of Lebanon, floated them down the Phoenician coast to Joppa, and thence hauled them over the hills to Jerusalem. Eighty thousand Israelites were reported to have been put to work in the stone quarries, and 70,000 toiled as burden-bearers. Thus the great Temple was completed at a cost far greater than the financial outlay—the cost of the life and liberty of exploited people. The ominous warning of Samuel had a ring of reality: if the people wanted a king like the surrounding nations to rule over them, they must reckon with the danger that the monarch's power would drastically limit their liberties, secularize their outlook, and undermine the very foundations of the covenant community.

It is no wonder, then, that the pent-up resentment of the people eventually exploded into revolution. The leader of the revolt was a man whom Solomon had appointed as an officer over one of the work gangs: a certain Jeroboam, son of Nebat, from Ephraim, one of the northern tribes. We have seen that even during David's reign the northern tribes, formerly under the crown of Saul, had attempted to secede from the united monarchy. Solomon's oppressive policies did nothing to eliminate this restiveness, and his death provided the spark that touched off the powder keg (see Chronological Chart 3, p. 258). Moreover, just as it was a prophet, Nathan, who had led the court intrigue that placed Solomon

---

[25] See R. de Vaux, *Ancient Israel* [113], pp. 133–35, who points out that Judah, the tribal area from which David had become king, was not incorporated into this system but had an administration of its own. See further G. E. Wright, "The Provinces of Solomon," *Eretz Israel*, 8 (1967), 58–68.

on the throne, so it was a prophet, Ahijah, from the former confederate center of Shiloh, who announced that Yahweh would "rend the kingdom out of the hand of Solomon," leaving only the tribe of Judah under the rule of a Davidic descendant (I Kings 11:29–39). Israel was to relearn under prophetic teaching the lesson that had been impressed upon its memory in the period of Moses and Joshua: the inescapable judgment and mercy of God in the historical struggle. The God who had rescued a people from the bondage of Egypt was able to deliver them from the tyranny of a king whose pretensions to absolute power were hidden behind the glorious façade of a state religion. For Israel's faith, unlike other religions of antiquity, did not promote and sanction the harmony of the existing order; rather, it promoted social change by emphasizing the conflict between God's will and human ambitions, between the kingdom of God and the kingdom of Israel. The God of Israel was involved in the political events that shook the very foundations of the kingdom created by David and Solomon.

Solomon's Broadmindedness

"Yahweh was angry with Solomon" (I Kings 11:9; cf. 9:1–9). This is the testimony of the Deuteronomistic historians who pondered the meaning of Solomon's reign. Solomon's kingdom was weighed in the balance of God and found wanting. To be sure, these historians have been quite lenient in evaluating Solomon's reign. They attributed his defects to his dotage, for "when Solomon was old, his wives turned away his heart after other gods; and his heart was not perfect with Yahweh his God, as was the heart of David, his father" (I Kings 11:4). To them, Solomon's weakness was an excessive broadmindedness, most evident with respect to his harem. It should be said that Solomon's possession of "seven hundred wives and three hundred concubines" was not evidence of mere sensuality. Many of his marriages were for the purpose of establishing close political and cultural ties with surrounding peoples. Thus his marriage with Pharaoh's daughter was a diplomatic marriage that linked Israel and Egypt together as allies and brought to Solomon the city of Gezer as a wedding dowry (I Kings 3:1; 9:16). Since marriages of this type were motivated primarily by political considerations, Solomon was quite willing for his foreign wives to practice their native religions, and he went so far as to build them special shrines in his capital city. To the Deuteronomistic historians this was carrying tolerance too far, for Israel's king was giving sanction to an idolatrous policy that diluted and perverted Israel's faith.

This judgment need not have been limited to Solomon's old age, for the record indicates that his entire reign tended toward religious syncretism—that is, the amalgamation of alien elements with Israel's native tradition. These foreign influences brought radical changes in the character of Israel's life. The former simplicities of Israel's agricultural society were swept away in the wave of Solomonic prosperity, bringing to some people sudden riches and royal favor and to others abject poverty and royal slavery. Jerusalem, the capital of the kingdom, became a cosmopolitan city into which caravans came from all parts of the world bringing new ideas and practices along with coveted wealth. The Temple itself, designed by foreign artisans, was the chief symbol of "the new look." Although Solomon probably regarded himself as a loyal worshiper of Yahweh, his broadminded hospitality led him to appropriate elements of the Baal religion and combine them with his Mosaic heritage. For instance, the "sea" (symbolic of the primeval ocean), which was supported by twelve bulls (I Kings 7:23–26), reflects fertility and mythological motifs of the Fertile Crescent. Apparently the Temple was intended to be a replica of Yahweh's heavenly abode, a microcosm of the macrocosm, in line with the ancient mythical view that a correspondence exists between the earthly and heavenly spheres.[26]

Finally, in his "largeness of mind" Solomon moved beyond the confines of Israel's Mosaic tradition to pursue the cosmopolitan wisdom that was fashionable in foreign circles, such as the Egyptian court. Indeed, Solomon was regarded as the patron of Israel's wisdom movement, a movement which played an increasingly important role in Israelite life and thought, beginning with the monarchy and even before (see further the discussion in Chapter 17). There is probably a solid basis for crediting Solomon with an avid interest in wisdom.[27] He was a skillful diplomat in his negotiations with Hiram of Tyre (I Kings 5:12; cf. 5:7), and he showed wisdom in other areas as well. His great wisdom is traditionally illustrated by his decision in the case of the two women who claimed the same baby (I Kings 3:16–28). The story goes that Solomon proposed to settle the argument by cutting the baby in two with a sword, giving half to one woman and half to the other. At this point the real mother of the child offered to surrender the baby, and Solomon, with psychological understanding of a mother's love, rendered the verdict in her favor. This folktale, one of the finest in the wisdom tradition, is rounded off with a statement of the community's response to the king's act:

> And all Israel heard of the judgment which the king had rendered; and they stood in awe of the king, because they perceived that the wisdom of God was in him, to render justice.
>
> —I KINGS 3:28 (RSV)

Here we have an excellent example of a popular story that must have circulated orally for many years before the editors of Kings picked it up as evidence that Yahweh had bestowed the gift of wisdom upon Solomon in answer to his "Deuteronomistic" prayer (I Kings 3:3–14). The story is important for understanding the place of wisdom in ancient Israel. In our way of thinking, Solomon was a

---

[26] See R. E. Clements, *God and Temple* [437], chap. 5; also M. Eliade, *Cosmos and History* [120], pp. 6–20.

[27] The origin of wisdom with Solomon is defended by Albrecht Alt, "Die Weisheit Salomos," in his *Kleine Schriften*, II (Munich, 1953), 90–99. However, R. B. Y. Scott, in his article "Solomon and the Beginnings of Wisdom in Israel," *Wisdom in Israel and in the Ancient Near East* [464], 262–79, traces the origin of the Israelite movement to the time of King Hezekiah (c. 700 B.C.E.).

shrewd judge of character and knew how to use a little practical psychology when the need arose. But in Israel's view psychological insight did not come simply with maturity or as a result of keen observation of human behavior. Rather, it was believed that Yahweh bestowed wisdom upon the sage, just as Yahweh gave "teaching" (*torah*) to the priest or the "word" to the prophet (see Jer. 18:18).

The editors of Kings have preserved other information, less legendary in character, about Solomon's famed wisdom. One passage (I Kings 4:29–34) says that "Solomon's wisdom surpassed the wisdom of all the people of the east [that is, the bedouin Arabs], and all the wisdom of Egypt," as well as the wisdom of the sons of Mahol, who may have been Edomite sages.[28] People from all lands came to hear the wisdom of Solomon, for "he was wiser than all other men":

> He spoke of trees, from the cedar that is in Lebanon to the hyssop that grows out of the wall; he spoke also of beasts, and of birds, and of reptiles, and of fish.
> —I KINGS 4:33 (RSV)

Now this does not mean that Solomon was a biologist. Rather, the sage, by studying the behavior of what we would call "nature," was given insight into correct human behavior, for ancient peoples did not draw the sharp distinction that we do between nature and human nature. The sage sought to gain insight into the divine order of creation, upon which the wellbeing of all existence—animal and human—depends. Psalm 104, which has affinities with Akhnaton's exquisite "Hymn to the Aton" and which parallels the Priestly creation story (Gen. 1:1–2:3), is a testimony to the profound influence of wisdom upon Israel's worship of Yahweh as creator.[29]

NEW HORIZONS OF FAITH

We can see, then, that in the age of Solomon profound changes were taking place in every aspect of Israel's life: political, economic, social, intellectual. The emphasis upon wisdom was only one symptom of the new way of life, which in the judgment of one Old Testament theologian, was fundamentally a transition from the "sacral" view which prevailed in the days of the Tribal Confederacy to a "secular" outlook that gained ascendancy during Solomon's reign.[30] Perhaps the adjective "secular" is too strong, for it may suggest the seculari-

[28] W. F. Albright, however, regards the sons of Mahol as Canaanite sages; see *Archaeology and the Religion of Israel* [cited under 111], pp. 127–28.

[29] Akhnaton's hymn is found in Pritchard, *Ancient Near Eastern Texts* [1], pp. 369–70. For a discussion of Psalm 104 and creation theology, see B. W. Anderson, *Creation in the Old Testament* [129], pp. 11–14.

[30] See Gerhard von Rad, "The Beginnings of Historical Writing in Ancient Israel," *Essays* [166], 166–204; *idem*, "The Joseph Narrative and Ancient Wisdom," 292–300.

zation of the modern world which leaves no room for God. In any case, it was no longer possible, at least in the "enlightened" circles of the Solomonic era, to be completely satisfied with the ancient, naive portrayal of Yahweh intervening in, and taking part directly, in Israel's history by special appearances, signs, and wonders. Yahweh's presence, according to the new theology, was veiled in the ordinary course of human events, in which actions have consequences (a fundamental theme of wisdom literature).

We have already seen this subtler understanding of Yahweh's activity in the Succession Narrative, in which the divine purpose is disclosed in the chain of actions and consequences in the Davidic family. The same understanding is found in the Joseph story, which seems to have been shaped in wisdom circles. In that story, too, Yahweh does not intervene directly or become manifest openly; rather, the divine purpose becomes evident more subtly in the drama of human relations (see above, p. 177).

This is the case, too, with the story of Ruth. This charming short story, which the narrator has placed in the rural setting of the ancient Tribal Confederacy ("In the days when the judges ruled . . . "), tells how Ruth, a Moabitess, was providentially led from her home country to Bethlehem of Judah, where she married an influential citizen, Boaz, and became the great-grandmother of David, Israel's greatest king. In this story, we find "no angel visitant, no opening of the skies," to quote the words of a modern hymn ("Spirit of God, Descend Upon My Heart")—but a beautiful story of how God works through the *ḥesed* (loyalty) of two women, Ruth and her mother-in-law Naomi.[31] The story was probably composed later than the period of the United Kingdom, but it surely is consonant with the spirit of the age of Solomon.[32]

Israel as a Nation

The age of Solomon, then, must be regarded ambivalently. In one sense, it opened up more spacious horizons than Israel had ever seen before and showed how Yahweh's providence works in a hidden way through ordinary human experiences. On the other hand, it was another chapter in the conflict between faith and culture, between Yahweh and the gods—a conflict that can be traced throughout Israel's history as a nation in Canaan.

The Deuteronomistic historians, who have presented this history to us in its present form, leave no doubt about where they stand. It was not Yahweh's intention that Israel should become a great nation, as nations measure greatness; rather—as affirmed in Solomon's "Deuteronomistic" prayer (I Kings 8:51, 53)—Israel was to be separated from other nations by a covenantal allegiance.

---

[31] See Katherine Sakenfeld, *Faithfulness in Action* [143]. On *ḥesed*, see Definition, Chapter 9, p. 308).

[32] See E. C. Campbell, *Ruth* [305], who observes that God's activity in this story is "a lightly exercised providential control." He suggests that the story may have originated in the Solomonic period and may have been fixed in writing in the ninth century.

From the very first, Israel's covenant emphasized Yahweh's uncompromising, "jealous" demand for absolute allegiance. It was difficult, however, to maintain faithfulness to the Mosaic tradition in the cultural crosscurrents of Canaan, where the gods of the Fertile Crescent made an irresistible claim upon people's lives. Incited by political aspirations and commercial expansion, the tendency of popular religion was toward tolerance and compromise—the very attitudes that were encouraged during the reign of Solomon. Had not this pursuit of the devices and desires of the people's hearts been rebuked and arrested by the prophets, Israel's distinctive faith would have fallen into oblivion along with the religions of the Fertile Crescent. Influenced by the convictions of Israel's prophets, the Deuteronomistic historians insisted that the regime of Solomon stood under divine judgment. Yahweh acted to stir up the revolutionary ferment, even to the point of raising up adversaries against Solomon (I Kings 11:14, 23).

In the judgment of many scholars, another perspective on Israel's role as a nation has been set forth in the masterful prose epic of the "Yahwist" (J). We have already referred to this epic, as well as that of the "Elohist" (E), in our study of the all-Israelite epic that began to take shape in the period of the Judges (Chapter 5). For generations Israel's oral traditions had been taking form at the various tribal shrines, especially at the confederate sanctuary at Shiloh. These traditions came to express the faith and worship of the covenant community, no less than the legends of King Arthur mirror the age of chivalry. But just as the age of chivalry came to an end in the social changes that brought about the decline of feudalism, so Israel's age of song and legend was superseded by the new way of life in the monarchy. The time was ripe for the sacred heritage to be reinterpreted so as to express the new nationalism. There is good reason to believe that this new situation was met by the anonymous author known as the Yahwist, who produced a monumental *literary* and *theological* work in written form, based on the story of Israel's life inherited from the days of the Tribal Confederacy.[33]

This hypothesis helps us to understand why at the outset of the ancestral history Yahweh makes the promise to Abraham that he and his descendants will become a great "nation" (*goy*, Gen. 12:2; 18:18; cf. 17:6, 16). The conviction that Israel is the *people* of Yahweh and Yahweh the God of Israel was fundamental to the ancient tradition and, as we have seen, was expressed in song and story (as, for instance, in the Song of Deborah, Judg. 5). The Yahwist, however, understands Israel's existence as a *nation* in the context of an unfolding plan that embraces all nations. In Yahweh's worldwide purpose Israel's role is to bring divine blessing upon all the families of the earth—a role that is thrown into the foreground of attention by the stories of primeval history that precede the call of Abraham. Israel, therefore, is chosen for a purpose. Yahweh's promise to Abraham will yield benefits for all humankind.

---

[33] This is the view of Gerhard von Rad in his commentary on Genesis [271], pp. 13–31. See also Peter Ellis, *The Theology of the Yahwist* [265], and H. W. Wolff, "The Kerygma of the Yahwist," in *The Vitality of Old Testament Traditions* [63], chap. 3.

We can understand the circumstances that prompted this historical vision during the Yahwist's time. In the era of David and Solomon, Israel was breaking out of its parochial ways of thinking, and was welcoming influences from the farthest parts of the world. In the very time when Israel's distinctive faith was in danger of being drowned by the new cosmopolitanism, advocated especially by Solomon, an unknown writer reinterpreted the Mosaic tradition in such a way as to make it profoundly relevant to the larger world in which Israel was to fulfill its special task in the unfolding drama of history. The breadth of the Yahwist's historical vision was not surpassed until centuries later, when a prophetic poet of the Exile, echoing the Yahwist's epic, proclaimed that in Yahweh's providential plan Israel was to be a light to the nations (Isa. 40–55).

CHAPTER 8

Prophetic Troublers of Israel

Today the term "prophecy" suggests a variety of meanings. We speak of prophets of the weather, prophets of the news, prophets who champion a social cause. Even when there is some interest in "biblical prophecy," popular understanding is distorted by preachers who sometimes give the impression that the biblical prophet gazed into God's crystal ball and predicted the shape of things to come. All this is evidence that many of us are woefully ignorant of the role of the Old Testament prophets and fail to understand properly and appreciate fully the remarkable spiritual legacy that we have received from them.

In this chapter we shall take up Israel's life-story where we left it at the end of the preceding chapter, and consider the rise of the prophetic movement against the background of the stormy events that followed the death of Solomon. But first let us raise a basic question: what was the role of a prophet in ancient Israelite society?

We can get some idea of how the prophet's role was understood in ancient Israel by glancing at a couple of passages which deal with the relationship between Moses and Aaron (Exod. 4:14–16; 7:1–2). Here the language is used figuratively. Moses was to be, as it were, "God" to Aaron, and Aaron was to be Moses' *nabi'*. That is, Moses was to tell Aaron what to say, and Aaron was to speak on behalf of Moses to Pharaoh. On the basis of this analogy, it is clear

Biblical readings: I Kings 12 through II Kings 8, with special attention to the Elijah stories. The account is paralleled in II Chronicles 10–21.

DEFINITION: "PROPHET"

Studies of words are interesting but do not necessarily throw light on the actual function of a person designated by a particular word. Our English word "prophet" comes to us from the Greek word *prophētēs,* which literally means one who *speaks for* another, especially for a deity. The corresponding Hebrew term is *nabî',* which is apparently related to the Akkadian verb *nabû,* meaning "to call, to announce, to name."

There is some uncertainty, however, as to whether the Hebrew form has an active meaning ("one who calls, an announcer") or a passive meaning ("one who is called"). In the former case, the emphasis would be on the role of a prophet to proclaim a message; in the latter, the stress would be on the prophet's vocation to be a messenger in the service of the deity. Both views are relevant for understanding Israelite prophecy, but one would have to turn to particular biblical texts to see how prophets actually function in different situations. In any case, the term refers to one who communicates the divine will. The prophet is an intermediary, a spokesperson—one who acts and speaks on behalf of Another.

---

that prophets were regarded as persons through whom God speaks to the people. Called to be God's spokespersons, they received the promise that God's "words" would be put in their mouths (see Jer. 1:9).

A clearer understanding of the role of a prophet may be obtained by considering the language used in communicating the divine will. Studies of the forms of prophetic speech have shown that prophets, Israelite and non-Israelite, often employed a "messenger style," which was well known in the ancient world.[1] For instance, when Jacob was returning to his homeland he bridged the distance between himself and his brother Esau by dispatching messengers.

> And Jacob sent messengers before him . . . instructing them,
> "Thus you shall say to my lord Esau:
> Thus says your servant Jacob, 'I have sojourned. . . . ' "
> —GENESIS 32:3–4

It is striking that almost the same language is used in prophetic oracles. The prophets understood themselves to be *sent.* They had received Yahweh's commission, "Go and say to my people." Moreover, a prophetic message often begins with the formula "Thus says Yahweh" and concludes with "the oracle of Yahweh" or "says Yahweh" (e.g., Amos 1:3–5; Jer. 2:1–3; Isa. 45:11–13). All of this indicates that the prophets thought of themselves as *messengers* sent to communicate "the word of Yahweh" to the people.[2] Their authority lay not in

---

[1] This is discussed by Claus Westermann in his analysis of the basic forms of prophetic speech [327], pp. 70–91. See also James F. Ross, "The Prophet as Yahweh's Messenger" [cited under 324].

[2] Martin Noth in his essay, "History and the Word of God in the Old Testament," [321], discusses parallels to the prophetic messenger speech in texts from Mari (pp. 183ff.). For example, in a dream the god Dagon says to a man: "Now go! I am sending you to Zimri-lim [the king of Mari] and you yourself shall say to him: 'Send your messengers to me . . . ' "

themselves—in their religious experience or in their opinions—but in the One who had sent them. Accordingly their message rang with an authority which could shake nations: "Thus says Yahweh!"

The purpose of God's speaking through a prophet was not to communicate information about a timetable of events for the distant future. To be sure, the prophets often made predictions, in the conviction that Yahweh was shaping the course of events leading from the present into the future. But these predictions, some of which came true and some of which did not, had reference to the immediate future, which impinged on the present. Just as a doctor's prediction that a patient has only a short time to live makes the patient's present moments more precious and serious, so the prophetic announcement of what God was about to do accented the urgency of the present. The prophets were primarily concerned with the present. Their task was to communicate God's message for *now*, and to summon the people to respond *today*.[3]

In the course of Israel's history there arose great prophets whose perception of God's "word" was deeper and more refined than that of many prophets whose names and oracles have not survived. Let us consider first, however, the origins of prophecy. In a broad sense, Israelite prophecy arose in connection with God's revelation in the Exodus; for, as we have seen (pp. 55–60), God not only delivered a band of slaves from servitude but also raised up a leader to proclaim the meaning of that historical experience. Moses, then, can be properly called a prophet (see Deut. 18:18; Hos. 12:13). Also, as we have noticed previously, the term "prophetess" (*nebî'ā*) was used to describe the leadership of two women: Miriam (Exod. 15:20) and Deborah (Judg. 4:4). In the time of Samuel, however, the word *nabî'* was applied to a special class of people in Israelite society. The prophets of that day were the immediate forerunners of the great prophets, of whom Elijah came to be regarded as the representative *par excellence*.

THE BACKGROUND OF PROPHECY

We first hear of this company of prophets in connection with the Philistines' attempt to overrun the territory of Israel (I Sam. 10:5–13). It was a time of great crisis, when the very existence of Israel hung in the balance. Shiloh, the confederate sanctuary, had been destroyed and the people were in despair. Samuel, the last judge of the Tribal Confederacy, attempted to rally the people to a militant devotion to Yahweh, as Deborah had done at the battle of Megiddo. He was supported by a band of prophets who evidently had been carrying on their prophetic activities for some time, for their presence in Israel seems to be taken for granted. After Samuel anointed Saul as leader over Israel, he enumerated the various "signs" that would show Yahweh's confirmation of his choice. One

---

[3] See Abraham J. Heschel, *The Prophets* [315], especially chap. 1.

of them was that Saul would come to the "hill of God" (that is, a religious "high place") near to a Philistine outpost.

> And as you come to the city you will meet a band of prophets coming down from the high place, with harp, tambourine, flute and lyre in their lead, and they will be prophesying [ecstatically]. Then the spirit of Yahweh will overpower you; you will prophesy [ecstatically] with them and be changed into another person.
>
> —I SAMUEL 10:5b–6

Spirit Possession

The Hebrew word that is here translated as "prophesy" has a stronger meaning than we give to that word. It means "to behave like a prophet, to prophesy ecstatically." Usually we use the word "ecstasy" to describe an experience of being overcome with an emotion so powerful that self-control or reason may be suspended.[4] In this case, however, the ecstasy arises not from mere emotional rapture but from the spirit (*rúaḥ*) of Yahweh which falls upon a person, takes control of the center of the self, and makes one an instrument of the divine will. No wonder Samuel promised that Saul would be turned into "another person": no longer would he be just Saul the son of Kish, but Saul *possessed* by Yahweh's spirit! In such a prophetic state unusual things happened, as we learn in another story which tells how Saul, again seized by prophetic ecstasy, stripped off his clothes and lay naked in a stunned condition all day and all night (I Sam. 19:19–24). These phenomena seem to correspond to prophetic behavior known in other cultures in which individuals acted in stereotyped ways so that observers would recognize that they were possessed by the divine spirit.[5]

Since the stories from I Samuel presuppose that ecstatic prophecy was already in full swing in Israel during the days of the early monarchy, we must look further back to find the origins of this movement. In Numbers 11:24–29 there is a curious story about how the spirit of Moses was transferred to the elders of Israel, causing them to prophesy ecstatically (the same verb as above is used). It is doubtful, however, whether this is an authentic episode from the Mosaic period. In the judgment of many scholars, this is another anachronism, that is, the storyteller's description of the Mosaic period in terms of the language and experience of a later time. Most likely, Israel first became acquainted with ecstatic prophecy in Canaan, where it was connected with Baal religion. The Egyptian story of Wen Amon (from the eleventh century B.C.E.) tells of a religious festival in the Phoenician port of Byblos where "the god seized one of

---

[4] The word comes from a Greek compound "to set or stand out," thus "to put out of place, derange, to be beside oneself."

[5] See the important essay by Robert R. Wilson, "Prophecy and Ecstasy: A Reexamination," *Journal of Biblical Literature* 98 (1979), 321–37. He argues that "at least some Israelite possession behavior did in fact follow patterns similar to those found in the possession behavior of modern prophets."

[the] youths and made him possessed"—that is, he fell into an ecstatic state.[6] Centuries later, prophets of Baal, imported from Phoenicia, worked themselves into an ecstatic frenzy on the top of Mount Carmel as they danced around the altar, cut themselves with knives, and raised their cultic shouts (I Kings 18:20–29). This type of orgiastic prophecy was also known in Asia Minor, from which it spread into the Mediterranean world and later took the form of the orgies of the cult of Dionysus.

Probably, then, Israel borrowed ecstatic prophecy from the Canaanite environment, as it did so much else. But in this case, too, what was borrowed was transformed. To be sure, there are certain external similarities between the Baal prophets, like those on Mount Carmel (I Kings 18), and the Israelite prophets of the early monarchy. Israel's prophets also went around in companies, delivering oracles when some inquirer sought a decision from God. Stimulated by the rhythm of music and bodily movements, the contagion of the prophetic ecstasy could carry away a person who fell in among them. According to an interesting passage in II Kings 3:15, Elisha, when asked for a word from Yahweh, first summoned a musician, "and when the minstrel played, the spirit of Yahweh came upon him." Under the influence of the divine spirit, the body was sometimes stimulated to hyperactivity, as in the case of Elijah, who ran before the king's chariot with superhuman energy (I Kings 18:46). But these are superficial similarities. The real difference between Israel's prophets and the prophets of Canaanite society was that the former were spokespersons of Yahweh who interpreted the promises and demands of the covenant.

Many of these early prophets belonged to guilds or schools, which were known as "the sons of the prophets." They lived together in communities, where they were under the leadership of a chief prophet who was apparently known as their "father" (II Kings 4:1). We catch brief glimpses of Elijah and Elisha, for instance, as leaders of prophetic communities at Bethel, Jericho, and Gilgal (II Kings 2:3, 4; 4:38). These guilds were not tied permanently to any one place but were free to travel around and deliver oracles as the occasion demanded. Apparently women were not excluded from these prophetic communities, to judge from the interesting story found in II Kings 4:1–7.

Cultic Prophets

In addition to these roving bands of ecstatics there were other prophets who were more closely tied to the great sanctuaries of Israel. Various studies have shown that sanctuaries like those at Bethel or Jerusalem had on their staff priests and prophets who served side by side in a joint ministry.[7] The "cultic prophets," as they have been called, had a special part in the services of worship.

---

[6] See Pritchard, *Ancient Near Eastern Texts* [1], pp. 25–29.

[7] See especially A. R. Johnson, *The Cultic Prophet in Ancient Israel* [316]; also R. E. Clements, *Prophecy and Covenant* [312], pp. 11–34. A good discussion of various types of "primitive prophets in ancient Israel" is given in J. Lindblom, *Prophecy in Ancient Israel* [317], chap. 2.

Regarded as experts in prayer, particularly intercessory prayer, they were called upon to bring the people's petitions before Yahweh. Moreover, as Yahweh's spokespersons, they communicated the divine answer to a particular petition, or indicated whether or not an offering was acceptable to the deity. On the occasion of the great religious festivals, such as the covenant-renewal festival, they may have had an important part in announcing the demands and promises of the covenant.

Increasingly we are coming to realize that these anonymous prophets had a great influence upon Israelite tradition. Even the forms of oracular speech which the great prophets used effectively may have been received, in some instances, from these prophetic ancestors. Oracles of cultic prophets, composed originally for use in situations of worship, may lie embedded in the body of prophetic literature which has been transmitted under the names of the classical prophets. And some of the psalms now found in the book of Psalms seem to reflect their role in Israel's worship (see Ps. 81:5b–16). In difficult times, when Israel was exposed to dangers from without and within, many of these unknown prophets must have been sincere and passionate interpreters of the covenant between Yahweh and Israel.

Prophets and Politics

As we have seen in the passage discussed above (I Sam. 10:5–13), prophecy was intimately associated with politics from the very first moment it appeared in Israel. The prophetic band was stationed right next to a Philistine garrison. Their purpose was to incite Israelites to engage in holy war against the Philistine foe, and to do this they must have sung, with the fervor of their ecstasy, war songs which aroused the people to action. (The author has witnessed this kind of dervish activity in modern Arab circles, where the purpose of singing and group dancing was to awaken patriotic feeling.) Like the charismatic judges of an earlier day, they were intoxicated with "enthusiasm"—a word that means literally to be inspired of God (Greek *entheos*).[8] Elijah and Elisha were such vigorous champions of Israel's faith that they were called "the chariots of Israel and its horsemen" (II Kings 2:12; 13:14).

The early prophets, however, were more than zealous champions of holy war. Primarily they were called to deliver Yahweh's word for a specific situation. In that time there were three accepted channels for ascertaining the divine will (I Sam. 28:6,15): dreams (particularly those experienced in a holy place), the sacred dice (Urim and Thummin) which were handled by the priests, and prophecy. Saul, according to I Sam. 28:6, had tried all three of these channels in the final hours of desperation and had received no answer. Of the two types of religious leaders—prophet and priest—the prophet was more suited to be the

---

[8] See Abraham J. Heschel, *The Prophets* [315], pp. 326–27. Heschel attempts to distinguish between "ecstasy" and "enthusiasm," but the line cannot be drawn sharply.

spokesperson for Yahweh in a time of political crisis. A priest could officiate at sacred rites, teach the people the traditions of the past, and manipulate the sacred lot in answer to yes-or-no questions. But the prophet, speaking under the influence of Yahweh's spirit, was able to interpret the meaning of events and to proclaim the will of God in concrete terms.

In the time of Saul, devotion to Yahweh, fired by the energy of prophetic enthusiasm, was Israel's bond of unity and strength in the struggle for survival. However, when Israel became a nation, with a monarchic form of government like the surrounding nations, the role of prophets in relation to the political establishment proved to be ambivalent. Some prophets, like Elijah, stood outside of the power structure and were viewed as enemies of the king (cf. I Kings 21:20). As radical critics of society, they advocated rapid, revolutionary social change. Other prophets operated within the social structure, advocating more orderly social transition.[9] In the time of David, as we have seen, the prophet Nathan achieved a position of great influence in the royal court. His oracle concerning Yahweh's covenant with David (II Sam. 7:11–17) had a lasting effect upon Israelite society, influencing other "establishment" prophets like Isaiah of Jerusalem. At the same time, Nathan did not hesitate to summon the king before the highest tribunal to hear the word of divine judgment against the misuse of royal power, as in the Bathsheba affair (II Sam. 12).

Israel's prophetic movement, then, belongs inseparably to the period of Israel's nationhood, when kings and queens sat upon the thrones of Israel and Judah. The prophets were not mystics or individualists who sought escape from society, but were members of communities that kept alive a tradition, gave the prophetic spokesperson support, and treasured the prophetic words. Above all, they addressed their oracles to Israel who, although having become a nation (*goy*), was called to be "the people of Yahweh." Since prophets differed in their relation to the structures of power and in the theological accents with which they spoke, sometimes they were at odds with one another over national policy. Thus arose the question, "Who speaks the word of Yahweh?"—or, in other terms, the relation between true and false prophecy.[10]

A HISTORIAN'S VIEW OF THE TIMES

In view of what has been said about the prophets' activity in the sphere of politics, it is necessary to consider the events that took place after Solomon's death. Specifically, we are interested in the period that extends from the split of the United Kingdom to the revolution of Jehu—that is, from about 922 to 842

---

[9] This is the thesis of Robert R. Wilson, *Prophecy and Society* [328], who draws a distinction between "central" and "peripheral" prophets with regard to their relation to the political establishment.

[10] See James Crenshaw, *Prophetic Conflict* [313].

B.C.E. From this period we have no literature that purports to have been written by prophets. Instead, the tradition about the prophets is interwoven with the historical narrative of the books of I and II Kings, which carries the story of Israel from the end of David's reign to the time just after the tragic fall of the nation in the year 587.

These books, it will be recalled, form the conclusion of the Deuteronomistic History that extends from the book of Joshua, with Deuteronomy (or a portion of it) as a preface.[11] As in the case of other periods covered by this work, the history of the monarchy is interpreted from the standpoint of the fundamental theological conviction of the Mosaic tradition: obedience to the covenant (as prescribed in the Deuteronomic law) yields the blessing of welfare and peace; disobedience invites the divine judgment of suffering and even expulsion from the land. To be in covenant with Yahweh requires that the people must love Yahweh with their whole being (Deut. 6:4); anything smacking of idolatry must be eradicated from the community. In order to keep Israel's society pure from the contaminating customs of surrounding peoples, the Deuteronomistic historians advocated the centralization of worship in Jerusalem and the closing up of all outlying sanctuaries ("high places") where popular syncretism and idolatry flourished. On the negative side, they stressed the sin of Jeroboam I who established rival sanctuaries, such as the one at Bethel, and they regarded all kings who tolerated these innovations as horrible sinners, regardless of how much they had to their credit on other points. On the positive side, they advocated the royal covenant theology of Judah, with its emphasis upon Yahweh's everlasting covenant with David and the choice of Zion as the central sanctuary. This historical perspective is set forth clearly in the summary found in II Kings 17:7–41, which reviews events from the establishment of the monarchy to the fall of the northern kingdom.[12]

Each northern and southern king is strictly judged by this Deuteronomistic standard of covenant obedience. As in the case of the stories of the judges, the historians follow a stereotyped procedure which, in its skeletal outline, varies only slightly in the case of each king of Israel or Judah.

Judah	*Israel*
1. In the_____year of so-and-so, king of Israel, so-and-so, king of Judah, began to reign.	1. In the_____year of so-and-so, king of Judah, so-and-so, king of Israel, began to reign.
2. Facts about his age, duration of reign, name, and queen mother.	2. Facts about the length of his reign and the place of his capital.

---

[11] See the discussion of the Deuteronomistic History above, pp. 122–123. Notice that the Deuteronomic law is specifically mentioned in II Kings 14:6; compare Deuteronomy 24:16.

[12] See Frank M. Cross, "The Themes of the Book of Kings and the Structure of the Deuteronomistic History" [112], especially the discussion of the themes of the historian, pp. 278–85. He advocates two editions of this history: an original version written just before the fall of the nation, and an updated expansion during the Exile.

3. Evaluation of his standing in comparison to "David his father."

3. Censure for the fact that "he did what was evil in the sight of Yahweh, and walked in the way of Jeroboam and his sin which he made Israel to sin."

4. "Now the rest of the acts of so-and-so . . . are they not written in the Book of Chronicles of the Kings of Judah?"

4. "Now the rest of the acts of so-and-so . . . are they not written in the Book of Chronicles of the Kings of Israel?"

5. Concluding statement that he slept with his ancestors, and so-and-so reigned in his stead.

5. Concluding statement that he slept with his ancestors, and so-and-so reigned in his stead.

The Deuteronomistic historians plainly tell readers that if they are interested in learning more about these kings, they may go to the royal library and consult the archives. Their purpose is to present to their own day the great lessons of the past in order that readers may understand and face the crisis in which they find themselves. They intend to show that these things did not happen by chance; rather, God was at work in the tragic career of Israel from the breakup of the Davidic kingdom and on, punishing the people for their repeated faithless behavior in spite of prophetic warnings and summoning them to turn from their evil ways (II Kings 17:13). So they go through the list of the kings, taking up a king of Israel and dating his reign in terms of the king of Judah who was reigning at the time; then they turn the spotlight on Judah and date the Judean king's reign by cross-reference to the date of the reigning king of Israel. This seems a somewhat confusing procedure, but it was a necessary one, since there was no standard calendar in those days. Not one king of Israel escapes the historians' blacklist, and their judgment falls pretty severely on the kings of Judah too. Only two southern kings (Hezekiah and Josiah) come off with a clean record; six receive a grade of only "passing," because they failed to remove the high places; and ten "flunk," because they "did what was evil in the sight of Yahweh."

Fortunately, the Deuteronomists often clothe this historical skeleton with flesh and blood by choosing stories and traditions derived from other sources. In presenting Solomon, as we have seen, they evidently drew on the royal archives known as the Book of the Acts of Solomon, and they probably had access to temple archives as well. In the history of the divided kingdom they refer frequently to two other sources: the Book of the Chronicles of the Kings of Israel, and the Book of the Chronicles of the Kings of Judah. No trace of these royal annals has ever been found. They perished long ago, and survive only in the fragmentary quotations of the Deuteronomistic History. In addition, this history incorporates certain legends that were drawn from popular tradition. The stories of Elijah and Elisha fall in the latter category, for they show no trace of Deuteronomistic bias.

With this background, let us survey what happened after the long reign of Solomon came to an end.

THE DIVIDED KINGDOM

The story opens in I Kings 12. We are told that Rehoboam, the son of Solomon, made a trip into northern territory to be installed as "king of Israel," although he was already recognized as king in Jerusalem. Here the word "Israel" refers to the ten northern tribes—not to the larger unity that David had forged out of the remnants of Saul's kingdom and his own tribe of Judah. Clearly, the deep rift within the covenant community, evident earlier during the period of the Tribal Confederacy, had been healed only superficially by the policies of David. It is significant that the gathering took place at Shechem, which was hallowed by unforgettable memories. It was at Shechem, near a sacred tree, that Abraham had built an altar to Yahweh (Gen. 12:6). Moreover, in the Jacob cycle, which was treasured in northern circles, Jacob's first holding in Canaan was at Shechem (Gen. 33:18–20). And above all, Shechem was the place where the Tribal Confederacy had been established (Josh. 24). At this ancient tribal gathering place, the northern tribes—acting with a show of independence—gathered to make Rehoboam their king.

The tribes of Israel, smarting under the whiplash that Solomon had laid upon them in his labor gangs, demanded that the yoke be lightened.[13] Solomon's tyrannical policy had fallen most heavily upon the prosperous northern tribes. But Rehoboam, shunning the advice of his older counselors and swayed by "progressive" young men, answered the Israelite ultimatum by saying that his father had lashed them with whips, but that he would chastise them with scorpions.

This was the match that touched off the explosion. Again the call to revolution was sounded, as it had been in David's time under Absalom and Sheba. In the ancient cry there was a nostalgia for the old days of tribal independence:

> What portion have we in David?
>   We have no inheritance in the son of Jesse.
> To your tents, O Israel!
>   Look now to your own house, David.
> —I KINGS 12:16 (RSV)

When Rehoboam indiscreetly sent Adoniram, the taskmaster in charge of forced labor, to bring the situation under control, Adoniram was stoned to death. The king jumped into his chariot and hastily fled to Jerusalem. Only the oracle of a prophet, Shemaiah (I Kings 12:22–24), prevented him from precipitating an immediate civil war.

---

[13] In *The People of the Covenant* [231], p. 177, Murray Newman points out that the "yoke" which the northerners wanted lightened was theological, too. Unable to accept the royal covenant theology (II Sam. 7) which promised divine authorization for the Davidic throne and dynasty, they insisted upon limitation of the king's sovereignty in the north, in accordance with their Mosaic covenant theology.

Jeroboam the First

At some point in the revolutionary movement, Jeroboam I, the son of Nebat, joined the plot to overthrow the kingdom—to "lift up his hand against the king" (I Kings 11:26). Jeroboam was an Ephraimite—a northerner—who had once been Solomon's taskmaster over forced labor in the northern provinces (I Kings 11:26–28). It is important to notice that the prophet Ahijah, from the former confederate center of Shiloh, was a chief conspirator in this plot. His prophecy that Yahweh was about to tear the ten northern tribes from Solomon and give them to Jeroboam (I Kings 11:29–39) poured fuel upon the fires of rebellion. When Solomon crushed the first stage of the revolt, Jeroboam fled to Egypt, where he was given political asylum by Pharaoh Shishak (I Kings 11:29–40). At the opportune moment after Solomon's death, Jeroboam returned and was proclaimed king over the northern tribes in about 922 B.C.E. Thereafter, these tribes were known as "Israel," as distinguished from "Judah," the tribe (along with Benjamin) that acknowledged allegiance to the Davidic dynasty.

The political situation at the time favored the northern tribes (Ephraim) in their secession. It is somewhat surprising that the empire of Solomon, fortified

---

DEFINITION "EPHRAIM AND JUDAH"

As we have noticed in the foregoing discussion, the term "Israel," which once referred to the whole people who were in covenant with Yahweh, is now being narrowed down to refer to a political entity, specifically the Northern Kingdom that parted company with the Davidic dynasty centered in Jerusalem. Thus the term was nationalized, as has occurred also in the case of the modern state which has taken the name Israel.

Often, however, the Northern Kingdom is referred to as Ephraim after Jeroboam's tribe, as in the poems of the northern prophet, Hosea (e.g. Hos. 12:1; 13:2). This prophet also uses the term Israel as a parallel (e.g. 10:1; 11:1), showing that the terms can be understood synonymously. Quite apart from the ideological claims on behalf of the northern state, undoubtedly the northerners believed that they were the true preservers of the Mosaic tradition that was dominant in the time of the Tribal Confederacy under the leadership of Joshua, also an Ephraimite.

The tensions between Ephraim (Israel) and Judah were exacerbated by the foolish policy of Rehoboam, who sought to crush rebellion within the Davidic empire by tough measures. However, the seeds of the tension between north and south, Ephraim and Judah, may be traced back to the time before the monarchy, when the Joseph tribes (Ephraim and Manasseh) had the ascendency over the tribe of Judah which may have entered the land separately. The rise of the tribe of Judah, especially under David and Solomon, temporarily smoothed over, but did not eliminate, deep-seated differences.

Despite the schism between north and south, Ephraim and Judah, the term Israel still retained its ancient significance of a people united in covenant solidarity with Yahweh. It is understandable, then, that prophets sometimes portrayed the future as a time of a new covenant, when political wounds would be healed and all Israel—north and south, Ephraim and Judah—would be united in a community transcending national rivalries (as in Jer. 31).

---

with the best military equipment of the day and policed by the king's officers, should collapse almost overnight. Rehoboam surely had the military power to strike against the revolutionaries before they had a chance to organize themselves and fortify their positions. He probably would have won had he acted quickly. The fact that he did not was undoubtedly due to a threatened attack from Egypt which caused him to forget about Ephraim (Israel) momentarily and to divert his energies to the protection of his borders to the south and west. The fortifications described in II Chron. 11:5–12 were built, according to the Chronicler's inference, in the expectation of an Egyptian invasion (II Chron. 12:2–4).

Egypt was showing signs of awakening from the political lethargy that had paralyzed it for three centuries, ever since the death of Merneptah in 1211 B.C.E. A new monarch had seized the throne—Shishak (c. 935–914), the founder of the Twenty-Second Dynasty. Dreaming of regaining Egypt's former position of prestige and power in the Fertile Crescent, he reversed the policy of diplomatic subservience that had been in force during the reign of David and most of the reign of Solomon, and began to meddle aggressively in Palestinian affairs. During Solomon's lifetime he had given refuge to political criminals, Jeroboam of North Israel and Hadad of Edom. The death of Solomon gave Shishak the opportunity to plot the disruption of Solomon's empire on the age-old political principle of "divide and conquer." So he gladly released Jeroboam to lead the seditionist movement, and began to prepare for the invasion of Palestine. Actually, Shishak was no fonder of Jeroboam than he was of Rehoboam, for when the Egyptian invasion came, just five years after the disruption of the United Kingdom (918), it swept like an avalanche over Edom, Philistia, Judah, and Is-

Chronological Chart 3

B.C.E.	Egypt	Palestine		Phoenicia	Mesopotamia
1000		THE UNITED KINGDOM			
	Decline	David, c. 1000–961		Hiram I,	Assyrian
		Solomon, c. 961–922		c. 969–936	Decline
	XXII Dynasty				
	Shishak I				
	(c. 935–914)				
		Division of the kingdom at			
(Iron Age)		death of Solomon, c. 922			
		THE DIVIDED KINGDOM			
	Shishak	Judah	Israel		
	invades Judah	DAVIDIC DYNASTY:			
	c. 918	Rehoboam,	Jeroboam I,		
		c. 922–915	c. 922–901		
		Abijah (Abijam),			
		c. 915–913			
900		Asa, c. 913–873	Nadab,		
			c. 901–900		

rael alike. In addition to the brief report in I Kings 14:25-28, we have the famous Karnak List of Asiatic countries that were conquered by Egyptian kings. This list was inscribed on the walls of the magnificent temple of Karnak, whose remains still stand outside Luxor.[14]

Jeroboam's Reform

While Rehoboam was busy with preparations for the threatened Egyptian invasion, Jeroboam took measures to strengthen his own kingdom. The Deuteronomistic historian, who regards Jeroboam as a *bête noire*, gives only a minimum of information about his reign. Most of the account is devoted to damning him for his blasphemous act in setting up rival shrines in the Northern Kingdom (all of I Kings 13 and 14 are tirades against Jeroboam). But by a critical appraisal of what is left (12:25-33)—which is precious little—we come to a more sympathetic understanding of Jeroboam's accomplishments.

To begin with, he strengthened his temporary capital, Shechem, and fortified Penuel on the other side of the Jordan. Since both of these sites figured prominently in ancient sacred traditions of Israel, and were especially identified with the northern patriarch Jacob (Gen. 32:22-32; 33:18-20; chap. 34), it is likely that Jeroboam was also trying to capitalize on the religious significance of these places. It is hardly accidental that he turned to Shechem, the first center of the old Israelite confederacy. He realized that something more than military measures was necessary to consolidate his people. The pull toward Jerusalem, the seat of Solomon's temple, could easily counteract the political independence of the North. So, just as David had attempted to unify his kingdom by bringing the Ark of the Covenant to Jerusalem, Jeroboam determined to provide a religious foundation for his kingdom. He established two shrines, one at Dan in the north of his kingdom, and the other at Bethel on the southern boundary, both of which had been places of pilgrimage for a long time. Also, he established a priesthood which claimed direct lineage from the Mosaic period. Finally, he instituted an annual Fall festival (the Feast of Ingathering—that is, a Thanksgiving) comparable to a festival that was celebrated in Judah at a slightly different time.

The Deuteronomistic historians were horrified at Jeroboam's innovations, especially the setting up of golden bulls in high places other than Jerusalem. Repeatedly in the books of Kings, they denounce Jeroboam as "the man who made Israel to sin." The language that is attributed to Jeroboam echoes the story of the worship of the Golden Calf in the wilderness period: "You have gone up to Jerusalem long enough. Behold your gods, O Israel, who brought you up out of the land of Egypt" (I Kings 12:28; see Exod. 32:4, 8)—surely a slanted version of Jeroboam's religious reform. Probably the Judean editors, swayed by anti-northern propaganda, have changed the tradition from "Behold your *God*," for

[14] See Pritchard, *Ancient Near Eastern Texts* [1], pp. 242-43, 263-64.

The Shechem Pass is the strategic gateway to the heart of Canaan. Located at the caravan crossroads between Mount Gerizim (left) and Mount Ebal (right), Shechem was the first center of the Israelite confederacy.

it is extremely doubtful that Jeroboam intended to introduce polytheism. As we have noticed in a previous connection (pp. 103–104), the setting up of the golden bulls probably did not have the sinister purpose that the historians saw in it. Jeroboam may have been returning to an old North Israelite tradition in which Yahweh, identified with El ("Bull 'El"), was represented standing invisibly on the back of a young bull. Modern defenders of this king argue that the practice was "no more idolatrous than the equally symbolic representation of Yahweh in the Temple of Solomon as an invisible Presence enthroned on the cherubim."[15] In any case, Jeroboam's intention—as the Deuteronomistic historians tacitly admit—was to connect the religion of the Northern Kingdom with the main stream of the Mosaic tradition, the chief theme of which was the Exodus from Egypt. As we shall see in Chapter 11, the traditions of the Tribal Confederacy—which was inaugurated in Shechem, the very place Jeroboam chose as his capital— were kept more alive in the North than in the Davidic circles of the South. Moreover, it has been plausibly suggested that in Jeroboam's time the northern (Elohist) version of the sacred history was written to express the nationalism of the independent state[16] (see pp. 289–290).

Jeroboam, then, had no idea of introducing the worship of new "gods"; rather, his intention was to renew Israel's devotion to the God of the covenant.

[15] W. F. Albright, *The Biblical Period* [90], p. 31; also his comments in *From the Stone Age* [111], pp. 203, 228–30. This view is supported substantially by Frank M. Cross, "Yahweh and 'El" [112], pp. 73–75. For a different assessment of Jeroboam's reform, see T. J. Meek, *Hebrew Origins* [97], chap. 5; Martin Noth, *Pentateuchal Traditions* [70], pp. 141–45.

[16] See Walter J. Harrelson [42], pp. 65, 199–200, who suggests that in retelling the "true" story of Yahweh's saving deeds the Elohist (E) tradition often retained more ancient material than the Yahwist (J).

The Storm God Hadad stands on the back of a bull, holding in each hand a pronged fork representing lightning. This bas-relief, found at Arslan-Tash in northern Syria, comes from the eighth century B.C.E. Jeroboam I may have intended the golden bull to be not an idol but a pedestal on which Yahweh stood invisibly.

However, his action in setting up the golden bulls was fraught with serious dangers in an environment where Canaanite religion was all too attractive. In the Ras Shamra literature (see pp. 186–189) the bull was associated not only with El, the high god of the pantheon, but also with Baal, the virile god of storm and fertility. Unwittingly, perhaps, Jeroboam was giving encouragement to the fusion of Israel's faith with Baal religion. It was a northern prophet, not a historian from the South, who first denounced the calf of Bethel, seeing in it the seductive idolatry that had perverted Israel's faith ever since the entrance into Canaan. According to the prophet Hosea, Yahweh reacts with loathing and rage to the "Calf of Samaria," the official image of the cult of North Israel (Hos. 8:5–6; 10:5–6).

The Rise of the House of Omri

Having finished the story of Jeroboam, the Deuteronomistic historians retrace their steps to summarize the reigns of two southern kings, Rehoboam and Abijah (or Abijam), who were contemporaries of Jeroboam. Finding nothing good to say about them, they finish them off quickly with characteristic Deuteronomistic judgments (I Kings 14:21–15:8). However, they do excerpt from the Book of the Chronicles of the Kings of Judah the notice about Shishak's invasion, because it shows Yahweh's retributive action against Rehoboam for his sins.

Next the historians turn to the reign of Asa of Judah, which overlapped the reign of Jeroboam (I Kings 15:9–24). Asa's reign provides a long dateline of about forty years on which to peg the reigns of contemporary kings of Israel—Nadab, Baasha, Elah, Zimri, Omri, and Ahab (I Kings 15:25–16:34). Thus the whole narrative leads up to the account of the reign of king Ahab, into which the Elijah stories have been inserted (see Chronological Chart 4, p. 269).

During these years (c. 900–850 B.C.E.) political tensions were becoming more acute in Palestine. For fifty years—ever since the split of Solomon's kingdom—civil war had gone on between Israel and Judah. Egypt was continuing to interfere, and new dangers from the North were beginning to be felt. Most imminent was the threat of Syria (Aram), whose traditional rivalry with Israel is celebrated in the Jacob-Laban stories of Genesis. No longer under subservience to Israel as was the case during the reign of David and part of the reign of Solomon, Syria took advantage of its strategic location at the commercial crossroads of the Fertile Crescent. Syrian kings looked with envious eyes on Israel's territory, especially the territory in Transjordan just south of the Syrian capital of Damascus. And in the farther background—ultimately to be a threat to Syria, Israel, Judah, and all the small nations of the Fertile Crescent—the Assyrian lion was pacing restlessly in its Mesopotamian lair. In about 870 B.C.E., Ashur-nasir-apal (884–860), awakening Assyria to its imperial ambitions after more than a century of lethargy, marched through northern Syria, and subjugated parts of Phoenicia.

Syrian Aggression

The trouble started during the reign of Asa of Judah (c. 913–873 B.C.E.). Asa was interested in religious reforms, for which he won the qualified praise of Deuteronomistic historians, and he probably helped to halt the tendency toward syncretism which had been encouraged under the reigns of Solomon and his immediate successors. We are told that Asa shook himself free from the control of his mother, deposing her from her regency and banning the worship of Asherah, the Canaanite mother goddess that the queen mother had sponsored (I Kings 15:13). But Asa had other problems—problems that could not be solved by religious reform. Israel, with whom Judah had waged intermittent war from

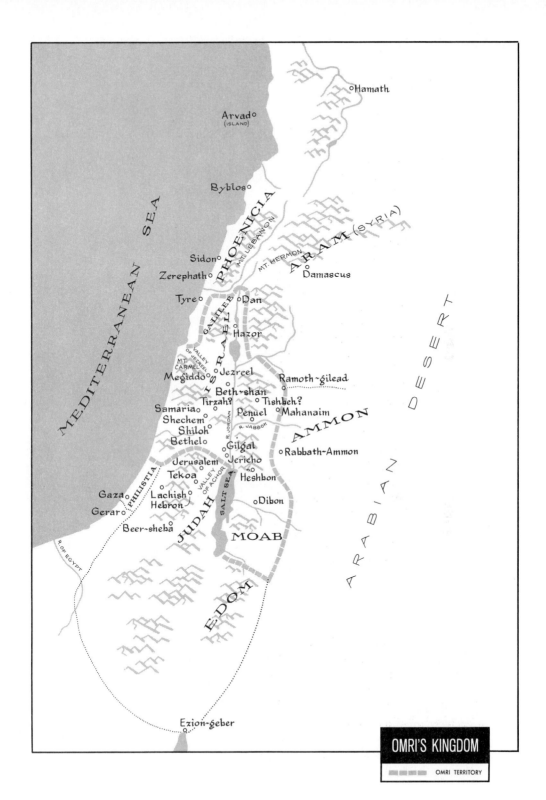

MEDITERRANEAN SEA

Hamath○

Arvad○
(ISLAND)

Byblos○

PHOENICIA

ARAM (SYRIA)

Sidon○

Zerephath○

MT. HERMON

Damascus○

Tyre○

Dan○

GALILEE

Hazor○

ISRAEL

VALLEY OF JEZREEL

MT. CARMEL

Jezreel○

Ramoth-gilead○

Megiddo○

Beth-shan○

Tirzah?○

Tishbeh?○

ARABIAN DESERT

Samaria○

Penuel○

Mahanaim○

Shechem○

R. JORDAN

R. JABBOK

AMMON

Shiloh○

Bethel○

Gilgal○

Jericho○

Rabbath-Ammon○

Jerusalem○

Tekoa○

VALLEY OF ACHOR

Heshbon○

SALT SEA

Gaza○

PHILISTIA

Lachish○

Hebron○

Dibon○

Gerar○

JUDAH

Beer-sheba○

MOAB

R. OF EGYPT

EDOM

Ezion-geber○

OMRI'S KINGDOM

▓▓ ▓▓ ▓▓ OMRI TERRITORY

The Stele of Mesha (king of Moab in the ninth century B.C.E.), on which the ruler boasts of his victory over the king of northern Israel. Discovered in 1868 at Dibon (Dibhan) in Transjordan, the stone was broken by some bedouin, and only fragments could be taken to the Louvre for restoration.

the time of the division of the monarchy, had become so strong that its king, Baasha, was able to blockade the northern avenues into Jerusalem. So Asa took a fateful step. He sent an appeal to Benhadad, king of Syria, to join him as an ally against Israel. The Syrian king gladly obliged by invading and devastating Galilee, and at the same time advancing his own political ambitions (c. 878).

In the resulting confusion, there was a rapid turnover of kings in Israel, owing to assassination, suicide, and intrigue. (One king, Zimri, who had murdered his predecessor, held the throne only seven days!) As often happens in such circumstances, the commander of the army, Omri, emerged from the struggle as the most powerful person. Omri came to the throne by a *coup d'état*.

The Deuteronomistic historians are unusually severe with Omri, insisting that he "did more evil than all who were before him." The account of his reign is limited to six verses (I Kings 16:23–28), most of it consisting of the usual Deu-teronomistic formulas. If we could look at the Book of the Chronicles of the Kings of Israel, to which we are referred, we would undoubtedly discover a man of tremendous political stature. He was able to do what none of his pred-ecessors had done: establish a dynasty of such prestige that Assyrian kings con-tinued to refer to the Northern Kingdom as "the land of the house of Omri" for many years after his death and the downfall of his dynasty. He initiated a period of collaboration with Judah—a collaboration that was later strengthened by intermarriage between the two royal houses. Thanks to the work of archae-ologists, we know a great deal more about Omri's reign than the scanty report in Kings tells us. In the Louvre Museum now stands the Moabite Stone, erected by Mesha, king of Moab (see II Kings 3:4), during the reign of the last king of the Omri dynasty. Boasting of his great accomplishments, Mesha says:

> As for Omri, king of Israel, he humbled Moab many years, for Chemosh [i.e., the god of Moab] was angry at his land. And his son [or, grandson] followed him and he also said, "I will humble Moab." In my time he spoke (thus), but I have triumphed over him and over his house, while Israel hath perished for ever![17]

Not only was Omri successful against the Moabites in Transjordan, but he was also able to keep the Syrians at bay, although at the price of ceding territory in Transjordan and granting the Syrians commercial concessions in Samaria (I Kings 20:34). His hand was strengthened, no doubt, by the close alliance he formed with Phoenicia, following the precedent of David and Solomon. This political union of two countries, whose common interest it was to hold Syria in check, was consummated by the marriage of Omri's son Ahab to the Phoenician king's daughter, Jezebel (I Kings 16:31). Here again he revived Solomon's policy of political marriage, although in this case—as we shall see—the marriage proved fateful for Israel.

So, in spite of the virtual silence of the book of Kings on Omri's reign, we have reason to believe that under his statesmanship Israel achieved great sta-bility and prosperity. During his twelve-year rule, Israel's political power ex-panded toward the Mediterranean and into Transjordan. Something like an economic boom must have followed in the wake of his vigorous political ex-ploits, with an inevitable widening of the gulf between the "haves" and the "have-nots," which was to persist in Israel's society until the time of Amos, a century later. The monument to Omri's political astuteness was the city of Sa-maria, the new capital that he began to build on a hilltop, and that was com-pleted by his son Ahab (I Kings 16:24).[18] The new site provided an excellent

---

[17] See Pritchard, *Ancient Near Eastern Texts* [1], pp. 320–21.

[18] Previously the northern capital had been located to the northeast at Tirzah (modern Tell el-Far'ah, which has been excavated under the direction of R. de Vaux). Because of military pressure Omri's predecessor, Jeroboam I, had been forced to move the capital from Shechem to Tirzah (see I Kings 14:17; 15:33).

The Hill of Samaria *on which Omri of Israel built his capital is seen in this southward-looking view. Because of the almost impregnable slopes of the hill and the strong fortifications surrounding it, the Assyrian armies had to lay siege to the city for three years before they were able to conquer it.*

view of the surrounding landscape; furthermore, the steep slopes of the hill made it difficult to capture by ancient military maneuvers. Omri's purchase of the hill of Samaria was a wise decision, for his capital, astride the main north-south highway, was strategically situated to watch any advance from Judah and to gain easy access to Phoenicia, with whom Israel was bound by dynastic marriage. This luxurious city has come to light under the excavator's spade: the masonry, fortifications, the palaces of Omri and Ahab, and even the ivory inlaid in the furniture and walls (see I Kings 22:39; Amos 3:15; 6:4). Apparently Omri imported Phoenician craftsmen to execute the art and architecture, as Solomon had done, for the remains show strong evidence of Phoenician style. Henceforth, Samaria was to be the symbol of the Northern Kingdom, just as Jerusalem was the symbol of the Southern.

Under Omri's son, Ahab—who also receives strong censure in the Deuteronomistic history—Israel's material progress continued. But international troubles were beginning to mount. By this time Egypt had sunk again into oblivion. But Syria (Aram) was on the move, expanding south into Transjordanian

*A **Cherub or Sphynx** set in an ivory plaque found during the excavation of Samaria. Although this piece comes from the ninth century B.C.E., the composite figure of the cherub—half human and half beast—was a familiar motif of ancient art. The fragments of ivory carvings, which are Phoenician in style, witness to the splendor of King Ahab's "house of ivory" (I Kings 22:39).*

territory traditionally claimed by Israel, and advancing up to the very gates of Samaria (I Kings 20). The southern king, Jehoshaphat (I Kings 22:41-46), reversed the foreign policy of his predecessor, Asa, and joined forces with Ahab to fight the Arameans in Transjordan in order to recover Ramoth-gilead (I Kings 22). It was in this battle, according to the story, that Ahab lost his life.

The Threat of Assyria

Just a few years before Ahab's death, however, the necessities of politics made Syria and Israel bedfellows. The Assyrians, intent on expanding to the Mediterranean, were beginning to pose a great threat to the petty kingdoms of Syria and Palestine. Syria, the nearest and most vulnerable, was the first to feel the threat of Assyrian expansion to the west. The Assyrian king, Shalmaneser III (c. 859–825), believing that the small western states would be easy prey, prepared to strike in 853 B.C.E. The battle was fought at Qarqar near Hamath, not far north of Damascus, against a coalition of western states. Benhadad of Syria had accomplished the diplomatic triumph of organizing the states, including his enemy Israel, to stop Assyrian aggression. Joining strong contingents from Syria and Hamath, "Ahab the Israelite" brought 10,000 foot soldiers and 2,000 chariots—the greatest number of chariots contributed by any of the allies, according to Shalmaneser's annals.[19] In the usual manner of war communiqués, the Assyrian boasted an overwhelming victory. But apparently the victory was not nearly so decisive as he claimed, for he withdrew and did not appear again in the west for several years. This event, however, was a shadow of things to come. From then on, as we shall see more clearly in the next chapter, Assyria's ambition to rule the Fertile Crescent was the darkest cloud on the political horizon of Israel and Judah.

Against this political background, there arose a succession of prophets who stood in the spiritual lineage of Moses and Samuel. Some of them are mentioned only briefly—like Ahijah from Shiloh, who led the revolt against Solomon (I Kings 11:29-39), and Jehu ben Hanani, who pronounced doom against King Baasha of Israel (I Kings 16:1-4). Our attention will focus on three outstanding Ephraimitic prophets who arose during the period of the Omri dynasty: Micaiah, Elijah, and Elisha.

ONE PROPHET AGAINST FOUR HUNDRED

One of the most vivid episodes in the history of prophecy is the story of Micaiah, the son of Imlah, a contemporary of Elijah. (Micaiah should not be confused with the later and better-known prophet, Micah.) It comes from the closing years of Ahab's reign, and properly should be considered after the Elijah narratives. But we shall look at it here because it shows how much the prophetic "schools" or guilds had been nationalized during the historical period that we have considered in this chapter.

The story of Micaiah in I Kings 22 should be read in connection with I Kings 20. The Deuteronomistic historians drew both these accounts from an independent source dealing with Ahab's wars. Their purpose in including them was to show how divine retribution finally descended upon Ahab, one of the members of the Deuteronomistic rogues' gallery. In describing the wars, they have given us a clear picture of the activity of "the sons of the prophets" (I Kings 20:35) at a time of military crisis, and have thrown into the foreground a great prophetic figure, Micaiah.

Chapter 20 takes us back to a time slightly before the battle of Qarqar, mentioned above. Even though Ahab's capital was besieged, he succeeded in turning the tables on the Syrian king at the battle of Aphek, forcing him to restore cities that Omri had ceded, and obtaining commercial concessions in Damascus. Ahab's act of mercy to the Syrian king was sharply rebuked by a member of a prophetic school who stood for a ruthless practice of holy war—the application of the sacrificial ban (ḥérem) against the enemy (see Definition p. 141). Despite this prophetic protest, it turned out that Ahab had been politically shrewd in making a covenant with Benhadad, for it was soon apparent that the

---

[19] See Pritchard, *Ancient Near Eastern Texts* [1], pp. 278-79.

western nations needed to stand together if they were to halt the Assyrian advance.

Then came the battle of Qarqar (853 B.C.E.), which the Deuteronomistic historians passed over in discreet silence because it did not serve their theological purpose. For three years the western military alliance against Assyria produced a truce between Israel and Syria (I Kings 22:1). But the friendship lasted no longer than the crisis. Shortly after the battle of Qarqar was fought to its indecisive finish, and after the Assyrians had withdrawn to face other problems, these two small nations resumed their bitter quarrel. The bone of contention was the city of Ramoth-gilead in Transjordan. Earlier, Omri had ceded this city along with others in order to hold Syria at bay. According to the agreement made after the battle of Aphek, Benhadad was to return them, but he had reneged. Ahab was eager to have possession of this city, which occupied a strategic position on the north-south commercial and military highway running through Transjordan.

As I Kings 22 opens, we see Ahab of Israel and Jehoshaphat of Judah taking counsel on a proposed joint military campaign. One of the accomplishments of the Omri dynasty had been to enter into friendly alliance with the Southern Kingdom, an alliance that was twice sealed by intermarriage. In this chapter,

Chronological Chart 4

B.C.E.	Egypt	Palestine		Mesopotamia	
		THE DIVIDED KINGDOM			
		Judah	Israel	Syria	Assyria
900		Asa, c. 913–873	Baasha, c. 900–877		Assyrian Revival
			Elah, c. 877–876		Adad-nirari II, c. 912–892
			Zimri, c. 876 (7 days)	Benhadad I, c. 885–870	Ashur-nasir-apal II, c. 884–860
				Benhadad II, c. 870–842	
			Omri Dynasty: Omri, c. 876–869		
	Egyptian Weakness	Jehoshaphat, c. 873–849	Ahab, c. 869–850		Shalmaneser III, c. 859–825
		Jehoram, c. 849–842	(Elijah, c. 850)		Battle of Qarqar, 853
		Ahaziah, c. 843/2	Ahaziah, c. 850–849		
850			Jehoram, c. 849–843/2	Hazael, c. 842–806	

however, Jehoshaphat's position suggests that he was almost a vassal of the more powerful and wealthier Northern Kingdom.

Jehoshaphat declared his willingness to go along with whatever Ahab had in mind, but slyly hoped that an oracle from Yahweh would render the proposed campaign unnecessary. Hence, as was customary when important military decisions were to be made, he suggested that they "inquire first for the word of Yahweh." Ahab complied by summoning about four hundred ecstatic prophets. Verses 10–12 give a vivid picture of these nationalistic dervishes working themselves into an ecstatic frenzy (the verb for "prophesying" in verse 10 means "prophesying ecstatically") before the two kings seated in state. Meanwhile, the prophets' ringleader—a certain Zedekiah—performed a symbolic action that was intended to dramatize the inevitable defeat of the Syrians. The "sons of the prophets" spoke "with one accord" (literally "with one mouth," vs. 13). According to the clear-cut verdict of these yes-men, the will of Yahweh and the purpose of the king coincided perfectly. Without any question, they agreed, Ahab would be successful in a campaign against Ramoth-gilead.

Suspicious of this verdict, the Judean king, Jehoshaphat, asked whether all the prophets had been heard from. It turned out that there was another prophet, Micaiah ben Imlah, who had not been called—for obvious reasons. "I hate him," said Ahab, "for he never prophesies good concerning me, but evil" (vs. 8). A revealing confession! Nevertheless, Micaiah was haled into the presence of the kings, after having been given a stern reminder that the majority was unanimously in favor of the military venture.

With a tone of sarcasm, Micaiah at first mocked and mimicked the optimistic prophecy of the four hundred. But Ahab, knowing that Micaiah was acting out of character, put him under oath to speak the truth in the name of Yahweh. This the prophet did in two oracles: One was a vision of Israel in leaderless rout, "scattered upon the mountains, as sheep that have no shepherd"— a prediction of the death of the Israelite king and the utter failure of the Syrian expedition. The other was a vision of Yahweh presiding over the heavenly court and commissioning a "spirit" to fill the prophets with a lying ecstasy. The reactions to Micaiah's unpleasant prophecy were what we might have expected: a slap on the face from Zedekiah, and an order snapped out by Ahab to "put this fellow in prison." The story goes on to relate how Micaiah's prophetic word was later vindicated. In spite of Ahab's disguise, an archer "drew his bow at a venture" and the king, mortally wounded, had to withdraw from the battle. Thus, in a seemingly chance occurrence the word of Yahweh through a prophet was fulfilled. In the narrator's perspective, history is governed by providence, not by chance.

I Kings 22 gives us a glimpse of a transitional moment in the history of prophecy. Micaiah vowed that "what Yahweh says to me, that will I speak"— even though it was diametrically opposed to the royal view and to the voice of the majority. He proclaimed God's judgment *against* the king—a message of doom—which in time was recognized as one of the badges of a true prophet of Yahweh (Jer. 28:8–9). With Micaiah, prophecy was no longer the echo of nationalism or the servant of the political establishment. Here we have a break with the professional prophets—a break that became sharper later when Amos disavowed any connection with the "sons of the prophets" (Amos 7:14). But in a deeper sense, prophets of Micaiah's type did not break with Israel's true prophetic tradition; they were indeed more sensitive to that tradition than the ecstatic prophets themselves. In prophets like Micaiah the ancient Mosaic faith came alive in the present with new meaning and power. This is clear in the case of the greatest ninth century prophet: Elijah (about 850 B.C.E.).[20]

ELIJAH, THE TISHBITE

We now turn backward from the end of Ahab's reign, with which I Kings 20 and 22 deal, to the fateful domestic crisis at the beginning of his rule. Our source for this period is the Elijah cycle, found chiefly in I Kings 17–19 and 21. Like the stories of Ahab's wars, this cycle is an independent unit of tradition that was incorporated into the Deuteronomistic History.[21] Notice that in this section the characteristic Deuteronomistic language is lacking, and the narrative betrays no "Deuteronomic" concern over the fact that Elijah built an altar on a "high place" (Carmel). Nor is Elijah rebuked for not having denounced the bull cult of Bethel, a subject on which the prophet is completely silent. Here we have prophetic legends that were preserved, no doubt, in the prophetic community with which Elijah was associated (II Kings 2:1–18).

The Elijah stories were not told with the precise, factual interest that a modern historian would display. They were tinted with the dye of the imagination and faith of Israel as they were remembered and elaborated in the oral tradition. Although many of them are based on actual circumstances, primarily they mirror the *experienced history* of Israel in one of its great crises. Not only do these stories record the terrific impression made by Elijah, the man of God, but they also portray the deepest dimension of Israel's history—its encounter with Yahweh in the political and cultural crisis of the time. This crisis came to a head as a result of the aggressiveness of Ahab's wife.

The French writer Pascal once said that the whole course of Western history was changed by the shape of Cleopatra's nose. We might say that the course of Israel's history was profoundly affected by the eccentricities of one person: Jezebel. It will be recalled that Omri, in order to strengthen relations between Israel and Phoenicia, had brought about the marriage of his son, Ahab, to Jezebel, the daughter of Ethbaal, king of Tyre. Had Ahab married someone else,

[20] See the discussion of the Micaiah story by Simon De Vries, *Prophet Against Prophet* [314], especially pp. 33–51.

[21] The Septuagint, the Greek translation of the Old Testament, places chapter 21 immediately after chapters 17–19, showing that these four chapters belong together as a single unit.

the whole story might have been different. The Deuteronomistic historians leave no doubt about their attitude toward the political marriage, for in marrying Jezebel, in their judgment, Ahab actually out-sinned Jeroboam (I Kings 16:31)!

Ahab immediately tried to make his bride at home in the new capital, Samaria, where he was continuing the building program initiated by Omri. Just as Solomon built shrines in Jerusalem for his foreign wives, so King Ahab built a ''temple of Baal,'' equipped with an altar and an image of Asherah, the mother goddess (I Kings 16:32–33). The Baal in this case was Baal-Melkart, the official protective deity of Tyre. This was the Phoenician version of the Canaanite nature religion, which we know best from the Ras Shamra literature. From the time of Israel's entrance into Canaan, this religion had been making subtle inroads into the covenant faith. Notice, however, that Baalism had now also acquired a political drive, for Phoenician imperialism was at its very height in the Mediterranean world. In antiquity, the way to acknowledge the political supremacy of another nation was to acknowledge and appropriate the religion of that country.

In fairness, though, Ahab seems to have had no idea of rejecting Yahweh, the God of Israel (contrary to the Deuteronomistic judgment of I Kings 16:31), for he gave his children names containing the sacred element *Yah* (Atal*iah*, Ahaz*iah*, *Jeh*oram), and—as we have seen in the story of Micaiah—later on in his reign he consulted the prophets of Yahweh. His position was one of tolerance; he merely wanted to give his wife freedom of worship, as Solomon had done with his foreign wives. But Jezebel was not one to retire into privacy. She was a proud, domineering woman who would stop at nothing to achieve her desired objective. A fanatical evangelist for her Phoenician religion, she inevitably came into conflict with the Yahweh prophets, who were equally passionate in their crusade for the covenant faith of Israel. She imported from Phoenicia a great number of Baal prophets and supported them out of the public treasury (I Kings 18:19). Moreover, she began an aggressive campaign to ''cut off the prophets of Yahweh.'' Taking advantage of the easy going tolerance and naive syncretism of the people, she tried to liquidate every vestige of Israel's traditional faith. The altars of Yahweh were torn down, the prophets were killed, and the remaining loyal adherents were driven underground. It was at this time of crisis that Elijah appeared in Israel to speak ''the word of Yahweh.''

The Contest on Carmel

The background of the first story in the Elijah cycle (I Kings 17 and 18) is a drought that paralyzed the country, as had happened periodically from time immemorial. Seen through a veil of legend, Elijah the Tishbite (that is, a native of the city Tishbeh in Gilead) suddenly appears on the scene like a meteor. The dramatic suddenness with which he is introduced suggests the impression he must have made on his contemporaries. Coming from across the Jordan, where he had lived a rough, seminomadic life on the edge of the desert, he must have been a strange sight in the cultured land of Israel—clothed in a garment of hair, wearing a leather girdle, and displaying his rugged strength (II Kings 1:8). His movements were so baffling that Obadiah, the king's servant, insisted that the spirit (or "wind") of Yahweh was wont to whisk him away to nobody-knows-where (I Kings 18:12). Elijah had a way of coming from nowhere to surprise people. According to the legend, his disappearance was just as mysterious as his lightning appearance, for—to use the language of the well-known spiritual—a fiery "sweet chariot," swinging low, carried him in a whirlwind to heaven (II Kings 2:11–12).

Elijah's first act was to announce a drought in the name of Yahweh—that is, to throw down the challenge to Baal in the sphere of his power—fertility (I Kings 17:1). The rest of chapter 17 is a series of vignettes showing the severity of the famine and the great miracles Elijah accomplished. These miracle stories, a favorite aspect of popular tradition that gathered around the prophet (see II Kings 1 and 2), need not be taken literally. The central concern of the stories is to portray Yahweh's authority over the fertility of the land, and to affirm that people's lives are wholly in Yahweh's hand. One of the most important features of this chapter is the claim that Yahweh controls fertility not only in Palestine but in Phoenicia as well—the special province of Baal-Melkart—for Elijah is shown ministering to a widow in the Phoenician town of Zarephath during the widespread famine.[22]

In I Kings 18, we find Elijah's encounter with Ahab the king. The king's first words were: "Is it you, you troubler of Israel?" He was thinking of the great disturbance that this prophetic "gadfly" had brought about by his senseless prophecy of drought—a drought that had hit Samaria so hard that the king and his steward had to scour the countryside to find enough fodder to keep the chariot horses alive. Elijah, however, turned Ahab's words against him, reminding him that the trouble had been brought about by his policy of supporting the worship of the Canaanite "Baals" (I Kings 18:18), who are here regarded as local manifestations of the Phoenician Baal, lord of sky and weather. The prophet announced that it is Yahweh, not Baal, who controls fertility. He challenged the "four hundred and fifty prophets of Baal and the four hundred prophets of Asherah" to a contest on the promontory of Mount Carmel, which juts out toward the Mediterranean Sea.

The description of the contest between the Baal prophets and the solitary prophet of Yahweh is one of the most dramatic accounts in the Bible. Elijah accuses the people of vacillating, of "limping with two different opinions" (RSV).

> Elijah stepped forward and said to the people, "How long will you sit on the fence? If [Yahweh] is God, follow him; but if Baal, then follow him."
> —I KINGS 18:21 (NEB)

---

[22] That this famine has a basis in fact is suggested by the first-century Jewish historian Josephus, who quotes the statement of Menander of Ephesus that there was a year of drought in the time of Ethbaal, father of Jezebel (*Antiquities of the Jews*, viii, 13, 2).

The people, according to the prophet, have been hopping on one foot, then the other. They wanted to keep one foot in the traditional faith of Israel and the other foot in the worship of Baal. This policy of syncretism had already had a long history, and had been encouraged among the people by Jeroboam's religious innovations. Finally Israel has come to the fork of the road, owing to the program of Jezebel. It is faced with a clear either-or question: either Yahweh, the God of the Mosaic covenant, or Baal, the Phoenician god of storm and fertility. Elijah puts the issue of monotheism in practical, not theoretical, terms. "If Yahweh is really God, then follow Yahweh; if Baal, then serve Baal." Deity makes a total claim upon human allegiance: heart, soul, and strength. Israel stood at the hour of decision. In the prophet Elijah the Mosaic tradition came alive with new power: Yahweh is the jealous God, who will tolerate no rival gods. The name Elijah, meaning "Yah(weh) is (my) God," was highly appropriate for this zealous prophetic champion of the Mosaic faith.

The object of the contest was to determine then and there who was Lord, who had the power to control rain and fertility. So both parties, the Baal prophets and the solitary Yahweh prophet, agreed to perform their respective rites with the understanding that "the God who answers by fire" is God. The Baal prophets lashed themselves into ecstatic frenzy as they performed their limping dance around the altar and shouted their ritual cries to Baal. With a touch of humor, the narrative portrays Elijah, serenely confident, laughing the Baal into meaningless unreality and taunting the Baal prophets with the jest that the heavens were unresponsive because, perhaps, Baal was relieving himself ("gone aside" is a euphemism), was on a business trip, or needed to be awakened from a reverie or from slumber. In spite of their ranting and raving, the ecstatic prophets were unsuccessful in ending the drought. The episode ends with the solemn words: "There was no voice; no one answered, no one heeded."

When Elijah stepped forward, his first act was to repair the abandoned altar of Yahweh—an act which signified a bold reclaiming of the cultic site for the God of Israel.[23] The ritual that followed (I Kings 18:32b–35) seems curious, for why would the prophet pour water on wood if he expected it to be consumed with fire? There have been various fantastic attempts to "explain" this—for instance, by saying that the "water" was actually inflammable naphtha from an oil geyser nearby! But the purpose of the act was clearly to bring on rain by sympathetic magic—by imitating the falling of rain. So Elijah, in a threefold ceremony, poured water on the wood until it filled the trench.

The upshot of Elijah's ritual is described in verses 36–40: the supernatural fire descended from heaven, the people were so awed by the spectacle that they

---

[23] Albrecht Alt, in his article dealing with the contest on Mount Carmel, "Das Gottesurteil auf dem Karmel," *Kleine Schriften zur Geschichte des Volkes Israel*, II (Munich, 1953), 135–49, argues that this area had come under the control of the Phoenicians in the past, who devoted the cult site to the worship of Baal. The Carmel contest, then, had political implications too: Elijah's victory dramatized the retaking of the territory in the name of Israel's God. For a discussion of the whole narrative, see H. H. Rowley, "Elijah on Mount Carmel" [325].

exclaimed, "It is Yahweh who is God," and the Baal prophets were condemned to the sacrificial ban (*ḥérem*). The real climax of the story, however, comes in verses 41–46, where the goal of the contest is realized: the drought is ended. Elijah proclaimed to Ahab that "there is a sound of the rushing of rain." Another rain ceremony, in which a servant was sent seven times to look toward the Mediterranean Sea while the prophet was prostrate in prayer, concluded with the announcement that a storm cloud—"a little cloud like a human hand"— was approaching. So while the storm gathered and the rain began to descend, Ahab hurried through the Valley of Jezreel lest his chariot bog down in the mud; and Elijah, with a terrific burst of ecstatic energy, ran before him.

The story of the drought belongs to the poetry of Israel's faith and should not be destroyed by modern rationalizations, such as construing the fire falling from heaven as the lightning of an electrical thunderstorm. In the Old Testament the symbolism of fire is frequently used to express the manifestation of God (for instance, the "burning bush"). Above all else, the narrator wants to communicate a sense of the active presence of Yahweh in that historical situation through the prophet, Elijah. In the various episodes of the story we view a great crisis in Israel's history as interpreted by prophetic faith.

The Flight to Mount Horeb

The dramatic description of the contest on Carmel—the participation of "all Israel" (I Kings 18:19, 20), the people's unanimous confession of faith in Yahweh, and the massacre of the Baal prophets—could easily give the impression that Baalism was destroyed once and for all. Actually, Elijah's victory was not that impressive. A few years later there were still enough Baal worshipers to fill a Baal temple (II Kings 10:21). The victory on Carmel was not the end of the war. Elijah was reminded of this by the fact that Jezebel was still on the throne, threatening to track him down.

The sequel to the Carmel episode is related in the legend of Elijah's flight from the territory of Ahab and Jezebel into the wilderness of southern Judah, a day's journey south of Beer-sheba, where he threw himself down beneath a lonely juniper tree. With profound insight the narrator portrays the doubt that shadows faith.[24] How could Yahweh really be sovereign when Jezebel's power was undiminished? The Elijah portrayed in I Kings 19:4 is a broken and fatigued man, running for his life and wishing to die because, in his efforts to crush the power of tyranny and idolatry, he had been no better than his forebears. The intent of the miracle story in verses 5–8, however, is to affirm that in his darkest hour Yahweh did not desert him, but mercifully supplied him with strength for a long journey that would lead to a new and keener sense of the sovereignty of God.

---

[24] See Robert Davidson, *Courage to Doubt* [134], pp. 95–99, for an illuminating interpretation of the Elijah narratives.

We are told that Elijah traveled "forty days and forty nights" (the traditional number for a long period of time) until he came to Horeb (Sinai), the sacred mountain of the covenant. On Horeb, a divine visitation (theophany) took place which the narrator describes with the revelation to Moses at Sinai/Horeb clearly in mind. The cave in which Elijah lodged recalls the cleft of the rock in which Moses was sheltered while Yahweh "passed by," showing the divine glory (Exod. 33:18–34:8). The Elijah narrative, too, says that Yahweh "passed by," and that this visitation was accompanied by earthquake, wind, and fire—the traditional phenomena of Yahweh's revelation on the sacred mountain (Exod. 19).

The whole narrative is an excellent illustration of "the contemporization of tradition."[25] The sacred heritage was not a mere archaeological item of the past; rather it was updated and made present in the current situation in which the people of God found themselves. Notice, however, that in the reinterpretation of the Mosaic tradition there is an important difference, almost a reversal of the traditional theophany. It is stated that Yahweh was *not* in the earthquake, wind, or fire—the traditional symbols of divine presence at Sinai/Horeb but in the lull that followed the tempestuous storm (cf. Ps. 107:29). The Hebrew words that are usually rendered "a still, small voice" refer to "a kind of silence so intense that you can hear it."[26] The "sounds of silence," to recall the title of a popular ballad, were understood to be the voice of the God of Exodus and Sinai who spoke with a new accent in the present.

The narrator goes on to say that when Elijah heard this voice of silence, speaking to him out of Israel's Mosaic tradition, he moved to the entrance of the cave. The ensuing dialogue introduces new dimensions of meaning. The question addressed to Elijah implies that he had no business out there in the safe mountain retreat, a fugitive from the places where history was being made. The prophet protests that he had been very jealous (the Hebrew word means both to be "jealous" and to be "zealous") for Yahweh. He had been a *zealot* for the Mosaic tradition, even though the people of Israel, under Jezebel's influence, had "forsaken your covenant,[27] thrown down your altars, and slain your prophets with the sword." But Elijah's brooding over his loneliness and over the threat to his life was quickly challenged by three divine orders, two of which involved his fomenting political revolutions. Although two of these commissions were carried out by Elisha, his prophetic successor, their mention here shows that Israel's faith finds expression in action rather than mere mystic contemplation. As in the case of Moses at the burning bush, Elijah realized afresh that Yahweh acts in the sphere of history, summoning a prophet to take part in

[25] Contemporizing the sacred heritage is one dimension of the "canonical criticism" advocated by James Sanders; see *Canon and Community* [521], especially chap. 2.

[26] R. Davidson, *Courage to Doubt* [134], p. 98.

[27] The Hebrew word translated "your covenant" is textually insecure; important versions read simply "forsaken you" (Yahweh) at I Kings 19:10, 14. Commentators admit, however, that the covenant tradition is implied in the whole narrative. See John Gray's commentary on I and II Kings [295], pp. 409–10.

the divine plan of action. Yahweh's plan called for returning to the land of Israel to incite a revolution. Elijah was told that although the revolution would make a clean sweep of the house of Omri and its supporters, Yahweh would nevertheless spare a faithful remnant—"seven thousand in Israel, all the knees that have not bowed to Baal."

It is significant that Elijah made a journey to Sinai, where Moses had received the revelation from Yahweh after the Exodus. In one sense, the whole prophetic movement, of which Elijah is the great exemplar, was a pilgrimage back to Sinai, to the source of Israel's faith. The prophets did not claim to be innovators—individuals who came forth with bright new ideas that would enable Israel to keep up to date in the onward march of culture. Rather, they demanded that Israel return to the wholehearted covenant allegiance demanded by the "jealousy" of Yahweh. They were reformers who took their stand on the ancient ground of Sinai. But in a deeper sense the prophetic movement was not a kind of archaism—a timid response to cultural crisis by retreating into the idealized past. In the message of the prophets the Mosaic past came alive in the present with new vitality and meaning, as we can see from the stories of Elijah. What was latent in the Mosaic tradition began to come to fullness, and Israel was given a deeper understanding of the implications of the covenant and of Yahweh's ways in history.

The Affair of Naboth's Vineyard

The third episode in the Elijah cycle (I Kings 21) apparently took place some years later. Ahab wanted to purchase the vineyard of Naboth, which adjoined his palace in the city of Jezreel (his second capital), so that he could enjoy more room. His terms were generous enough, but Naboth refused to sell for one reason: it was a family estate. Properly speaking, it was not Naboth's "private property" to dispose of as he pleased. It belonged to the whole family or clan through whom it had been passed down from generation to generation as a sacred inheritance. His refusal—"Yahweh forbid that I should give you the inheritance of my ancestors"—revealed an attitude toward land that was unique with Israel. According to this view, the real owner of the land is Yahweh. Fulfilling the promises made to the ancestors of Israel, Yahweh had brought the Israelites into a country where they could settle down and had given the land to various tribes and clans. They were to be stewards of Yahweh's property, administering it for the welfare of the whole community. So land-grabbing and private speculation were ruled out by the very nature of the covenant community. Naboth was only reaffirming the ancient basis of Israel's land tenure when he insisted that he did not have the freedom to sell the ancestral estate.[28]

Ahab recognized the validity of Naboth's position, although it made him very sullen. But Jezebel, who had been nurtured in the commercial civilization of Phoenicia, had other conceptions of property. Her Baal religion placed no

---

[28] See Walter Eichrodt, "Revelation and Responsibility," *Interpretation*, III (1949), 393–94.

limitations on the exercise of royal power. "Do you now govern Israel?" she asked Ahab. She promised to get Naboth's vineyard for him—in her own way. At her direction, Naboth was accused by two "good-for-nothings" of "cursing God and the king" (that is, of blasphemy and treason), and, with no word of defense spoken on his behalf, Naboth was stoned to death. Evidently Naboth's sons were done away with too (II Kings 9:26). The murder had a pretense of legality—enough to salve the consciences of those who had a hand in the treacherous deed. So, with Naboth and his sons out of the way, Ahab thought he was free to take possession of the vineyard.

But Ahab had yet to stand before the highest tribunal, for "the word of Yahweh came to Elijah the Tishbite." In the vineyard that Ahab had gone to claim as his own, there occurred another dramatic face-to-face encounter of prophet and king. Like the ground stained with the blood of Abel, this outrageous crime was crying to Yahweh for requital, and the prophet thundered out the impending divine judgment. Stinging under the sharp words of the prophetic gadfly, the king could only mutter, remembering his past associations with Elijah, "Have you found me, O my enemy?" The story concludes with a vivid description of Ahab's penitence, which reminds us of David's remorse after his encounter with Nathan (I Kings 21:27–29; most of verses 20b–26 are Deuteronomistic comments).

The Naboth incident provides an excellent preface to the social message of the prophets of a later period. Here we see the Baal religion and the Yahweh faith in opposition, not in a dramatic contest on Carmel but in the field of social relationships. The great Israelite prophets were champions of the stern ethical demands of the ancient Mosaic tradition. As we saw in Chapter 3, Israel's covenant obedience was motivated by gratitude for the great acts of liberation that Yahweh had wrought on behalf of an oppressed people. Yahweh had created a covenant community in which every person stood equal before the law— whether rich or poor, king or private citizen. The whole community was responsible to the sovereign will of Yahweh as expressed in the absolute laws that had been handed down from the wilderness period and refined by legal usage. And when the justice of a member of the community was downtrodden by the powerful, Yahweh intervened to defend the weak and the defenseless and to restore the order and familial solidarity of the covenant community. The Baal religion tended to support the *status quo*, with the aristocracy on top. But the Yahweh faith, as revived in the prophet Elijah, supplied the energy for a protest against the evils of a commercial civilization and for social reform.

ELISHA AND THE CLOSING YEARS
OF THE OMRI DYNASTY

At the opening of the book of Second Kings (chapters 2–9; 13:14–21), we find the stories dealing with Elisha, upon whom Elijah's prophetic mantle had fallen. The Elisha cycle (as well as the Elijah legends in II Kings 1) represents a type of prophetic tradition different from the great Elijah narratives we have been considering. Here is a popular lore that is filled with wonder tales: the rolling back of the Jordan by Elijah's mantle, the magical sweetening of water, the deception of the Moabites with a mirage of blood red water, the restoration of the Shunammite woman's child from the dead, the incident of the floating axe-head, and so on. Stories like these delighted the popular imagination and no doubt were told and retold by the members of the prophetic order with which Elisha was intimately associated. Fanciful though they are, they show us Elisha as a prophet concerned for the people, and they record the conviction of those who knew from his deeds that "the word of Yahweh (was) with him" (II Kings 3:12).

The stories are told against the background of the political events in which Israel was involved during the closing years of the Omri dynasty, especially the reign of J(eh)oram, king of Israel. In this period (c. 849–842 B.C.E.) Moab revolted against Israel—a fact that is confirmed by the Moabite Stone (see pp. 264–265), which makes the extravagant claim that Mesha, the Moabite king, subjected Israel to the sacrificial ban (*ḥérem*) of the god Chemosh, so that "Israel perished forever."[29] The Israelite account, though adorned with fanciful elements, is probably correct in reporting that the Moabite king sought victory by sacrificing his eldest son to the Moabite god Chemosh upon the city wall. As a result, so the historian interprets, "there came great wrath upon Israel" (II Kings 3:4–27).

Most of the stories, however, reflect the conditions of the continuing wars between Syria and Israel. A magnificent illustration is the charming story of Naaman, the commander of the Syrian army, who, at the suggestion of a little slave girl whom the Syrians had carried off from Israel during a raid, made the trip into Israelite territory to seek Elisha, and there became convinced that "there is no God in all the earth but in Israel" (II Kings 5). The story shows how people could believe, even under the trying conditions of war, that the enemy was included within the sovereignty of Yahweh.

According to the account in II Kings 8:7–15, Elisha journeyed to Damascus, the capital of Syria. While he was there, King Benhadad, suffering from sickness, sent one of his officers, Hazael, to ask the prophet whether he would recover. In a prophetic trance, Elisha predicted that Hazael would be the next king of Syria and that he would bring great military calamity to Israel. Under the authority of this prophetic word, Hazael murdered Benhadad the very next day, thus bringing about one of the revolutions that Elijah was to foment (I Kings 19:15–16). The second revolution was brought about when Elisha summoned one of the "sons of the prophets" to anoint Jehu as king over Israel (II Kings 9:1–13). With Jehu's rise to power, the Omri dynasty was brought to an end in a terrible bloodbath, and a new chapter in Israel's history began.

---

[29] In the Moabite text, "son" probably means Omri's "grandson." The revolt occurred in Jehoram's reign, not Ahab's.

CHAPTER 9

Fallen Is
the Virgin Israel

Today we tend to value tolerance so highly that we sometimes advocate indifference toward competing religious loyalties. We are likely to sympathize with Solomon's cosmopolitanism, or even with the compromising attitude of Ahab's generation, which teetered back and forth between opposing views. But, as we have seen, Israel's prophets attacked the tolerant syncretism of the time and insisted on an ardent devotion to Yahweh. It has been rightly observed that ''intolerance in religion was not a characteristic of ancient peoples, and was only introduced into Israel by the prophets.''[1] The flame of their conviction was kindled at the ancient sources of the Mosaic faith, and burst forth like a consuming fire at a time when the nation was in danger of being engulfed by Canaanite culture.

In the previous chapter we were primarily interested in the Northern Kingdom, whose prosperity and political power overshadowed that of Judah. To be sure, in the reign of Jehoshaphat, a contemporary of Omri, Judah enjoyed a resurgence of political and commercial power. The policy of peaceful collaboration with Israel, sealed by intermarriage between the royal houses, enabled Judah to recover from the enervating civil wars that had sapped its energies ever since the division of Solomon's kingdom. But Judah was still the weaker

Biblical readings: The books of Amos and Hosea, and the background material in II Kings 9–17. The account of II Kings is paralleled in II Chronicles 22–25.

[1] T. J. Meek, *Hebrew Origins* [97], p. 169.

of the twin kingdoms, especially during the period of the powerful Omri dynasty. In this chapter, the spotlight again falls on the kingdom of Israel during its next dynasty, that of Jehu. Toward the end of the Jehu dynasty, the star of Israel reached its zenith of glory, only to plunge like a meteor into oblivion. The main sources for our study are found in a section of the Deuteronomistic History (II Kings 9–17) and, above all, in the written prophecies of Amos and Hosea. We shall see how the reforming zeal of the prophets of the ninth century— Elijah, Micaiah, and Elisha—was continued and deepened by the prophets of the eighth.

THE REVOLUTION OF JEHU

Compared with the stability of the Southern Kingdom of Judah, which had a single dynasty from the time of David to its very end, the Northern Kingdom of Israel had a checkered political career. Political unrest and intrigue had kept both Jeroboam I and Baasha from founding a dynasty. And the dynasty of Omri lasted only for the reigns of four kings, to be superseded by the five-king dynasty of Jehu. Then political instability returned again, until the fall of the nation in 721 B.C.E. The political differences between the two kingdoms, as we have previously noticed, were rooted in different "ideologies." The continuity of the Davidic dynasty was supported by the view that Yahweh had made a covenant to maintain the Davidic throne. This view provided a basis for the transfer of power from one royal administration to the next. In the Northern Kingdom, however, there was greater political instability, owing to the persistence of the old "democratic" ideal of the Tribal Confederacy. Northerners believed that Yahweh's spirit was poured upon an individual, but not a dynasty—and this view could foster revolution.

The story of the Jehu dynasty opens in II Kings 9. Elijah, as we have seen, set in motion the forces that were to overthrow the Omri dynasty by revolution. In this passage, Elisha commissions one of the prophetic band to seek out Jehu, the army commander who had resumed the attempt to take Ramoth-gilead from Syria, and to anoint him king of Israel. The word of Yahweh coming from this ecstatic "madman," as he is called (II Kings 9:11), was all that was needed to light the fuse of revolt. Supported by the power of the mutinous army, Jehu was proclaimed king with great fanfare.

Jehu's purge of Israel after he took the throne was both thoroughgoing and brutal. The memory of the gory details, which are given in the old story that has been slightly touched up with Deuteronomistic comments (II Kings 9:7–10a), sent a shudder through future generations, as we shall see in the book of Hosea. Riding furiously in his chariot—a trait that has become proverbial for modern speed demons ("sons of Jehu")—Jehu came to Jezreel, where Joram, the king of Israel, was nursing wounds received in the Syrian battle, and sent an arrow through the heart of the fugitive king. With a sense of poetic justice,

Jehu ordered Joram's body to be cast into Naboth's vineyard—an act designed, no doubt, to win over the people, who had been suffering under the economic oppression of the nobility and merchant class during the time of the Omri dynasty. But Jehu was not satisfied to limit the purge to Israel; so he murdered Ahaziah of Judah, who had come to visit his sick uncle, and later massacred Ahaziah's brothers, who also had come for a visit. Then Jezebel, whose last queenly act was to paint her eyebrows and adorn her head, was tossed out of a window and mangled beyond recognition. Finally, to cap the gory climax, Jehu had all seventy sons of Ahab decapitated, thus removing all claimants to the throne (see Chronological Chart 5, p. 304).

The Religious Side of the Revolution

This was more than a typical *coup d' état*. Although the more sensitive Israelites must have cringed at Jehu's brutal excesses and brazen callousness (see II Kings 9:34: "He went in and ate and drank"), Jehu himself sincerely believed that he was carrying out the religious revolution called for by Elijah and Elisha. True, his butchery of the whole house of Ahab was motivated by political ambition, and he shrewdly capitalized on the revolutionary ferment within the army and the widespread economic unrest in the land. But he was also influenced by religious considerations, and undoubtedly intended the massacre as an application of the *ḥérem* against an evil family, as Achan's household had been destroyed in the time of Joshua (Josh. 7:24–26). Elijah himself, after all, had demanded the ruthless extermination of the prophets of Baal after the Carmel contest.

That the revolution was in part a religious development is clear, not only in Jehu's being anointed by an ecstatic prophet, but also in the collaboration of Jehonadab, the son of Rechab (II Kings 10:15–17). This man was the head of a family that was known for its passionate devotion to the tradition of the wilderness, in opposition to the agricultural ways of Canaan. He was a descendant of the Kenites (Midianites), the nomadic people who influenced and supported Moses during the wilderness period. And Jehonadab's descendants of a later generation, known as Rechabites (Jer. 35), perpetuated their ancestors' puritanical devotion to the ancient ways of the wilderness. Under a vow, which they had received from Jehonadab, they refused to drink wine, cultivate vineyards, build houses, or till the soil. Dwelling in tents as their nomadic ancestors had, they stood for the pristine purity of the Mosaic tradition of the wilderness—a purity which, they maintained, had been defiled by the agrarian culture of Canaan.

According to the story, Jehu invited Jehonadab to join him in his work of extermination. "Come with me," said Jehu, "and see my zeal for Yahweh." Jehu showed his zeal for the Yahweh faith by slaughtering the remnants of Ahab's house, according to the prophetic word of Elijah. And Jehonadab, a representative of the conservative, nomadic tradition of Israel, endorsed Jehu's purge by riding with him in his chariot.

Jehonadab also matched Jehu's zeal for Yahweh by joining in the extermination of the Baal worshipers (II Kings 10:18–27). With cunningly concealed
sarcasm, Jehu announced that he was planning to make a great sacrifice to the
Phoenician deity, Baal-Melkart, but the "sacrifice" turned out to be an application of the sacrificial ban (*ḥérem*) to the devotees assembled in the temple of
Baal. The holocaust was completed by burning the "pillar" (perhaps this was
the *Asherah*, an image of the mother goddess), demolishing the temple, and
converting the place into a latrine. Notice that the Deuteronomistic historians
are somewhat impressed by Jehu's zeal, and not the least bit horrified at the
ruthless destruction of the house of Ahab and the Baal worshipers. They denounce Jehu, despite his fanatical devotion to Yahweh, for not removing the
idolatrous shrines that Jeroboam I had established at Dan and Bethel.

Jehu's revolution had serious repercussions in the Southern Kingdom. The
mother of the Judean king Ahaziah, who had been slain by Jehu, was Athaliah,
the daughter of Ahab. Despite her Yahweh name (Athal-iah = "Yah[weh] is
exalted"), she was evidently a devotee of Baal-Melkart and, like Jezebel in the
north, had helped propagate this religion in Judah (see II Kings 11:18). When
she heard of her son's death, she liquidated the male members of the Davidic
line and usurped the throne. But she missed one person: the infant Joash (or
Jehoash), who was spirited away and hidden by the priests in the Temple. In
the north, it was the prophets who led the revolution against the Phoenician
Baal; in the south, however, revolution was fomented in the priestly circles of
the Temple with the cooperation of "the people of the land"—that is, the conservative landowners who lived outside Jerusalem. After a covenant ceremony
involving Yahweh and the people on the one hand and the people and the king
on the other (II Kings 11:17), the temple of Baal was destroyed, and both Athal-
iah and the Baal priest Mattan were assassinated. Thus Joash took his place
along with Asa as one of the reforming kings of Judah, and thereby won the
moderate praise of the Deuteronomistic historians (II Kings 12:1–3).

Problems of Foreign Policy

Once the fires of revolution had died down in the north, Jehu was faced with
political problems that proved too much for him to handle. His cold-blooded
murder of Ahaziah and the rise of the new regime in Judah had alienated the
Southern Kingdom, and his liquidation of the devotees of the Phoenician Baal
had no doubt cut off any support from Phoenicia. Isolated from the political
allies that the Omri dynasty had counted on in its foreign policy, the Northern
Kingdom was now more vulnerable to attack from Syria than ever before. The
Syrian king, Hazael, quick to take advantage of the situation, swept down
through Transjordan (II Kings 10:32–33). In 841 B.C.E., Jehu sensed his hopeless
plight and, anxious to save his throne at any cost, paid tribute to the Assyrian
monarch, Shalmaneser III, who by that time had recuperated from the battle of
Qarqar and was renewing his march into the west. This political event is ignored
in the biblical account, but it is mentioned in the famous Black Obelisk of Shal-

The Black Obelisk of Shalmaneser III (859–825 B.C.E.) portrays scenes of tribute being brought by representatives of various countries, including Jehu of Israel, to the Assyrian king. About six and a half feet high, the obelisk once stood in the public square of Nimrud, the city (about 25 miles south of Nineveh) where the king's palace was located. Commemorating the events of his reign, each of the five panels depicts a region from which tribute was brought.

maneser III, which depicts Jehu, at the head of an Israelite delegation, kneeling before "the mighty king, king of the universe, king without a rival, the autocrat, the powerful one of the four regions of the world"—as Shalmaneser modestly described himself. The inscription records the "tribute of Jehu, son of Omri" (for the Assyrians continued to designate Israelite kings after the name of Omri).[2]

²See Pritchard, *Ancient Near Eastern Texts* [1], p. 280.

"Jehu, Son of Omri" is shown kneeling before the Assyrian king in the second panel from the top of the obelisk. On the other faces of this panel, which run around the four sides of the obelisk as a continuous frieze, thirteen Israelite porters bear the tribute. The king holds a bowl in his hand, and an attendant shades his head with a parasol.

The Assyrian advance relieved the pressure on Israel for the time being, for Syria had to meet this threat to its Mesopotamian border. Within a few years, however, internal problems forced Assyria to shelve plans for expansion into the west for a generation. Hazael capitalized on this good luck (after the year 837 B.C.E.) and sent his armies in lightning thrusts to the south (see Amos 1:3). During the reign of Jehoahaz, son of Jehu, Israel's armaments were reduced to the barest minimum (II Kings 13:7), for, as the historian says with some exaggeration, "the king of Syria had destroyed them and made them like the dust at threshing." At the same time, during the reign of the contemporary Judean king Joash, the Syrians swept down the Philistine coast and were stopped from attacking Jerusalem only when the royal and temple treasures were turned over to them (II Kings 12:17–18).

Then, in the year 805, the tide turned. The Deuteronomistic interpreter states that "Hazael king of Syria oppressed Israel all the days of Jehoahaz; but Yahweh was gracious to them and had compassion on them." As a result of this divine favor, when the new Syrian king, Benhadad, the son of Hazael, came to the throne, Jehoash of Israel (who had the same name as the contemporary Judean king) recovered from the Syrians the cities that previously had been lost in war (II Kings 13:22–25). This turn of affairs was due less to the energetic warfare of the new Israelite king than to another surge of Assyrian power into Syria. In the year 805, a new Assyrian monarch, Adad-nirari III, resumed the attack on Syria and in a short time so crippled the neighboring state that it was no longer a threat to Israel. However, the momentum of the Assyrian advance was spent in this campaign; and for fifty years Israel did not have to fear invasion from beyond the Euphrates.

So with Assyria having troubles at home, and with Syria barely able to maintain itself as a state, J(eh)oash of Israel inherited the most favorable political situation in the entire history of the Northern Kingdom. His program of political expansion was challenged only by the kingdom of Judah, whose king, Amaziah, riding high on the wave of victory over Edom, insisted on trying to settle a score with the Jehu dynasty. It was a foolhardy move, as the fable about the thistle and the cedar shows (II Kings 14:8–10). The Israelite king soundly whipped the Judean state and reduced it to vassalage, thus preparing the way for the glorious era of Jeroboam II, the greatest king of the Jehu dynasty.

THE AGE OF JEROBOAM II

The Deuteronomistic historians dismiss the reign of Jeroboam II with a scant seven verses, most of which consist of the usual monotonous formulas (II Kings 14:23–29). They do excerpt from the Book of the Chronicles of the Kings of Israel the notice that Jeroboam "restored the border of Israel from the entrance of Hamath as far as the Sea of the Arabah." The "entrance of Hamath," the northernmost boundary of Solomon's kingdom (I Kings 8:65), refers to the pass between Mount Lebanon and Mount Hermon, which can be located on a map by drawing a line straight across from Damascus to Sidon. The "Sea of the Arabah" refers to the Dead Sea, named after the low desert plain that extends from the Jordan valley to the Gulf of Aqabah. Thus Jeroboam II extended his kingdom northward into the orbit of Hamath and Syria, and southward into territory that encroached upon Judah.[3] Never before had an Israelite king held undisputed sway over so large a kingdom. And once again, this nationalistic revival was inspired by a prophet—Jonah, the son of Amittai, under whose name the book of Jonah was later written (see pp. 605–607).

A blanket of Deuteronomistic silence also falls upon the reign of Azariah (Uzziah), Jeroboam's contemporary in Judah (II Kings 14:21–22; 15:1–7). Under his reign and that of his son and coregent, Jotham, however, Judah also experienced a national revival, as we know from the apparently authentic report by the Chronicler (II Chron. 26). Having enlarged and modernized his army, Uzziah carried out conquests on both sides of the Jordan. The cities of the Philistine plain were subjected, as were the peoples of Transjordan. Moreover, the Negeb to the south was brought into the orbit of Judean control, enabling Uzziah to build Elath (II Kings 14:22) near Ezion-geber, and to restore the avenues of commerce into the Arabian world that Solomon had opened up two centuries be-

---

[3] The statement in II Kings 14:28—"he recovered for Israel Damascus and Hamath, which had belonged to Judah"—is very obscure.

The Classical Age of Israelite Prophecy*

	North	South
Middle and Late Eighth Century B.C.E.	Amos (c. 750) Hosea (c. 745)	
		Isaiah (c. 742–700) Micah (c. 722–701)
Late Seventh Century		Zephaniah (c. 628–622) Jeremiah (c. 626–587) Nahum (c. 612) Habakkuk (c. 605)
Sixth Century		Ezekiel (c. 593–573) Obadiah (after 587) II Isaiah (c. 540)
Period of Restoration		Haggai (c. 520–515) Zechariah (c. 520–515) Joel (c. 500–350) Malachi (c. 500–450)

*This outline gives the sequence of the prophetic figures, but does not take into consideration the later updating of their prophecy in prophetic circles.

fore. Thus under Jeroboam II and Uzziah the twin kingdoms of Israel and Judah controlled almost the full sweep of Solomon's empire "from the entrance of Hamath to the Brook of Egypt" (I Kings 8:65). Judah, however, did not reach the peak of its political and economic power until the stronger Northern Kingdom had begun to decline after the death of Jeroboam II. So we shall postpone further discussion of Judah until the next chapter, in order that we may consider the last and most glorious era of North Israel. This period marked the beginning of the classical age of Israelite prophecy, which will engage our attention in this and subsequent chapters.

A Time of Prosperity

In spite of the silence of the Deuteronomistic historians, we know a great deal about the long reign of Jeroboam II, not only from the books of Amos and Hosea, but also from archaeological findings. A vivid picture of the material prosperity of this period has been provided by excavations at Megiddo and Samaria (see pp. 266–267).[4] Especially at Samaria we see signs of the prosperity and cultural achievement that prompted Amos, a prophet of the mid-eighth century, to denounce "those who feel secure on the mountain of Samaria" (Amos 6:1). The beautiful ivories, the luxurious summer and winter homes (Amos 3:15), the impressive fortifications, the teeming marketplaces—all filled Amos with disgust, and led him to proclaim that Yahweh too loathed the whole spectacle. Unlike the "Unmoved Mover" of classical Greek philosophy, who is character-

---

[4] See Kathleen Kenyon, *Archaeology in the Holy Land* [105], chap. 11.

ized by apathy (lack of emotion) and is uninvolved in the human situation, the God of Amos is involved and reacts with passion:[5]

> I loathe the pride of Jacob,
> I hate his palaces,
> and I am going to hand over the city [Samaria]
>   and all it contains.
>
> —AMOS 6:8

The books of Amos and Hosea provide a clear picture of the economic injustices that followed in the wake of generations of intimate cultural relations with the mercantile economy of Phoenicia. During the reign of Jeroboam II, the commercial and colonial activity of the Phoenicians was at its peak in the Mediterranean world, and Israel shared in the profits that flowed from the exchange of goods and services. Moreover, Jeroboam's conquests in Transjordan (the cities of Lo-debar and Karnaim mentioned in Amos 6:13) put him in a position to control the trade route from Syria and evidently the commercial highways from Arabia. Thus Samaria, the luxurious capital, became a great center of wealth. But the price for this prosperity was high, for an oppressive social pyramid grew up with the royal courtiers and the merchant class at the top and the great mass of people ground into poverty at the bottom. The heinous crime committed by Ahab against Naboth was perpetrated on a wider scale, as economic tyrants— with the sanction of corrupt courts (Amos 5:10–13)—"bought the poor for silver, and the needy for a pair of sandals" (Amos 8:6; see 2:6). Amos felt that these crimes would have been shocking to any of Israel's neighbors who had an elemental sense of justice:

> Proclaim it to the palaces in Assyria,*
>   and to the strongholds in the land of Egypt,
> saying:
>   "Gather together upon the hill* of Samaria,
>   and see the terrible disorder in that city,
>   and the oppression within it!
>   They don't know how to do right,"
>   —the utterance of Yahweh—
>   "they who accumulate violence and force in their palaces."
>
> —AMOS 3:9–10

*Reading with the Greek translation (Septuagint).

The prophetic books of Amos and Hosea also give a clear picture of the popular religion of the time and tend to support the Deuteronomistic judgment that the ways of Jeroboam I were perpetuated in his namesake. Baalism was too deeply rooted in the Northern Kingdom, which was directly exposed to the culture of the Fertile Crescent, to be eradicated even by measures as thorough-

---

[5] For a discussion of "the pathos of God," including the pathos of indignation, see Abraham J. Heschel, *The Prophets* [315], especially chaps. 11, 12.

going as those of Jehu. Hosea, a contemporary of Amos, excoriated Israel for supposing that its prosperity sprang from the worship of the Baals, the local representatives of the Canaanite storm god who allegedly granted the blessings of agriculture (Hosea 2:2–13). He poured scorn upon the Baal festivals (2:13), the practice of temple prostitution (4:14), sacrifice at the high places (4:13), and the worship of images in the form of bulls (13:1–2). Twice the golden bull, which Jeroboam I installed in Bethel as a symbol of Yahweh's presence (see pp. 259–261), came in for the strongest censure (8:5; 10:5).

The Northern Mosaic Tradition

The Yahweh faith was by no means dead, however. In the worship centers, the Mosaic tradition was kept alive through ceremonies of covenant renewal like the one Joshua inaugurated at Shechem (Josh. 24). In the villages, a class of teaching priests, known as Levites, proclaimed and expounded the great convictions of Israel's faith. So when prophets like Amos and Hosea appeared in the Northern Kingdom, they did not speak in a vacuum, for they could appeal to the people on the basis of a common religious heritage. Indeed, these prophets did not claim to introduce the people to new doctrines that had never been heard of before. Rather, their task was to recall their hearers to the memory of events they had all but forgotten and to convictions that formed the basis of the whole community of Yahweh.

In the Northern Kingdom this religious heritage, in the judgment of many scholars, found expression in an Ephraimitic version of Israel's sacred history, the so-called Elohist (E) narrative. This epic narrative, which now survives only in fragmentary form, presumably was composed in the ninth century to express the national consciousness of the newly formed Kingdom of Israel under Jeroboam I (c. 922–901 B.C.E.), possibly in the time of Elijah (c. 850) when Phoenician culture presented a challenge to Israel. Whatever the date of literary composition, the narrative cycle goes back to an oral tradition that flourished in the period of the Tribal Confederacy. The common oral tradition was given a special stamp in the circle of the northern tribes, just as it received a distinctive Judean impression from the so-called Yahwist (J) in the age of Solomon, as we noticed previously (pp. 245–246). By the time of Amos and Hosea in the eighth century, this northern version of the Israelite epic was well known in Ephraim (Israel). Indeed, it was a point of contact when prophets addressed the people (e.g. Amos 2:9–10; Hosea 12:2–6).

This hypothesis may provide another example of how the sacred heritage was contemporized during the ongoing pilgrimage of the people. The Elohist narrative rehearses the sacred history of Israel, with special emphasis upon the call to the obedience of faith (the "fear of God") and the mediatorial role of the Mosaic prophet. If written down in the time of Elijah, when Israelites were tempted to follow the easy way of religious syncretism, it provided a forceful

DEFINITION: "ELOHIST"

This version of the Israelite tradition is designated by the symbol "E" because, for one reason, it shows an Ephraimitic, or North-Israelite, slant. This is evidenced by the prominence given to northern figures like Joseph, his mother Rachel, and his son Ephraim (Gen. 48:20), and also by the interest in northern shrines like Bethel (Gen. 28:17–22) and Shechem (Gen. 33:18–20). Moreover, this narrative shows peculiarities of vocabulary, like the use of "Horeb" for the sacred mountain (the southern or "J" tradition prefers "Sinai") and "Amorites" for the natives of Canaan (the other tradition favors "Canaanites"). Finally, this tradition apparently prefers to use the word 'Elohim for God instead of Yahweh in the stories dealing with the pre-Mosaic period.

According to the literary analysis that prevailed during the early twentieth century, this "source" or "tradition" survives only in fragmentary form; the Epic was reshaped by southern or Judean editors, especially after the fall of the Northern Kingdom in 721 B.C.E. In the contemporizing and editing of traditions, preference was given to the southern or Judean version, with the result that it is often difficult to reconstruct a continuous Ephraimitic (or Elohistic) narrative. Indeed, for a good number of years the Elohist hypothesis has been regarded as the Achilles' Heel of the whole literary analysis of the Pentateuch. Nevertheless, a number of scholars, whose ranks may be dwindling, still maintain that what is left of the Ephraimitic tradition, even after Judean editing, stands out sharply enough for us to get some idea of its distinctive character.[6]

In this view, the Elohist narrative starts with the call of Abraham (Gen. 15) and from this point follows the general outline of the Old Epic tradition through the rest of Genesis, Exodus, and Numbers. Special nuances of this tradition are said to be the motif of the "fear" or obedience of God as illustrated in the story of Abraham's sacrifice of Isaac (Gen. 22; note vs. 12) and the special status of Moses who, as a prophet, acts as a mediator between God and people (Num. 12:7–8; Deut. 34:10–12, presumably an Elohist passage). In Ephraimitic tradition, Moses is regarded as the prophet *par excellence* and the first in a succession of prophets "like Moses" (see Hos. 12:13; Jer. 15:1; cf. Deut. 18:15–22).[7]

call to radical obedience and a powerful reinterpretation of the Mosaic heritage.

In any case, whatever the distinctive literary and theological traits of the Ephraimitic and Judean (Elohist and Yahwist) versions, both traditions agree on the fundamental convictions which bound together the twin kingdoms, Israel and Judah, in the common worship of Yahweh. Sharing these convictions, Amos—a southerner and perhaps a representative of Judean (Zion) theology—journeyed to Bethel in the Ephraimitic hill country to hurl his protest against the people's way of life and to recall Israel to a worship and lifestyle consonant with the Mosaic covenant tradition.

---

[6] See Hans Walter Wolff, "The Elohistic Fragments in the Pentateuch," *Interpretation* 26 (1972), 158–73; also in *The Vitality of Old Testament Traditions* [63], chap. 4.

[7] See Robert R. Wilson, *Prophecy and Society* [328], pp. 159–66 and *passim*, for a discussion of how the Ephraimitic view of the Mosaic prophet was expanded by the Deuteronomistic circle to mean a succession of prophets "like Moses."

THE HERDSMAN FROM TEKOA

We know very little about Amos, for the book that bears his name stresses the "word of Yahweh" spoken by the prophet, rather than biographical facts about the man himself. The heading of the book of Amos (1:1), which was added by a later editor, tells us that Amos came from among shepherds of Tekoa,[8] a village lying a few miles south of Jerusalem, and that he was active during the reign of two contemporary kings, Uzziah of Judah and Jeroboam II of Israel. We could date his career more precisely if we were sure of the meaning of the chronological reference, "two years before the earthquake" (see Zech. 14:5). In any case, Amos was active in the Northern Kingdom during the height of the reign of Jeroboam II, some time before Jeroboam's death in 746 B.C.E. A date of about 750 fits the conditions reflected in the book.

A clearer picture of Amos' background is given in the prose passage found in Amos 7:10–15, which records the dramatic encounter between Amos and Amaziah, the chief priest of the Bethel temple—the royal sanctuary which Jeroboam I had once established as one of the national shrines of the Northern Kingdom. Here we are told that Amos was a native of Judah where he had been a herdsman and a "dresser of sycamore trees." (The latter expression refers to the puncturing of the fig-like fruit so that the insects that form on the inside may be released.) The appearance of this southerner in the Northern Kingdom discloses that the division between Israel and Judah was primarily political, and that the two nations were actually bound together as *one* covenant people with a common religious tradition. Amaziah, assuming that Amos was just a "visionary" (*ḥozeh*) who earned his living by his religious trade (see I Sam. 9:8; I Kings 14:2; II Kings 8:8), warned him to return to Judah and there "eat bread"— that is, seek fees for his prophetic oracles. Amos, however, replied:

> I am not a prophet [*nabî'*],
>   Nor one of the sons of the prophets;
> rather, I am a herdsman,
>   and a dresser of sycamore trees.
> However, Yahweh took me from behind the flock,
>   and Yahweh said to me:
> Go! Prophesy to my people Israel.
>   —AMOS 7:14–15

The meaning of Amos' reply to Amaziah is not altogether clear. According to one interpretation, the priest recognizes Amos to be a "visionary" (*ḥôzeh*), a

---

[8] Some scholars say that Amos was at home in the atmosphere of traditional wisdom which was esteemed in nomadic clans and small towns like Tekoa. See H. W. Wolff, *Amos, the Prophet* [337] and Samuel Terrien, "Amos and Wisdom," *Israel's Prophetic Heritage* [152], 108–15. Doubtless Amos was influenced by this tradition, as evidenced by his use of literary forms and expressions characteristic of Wisdom. But the wisdom movement exerted an influence upon other prophets too and was undoubtedly a major ingredient in Israelite society (see Jer. 18:18), at least from the time of Solomon.

term used to refer to the prophetic office in southern circles, and tells him to go back to Judah where prophets of this type belong. Amos answers by using the word *nabî'* ("prophet"), a term current in northern circles to designate a Moses-like prophet who found support in a prophetic community ("sons of the prophets"). Following this line of thought, was Amos merely disavowing that he was a northern (Ephraimitic) style prophet like Moses? Or was he saying that he was not a prophet in any sense, northern or southern?[9] The latter seems to be the case. Amos was only a layperson whose work had been interrupted by a divine commission that came to him with the irresistible power of Yahweh's spirit (see Amos 3:8). In other words, this was prophecy of such a different type that the usual terms for "prophet" did not adequately express his understanding of his task.

Amos is the first in an extraordinary series of prophets whose oracles have been left to us in written form. The prophets who preceded him, like Elijah and Elisha, are known to us only through the oral tradition in which the memory of their words and acts was preserved. With Amos, however, we have the actual "words which he saw," as the heading of the book puts it. The book of Amos is a compilation of little units or "oracles," spoken by the prophet on different occasions, and compiled by Amos himself or by the circle of the prophets who treasured them. Amos delivered these oracles in various situations over a fairly brief span of time during his preaching at Bethel (7:13) and possibly at Samaria (4:1). He directed his message primarily to the Northern Kingdom; but, since he was a southerner, the twin kingdom of Judah was also in his mind (6:1, 2; 8:14). He was concerned about "the whole family which Yahweh brought out of Egypt" (3:1).

Yahweh's Sovereignty over the Nations

In reading the book of Amos, we must remember the political situation at the time. As we have seen, in the age of Jeroboam II Israel was able to flex its military muscles and expand because Syria had been weakened and the Assyrian lion was confined to its distant lair. The whole picture was soon to change, however, with the rise to power of an Assyrian usurper, Tiglath-pileser III (c. 745–727 B.C.E.). With amazing speed and energy he resumed the Assyrian advance, which had been slowed to a halt shortly after Assyria's crippling attacks on Syria in the year 805, and soon he was marching into Palestine, conquering

---

[9] See Robert R. Wilson, *Prophecy and Society* [328], pp. 269–70. Some scholars argue that the reply should be translated in the past tense, "I was no prophet, nor a member of a prophetic guild, . . ." implying that Amos was not a member of a prophetic order when Yahweh called him but that he is actually one now by his own admission. See R. E. Clements, *Prophecy and Covenant* [312], pp. 35–38. It is possible to translate the Hebrew that way, although the interpretation curiously inverts the negative statement of vs. 14a into positive agreement with Amaziah. However, this translation makes Amos' statement somewhat awkward as a reply. Amaziah had accused Amos of being a seer (*hôzeh*) in the present, not in the past, and Amos' reply to this charge would appropriately express his *present* self-understanding.

everything before him. These events are clearly reflected in the book of Hosea. But in the time of Amos, Assyria's threat to Israel was still only "a little cloud" on the horizon "the size of a human hand" (cf. I Kings 18:44). With great seriousness, which differed radically from the complacency and self-confidence of Samaria and Judah, Amos saw that trouble was brewing—not just because of Assyria's imperial ambitions, but also because Yahweh was at work in the political arena. Amos shocked his contemporaries with the hard-hitting language of history—of the sword's brutalities, captivity, desolate cities, political collapse. His role as a prophet was to interpret these ominous events in which Yahweh was acting, just as Yahweh had acted in Israel's history in the past.

As the book of Amos opens, we hear that Yahweh is at work among the nations. In the section on "Yahweh's Judgment Against the Nations" (Amos 1:3-2:3) Amos may have adopted a cultic "execration" form which was used in the temple to pronounce divine judgment upon the enemies who threaten Yahweh's chosen people.[10] If so, Amos has given the form a completely new twist. The prophet arouses attention by throwing the spotlight of divine judgment upon the small nations that surrounded Israel: Syria, Philistia, Tyre, Ammon, Moab.[11] Amos affirms that Yahweh is sovereign over these enemies and rivals of Israel. Because of their war atrocities a divine fire will break out against their proud palaces and fortifications. But then comes the surprise. What Israel least expected or wanted to hear was the prophetic announcement that the same fire would consume the people of Yahweh's choice because of the atrocities committed in peace and prosperity. Thus the climax of the series of divine judgments is the startling announcement that Yahweh's wrath is also directed against the people of Israel (2:6-8).

It is just at this point, where Amos is affirming the universal sovereignty of Yahweh, that we become most aware of the covenant tradition in which the prophet was rooted. He did not claim to say anything new, although certainly he spoke with a disturbingly new accent. Echoing Israel's confessional affirmation (Deut. 26:5-9; Josh. 24:2-13), he appealed to the memory of events enshrined in Israelite tradition. Just as Americans reflect on the meaning of a world crisis in the light of a common memory of their past, so Amos interpreted Israel's crisis in the light of a shared memory of the events that had made Israel Yahweh's people with a special task and destiny. He summoned the people to remember the events of their sacred history: how Yahweh had brought them out of the land of Egypt, had guided them in the wilderness, had enabled them to possess the "land of the Amorites," and had raised up prophets and Nazir-

---

[10] See especially A. Bentzen, *The Ritual Background of Amos* 1.2–2.16, Oudtestamentische Studiën, VIII (Leiden: Brill, 1950), 85–99.

[11] Some scholars question the originality of three oracles—those against Phoenicia (Amos 1:9-10), Edom (Amos 1:11-12), and Judah (Amos 2:4-5)—because they are cast in a somewhat different form and lack a specific portrayal of impending punishment. The oracle against Judah, however, may have replaced an earlier oracle, for it is hard to believe that the prophet would have omitted his own home country.

ites to keep them faithful to their God (Amos 2:9–11).[12] In short, the prophet was proclaiming the "word of the Lord" within the context of Israel's sacred story. According to his witness, God speaks in the present through the remembrance and appropriation of the tradition.

Covenant Promises and Threats

This appeal to Israelite tradition, and to the great convictions that were stamped indelibly on the national epics current in the northern and southern kingdoms (J and E), shows that Amos was a vigorous upholder of the Mosaic tradition. That the conclusions which Amos and the people drew from their common convictions were very different, however, is seen in their contrasting attitudes toward Israel's election by Yahweh. The keynote of Amos' prophecy is struck in Amos 3:1–8, a passage which begins by recalling the crucial event of Israel's history: the Exodus from Egypt. It was through Yahweh's action in this event that Israel had become a community, a "whole family" bound together by the bonds of religious loyalty. Israel was "the people of Yahweh." It was also through that event that Yahweh had entered into a covenant relationship with Israel: "You only have I known of all the families of the earth. . . . " The verb "know" (*yada'*) refers to the closest kind of personal relationship. In some contexts the verb is used for the intimate union between husband and wife (e.g., Gen. 4:1); but here it reflects ancient covenant (or treaty) language, in which a Suzerain "knows" (that is, enters into covenant relationship with) a vassal, who in turn is obligated to "know" (or recognize) the legitimate authority of the Suzerain (see pp. 98–101).[13] Yahweh, then, was "the God of Israel." As we have seen before, this covenant formula—"Yahweh the God of Israel, and Israel the people of Yahweh"—is the very heart of the covenant faith.

This conviction, however, led the people to an attitude against which Amos protested with all his might. Reasoning from Yahweh's special calling, the people felt that they could go on to say: "Therefore, Yahweh will give us prosperity, victory, and prestige among the nations." After all, they thought, the covenant included Yahweh's promises of blessing! So, flushed with the national revival and economic boom of the age of Jeroboam II, they anticipated the "Day of Yahweh." Apparently this festal Day was celebrated annually during the Fall covenant festival, that is, at the turn of the year. In popular belief this New Year's Day was an anticipation and foretaste of the great Day of Yahweh, a final climax of history when Yahweh would fulfill the promises of the covenant and crown Israel with glory and honor. This attitude shows through in the oracle

---

[12] The Nazirites (literally, "separated ones") were individuals who took special vows of consecration to Yahweh. Their abstinence from wine was a protest against Canaanite culture in the spirit of Israel's wilderness tradition.

[13] See Herbert B. Huffmon, "The Treaty Background of Hebrew Yada'," *Bulletin of the American Schools of Oriental Research*, 181 (1966), 31–37; summarized in Delbert R. Hillers, *Covenant* [225], chap. 6.

found in Amos 5:18–20, where it is said that the people were "desiring" the Day of Yahweh, confident that it would be a day of "light"—that is, a time of victory and blessing. Religion went hand in hand with nationalism. Indeed, in that time there was a great religious revival. Amos paints vivid pictures of a people thronging to the shrines to worship (4:4–5; 5:21–23), although they could scarcely wait for the services to be over so that they could get back to their money making (8:4–6). Over and over again they were saying to one another that they were not really on "the eve of destruction."

According to the Mosaic tradition as remembered in the north, however, the covenant did not give an unconditional guarantee for the future. The covenant rested upon a fundamental condition: "*If* you will obey my voice and keep my covenant you shall be my own possession among all peoples" (Exod. 19:5). It included blessings for obedience, to be sure, but it also included threats in the form of curses upon disobedience (see above, pp. 147–150).[14] Standing in this covenant tradition, and aware of the serious threats of divine judgment that it held forth, Amos reversed the popular logic of his time, saying: Yahweh has "known" only Israel of all the families of the earth; *therefore,* Israel will be punished for its iniquities. Israel's special calling, said Amos, does not entitle it to special privilege, but only to greater responsibility. In fact, he censured Israel far more heavily than any of the surrounding nations precisely *because* Israel alone had been called into a special relationship with God and had received, through its historical experience, the teaching concerning God's will. Having seen the light, however, the people preferred the darkness to cover up evil doings. Consequently, said Amos, "the Day of Yahweh" would prove to be the night of gloom:

> Trouble for those who are waiting so longingly for the day of Yahweh!
>   What will this day of Yahweh mean for you?
> It will mean darkness, not light,
>   as when a man escapes a lion's mouth,
>   only to meet a bear;
>   he enters his house and puts his hand on the wall,
>   only for a snake to bite him.
> Will not the day of Yahweh be darkness, not light?
> It will all be gloom, without a single ray of light.
>
> —AMOS 5:18–20 (JB)

Amos became more specific: Yahweh, who supervised the affairs of all peoples, was about to raise up a nation to be the instrument of divine judgment (6:14).

[14] R. E. Clements, *Prophecy and Covenant* [312], pp. 39–44, has an excellent discussion of "the curse of the law" which was rooted in the covenant cult and, under Amos' prophetic interpretation, was transformed into a message of doom. He argues that Amos has taken the covenant threat and radically reinterpreted it to mean not just the purging of sinners within Israel, but the end of Israel absolutely. See further D. R. Hillers, *Treaty-Curses and the Old Testament Prophecy* (Rome: Pontifical Biblical Institute, 1964), who points out that the curses of Israel's covenant are paralleled by the curses (e.g., captivity, exile) of ancient Near Eastern treaties.

So critical was Amos of the belief in Israel's election that in one passage he seems to renounce the doctrine altogether:

> "O Israelites, aren't you the same to me as the Ethiopians?"
> —the utterance of Yahweh.
> "Didn't I bring Israel up from the land of Egypt,
>   as well as the Philistines from Caphtor and the Syrians from Kir?"
> —AMOS 9:7

Two of the peoples referred to, the Syrians and the Philistines, had been Israel's worst enemies; and yet, says the prophet, Yahweh—the Sovereign of all the nations—has brought these peoples to their national homelands, just as Israel was brought out of Egypt into Canaan. In this instance the prophet repudiated Israel's notion that Yahweh is a national god, to be mobilized for the service of Israel's interests. Insofar as the doctrine of election meant that God serves Israel, rather than that Israel is called to serve God, it was in error.

The two oracles about divine election just considered (Amos 3:2 and 9:7) were undoubtedly delivered at different times. Amos was not a systematic theologian, but a prophet who delivered the word that needed to be heard at the moment. Even so, it is doubtful whether there is a fundamental inconsistency between the two statements. What Amos says in 9:7 is that Yahweh is surely active in the histories of other nations, even though they are not aware of this divine guidance and judgment. Although they suppose that they are "known" by other gods, they are actually embraced within the sovereign control of the sole God, Yahweh. But with Israel it is different. This people has been "known" by Yahweh in the context of a personal, covenantal relationship. Through crucial historical experiences, indelibly imprinted upon their memory, they have come to know who God is and the lifestyle God demands. Therefore, because the people of Yahweh could not plead ignorance, they must stand under a more severe judgment than any other nation.

The Threat of Doom

Amos spoke in accents of doom. Scarcely a ray of light breaks through the dark clouds he saw on the horizon. So certain was he of the impending catastrophe, which actually took place a generation later when the Northern Kingdom was destroyed by Assyria, that he sang a funeral dirge over Israel. This little lamentation (*qinah*) appears in a special 3–2 qinah-meter, and imitates the dirges that mourners wailed at the scene of death:

> Fállen, no móre to ríse,
>   is Vírgin Iśrael;
> Forlórn upón her sóil,
>   nóne to líft her.
> —AMOS 5:2

The same theme is struck in a series of five prophetic visions, in which everyday objects are transfigured with religious significance. Four of the visions are introduced by the words, "Yahweh showed me." In the first, Amos is shown a locust plague about to consume the crop after the king has taken the first mowing for his tax (7:1–3). In the second, he sees a supernatural fire that has already licked up the subterranean waters which irrigate the earth and is about to consume the soil necessary for human livelihood (7:4–6). In both cases, Amos is sensitive to the plight of Israel and intercedes on behalf of the people. So far, there still seems to be hope for Israel. But not in the remaining visions. A plumb-line, used by carpenters for construction, becomes the sign of the destruction that Yahweh will accomplish in the midst of "my people, Israel" (7:7–9). A basket of summer fruit (*qáyitz*), by a play on words, becomes a sign that "the end (*qētz*) has come upon my people Israel" (8:1–2). And finally a vision of Yahweh destroying the worshipers in the Temple (which reminds us of Jehu's purge of the Baal worshipers) fades into the judgment of Yahweh from which there is no escape, whether in the heights or the depths (9:1–4). The last clearly authentic word in the book of Amos is one of utter doom:

> Behold, the eyes of Lord Yahweh
>   are upon the sinful kingdom,
> and I will obliterate it from the
>   surface of the ground.
>   —AMOS 9:8

This final prediction of the end of Israel had nothing to do with political fatalism. True, from a purely military point of view, Israel had no more chance of withstanding the Assyrian colossus than, say, Finland would have against Russia. But Amos was not thinking of comparative military strength. Nor did his message of doom spring from social despair, for the age of Jeroboam II was one of great political confidence. It rested solely on his conviction that although Israel seemed healthy outwardly, inwardly it was diseased with a spreading cancer. Israel was not merely guilty of social crimes; it stood accused of unfaithfulness to its calling as the people of Yahweh. In the economy of God, such a society could not long endure.

Symptoms of Sickness

To Amos this unfaithfulness was shockingly evident in the evils of the flourishing urban society. He pointed out the social injustices of his day with such severity that Amaziah regarded his message as high treason and insisted that "the land is not able to bear all his words" (Amos 7:10). Wealthy merchants, lusting for economic power, were ruthlessly trampling on the heads of the poor and defenseless. Public leaders, reveling in luxury and corrupted by indulgence, were lying on beds of ease—unconcerned over "the ruin of Joseph" (6:1–7). The sophisticated ladies, whom Amos—in the rough language of a herdsman—compares to the fat, sleek cows of Bashan, were selfishly urging their husbands on (4:1-3). Law courts were used to serve the vested interests of the commercial class. Religion had no word of protest against the inhumanities that were being perpetrated in the very shadow of the temples at Bethel, Gilgal, Dan, and Samaria. To Amos, all these things were symptoms of a deep "sickness unto death": Israel's estrangement from Yahweh and the surrender of its covenant calling. Boldly, the prophet declared that Yahweh "hates," "despises," "abhors" the whole scene:

> Take away from me the noise of your songs;
>   to the melody of your harps I will not listen.
> But let justice roll down like waters,
>   and righteousness like an ever-flowing stream.
> —AMOS 5:23–24 (RSV)

This passage shows us that Amos was opposed to the forms in which people acted out their worship of God, and other passages strengthen this impression. Turning back to the Mosaic period, Amos asks the rhetorical question (which seems to call for a negative answer): "Did you bring to me sacrifices and offerings the forty years in the wilderness, O house of Israel?" (Amos 5:25). He is merciless in his attack on the shrines, especially the royal shrine of Jeroboam II at Bethel (3:14; 7:7-9, 10-17; 9:1). It is very doubtful, however, that he intended a wholesale abolition of the system of worship. Rather, Amos was probably demanding that the cult be purified, for it had become so contaminated by pagan thought and practice that the people had become indifferent to the true worship of Yahweh and to Yahweh's ethical demands. The prophet's standard—Yahweh's revelation in the Mosaic period—demanded that everything be swept away that did not conform to the proper worship of Yahweh. Amos felt that the existing cult was the source of Israel's sickness, and that divine surgery had to be applied radically to the source of the cancerous corruption: the temples and their system of worship (see the vision in 9:1). For the way people worship, and their theological convictions concerning God, determine the attitudes and the lifestyle of the community.

A Call to Repentance

And yet the divine purpose was not that of mere destruction. Yahweh was active in the midst of the people, said Amos, in order that Israel might turn from its evil ways and "return" to Yahweh. This is the meaning of repentance: it is a return (teshubah) to the One who is the source of Israel's life, a redirection of the will in response to the jealous claim that Yahweh makes upon people's allegiance, and a corresponding change of lifestyle. In a striking series of oracles, each of which ends with the refrain "yet you did not return to me," Amos affirms that repentance had been the divine purpose behind the calamities that had befallen Israel (Amos 4:6-12). But Yahweh had failed in every attempt, for

Israel was stubbornly set in its rebellious ways. The prophet warns that even more terrible events could be expected in the near future:

> Assuredly,
> Because I am doing that to you,
> Even so will I act toward you, O Israel—
> Prepare to meet your God, O Israel!
> —AMOS 4:12 (TNK)

Amos did not specify when or where this rendezvous would take place, but he was sure that it would take place soon, and in the arena of history. The end of Israel would be a great tragedy, but it would be a *meaningful* tragedy, and Israel would be completely responsible for it. People can choose whom or what they will serve, but they cannot escape the consequences of their choice.

The purpose of Amos' preaching, then, was to give people an opportunity for the reformation and reorientation of their lives. He proclaimed what Yahweh was about to do in the future in order to show how urgent it was to face the demand for change of lifestyle—and face it now. Tomorrow, he said, might be too late; *today* is the time for decision, repentance, and change. The end is at hand! Therefore, "seek Yahweh and live"—this was his appeal as the approaching judgment thundered nearer and nearer.[15]

There was little chance, however, that the people of Israel, enslaved by habit and blinded by complacency, would listen to Amos and mend their ways. But the prophet was no fatalist. He admitted that there was a slim possibility that a few (a remnant) might take his warnings to heart and "return" to Yahweh:

> Seek good, and not evil,
>   so that you may live,
> and that Yahweh, God of Hosts, may be with you,
>   as you maintain.
> Despise evil, and love good,
>   and establish justice in courts of law.
> It may be that Yahweh, God of Hosts, will be gracious
>   to the remnant of Joseph.
> —AMOS 5:14–15

This, however, was a "maybe," which rested on the unpredictable response of the people and, above all, on the incalculable grace of God.

Here is a slight indication that the message of doom was not Yahweh's last word, as later prophets recognized more clearly. In making his heavy emphasis upon doom, Amos leaned over backward to counteract the false optimism of his time. Later on, when the desperate political situation drove people to fa-

---

[15] See further, "Turning Away and Turning Around," in B. W. Anderson, *The Eighth Century Prophets* [329], chap. 3.

Tiglath-pileser III (745–727 B.C.E.) riding in his royal chariot, accompanied by his driver and an attendant who shades his head with an umbrella. The king apparently raises his hand in a salute. The inscription indicates that the scene is connected with the Assyrian deportation of inhabitants from Astartu, the fortified hilltop city (east of the Sea of Galilee) called Ashtaroth in the Bible (Deut. 1:4).

naticism or despair, the prophets were to proclaim a message of hope. But the age of Jeroboam II did not need to hear the divine promise, for the people already believed that "God is with us" (Amos 5:14).[16] What they needed to hear was the word of divine judgment that would shatter their complacency and false security. Then, perhaps, they would understand that the promise rests, not on

[16] This is the literal meaning of Immanuel—the name that the prophet Isaiah later introduced (see pp. 331–333).

political and economic fortunes, but on the gracious dealings of God with the people.

THE PROPHECY OF HOSEA

Now let us take up the narrative in II Kings where we left off, and follow the thread of the history of the Northern Kingdom (II Kings 15–17). After the death of Jeroboam II in 746 B.C.E. came catastrophe. Shortly afterward (c. 745), Tiglath-pileser III, whose official throne-name was Pulu, and who is referred to as Pul in the biblical account, seized the Assyrian throne. He awakened Assyria from fifty years of lethargy and set a military program in motion that led ultimately to the conquest of Egypt. Under a line of vigorous rulers, Assyria moved toward a goal that had been in the mind of its kings from the time of the thirteenth century: the domination of the Fertile Crescent, the lifeline of the ancient world.

Tiglath-pileser lost no time in setting out on the path of conquest. After conquering Babylonia and incorporating it into his empire, he marched toward the Mediterranean and sent terror through all of Syria and Palestine. One reason for fear was his introduction of a new military policy, shrewdly calculated to crush nationalism and to hold captive countries firmly in control. This was the

Assyrian Scribes Counting Spoil taken from a captured city in a palm-growing region. A battering ram (left) has partly penetrated the double wall with turreted towers. Women and children are taken from the city in ox-drawn carts (men would have to walk), and sheep and cattle are driven away by the captors. Two scribes (upper center) use writing instruments and tablets to record the spoil. Deportation of conquered peoples was an Assyrian military policy.

policy of uprooting conquered populations from their homeland and exiling them to remote parts of the Assyrian empire. Their land was resettled with foreign colonists and was incorporated into the system of Assyrian provinces. Israel, like other small nations, was destined to learn by bitter experience the meaning of the word "exile."

Neither Israel nor Judah could escape involvement in these political events, although Judah—as we shall see in the next chapter—managed to maintain far greater stability than the Northern Kingdom. Israel's political anxiety was reflected in the confused domestic events described briefly in II Kings with the usual Deuteronomistic flourishes. Zechariah, the last king of the Jehu dynasty, was murdered after only six months on the throne. His assassin, Shallum, was struck down by Menahem after one month's reign, and cities that resisted this latest usurper were treated with savage ferocity. Menahem, after ten years of rule purchased by appeasement of Assyria, died in his bed, but his son Pekahiah held out for only two years before he fell victim to the conspiracy of Pekah, the army commander. Pekah held the throne for a few precarious years, only to be knifed by Hoshea.[17] And Hoshea, the last king of Israel, died in chains (see Chronological Chart 6, p. 332). Never before in the history of the Northern Kingdom had there been such a tangle of murder and intrigue. Hosea vividly describes the sorry situation:

> On the day of our king the princes became sick
>   with the heat of wine;
>   he stretched out his hand with mockers.
> For like an oven their hearts burn with intrigue;
>   all night their anger smolders;
>   in the morning it blazes like a flaming fire.
> All of them are hot as an oven,
>   and they devour their rulers.
> All their kings have fallen;
>   and none of them calls upon me.
>   —HOSEA 7:5–7 (RSV; see all of 6:11–7:7)

It was during the reign of Menahem (c. 745–738 B.C.E.) that Israel courted Assyrian favor. This was politically expedient, for in the very year that Menahem usurped the throne, Tiglath-pileser's armies began to invade the land. Menahem had to surrender the northern part of his kingdom (Galilee) and, in addition, he paid a heavy tribute to the Assyrian monarch "that he might help him to confirm his hold of the royal power" (II Kings 15:19). In his annals, Tiglath-pileser recorded that he received tribute from "Menahem of Samaria," along with gifts from numerous other peoples.[18] Menahem's policy of appease-

---

[17] According to II Kings 15:27, Pekah reigned for twenty years, but this figure is too high, as historians point out, for Samaria's fall occurred less than twenty years after the beginning of his reign. John Bright suggests, *History* [91], p. 273 (n. 8), that Pekah may have claimed that his rule began before he seized the throne and that he may have exercised some authority in Gilead (II Kings 15:25) ever since Jeroboam's death.

[18] See Pritchard, *Ancient Near Eastern Texts* [1], pp. 283.

THE ASSYRIAN EMPIRE

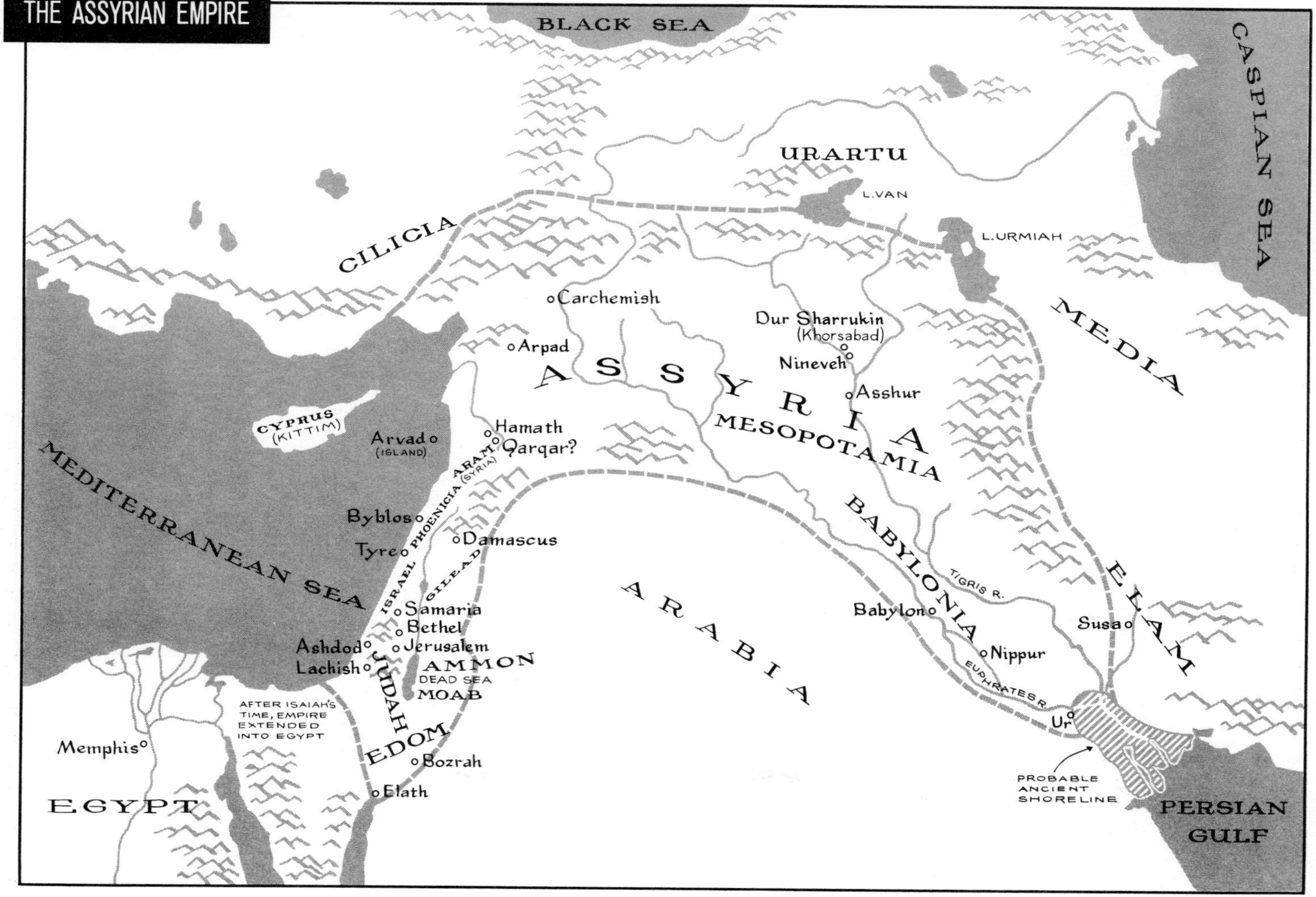

Map labels:
CASPIAN SEA
MEDIA
ELAM
PERSIAN GULF
Susa
Ur
PROBABLE ANCIENT SHORELINE
URARTU
L. URMIAH
L. VAN
Dur Sharrukin (Khorsabad)
Nineveh
Asshur
ASSYRIA
MESOPOTAMIA
BABYLONIA
TIGRIS R.
EUPHRATES R.
Nippur
Babylon
ARABIA
BLACK SEA
Carchemish
Arpad
Hamath
Qarqar?
ARAM (SYRIA)
Damascus
GILEAD
Samaria
Bethel
Jerusalem
AMMON
DEAD SEA
MOAB
JUDAH
EDOM
Bozrah
Elath
Arvad (ISLAND)
Byblos
Tyre
Ashdod
Lachish
ISRAEL
PHOENICIA
CYPRUS (KITTIM)
MEDITERRANEAN SEA
AFTER ISAIAH'S TIME, EMPIRE EXTENDED INTO EGYPT
Memphis
EGYPT

303

ment succeeded for the time being and the Assyrians marched away, allowing the Israelite king to keep his throne. However, his capitulation was highly unpopular, for the wealthy class was heavily taxed to pay for it, and the fires of resentment and revolt were fanned even more briskly. Before we consider the attempts to throw off the Assyrian yoke, let us turn to the prophet Hosea.

Hosea's Optimism of Grace

Hosea's prophetic career overlapped two eras: the last part of the age of Jeroboam II and the period of political instability that followed his death in 746 B.C.E. Hosea's earliest prophecy, found in Hosea 1–3, was apparently delivered in the very year of Jeroboam's death, for according to these chapters the dynasty of Jehu was still in existence (see 1:4). The heading of the book (1:1), which in its present form comes from a later Judean editor, states that Hosea prophesied "in the days of Jeroboam," and adds that his career embraced the reigns of four Judean kings, the last being Hezekiah (c. 715–687). The latter statement is probably inaccurate, for it is doubtful whether Hosea was prophesying as late as the fall of the Northern Kingdom in the year 721. His career lasted for at least ten years after the death of Jeroboam, however, for the second major section of the book (chapters 4–14) reflects the turbulent conditions of that period. According to these chapters, the dynasty of Jehu had fallen; kings followed one another in rapid succession as "the land devours its rulers"; and the country was filled with confusion, demoralization, and anxiety because of international developments.

Chronological Chart 5

B.C.E.	Egypt	Palestine		Mesopotamia	
		THE DIVIDED MONARCHY			
		Judah	Israel	Syria	Assyria
850		Athaliah, c. 842–837	Jehu Dynasty:	Hazael, c. 842–806	Shalmaneser III, c. 859–825
	Decline	Joash, c. 837–800	Jehu, c. 843/2–815		(Jehu pays tribute, 841) Shamshi-Adad V, c. 824–812
			Joahaz, c. 815–801		Adad-nirari III, c. 811–784
		Amaziah, c. 800–783	Jehoash, c. 802–786		
		Uzziah (Azariah), c. 783–742	Jeroboam II, c. 786–746 (Amos, c. 750) (Hosea, c. 745)	Decline	
c. 750			Zechariah (6 mos.) c. 746–745		Tiglath-pileser III, c. 745–727

Like the book of Amos, the book of Hosea is a compilation of brief oracles delivered at different times and linked together in their present arrangement either by the prophet himself or by his disciples. Consequently, the same prophetic themes are repeated over and over again, with variations from situation to situation. The text has not been preserved as well as that of Amos. In chapters 4–14 the text is often so corrupt that the translator must turn to other ancient versions or resort to conjecture (see the footnotes of the Revised Standard Version). Moreover, several additions have been made to Hosea's oracles, the most obvious of which is the concluding exhortation in Hosea 14:9.

Hosea, like Amos, was a prophet of doom. But unlike Amos, who announced that the Day of Yahweh would be a day of pitch-darkness, Hosea balanced the word of divine judgment with the promise of restoration and renewal. He, too, saw the coming of the Day of Darkness, but he proclaimed that despite the total eclipse the sun was still shining. Hosea's qualified optimism was not due to any improvement in the political or religious situation since the time of Amos a few years earlier, for actually affairs had gone from bad to worse in the Northern Kingdom. Hosea insisted that Israel was prematurely senile and approaching death—"grey hairs" were scattered upon Ephraim (Hosea 7:8–9). His message was an "optimism of grace," for Israel's hope was grounded solely in the constancy of Yahweh's love for the people. This was made clear to Hosea by his marriage experience, which became a "living parable" of the relation between Yahweh and Israel.

Hosea's Marriage

The key to the interpretation of Hosea's message is the story of his marriage with Gomer. This story, however, which is found in the first three chapters of the book of Hosea, presents one of the most difficult problems in biblical studies. For one thing, Hosea was not primarily interested in giving biographical data. Certainly he did not write a "true confession" after the manner of modern love romances. As in the case of Amos, the man recedes behind the word he proclaims. He gives only enough details about his marriage to symbolize the story of Yahweh's relation to Israel, which occupies the center of his attention.

What was the marital experience on which the prophet based his parable? Notice that there are different types of material in chapters 1–3: chapter 1 is written in the third person in the style of "biography," and chapter 3 is written in the first person in the style of "autobiography." The problem is this: Do chapters 1 and 3 represent a sequence of events in the prophet's experience with one woman, Gomer? Because the unnamed woman of chapter 3 is not explicitly identified with Gomer, some scholars think that the autobiographical chapter tells of Hosea's relation to another woman.

The balance of probability is on the side of the view that these chapters recount Hosea's experience with a single woman. If another woman were introduced in chapter 3, we would expect more explicit mention of it. We cannot escape the impression that the language of verses 1 and 2 takes it for granted that the woman has already been mentioned. Moreover, the analogy with Israel (Hosea 3:1b) suggests that the prophet is to be reconciled with the estranged Gomer, just as Yahweh takes back the same alienated people. In chapter 1 the theme is the faithlessness of Israel; in chapter 3 it is the steadfastness of Yahweh's love in the face of infidelity. These themes are not based on one event of Hosea's life, but on a sequence of events in his relation with Gomer.

Forgetting for a moment the troublesome second verse of chapter 1, we may reconstruct the events as follows: In good faith, Hosea married a woman who bore him three children. Just as Isaiah gave symbolic names to his children (Isa. 7:3; 8:3), so Hosea gave significant names to his, in order that they might be "walking signs" of Yahweh's word to Israel. The first son was named Jezreel, in recollection of the place where Jehu carried out his terrible blood purge (II Kings 9)—a sign that "in a little while" Yahweh would punish the house of Jehu for those monstrous atrocities. The second child, a daughter, was named "Not-pitied," a symbol that Yahweh's patience with Israel had been exhausted. And the third child, a son, was called "Not-my-people," a sign that Yahweh had dissolved the covenant bond and rejected the people. Then the prophet's attention shifted from the children to their mother, who had proved unfaithful to the marriage bond (as suggested in Hosea 2:2). Reading between the lines—for at this point we leave the biographical narrative and turn to the prophetic sermon in chapter 2 about the rejection of Yahweh's harlotrous wife, Israel—we must assume that Hosea divorced Gomer because of her unfaithfulness (2:2). But despite her disloyalty, Hosea was ready to go beyond the law and forgive. So, in chapter 3, we read that Hosea ransomed her and, after a period of discipline, restored her as his wife.

Hosea 1:2, then, which is a kind of second introduction, is the prophet's later interpretation of what had happened. When he married Gomer she was not yet a harlot, although—looking at the matter in retrospect—she was clearly destined to become one. Since in the prophetic view a divine purpose was discernible in life's varied experiences, Hosea insisted that all this had happened at Yahweh's command. He was ordered to take "a wife of harlotry and have children of harlotry," that is, children who share the defect of their mother. And once he had reflected on Israel's relation to Yahweh, the meaning of his own marriage became clear: "for the land commits great harlotry by forsaking Yahweh."

Since Hosea's only reason for mentioning his private life was to draw a living analogy of Yahweh's covenant with Israel, let us turn to the story of the "marriage" between Yahweh and Israel.

The Broken Covenant

No prophet was more profoundly aware of the Mosaic past than was Hosea. The memory of the Exodus, the sojourn in the wilderness, the covenant at

Horeb, and the occupation of Canaan were always in his mind as he interpreted the events and conditions of his time. In fact, he understood himself to be a successor of Moses, the great interpreter and mediator of the covenant.[19] Since Hosea was a native of the Northern Kingdom, chances are that he was nurtured in the northern (Ephraimitic) cycle of tradition presented in the so-called Elohistic epic (see Definition, p. 290).

In Hosea's thinking one thing stood out in the whole epic tradition: Yahweh's gracious choice of Israel manifested in the liberating experience of the Exodus. Israel's knowledge of God was based on that "root experience": "I am Yahweh your God from the land of Egypt" (Hosea 12:9; 13:4–5). It was in the wilderness that Yahweh *found* Israel, like grapes on a vine (9:10). And the Exodus was the sign of a special relation between God and people, on the analogy of a parent and child:

> When Israel was a boy I loved him;
> I called my son out of Egypt.
> —HOSEA 11:1 (NEB)

The analogy of Israel as the "son" of God is also found in the Old Epic tradition (Exod. 4:22). But Hosea was the first Israelite prophet to interpret the covenant by means of the analogy of the relation between a husband and wife. To be sure, the conception of sacred marriage was well-known in antiquity. The mythological dramas of the fertility religions portrayed the loves and marriages of the gods and the goddesses, and in Canaanite temples the sacred marriage was enacted through ritual prostitution (see pp. 184–186). In a day when sex was glorified by nature religions, Hosea's use of the image of sacred marriage was a bold reinterpretation of Israel's faith. The way Hosea used the comparison, however, was completely new. Instead of explaining the divine marriage by referring to the cycles of nature, he spoke of a *historical* marriage made in the wilderness between God and a people. And the meaning of this marriage was disclosed to him, not by reflecting on the marriage of a god and a goddess, but by a deep understanding of his own relationship to Gomer.

Just as Gomer played the harlot, so Israel had broken the covenant. According to Hosea, this was the real historical tragedy, and all the contemporary troubles of Israel were only symptoms of it. The "wife" whom Yahweh had chosen and betrothed had become a whore. A "spirit of harlotry" had inflamed the people, and they had become estranged from their God (Hosea 4:12). Hosea's critique of Israel's society went far deeper than a mere condemnation of social immorality, political confusion, or religious formalism. He was concerned with human motives, with the devotion of the heart, with the values in which people place their trust. Hence, echoing the criticism made by leaders of the old Tribal Confederacy (see pp. 207–210), he condemned the institution of the mon-

---

[19] See James Muilenburg, "The 'Office' of the Prophet in Ancient Israel," *The Bible in Modern Scholarship,* [161], 94.

archy, seeing in it a symptom of a harlotrous spirit. Saul's hometown of Gibeah and his coronation at Gilgal were evidences of Israel's determination to reject Yahweh as king (8:4; 9:15; 10:3, 9). The consequences of Israel's betrayal of the covenant were to be seen in the regicides (7:3–7), the feverish foreign policy aimed at courting Egypt or Assyria (7:11), and the foolish reliance upon arms and fortifications (8:14). Stubborn and determined, Israel had insisted on being "like the nations," and as a result it was "swallowed up" among the nations (8:8) and "strangers" were consuming its strength (7:8–9).

This harlotrous spirit had led the people into a false and idolatrous religion. Like the other great prophets, Hosea knew that religion was not necessarily a good thing, for it could be a way of betraying God, a manifestation of sin. In Hosea's time, popular religion, corrupted by the fertility cult of Canaan, provided a means of obtaining the good things of nature and tethering God to human interests. People thronged to the temples, not to acknowledge gratefully their utter dependence upon the God who had brought them out of Egypt, but rather to "get something out of religion"—harmony, security, prosperity, and welfare. The priests and the prophets, exploiting the upsurge of religious in-

---

DEFINITION: "ḤÉSED"

This word is exceedingly difficult to render into English, as evident in various translations of the term in Hosea 6:6: "mercy" (King James Version), "steadfast love" (Revised Standard Version), "goodness" (American Jewish Translation), "loyalty" (New English Bible), etc.

Studies of the term have shown that, at the human level, it applies to relationships in which one party is "superior" in the sense of having more power or influence by virtue of social position, although one's status could be altered by shifting circumstances. A good illustration is the friendship between David and Jonathan. At one point David says to Jonathan: "Deal faithfully [show ḥésed] with your servant, since you have taken your servant into a covenant of [Yahweh] with you" (I Sam. 20:8a, TNK). As long as Jonathan had the superior position (son of the king), it was his obligation in the sacred covenant of friendship to help David to escape from his father's evil designs. But Jonathan asked David to promise that, when their roles were reversed and David came to power, David would manifest loyalty (ḥésed) to him (I Sam. 20:12–17). David's obligation of friendship lasted even beyond Jonathan's death, for he was determined to "show ḥésed" to other members of Saul's family for the sake of Jonathan (II Sam. 9:1, 3, 7).

Ḥésed, then, is loyalty manifested by a stronger party toward someone who is in a weaker position (compare the suzerain-vassal treaty relationship above, pp. 98–101). It is not a virtue or personality trait but rather it is something to be *done*, which accounts for the accompanying verbs "do," "maintain," "love," ḥésed. We must not think, however, of *noblesse oblige*, that is, people of high standing behaving nobly toward inferiors in a condescending manner, as when the rich give alms to the poor. Rather, loyalty arises from the relationship itself, not from any external legal obligation or social custom. It is an act of inner faithfulness and therefore of grace. One is free to be loyal or not to be loyal, although the weaker party in the relationship, in a time of distress, may have no other source of help. See further Katherine D. Sakenfeld, *Faithfulness in Action* [143].[20]

---

terest, actually contributed to Israel's harlotry. Priests were "feeding on the sin" of Yahweh's people (Hosea 4:7–10).

Israel's fidelity, then, was that of a fickle wife. It lacked the steadfastness, the truthworthiness of true covenant love. In Hosea's native language, Israel lacked *ḥésed*, covenant faithfulness.

It is, above all, Yahweh who, according to Israel's ancient confession, "abounds in *ḥésed* and faithfulness" (Exod. 34:6; cf. Ps. 103:8). As the Sovereign who initiated the covenant relationship, Yahweh displays constancy in dealing with the people Israel—not because Yahweh is bound by law or necessity but solely by virtue of divine grace (freedom) and commitment. The relationship is not characterized by caprice but by steadfastness and trustworthiness. Hosea also applies this term to *Israel's* covenant relationship to Yahweh, suggesting that the people should display a constancy corresponding to Yahweh's covenant loyalty. But, in the prophet's vivid figures, Israel's *ḥésed* was like a transient morning cloud, or like the dew that evaporates quickly (Hosea 6:4). Hence Yahweh scorned the existing forms of worship:

> For I desire steadfast love [*ḥésed*] and not sacrifice,
> the knowledge of God, rather than burnt offerings.
> —HOSEA 6:6 [RSV]

We probably should not press Hosea's words to mean that he was opposed to formal worship. But clearly he was opposed to forms that were devoid of the spirit of true faithfulness to the God of the covenant. Jesus twice asked his hearers to go and reread Hosea 6:6 when he was accused of breaking the formal rules of orthodoxy (cf. Matt. 9:13 and 12:7).

The Inner Flaw

In the key sentence Hosea 6:6, Hosea draws a poetic parallel between two important words. The first is *ḥésed*, which we have already discussed. The second term, which overlaps in meaning, is "the knowledge of God." Hosea insisted that Israel did not *know* God (see 4:1, 6, 11), and that this deficiency was the root of its problem. We must be on guard against reading into the book of Hosea modern conceptions of knowledge. Hosea was speaking about a kind of knowledge that is intrinsic to the covenant relationship: a knowing God which is the response to being known (chosen) by God (Amos 3:2). Here we find ourselves again in the context of the suzerainty treaty form (see above, pp. 98–101). In Hittite and Akkadian texts the verb "know" is used in two ways: it may refer to the suzerain who "recognizes" ("knows") his vassal and the vassal who "recognizes" his lord; or it may refer to "recognizing" (acknowledging) that

---

[20] This definition is excerpted with some changes from the author's book, *The Eighth Century Prophets* [329], pp. 48–49.

treaty stipulations are binding.[21] Given this background, it is not surprising that Hosea puts *ḥésed* (loyalty) and "knowledge of God" in poetic parallelism. He is speaking about Israel's covenant responsibility to recognize and be loyal to Yahweh, its exclusive Sovereign. The meaning of "know" for both parties of the covenant is brought out in this passage:

> Yet I am Yahweh your God
>   ever since the land of Egypt.
> You know no God but me,
>   and besides me there is no savior.
> I knew you in the wilderness,
>   in the land of drought.
>   —HOSEA 13:4–5

On the human side such knowledge has two aspects. On the one hand, this is a *theological* knowledge which can be taught by parents in the home (Deut. 6:20–25) or by cultic officials at the sanctuaries, especially at the covenant-renewal festivals. It is the knowledge of who God is (Hos. 13:4), what God has done for Israel, and what God requires of the people—in short, a knowledge of the covenant tradition. When this understanding is lacking, the people turn to strange gods and break the laws of the covenant that are epitomized in the Ten Commandments.[22] Hosea lays the blame for this state of affairs at the door of the priests and prophets, whose duty it was to instruct the people in what the covenant means (4:5–6). On the other hand, this is a knowledge which includes the *will* as well as the mind. Hosea was talking about the knowledge of the heart[23]—that is, the response of the *whole person* to God's love. To know Yahweh means to respond to the claim Yahweh makes upon one's devotion, to obey Yahweh's will in society where the poor and needy cry for help (see Jer. 22:16). So in observing that Israel lacked knowledge of God, Hosea affirmed that the people did not *acknowledge* God. The covenant was broken. Israel, the "wife," was estranged from her "husband."

> Their deeds do not allow them
>   to return to their God;
> For the spirit of harlotry is within them,
>   and they do not know Yahweh.
>   —HOSEA 5:4

---

[21] See Delbert R. Hillers, *Covenant* [225], pp. 120–23.

[22] The Decalogue is specifically referred to in Hosea 4:2 (prohibitions against lying, killing, stealing, and adultery). The whole passage (4:1–10) is cast in the form of a legal controversy or lawsuit, in which one covenant partner accuses the other of violation of the covenant. On this form see, for instance, Herbert B. Huffmon, "The Covenant Lawsuit in the Prophets," in *Journal of Biblical Literature*, LXXVIII (1959), 285–95; also B. Gemser, "The *Rîb*—or Controversy—Pattern in Hebrew Mentality" [464], pp. 120–37.

[23] In the anthropology of ancient Israel, the heart is the organ of thinking, willing, and feeling.

In the end, when God's purpose wins out, the covenant will be restored, and then Israel will "know Yahweh" (2:20).[24]

Not only did Hosea expose the inner motives of Israel's contemporary life, but also he saw clearly that behind Israel's infidelity lay a pattern of thought and action that had been deeply ingrained in the people ever since their entrance into Canaan. In earlier chapters, we have described the transition from the pastoral life of the wilderness to the agricultural life of Canaan—a transition that accentuated the problem of the relation between faith and culture. According to Hosea, in the wilderness Yahweh had entered into covenant with a bride who was destined to prove unfaithful. Indeed, the "honeymoon" in the wilderness, the time of Israel's fidelity, was all too brief. No sooner had Israel set foot on the soil of Canaan than she began to deck herself alluringly in a harlot's attire and to pursue her "lovers," the nature gods of Canaan who promised the "harlot's hire" of prosperity and security. This is the theme of the prophetic sermon in Hosea 2. The infiltration of Baal worship had taken place so slowly and subtly through the years that in popular religion Yahweh and Baal had become identified. No longer did the people see the difference between the story of Yahweh, that centered in the liberating event of the Exodus, and the story of the loves and wars of Baal and his female counterpart. They did not realize that the very gifts of fertility that were sought from the Baal had been mercifully provided by the God who brought Israel up out of the land of Egypt!

So, from the very first, Israel's history was a sordid and shameful story of the betrayal of Yahweh's love. Throughout the years, the people had pursued the devices and desires of their own hearts, and now they were caught in the coils of a sinful history from which they could not extricate themselves. Israel was in bondage to habitual ways of thinking and to established patterns of behavior. "Their deeds," said Hosea, "do not permit them to return to their God" (Hosea 5:4). So enslaved were the people to false loyalties that it was almost useless to appeal to them: "Ephraim is joined to idols, let him alone" (4:17). Every aspect of Israel's corporate life—politics, economics, religion—was tainted with the ideology of a false allegiance, a misdirected will, a vicious style of behavior. We might liken the situation to the plight of persons who are so completely enslaved by habitual ways of thinking and living that they lack both the imagination and the willpower to change themselves. And just as a great crisis in an individual's life sometimes makes possible a new beginning, so Hosea believed that the historical catastrophe about to befall the nation was intended by God as an opportunity for Israel to recover its health.

The Triumph of Love

Like Amos, Hosea spoke in accents of terrible doom as he described the threat from Assyria. The three children born to Gomer were given names that signified

---

[24] In the last days, according to Jeremiah's prophecy of the "new covenant" (Jer. 31:31–34), knowledge of Yahweh will come from the heart, not from teaching (see pp. 421–423).

Yahweh's judgment, and the youngest child in particular stood for Yahweh's termination of the covenant relationship: "You are not my people and I am not your God" (Hosea 1:9). Furthermore, the prophetic sermon in Chapter 2 begins with Yahweh's announcement of divorce from Israel, the harlotrous mother of harlotrous children: "She is not my wife, and I am not her husband" (2:2). Elsewhere, even stronger, fiercer language is used. Yahweh is compared to a wild animal that pounces on the human prey (5:14; 13:7–8), to moth or dry rot that destroys the social fabric (5:12). If the people try to seek Yahweh, it will be in vain (5:6); Yahweh will love them no more (9:15). A faithless people deserves a treatment no better than Gomer deserved: to be rejected.

This is shocking language—even to modern ears. The purpose of these harsh metaphors, however, was to create a kind of "future shock," that is, to awaken people to the urgency of the present in view of the impending judgment of God. Eighth century prophets perceived that, in one sense, the imminent calamity would be the result of the people's actions: their foolish lifestyle and suicidal foreign policy. "They sow the wind," said Hosea, "and they shall reap the whirlwind" (Hosea 8:7). Actions inexorably draw upon themselves consequences. In another sense, however, God did not merely ordain moral laws which, like the law of gravity, people may break at their own risk. Rather, these prophets announced that God *personally* was acting in the social sphere, using agencies (like Assyria) to bring people to their senses. Like a New Testament writer, they knew that "it is a terrible thing to fall into the hands of the living God" (Hebrews 10:31). The absolute sovereignty of God in human affairs, on the one hand, and full human responsibility on the other, are equally important tenets of prophetic faith, even though the paradox may be difficult for us to grasp.

The deepest note struck in the book of Hosea is the proclamation that God's "wrath" or judgment is redemptive. God's purpose is not to destroy, but to heal. Through historical crises that shake the very foundations of human self-sufficiency, Yahweh acts to free people from their enslavement to false allegiances and to restore them to freedom in the covenant loyalty. Just as Hosea's love was greater and deeper than Gomer's infidelity, so Yahweh's love for Israel is truly steadfast. It is a divine love that will not let the people go, despite their fickleness and harlotry. Yahweh's "wrath" is not capricious, vindictive, and destructive; it is the expression of a holy love which seeks to break the chains of Israel's bondage and to emancipate them for a new life, a new covenant. According to Hosea, this new freedom will come only when God acts to destroy the idols in which people place their trust so that the "wife," Israel, may stand naked and humiliated in the presence of her lovers (see Hosea 2:2–13). Then Israel will have the opportunity to *be Israel,* to be the people of the covenant, living in grateful dependence upon the God who redeemed them from Egypt and who constantly supplies their needs in the land of Canaan.

Parental Discipline

The holiness of Yahweh's love, which includes both judgment and mercy, is magnificently portrayed in Hosea 11, where the figure changes from the relationship between husband and wife to the relationship between parent and child. There we read that the creative, nurturing love of Yahweh is behind and within Israel's whole history, right from the very first, giving meaning and purpose to its life. The first part of the poem (verses 1–4) announces that Israel, Yahweh's "son" (cf. Exod. 4:22–23), was loved into being, and that Yahweh, like a parent, had gathered the child in a compassionate embrace and taught it how to walk. (In verse 4, the figure suddenly shifts to a farmer who gently leads and cares for an animal.) The theme of the next section (verses 5–7) is that Yahweh's patience is exhausted in dealing with this refractory child. Israel must be disciplined, and the punishment will come from Egypt or Assyria, the very nations to whom they were turning for political salvation. However, divine judgment is not the last word, as we read in the next section (verses 8–9). For even in the hour of catastrophe Yahweh does not abandon the people, nor does divine love for them cease. It is not Yahweh's will that Israel be destroyed as Admah and Zeboim were leveled during the holocaust of Sodom and Gomorrah (see Gen. 19:24–25; Deut. 29:23). Rather, the purpose behind Yahweh's judgment is love, like that of a parent who lovingly disciplines a wayward child. These verses passionately describe a struggle, as it were, within the heart of God—a struggle that doubtless reflects the agony of Hosea's experience with Gomer. But the triumph is on the side of the love that will not let Israel go. In the last analysis, mere words fail to plumb the depths of this holy love:

> for I am God and not man,
>   the Holy One in your midst,
>   and I will not come to destroy.
>   —HOSEA 11:9b (RSV)

To us, the "wrath" and the "love" of God may seem contradictory, but to Hosea God's *pathos*—to use Abraham Heschel's expression again—surpasses the logic of human understanding.[25] God's relationship with Israel has both the dark side of judgment and the bright side of the promise of renewal (see verses 10–11). Israel would come to learn, as did the poet Frances Thompson out of bitter personal experience, that its gloom after all was but "the shade of His Hand outstretched caressingly."[26]

---

[25] Abraham J. Heschel, *The Prophets* [315], chap. 3.
[26] See Francis Thompson, "The Hound of Heaven."

The Renewal of the Covenant

Let us return, now, to the story of Gomer in Hosea 3. Hosea continued to love his wife even though she proved unfaithful. In this experience, Hosea found an analogy of the relation between Yahweh and Israel, for Yahweh, too, steadfastly loved the people even though they turned to other gods (Hosea 3:1). (The phrase "cakes of raisins" refers to food used in the Baal fertility cult.) So Hosea ransomed her and restored her unto himself, although disciplining her "for many days." Israel also had to go through a period of discipline and quarantine—"without king or prince, without sacrifice or pillar, without ephod or teraphim" (Hosea 3:4). The deprivation would be primarily political and religious, the very areas that had been corroded by the culture of Canaan. Then, after "many days" of cleansing and purgation, there would be a new beginning, a new relationship. For Israel would return (or "repent") and seek Yahweh their God.[27]

This theme of discipline through suffering is developed at great length in Chapter 2. In vivid language Hosea speaks of the exposure of Israel's harlotry and the frustration of all attempts to pursue "her lovers." However, Yahweh's purpose throughout is reconciliation:

> So, I am going to allure her,
>   and lead her into the wilderness,
>   and speak to her heart.
> From there I will give her her vineyards,
>   and the Valley of Achor as a gateway of hope.
> There she will respond as in the days of her youth,
>   as in the time when she came out of the land of Egypt.
> —HOSEA 2:14–15

Just as life had been given to Israel in the ancient wilderness, so it will be in the wilderness—away from all the temptations of culture—that its life will be renewed. Probably the Valley of Achor was located in the wilderness of Judah, on a plateau overlooking the Dead Sea. At its eastern rim, the brook Qumran plunges through a gorge and descends abruptly to the Jordan Valley, passing by the site which, centuries after Hosea's time, was to be the headquarters of an Essene community which also spoke of a new covenant in the wilderness. Even today the visitor to the valley, just above the cliffs of Qumran, is impressed with the stark contrast between the elemental simplicity of this barren place and the fertility of the hill country where great cities once stood as proud symbols of human culture. Life in the wilderness is precarious, and here the person of

---

[27] In Hosea 3:5, the phrase "and David their King" is obviously a gloss by a later editor of the Southern Kingdom. Elsewhere the book has been touched up with Judean additions: 1:7, 4:15, 11:12b. Some scholars argue that all references to Judah are spurious. However, it is probable that Hosea, like Amos, applied his message both to Israel and Judah.

faith is reminded that life depends on God's mercies.[28] Significantly, Hosea saw the wilderness as the place of a new beginning. Yahweh, he prophesied, personally would lure the people into the wilderness. To Israel, stripped of all false securities and purged of all cultural pretentions, Yahweh would "speak tenderly," or, as the Hebrew says, "speak to her heart." There Israel would receive back its vineyards and learn that all the blessings of culture are gifts of God's grace. There the people would enter a door of hope, leading into a meaningful and secure future within the love of God.

To sum up, the wilderness was to be the scene of the renewal of the covenant, and there the long history of the broken covenant would be ended. In the wilderness, Israel would *answer* Yahweh's overture of love, as the people had responded in trust and gratitude at the time of the Exodus. There Yahweh would restore Israel to the relationship of a wife, betrothing her in righteousness and in justice, in covenant faithfulness (*ḥésed*) and in mercy. For Israel's persistent infidelity would be conquered by a stronger and deeper love, and Israel would *know* Yahweh in the relationship of a new covenant (Hosea 2:19–20).

THE FALL OF SAMARIA

Hosea's hope, as we have seen, rested on an "optimism of grace," not on political probabilities. To be sure, his message of doom was called forth by Israel's precarious position directly in the path of Assyria's advance across the Fertile Crescent toward Egypt. Politically, little Israel did not have a chance, especially when the leaders of the nation were pursuing suicidal foreign and domestic policies. But to Hosea the political crisis had another dimension. Within the events of the time he saw the activity of God in judgment and renewal.

We are not sure how long Hosea's prophetic career continued. Some scholars believe that he was active in 735–733 B.C.E. during the alliance between Syria and Israel (to be discussed in the next chapter), and suggest that Hosea 5:8–14 reflects an invasion by the Southern Kingdom into Israel at that time.[29] In any case, his ministry, especially as reflected in chapters 4–14, extended into the turbulent period of the last days of the Northern Kingdom.

Events moved rapidly toward disaster. Tiglath-pileser's death in 727 B.C.E. gave Israel an opportunity to revolt (see Chronological Chart 6, p. 332). King Hoshea of Israel, hoping that the new Assyrian emperor would not be strong enough to keep his far-flung empire under control, and foolishly relying on the "weak reed" of Egypt, refused to pay tribute in about the year 724. But the new

---

[28] On the spiritual meaning of life in the wilderness, see especially Walter Brueggemann, *The Land* [237], pp. 28–44.

[29] This view has been advanced by Albrecht Alt, "Hosea 5, 8–6, 6"—an article which now appears in his *Kleine Schriften zur Geschichte des Volkes Israel*, II (Munich, 1953), 163–87. See further James M. Ward, *Hosea* [345], on this passage.

Sargon II (721–705 b.c.e.) was the conqueror of Samaria. Here he is shown wearing the royal headdress, long hair and curled beard, and a cruciform earring. This bust was found at Dur-Sharruken (Khorsabad), the city the ruler built as his residence a few miles east of Nineveh.

Assyrian king, Shalmaneser V (c. 726–722), quickly attacked Samaria. He died during the battle, and his successor Sargon II (c. 721–705) inherited the task of finishing the job. Then, in the first months of the year 721, after a three-year siege, Samaria fell. According to Sargon's annals, he deported 27,290 Israelites into the region of Persia (see II Kings 17:6) and repopulated Israel with colonists from Babylonia, Elam, and Syria.[30] The words of Amos' dirge had been translated into historical reality: "Fallen is the virgin Israel."

So far as we know, Hosea did not live through this final tragedy. But his prophecy was not forgotten. It was preserved in prophetic circles and eventually was edited and cherished in the Southern Kingdom of Judah where it was contemporized with new meaning.

---

[30] See Pritchard, *Ancient Near Eastern Texts* [1], pp. 284–87.

CHAPTER 10

Judah's Covenant with Death

All the great prophets we have considered up to this point—Elijah, Elisha, Micaiah, Amos, and Hosea—were active in the Northern Kingdom, which parted with the Davidic empire after Solomon's death. It is true that prophets were active in Judah during the same period, for the record speaks of obscure figures like Azariah (II Chron. 15:1-7), Hanani (II Chron. 16:7-10), and Jehu, the son of Hanani (I Kings 16:1-4; II Chron. 19:2). But none of these individuals could hold a candle to the prophets of the kingdom of Israel, whose spiritual stature matched the great crises of their time. It must have seemed that all the big issues were being decided in the north. Even Amos, a southerner, chose to deliver his message in Bethel, the seat of the royal sanctuary of Jeroboam II.

In politics, as well as prophecy, the kingdom of Israel stayed in the lead after the split of the United Kingdom. Occasionally, of course, when Israel was temporarily weakened by domestic troubles or by the intervention of a foreign power, Judah was able to achieve a position of equality. But on the whole Judah was overshadowed by the stronger and wealthier twin kingdom to the north. Whereas Judah was comparatively isolated in the hill country, off the main roads of the ancient world, Israel stood squarely in the path of history. Situated geographically astride the crossroads of commerce between Egypt and Mesopotamia, the Northern Kingdom inevitably played a leading role in Palestine.

Biblical readings: Of the prophetic literature dealt with in this chapter it is especially important to read at least Isaiah 1–11 and 28–32, and Micah 1–3 and 6:1–8. The historical background is sketched in II Kings 15:32–20:21 (paralleled in II Chronicles 26–32).

Providentially, a succession of great prophets appeared on the stage of history at the very time when this nation was recognized as a leader among the small nations.

When "the wide land of the house of Omri," as Sargon II called the kingdom of Israel,[1] was swallowed up in the Assyrian empire, the prophetic succession was continued in Judah.[2] Here too the story of the prophets is intertwined with the account of the political fortunes of the nation, down to the time when it collapsed under the attack of the Babylonian armies. Let us begin by considering the long and prosperous reign of Uzziah, or Azariah (c. 783–742 B.C.E.), which paralleled the glorious era of Jeroboam II in the Northern Kingdom of Israel.

THE REIGN OF UZZIAH

In contrast to the political restlessness and economic discontent manifest during the history of the Northern Kingdom, Judah was able to achieve a remarkable degree of political and economic stability. A single dynasty, that of David, remained on the throne of Jerusalem throughout the whole period, while the sequence of Israelite kings was punctuated by violence and intrigue. Unlike Israel, where swift economic changes led to the erection of an unstable social pyramid, Judah moved fairly smoothly from the simplicities of the old tribal order to the more advanced economy of town life. In the process, this state preserved an astonishing degree of social equilibrium. True, the Northern Kingdom had no monopoly on evil. Judean prophets saw plenty of evidence that rapacious landlords were swallowing up the holdings of small farmers (Isa. 5:8–10; Mic. 2:1–2), that the rich were skinning the backs of the poor (Isa. 10:1–2; Mic. 3:1–4), and that flagrant social injustices were smoothed over with a veneer of religious piety (Isa. 1:10–17). Nevertheless, the social order was relatively stable, and this stability—symbolized by the Davidic crown—is important to keep in mind as we approach the book of Isaiah. As we have already observed, this political stability was abetted by the theological conviction that Yahweh had made a special covenant with David, promising to uphold his throne and to establish his descendants after him (see pp. 230–234).

Under Uzziah, Judah reached the very peak of its economic and military power. The brief report in II Kings 15:1–7, supplemented by the longer account in II Chronicles 26, gives us a picture of Uzziah's extraordinary accomplishments: the modernization of the army; his conquests in the Philistine plain,

---

[1] This expression is used in Sargon's report of the conquest of Samaria (see Pritchard, *Ancient Near Eastern Texts* [1], pp. 284–85). As we noticed earlier, it had been customary for Assyrians to name the land of Israel in honor of Omri. Even Jehu was called "son of Omri" in Assyrian records.

[2] See Robert R. Wilson, *Prophecy and Society* [328], chap. 5 on prophecy in the Ephraimite tradition and chap. 6 on prophecy in the Judean tradition.

which put him in control of the main commercial highways; his commercial expansion into Arabia; his reconstruction of the trade-route seaport city of Elath (formerly Ezion-geber); and his development of agriculture, for, we are told, "he loved the soil."

To Judeans, the only disturbing event in Uzziah's reign was that in about 750 B.C.E. their beloved king was stricken with the dread disease of leprosy. He had to be confined to a separate house, and his son, Jotham, appeared in public as regent. But not even this loathsome disease, which the Judean historian interprets as a sign of Yahweh's disfavor, eclipsed the glory and fame of Uzziah. Even after his confinement, he continued to be the recognized ruler, and his name remained a symbol of the strength and stability of Judah (see Isa. 6:1). As the kingdom of Israel swiftly declined after the death of Jeroboam II, Judah rose to a position of power and influence second only to that of the era of David and Solomon. The only cloud on the horizon was the threat of Assyrian imperialism.

The Assyrian threat was, of course, no new development. As we have seen, the dominant theme of international politics, from the thirteenth century on, was the rise of Assyria and its ambition to establish an empire encompassing the whole Fertile Crescent. With the rise of Tiglath-pileser III to power, this threat became an ominous reality. Once the Assyrian war machine was rolling, it did not stop until, under one of Tiglath-pileser's successors, it reached the valley of the Nile (see map, p. 303).

In such a time, filled with political promise and ominous with impending catastrophe, Isaiah was called to be a prophet. His call came in 742 B.C.E.—the year in which King Uzziah died and Tiglath-pileser finished his siege of Arpad, the capital of a province in northern Syria. Isaiah's prophetic career lasted more than forty years, and during that time the political map of the world changed. Crisis followed crisis. The first major political event occurred in the year 735 when the armies of Syria and north Israel invaded Judean soil to force Judah to enter a coalition, organized for the purpose of stopping the Assyrian advance, after the manner of the western alliance that fought Assyria at Qarqar (see p. 269). It was a futile enterprise, for in 733–732 Tiglath-pileser conquered Syria and swept down through Gilead, Galilee, and the Plain of Sharon.

The second major event of Isaiah's career occurred when Shalmaneser V, the successor of Tiglath-pileser, was provoked by Israel's insurgence to visit Palestine again, this time to lay siege to Samaria, the capital of the Northern Kingdom (722–721 B.C.E.). Then, later on, during the reign of the next Assyrian king, Sargon II, the Assyrian army marched down along the coastal highway of Palestine to put down another anti-Assyrian revolt, this time localized in the Philistine city of Ashdod (712). Finally, toward the close of his ministry, Isaiah saw Judah's foolish attempt to conspire against Assyria and lived through the terrible days of Sennacherib's invasion in the year 701 (see Chronological Chart 6, p. 332).

Through all these crises, the prophet maintained that an alliance against

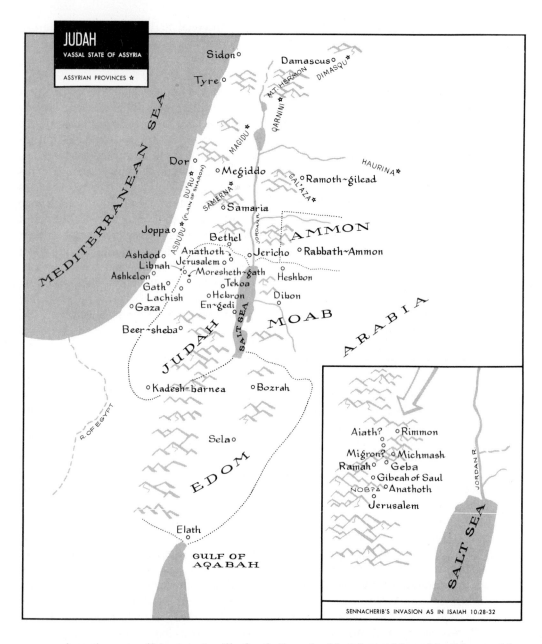

JUDAH
VASSAL STATE OF ASSYRIA

ASSYRIAN PROVINCES ✿

SENNACHERIB'S INVASION AS IN ISAIAH 10:28-32

Assyria was a "covenant with death," as the kingdom of Israel had learned by bitter experience. And yet Isaiah was no mere political analyst. In the historical arena, where nations vied for power, he discerned the activity of Yahweh, the Sovereign of Israel and the nations. His task as prophet was to interpret what Yahweh was saying and doing in the tense political events of the time.

THE BOOK OF ISAIAH

Before we turn to the message of Isaiah, we must first consider the book itself. The present book of Isaiah has sixty-six chapters. It is commonly agreed, however, that not all this material comes from the eighth-century prophet. A nucleus of this big book does come from Isaiah, but a great deal of the material comes from others who were disciples and interpreters of the prophet. Again we must remember that our conception of "authorship" did not prevail in the biblical period. In a day when it was impossible to "publish" books for general circulation and when copyrights were unheard of, the only way to preserve prophetic material was to deposit it within a circle of followers who faithfully remembered the words of their leader and recorded the tradition for posterity.

Isaiah gives us a picture of how his message was handed on. Early in his ministry, when his message to Judah had fallen on deaf ears, he withdrew from public life in order to "bind up the testimony" and to "seal the teaching among [his] disciples" (Isa. 8:16–18; cf. 30:8). If the present was a time of "the eclipse of God," when Yahweh was "hiding his face from the house of Jacob," as he put it (Isa. 8:17), then he would wait for Yahweh to come in glory and to speak with power. Apparently, then, Isaiah deposited his oracles for safekeeping within the faithful prophetic community. There they were treasured, revised in the light of Isaiah's later teaching, and, after his death, handed on by his disciples. Thus the tradition was kept alive. It included not only Isaiah's original words, but also other accumulated materials which, in the conviction of his followers, were in keeping with his teaching. We have already seen that this is what happened with the teachings of Moses. The Mosaic tradition, finally compiled in the Pentateuch, included not only the original traditions of the Mosaic period but also an accumulation of later traditions that had clustered around the great name of Moses.

In the Hebrew Bible the writings of the prophets are contained in four major scrolls: the book of Isaiah, the book of Jeremiah, the book of Ezekiel, and the book of the Twelve. Together, these scrolls make up the "Latter Prophets," as distinguished from the "Former Prophets" (see the table on p. 123). All four scrolls are approximately the same length. Apparently the size of a manageable scroll was one factor that controlled the amount of material to be included. The book of the Twelve, for instance, contains twelve small prophetic books—Hosea, Joel, Amos, Obadiah, Jonah, Micah, Nahum, Habakkuk, Zephaniah, Haggai, Zechariah, and Malachi. They are arranged in a single scroll, not on the basis of chronology or of relative importance, but because together the writings associated with the names of these prophets fill out a scroll. Like the book of the Twelve, the scrolls of Isaiah, Jeremiah, and Ezekiel are really prophetic collections, even though they are gathered under the name of a single prophet.

One of the primary tasks of biblical criticism is to understand these "books" in the final form that they have been given. Usually, however, the final text is the end result of a dynamic history of traditions, during which an original nucleus of material was interpreted and contemporized as it was passed on from generation to generation. Our understanding of a particular "book," such as the scroll of Isaiah, is enriched by discerning that the final text contains various levels of tradition, each of which—like voices in a choir—contribute to the completed production.[3]

A Breakdown of the Material in Isaiah

Let us examine the kinds of material included in the Isaiah scroll. First of all, it is generally agreed that chapters 40–66 do not belong to the Isaiah who prophesied in Jerusalem in the eighth century. As we shall see in Chapter 14, these chapters reflect a historical situation that existed about two centuries later: when Judah had fallen, when the people were in exile, and when Babylonia—then the superpower in the world—was about to fall before the rising empire of Persia. This material, or at least much of it, is usually attributed to "Second Isaiah." This scholarly nickname does not mean that the writer was actually named Isaiah, but merely that this anonymous prophet's writings are included in the same scroll with those of "First Isaiah"—that is, Isaiah of Jerusalem.

The genuine writings of Isaiah, then, are found in the first thirty-nine chapters of the book. A variety of material is contained even in these chapters, however. Chapters 36–39 have been lifted, with some modifications, from II Kings 18:13–20:19, which relate incidents that happened during the latter part of Isaiah's ministry. Chapters 34 and 35, the first a passage of doom and the second a passage of hope, are more like the poems of Second Isaiah than like the preceding material in the book of Isaiah. Scholars generally agree that these two chapters, which deal with the end-time, do not come from the eighth century Isaiah. Moving backward a bit further, chapters 24–27 (often called "the little apocalypse") seem to reflect a later stage in the Isaiah tradition. So, by a process of elimination, we are left with three sections of the book of Isaiah that contain the prophecies of Isaiah of Jerusalem:

A. Chapters 1–11—a series of prophetic oracles and prophetic narratives. A compiler added chapter 12, a hymn of praise (psalm), to round off this section.

B. Chapters 13–23—a series of oracles against foreign nations. Many scholars believe that only a fraction of this material comes from Isaiah, however.

C. Chapters 28–32—a series of prophetic oracles. Chapter 33, which completes this section, is a late prophetic liturgy.

---

[3] The call to go beyond past biblical criticism and consider the book of Isaiah as a canonical unity was issued by Brevard Childs, *Introduction* [37], pp. 325–38. See further R. E. Clements, "The Unity of the Book of Isaiah," *Interpretation*, 36 (1982), 117–129, and "Beyond Tradition History: Deutero-Isaianic Development of First Isaiah's Themes," *Journal for the Study of the Old Testament*, 31 (1985), 95–113; also Walter Brueggemann, "Unity and Dynamic in the Isaiah Tradition," *Journal for the Study of the Old Testament*, 29 (1984), 89–107. On "canonical criticism," see Definition, Chapter 18, p. 639.

So the study of Isaiah is not so big a job as it would seem on first opening the book of Isaiah! At the most, we must tackle twenty-nine chapters, and, since for our purposes the section on the foreign nations (B) can be set aside temporarily, only eighteen chapters are left.

By narrowing our attention to these two sections—chapters 1–11 (A) and chapters 28–32 (C)—our study of the long career of Isaiah is greatly simplified, for each of these sections comes from a fairly well-defined period in the prophet's ministry. In general, chapters 1–11 reflect the early period of Isaiah, from the death of Uzziah to the time of the Syro-Israelite alliance—or about ten years (c. 742–732 B.C.E.). And chapters 28–32 reflect the later period of the prophet's career, from the accession of king Hezekiah of Judah to the great crisis brought on by Sennacherib's invasion of Judah—or about fourteen years (c. 715–701). These two major sections provide a convenient approach to the study of Isaiah. Let us look first at section A of our outline, beginning with the prophetic memoirs found in Isaiah 6:1–8:18, and then move on to the oracles of Isaiah's early career.

Isaiah's Early Ministry

Not very much is known about Isaiah's background. He was obviously a man of the city, which accounts for the great number of urban metaphors he used, and he may have grown up in the privileged circles of Jerusalem. Above all, the city of Jerusalem had a deep place in his affection. For Jerusalem was the place of Yahweh's Temple, the seat of David's throne, and the city hallowed with many sacred memories. Oddly enough, Israel's wilderness tradition, which loomed so large in the message of prophets like Amos and Hosea, seems to have had no great influence on Isaiah's prophecy. On the Exodus and the other great themes of Israel's sacred history he is virtually silent, even though he was obviously aware of these traditions.[4] Isaiah seems to have been nurtured in circles that stressed the special relationship between Yahweh and the Davidic dynasty (see II Sam. 7). In view of his absorbing interest in Davidic theology, it is not surprising that he is regarded as the chief exponent of the hope for a coming Messiah (literally: "Anointed One") of David's lineage. (See Definition, p. 233).

The Kingship of Yahweh

The account of Isaiah's call to be a prophet is one of the classic passages in prophetic literature (Isa. 6). In a few verses of prose that verge on poetic sub-

---

[4] The Exodus is referred to explicitly in Isa. 10:24–26 and 11:16—passages which, in the judgment of some scholars, come from later Isaianic tradition. On the affinities between Isaiah's message and the Mosaic covenant tradition, see Walther Eichrodt, ''Prophet and Covenant: Observations on the Exegesis of Isaiah,'' in *Proclamation and Presence* [158], 167–88. Jon D. Levenson maintains that the ''Sinai'' and ''Zion'' traditions, though separate in origin, actually supplement one another [140], pp. 187–219.

limity we are ushered into the worship experience which provided both the motive and the content for his preaching. The account in its present form, of course, is written in retrospect. Although it points back to a time when he was a very young man, it carries the overtones of his later experiences, especially his bewilderment over the people's dullness and blindness. This, in part, is why the prophetic commission is described in such bleak and unpromising terms (Isa. 6:9–13; see 29:9–12, an oracle from his later ministry). As a whole, however, the passage is a vivid portrayal of the great moment of decision in Isaiah's life, an experience that was to persist at the center of his message.

Notice the time and the place. It was a critical time, heavy with urgency and foreboding. That is the meaning of the reference to Uzziah's death. Uzziah had been a strong king, and even while his son Jotham was acting as regent Uzziah remained a pillar of strength for the people. Since kingship is more or less alien to our experience, it is difficult for us to appreciate the significance of the king in ancient society. "Just as the house is centered in the father," writes an eminent authority on ancient Israelite life, "so the soul of the people is centered in the king."[5] From the king's person blessing and strength went out through the whole nation, like life-giving sap through the branches of a tree. Hence Uzziah's death was an event that touched the life of the people, especially in view of the weakness of his son Jotham and the menacing shadow of Assyria. In such an hour, says the prophet, "I saw *the* King." His testimony implies that his people were ultimately dependent, not upon the Davidic king enthroned in Jerusalem, but upon the cosmic King, Yahweh of hosts (i.e. of heavenly armies; cf. Judg. 5:20).

The place of Isaiah's vision was the Temple of Solomon. Here, in a priestly setting of worship with which the prophet had grown familiar through the years,[6] he beheld a vision of Yahweh sitting on a heavenly throne, high and lifted up, while the chamber rang with the "holy, holy, holy" which is heard in anthems of worship even today. This theme of Yahweh's enthronement as King over the earth and the whole universe was especially at home in the Jerusalem cult. The exclamation, "Yahweh is king!" sounded forth on the New Year's Day of the Autumn Festival, when worshipers sang hymns which portray Yahweh as robed in majesty, exalted in "the beauty of holiness," and enthroned over the whole creation as Judge and Arbiter of the destinies of the peoples.[7]

---

[5] Johannes Pedersen, *Israel* [117], I–II, 275.

[6] It has been suggested that Isaiah himself was a priest or a temple prophet (see R. B. Y. Scott, *Interpreter's Bible*, V, 207–208). Since ordinary worshipers did not enter the Temple but stood outside before the high altar of sacrifice, this is possible; but it is sufficient to say that Isaiah, like other great prophets—Samuel (at Shiloh), Jeremiah, and Ezekiel—was influenced by the priestly tradition.

[7] The so-called Enthronement Psalms (Pss. 47, 93, 96–99) will be discussed in Chapter 16. An excellent discussion of Zion theology is given by Bennie Ollenburger, *Zion, the City of the Great King* [352].

The Prophet in the Heavenly Council

In this setting, the elements of the temple service—the antiphonal singing, the altar with its red-hot stones, the incense smoke that filled the sanctuary, the mysterious depths of the Holy of Holies—are transfigured. Even the temple itself was suffused with celestial glory, for Isaiah's vision presupposes the ancient view that the Jerusalem temple was a microcosm of the macrocosm—that is, an earthly replica of the heavenly Temple. This view enabled people to believe that Yahweh is truly present in Mount Zion and at the same time is the transcendent God, enthroned on high.[8] (See the reconstruction of the temple, p. 238.)

In the prophet's vision, the earthly temple suddenly enlarges and he finds himself standing in a spacious heavenly temple. He sees Yahweh seated upon a great throne, clothed in a majestic robe whose skirt fills the temple. A thrice-holy anthem resounds in the temple, and the visible radiance ("glory") of the King fills the whole earth. Yahweh is not only Israel's King, but the King *par excellence*, upon whose sovereignty the destinies of all peoples depend. With appropriate poetic reserve, Isaiah makes no attempt to describe Yahweh's appearance; but the imagery communicates the overpowering and awesome effect of divine sovereignty. Surrounding the throne are unearthly *seraphim*, like the strange figures—half-human and half-animal—which ancient people portrayed as attendants of the deity's sanctuary. Their three pairs of wings express symbolically the appropriate responses to Yahweh's presence: with one pair they shield their faces from the King's blinding glory, with the second pair they hide their nakedness from God's holy purity, and with the third pair they fly to do their appointed tasks.

So the narrative suggests that the prophet, entering through the vestibule of Solomon's Temple, stands in Yahweh's celestial throne room, where the heavenly host surround the King. One of the recurrent themes in the Old Testament is the picture of the Heavenly Council presided over by Yahweh—as in Micaiah's vision, for example: "I saw Yahweh sitting upon his throne, and all the host of heaven standing by him on his right hand and on his left" (I Kings 22:19; see pp. 268–271).[9] Yahweh's speech employs the plural "us" (Isa. 6:8), a pronoun that includes the surrounding Council, the "heavenly host," to whom and for whom Yahweh speaks. Isaiah, then, is drawn into Yahweh's Heavenly Council where the divine decrees are announced and where messengers are sent

---

[8] See R. E. Clements, *God and Temple* [437], chap. 5.

[9] See the prologue to the book of Job, and also various Psalms where the angelic hosts are summoned to praise Yahweh as "a great king above all gods" (Ps. 82:5–7; 95:3; 103:19–22; 148:2). A good discussion of the Heavenly Council is found in G. E. Wright, *The Old Testament Against Its Environment* [289], pp. 30–41. See also H. Wheeler Robinson, "The Council of Yahweh," in *Journal of Theological Studies*, XLV (1944), 151–57.

forth to execute them.[10] In a visionary moment he is permitted to behold what is veiled to the sight of mortals, (see Exod. 33:20), for he exclaims that with his own eyes he has seen the celestial King.

Called to Be the King's Messenger

His first response—already symbolized in the attitude of the seraphim in the King's presence—is to cry out that he is an "unclean" person and a member of an "unclean" people (verse 5). This response is evoked by an overwhelming sense of the holiness of Yahweh, a fundamental aspect of Israel's experience of the presence of God in the world, portrayed classically in the story of the Sinai revelation (Exod. 19). Yahweh's holiness means, first of all, that Yahweh is "God and not a human being" (Hos. 11:9)—the God who completely transcends the human world and is therefore beyond all human analogies or categories. Although active within the human world, Yahweh cannot be domesticated within it or manipulated and controlled according to human purposes (remember the story of the Golden Calf, Exod. 32). Yahweh is the One who is God absolutely, before whom all beings stand in judgment and upon whom everything that exists is dependent. Moreover, in Isaiah's message holiness is not limited to the sublimity of God as contrasted with human creatureliness; it also means the awful contrast between God's purity and human sinfulness. As "the Holy One of Israel"—a favorite expression of the prophet—Yahweh is exalted in righteousness (Isa. 5:16). In Yahweh's presence, nothing unclean, nothing unrighteous, nothing idolatrous can survive. So, in the moment when the threshold of the Temple shakes at the sound of the seraphim's anthem, Isaiah confesses that he is a member of a community in which there is no health (see Isa. 1:4–9), and he links himself with his people in a woeful cry of dereliction: "Woe is me! For I am lost!"

In his vision one of the heavenly "priests" (a seraph) takes from the altar a glowing stone and purges his unclean lips:

> Behold, this has touched your lips;
> your guilt is taken away,
> and your sin forgiven.
> —ISAIAH 6:7 (RSV)

Here a new note is introduced into prophecy: the prophet himself needs purification before he can be God's messenger. Amos had prayed that Yahweh would forgive the people (Amos 7:1-6), but Isaiah begins his prophetic career as a person who has been forgiven. And no sooner is he "consecrated"—that

---

[10] The prophet understands himself to be God's messenger (see pp. 248–249), sent to deliver a message to the people. The prophet's source of authority, according to some passages, was located in Yahweh's Heavenly Council (Jer. 23:18, 22). On this point see James F. Ross, "The Prophet as Yahweh's Messenger" [cited under 324], 102–6.

is, made holy or cleansed for God's service—than Yahweh, speaking in a manner which includes the whole Heavenly Council, says: "Whom shall I send, and who will go for us?" Isaiah volunteers, only to receive a commission so unbearable that he cries out, asking how long it must go on. The answer is that he is to proclaim Yahweh's word to a people whose heart[11] is fat (insensitive), whose ears are heavy (dull), and whose eyes are blind (verses 9–10).

This is a very puzzling command. As we have said, Isaiah's memory of his call seems to be colored by his later experiences of failure. And yet more is expressed in this language than the mood of later discouragement. Isaiah, like other prophets, believed that all events came from the hand of God. Although we would regard the developments of Isaiah's career as stemming from human sources, for which a cause-and-effect explanation could be found in the social situation, the prophet insisted that these experiences happened within the divine purpose; God was not taken by surprise, as it were. It was known in advance that the prophetic word would have the effect that it did among a *rebellious* people (see Isa. 1:2–3). For as excessive light can blind the eyes, or excessive sound can be deafening, so the words and signs of the prophet would increase the people's blindness to Yahweh's acts and their deafness to Yahweh's words, although, strictly speaking, that was not the intention of the prophet's activity. Yet, if we are correct in interpreting the severe passage of doom (verses 11–13), the darkness is illumined by a ray of light, for it is said that after the fire of divine judgment has swept through the land a "stump" will remain. And just as a new branch sprouts from a stump that stands in a burned forest, so new life will begin in a remnant of the people.

The Day of Yahweh

Before going on to the prophetic memoirs in chapters 7 and 8, it is appropriate to look back from chapter 6 to the preceding chapters, which, for the most part, reflect Isaiah's early ministry.[12] In these chapters the themes of Isaiah's vision are elaborated. In various ways and situations the prophet reaffirmed that Yahweh is enthroned, high and lifted up, above all the tumult of history and the feverish strivings of the nations. As with Amos, the Day of Yahweh will not be light, but darkness—a day of judgment against all symbols of human pride and self-sufficiency: against silver and gold, horses and chariots, fortified cities, and stately ships that sail to faraway places (2:6–21). These cultural treasures are not bad in themselves; but when they are "lifted up" like the proud cedars of Lebanon, people begin to place their trust in them, and they become objects of

[11] "Heart" refers to the inward center of the person, not to mere feelings or emotions. In Hebrew a person thinks in the heart, and loves with the heart.

[12] Not all of chapter 1 comes from this period, for verses 7–9 refer to the isolation of Jerusalem during the siege of Sennacherib. Indeed, some scholars maintain that the whole chapter is a later editorial introduction, designed to introduce the themes that are announced in the entire Isaiah tradition, Isa. 1–66; see Brevard Childs, *Introduction* [37], p. 331 (referring to the view of G. Fohrer).

idolatry—for idolatry is trusting in anything less than God. The time will come, says the prophet, when people will cast their idols to the moles and the bats. The oracles of doom are punctuated with this refrain:

> Human haughtiness will be humbled,
>   human pride will be abased,
> And Yahweh alone will be exalted in that day.
> —ISAIAH 2:17

That Yahweh comes to judge the people is the theme of Isaiah's famous Song of the Vineyard (Isa. 5:1–7). The prophet begins by singing a vineyard song, like the popular ballads that were sung at the autumn vintage festivals. It is possible that Isaiah posed as a singer in order to catch the attention of the crowds on their way to the Temple to celebrate the gathering of the harvest. He tells about his disappointment. He had done everything possible to insure a good harvest, only to find that his vineyard yielded wild grapes. He asks his hearers what had gone wrong; after all, what more could he have done? Then he announces what he is going to do: he will tear down the vines and let the vineyard become a briar patch. Suddenly, the unexpected point of the song is plunged into the people's heart, for it turns out that Yahweh is the speaker and that the song is about Yahweh's chosen people: "the vineyard of Yahweh of hosts." With a play on words, the prophet announces Yahweh's indignant disappointment:

> He looked for justice [*mishpaṭ*],
>   and behold, bloodshed [*mispaḥ*];
> for righteousness [*zedaqah*],
>   but behold, distress [*ze'aqah*].

It is impossible to reproduce the force of the Hebrew assonance in English, but word-pairs like justice/distress and right/riot give a rough idea. The following oracles (5:8–24) elaborate further the woes of a people guilty of the most flagrant injustice and exploitation.

Isaiah's earliest message, then, was one of doom, in keeping with the commission given to him in chapter 6. Yahweh announces a covenant lawsuit[13] against the people Israel, summoning them to stand trial before their Judge (Isa. 1:18–20; 3:13–15). Arraigned before Yahweh's holy presence, the prophet had to say on their behalf that they were "unclean"—indeed, that there was no health in them (1:4–6). And yet, Yahweh's purpose was not just destructive: it was to restore Israel to health, to make Israel a holy people fit to serve the King. Just as Isaiah was cleansed by forgiveness, so—according to the prophet's interpretation—Yahweh was seeking to purify the people as by fire. Through the terrible sufferings of the time, Yahweh was purging away the dross and alloy

---

[13] See pp. 339–340 where the structure of the covenant lawsuit (*rîb*) is given.

so that Jerusalem might become the New Jerusalem: the city of righteousness (1:24–26).

The Syro-Israelite Alliance

Now it is appropriate to return to the prophetic memoirs found in chapters 7 and 8.[14] A few years after Isaiah's call, his wife, the "prophetess" referred to in Isaiah 8:3, gave birth to a boy, who was named Shear-yashub (7:3). Just as Hosea gave symbolic names to his children, so Isaiah's child was a living sign from Yahweh, a visible confirmation of the message of the prophet. Literally, the name means "A remnant shall return" (that is, "turn to God," "repent," as in 6:10). Although in one sense, this phrase carried a negative meaning ("*Only* a remnant shall return," as in 10:22–23), in another sense it concealed a promise ("A remnant *shall* return"), just as doom and hope seem to be blended together in the concluding verses of chapter 6.

This sign-child figures prominently in a scene in the prophetic memoir found in chapter 7. The material in chapters 7 and 8 deals with the Syro-Israelite crisis that occurred in 733–732 B.C.E., which we have already touched on in connection with Hosea (pp. 315–316). Uzziah's regent, who had become king in his own right after his father's death, had been succeeded on the throne of Judah by Ahaz (c. 735–715). This youthful king was no match for the political troubles he inherited. A plot was afoot among the small western states to stop the advance of Assyria. Apparently they hoped that by pooling their efforts they might duplicate the feat of the western allies more than a century earlier, when the Assyrian armies were temporarily turned back at Qarqar. This international conspiracy made the one-time enemies—Israel (the Northern Kingdom) and Syria—political bedfellows for a very short time. Initially, the Assyrian king, Tiglath-pileser III, was recognized by the western nations. Therefore, in the year 738 Menahem, king of Israel, joined with Rezin of Damascus to pay tribute to the Assyrian victor (II Kings 15:19–20). This capitulation to Assyria enabled Menahem and his son Pekahiah to stay in power, but it was highly unpopular, especially since the tribute was raised by heavy taxes on the rich. The time was ripe for revolution. An army captain, Pekah, the son of Remaliah, murdered Pekahiah in the year 737 and shortly thereafter, while Tiglath-pileser was occupied in the north, conspired with Rezin of Damascus to form an anti-Assyrian coalition. The two kingdoms joined in an attack on Judah in an attempt to replace Ahaz with a non-Davidic puppet king on the Judean throne (Isa. 7:6).

---

[14] These memoirs are found in the so-called "book of testimony," which Isaiah and his disciples may have composed after the events referred to in it (see Isa. 8:16). It includes: the account of Isaiah's call (chap. 6), his counsel to Ahaz (chap. 7), the consequences of his spurned counsel (chap. 8), and an oracle of promise to Judah (9:1–7). When this "book of testimony" (6:1–9:7) was inserted into the heart of chapters 2–11, the continuity of the material was disturbed. Thus the refrain in 5:25 continues in 9:12, 17, 21, and 10:4; and the sevenfold "woes" begin in 5:8 and are resumed in 10:1–19. See Otto Kaiser, *Isaiah* 1–12 [350], pp. 64–65.

Ahaz was in a tight spot, for he had come to the throne of Judah in one of the gravest crises of Judean history. From a purely political standpoint he deserves our sympathy, even though as a leader he was weak and vacillating. The presence of the invading armies on his soil filled him with panic: "his heart and the heart of his people shook as the trees of the forest shake before the wind." Terror-stricken, he burned his son as an offering in the Valley of Hinnom just outside the city (II Kings 16:3), hoping by this pagan rite to assuage the divine wrath that had come upon the city (compare the action of the Moabite king, II Kings 3:26–27). The situation was desperate. As a responsible political leader, Ahaz had to choose between accepting defeat at the hands of the invaders or appealing for outside help. Thoughts like these must have been in his mind as he went out to inspect the city's water supply, which was essential to Jerusalem's ability to hold out during a siege. It was at that moment that Isaiah confronted Ahaz, accompanied by his little boy, Shear-yashub (meaning, "A remnant shall return").

Harassed as he was, Ahaz must have regarded Isaiah's counsel as an irrelevant interruption. But Isaiah's message was simple, apparently too simple: "Trust in Yahweh; be quiet and keep calm." The appropriate response to the crisis, he said, was relaxed confidence, not feverish anxiety over the defenses of Jerusalem. Isaiah evidently was thinking of the weakness of the Syro-Israelite alliance, whose kings were "two smoldering stumps of firebrands," almost burned out; and he probably realized that for Judah to become involved in the international rivalries of the time would be suicidal, as subsequent events were to show in the case of the Northern Kingdom. But he viewed the crisis in a wider and deeper perspective than that of mere diplomacy and fortifications. For beyond the political schemes of nations was the sovereign activity of God, whose purpose shapes the course of events. The head of Ephraim is Pekah, and the head of Damascus is Rezin, *but these are men, not God!* Their plan to place a puppet king on Judah's throne ("the son of Tabeel," probably an Aramean) will fail, for Yahweh is bound in covenant loyalty (*ḥésed*) to David and David's descendants. So Isaiah affirms that the greatest resource in time of trouble is faith— absolute trust in and dependence upon God (see Ps. 46:8–10). He underscores his message of faith with a play on words (Isa. 7:9b), which may be paraphrased: "If your faith is not sure (*ta'aminu*), your throne will not be secure (*te'amenu*)."[15] Abandon human *alliance*, exclaims Isaiah, and place your *reliance* on Yahweh, whose sovereign will controls human affairs! Such faith demands a complete and firm commitment of one's whole being to God, in the confidence that Yahweh is the true King (see also Isa. 28:16; 30:15).[16]

---

[15] Both words are derived from the verb *'amen* which means "to be firm, to be sure," from which comes the meaning "to trust, to believe." NAB translates: "Unless your faith is firm you shall not be firm!"

[16] Martin Buber's term for Isaiah's attitude is "theopolitics"—that is, the attempt to bring Israel in a specific situation so completely under the divine sovereignty that it accepts its historical task: "to become the beginning of the kingdom of God." *The Prophetic Faith* [311], p. 135.

Specifically, Isaiah's advice in that political situation called for Ahaz to cancel his plan to ask for Assyrian intervention on behalf of besieged Judah. It was the prophet's conviction that Yahweh would overthrow the Syro-Israelite alliance by bringing Assyria against these foolish nations. The word of faith, then, was politically relevent in that situation. But Ahaz could not believe this. So later on, when the king was mapping out a political strategy with his advisers, Isaiah came to him again with the offer of a "sign."

The Sign of Immanuel

Here it is appropriate to call to mind our earlier discussion about the meaning of signs (see Definition, p. 74). According to the Exodus tradition, Moses performed signs in the sight of Pharaoh, and according to the New Testament Jesus performed signs (*semeia*). In the Bible a sign does not stand by itself; rather, it is closely linked to the prophetic word, as in Isaiah 7. The purpose of a sign is to make visible, to confirm dramatically, the truth and power of Yahweh's word spoken by a prophet. The sign does not have to be a stupendous "miracle," in our sense of the word, for its significance is not so much its unusual character as its power to confirm a prophetic word spoken in threat or promise. In other instances, Isaiah's symbolic act of going about naked and barefoot (Isa. 20), or his children who were present with him (8:18), are called signs. The ability to see signs is an indication of something that we have found to be characteristic of Israel's faith, a vivid sense of divine activity in the realm of human affairs. God is *with us*—not aloof from the scene of history. Thus, not only can God's word be *heard* through the prophetic message, but also God's action can be *seen* in signs that the prophet points to or acts out.

Remember that Isaiah was commissioned to speak to a people who could neither hear Yahweh's word nor see the signs of Yahweh's activity (Isa. 6:9). Ahaz had already failed to hear. So Isaiah said that Yahweh would confirm the prophetic word by any sign the king might choose. But evidently Ahaz had already decided to take another course of action, so he declined with a pretense of piety: he would not put Yahweh to the test. Exasperated by the king's sacrifice of faith on the altar of political expedience, Isaiah tersely announced that Yahweh would nevertheless give "the house [dynasty] of David" a sign—a sign that would confirm the word of doom upon the Syro-Israelite alliance and at the same time confirm Yahweh's promises of grace to David.

The sign promised was the birth of a child whose name would be Immanuel, which in Hebrew means, "God [is] with us." The language presupposes that the mother is already, or soon will be, pregnant; the child will be born in the near future.

> The maiden is with child and will soon give birth to a son whom she will call Immanuel.
>
> —ISAIAH 7:14 (JB; see also NEB)

Chronological Chart 6

B.C.E.	EGYPT	PALESTINE — DIVIDED KINGDOM		SYRIA	MESOPOTAMIA
		JUDAH	ISRAEL		ASSYRIA
750	Decline	Jotham (regent), c. 750–742	Shallum (1 mo.), c. 745		Tiglath-pileser III, c. 745–727
		Jotham (king), c. 742–735 (Isaiah, c. 742–700)	Menahem, c. 745–737 Pekahiah, c. 737–736 Pekah, c. 736–732	Rezin, c. 740–732	EXPANSION OF ASSYRIAN EMPIRE
		Jehoahaz (Ahaz), c. 735–715 Invasion by Syro-Israelite Alliance, 735	SYRO-ISRAELITE ALLIANCE		Siege of Damascus, 732 Shalmaneser V, 726–722
			Hoshea, c. 732–724	FALL OF SYRIA 732	
		(Micah: before 722 to c. 701)	FALL OF SAMARIA 722–721		Siege of Samaria, 722/721
	XXV Dynasty (Ethiopian) c. 716–663	JUDAH			Sargon II, 721–705 Siege of Ashdod, 712 Sennacherib, 704–681
700		Hezekiah, c. 715–687/6			Invasion of Palestine, 701

Even before the child reaches the age of choosing between good and evil, the Syro-Israelite alliance will have been broken up and the king of Assyria will have wrought havoc upon Judah. At that time Judah will be reduced to a primitive pastoral state in which the people will live on curds and honey. Yahweh will "shave" Judah with an Assyrian razor. In other words, Isaiah promised Ahaz that Yahweh would bring immediate relief from the Syro-Israelite threat, but announced that the deliverance would be followed by even greater disaster for Judah (7:15–24).

A great deal of interest has centered in the Immanuel prophecy of Isaiah 7:14. In the New Testament period it was believed that the prophecy was fulfilled in Jesus Christ, to whom was given the name "God is with us." Moreover, in some circles the passage was appealed to in support of the Virgin Birth (Matt. 1:23). While it is beyond our purpose to consider the validity of this belief, we do want to understand what Isaiah meant in the concrete political situation we have been discussing. Let us consider briefly the meaning of Isaiah's words.

First of all, the sign is the child himself—not the manner of his birth. To be sure, the prophet had explicitly said that Ahaz could ask for anything—"let it be deep as Sheol or high as heaven" (Isa. 7:11)—on the assumption that all things are possible with God. Ahaz refused to ask, so Isaiah announced the *timely* birth of a child to a "young woman" of marriageable age (see the Revised Standard Version).[17] The prophet, then, pointed to the advent of a child in the immediate future who would grow up among his people as a pledge that "God is with us."

The Davidic Heir Apparent

Moreover, Isaiah apparently indicated that the child would come from a particular family. In the Hebrew text he uses the definite article, saying, "*The* maiden is pregnant," as though he were referring to a particular woman, already known to Ahaz. It has even been suggested that the woman was the queen and that the child was Hezekiah, Ahaz's son and successor. Whether or not this is true, it seems that Isaiah was thinking of a son of the house of David, although surely the messianic implications of his prophecy were not fully developed until later in his ministry. The well-known poem in Isaiah 9:1–7, perhaps written later in his career, clearly says that the wonder child will sit upon the throne of David.

How, then, does the imminent birth of the Davidic child relate to the political crisis of the Syro-Israelite alliance? In contrast to Ahaz, the king who shows no faith, Isaiah pictures the advent of a child-king who in due time will *faithfully* exercise the task of government. Initially, the Immanuel child will live in a time

---

[17] Apparently this is the meaning of the Hebrew word *'almah*, which is used in the Hebrew Bible without prejudice as to a maiden's virginity (for instance, Gen. 24:43; Exod. 2:8; Prov. 30:19). The usual word for "virgin" is *bethulah*. In this passage, the Septuagint translators render *parthenos*. Normally, this is the translation of *bethulah* in the Septuagint, but it is also used for *'almah* in Gen. 24:43; cf. 34:3. This simply shows that the Septuagint used the word freely, and did not necessarily imply literal virginity in Isa. 7:14. Other Greek versions render "maiden" (*neanis*) here, which is more accurate.

of great woe, for before he is very old, the Assyrian invasion will sweep through the land, converting it into a wilderness (Isa. 7:16–17).[18] And yet, to those who have eyes to see, his presence will be a sign, an assurance that God is leading the people through the fire of divine judgment to the dawn of a new day. The child will share his people's sufferings, will live with them in the wilderness of destruction. But, as in the prophecy of Hosea, "wilderness" will have a double meaning. It will be both the time of judgment, and the opportunity for a new beginning. The fact that the child will eat milk and honey—the food of Paradise which tradition associated with the Promised Land ("the land flowing with milk and honey")—suggests that he will be a sign of the promised future, which lies on the other side of the dark days ahead. For Yahweh's purpose is not to destroy, but to refine and cleanse a remnant of the people. Once the Assyrian yoke is removed, the child will ascend the throne as the agent of God's rule over the people. Then the meaning of his name, Immanuel, will be clearly understood.

So, although Isaiah was not looking into the distant future, it is difficult to resist the conclusion that he meant the child as a "messianic" figure, although it must be pointed out that in Isaiah's time the word "Messiah" ("the Anointed One") referred to the reigning king. (See Definition, Chapter 7, p. 233). If so, the messianic poem in Isaiah 9:1–7 fits in with the theme of his prophecy (see also Isa. 11:1–9). Like his initial prophecy to Ahaz, this passage begins with a picture of doom and darkness, a reminiscence of the terrible destruction wrought by Tiglath-pileser in 733–32 B.C.E. in the territory of Zebulun and Naphtali (Galilee) when these tribal areas were incorporated into the Assyrian empire (II Kings 15:29).[19] But the darkness is illumined by a great light:

> For to us a child is born,
>   to us a son is given;
> And the government will be upon his shoulder,
>   and his name will be called
> "Wonderful Counselor, Mighty God,
>   Everlasting Father, Prince of Peace."
>   —ISAIAH 9:6 (RSV)

From Isaiah this prophecy passed into the stream of prophetic tradition and eventually was transposed into a new key in the Christian gospel (see Matt. 4:15–16).[20]

[18] In Isa. 8:8 this devastated land is referred to as Immanuel's land. Here again the reference is to the child-king. See also the saying "God is with us" in 8:10.

[19] The reference to Tiglath-pileser's conquest of Galilee places this oracle (Isa. 9:1–7) early in the career of Isaiah, according to the judgment of Albrecht Alt in his article, "Jes. 8:23–9:6," now found in his *Kleine Schriften*, II (1953), pp. 206–25. Since the Assyrian king took this territory in 733–732 B.C.E., Alt dates the oracle sometime between the years 732–722. He believes that it was intended as a prophecy of the expulsion of Assyrian forces and the restoration of a United Kingdom under Davidic rule.

[20] It must be admitted that the interpretation of the Immanuel prophecy is exceedingly difficult and that a wide variety of views have been expressed. See the brief treatment of the problem by C. R. North, "Immanuel," in the *Interpreter's Dictionary* [25] and the literature cited at the end of the article; in addition, J. J. Scullion, "Approach to the Understanding of Is. 7:10–17," *Journal of Biblical Literature*, 87 (1968), 288–300, and Joseph Jensen, *Isaiah 1–39* [349], pp. 90–98.

The Waters of Shiloah That Flow Softly

We turn now to the rest of Isaiah's memoirs in chapter 8. At the outset of the chapter, Isaiah is still warning about the swift doom that will overtake the Syro-Israelite coalition. Some time after his encounter with Ahaz, a second son was born to Isaiah's wife, to whom was given the frightening name: Maher-shalal-hash-baz—that is, "The spoil speeds, the prey hastens." The prophet declared that before this sign-child learned how to say "Daddy" and "Mama"—to modernize a bit—the Assyrian king would plunder Samaria and Damascus. Even before the child was born, this same ominous message was written conspicuously on a tablet and properly "notarized," in order to remind people in the future, when the anti-Assyrian coalition was finally overthrown, that God had given true words and signs to the prophet (Isa. 8:1-4).

But the words and the signs were of no avail, for Ahaz lacked the kind of faith the prophet called for. Ahaz had to be "practical" in facing the political realities of the moment, or so he would have said in self-defense. Already the king of Edom, taking advantage of Judah's plight, had recovered the seaport of Elath, which Uzziah had won (II Kings 16:6). Action was imperative. Only two alternatives were open, and neither one was desirable. Either Ahaz could surrender to the forces of Syria and Israel, in which case he might lose his throne and would surely risk being on the wrong side in a showdown with Assyria; or else he could throw in his lot with Assyria, in which case Judah would become a vassal state of the Assyrian empire. He chose the latter course. According to the record in II Kings 16, he appealed for help to the Assyrian king, emptying the treasuries of the Temple and his palace to court his favor. Tiglath-pileser was more than glad to come to the rescue. Damascus was overthrown, Rezin was killed, and Syria was subdivided into provinces of the Assyrian empire. A good part of the state of Israel was annexed (II Kings 15:29; cf. Isa. 9:1), leaving Israel only a strip of land from the plain of Jezreel to the Judean frontier. Ahaz went to Damascus to pay homage to Tiglath-pileser and to congratulate him on his victories. While there, he obtained the blueprint for an Assyrian altar, which he promptly ordered constructed in the Temple at Jerusalem (II Kings 16:10-18). In a day when religion and politics were inseparable, there was no clearer way to demonstrate that Judah had become an Assyrian vassal. The record in II Chronicles 28:16-27 shows further how greatly the kingdom suffered under this royal weakling.

To Isaiah, Ahaz's action was final proof of the lack of faith for which Judah would pay the consequences. In a vivid figure of speech, Isaiah denounced the people for rejecting "the waters of Shiloah that flow softly" in order to show their confidence in the mighty Euphrates of Assyria. Shiloah was a little aqueduct that carried water from the Spring of Gihon to a pool inside the city wall of Jerusalem—probably the very waterworks that Ahaz was examining when Isaiah went out to meet him (Isa. 7:3). This gentle stream was to Isaiah a symbol of quiet and confident faith in Yahweh, whose kingdom is more powerful and everlasting than the mightiest empires. As he had warned, "If you will not have faith, you shall surely not be established'' (7:9). The Assyrians, like a flood overflowing from the Euphrates, would sweep through the land, devastating not only Syria and Israel, but Judah as well.

Binding Up the Testimony

Isaiah, then, was met by the stubborn resistance of a faithless generation. The words that should have awakened faith fell on deaf ears. The signs that should have made the truth visible were held up before blind eyes. But the prophetic words and signs had not been given in vain, for, in the conviction of the prophet, the future was in the control of ''Yahweh of hosts,'' the heavenly Warrior-King. It was evidently at this time, just after Ahaz's overture to Assyria, that Isaiah separated himself from his unheeding fellow citizens and withdrew into the prophetic circle. According to Isaiah, the action was taken under Yahweh's pressure, for ''Yahweh spoke to me with his strong hand upon me and warned me not to walk in the way of this people'' (Isa. 8:11). He told the prophetic community that they were to ''conspire'' with God, not to join the political conspiracy; and they were to ''fear'' Yahweh of hosts, not to have the kind of fear (panic) that drives a nation to political suicide.[21] This faithful community, the prophetic remnant, was to be separated from the rest of the nation by a different allegiance. They were to trust in Yahweh and wait expectantly for the fulfillment of the divine purpose in history.

So Isaiah took his place within this ''community,'' the nucleus of the New Israel. His prophetic *torah*, or teaching, was sealed, or entrusted, among his disciples until a future day when Yahweh would make its truth plain. The prophet himself, as well as his children, were signs that Yahweh had given, and some day these signs would be understood. In such a rebellious time, a few people of faith turned to the future in patient hope. ''I will wait for Yahweh, who is hiding his face from the house of Jacob, and I will hope in him'' (Isa. 8:17). The command to ''bind up the testimony'' among Isaiah's disciples probably resulted in the composition of the Book of Testimony (6:1–9:7) which included not only the prophet's early memoirs, but also, as we have seen, the magnificent promise of the coming of a Davidic King and the dawning of a new day.

Evidently Isaiah emerged from the prophetic circle to address himself to the second great political crisis of his career, the imminent fall of the Northern Kingdom. As events rushed on toward the final Assyrian blow against Samaria in 722–721 B.C.E., he spoke out against ''the fading flower of Ephraim's glorious beauty'' in oracles that are now scattered in various parts of the book (9:8–10:4; 17:1–11; 28:1–4). Of these oracles the most forceful is the series found in 9:8–10:4, with which is to be included the oracle in 5:26–30. Blow after blow of divine

---

[21] The verbs of verses 12 and 13 are in the plural, indicating that they refer to the prophetic circle.

judgment shatters the people, but in vain. They do not learn the severe discipline of history. Ending with a refrain, which grows ominous with repetition, each strophe discloses that Yahweh's hand is poised, ready to strike:

> For all this Yahweh's anger is not turned away,
>   and his hand is stretched out still.

Since we know very little about Isaiah's activity during the remainder of the reign of Ahaz, however, this is an appropriate point to turn to his great contemporary, the prophet Micah, whose earliest oracles were delivered before the fall of Samaria.

MICAH, A RURAL PROPHET

Other than the fact that Micah's hometown was Moresheth-gath, a small village in the hills about twenty-five miles southwest of Jerusalem, we know little about him. Unlike the city-bred Isaiah, Micah was a country prophet who spoke for the poor farmers who were suffering at the hands of the powerful landlords. In many respects he reminds us of Amos, also a prophet of social justice. But his message of divine judgment, evoked by the inexorable march of Assyria, is especially akin to the message of judgment and renewal proclaimed by Isaiah. Indeed, it has even been suggested that Micah was one of Isaiah's disciples. Although this is doubtful, it is appropriate to link the two prophets together in considering the fateful events that engulfed Judah toward the end of the eighth century B.C.E. Micah's career seems to have spanned the events from the fall of Samaria in 721 to the arrival of the Assyrians at the gates of Jerusalem in 701.

In its present form, the book of Micah, like that of Isaiah, comes from a prophetic school that preserved and expanded the poems of the eighth century prophet. The book displays a two-beat rhythm of doom and hope, of judgment and renewal which is characteristic of the message of the prophets. This rhythm is evident in the architecture of the book:[22]

Part I: Oracles of judgment (chs. 1–3)
         Oracles of salvation (chs. 4–5)
Part II: Oracles of judgment (6:1–7:7)
         Oracles of salvation (7:8–20)

The reference to exile in Babylonia (Micah 4:8) is one of various indications that the original oracles of Micah, which are concentrated especially in chapters 1–3, have been expanded and updated to speak to the situation after the fall of Jerusalem.

---

[22] On the structure of the book of Micah and the editing of Micah's oracles, see James L. Mays, *Micah* [358], pp. 2–12, 21–33.

Micah's first oracle of judgment (Micah 1:2–7) uses the imagery of a court trial (*rîb*), announced from Yahweh's "holy temple" or cosmic citadel. The earth and all its inhabitants are summoned to hear the indictment and the verdict against both houses of Israel—the north (Samaria) and the south (Judah). The mountains melt and the valleys divide as Yahweh, coming in awesome theophany from the cosmic temple, treads in gigantic steps upon the high places of the earth. The prophet insists that the capital cities are the source of the cancerous corruption that arouses Yahweh to come as Judge.

> All this is because of the transgression of Jacob,
>   because of the sins of the house of Israel.
> What is the transgression of Jacob?
>   Is it not Samaria?
> And what is the sin of Judah?
>   Is it not Jerusalem?
>   —MICAH 1:5

Here the Assyrian devastation of Samaria in 721 B.C.E. is perceived to be an expression of the judgment of God in human affairs.

In the ensuing poem, cast in the form of a dirge (Micah 1:8–16), Micah goes on to say that the fate of Samaria is also in store for Judah. In a vivid passage, in which the Hebrew contains wordplays on the names of various cities and towns (verses 10–16), the prophet portrays the Assyrian avalanche sweeping through Judah, causing suffering that "has reached to the gate of my people, to Jerusalem" (1:9). Clearly this poem reflects the crisis of the year 701 when Sennacherib invaded Judah, engulfing fortified cities like Lachish and villages like Micah's own home town of Moresheth near Gath. (See below, p. 347.)

Filled with the divine charisma ("spirit," Micah 3:9), in contrast to the popular prophets who preached a message that buttered their bread (3:5–8), this austere prophet felt compelled to announce the consequences of the people's behavior. Unlike Isaiah, Micah did not believe that Jerusalem would be spared, for it was "built with blood" (3:10). This city was the scene of outrageous social injustice, a place where people lay awake at nights devising wickedness (chapter 2). The civil and religious leaders were to blame for the sad state of affairs, for they should have known what Yahweh demands of the people (chapter 3). What good is it, the prophet asks, to "lean upon Yahweh" and to say that no evil will befall us because Yahweh is "in our midst" (a reference to the "Immanuel" theme)? Yahweh's indictment against Jerusalem, as in the case of Samaria (1:6), issues in an ominous "therefore":

> Therefore, on account of your deeds,
>   Zion will be ploughed as a field,
> Jerusalem will be a rubble heap,
>   and the Temple mount a wooded height.
>   —MICAH 3:12

This announcement was quoted a century later, when Jeremiah's life was in jeopardy because he made a similar prediction about Jerusalem and its Temple (see Jer. 26:18-19). According to the passage in Jeremiah, the oracle was first delivered in the time of King Hezekiah (c. 715-687/6 B.C.E.), who succeeded Ahaz to the throne of Judah.

Micah's bold prophesy against Zion cannot be explained wholly by saying that, unlike the city-bred Isaiah, he came from the country and therefore could criticize the Davidic City with cool detachment. There must have been also profound *theological* differences between the two prophets, despite the fact that both books bearing their names now contain the famous prophecy concerning the elevation of Zion "in the last days."[23] It is significant that in the indisputably original oracles of Micah there is not a single reference to the Davidic covenant theology, which guaranteed the permanence of the Davidic dynasty and the security of the Davidic City. Even the "messianic" passage in Micah 5:2-6, which in the New Testament is interpreted to refer to the birth of Jesus (Matt. 2:6), announces that the coming ruler will be born, not in the royal court of Jerusalem, but in Bethlehem among the humble clans of Judah, where David got his start.[24] Micah seems not to have been nurtured in court theology but rather in the Exodus tradition, which was kept alive in the rural areas of Judah. It is not surprising, therefore, that in the passage in Micah 6:1-8, which is often hailed as the epitome of the message of the eighth-century prophets, Micah turns to Israel's sacred history which centers in the Exodus.[25]

Like the opening oracle of the book of Micah, this passage employs the imagery of a controversy in a law court, a familiar theme of prophecy, as we have seen. Notice the dramatic structure of the "covenant lawsuit" (*rîb*):

A. SUMMONS (VERSES 1-2)   The trial opens with a summons by the prophet who acts as Yahweh's prosecuting attorney. The mountains are the witnesses: before them Israel is to present its case, and they are to hear the controversy between God and people.

B. THE PLAINTIFF'S CHARGE (VERSES 3-5)   Then Yahweh, through the prophetic attorney, raises a complaint. Significantly, however, Yahweh appeals to

[23] This oracle is found in both Micah 4:1-4 and Isa. 2:2-4, with only slight variation. Isaiah clearly has the greater claim upon the oracle in view of his Zion-centered message. But it is possible that an independent oracle has been added to both prophetic books by compilers.

[24] The prophecies of a glorious future found in Micah 4:1-5:9 may reflect the message of Micah at points, but they have been reworked by later prophetic circles, as is evident from the references to the Babylonian exile (e.g., 4:10).

[25] Micah's prophecies are concentrated in chapters 1-3, though other oracles from him are found in 5:10-7:7. The arguments for denying 6:1-8 to Micah are not decisive. The reference to child sacrifice (vs. 7), was not only familiar from tradition, like that of Gen. 22, but perhaps was immediately based on the action of King Ahaz under stress (II Kings 16:3). And the evangelical appeal of these verses is similar to passages in Amos (e.g., Amos 2:9-11), who also spoke in accents of doom.

Israel's historical traditions—not to laws written in a statute book. The appeal is based on events that have manifested Yahweh's *ḥésed* or covenant grace toward the people, beginning with the Exodus from Egypt and culminating in the occupation of the promised land. These events constitute the very foundation of the covenant community. The clear implication is that because the people Israel has forgotten the great deeds that Yahweh had done on their behalf, they no longer know what the Suzerain requires of the vassal. The prophet is appalled at the incongruity between Yahweh's benevolent actions and Israel's conduct.

C. THE DEFENDANT'S PLEA (VERSES 6–7) At last the defendant, Israel, speaks. But before Yahweh, Israel has no case to plead, save to confess humbly that its actions are inconsistent with Yahweh's saving acts in history and a betrayal of the covenant. Burnt offerings, rivers of oil, even the most costly sacrifice of the firstborn—these things do not satisfy the demands of the covenant. In view of what Yahweh has done for Israel, such responses are empty mockery and wearisome offense.

D. THE INDICTMENT (VERSE 8) The passage reaches a climax as the prophetic attorney proclaims that Yahweh has shown what is "good"—that is, the good relations of the covenant:

> What does Yahweh require of you
>   but to do justice, and to love kindness,[26]
> and to walk humbly with your God?
> —MICAH 6:8 (RSV)

Here we find, expressed in a single sentence, Amos' demand for justice, Hosea's appeal for the faithfulness that binds people in covenant with God and with one another, and Isaiah's plea for the quiet faith of the "humble walk" with God.

In this poetic unit, the verdict of the Judge is not given. It is appropriate, however, that the covenant lawsuit is followed, in the present arrangement of the material, by an oracle of divine judgment (Micah 6:9–16) with its characteristic "therefore" (vs. 13) which announces the consequences of human behavior. Micah pointedly likens the sins of Judah to the crimes committed by the dynasty of Omri, particularly the deeds of Ahab (vs. 16).

---

[26] The word translated "kindness" is *ḥésed*, the same word that we have met in our study of Hosea (see Definition, p. 308). It refers to a covenant relationship that is steadfast and that finds expression in acts of mercy. On the "covenant lawsuit," see further Delbert R. Hillers, *Covenant* [225], pp. 124ff.

ISAIAH'S LATER CAREER

As we have seen, Isaiah seems not to have been very active in public after the Syro-Israelite crisis. Indeed, it has been suggested that during most of the remainder of Ahaz's reign he withdrew into the circle of the prophetic community. However that may be, the death of Ahaz inaugurated a new period of his prophetic activity. It must have seemed to Isaiah, at least for a moment, that the time had come to break the "seal" from the prophetic testimony, in the expectation that Hezekiah would give a more favorable hearing than had his father.

The Age of Hezekiah

The accession of Hezekiah in 715 B.C.E. marked a turning point in Judean affairs. Ahaz had been a weak king, a servile and frightened vassal of Assyria. Hezekiah, however, was a wise and vigorous leader, whose policies brought about a religious reformation and a stiffening of Judah's attitude toward Assyria. In II Kings 18, the Deuteronomistic editor gives unqualified approval to his reign, comparing him to David and saying that "there was none like him among all the kings of Judah after him, nor among those who were before him." This tribute, of course, was based on the Deuteronomic premise that the true worship of Yahweh must be centralized in Jerusalem.

One of Hezekiah's accomplishments was his great religious reform, which led to the suppression of local shrines ("high places"), the centers of the Canaanized popular religion that had threatened Israel's faith from the very first. Not satisfied with destroying the sacred objects in these local sanctuaries—the altars, the sacred pillars, and the Asherah—Hezekiah carried the reform right into the Temple of Jerusalem. At his orders, the copper serpent, Nehushtan, which had been an object of veneration for centuries, was shattered (II Kings 18:4). According to the tradition, it had been made by Moses himself (Num. 21:4–9). Hezekiah's aim was to purify Judah's worship and to concentrate it in the Temple of Jerusalem. His sweeping reform prepared the way for the Deuteronomic Reform, to be considered in the next chapter. Surprisingly, Isaiah makes no reference to Hezekiah's reform, although it may have been one of the factors that led the prophet to break his long silence and to reappear in public.

As in the case of other religious revivals in Israel, so here we find that Hezekiah's religious reform had certain political implications. When he ascended the throne, Judah was growing restive under the Assyrian yoke. Ahaz's appeasement policy, symbolized by the installation of an Assyrian altar in the Temple, had proved unpopular, especially among those who had to dig down into their pockets to pay heavy taxes for Assyrian tribute. Hezekiah's purification of worship, including no doubt the removal of Assyrian cult objects from the Temple, was a stimulus to Judean nationalism, for he was virtually declaring independence from Assyrian domination and throwing his weight behind the

The Siloam Tunnel was carved through 1,777 feet of solid rock for the purpose of bringing water from a spring outside Jerusalem to a pool inside the city wall. On the wall of the tunnel an inscription was found that described how the workers started at both ends and met in the middle after following a winding route.

revolutionary spirit of the day. He got away with this nationalistic policy for the time being, because Sargon, the Assyrian king, was busy waging war in the mountains of northern Mesopotamia.

A symbol of Hezekiah's political energy was the construction of the Siloam tunnel later in his reign, when political tensions were high (II Kings 20:20; cf. II Chron. 32:30). Ahaz, it will be remembered, had been worried about Jerusalem's fresh water supply—one of the city's main defenses—during the Syro-Israelite crisis. So long as the city water had to be brought in through a conduit from the Spring of Gihon (or Virgin's Spring) outside the city wall, to the Pool of Siloam inside the wall, Jerusalem was vulnerable to the enemy. Hezekiah overcame this problem by a remarkable engineering feat. A tunnel more than 1,700 feet long was cut through solid rock from the spring to the pool. Workers equipped with wedges, hammers, and picks started boring at both ends simultaneously, and after some winding met in the middle. Up until recent times (as the author knows by personal experience), visitors have been able to walk through this tunnel, if they were willing to wade knee-deep in cold spring water, and they have been able to see the slanting pick marks where the workers met in the middle. The famous Siloam inscription, which has been cut from the wall and taken to the museum at Istanbul, tells the story of the boring, saying that "while there was yet three cubits to be bored through, there was heard the voice of one calling unto another."[27] Besides this work, Hezekiah extended the walls and strengthened the fortifications of Jerusalem (II Chron. 32:5).

Hezekiah was first tempted to join the rising rebellion against Assyria in the year 712 B.C.E. The revolution, instigated by Egyptian intrigue, broke out in the Philistine city of Ashdod (Isa. 14:28–32), which had been a hotbed of revolution for several years. Afraid of being overrun by Assyria, Egypt fanned the fires of revolution. At this time, Isaiah was commanded to perform a "sign" to dramatize Yahweh's judgment against the conspiracy (chapter 20). He was to go naked and barefoot through the streets of Jerusalem, clad only in the loincloth of a prisoner of war, to signify that Assyria would lead Egypt and Ethiopia away into exile.[28] As matters turned out, Isaiah's prophecy did not apply to Egypt, for Egypt left the Philistines in the lurch at the last moment. Sargon's armies pointed up the folly of revolution by destroying Ashdod and two other Philistine cities, and by converting the Philistine coast into an Assyrian province. Although Sargon accused Judah of having a hand in the revolt, evidently Hezekiah had avoided becoming deeply involved, possibly as a result of Isaiah's influence. In any case, Assyria did not invade Judah. The prophet Micah was still active at this time. Ashdod and Gath, two of the Philistine cities sacked by the Assyrians, were only a short distance from his hometown. The distant sound of marching armies during this invasion prompted him to say that Moreshethgath (near Gath) would fall to Assyria (Mic. 1:15).

Living in Revolutionary Times

The death of Sargon in 705 B.C.E. set off a chain reaction of revolution throughout the whole Assyrian empire. To a political observer of the time, it must have seemed that the empire, founded by the power of the sword and upheld by the ruthless suppression of nationalism, was about to explode into fragments. This time the revolution centered in the eastern part of the empire, in the province of Babylonia. The leader was the king of Babylonia, Marduk-apal-iddina, who is referred to in the Old Testament as Merodach-baladan (II Kings 20:12 = Isa. 39:1). Something of a political genius, he might have established a Babylonian empire had the political situation been more favorable, but this dream was not realized until a century later.

Merodach-baladan, believing that the best way to win his political objectives was to stir up trouble for Sennacherib, kindled the fires of revolt throughout the whole Assyrian empire. He consolidated the revolutionary forces in his own area, and then sent embassies into Palestine. The story of the embassy to

---

[27] See Pritchard, *Ancient Near Eastern Texts* [1], p. 321.
[28] Ethiopia is mentioned because the new Egyptian dynasty was Ethiopian.

Hezekiah, and Isaiah's vehement protest against it, is given in II Kings 20:12–19 (= Isa. 39:1–8). Egypt, too, was experiencing a national revival at the time, under the leadership of an energetic Ethiopian king named Shabako, the founder of the Twenty-fifth Dynasty. The oracle in Isaiah 18, which apparently comes from this period, speaks about the coming of Shabako's ambassadors to secure Hezekiah's participation in the general revolt. Egypt wanted to recover its ancient imperial glory, and through diplomatic intrigue it hoped to bring about Assyria's collapse.

When all Judah's neighbors, with few exceptions, were jumping on the revolutionary band wagon, Hezekiah simply could not resist the temptation to join in. This time he went all out for the revolution. He even threw his army against Philistia (II Kings 18:8) when several Philistine kings refused to join the conspiracy, and, as we know from Sennacherib's annals, took Padi, king of the Philistine city of Ekron, back to Jerusalem as a prisoner.

In this hour of fateful decision, Isaiah counseled the Judean king, as he

A Boundary Stone named after Merodach-baladan II, the king who aspired to build a Babylonian empire in Isaiah's time. The king is presenting an official (the smaller figure) with a land grant. At the top are four shrines with the emblems of Babylonian deities. The triangular symbol at the right—resting upon a shrine and a straight-horned dragon—is that of the god Marduk.

had counseled Ahaz before, to stay out of the revolution. As we have said, most of the prophetic oracles found in chapters 28–33 reflect this period, the last five years of the eighth century. Isaiah's advice was not based merely on the shrewd political calculation that Assyria would eventually win. As a political observer, he was perhaps no wiser than others at the time who came to a different conclusion about the best course of action. Isaiah's greatness as a prophet does not lie primarily in his political astuteness but in the religious perspective from which he viewed the international scene.

In Quietness and Confidence Is Strength

Uppermost in his mind was the conviction that Yahweh was in control and that Assyria was called to serve Yahweh's purpose. Isaiah elaborates this conviction in a magnificent oracle in the earlier section of the book of Isaiah, 10:5–19, where the Assyrian is hailed as "the rod of Yahweh's anger":

> Ah, Assyria, the rod of my anger,
>   the staff of my fury!
> Against a godless nation I send him,
>   and against the people of my wrath
>   I command him,
> to take spoil and seize plunder,
>   and to tread them down like the
>   mire of the streets.
> —ISAIAH 10:5–6 (RSV)

To be sure, the Assyrian dictator does not realize that he is an instrument in the hand of God, for he supposes that he is pursuing his own political objectives. Nevertheless, behind the inexorable Assyrian advance is the overruling sovereignty of God who, as one of the psalmists said, makes even the wrath of the enemy serve the divine purpose (Ps. 76:10, RSV). History is not governed by caprice or by the nation that possesses the largest battalions. The terrible havoc wrought by the Assyrian invaders, when seen in prophetic perspective, is the sign of God's judgment in human affairs, which even the people of Yahweh's choice cannot escape. However, when Yahweh's work on Mount Zion is finished, then the king of Assyria will be punished for his "arrogant boasting" and his "haughty pride" (Isa. 10:12). It is folly for the axe to boast over the person who uses it, or for the rod to vaunt over the one who wields it! In due time Yahweh "will trample the Assyrian underfoot" and the yoke of tyranny will be lifted from the people (see 14:24–27). Even the most powerful empire must learn that it is Yahweh who is King, and that the tumultuous stream of history cannot break beyond the banks of God's purpose. Hence people of faith should willingly submit, not to the Assyrian yoke, but to the yoke of Yahweh's kingdom. They should accept the judgment of God as a call to purge the flagrant wrongs from society, and should wait patiently for the time when Yahweh will humble the pride of the mighty.

It was out of this conviction that Isaiah advised Hezekiah to shun the revolution against Assyria. Human power cannot stay the Assyrian advance any more than it can prevent Yahweh's coming to judge and rebuke the people of Israel. Like Hosea, Isaiah condemned political alliances, calling them a "covenant with death" (Isa. 28:18). When the "overwhelming scourge" passes through the land, Judah will be inundated, for Yahweh will perform a "strange work," one that will utterly confound all human plans and hopes (28:14–22). In particular Isaiah condemned the favorable reception given the Egyptian envoys mentioned in Isaiah 18, just as he had denounced Hezekiah's secret negotiations with Merodach-baladan (II Kings 20:12–19). He denounced those who went down to Egypt for help, trusting in "chariots because they are many" and "horsemen because they are very strong" (Isa. 31:1–3), for

> the Egyptians are human beings, and not God;
> and their horses are flesh, and not spirit.
> —ISAIAH 31:3

Such political efforts, according to the prophet, were clear evidence that people did not trust "the Holy One of Israel." In Isaiah 30:1–15, he stresses the folly of taking refuge in "the shadow of Egypt." Echoing his earlier advice to Ahaz (7:9), Isaiah here gives the supreme summary of the meaning of faith:

> In returning and rest you shall be saved;
> in quietness and in trust shall be your strength.
> —ISAIAH 30:15 (RSV)

Judah's security lies not in politics—in being a nation like other nations—but rather in returning to, and in depending upon, Yahweh—confident that deliverance will come from God alone in God's good time. But to the prophetic call for faith the people answered a flat "No" (30:16). They wanted to ride on horses. They would ride, all right—in flight from swift horsemen. And if they could not hear the call to repentance in plain-spoken Hebrew, then they would have to listen to Yahweh speaking to them in the strange babble of a barbarian tongue (28:7–13). From the beginning to the end of his ministry, Isaiah was baffled by the people's inability to hear what Yahweh was saying in the events of the time. Yahweh had spoken of "rest to the weary"—the rest and repose of a steady and serene faith in a day of political anxiety and tumult; "yet they could not hear" (28:12).

More and more, however, Isaiah came to believe that a remnant of the faithful would hear and would be saved from the impending destruction. For Yahweh would lay in Jerusalem a foundation for "the faithful city" (see Isa. 1:26), a precious and well-tested cornerstone composed of a remnant whose strength is a quiet and patient trust in God:

See, I lay stone in Zion,
   a tested stone,
a precious cornerstone for a sure foundation;
   the one who trusts will never be dismayed.
I will make justice the measuring line
   and righteousness the plumbline.
                                   —ISAIAH 28:16–17a (NIV)

This appeal for steady faith in Yahweh, the cosmic King of the world and the Holy One of Israel, was the prophet's central theme.

Shut Up Like a Bird in a Cage

Sennacherib moved quickly to crush the rebellion that threatened his empire. First he decisively defeated Merodach-baladan of Babylonia and all his allies. Then, having restored order throughout Mesopotamia by the year 703 B.C.E., he launched a victorious campaign into the west. He marched triumphantly through Phoenicia and into the Philistine plain, where he destroyed a large Egyptian army at the Philistine city of Ekron. Micah 1:10–16 reflects the inexorable Assyrian advance, before which all the cities in his neighborhood—including the fortress of Lachish—fell one by one. Evidently one Assyrian army moved inland, through the hill country of Samaria and Judah, and approached Jerusalem from the north. The route of the Assyrian advance is reported in Isaiah 10:28–31, a passage that gives us a vivid impression of the lightning speed with which the cities were conquered. According to Sennacherib's annals, forty-six of Hezekiah's fortified cities were taken, as well as numerous small cities in the neighborhood, and 200,150 people were taken captive (cf. II Kings 18:13). (See map, p. 320.) The report in II Kings 18:13–16 agrees essentially with the Assyrian account.[29]

During the invasion of 701 B.C.E., Jerusalem was cut off from all outside help.[30] Sennacherib says that Hezekiah "like a caged bird, I shut up in Jerusalem, his royal city." In even stronger terms, Isaiah compared the catastrophe to the destruction of Sodom and Gomorrah. Isaiah 1:4–9 apparently springs from this crisis. Why, he asks, does Judah continue to revolt? The country is stricken, like a sick person, from head to toe; aliens are devouring the land; and Zion is left isolated and alone, "like a booth in a vineyard, like a lodge in a cucumber field."

---

[29] See Pritchard, *Ancient Near Eastern Texts* [1], pp. 287–88.

[30] Certain difficulties in the biblical text have led scholars to advance the hypothesis that Sennacherib actually invaded Judah twice, once in 701 and again after 691 when another rebellion flared up in the west, and that it was on the latter occasion that Jerusalem was miraculously spared. John Bright, *History* [91], pp. 285–288, 298–309, favors this view, although he admits that Assyrian inscriptions do not mention the supposed second campaign. See the criticism of this view by Brevard S. Childs, *Isaiah and the Assyrian Crisis* [347], especially pp. 118–20.

Sennacherib's Clay Prism announces his victory over Palestinian forces and their Egyptian allies. The hexagonal artifact tells how he overran Judah and shut up Hezekiah "like a caged bird" in his royal city, Jerusalem.

Strangely, Jerusalem did not suffer the complete destruction of Sodom and Gomorrah, for Yahweh mercifully spared the city and left "a few survivors" (Isa. 1:9). The story of this unexpected, marvelous turn of events is related in II Kings 18 and 19 (= Isa. 36–37). During the siege of Lachish, Sennacherib sent a delegation, led by the Rabshakeh (a title meaning "chief deputy"), to Jerusalem to demand unconditional surrender. The story is told so vividly that we can almost imagine ourselves on the walls with the city's defenders, witnessing the episode. We see the Rabshakeh standing off at some distance, with a detachment of the powerful Assyrian army behind him. Through the tensely silent air comes the shrewd propaganda speech of the Rabshakeh, threatening to have a deadlier effect on the stout morale of the city's defenders than the Assyrian swords themselves. In alarm, the Judean officials ask him to speak in Aramaic, the language of international diplomacy (see Definition, p. 508), lest his unanswerable challenge be heard by the civilian population. But this confession of weakness only incites the Rabshakeh to press his arguments with greater force. In effect, he says that the people are fighting for a lost cause. They have everything to gain and little to lose by discarding Hezekiah and surrendering unconditionally to the powerful army of Sennacherib.

Isaiah's Message During the Invasion

Now comes a surprise: Isaiah counsels against capitulating to Assyria. In view of his earlier message that the Assyrian was the rod of Yahweh's anger, this may seem like an about face. But we must remember that Isaiah was not a politician who based his message on the relative strength of Assyria and the powers ranged against it. To us it seems reasonable that Judah, situated off the beaten path of world conquerors, could have escaped trouble by following a policy of noninterference. This may have been in the background of Isaiah's mind in earlier situations, but if so he gives no hint of it. His perspective was *religious*, not political. He believed firmly that Assyria was an instrument in Yahweh's hand. And although for a time Yahweh wielded that instrument to judge the citizens of Judah, Isaiah believed that it would be cast aside when Yahweh's "strange work" in Jerusalem was finished (cf. Isa. 28:21). Because Assyria's power was given to it by God, that power could be checked or taken away when God chose to do so.

Isaiah and Micah proclaimed different messages during the crisis of Sennacherib's invasion. With unyielding conviction, Micah insisted that Zion would be "plowed like a field" (Mic. 3:12). Isaiah, on the other hand, declared that Zion could not fall. This claim, however, must be viewed within the total context of Isaiah's prophetic ministry. As we have seen, he believed that Yahweh's saving purpose in history was tied up especially with the city of Jerusalem. For Jerusalem was the place of the Temple, in which the Ark rested. Jerusalem was the city that Yahweh had founded (Isa. 14:32); Mount Zion was "the place of the name of Yahweh of hosts" (18:7). It was in Jerusalem's Temple that Isaiah had seen the vision of Yahweh, the King. Moreover, Jerusalem was the City of David. And the Davidic dynasty, which had survived through three troubled centuries of history, was the sign of a social stability that Yahweh had given.

All these convictions, however, had their roots in a royal theology which developed in Jerusalem under the influence of Nathan's prophecy to David. This oracle (II Sam. 7), it will be recalled, announced Yahweh's *unconditional* promise to maintain the Davidic throne, regardless of the merit or demerit of Israel's kings. In Northern Israel, where the contingency of the Mosaic covenant was stressed, prophets like Amos or Hosea could announce that Israel's disobedience was sufficient ground for Yahweh to bring Israel's history to an end. Isaiah took his cue, however, from Yahweh's promises of grace to David and, through the Davidic king, to the whole people. This did not mean soft-pedaling the call to repentance and reform. As we have seen, Isaiah was the equal of Amos in his radical criticism of society and his urgent demand for reform. Yet he believed that, in the last analysis, the hope for the future rested not on the behavior of the people or the greatness of their king, but solely on Yahweh's covenant commitment to David and Yahweh's loyalty to that commitment through thick and thin.

The Siege of Lachish, depicted on a large frieze found in Sennacherib's palace at Nineveh. From towers along the city's double walls, the defenders shoot arrows and hurl stones and lighted firebrands at the attackers. The Assyrians have thrown up a log incline for their battering ram, whose long ramrod is pointed at a part of the gate tower. Spearmen (left) carrying wicker shields advance behind the siege engine and, on a higher level, bowmen, protected by a large wicker shield, send volleys of arrows into the city.

A Reconstruction of the battle for Lachish. The fighting centers around the gate tower, which has three windows near its fortified top. Soldiers defend the battlement, while inhabitants of the city escape with their possessions through a doorway in the side of the tower. In the lower center three naked victims have been impaled on pointed wooden stakes.

It is not surprising, then, for Isaiah to insist that Yahweh's purpose was not to eradicate Jerusalem, but to build a new Jerusalem on the foundation of a righteous and faithful remnant. Yahweh's purpose called for a holy people and a holy city. The doctrine of the remnant also had a positive meaning: a remnant shall return (repent) and "lean upon Yahweh" (Isa. 10:20–21). Yahweh would spare Zion "for my own sake and for the sake of my servant David" (37:33–35), according to the tenets of the royal covenant theology.[31]

So, when we consider Isaiah's message as a whole, his stand during the invasion of Sennacherib turns out to be religiously consistent. We must be on guard against forcing the prophet's pronouncements into our own patterns of logic, or even assuming that all prophets said exactly the same thing about Jerusalem. *The prophets always addressed themselves to the situation at hand.* And Isaiah, in 701 B.C.E., was called to speak to *that* situation, not to the earlier situation of the Syro-Israelite war or the later situation of Jeremiah's day. Experience had led him to realize, perhaps more deeply than in his earlier career, that behind and within Yahweh's judgment was the divine will to deliver and renew. Hence the oracles from the stormy final years of Isaiah's ministry stressed Yahweh's saving power. On the completion of the *opus alienum*, God's "strange work" of purifying judgment on Mount Zion (Isa. 28:21), the arrogant Assyrian empire will be punished. The Assyrians will fall "by a sword not of human making," for Yahweh "will come down to fight upon Mount Zion" and, like hovering birds, "will protect Jerusalem" (31:4–9). Since it is Yahweh who is encamped against Jerusalem, the proud nations that fight against Mount Zion will be like a hungry man who dreams that he is eating, only to awake and find that his hunger is not satisfied (28:1–8). Yahweh comes from afar to sift the nations with the sieve of destruction, and the Assyrians will be terror-stricken at Yahweh's mighty arm and furious voice (30:27–33). This appearance will be the final reminder that Yahweh, and not Assyria or any other human power, is the Ruler of history.

The Deliverance of Jerusalem

According to the narrative in II Kings 19 (paralleled in Isa. 37), when the challenge of the Rabshakeh was reported to Hezekiah, the king was filled with despair. "This day is a day of distress, of rebuke, and disgrace; children have come to the birth, and there is no strength to bring them forth" (vs. 3). Isaiah, following an urgent word from the king, delivered an oracle against the arrogance of the Assyrian king (II Kings 19:20–28). To this prophetic word is linked another "sign," that a remnant will be saved and that after three years conditions in the land will return to normal (verses 29–31).

---

[31] The latter passage comes from the section (Isa. 36–39) excerpted from II Kings 18–19, which may give a slightly different view of Isaiah's stand in the crisis. See Brevard S. Childs, *Isaiah and the Assyrian Crisis* [347], pp. 69–103.

The oracle against Assyria is in keeping with the prophetic message of Isaiah in 10:5–16, but the rest of the story (verses 32–37) teems with difficulties. It is quite true that the Assyrian armies departed without laying siege to Jerusalem, precisely as Isaiah predicted in verses 32–34. However, this "answer to prayer" was explained on the basis of a legend: Sennacherib's army was decimated by the Angel of Yahweh during the night, prompting Sennacherib to return to his capital, where he was assassinated by one of his sons (II Kings 19:35–37). Possibly this refers to a disease or pestilence that spread through the Assyrian army, although Sennacherib's annals do not mention this. More likely, Sennacherib heard "a rumor," as Isaiah is said to have predicted elsewhere, which prompted him to hasten back to his home base (II Kings 19:7). The rumor proved to be word of a new uprising in Babylonia. So Sennacherib hastily withdrew to deal with a trouble spot that was potentially more dangerous than the little kingdom of Judah. Anyway, he had accomplished his objectives in Palestine: Egypt had been dealt a staggering blow; the anti-Assyrian coalition, inspired by Egypt, had been broken up. Hezekiah, secure in his mountain fortress, had seen his land diminished and had yielded to Assyrian demands by paying a handsome tribute to the Assyrian king during his stay at Lachish. The payment of the tribute is described in detail in II Kings 18:14–16 and is corroborated by Sennacherib's own account of his western campaign. So why should Sennacherib waste time and manpower on a costly siege of Jerusalem, especially when there were other, more pressing matters to attend to?

Whatever the explanation of Sennacherib's sudden withdrawal, the event made a deep impression upon Judean memory. The fact that Yahweh had spared Jerusalem in that crisis came to mean in popular thought that Yahweh would spare Jerusalem under any circumstances. Zion would stand forever! It is inconceivable that Isaiah would have agreed, for his message, like that of earlier prophets, included a condition:

> If you are willing and obedient,
>   you shall eat the good of the land;
> But if you refuse and rebel,
>   you shall be devoured by the sword.
>   —ISAIAH 1:19–20 (RSV)

It may be that Isaiah 22:1–14 comes from the time when the Assyrian armies withdrew from Jerusalem. If so, it gives us a picture of the wild abandon of those who went up to the housetop "full of shoutings." In the midst of the victory celebration, Isaiah stands alone, weeping for "the destruction of the daughter of my people."

After the tumultuous events of the end of the eighth century, Isaiah drops out of view. Whether he was active during the closing years of Hezekiah's reign (Hezekiah died in 687/6 B.C.E.) we do not know. Tradition has it that he was martyred during the reactionary reign of Hezekiah's successor, Manasseh. It

Sennacherib's Camp at Lachish (II Kings 18:14). Against a background of palm trees and grapevines, the king is seated on his throne and fanned by servants. Immediately behind his officers, who present the booty of Lachish, hapless citizens of the town prostrate themselves (left). To the right of the throne is the royal tent, pitched on a wooded hill.

may be that Isaiah turned his attention to his disciples, giving fresh impetus to the extensive tradition that is associated with his name and, within that prophetic community, waited patiently for God's purpose to be realized. In any event, long after the Assyrian empire had become a mere memory, Isaiah's conception of Yahweh's remnant—the "church" within the nation—exerted its influence upon Israel and eventually upon the community gathered around Jesus of Nazareth.

CHAPTER 11

The Rediscovery
of Mosaic Torah

In times of insecurity, when the foundations of life are severely shaken, people often turn to the past to regain perspective and wistfully long for "the good old days gone by." In our time, for instance, the world crisis has sometimes stimulated nations to study their past with new interest, and it has prompted people to search for their "roots" by inquiring into their genealogies or the tradition in which they stand. The same situation arose in the kingdom of Judah during the seventh century B.C.E. At that time there was a "nostalgic revival of interest in the past."[1] This interest, which is clearly seen in the literature of the period, reflected a general tendency that was evident in the whole ancient Near East. The spirit of the times was well summed up by Jeremiah:

> Stand by the roads and consider,
> Inquire about ancient paths:
> Which is the road to happiness?
> Travel it, and find tranquility for yourselves.
> —JEREMIAH 6:16 (TNK)

Biblical readings: The historical background is presented in the important chapters, II Kings 21–23 (paralleled in II Chron. 33–35). A great deal of literature comes from this period. We shall deal with the "Mosaic" sermon found in Deuteronomy 4:44 through chapter 26; read at least through chapter 11. Then read the following prophetic literature: Zephaniah 1–3, Jeremiah 1:1–4:4 (his early prophecies), Nahum, and Habakkuk 1–2.

[1] W. F. Albright, *From the Stone Age* [111], pp. 240–44.

DIFFERING VIEWS OF THE COVENANT

We have already detected some of this nostalgia for the past in the prophet Isaiah, for whom the Golden Age was the glorious reign of David. Isaiah felt that the establishment of Jerusalem was "the beginning," the decisive time of the past, and that Yahweh's purpose in history was to restore Zion "as at the beginning" (Isa. 1:26). Isaiah's concern for Davidic tradition was a unique development in prophecy, for he apparently paid little attention to the great formative period of the Exodus and the Sinai covenant. In this respect, as we have seen, he differed from the prophets of the Northern Kingdom. Hosea, for instance, had traced Israel's beginning to the time of the Exodus and had affirmed that the goal of Israel's history would be a renewal of the covenant made in the wilderness. And Elijah's flight to Mount Horeb, the sacred mountain of the Mosaic covenant, was a symbol of the prophetic spirit in the Northern Kingdom.

In the kingdom of Judah, as we have observed at various points along the way, there developed a conception of the covenant that was fundamentally different from the northern Mosaic tradition.[2] David, the architect of the United Kingdom, had tried to unify the twelve tribes under his rule by taking over the religious traditions and symbols of the old Tribal Confederacy. But in the circle of the Davidic court a new theology developed, one that took its place alongside of the covenant faith that had been inherited from the Mosaic period. According to this view, Yahweh made an absolute commitment to David, sealed by a solemn oath, and promised to preserve the Davidic line and spare the Davidic kingdom "for the sake of my servant David," as Isaiah is reported to have said (Isa. 37:35). The promises of grace to David (II Sam. 7), as we have seen earlier (see above, pp. 230–234), did not exempt corrupt administrations from punishment, but at least there was a guarantee of dynastic continuity. By contrast, the Mosaic covenant held out the possibility that the relationship between God and people could be dissolved (Hosea 1:9) and that the "end" could come upon the people Israel (Amos 8:2).[3]

In past chapters, as we have surveyed the history of Israel and Judah, we have seen that the differences between the twin kingdoms were both political and theological. The theology of kingship, which centered in Yahweh's covenant with David, provided the theological foundation for the stability of Judah, with its unbroken succession of Davidic kings on the throne of Jerusalem. In the north, however, where no single dynasty was able to maintain itself throughout the history of the kingdom of Israel, the traditions of the ancient Tribal Confederacy were kept alive. There the remembrance of the old days of

---

[2] See the important study by George E. Mendenhall, *Law and Covenant* [229], pp. 44–50; also his article, "Covenant," *Interpreter's Dictionary* [25].

[3] The theological differences between these two covenant traditions are set forth clearly by J. Coert Rylaarsdam, "The Two Covenants" [304]. The interaction of the two covenant traditions is considered by B. W. Anderson, "Exodus and Covenant in Second Isaiah and Prophetic Tradition," *Magnalia Dei* [157], 339–360.

tribal independence contributed to the revolutionary ferment which brought about the downfall of kings; and there the accent fell upon the covenant made at Sinai, one that was based on the great saving acts of Yahweh which placed a grateful people under obligation to serve their covenant Suzerain. Recall at this point our consideration of the "suzerainty" covenant or treaty (pp. 98–101) with its emphasis upon the responsibility of the people and the possible termination of the relationship in the event of infidelity.

The most significant development within Judah during the seventh century B.C.E. was "the rediscovery of Moses," and the greatest literary monument to this revival of interest is the book of Deuteronomy. "Ask now of the days that are past," is a characteristic appeal of Deuteronomy (4:32). But, as the context of this passage (verses 32–40)—one of the finest in Deuteronomistic literature—indicates, the decisive period of the past was not the Golden Age of David's rule, but the time of the Exodus when Yahweh redeemed Israel "by trials, by signs, by wonders, and by war, by a mighty hand and an outstretched arm, and by great terrors, according to all that Yahweh your God did for you in Egypt before your eyes." The event of the Exodus, which fired the imagination and excited the wonder of the Deuteronomists, provided the source of Israel's knowledge of God, the foundation of the covenant community, and the motivation for fulfilling the obligations of the covenant.

MANASSEH, THE VILLAIN OF JUDAH

Let us look briefly at the historical background of the rediscovery of the Mosaic Torah or Teaching.

In recounting the events of Judah after the death of King Hezekiah, the Deuteronomistic historian portrays Manasseh as the arch-villain of the whole gallery of Davidic kings. What Jeroboam I was to the kingdom of Israel, Manasseh was to the kingdom of Judah. It was he who reversed the religious reforms made under Hezekiah and "seduced" the people into doing more evil than the surrounding nations (II Kings 21:2–15). His long reign (c. 687/6–642) was painted as the darkest period of Judean history. Later historians, writing after the final fall of Jerusalem in the early sixth century B.C.E., held him responsible for provoking Yahweh into bringing judgment upon the nation (II Kings 23:26–27; 24:3–4; cf. Jer. 15:4).

The reign of Manasseh, however, was an important traditional link between the great eighth-century prophets and the revival of prophecy at the end of the seventh century. So it should be viewed in a larger and perhaps a more sympathetic perspective than that of the critical report given in II Kings 21. This report makes no allusion to the great political fact that overshadowed the life and thought of Judah during Manasseh's entire reign: Assyria's victorious advance toward Egypt and its almost undisputed sway over the whole Fertile Cres-

DEFINITION: "DEUTERONOMISTIC HISTORY"

Previously we have noticed the distinction between two adjectives: "Deuteronomic," referring to the Deuteronomic Torah (Deut. 5–28), and "Deuteronomistic," referring to the Deuteronomistic History extending from Joshua through II Kings (see Definition, p. 183). This history work also includes the framework to the present book of Deuteronomy (chaps. 1–4 and 27–30). Indeed, Deuteronomy chapters 1–4 serve as an introduction to both the book of Deuteronomy itself and to the whole Deuteronomistic History.

The last event reported in the Deuteronomistic History proper (Joshua through II Kings) is the release of the Davidic king Jehoiachin from Babylonian imprisonment in 561 B.C.E. (II Kings 25:27–30). There is no mention of the rise of Cyrus of Persia or his conquest of Babylon (c. 539). This indicates that the history, in its final form, was finished after Jehoiachin's release, perhaps around 550. Some scholars maintain, however, that the Deuteronomistic History appeared in two versions, one composed during the late monarchy to express the hopes for national revival centering in King Josiah, and the other written (or "overwritten") to make the history "relevant to exiles for whom the bright expectations of the Josianic era were hopelessly past."[4] Notice the references to "the First Deuteronomist" and "the Second Deuteronomist" in the Oxford Annotated Bible (RSV). If this hypothesis is correct, we have another instance of the updating or contemporizing of tradition which was characteristic of the Israelite community.

In the section of the Deuteronomistic History found in I–II Kings, two theological themes are interwoven. The dominant one, set forth in the theological introduction to the whole history (Deut. 1–4), is the call to be faithful to Yahweh's covenant with Israel, under the sanctions of blessing and curse. The consequences of failure in this responsibility are spelled out, for instance, in the discourse on the fall of Samaria, II Kings 17:1–23. A secondary theme is Yahweh's promises of grace to David (II Sam. 7) which guarantee a future in spite of human failure, "for the sake of David my servant and for the sake of Jerusalem which I have chosen" (I Kings 11:13; cf. 15:4; II Kings 8:19; 20:6 etc.). With impressive counterpoint, the historian has interwoven these two themes, one centering in Moses and the other in David, in the attempt to understand Israel's history of failure in the promised land and to espouse hope in a king of the Davidic line.

cent. It was during the reign of Manasseh that Assyria reached the very pinnacle of its imperial power and glory. To be sure, even in the early part of the seventh century, there were signs that the empire was built on shaky foundations. The murder of Sennacherib in 681 B.C.E. touched off a new revolution in Mesopotamia, and for a while it seemed as if the staggering empire, held together by the power of the sword and a system of vassal provinces, would fall. But the next Assyrian monarch, Esarhaddon (c. 680–669) proved equal to the situation. After putting down all revolts, he marched into Egypt in the year 671, captured the city of Memphis, and took captive Tirhakah, the king of Egypt and Ethiopia. Esarhaddon's triumph is vividly portrayed on a stele in which he is represented

---

[4] See Frank M. Cross, "The Themes of the Book of Kings and the Structure of the Deuteronomistic History" [112], pp. 278–289.

The Stele of Esarhaddon was erected in northern Syria to commemorate that ruler's conquest of Egypt. With his right hand the king offers a libation to deities pictured (at top, riding on animals) next to their respective symbols—the crescent, winged sun disc, star, and lance. In his left hand he grips a mace and holds ropes on which two prisoners are leashed. The one kneeling is doubtless Pharaoh Tirhakah, whose decisive defeat is described on the inscription written across the lower half of this stele, found at Zinjirli in North Syria.

standing before Assyrian religious symbols, while he holds two kneeling captives by ropes, one of whom is identified as Tirhakah.

The next Assyrian king, Ashurbanapal (c. 668–627 B.C.E.) was able to hold his father's empire together during the first part of his reign. The city of Thebes in Upper Egypt was destroyed and for a short while Egypt was held within the Assyrian orbit of power. Thus Assyria had succeeded at last in building the greatest empire of that time. But as time passed it became clear that the sprawling empire was slipping out of control. In 652, revolt broke out again in Babylonia, this time under the leadership of a brother of the Assyrian emperor who had been appointed ruler of that vassal kingdom. With great effort, Ashurbanapal restored order, but not before the flames of revolution had spread through-

Shamash, the Sun God, *enthroned in his shrine (right) above the heavenly ocean represented by the wavy lines and four inset stars at the base of the picture. Above his head are the emblems of astral deities: the crescent (Sin), sun-disc (Shamash), and eight-pointed star (Ishtar). The Babylonian king Nabuapaliddin (middle figure in the trio, left), who endowed the sun temple at Sippar in the ninth century B.C.E., is escorted before an altar on which is a large sun-disc. The altar is supported by ropes held by attendant deities on the roof. Astral motifs were characteristic of ancient Assyrian and Babylonian religion.*

out the Fertile Crescent. Other events conspired against Assyria. About 664, Egypt rose up under Psammetichus I (c. 664–610), founder of the Twenty-sixth Dynasty, and threw out the detested Assyrian army of occupation, thus inaugurating a brief Egyptian revival. To add to Assyria's troubles, hordes of invaders known as Scythians and Cimmerians were pouring into Mesopotamia from beyond the Caucasus mountains, and the Medes were beginning to consolidate their position in the highlands of Iran. Plainly, Assyria's days of imperial rule were numbered. The time was not far off when the Judean prophet Nahum would vent his people's spleen against Assyrian oppression, announcing that the Assyrian capital of Nineveh would be overtaken by the same destruction that Assyria had visited upon Thebes (Nahum 3:8).

But all through the reign of Manasseh the powerful Assyrian empire was still intact. Like Ahaz before him, Manasseh believed that the best political policy was for Judah to play ball with Assyria as a faithful underling. There is some evidence that Manasseh was once taken captive to Babylon, presumably because of his part in an insurrection (II Chron. 33:10–13).[5] If he tried to revolt, however, he failed completely. In any event, most scholars doubt the historicity of this account, for which there is no parallel in II Kings or in the Assyrian annals. Chances are that Manasseh bought peace and at the same time made his own throne secure by playing the part of an obsequious vassal. This expedient policy paid off, for while the Assyrian armies were marching up and down Palestine on their way to Egypt, the vassal state of Judah seems to have been left unmolested. (See maps on pp. 303 and 320.)

Judah's Dark Age

II Kings 21 points up Manasseh's domestic policy, which reflected the religious and social consequences of his capitulation to Assyria. Every one of his acts infuriated the minority who still remembered the great wave of religious enthusiasm created by Hezekiah's reforms. It is reported that "he rebuilt the high places which Hezekiah his father had destroyed"—that is, he reopened the local pagan shrines in communities outside Jerusalem. He brazenly sponsored a program to amalgamate the worship of Yahweh with Baal nature religion. Yahweh was worshiped at "altars of Baal"; an emblem of the mother-goddess, an Asherah, was made; and sacred prostitution was practiced (II Kings 23:7). Thus the paganization of Israel's worship, which had been a threat ever since the time of judges, was given free rein under royal sanction and patronage.

Moreover, the doors were thrown open to other pagan influences. The astral cult of Mesopotamia, referred to as "the worship of all the host of heaven" (the sun, moon, and stars were identified as deities) was introduced—clear evidence of the cultural influence that accompanied Assyrian political supremacy. To make matters worse, these pagan practices were admitted into the Temple of Jerusalem, the central sanctuary that Hezekiah had tried to purify of all alien defilement. Then, as if attempting to dredge up the foulest practices of the past, Manasseh revived the old cult of the dead (necromancy), which even Saul in his saner moments had suppressed and which Isaiah had vehemently condemned (Isa. 8:19). In this respect, too, Manasseh was showing his capitulation to Assyria, which gave official sanction to astrology, magic, and divination. And as a final concession to paganism, he resorted to the barbarous practice of human sacrifice. Following the precedent of Ahaz (II Kings 16:3), he "burned his son as an offering," evidently in an attempt to court divine favor in an emergency (see Jer. 7:31).

The historian of II Kings compares Manasseh's reign with the time of Ahab and Jezebel, when paganism was sponsored and propagated by the crown. As

---

[5] The account in II Chronicles also states that while in exile the sinful king "humbled himself greatly before the God of his ancestors" and repented. The reference to his prayer (II Chron. 33:19) prompted the composition, sometime during the last two centuries B.C.E., of "The Prayer of Manasseh." This is included in the Protestant Apocrypha; it is not contained in the Roman Catholic canon.

Chronological Chart 7

B.C.E.	EGYPT	PALESTINE	MESOPOTAMIA
		JUDAH	ASSYRIA
700	XXV Dynasty, c. 716/15–663 (Ethiopian)	Manasseh, 687/6–642	Sennacherib, 704–681 Esarhaddon, 680–669 Invasion of Egypt, 671
	Tirhakah, c. 685–664 Invasion by Assyria, 671 Sack of Thebes, 663, by Ashurbanapal	Amon, 642–640 Josiah, 640–609 First show of Judean independence, 629 (*Zephaniah*, c. 628–622) (*Jeremiah*, c. 626–587) Josiah's "Deuteronomic Reform," 621	Ashurbanapal, 668–627 RISE OF BABYLONIA Nabopolassar, 626–605
	XXVI Dynasty, c. 664–525 Psammetichus I c. 664–610 Necho II, 610–593	Death of Josiah at Megiddo, 609 Jehoahaz II (Shallum), 609 (3 mos.) Jehoiakim (Eliakim), 609–598/7 (*Habakkuk*, c. 605)	Fall of Ashur to Medes, 614 Fall of Nineveh to Medes and Babylonians, 612 Babylonian defeat of Assyrians and Egyptians at Haran, 609 Nebuchadrezzar, 605/4–562 Battle of Carchemish, 605
600			FALL OF ASSYRIA

in Ahab's time, the pagan practices were probably welcomed by many of the people, who saw no difficulty in worshiping Yahweh and at the same time appropriating practices that were fashionable throughout the Assyrian empire. But there was one great difference between the time of Ahab and that of Manasseh: in Manasseh's day there was no Elijah to rebuke the people boldly for deviating from the Mosaic tradition, and to summon them to a renewed loyalty to the jealous God of the covenant. In part, the weakness of the prophets, who are mentioned anonymously in II Kings 21:10–15, may have been due to Manasseh's police-state measures, for we are told that he "shed very much innocent blood, till he had filled Jerusalem from one end to another." Some have suggested that he tried to liquidate the prophets; and, as we have seen, according to tradition Isaiah was martyred at this time.[6] But this charge against Manasseh is only an inference, for which there is no real basis in the biblical record. It is hard to believe that if a prophet like Elijah had appeared, or if an organized purge of the prophets had been carried out, all record of such events would have disappeared. Quite possibly the historian has exaggerated his account of

[6] See the late apocryphal work, *The Martyrdom of Isaiah*, from about the first century C.E.

Manasseh's reign somewhat in order to make him show up as badly as possible in comparison with the reforming kings, Hezekiah and Josiah. Nevertheless, after due allowance is made for the bias of the Deuteronomistic historian, it is clear that his verdict is substantially correct. Manasseh's desertion of Yahweh plunged Judah into the "dark age" of its history, for he bought peace at the terrible cost of surrendering Israel's distinctive religious heritage.

Anonymous Devotees of Yahweh

However, the faithful devotees of Yahweh were far from inactive under Manasseh's rule. Not too many years after Manasseh's death, Jeremiah commended the Rechabites (see pp. 282–283) for their fidelity to their religious vows in protest against the sellout of the ancient Mosaic faith (Jer. 35). This group, and others like them, must have annoyed Manasseh's party no end. Moreover, Manasseh's submission to Assyria must have galled all patriotic Judeans who were eager to throw off the Assyrian yoke. The smouldering fires of nationalism were kept alive, we may be sure, by prophets and priests who preserved and handed on the religious traditions of the past, especially by an order of teaching and preaching priests, known as Levites, who were active in the towns and the country area.[7] The oracles of the northern prophet Hosea, preserved in Judah after the fall of Samaria, were updated to apply to the southern kingdom as is evident from editorial touches here and there (e.g. Hos. 1:7; 4:15a). The Ephraimitic or Elohist version of the Old Epic tradition (see pp. 289–290) was inherited and, at least in part, preserved in Judah. Thus throughout the "dark age" of Manasseh, the all-Israelite Epic (JE) that included the traditions of the Northern and Southern Kingdoms continued to thrive and expand (see Chapter 5).

If we knew more about the period of Manasseh, we might find that many of the anonymous prophecies that are now mingled among the writings of the great prophets were composed at this time. For instance, portions of the book of Isaiah, which apparently come from a time before Second Isaiah, were probably produced then, and may well have come from the circle of disciples among whom Isaiah had deposited his original teaching. This was a reactionary period—a time when the prophets went into retreat—so it would have been appropriate for them to cherish and reflect upon the tradition, waiting and hoping for the time when Yahweh's "face" would no longer be hidden from Israel (Isa. 8:16–17). If so, Manasseh's time was an age of anonymous prophecy when persons of faith trusted in Yahweh's promise to overthrow the proud oppressors and to renew and restore the people.

---

[7] The role of the Levitical priests in the country outside Jerusalem has been stressed by Gerhard von Rad, *Studies in Deuteronomy* [cited under 367].

NEW OUTBURSTS OF PROPHECY

So the reign of Manasseh, horrible as it appeared to the Deuteronomistic historians, was not a time of complete decadence. Deep within the life of Judah a prophetic ferment was stirring, and people were turning to the past to rediscover the meaning of the Mosaic heritage. In anonymous circles, the way was being prepared for the national and religious renaissance that took place in Judah in the last quarter of the seventh century B.C.E. This Judean revival was made possible by changes in the international situation after the death of Assyria's last great king, Ashurbanapal, about the year 627.

Even before Ashurbanapal's death, trouble had been brewing for Assyria, as was evident in the abortive revolt in Babylonia and the revival of Egyptian nationalism. With lightning speed, rumors of Assyria's weakness spread throughout the Fertile Crescent and excited great restlessness among satellite nations. When Manasseh died (c. 642 B.C.E.), his son, Amon, continued his father's pro-Assyrian policy, but after a brief reign of two years he was murdered during a patriotic revolt. He was succeeded by the boy-king, Josiah (c. 640–600), who came to the throne when he was eight years old, about seven years before the death of Ashurbanapal. So by the time Ashurbanapal died, Josiah was ready to take over the reins of government. And the time was ripe for a radical change in Judah's policy.

The Prophet Zephaniah

Not long after the death of Ashurbanapal, the long prophetic silence that had lasted for three-quarters of a century was broken by two prophets who raised their voices publicly against the apostasy and degeneracy of Judah. The first was Zephaniah, possibly a descendant of the reforming king Hezekiah, according to the heading of the book that bears his name (Zeph. 1:1). It is impossible to date Zephaniah's career exactly, although his attack upon corruptions in worship suggests a time before Josiah's great reform in 621 B.C.E., to be discussed presently. He must have been a citizen of Jerusalem, for he mentions the districts of the city by name (Zeph. 1:10–11); indeed, he seems to have been part of the Jerusalem "establishment."[8]

Zephaniah's devastating message pierced the complacent atmosphere of Jerusalem like a trumpet blast. The central theme of his prophecy, the nearness of the Day of Yahweh, echoed a note struck earlier by Amos and Isaiah. Yahweh's Day would be "a day of wrath . . . a day of distress and anguish, a day of ruin and devastation, a day of darkness and gloom, a day of clouds and thick

---

[8] See Robert R. Wilson, *Prophecy and Society* [328], pp. 279–282, who maintains that Zephaniah stood within Jerusalem (Zion) traditions but was influenced by Josiah's "Deuteronomic" Reform.

Ashurbanapal's Horsemen battle camel-riding Arabs in this vivid action scene. Besides fighting wars on several fronts, Ashurbanapal was also a patron of culture, as shown by the excavations of his palace and royal library at Nineveh, where this artistic relief was found.

Ashurbanapal Drinks a Toast *to a victory in war. The last great king of Assyria, reclining upon a high couch while banqueting in his royal garden, is joined in the quaffing by his queen, seated facing him on a throne. Attendants fan the couple and provide music and delicacies. From the tree just in front of the harpist (left) hangs a man's head, perhaps that of the Elamite king just conquered. This mixture of culture and brutality was characteristic of Ashurbanapal's reign.*

darkness, a day of trumpet blast and battle cry" (Zeph. 1:15–16). Isaiah had said that the Day of Yahweh would be ushered in by an Assyrian invasion; but by the time of Zephaniah the whole political situation had changed. The proud capital of Nineveh was about to be turned into a wilderness (2:13–15); Assyria would soon taste the bitter suffering it had inflicted on others. At first it may seem strange that these two prophets should change the *political* focus of their messages. But remember that the prophets were not political forecasters, concerned only with tracing political developments. They viewed the historical scene from the perspective of faith in God, whose purpose is made known in, but is not identical with, political crises at definite moments of history. Since they were concerned with what Yahweh was saying and doing in the concrete situation at hand, they did not think it was inconsistent for the agent of divine judgment to vary from time to time. Notice that Zephaniah is rather vague about political details. Although he vividly describes the invasion that sweeps down out of the north, reducing the Assyrian capital of Nineveh to a dry waste (2:13–15) and approaching the Fish Gate of Jerusalem (1:10), he does not clearly identify the aggressor, the new "rod" of Yahweh's judgment. Some scholars have felt that he may have had in mind Scythian hordes who, along with other peoples, contributed to the ferment of the time.[9] In any case, behind and within the whole political upheaval that hastened the downfall of the Assyrian empire, Zephaniah saw the judgment of Yahweh in the affairs of history.

[9] The theory of a Scythian invasion which swept as far as the border of Egypt is based on the Greek historian Herodotus' report (*Persian Wars,* I, 104–106); but, in the judgment of recent historians, this report must be taken with a grain of salt (e.g., John Bright, *History* [91], p. 315).

Zephaniah spoke with a sense of urgency that was to be matched later by Jesus' proclamation that "the Kingdom of God is at hand." "The great day of Yahweh is near, near and hastening fast" (Zeph. 1:14). Events were hastening toward catastrophe; the clock was nearing midnight. Therefore, he summoned people to decision and repentance while they still had a chance. In scathing language he denounced the pagan practices which, under the influence of Manasseh, had defiled Judah and Jerusalem. He condemned Baal worship "in this place" (that is, in the city of Jerusalem); the astral cult—an importation from Assyria—which was practiced on the roof of the Temple; and the linking together of Yahweh and Milcom (the god of Ammon) (1:4–6). Even worse was the people's easy-going complacency, based on the preposterous notion that Yahweh has no sway over history and is impotent to do either good or evil (1:12). In one breath Zephaniah condemned the whole leadership of the nation: politicians and judges, priests and prophets, whom he likened to predatory "roaring lions," and "evening wolves" (3:3–4). Jerusalem, said Zephaniah, is a "rebellious city," impervious to Yahweh's word and lacking in faith. His prophetic task was to interpret the world crisis as God's action in history.

The prophet held out no hope that "the shameless nation," so deeply stained with paganism and so firmly entrenched in rebellion, would reform. Rather, Judah along with the other nations of the world would be consumed by "the fire of Yahweh's jealous wrath." Like Isaiah, he appealed for a remnant to repent and to seek refuge in Yahweh:

> Seek Yahweh,
>   all you, the humble of the earth,
>   who obey his commands.
> Seek integrity, seek humility;
>   you may perhaps find shelter
>   on the day of the anger of Yahweh.
>   —ZEPHANIAH 2:3 (JB)

Since Yahweh's purpose was not utter destruction but the cleansing and renewal of the people, Zephaniah announced that a remnant would be saved from the catastrophe (cf. 1:7)—"a people humble and lowly" who would live in sincerity and security (3:8–13).

The Prophet Jeremiah

The second prophetic voice heard in the early years of Josiah's reign was that of Jeremiah. A full discussion of his long career will be postponed until the next chapter, but here we shall look for a bit at the early years of his ministry, which overlapped that of his contemporary, Zephaniah. According to the heading of the book of Jeremiah, he began to prophecy in the thirteenth year of Josiah's reign—that is, about the year 626.[10] He was nurtured in the great traditions of Israel, for he is said to have come from a priestly family of Anathoth, a village about four miles northeast of Jerusalem. According to I Kings 2:26-27, Anathoth was the family residence of the priest Abiathar, a descendant of Eli whom Solomon expelled because of his complicity in Adonijah's attempt to seize the crown. Possibly Jeremiah could trace his priestly ancestry back to Eli, the custodian of the Ark in the old Confederate sanctuary of Shiloh. As we shall see later, the recollection of the fall of Shiloh, an event which virtually brought the former Israelite Confederacy to an end (see above, pp. 204-205), made a deep impression on Jeremiah's thought.

The materials in the first three chapters of the book of Jeremiah have been revised and reinterpreted in the light of later events in the prophet's ministry. But even so, these chapters (especially 2 and 3) give us important information about his career before the Deuteronomic Reformation of 621 B.C.E.

Evidently he was a very young man at the time of his call (c. 626) for he protested to Yahweh that he was a mere "lad" (Jer. 1:6). The interior struggle recorded in the first chapter is played out under the ominous shadow of international events. It was a restless, uncertain time, yet pregnant with the hope of national liberation. Not long before, Ashurbanapal's death had set off a chain reaction of events. Babylonia, under Nabopolassar (c. 626-605), had at last gained independence after years of futile effort. Media had revolted under Cyaxares. Scythian hordes were on the move in the north. Egypt, like the famed phoenix bird, was rising from the ashes. Great nations were stirring—watching for the opportune moment to strike a deathblow to the tottering Assyrian giant, each hoping to become the new master of the world. The old world order, which for over two centuries had been held together by Assyrian might, was crumbling. It was in this eventful hour of history that "the word of Yahweh" came to Jeremiah.

The Power That Destroys Rebuilds

In the story of Jeremiah's call, vividly presented in the form of a dialogue with Yahweh (Jer. 1:4-19), we are told how irresistibly Yahweh's word came to him (see 5:14; 23:29). Throughout his career, Jeremiah himself had to struggle with the mighty power of Yahweh's word, but he could not refrain from speaking it. In retrospect, he saw that his whole life, right back to the time when he was still in his mother's womb, was part of Yahweh's plan. This was the meaning of his life: to be "a prophet to the nations," consecrated for a "political office" in Yahweh's world government.[11] Like Moses (see Exod. 3 and 4), he shrank

---

[10] Some scholars, doubting that Jeremiah was active during Josiah's reform (621 B.C.E.), suggest changing "thirteenth year" to "twenty-third year." According to this view, which is improbable, the prophet's call occurred in the year 617.

[11] On the "political office" of the prophets, see G. E. Wright, "The Nations in Hebrew Prophecy," *Encounter*, 26 (1965), 225-37.

from the great task, not only because he was too young—perhaps not yet twenty years old—but also because he felt that he was the last man on earth to be chosen for such work. However, his attempts at evasion were in vain. His strength, after all, did not lie in his youth but in the power of the One who spoke through him, of the Sovereign who sent him. He was to be the servant of Yahweh's word that "makes history," the word that is filled with power to destroy and to rebuild (Jer. 1:10). In their feverish struggle to gain control of history, the nations had to know that Yahweh controls human affairs. So in vivid language the narrative portrays Yahweh touching the prophet's mouth, not to cleanse (as in Isaiah's vision), but to empower him to speak:

> Then Yahweh reached out his hand and touched my mouth,
>   saying to me:
>   "Look! I have put my words in your mouth.
>   You see, this day I have set you
>   over nations and over kingdoms,
>   to tear up and to pull down,
>   to demolish and to overthrow,
>   to build and to plant.
>   —JEREMIAH 1:9–10

In Jeremiah's message we are made aware, more clearly and deeply than in the case of any other prophet, that Yahweh's word is not only sovereign over the nations but also over the interior life of the prophet himself.

The ensuing passage relates two visions in a question-and-answer style that is reminiscent of the visions of Amos (Amos 7:7–9; 8:1–3). The first one, like Amos' vision of the basket of summer fruit, employs the favorite prophetic device of a play on words. In Hebrew there is close similarity between "al-mond" (*shāqēd*) and the participle "watching" (*shôqēd*). According to some interpreters, the almond branch, which in Hebrew means "waker" or "watcher" because it "wakes to blossom as early as February," suggests to the prophet that God is the Waker or Watcher, "who slumbers not nor sleeps, but proceeds to judgment."[12] The emphasis, however, probably is more on the sound of the words than on the association of ideas. The striking assonance of the Hebrew words was enough to evoke the conviction that Yahweh is "watching over his word"—that is, acting to bring the divine purpose to fruition (see Isa. 55:10–11). It was as if someone today, gazing intently at a watch, were to realize that God is "watching" (keeping alert), in order to bring a plan to fulfillment.

The second vision brings out what is implicit in the first one: Yahweh's historical purpose is ominous for Judah, for judgment is at hand. The prophet sees an ordinary cooking pot. Although the details are not too clear, it may be

---

[12] So H. Wheeler Robinson, *The Cross in the Old Testament* (Philadelphia: Westminister, 1955), p. 143.

that the pot is boiling in the north, with its mouth tilted south and pouring out an evil brew upon the land. In any case, the meaning is clear enough: It is from the north that an avalanche of evil will come upon the inhabitants of the land. Some think that in this passage, and in the original version of Jeremiah 4:5–6:26, the foe from the north was the Scythians (see, however, the foregoing discussion of Zephaniah). But whatever the historical agency, Jeremiah was convinced that Yahweh was the real foe who was coming to execute judgment against the whole land. Yahweh's word, spoken by this prophet, was *against* the kings of Judah, its princes, its priests, and the people of the land (verse 18).

Jeremiah's Early Preaching

The content of Jeremiah's message, delivered in the years between his call and the Deuteronomic Reformation, is set forth in a series of oracles now contained in Jeremiah 2:1–4:4.[13] Here the Mosaic tradition is revived with a depth of understanding that is matched only by the prophet Hosea. Indeed, the affinities between the second chapter of Jeremiah and the prophecy of Hosea are so striking that we may surmise that Jeremiah knew and was influenced by Hosea's message, which by that time had become the possession of the kingdom of Judah. Jeremiah's memory goes back to the great formative period of Israel's past: the Exodus and the sojourn in the wilderness. This was the time of Israel's covenant faithfulness (*ḥésed*),[14] when the "bride" Israel was in love with her husband (verses 1–3). In the honeymoon of her "youth," Israel responded with her whole being to Yahweh's historical revelation. But since then things have changed. Using the form of the *rîb*, or "covenant lawsuit" (2:4–13), which we have encountered before (see pp. 339–340), the prophet acts as Yahweh's prosecuting attorney. After the court is convened (verse 4), Yahweh the Plaintiff makes the charge: Israel's life in Canaan had been a history of unfaithfulness, with no sense of gratitude for Yahweh's past deeds of benevolence and continuing providence (verses 5–7). The leaders of the people—the priests, the rulers, the prophets—have failed to acknowledge the suzerainty of Yahweh (verse 8). The lawsuit reaches a resounding climax in the indictment against Israel (verses 9–13). To the prophetic attorney the whole thing was fantastic—for no other nation had ever repudiated its gods, even though they were really not gods at all, in order to follow after "emptiness" and thus become empty—"hollow" people (see vs. 5b)! It was just as appalling as if Jerusalem had rejected a supply of fresh water in order to store up water in cisterns that were no better than sieves! An appeal is made to the "jury"—the heavens:

---

[13] However, references to Egypt in 2:14–17 and 2:29–37 indicate that these passages were reworked in a time after the year 609 B.C.E., when the Egyptians were victorious over Josiah at Megiddo.

[14] In the Revised Standard Version of 2:2 *ḥésed* is translated as "devotion." On this covenant term, see Definition, Chapter 9, p. 308.

> Stand aghast, you heavens, at this!
>   Be astounded—utterly appalled,
>   says Yahweh.
> For a double evil have my people committed:
>   Me they have rejected,
>   the fountain of living water,
>   only to hew out cisterns for themselves,
>   broken cisterns that cannot hold water.
>   —JEREMIAH 2:12–13

In further elaboration of this theme, Jeremiah likened Israel to a faithless wife who leaves her husband (Jer. 3:19–20). Indeed, Israel is no better than a common harlot driven by lusts as strong as those of an animal in heat (2:20–25). Israel's lifestyle has polluted the land, Yahweh's heritage, for Israel's harlotry is practiced "upon every high hill and every green tree" where people worship Baal at local sanctuaries. Like Lady Macbeth, the stain of Israel's sin cannot be washed from her body even by the most powerful detergent; her skirts are soiled with "the life-blood of guiltless poor." Therefore, a divorce must take place (3:1–15). For Judah has not learned the lesson of the history of the Northern Kingdom, which ended in a decree of divorce written in the visible language of tragic events. "Faithless Israel has shown herself less guilty than false Judah!" She stands condemned for the most flagrant betrayal of the love that had called, redeemed, and sustained her throughout her history (3:6–14). Nevertheless, there is still time for repentance (that is, for a change of lifestyle), said the prophet. For in the events of history Yahweh is pleading with the faithless people to return ("repent"), to acknowledge their true Lord. It is Yahweh's purpose to heal the broken relationship (3:22) and to effect an inward transformation of the heart. Notice the conditional "if" of the Mosaic covenant which introduces the plea for repentance (4:1–4). *If* Israel turns around and returns to the covenant relationship with Yahweh, then the ancient promise to Abraham will come into effect: Nations will bless themselves in the name of the God of Israel (4:2). (On "repentance," see Definition, Chapter 12, p. 401)

Thus Jeremiah, like his contemporary Zephaniah, protested against the syncretism that had all but erased the distinctive elements of Israel's faith. He called for a reformation—not just a superficial reform of traditional rites and practices, but a reformation that begins in the heart, the seat of human loyalties and affections. He called for a "circumcision of the heart,"[15] for a breaking up of the fallow ground that had encrusted the life of the people (Jer. 4:3–4). In a time when Israel's sacred past was neglected and forgotten, the Mosaic faith of the ancient wilderness was revived with new depth and power through the message of Jeremiah.

---

[15] This expression, found also in Deuteronomy 10:16 and 30:6, is a metaphor for opening the "heart," the center of one's being, so that it may be humbly submissive to the will of God. The "uncircumcised heart" (Jer. 9:26) is one that is hardened in stubborn rebellion.

THE DEUTERONOMIC REFORMATION

The break-up of the world order, expected by Zephaniah and by Jeremiah, did not take place overnight. Instead, the course of events in the decades after the death of Ashurbanapal seemed to favor a renaissance of Judean nationalism. The youthful Josiah, capitalizing on Assyria's impotence to restore order in the Fertile Crescent, took the initiative in removing every sign of Assyrian domination in Palestine. According to Chronicles, which seems trustworthy in this instance, Josiah's first efforts at reform began in the twelfth year of his reign (629 B.C.E.), six years before the Deuteronomic Reformation (II Chron. 34:3). At that time, he expanded his influence into the territory of the former Northern Kingdom, which had become the Assyrian provinces of Megiddo and Samaria. Evidently Judah's aspiration to restore a United Kingdom under a Davidic king was intensified by the political situation of the day, and Josiah was eager to translate this nationalistic dream into reality.

The Discovery of the Book of Torah

In the following years, Josiah probably stepped up his program of nationalistic reform, especially with the rise to power of Nabopolassar (c. 626–605), who led the Babylonians to independence. And just as Hezekiah expressed his stiffening attitude toward Assyria by attempting to cleanse Judean worship of Assyrian and other alien elements, so Josiah's nationalism was accompanied by religious reform. In this reform he was supported by the conservative landowners of Judah, referred to in II Kings 11:14, 20 as "the people of the land," who had been hostile to Manasseh's appeasement of Assyria and longed for national independence (see II Kings 21:23–24).[16] Indeed, this reform was probably already underway when a remarkable discovery was made in the eighteenth year of his reign—that is, 621 B.C.E. We miss the import of the account in II Kings 22 if we fail to read it in the political context of the time. According to the story, a manuscript—"the book of the Torah"—was found when repairs were being made on the Temple of Jerusalem. Perhaps these were not routine repairs, but repairs designed to remove from the Temple all traces of Assyrian and other alien influences. In any case, when Josiah's secretary came to the Temple to supervise the payment of the workers' wages, he was informed of this "archaeological discovery" and he immediately brought the matter to Josiah's attention.

When the contents of the document were read to Josiah, he tore his garments—a gesture of consternation or despair. Urgently he demanded that the High Priest verify the authenticity of the manuscript. This was done, not by trying to determine its age and authorship (as we would do), but by consulting Huldah the prophetess. Her oracular response cut to the quick: Because of the

---

[16] Jehoash, in an earlier period, likewise had gained the support of this group. In cooperation with the High Priest, Johoiada, they elevated the king to the throne (II Kings 11:17–21; see p. 283).

violation of the words of the book, Yahweh would bring evil upon Jerusalem, making it "a desolation and a curse." At this point, Josiah summoned the people to the Temple for a ceremony of covenant renewal. He read "the book of the covenant" to them (the same book referred to above), and on the basis of this Torah the people made a covenant before Yahweh to walk after Yahweh and to be obedient to the covenant commandments. The ceremony calls to mind the story in Joshua 24 about the convocation "before God" at Shechem, the ritual of covenant renewal, and "the book of the Torah of God" in which the Shechem covenant was recorded. It also recalls the ancient covenant ceremony in Exodus 24:3–8, when Moses read to the people "the book of the covenant."

This covenant ceremony was followed by a great royal reform, similar to that of Hezekiah almost a century earlier but carried out with greater energy and thoroughness (II Kings 23). The finding of the Book of the Torah at the opportune moment accelerated and gave direction to the reform that Josiah had initiated some years earlier. Behind Josiah's house-cleaning was the desire to recover Judah's vitality and strength and to avoid the curse that the Torah invoked upon the nation when it disobeyed Yahweh's commandments (see Deut. 11:26–32; chap. 28). Accordingly, the paganism against which Zephaniah had protested (Zeph. 1:4–6) was abolished: the Canaanite Baal worship, the Assyrian astral cult, and the worship of other deities such as the Ammonite Milcom. Into the ash heap went all foreign objects found in the Temple: the appurtenances of the male god Baal and the mother goddess Asherah, the horses dedicated to the sun, and the astral altars on the roof. The practices of sacred prostitution, child sacrifice in the Valley of Hinnom, and the consultation of mediums and wizards were discontinued. And Josiah's reform did not stop with the cleansing of the Jerusalem Temple. The outlying sanctuaries, or "high places," which had been hotbeds of pagan religion, were destroyed and defiled, and their idolatrous priests were deposed.[17] Finally, Josiah's reform was carried into the area of the former Northern Kingdom, then nominally under Assyrian control. The rival temple of Bethel was destroyed, along with other outlying high places. Josiah's declaration of independence from Assyria could hardly have been made in clearer terms!

One feature of Josiah's reform deserves special attention. According to II Kings 23:8–9, the Yahweh priests in the cities of Judah were put out of business when the local shrines were abolished. We are told, however, that "the priests of the high places did not come up to the altar of Yahweh in Jerusalem, but they ate unleavened bread among their brethren" (verse 9). Clearly, the most drastic aspect of the reform, although it had been anticipated by Hezekiah, was that worship was to be concentrated in the Jerusalem Temple, the central sanctuary for all Judah, where it could be rigorously watched by the official priesthood.

---

[17] Some maintain that the sanctuary of Arad was destroyed at this time. See Yohanan Aharoni, "The Israelite Sanctuary at Arad," *New Directions in Biblical Archaeology* [104], 25–39. But as noted in an earlier chapter (p. 237, n. 23), it is not certain that the Arad structure was a temple.

In this way the faith of Israel could be kept free from the defilement of pagan ways and practices.

Josiah's reform, then, represented a break with Assyria, whose cultural influence had been deeply impressed upon Judah during the reign of Manasseh. Religiously, it involved a repudiation of what in those days might have been called "modernism": the attempt to conform to the religious fashions of the Assyrian empire and to blend Israel's religion and other religions into a coat of many colors. Josiah's reform was essentially conservative, for it sought to return to and conserve the distinctive elements of Israel's faith, rather than capitulate to the cultural pressures of the world. The reform was based on the conviction that unless the people repudiated the syncretism that sapped their vitality, Judah would go the way of the Northern Kingdom, which had been destroyed because the sacred past—the past of the Exodus and the covenant of the wilderness—had been forgotten. So by means of the ancient ceremony of covenant renewal a serious effort was made to recover the past and to restore its meaning in the present. In keeping with this effort, Josiah ordered that the long-neglected feast of the Mosaic period, the Passover, be reinstituted (II Kings 23:22–23).

The Deuteronomic Basis of Josiah's Reform

We now come to a major question: What document was it that was discovered in the Temple and read in the ceremony of covenant renewal? Is this book of the Torah still preserved somewhere in the Hebrew Bible? It stands to reason—at least the "reason" of critical scholarship—that it could not be the Pentateuch, for this was not completed until quite a bit later than Josiah's reform. Other legal collections within the Pentateuch—for instance, the so-called Covenant Code in Exodus 20:23–23:19, or the Holiness Code in Leviticus 17–26—hardly fit the situation. If the Torah found in the Temple during Josiah's reign is still extant, it must be a book that strongly condemns the paganisms of the Manasseh era, demands centralization of worship in Jerusalem, and solemnly warns that unswerving loyalty to Yahweh alone is the sole basis of the nation's existence.

These specifications are met by a body of law that is now found in chapters 12 to 26 of the book of Deuteronomy. When we read these chapters through with the story of II Kings 22–23 in mind, we are immediately struck by the correspondence between this Deuteronomic Code and the reform measures of Josiah. This is clear, for instance, in chapter 12, where it is stated that all the local high places must be abolished, and that the worship of Yahweh must be confined to the central sanctuary, "the place which Yahweh your God shall choose." Moreover, the Deuteronomic Code stipulates that while animals can be slaughtered for meat in any city, sacrifice to Yahweh is confined to the central sanctuary (Deut. 12:13–14; 16:5–6) and, further, that the people must make pilgrimages to the central sanctuary to celebrate the great religious festivals (16:1–5). In Deuteronomy 18:1–8 it is said that the country priests, who would lose their jobs with the closing of the local sanctuaries, are entitled to minister in the central sanctuary, although the writer in II Kings, who evidently knew that it was impractical for all these priests to join the Jerusalem temple staff, states that they found their livelihood by sojourning in the midst of their own people (II Kings 23:9). We cannot pursue these parallels any further at this point. Suffice it to say that since suggestions made by early church leaders of the fourth century C.E. (Athanasius, Chrysostom, Jerome), and especially since scholarly advances made during the nineteenth century, it has been held that Josiah's reform was based on the Code of Deuteronomy in some form. For that reason, it is called the Deuteronomic Reformation. As we have seen in earlier chapters, historians who took the theological convictions of the Deuteronomic Reformation seriously produced a comprehensive "Deuteronomistic" history of Israel from the Mosaic period to the final fall of the nation (Deuteronomy through II Kings).

Both in form and content the Deuteronomic Code shows dependence on an old legal tradition, although the tradition is recast and reinterpreted for the seventh century B.C.E.[18] Indeed, it is probable that Deuteronomic Torah goes back ultimately to a northern covenant tradition which had been preserved and interpreted by Levite teachers in North Israel. In the Deuteronomic Code, Jerusalem is not explicitly identified as the central sanctuary even though Josiah so identified it for his own reforming purposes. Originally, the Deuteronomic authors may have had in mind the city of Shechem, the scene of the covenant renewal under Joshua, and the city chosen by Jeroboam I as his first capital.

So the nucleus of Deuteronomy, chapters 12–26, has a long history behind it, even though it was kept in the Jerusalem Temple during the reactionary reign of Manasseh, and later was "found" at the appropriate time during Josiah's reign. If it also contained chapter 28, as it probably did, we can understand why the reading of "the blessings and the curses" led to Josiah's consternation and contrition. Moreover, it is probable that other sermonic material was included in the book presented to Josiah, but this question necessitates a brief consideration of the structure and contents of the whole book of Deuteronomy.

THE BOOK OF DEUTERONOMY

The book of Deuteronomy merits special attention in view of its great importance in Judean faith and worship. The publication of this book under state sponsorship during Josiah's reign was the first serious step toward the creation of an official canon of sacred literature that would be binding upon the whole people in matters of faith and conduct. Later on, as we shall see, the concept of an authoritative Torah, or Teaching, was extended to include not only Deu-

---

[18] The laws in Deuteronomy 12–26 show many similarities to the Covenant Code of Exodus 20:23–23:19, as can be seen by consulting the table given in S. R. Driver's *Introduction* [38], pp. 73–75. Moreover, many of the laws are cast in the "conditional" (casuistic) style of Near Eastern jurisprudence which influenced Israel during the settlement in Canaan. See above, pp. 95–98, 149–150.

teronomy but also the Priestly edition of the Old Epic tradition (JE)—that is, the whole Pentateuch (see Chapter 13). Deuteronomy nourished and deepened faith in Yahweh during the critical period of the collapse of the Assyrian empire and in subsequent generations. Significantly, it is one of the Old Testament books most frequently quoted in the New Testament. The First Great Commandment, which Jesus affirmed to be the fulfillment of the whole Torah, is a direct quotation from Deuteronomy 6:5 (Mk. 12:30 = Matt. 22:37 and Lk. 10:27). And the Second Commandment, although it is quoted directly from Leviticus 19:18, is implicit in the Deuteronomic conception of neighborly love (see Deut. 10:19). Moreover, Jesus' answers to the Tempter, as recorded in the Gospels (Matt. 4:1-10 = Lk. 4:1-13), were couched in terms of Israel's trials of faith as recorded in Deuteronomy 6-8 (see 6:13, 16; 8:3).

In its present form, the whole book of Deuteronomy purports to be a sermon given by Moses to Israel in Moab, just before the people crossed over the Jordan River to take possession of the Promised Land. As they stand on the threshold of a new life, with all its opportunities and dangers, Moses exhorts them to remember Yahweh's gracious acts made known in the Exodus and the wilderness sojourn, and to hold firm to their covenant pledge when they are confronted with the temptations of the land of Canaan. This sermon is made all the more forceful and relevant because it actually reflects Israel's temptations to compromise its faith with Canaanite culture, from the earliest days of the Conquest to the recent heyday of paganism under Manasseh.[19]

Closer inspection of the book shows, however, that it is not all of one piece. Around the nucleus of laws collected in chapters 12-26 are clustered no less than three "Mosaic addresses." The structure of the book may be outlined as follows:

A. The First Address (chapters 1-4)
    1. Introduction (1:1-5)
    2. Moses' summary of events since the departure from Mount Horeb (1:6-3:29)
    3. Moses' exhortation to Israel (4:1-40)
    4. Appendix (4:41-43)
B. The Second Address (chapters 5-26 and 28)
    1. Introduction (4:44-49)
    2. Moses' exhortation to Israel (chapters 5-11)
    3. The exposition of the Law (chapters 12-26)
    4. Conclusion (chapter 28)
C. The Third Address (chapters 29-30)
D. Supplements
    1. The Shechem covenant ceremony (chapter 27)
    2. Moses' last instructions (chapter 31)
    3. Old poetry: the Song of Moses (chapter 32) and the Blessing of Moses (chapter 33)
    4. Narrative of Moses' death (chapter 34)

---

[19] Remember that the term "Israel" actually embraces the two kingdoms of Israel, Ephraim and Judah, making it possible to refer to them as "the two houses of Israel" (see Isa. 8:14). Thus, even after the Northern Kingdom had fallen, the term still applied to Judah. See Definition, p. 6.

The main address—the one on which we shall concentrate here—is section B of the above outline. It is generally agreed that this is the oldest edition of Moses' ''sermon'' to Israel, although we cannot be absolutely sure whether the sermonic material which frames the law code (chapters 12–26) was composed before or after Josiah's reform. Without attempting to go into this critical question, we shall assume that at least this section should be read as a unified whole and that probably this was substantially the book that was presented to Josiah.[20]

Moses' Sermon to Israel

One of the first things we notice in this passage is that Moses' farewell address is presented in a distinctive literary style. If we were to compare a Deuteronomic passage (for instance, Deut. 10:12–22) with a typical selection from either the Old Epic tradition or the Priestly Writing, the differences would be apparent immediately. Here we find not the chaste style of a narrator or the formulaic prose of a priest concerned with cultic matters, but that of a preacher who uses skillful oratory to move his congregation to consider issues of life-and-death urgency. Very often the sentences are long flights of eloquent and impressive prose. As though trying to drive home the message to his hearers, the preacher piles clause upon clause in a manner that seems repetitious. Throughout the sermon appear characteristic turns of speech that we have already encountered in the Deuteronomistic History: ''To go after [or serve] other gods''; ''to hearken to the voice of Yahweh''; ''that you may prolong your days in the land''; ''that it may be well with you''; ''to do that which is evil (or good) in the eyes of Yahweh.''[21]

This new literary style, found in the Deuteronomic literature and the prose sections of Jeremiah, seems to have been characteristic of the late seventh and early sixth centuries B.C.E. The Lachish Letters, a series of inscribed potsherds found in 1935 and dating from the time just before the fall of Jerusalem, strengthen the opinion that this ''rhetorical prose'' was the literary fashion of the period.[22] Although the *style* belongs to the Deuteronomic period, the *content* is much older. At several points the pattern and content of the Mosaic sermon (especially chapters 29 and 30) suggest that this material has come out of a covenant-renewal ceremony, initiated by Joshua at Shechem, practiced at the old central sanctuary of Shiloh during the period of the Tribal Confederacy, and

[20] See the critical discussion by G. E. Wright, *Interpreter's Bible*, II [16], 311–30, who argues that Josiah's lawbook may have included virtually the whole of 4:44–30:20 (that is, sections B and C) and that most of the material in section A was added later as a preface to the Deuteronomistic History of Israel, which extends from Deuteronomy through II Kings.

[21] The closest affinities to Deuteronomic style are found in the northern Elohist tradition (E)—as evidenced, for example, by the fact that Deuteronomy, like the Elohist, calls the sacred mountain Horeb instead of Sinai (J and P), and refers to the natives of the Promised Land as Amorites rather than as Canaanites. On the Elohist narrative, see Definition, p. 289.

[22] For the Lachish Letters, see Pritchard, *Ancient Near Eastern Texts* [1], pp. 321–322. On the style and theology of Deuteronomy see further, Moshe Weinfeld, *Deuteronomy* [369].

preserved in the Northern Kingdom. When it was used later as the basis of Josiah's reform, the old covenant tradition was written down and expanded in the language of the time.

Although the author of Deuteronomy remains anonymous, as is true of so much Old Testament literature, placing the address in the mouth of Moses is not a complete literary fiction. For Deuteronomy is essentially a revival of Mosaic teaching as it was understood in the seventh century B.C.E. To be sure, it does not contain the verbatim utterances of Moses; but the atmosphere is that of the Mosaic faith, though charged with the religious and ethical insights of the prophetic movement. Like the prophets themselves, the Deuteronomic Torah does not pretend to lead Israel forward to new heights of religious development, but to recall the people to the original faith of the Mosaic period. This is a program of reform, not innovation. Hence the address appropriately is ascribed to Moses.

The title of the book is evidently derived from the passage in Deut. 17:14–20, which stipulates that the king must have at hand ''a copy of this law'' all the days of his life and must conduct himself in obedience to it. The Greek translation (Septuagint), from which come our present names for the books of the Pentateuch, reproduces this phrase as ''this second law'' (*to deuteronomion touto*). The Hebrew title is simply ''these are the words,'' the opening phrase of the book (1:1). So the Greek title designates the book according to its central theme: the ''seconding'' or repetition of the original law given by Moses. As the contents of Deuteronomy disclose, however, the modern word ''law,'' which reflects Greek *nomos* and Latin *lex,* is inadequate to cover the full meaning of the Hebrew word *torah.* Literally, *torah* means ''teaching,'' perhaps even ''revelation.'' Deuteronomy does contain what we would call ''law,'' but the book is not narrowly confined to legal matters. It is fundamentally a teaching or ''exposition'' (see 1:5) of the basis and demands of Israel's covenant faith, and as such is directed not to professional administrators of law or to priests, but to the whole lay community of Israel. It is not a code of rules, but ''a preaching, a proclamation and exposition of the faith of the nation,'' which includes both the ''good news'' (gospel) of Yahweh's liberating deeds and the requirements that are binding upon the people who have been liberated.[23] Therefore, the term Torah covers not only the so-called ''code'' in chapters 12–26 but also the whole Mosaic address.

THE RENEWAL OF THE COVENANT

Let us glance briefly at the contents of Moses' address to Israel. It begins with an imperative that resounds like a trumpet call through the whole sermon:

[23] See the excellent treatment of Deuteronomy by G. E. Wright, *Interpreter's Bible,* II [16], especially pp. 311–14.

"Hear, O Israel" (Deut. 5:1). A message is being proclaimed with great urgency, and the community is called to listen. Moses is speaking to the Israelite community in Transjordan at a time when the memory of the Exodus is still fresh and the people face the hazards of entering Canaan. But it is soon quite clear that the message is not addressed to a generation long ago, but to "this day" when Israel stands before God. Moses is speaking *today*. The present generation was actually *there* when the covenant was made, just as a Christian, singing the well-known spiritual, can testify that "I was there when they crucified my Lord." Notice the contemporary accent of the language:

> Yahweh our God made a covenant with us at Horeb. It was not with our ancestors that Yahweh made this covenant but rather with us, all of us here, all of us who are living today.
>
> —DEUTERONOMY 5:2–3 (see also 29:10–15)

Every generation of Israel is involved in the covenant made at Mount Horeb. Therefore, when the covenant is renewed, the decisive moment of the past is "made present," contemporized. Deuteronomy does not advocate a retreat from the tumult of the present into a golden age of the past. Rather, it deals vigorously with the challenge of the present crisis, and with Israel's responsibilities and destiny in Yahweh's purpose. But, according to this sermon, the Mosaic past must come alive in the present if Israel is to have any future at all in the land that Yahweh has given. Hence the appeal for covenant renewal is made with life-or-death urgency. Another passage in the Third Address (30:15–20), which may have been used as a liturgy of covenant renewal, strikes the same serious and urgent note:

> I call heaven and earth to witness against you this day, that I have set before you life and death, blessing and curse; therefore choose life. . . .
>
> —DEUTERONOMY 30:19

This is a forceful restatement of Joshua's message before the ancient assembly at Shechem: "Choose this day whom you will serve" (Josh. 24:15).

The Fulfillment of the Law

Having sounded this keynote, the speaker immediately turns attention to the requirements that are binding upon the covenant community. These are summed up in the Ten Commandments (literally: "the ten words"), which are given in Chapter 5 with slight variation from the version in Exodus 20. The essence of the commandments, however, is given in Deuteronomy 6:4–5, where the first commandment of the Decalogue is presented in a positive, rather than a negative, form. This terse summary—known as the Shema, from the opening Hebrew verb (*shema'* = "hear")—was regarded by the rabbis and by Jesus as the core of the Law. It states that Israel's first responsibility is to love God with its whole being—"with all your heart, and with all your soul ["self"], and with all your might."[24] This does not mean that one should love God in different ways, for these terms overlap in meaning. Israel is to love God in one way: with the unswerving, complete, steadfast loyalty that is the very foundation of the covenant community.

The emphasis upon love is one of the characteristic themes of Deuteronomy. In this respect, Deuteronomy, influenced in part by Hosea's message, returns to and deepens the meaning of the original Mosaic covenant.[25] Yahweh's gracious and undeserved love, manifested in deeds of benevolence on behalf of Israel (Deut. 6:20-23), should awaken Israel's response: love of God and, as a corollary, love of neighbors. Notice, however, that Deuteronomy actually revives the original Mosaic tradition in which Israel's "gospel"—the good news of what Yahweh had done on behalf of a people in bondage (Exod. 1-15)— provided the motive for accepting the obligations of the covenant (see pp. 91-92). According to Deuteronomy, Israel is to love God, not for an ulterior motive, but solely because Yahweh first loved them. Love is "the fulfillment of the law." However, Israel's love of God must be combined with reverence ("fear," "obedience") for Yahweh is a "jealous" God who will not tolerate turning to other gods (Deut. 6:10-15). Yahweh's love is a holy love, a wrathful love, that will become a consuming fire to those who are unfaithful to the covenant relationship.

The Choice of Israel

In the following chapters (7-9), the speaker shows what is meant by Yahweh's choice of Israel. Israel is a *holy people*. The basis of the community is a unique relationship to Yahweh, the Holy God. According to Deuteronomy, this is what makes Israel different from other nations:

> For you are a people holy to Yahweh, your God. You Yahweh your God has chosen to be his very own possession out of all the peoples that are on the surface of the earth.
>
> —DEUTERONOMY 7:6

Negatively, this means that Israel has been *separated from* the nations. Therefore, the people are not to intermarry with them or to adopt their cultural

---

[24] The New Testament quotation of this commandment adds "the mind" in order to bring out what is meant by the Hebrew word "heart." As we have noticed before, the word *néfesh*, often translated "soul," does not mean soul in the Greek sense, but refers to the whole person, the self.

[25] William L. Moran, in an article on "The Ancient Near Eastern Background of the Love of God in Deuteronomy" (*Catholic Biblical Quarterly*, XXV [1963], pp. 77-87), argues that whereas Hosea spoke of Yahweh's love for Israel but never of Israel's love for Yahweh, Deuteronomy actually harks back to the ancient suzerainty covenant, within which the "vassal" was commanded to love the sovereign who had performed deeds of benevolence.

ways, lest the gods of the nations seduce them from loyalty to Yahweh. This is put so strongly that Israel is enjoined to practice the *ḥerem* of holy war (see Definition, p. 141)—that is, to consign the inhabitants of Canaan to total destruction as a sacrifice to Yahweh (Deut. 7:1–5). Holiness demands purity, so the cult must be purified and all alien elements must be removed from the covenant community.

Positively, Israel has been *separated for* special service to Yahweh. Here the speaker presents one of the finest treatments of Israel's special calling in the Old Testament, although it lacks the universal breadth of the Old Epic tradition (Gen. 12:1–3). Israel did not first choose; Israel was chosen (cf. Exod. 19:3–6). The initiative was with Yahweh. In marvelous grace Yahweh selected this people, not because they were stronger or more numerous than others, but solely because Yahweh fell in love with a small, insignificant band of slaves in Egypt (cf. Hos. 11:1). Therefore, Israel has no reason for boasting of its righteousness or superiority to other people. Election is an act of divine grace that should evoke consecrated service rather than the proud feeling of being God's favorite (Deut. 7:6–11). The conquest and the inheritance of Canaan are reviewed in the light of this conviction (7:12–26).

As the sermon continues, we realize that Moses is speaking about the "temptations of culture" that Israel experienced throughout its history as an independent nation. One temptation was to suppose in *self-sufficiency* that "my power and the might of my hand have gotten me this wealth" (Deut. 8:17). The community is urged to remember the wilderness sojourn, when Yahweh graciously led them for forty years, allowing them to hunger and feeding them with manna so that they might know that "human beings [*ha-'adam*] do not live by bread alone but they live by everything that proceeds from the mouth of Yahweh" (8:3). In the spirit of the prophet Hosea, the speaker affirms that the sufferings of the wilderness period were a form of discipline, like the loving discipline that a parent inflicts upon a child. The purpose was to "humble" Israel, to test the loyalty of Israel's heart. In this way the people were awakened to the realization that "life" is not subject to human control, but is a gift received only by those who acknowledge their constant dependence upon God.

The second cultural temptation was that of *self-righteousness*, the proud belief of a victorious people that "it is because of my righteousness that Yahweh has brought me in to possess this land" (Deut. 9:4). The speaker reminds Israel that victory in Canaan does not rest upon its righteousness, but upon the corruption and wickedness of the peoples of the land, and especially upon Yahweh's faithfulness to the promise made to the ancestors (9:5). Israel has no claim upon Yahweh because of moral virtue or special religious insight. Indeed, the wilderness sojourn, contrary to Hosea's idealized treatment of it, was not a honeymoon of covenant faithfulness, but a time of ingratitude and rebellion. Israel is "a stubborn people" by nature. Moses is represented as saying: "You have been rebellious against Yahweh from the day that I knew you" (9:24)—a statement that is not intended to apply just to the generation of the wilderness but to the whole course of Israel's history from the Exodus to the time of Josiah. Had it not been for Moses' intercession on behalf of Israel, Yahweh would have destroyed the people in the wilderness and fashioned some better instrument to use in history. Israel's preservation, so the speaker emphasizes, is due solely to Yahweh's freely bestowed grace and love (9:6–10:11).

Israel's Social Responsibilities

The climax and epitome of the sermon are reached in Deuteronomy 10:12–22. Here the speaker again strikes the note with which the sermon began, one that also reverberates in the great prophetic summary found in Micah 6:8. In answer to the question, "What does Yahweh require of you?," Israel is reminded that its calling is to be an obedient people, fearing Yahweh who is Sovereign of heaven and earth and loving the One who first loved them. Thus the basis for ethical responsibility is not dutiful obedience to a law code, but an inward, personal response to Yahweh's sovereign deeds of kindness and benevolence.

Moreover, Yahweh's righteous activity on behalf of the weak and oppressed has shown the way in which Israel should walk. In Yahweh's sovereign rule, love and justice are perfectly combined. Israel's God, "God of gods and Lord of lords, the great, the mighty, and the terrible God," has not only demonstrated love for Israel but also has manifested divine love through the exercise of justice on behalf of oppressed slaves. Hence Yahweh is the champion of those who are legally weak or helpless: the orphan, the widow, the resident alien. Yahweh shows no partiality; everyone stands equal before the divine Judge. Because Yahweh acts this way, Israel must imitate this manner of dealing with people. Here we find the basis of the "humanitarianism" that infuses the laws found in Deuteronomy 12–26. The justice of the weak members of society must be defended, for Israelites must remember that they were once slaves in Egypt whom God set free (15:1–18). Every member of the community—high or low, rich or poor, bond or free—must be accorded equality before the law (16:18–20). This emphasis puts Israelite legislation on a higher plane than other codes of the Near East, which favored the aristocratic class. Any exploitation of a fellow Israelite is ruled out, whether through murder, adultery, theft, dishonesty, false witness, or the taking of interest. The sanctities of the family are to be protected. Injustice in any form defiles the covenant community. The righteousness of God demands, negatively, the abolition of anything that defiles the community, even to the point of imposing the severest penalties, as in the case of idolatry (13:1–18; 17:2–7) or sexual abuses (22:13–25). And, positively, it means imitating God's dealings in order that a spirit of love and solidarity may pervade the community.[26]

[26] See the perceptive essay by Lawrence E. Toombs, "Love and Justice in Deuteronomy," in *Interpretation*, 19 (1965), 399–411. Here it is argued that the Deuteronomist's understanding of the law is one which avoids the Scylla of restricting law to the secular sphere, and the Charybdis of a legalism which identifies the Law with the whole will of God.

In chapters 11 and 28, which are separated from one another by the exposition of specific laws, Israel is reminded that its future depends on how it responds to Yahweh's requirements. The people are confronted with a crucial decision, with the alternatives of the blessing or the curse. If Israel obeys faithfully, it will be strong in the land and will be blessed with fertility and welfare. But if Israel stubbornly turns aside to serve the gods of the land, Yahweh's anger will break forth and the people will be visited with all kinds of calamities and will quickly perish from the land.

Thus the governing purpose of Deuteronomy is to summon Israel to a renewal of the covenant with Yahweh. Although this literature has behind it a long tradition of covenant-renewal ritual, its immediate background is the cultural situation of the seventh century, when Israel's faith was corroded by the Canaanite nature cult and by Assyrian religious practices. The writer demands exclusive loyalty to Yahweh as the condition for national welfare and survival. In that situation, when powerful religious loyalties were contending for the devotion of the human heart, the Deuteronomic writer summoned Israel to decision, to whole-hearted commitment to Yahweh whose gracious love was made known in "saving deeds" of historical deliverance and guidance.

INADEQUACIES OF THE REFORM

For a while, the Deuteronomic Reformation made a deep impression upon the life and thought of Judah, as can be seen from the dominance of the Deuteronomic viewpoint in the Deuteronomistic History of Israel that we have dealt with from time to time. The reform movement sincerely attempted to take prophetic teachings seriously and to return to the covenant faith of Moses. But alas, social reforms—even when sanctioned by the government and supported by popular approval—last only as long as the inward change in the hearts of the people persists. Josiah's reform, as we have seen, reflected the political climate of the time. Inspired to a great degree by the nationalistic spirit of rebellion against foreign rule, it could flourish only as long as the political situation that occasioned it.

Theological Flaws

Evidently Jeremiah supported the Deuteronomic Reformation for a time, although his attitude is not as clear as we might wish.[27] His interest in the reform

---

[27] For a defense of Jeremiah's support of the Reformation, see H. H. Rowley, "The Prophet Jeremiah and the Book of Deuteronomy," in the book edited by the same author, *Studies in Old Testament Prophecy* (Edinburgh: T. & T. Clark, 1950), 157–74. See also essays on this subject by Henri Cazelles and J. P. Hyatt in Perdue and Kovacs, eds., *A Prophet to the Nations* [382], pp. 89–111, 113–27. For William Holladay's interesting view, based on the premise that Jeremiah began to preach not in 627 B.C.E. but during the reign of Jehoiakim (c. 609–598), see *Jeremiah: Spokesman Out of Time* [cited under 378], chap. 2.

movement would certainly have been in keeping with his concern for the Mosaic tradition. In Jeremiah 11:1–13 we are told that the prophet went through the streets of Jerusalem appealing for acceptance of "this covenant." The language of the passage strongly suggests that in his early career he supported the Deuteronomic Covenant, which was a renewal of the Sinai Covenant (see vs. 7). In the same chapter (verses 18–23), we are told that Jeremiah's kinsmen of Anathoth plotted to take his life. The reason may have been that this priestly family, which was associated with the local shrine, resented Jeremiah's support of a program that would put them out of their jobs by centralizing worship in Jerusalem, where the royal priesthood was in control.[28] Moreover, even in his later career, Jeremiah held Josiah in high esteem for his vigorous administration of justice (Jer. 22:15–16). In any case, if Jeremiah supported the reform at first, he must have soon turned against it. He came to see that it did not result in a circumcision of the heart or a breaking up of fallow ground, as Deuteronomy advocated (Jer. 10:16), but yielded only a defiant nationalism and an external piety. Centralizing worship in Jerusalem only made people think that they were secure because Yahweh was present in their midst. Moreover, the Torah was being twisted into a way to "get something out of religion," to maintain the *status quo*. Jeremiah denounced spurious wisdom based on the Torah:

> How dare you say: We are wise,
> and we possess the Law [Torah] of Yahweh?
> But look how it has been falsified
> by the lying pen of the scribes.
> —JEREMIAH 8:8 (JB)

This sounds like the outburst of a person disillusioned by a reform that had failed to achieve a genuine spiritual renewal of the covenant. His prophecy of the "new covenant," which we shall consider in the next chapter, must have been influenced partly by the failure of the Deuteronomic Reform.

One of the greatest defects of Deuteronomic theology was that it oversimplified the ways of God in history. The Deuteronomic doctrine of divine justice makes things too neat: obey Yahweh and all will go well; disobey and hardship will come. It may be that the original version of Deuteronomy understood this truth more profoundly, but as it was worked out by the writer who left us the Deuteronomistic History, it sounds suspiciously like the "success philosophy" which even today is the basis of much popular religion. Of course, the belief in divine reward (blessing) and divine punishment (judgment) had been fundamental in Israel's faith right from the very first. But Isaiah, like the other great prophets, put into the foreground an important qualification: "*If* you are willing and obedient, you shall eat the good of the land" (Isa. 1:19). In Deuteronomy,

---

[28] Deuteronomy 18:6–8 specifies that village priests had a right to be included on the Jerusalem staff, but this proved impractical (II Kings 23:9). The Jerusalem hierarchy would naturally oppose the intrusion of outside priests.

however, something new was added—the belief that obedience or disobedience could be measured by a code of rules set down in a book, the Book of the Torah. Joshua, according to the Deteronomic history, was promised success in the invasion of Canaan *if* he would study faithfully "this book of the law"—the Deuteronomic Torah:

> Let not this Book of the Teaching cease from your lips, but recite it day and night, so that you may observe faithfully all that is written in it. Only then will you prosper in your undertakings and only then will you be successful.
> —JOSHUA 1:8 (TNK)

Now, in defense of Deuteronomy we must say that it was not the intention of the Mosaic address to encourage a bargain counter religion. This address is concerned primarily with personal relationship to Yahweh, rather than with personal profit gained by obeying religious rules. True, it was believed that the covenant relationship would result in concrete blessings in the daily life of the people. The Old Testament does not make our artificial distinction between "material" and "spiritual" blessings—the latter being confined to the inner blessings of peace of mind, fortitude, patience, and so on. There is a healthy spiritual "materialism" in Deuteronomy. Just as the marriage covenant yields the blessings of home life, so Israel's covenant with Yahweh yielded the divine promise of tangible blessings: security in the land, abundant crops, annual rainfall, long life. But the danger was that the people would renew the covenant *for the purpose of* obtaining these blessings or—to use recurring Deuteronomic phrases—"in order that it may be well with you," or "in order that your days may be long upon the land which Yahweh your God gives you." And because faith did not always bring people what they expected or wanted, a huge question arose with which later generations, influenced by the Deuteronomic view, had to struggle: If people obey the laws of God and are recompensed with suffering or hardship, how can God be just?

A Period of Disillusionment

The easy moral logic of the Deuteronomic view was put to severe strain in the years following Josiah's reform. As we have seen, Josiah dreamed of restoring a United Kingdom under the single religious and political capital of Jerusalem. The Deuteronomic Reformation, viewed politically, was an attempt to consolidate and revitalize his expanded kingdom. Josiah evidently grew bolder and bolder as Assyria's star sank into political darkness. Thanks to the discovery of a Babylonian clay tablet, now in the British Museum, the story of the final death throes of Assyria can be told.[29] In 612 B.C.E., the Assyrian capital of Nineveh fell before the combined assault of the Babylonians, Medes, and Scythians. In retreat, the Assyrians tried to make a last-ditch stand at Haran, whence their cap-

---

[29] See J. Pritchard, *Ancient Near Eastern Texts* [1], pp. 303–5.

ital had been moved, but this city too was captured by Scythian forces (see the prediction of Zephaniah 2:13–15).

The prophecy of Nahum, which comes from this period, gives powerful expression to the pent-up feelings of bitterness and hatred which Assyrian occupation had engendered in Judean hearts. Anticipating the fall of the capital city of Nineveh (612 B.C.E.), this "cultic" prophet uses an acrostic (alphabetic) psalm to portray Yahweh's coming in a storm to rescue the faithful (chap. 1). He vividly describes the enemy attack upon the city as the battle rages through the streets (chap. 2), and he pronounces a terrible invective upon "the bloody city" (chap. 3). With more patriotic zeal than prophetic insight into the tragic dimension of history, he insists that Nineveh is about to get the same treatment as Assyrian kings had once given to Thebes, the capital of Egypt (Nahum 3:8), when Esarhaddon conquered the city in the year 669 and Ashurbanapal delivered the *coup de grâce* in 663. At last Assyria is going to taste to the full the suffering that it had inflicted upon other peoples, and there will be no one to feel sorry:

> Your shepherds are asleep,
>   O king of Assyria;
>   your nobles slumber.
> Your people are scattered on the mountains
>   with none to gather them.
> There is no assuaging your hurt,
>   your wound is grievous.
> All who hear the news of you
>   clap their hands over you.
> For upon whom has not come
>   your unceasing evil?
>   —NAHUM 3:18–19 (RSV)

Then came a sudden turn of affairs, the result of a political somersault on the part of Egypt. Pharaoh Necho (c. 610–594), the son of Psammetichus I, decided belatedly to come to the rescue of Egypt's former enemy, Assyria—the same enemy that had sacked Thebes not many years before. From Egypt's standpoint, it was expedient to have a weak Assyria as a buffer against more dangerous foes in the north; moreover, Necho was eager to bring Syria and Palestine back into Egypt's orbit of power as in the days of its imperial glory. So in the year 609 Necho's army marched north to salvage the last remnants of the Assyrian empire. He was intercepted at the pass of Megiddo (see p. 197) by Josiah, who gambled on achieving his goal of a United Kingdom by throwing in his lot with the Babylonians. In the ensuing battle, Josiah was defeated, and evidently executed for his conspiracy with Babylonia. Judah was made a vassal of Egypt (II Kings 23:29–30), and Necho continued his march to the Euphrates to challenge Babylonia. The issue was decided in the year 605 at the battle of Carchemish, when Necho's army was decisively defeated by Babylonian forces under the command of the crown prince, Nebuchadrezzar II. (The name of the Babylonian prince is oftentimes spelled Nebuchad*n*ezzar.)[30] The Egyptian army, now in full retreat, was chased across Palestine to the borders of Egypt. Fleeing before its victorious enemies, Egypt made "a sound like a serpent gliding away" (Jer. 46). This was Egypt's last attempt to establish an empire in the Fertile Crescent. The fall of Nineveh and the victory at Carchemish made it clear that Babylonia was the new ruler of the world.

These developments must have profoundly shaken the morale of the people, whose hopes had been kindled by Josiah's reform. Good king Josiah, not yet forty years old, was dead, and Jeremiah must have shared the general sorrow (Jer. 22:10; and see II Chron. 35:24f.)[31] The dream of a Davidic kingdom that would include both Israel and Judah was shattered. Temporary respite from the yoke of Assyrian oppression was followed, after a brief interval of Egyptian rule, by the imposition of a Babylonian yoke not a bit lighter or more merciful. In the popular view, Yahweh's justice meant that good consequences would come from good actions, that obedience would result in security on the land, victory against foes, and abundant life. But the cruel facts of history contradicted this belief. No wonder that the first, fine rapture of the Deuteronomic Reform was soon spent! In the judgment of many scholars, the accomplishments of the reformers were erased in a short time, just as Hezekiah's reform had been eclipsed during the reign of Manasseh.[32] As we learn from the prophets of this period, Jeremiah and Ezekiel, the Mosaic faith was forgotten, or compromised with the pagan ways of the world. Once again there was a reversion to the easy tolerance of syncretism. The tragedy of the time called for a deeper understanding of the meaning of Israel's covenant with Yahweh.

HABAKKUK'S WATCHTOWER OF FAITH

The strongest challenge to a simple view of God's justice in history was given by the prophet Habakkuk. His prophecy, found essentially in chapters 1 and 2 of the book, dates from a time just after the battle of Carchemish in 605 B.C.E., the event that established Nebuchadrezzar as world ruler.[33] In these chapters

---

[30] Nebuchadrezzar is perhaps the more proper spelling of the Akkadian name, *Nabukudurri-usur*. See the *Interpreter's Dictionary of the Bible* [25] under this name.

[31] Stanley B. Frost, in an article, "The Death of Josiah: A Conspiracy of Silence," *Journal of Biblical Literature*, 87 (1968), 369–82, maintains that Josiah's death was not only a challenge to Davidic theology but also to Mosaic (Deuteronomic) theology and therefore could not be dealt with in the traditional manner of Israelite historiography.

[32] See, however, M. Weinfeld, *Deuteronomy* [369], who maintains that many of the reforms remained in effect.

[33] Most scholars believe that the psalm in chapter 3, though appropriate here, comes from another hand. W. F. Albright, however, regards the book as "substantially the work of a single author" in his study, "The Psalm of Habakkuk," in *Studies in Old Testament Prophecy* [368], 1–18. See further Donald E. Gowan, *The Triumph of Faith in Habakkuk* [387].

we find a dialogue in two cycles between the prophet and Yahweh (Hab. 1:2–2:5). The prophet's poignant complaint, which echoes the anguished "How long?" of psalms of lament (see below, chap. 16), is evoked by the social violence which seems to mean that God has forsaken the people.

> How long, Yahweh, must I cry for help,
>   and you don't answer?
> shall I cry to you "Violence!"
>   and you will not deliver?
> Why do you make me see evil,
>   make me look upon trouble?
> Destruction and violence are at hand,
>   controversy and contention arise.
> Therefore torah is feeble,
>   and justice does not achieve its end.
> Hence the wicked gang up around the righteous,
>   and on account of this justice is miscarried.
>   —HABAKKUK 1:2–4

The answer is that Yahweh is doing something almost unbelievable, namely, raising up the Chaldeans (that is, the Babylonians)—"that bitter and hasty nation" (Hab. 1:5–11). But this hardly answers the prophet's question, for the new world power represented a continuation of the monstrous, lawless evil that Assyria had unleashed. The prophet wonders whether history does justify the righteous, or whether brute power is really the factor that determines human destiny. To him it is strange that when Yahweh is the Ruler of history, the Chaldeans can sweep like a wild avalanche over the world, destroying all patterns of meaning and defying the most elementary human justice. These ruthless invaders rule by defining justice in their own terms (1:7); they are "guilty men, whose own might is their god" (1:11, RSV). Not that Yahweh's people are guiltless! But at least they are "more righteous" than this nation, which is a law unto itself. Divine judgment, which other prophets had proclaimed in times of invasion, makes no sense if faith cannot discern some purpose in historical events.

So once again the prophet raises his complaint (1:12–17):

> You whose eyes are too pure to look upon evil,
>   and who cannot countenance wrong,
> why do you countenance treacherous people,
>   and are silent when the wicked devour
>   those who are more righteous than they?
>   —HABAKKUK 1:13

Habakkuk's question becomes even more acute if, as some scholars hold, he has in mind, especially in 2:6–20, not only the enemy without but also the enemy within—namely, the wicked and worthless king Jehoiakim (see Jer. 22:13–

19).[34] In any event, the prophet takes his stand on his "watchtower of faith" to await Yahweh's answer. But no immediate answer is given. The answer that comes (2:1–5) lifts his eyes to the horizons of the future, when God's purpose ultimately will be realized, even though from a human standpoint the time will be slow in coming. In the meantime, when God's presence in history is eclipsed, one must live in the courage of faith.

> Behold, he whose soul is not upright in him shall fail,
>   but the righteous shall live by his faith.
> —HABAKKUK 2:4 (RSV)

According to this answer, the righteous person must face the enigmas of history in faith (or better, "faithfulness")—that is, by living and acting faithfully, confident that the issues are in God's hands and waiting patiently for the time when God's sovereignty will be made clear (cf. Isa. 8:16–18). The answer to Habakkuk's question was to be pondered deeply in the tragic era that lay ahead, and eventually was reinterpreted in the New Testament by Paul in his doctrine of "justification by faith" (Rom. 1:17; Gal. 3:11).

FAITH AND NATIONALISM

Looking back over this chapter, one fact stands out above all: the rediscovery of the Mosaic heritage was accompanied by an upsurge of nationalism. Josiah's reform went far toward removing the religious influences of the Fertile Crescent which, like a cancer, had weakened Israel's vitality, making it the victim of Manasseh's reactionary policies. As in the period of the ancient Tribal Confederacy, Israel became strong when the people were loyal to their covenant pledge to Yahweh. But the Reform was infected with nationalism. The centralization of worship in the Jerusalem Temple, though it purified the land of pagan religious practices, actually led to a proud confidence that God was on the side of the people and that no evil could befall them. As we shall see in the next chapter, the pride of nationalism died hard in the turbulent events that rolled over Judah like an avalanche toward the end of the seventh century. Yet ironically, it was the revival of the covenant faith in a time of nationalism that made possible the understanding of the death of the nation. Israel was a covenant community before the rise of the nation; and the nation would have to be dissolved before people could understand again the meaning of the covenant.

---

[34] This view is maintained in an extreme fashion by Paul Humbert, *Problèmes du livre d'Habacuc* (Neûchatel: Université, 1944), who argues that the prophet used international references to veil his attack against Jehoiakim. See the discussion by Walter J. Harrelson [42], pp. 375–78, who judiciously combines both the external and internal threats.

CHAPTER 12

The Doom
of the Nation

The reform of Josiah, as we have seen, was borne on a wave of nationalism that swept through Judah during the last days of the Assyrian empire. For a while it seemed as though the people were standing on the threshold of a Golden Age like the glorious era of David's empire. But the patriots were awakened from their daydream by the shock of a swift succession of events, beginning with the untimely death of Josiah and culminating in the fall of the nation and the carrying off into exile of part of the population. Nationalism died hard during those crowded years, for many prophets flourished by preaching a comfortable message of peace when there was no peace, by promising that affairs would soon return to the good old days of national glory. These prophets won great applause at the time for their cheering message. But in the long run the deepest impression was made by the prophets whose sharp words punctured the illusions of the time and summoned people to face the realities of their history.

We are fortunate to have the lengthy testimony of two great prophets who lived through this era of national cataclysm—Jeremiah and Ezekiel. Both men came from priestly families; and although they differed greatly in temperament and outlook, they supplemented each other as had Amos and Hosea, who also prophesied in a time of national downfall. Their task was to speak to the crisis

Biblical readings: Primary attention should be given to the prophecies of Jeremiah's later career found in Jeremiah 4–25. These oracles are supplemented by the biographical narratives of chapters 26–45. The history of the period is sketched in II Kings 24–25 (paralleled in II Chronicles 36), and the mood stimulated by the fall of the nation is poignantly expressed in the book of Lamentations.

of their time by reflecting upon and reinterpreting the religious traditions that they had received and in which they stood.

THE SUFFERING PROPHET

Postponing discussion of Ezekiel until the next chapter, we shall turn our attention first to Jeremiah, whose early career we have already traced in the previous chapter. His prophetic activity spanned forty years (c. 626–587 B.C.E.), fateful years in the history of the Southern Kingdom. Later tradition tended to portray him as a "weeping prophet," a reputation that led to the invention of our word "jeremiad" for a doleful lament or complaint. But this portrait is overdrawn, for certainly Jeremiah's message had in it all the iron severity of Amos or Isaiah. Like his prophetic predecessors, Jeremiah announced that the Day of Yahweh, for which the people waited expectantly, would not be a day of victory and rejoicing, but a dark, bitter day of doom and gloom. But Jeremiah identified himself with his message and with his people in a more personal way than any other prophet. This helps to explain why we know more about Jeremiah *the man* than about any other Old Testament figure, with the possible exception of David. If Jeremiah was as staunch as "a fortified city, an iron pillar, and bronze walls" (Jer. 1:18), he was also as sensitive as a mother bereft of her children. His career was intimately tied up with the tragedy of Jerusalem, a tragedy that was intensified by the very words he felt compelled to speak in the name of Yahweh. The wound of his people cut deeply into his own heart, prompting him to mix with his prophecies of doom outcries of agony and grief (see 8:18–22). Although he was not the author of the elegies found in the book of Lamentations, which vividly reflect the mood of the time, it is appropriate that these poems were attributed to him.[1] His career was a *via crucis*—a course that led through suffering toward ultimate vindication. It is not without reason that some of Jesus' contemporaries thought that perhaps he was another Jeremiah (Matt. 16:14).

THE BOOK OF JEREMIAH

Before turning to Jeremiah's later career, let us glance briefly at the book itself. Readers who turn to it for the first time may find themselves in a maze of confusion. A modern novel on Jeremiah, like Franz Werfel's *Hearken Unto the Voice*, would tell the story in a more orderly fashion, following a chronological timeline throughout the prophet's career from beginning to end. And a modern theologian, seeking to present the prophet's message, would at least arrange the materials in a pattern according to subject or topic. But in the book of Jer-

---

[1] Several authors were evidently responsible for the book of Lamentations. Chapters 2 and 4 may have been written by eyewitnesses of the fall of Jerusalem; chapters 1 and 3 may have been inspired by the book of Jeremiah. With the exception of chapter 5, these poems are in the *qinah* or elegiac 3/2 meter (see p. 296) that Jeremiah and Ezekiel used effectively.

emiah there is no clear principle of organization or development. There is some evidence that the compilers have tried to group materials according to the early, middle, and later periods of Jeremiah's ministry; usually, however, they have not bothered to date materials in sequence or to give dates at all. And sometimes materials belonging to the same date are widely separated from each other, for instance, Jeremiah's temple sermon (Jer. 7) and the account of the audience response to it (Jer. 26). The picture is further complicated by the fact that the Greek translation of the Old Testament, the Septuagint, not only displays different readings and different arrangement of the material but also is about one-eighth shorter than the received Hebrew text.

These difficulties only indicate that the book of Jeremiah, like other prophetic literature, has undergone a complicated history before reaching its present canonical form. Fortunately, however, it is possible to provide a rough map that will enable the reader to find a way through the fifty-two chapters of the book.

1. Chapters 1–25. This section stands out as a separate block of material. In the main, it is composed of prophetic oracles, although now and then biographical or autobiographical passages are found (e.g. 1:4–19; 7:1–15; 11:1–17; 13:1–11).
2. Chapters 26–45. In contrast to the preceding section, this one is composed largely of biographical narratives about Jeremiah, interspersed occasionally with prophetic sermons. It falls into two subdivisions:
   a. Prophecies of judgment and hope (chapters 26–35). Inserted into this section is "The Little Book of Comfort" (chaps. 30–33), partly poetic material.
   b. Narratives dealing with the latest recorded events in Jeremiah's life (chaps. 36–45).
3. Chapters 46–51. This section consists of oracles against the nations. Although according to chapter 1 Jeremiah was called to be "a prophet to the nations," some of this material comes from other writers.
4. Chapter 52. The story of the fall of Jerusalem, extracted from II Kings 24:18–25:30, is fittingly placed here as a historical conclusion.

For our purpose, sections 1 and 2 are relevant, and section 1 is the more important for a first reading.[2] Notice that, in general, the distinguishing feature of section 1 is its poetic form. On the other hand, section 2 is largely in prose. Right away we are confronted with one of the major problems of the book: the relation between the poetry and the prose.

Literary critics have attacked this problem by singling out three basic types of material or "levels of tradition" in the book of Jeremiah.

A.   *Poetry of Jeremiah,* found chiefly in chapters 1–25 (section 1). Often these religious lyrics are cast in a 3/2 *qinah* meter (see Jer. 9:20–21), the mournful cadence so appropriate for expressing sorrow (as in Amos 5:2 and Lamentations). Some scholars have gone so far as to insist that Jeremiah's genuine oracles are found only in the poetic sections, in which case the symbol A stands for "authentic."

---

[2] That these are separate units of the book is suggested by the fact that the Septuagint places section C between sections A and B (that is, after 25:13).

B.   *Biographical prose,* found chiefly in chapters 26–45 (section 2), but also interspersed among the poetic materials of section 1. Many of these narratives seem to represent the memoirs of Baruch,[3] Jeremiah's faithful disciple and secretary, to whom a special oracle is directed (chap. 45) at the very end of this prose section (chaps. 26–45). Thus the symbol B stands for Baruch's biography.

C.   *Contributions by the Compiler (Redactor).* Frequently the prose sections of the book of Jeremiah resemble the language and literary style of Deuteronomy and the Deuteronomistic History, for instance in the Temple Sermon (7:1–15) or the passage about Jeremiah's support of Josiah's covenant reform (11:1–6). Indeed, Jeremiah is portrayed as a prophetic preacher of the type highlighted in Deuteronomic tradition (Deut. 18:15–22; cf. II Kings 17:13–18). Passages of this kind may well preserve the substance of Jeremiah's message, but they also show that the book in its present form has been compiled by redactors of, or akin to, the Deuteronomistic school. Hence the symbol C stands for the compiler of the book.

DEFINITION: "REDACTION CRITICISM"

Franz Rosenzweig, a distinguished philosopher of Judaism, once observed that the sign "R," used for Redactor by critical scholars, must not be underrated. The sign, he said, should be construed to mean "Rabbenu," which in Hebrew means "our master," for we are dependent on the Redactor who has given us the scriptures in their final form. In recent years more and more attention has focused on the final shaping, or redaction, of biblical books.

Redaction criticism is concerned mainly about two things. First, it wants to understand how various literary units function in the present arrangement of the biblical text. In this view, a biblical book is not thrown together haphazardly, but displays an overall structure or "architecture." Hence it is important to see the parts in relation to the whole. Secondly, redaction criticism wants to understand, if possible, the social situation in which the text was given its final shape and to which it was addressed. In this view, older traditions were brought together and updated for the purpose of speaking to a new situation in the life of the people Israel.

In the case of Jeremiah, this means that it is not enough to inquire for the historical Jeremiah, whose message is found authentically in poetic materials and is echoed in prose sections. We must also inquire into the theological message of the final form of the book given to us by the redactor, and this means that we must read particular literary units (such as the "confessions" of Jeremiah) in their given literary context. Moreover, we must inquire into the social situation of the (Deuteronomistic) redaction of the Jeremiah tradition preserved in poetic materials and refracted in prose narratives. Redaction criticism has helped us to understand that the purpose of the final level of tradition in Jeremiah (level C, which is often assigned to the Deuteronomistic redactor) was to relate Jeremiah's preaching to a new situation, that of people who had been exiled from Jerusalem in the catastrophic event of 587 B.C.E. In this view, the book of Jeremiah in its redacted and final form was not addressed just to the political realities of the state of Judah in its final days. It was a new form of proclamation: "preaching to the exiles" who had been uprooted from their homeland and needed to hear the "word of Yahweh," spoken through the prophet Jeremiah, addressed to them in their new situation.[4]

---

[3] The book of Baruch is in both the Roman Catholic canon and the Protestant Apocrypha (see Chart, pp. 4–5); it purports to have been composed by Jeremiah's disciple in 582 B.C.E., five years after the fall of Jerusalem to the Babylonians. However, the book was written much later and indeed seems to reflect the destruction of Jerusalem by the Romans in 70 C.E.

[4] This is the view of E. W. Nicholson, *Preaching to the Exiles* [365]; also J. P. Hyatt, "The

The Burning of the Prophet's Scroll

An interesting account found in Baruch's Memoirs (chapter 36) throws light on a major development in Jeremiah's preaching career: the shift from preaching orally (as reflected in poetic oracles) to a written form of proclamation.[5] The story is placed in the fourth year of King Jehoiakim (605 B.C.E.), the son of Josiah whom the Egyptians had elevated to the throne after Josiah was killed at Megiddo (see p. 387). The battle of Carchemish in the year 605 had changed the political picture, and the time was ripe for the prophet to restate his message. Earlier—possibly under the influence of rumors about commotion caused by Scythian raiders in upper Mesopotamia[6]—he had spoken vaguely of a threat from the north; now he could identify the northern foe as Babylonia. He hoped that the publication of his oracles, which up to that time had been preserved in his memory and that of his followers, would awaken the people to the seriousness of their situation and encourage them to amend their ways. With this practical purpose in mind, Jeremiah dictated the oracles he had spoken during the twenty-three years that had elapsed since his call. His secretary, Baruch, took down the dictation, writing with ink on a scroll (cf. chapter 45).

Since Jeremiah was barred from the Temple at that time, Baruch was sent in his place to read the scroll before all the people who had assembled for a fast day. Jeremiah's warning that Yahweh would display wrath against Judah by sending the Babylonian invader must have sounded like high treason. Alarmed, the royal officials advised Jeremiah and Baruch to go into hiding while the scroll was brought to the attention of King Jehoiakim. The haughty king's reaction was typical. We see him sitting in his luxurious winter palace, toasting himself before a fire burning in the brazier. As each few columns of the scroll were read, the king would reach over with his famous penknife, slash off the portion of the manuscript that had been read, and contemptuously toss it into the fire. And so it went, despite the protest of some of the princes, until the whole scroll had been shredded and burned. But this was not the end of the matter. Safe from arrest by the king, Jeremiah began his literary work all over. This time, we are told, he not only dictated the contents of the original scroll but also produced an enlarged edition, for "many similar words were added" (Jer. 36:32).

Deuteronomic Edition of Jeremiah," *Vanderbilt Studies in the Humanities*, Vol. I (Nashville, 1951), 71–95; Winifried Thiel, *Die deuteronomistische Redaktion von Jeremia 1–25*, WMANT 41 (Neukirchen-Vluyn: Neukirchener Verlag, 1973). Other scholars oppose the hypothesis of Deuteronomistic editorship, e.g., John Bright, "The Date of the Prose Sermons of Jeremiah" [360]; William Holladay, "A Fresh Look at 'source B' and 'source C' in Jeremiah," *Vetus Testamentum*, 25 (1975), 394–412; *The Architecture of Jeremiah 1–20* [378].

[5] For further discussion of this transition, see Brevard Childs, *Introduction* [37], pp. 345–347.

[6] The question of the identity of the foe from the north is reviewed by H. H. Rowley in "The Early Prophecies of Jeremiah in their Setting" [383], pp. 206–20.

Besides giving us a glimpse into one of the episodes of Jeremiah's career, this story helps us to understand how the book of Jeremiah took shape. The nucleus of the book is the enlarged scroll, which is written in the first person, as we would expect if the oracles had been taken down at dictation. These oracles are dominated by the practical purpose of awakening the people to the meaning of the Babylonian threat. To be sure, the scroll contained numerous oracles from Jeremiah's early period; for instance, the oracles found in Jeremiah 1:1–4:4 (see pp. 368–372) and possibly the account of Jeremiah's support of the Deuteronomic Reform in chapter 11. But these prophecies were reworked in the light of events that were fresh in Jeremiah's mind.[7] In addition, Jeremiah included many other oracles of more recent origin. The upshot of all this is that it would be an idle exercise of the imagination to try to reconstruct the contents of the original scroll that was burned.

Of course, the traditioning process did not come to an end once the second scroll had been dictated. We may imagine that Jeremiah paused from time to time to dictate more oracles, thus expanding the scroll still further. And other oracles and narratives, now found in section 1, were added subsequently by Baruch and later prophetic disciples. Then, toward the end of Jeremiah's career, Baruch composed his biography of Jeremiah, using the third rather than the first person. As we have seen, most of the narratives are contained in section 2, although some are found in the latter part of section 1, beginning with chapter 19. Finally, the redactor, probably of the Deuteronomistic school, gave the Jeremiah traditions final shape as a book during the period of the Exile.

IN THE REIGN OF JEHOIAKIM

The reading of Jeremiah's scroll before Jehoiakim gives us a convenient point from which to consider first his message during the early part of Jehoiakim's reign, and then to deal with his career after he was driven into hiding by the king. Let us begin by considering the experiences that were still fresh in the prophet's memory as he revised and expanded his prophecies in the year 605 (see Chronological Chart 7, p. 363).

A new phase of Jeremiah's career began in the year 609, when Josiah was killed as a result of his attempt to halt the Egyptian army at Megiddo. Josiah's immediate successor to the throne was his son Jehoahaz (referred to as Shallum in Jer. 22:10–12). The reign of Jehoahaz need not detain us, however, for he was removed from the scene by the Egyptians after only three months. In his place, the Egyptians elevated to the throne another son of Josiah, and changed his

---

[7] For instance, the references to Egypt in Jer. 2:14–19 and 2:36–37 reflect the situation during c. 609–605 B.C.E. when Judah was temporarily a vassal of Pharaoh Necho (see pp. 387–388).

name from Eliakim to Jehoiakim (II Kings 23:31–36). The fact that he was set up by a foreign conqueror shows that he was a puppet of Pharaoh Necho. His first act in office was to impose a heavy tax upon the people of Judah in order to raise a tribute for Egypt (II Kings 23:35).

In almost every respect, Jehoiakim (c. 609–598 B.C.E.) was a different man from his father, Josiah. If his father wanted to model his reign after David, then Jehoiakim's ambition was to be another Solomon. Jeremiah draws a sharp contrast between the two rulers in his oracle in Jeremiah 22:13–19. Jehoiakim was a typical tyrant—cruel, selfish, and indulgent. Like Solomon, he subjected his people to forced labor to build his magnificent palaces (22:13). To him, being a king meant living in luxurious style (22:15). Heedless of the prophetic reminder that to "know" ("recognize," "be loyal to") Yahweh is to do justice, he recklessly oppressed his people and shed much innocent blood (22:16–17). Those who opposed him courted death, for he feared neither God nor man. He was the only Judean king, so far as we know, who dared to put a prophet of Yahweh to death (26:20–23). During the brief interlude of Egyptian control of Palestine— that is, between the death of Josiah and the battle of Carchemish (c. 609–605)— Jehoiakim expediently followed a pro-Egyptian policy in order to keep himself in power.

The Temple as a Den of Robbers

Jeremiah stepped into the public arena at the beginning of Jehoiakim's reign. Perhaps as a result of his growing disillusionment about Josiah's reform program, he had been on the sidelines for several years. If so, he was at last "full of the wrath of Yahweh, weary of holding it in" (Jer. 6:11). In the first year of Jehoiakim's reign (see 26:1), Jeremiah made a bold public appeal in the Temple— the very shrine that had become the center of religious zeal as a result of the Deuteronomic Reform. His Temple Sermon is given to us in two versions. The first, found in Jeremiah's scroll (chapter 7), gives a full account of what he said on the occasion. The second, found in Baruch's Memoirs (chapter 26), gives only a brief summary of Jeremiah's message and concentrates rather on audience response. We must read both chapters together if we are to see the complete picture.[8]

In addition to playing the tyrant, Jehoiakim revived the paganism that his father had tried to eliminate. Evidently the people, disillusioned with the Deuteronomic Reform, were turning enthusiastically to their former ways. Every member of the family, we are told, had a part in making cakes for Ishtar, Queen of Heaven—the mother-goddess worshiped in Assyria and Babylonia (Jer. 7:18). The barbarous rite of child sacrifice was practiced in the Valley of Hinnom (To-

---

[8] The reason for the separation of these two accounts, which supplement one another, is probably to be found in the redactor's plan.

pheth), south of the city, and pagan abominations (idols) were set up in the Temple (verses 30–31; 19:5).[9] To make matters worse, social abominations were perpetrated in the very shadow of the Temple; and the people supposed they could get away with these crimes as long as they went through the formalities of worship (verses 8–10).

All these things rankled in Jeremiah's heart that day when he stood in the Temple court watching the people entering to worship. He began his message with a sharp summons: "Amend your ways and your doings!" Notice that Jeremiah, true to the Mosaic tradition, used the conditional "if" (verses 5–7) and appealed to covenant law, the Decalogue (verses 8–10). He challenged one of the premises of Davidic covenant theology: the Temple as the place of Yahweh's presence. There was no point in chanting glib words about the Temple being a sanctuary of refuge (cf. Ps. 46) when it had become—as Jesus was to say many years later—a den to harbor thieves (Mark 11:17). After all, what had happened to Shiloh, the central sanctuary of the old Tribal Confederacy? (See pp. 204–205.) The Temple was no bulwark of security, no guarantee that "God is with us" to see that no harm would come. For, the prophet threatened, the Temple would fall and Judah would go into exile along with the Northern Kingdom. In another oracle, Jeremiah repudiated the practice of sacrifice. Yahweh, he said, had not commanded the people to offer sacrifices on the day Israel came out of Egypt, but rather had asked for a loyal and obedient heart so that the covenant promise might be fulfilled: "I will be your God and you shall be my people" (verses 21–23). Faithfulness within the covenant relationship was fundamental.

According to chapter 26, Jeremiah's sermon created an uproar. Some people must have been shocked by the way he challenged the royal covenant theology, with its divine guarantee of support for the Davidic king and its assurance of Yahweh's presence in the Jerusalem Temple. Like some of his prophetic predecessors, he took his stand upon the covenant tradition rooted in the Exodus and the experiences of the wilderness. Had not some elders appealed to the precedent of Micah, who a hundred years before had prophesied the fall of Jerusalem and the Temple, Jeremiah would have lost his life like the hapless prophet Uriah. Even more important in saving Jeremiah from the wrath of the king was the support of Ahikam, son of Shaphan, a prince of great political influence (Jer. 26:24). More than once, a member of the family of Shaphan stood on Jeremiah's side in a time of need.

The comparison with Micah was apt, for, like other prophets who had gone before him, Jeremiah also prophesied doom (see Jer. 28:8–9). The first effect of Yahweh's word—that is, the divine intention—was "to pluck up and to break down, to destroy and to overthrow" (1:10). To be sure, judgment was not the last word, for Yahweh's intention was also "to build and to plant." But

---

[9] The same picture is presented in Ezek. 16:20–21; 20:26, 31; 23:29.

the rebuilding would come only after the destruction. "Is not my word like fire, says Yahweh, and like a hammer that breaks the rock in pieces?" (23:29).

The Balm of Gilead

Jeremiah's word of doom seemed incredible both to the king and the people. They believed that their reliance upon Egypt was only a temporary device to protect them from the storm arising out of the north (see Jer. 2:16, 18, 36–37). It is not surprising, then, that Jeremiah's greatest adversaries were the popular prophets who promised a shortcut to divine restoration without going through the valley of judgment. Like spiritual quacks, they were crying "peace, peace" when there was no peace and trying to "heal the wound of the people lightly" by remedies that did not touch the root of the trouble (6:13–15; cf. 5:12–13, 30–31; 14:13–16; 23:9–40). Jeremiah accused these prophets of lacking the proper credentials to speak, for they had not stood in "the Council of Yahweh," as had great prophets like Micaiah and Isaiah (see pp. 325–326). He said that they were filling the people with vain hopes, deceiving their hearers with lies, and stealing Yahweh's words from one another. Between them and the true order of Yahweh prophets there was no more similarity than between straw and wheat (23:28). For Yahweh's word brings not peace, but a sword—the sword that cuts like a surgeon's knife to the seat of the malignant cancer and makes possible a deep inward healing. To Jeremiah's poignant question, "Is there no balm in Gilead?" (8:22)—a region famous for its healing ointments—came the answer that Yahweh's judgment was the beginning of restoration to health.

Jeremiah agonized over the people's incurable sickness. They were, he said, a people with "a stubborn and rebellious heart" (Jer. 5:23). All Yahweh's discipline had failed. The word of the prophets had fallen on deaf ears; indeed, it had become an object of scorn to the people (6:10). With searching insight, anticipated by Hosea, Jeremiah perceived that the problem lay *within*—in the heart. To be sure, Israel's "sickness unto death" showed itself outwardly in many ways. The people were putting their trust in institutions: the Ark (3:16), the rite of circumcision (4:4), the Torah (8:8), sacrifice (7:21–26), the Temple itself (7:4). Moreover, the social bond of the covenant community was fractured. Every brother, said Jeremiah, was another deceitful Jacob (9:4–6). No one could be trusted, and oppression was heaped up like a pyramid. The people were like "well-fed stallions," each neighing for his neighbor's wife (5:8) and showing no concern for the defenseless victims of society (5:28). Blind nationalism, excited by the deceitful prophets, was rampant. And idolatry was practiced not only in the Temple but also on every high hill and under every green tree.

But these were only the outward symptoms of a problem rooted in the heart, the seat of human loyalties and devotion. Anticipating modern depth psychology, Jeremiah pointed out that the heart can cover up and justify ("rationalize") its real motives:

> The heart is deceitful above all things,
> and desperately corrupt;
> who can understand it?
> —JEREMIAH 17:9 (RSV)

Yet there is no hiding place from the God who "probes the heart" in order to repay people with "the fruit of their deeds" (17:10). The God whom Israel worships is not a god who is "at hand" (a "value" created by human need or a fancy of human wishful thinking) but the God who is "far off," transcendent, and therefore the inescapable Judge of human motives and actions (23:23–24; see the exquisite treatment of this theme in Ps. 139). In the awful exposure of divine scrutiny, the people's real condition comes to light. Yahweh's "eyes" look for truth (Jer. 5:3), for the inner integrity that is based on a true relationship to God and neighbors in the covenant. But instead, Yahweh finds inner deceit, a chronic falseness evident throughout Israel's long history in Canaan. Shifting the figure of speech, Jeremiah stresses the deep-seated and elusive nature of the problem. If one were to run through the streets of Jerusalem, like Diogenes in Athens, seeking for a single just individual, such a person could not be found (5:1–3). Indeed, things are approaching a state of chaos; for every person recklessly follows a self-determined course, like a horse wildly plunging into battle (8:6). Although the birds follow their homing instincts, Israel has no instinct for the covenant relationship (8:7). Yahweh has set a bound for the restless waves of the sea, but Israel's rebellion goes beyond all bounds (5:20–29). Indeed, Israel's sin is deeply engraved upon the heart as though with a pen of iron or a diamond point (17:1–4). The people can no more change their accustomed evil ways than Ethiopians can change their skin or the leopards their spots (13:23). Sin has become so "natural" that the people do not even know how to blush for it (8:12).

The catharsis—to use the language of psychology—had to come through crisis and catastrophe that would shock and shake the people to a new awareness. In the past, according to Jeremiah, Yahweh had shown forbearance. "Rising up early," to use the poetic expression for divine persistence, Yahweh had sent "his servants, the prophets." Moreover, Yahweh had tried the "shock treatment" of calamity with the purpose of bringing the people to their senses, but in vain. The people's hardness of heart was, according to Jeremiah, a puzzle to God; for ordinarily if somebody falls down that person rises again, or if someone turns away that one comes back (Jer. 8:4–7). Not so in Israel's case, however. Despite all warnings and chastening experiences the people had *refused* to "return" (that is, repent). At last Yahweh's patience was exhausted. "Weary of relenting" (15:6), Yahweh had resolved to pour out divine wrath upon the people, destroying their idols and shaking the foundations of their existence.

Jeremiah perceived that God is at work in human history, dealing with the recalcitrant stuff of human nature. This conviction is vividly emphasized in the oracle that Jeremiah received in the potter's house (chap. 18)—an oracle that may have formed the pungent climax of Jeremiah's scroll dictated to Baruch and, in any case, has a strategic position in the redaction of the materials.[10] Seeing a potter seated in his pit, his feet spinning the wheel and his hands deftly molding the clay, Jeremiah was reminded that Israel was like clay in the divine potter's hand. If the vessel was spoiled, owing to some imperfection or unmalleability of the material, it could be reworked into another vessel as the potter saw fit. And so it was with Israel. If a nation refused to be molded by the divine design, and insisted on following its own devices, then Yahweh would "repent" of the good planned for them and visit the nation with destruction.

Notice that the threatened catastrophe is to come as a result of human recalcitrance, not as a result of the arbitrary, capricious wrath of the potter. Again and again the prophet reminded the people that the imminent tragedy would be the consequence of their own actions:

> Your ways and your doings
>   have brought this upon you.
> This is your doom, and it is bitter;
>   it has reached your very heart.
> —JEREMIAH 4:18 (RSV)

DEFINITION: "REPENT"

A key word in Jeremiah's theological vocabulary is the verb of turning, *shûb*, found for instance in the passage cited above: Jeremiah 8:4–5.

The people's "turning" may have two meanings, the obverse and reverse of the same coin. On the one hand, it may be a "turning away"—that is, a defection from loyalty to the God of the covenant ("apostasy"), and hence a turning to some other loyalty, to some other "God-story." This meaning is suggested in 8:5: "Why does this people persist in apostasy [turning away], in continuous apostasy?" (JB).

The same passage indicates another meaning of turning: "They cling to illusion, they refuse to come back" (JB). This "coming back" is, in the positive sense of the Hebrew word, "turning around"—a return to the covenant relationship with Yahweh, specifically to the story which portrays Yahweh's liberating work and which evokes the people's response. The turning again to Yahweh, or return, therefore, is "repentance," that is, a reorientation and change of lifestyle.

In Jeremiah 18 (the parable of the potter and the clay) another Hebrew verb is used for God's "repentance" (*niham*). In this case, the idea is that God is not bound inflexibly to an announced course of action but, if the people "turn" (*shûb*, "repent" as in Jer. 18:8, 11b), there will be a free response on the divine side. Responding to the people's repentance, God will have a "change of mind" or will "relent" from bringing judgment upon them. Thus God's impending judgment is not to be identified with the inexorable Fate of Greek tragedies.

See further "Turning Away and Turning Around," in B. W. Anderson, *The Eighth Century Prophets* [329], chap. 3.

---

[10] See Kathleen M. O'Connor, *The Confessions of Jeremiah* [381], chap. 8.

In one sense, the "wrath of God" is not so much God's intervention to punish as it is *withdrawal* from a rebellious people, leaving them to suffer the destructive consequences of their own actions and attitudes. It is, one might say, a kind of self-destruction. God's sovereignty in human affairs means that people cannot live with impunity, but the punishment is only "the fruit of their devices" (6:19). Therefore, in the very passage where Jeremiah proclaims the sovereignty of the potter over the clay, his word is accompanied by an urgent plea that the people amend their ways and doings while there is still time. Divine sovereignty does not erase human responsibility.

The Foe from the North

During the reign of Jehoiakim, Jeremiah saw the judgment of God taking political shape in international developments. At the time of his call, when he had a vision of a boiling cauldron pouring out evil upon Palestine, he spoke of some foe from the north. Beginning with the battle of Carchemish in 605 B.C.E., however, the northern foe came clearly into focus: the cauldron was boiling over from the land of Babylonia.

Scattered through chapters 1–18 are a number of prophetic oracles occasioned by the advance of Babylonia, most of them from the latter part of Jehoiakim's reign, after the battle of Carchemish. The cycle in chapter 4 is an excellent example of the poems on "the foe from the north." As expressions of intense feeling, these lyrics are unsurpassed in the Old Testament. With urgent voice Jeremiah sounds the battle alarm, crying to the people to flee to the fortified cities for safety (Jer. 4:5–8). He sees the army approaching in chariots like the whirlwind and cries out to Jerusalem to repent while there is still time (5:13–18). His heart beats wildly as he hears the enemy trumpet and sees disaster suddenly overwhelm the land (5:19–22). He hears Jerusalem's death cry, like the piercing shriek of a woman in travail (4:29–31). Like Jesus later, he weeps over the fate of Jerusalem (see 8:18–9:3). Reading these moving poems, one has the impression that all the suffering of the people of Israel flowed through the channel of a single heart. No other prophet of the Old Testament period was more personally identified with people or felt more keenly the "giant agony" of their tragedy.

Included with the poems of chapter 4 is a powerful lyric on "the return of chaos." In a terrifying vision, Jeremiah sees the earth—"as if struck by a mighty nuclear bomb," as one commentator puts it—returning to chaos like that which prevailed before the Creation: the "waste and void" of Genesis 1:2.[11]

---

[11] The comment is that of Victor R. Gold, *Oxford Annotated Bible* [10], *in loco*. The expression "waste and void" in 4:23 (*tohu wa-bohu*) is exactly the same as in the Priestly creation story (Gen. 1:2). See the interpretation of Jeremiah's poem on the return of chaos by a Japanese theologian, Kosuke Koyama, *Mount Fuji and Mount Sinai* (Maryknoll, N.Y.: Orbis Books, 1985), chaps. 3 and 5.

I looked upon the earth, and lo, a chaotic waste,
  and unto the heavens, and their light was gone.
I looked on the mountains, and lo, they were quaking,
  and all the hills were trembling.
I looked, and lo, there was no human being,
  and all the birds of the sky had vanished.
I looked, and lo, the orchard land was wilderness,
  before Yahweh, before his burning wrath.
                              —JEREMIAH 4:23–26

To Jeremiah, the catastrophe was of cosmic proportions, like the Deluge of Noah's time which threatened to convert the world into pre-creation chaos. His deep sense of universal disorder is echoed in modern literature that speaks of the wasteland, the threat of "nonbeing," "The Day After," the void.

Signs of Doom

Jeremiah's words of impending doom were accompanied by signs, one of the most enigmatic of which is described in Jer. 13:1–11. According to the story, Jeremiah bought a linen waistcloth and wore it "to the Euphrates,"[12] where he hid it in a cleft of a rock. Later, when he found that the cloth was spoiled and good for nothing, he was told that Yahweh would spoil the pride of the people, even though they had clung to their God as closely as a garment. On another occasion, Jeremiah was commanded to buy a clay flask and to break it publicly in the Valley of Hinnom, the place where human sacrifice was practiced. In this way he dramatically demonstrated that Jerusalem would be broken into fragments, and that the destruction would be so great that the accursed valley would have to be used for a burial place (chapter 19). These signs or "enacted words" had an ominous significance, for Jeremiah portrayed *what Yahweh was about to do*. It is understandable that later, when Jeremiah repeated his message of doom against the Temple itself, Pashhur, the priest, seized him, flogged him, and put him in stocks for the night (20:1–6). In spite of the people's heedlessness, however, Jeremiah believed that Yahweh's word was the power that shaped the course of events. Yahweh was "watchful" to bring the divine word to pass (see 1:12, AJT).

Then came the battle of Carchemish, in which Egypt was decisively defeated and from which Babylonia emerged as the dominant world power.[13] From this fateful period comes the important prophecy of Jeremiah 25:1–13. In its present form, it is dated in the fourth year of Jehoiakim (605 B.C.E.), the same year the scroll was burned. Certain problems make it difficult to ascribe this

---

[12] It is difficult to understand this sign if it involves trips to the Euphrates (700 miles round trip). Probably Jeremiah went to Parah (modern 'Ain Farah), a short journey northeast from his home town of Anathoth. In Hebrew "to the Euphrates" and "to Parah" are spelled the same. See the commentary by John Bright [375], p. 96.

[13] Jeremiah's oracle against Egypt (Jer. 46:1–12) was delivered shortly after the battle of Carchemish.

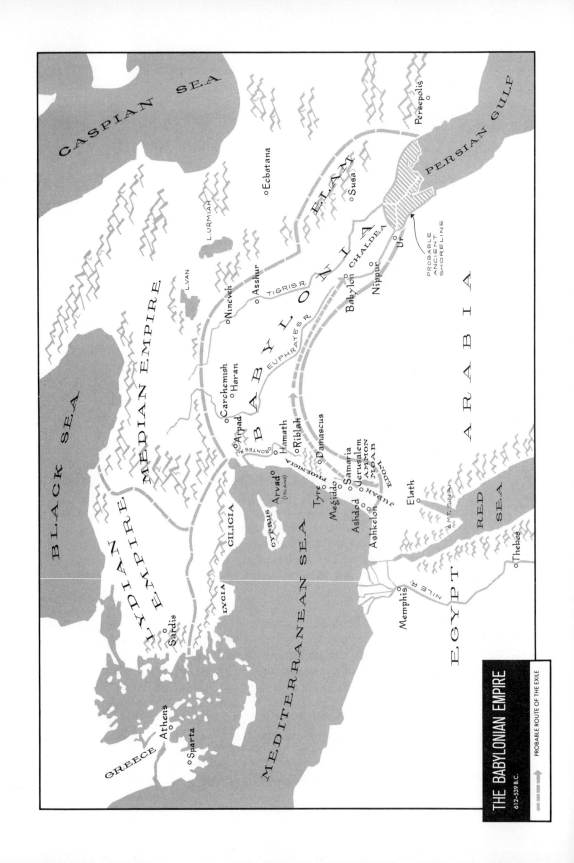

CASPIAN SEA

BLACK SEA

MEDIAN EMPIRE

LYDIAN EMPIRE

Ecbatana

LURMIAH

L.VAN

Nineveh

Asshur

TIGRIS R.

Carchemish

Haran

Arpad

ORONTES R.

Hamath

Riblah

Damascus

Sardis

LYCIA

CILICIA

CYPRUS

Arvad
(ISLAND)

PHOENICIA

Tyre

Megiddo

Samaria

Jerusalem

AMMON

MOAB

EDOM

Ashdod

Ashkelon

HVANE

Elath

MT. SINAI

Athens

Sparta

GREECE

MEDITERRANEAN SEA

EGYPT

NILE R.

Memphis

Thebes

RED SEA

ARABIA

BABYLONIA

EUPHRATES R.

CHALDEA

Babylon

Nippur

Ur

ELAM

Susa

Persepolis

PERSIAN GULF

PROBABLE
ANCIENT
SHORELINE

THE BABYLONIAN EMPIRE

612–539 B.C.

PROBABLE ROUTE OF THE EXILE

passage to Jeremiah just as it stands, and the Septuagint (Greek) version, which is much shorter, may have a greater claim to authenticity. The Greek version makes no reference to Nebuchadrezzar or Babylonia, and concludes with the words of verse 13: "I will bring upon that land [Judah] all the words which I have uttered against it, everything written in this book, which Jeremiah prophesied against all the nations." Moreover, the Greek version has the oracles against the foreign nations right after this sentence (verse 13), where they appropriately belong, rather than after Baruch's Memoirs (chapters 26–45) as in the Hebrew Bible.

Aside from these differences between the Hebrew and Greek texts, the story rings true to the message of Jeremiah. In the shorter version, this story may have been the conclusion of the scroll that Jeremiah dictated to Baruch.[14] Astonished at the people's refusal to heed the warnings of his twenty-three year ministry, the prophet announced that Yahweh would send "a family from the north" (Septuagint) to devastate the whole region and reduce Judah to utter ruin. The people would serve the conqueror for seventy years—a round number (the proverbial span of a human life) not intended to be taken literally. During this long period, the end of which would be seen by no person then living, the ordinary affairs of life would be interrupted, for Yahweh would banish "the voice of mirth and the voice of gladness, the voice of the bridegroom and the bride, the grinding of the millstones and the light of the lamp."

Evidently this dire prophecy of a Babylonian invasion, following closely in the wake of Babylonia's victory at Carchemish, was the theme of the scroll that infuriated Jehoiakim (Jer. 36:29). Certainly the king's feelings were not soothed by the announcement that he—an Egyptian vassal—would die a shameful death (36:30–31) and that, as Jeremiah said in another oracle, he would be buried "with the burial of an ass" (22:18–19). This was simply more than a king could stand.

JEREMIAH'S CONFESSIONS

We have turned in a circle back to where we started earlier: the burning of Jeremiah's scroll by Jehoiakim. The sequence of events that we have considered so far may be outlined as follows:

609 B.C.E. Death of Josiah at Megiddo
Jeremiah's Temple Sermon
605 B.C.E. The Battle of Carchemish
The burning of Jeremiah's scroll

Starting with the last episode, we have looked back over Jeremiah's ministry during these years and have considered the content of his enlarged scroll

---

[14] For the short text, see John Skinner, *Prophecy and Religion* [384], pp. 240–41.

of prophecy. Now we shall move ahead from the year 605 to the last decades of Jeremiah's career.

Hunted as a public enemy and traitor to the king, Jeremiah may have gone into seclusion for some time. From this "period of silence" may have come a remarkable series of lyrics, usually referred to as the Confessions of Jeremiah. Actually, these intimate outpourings of the prophet's restless heart, similar in type to the *Confessions* of Augustine, came from several occasions in the prophet's career. It may be that Jeremiah dictated them to Baruch during the time when he was a fugitive from Jehoiakim's police. In any event, it is appropriate for us to consider them at this point.

These personal outcries are without parallel in the writings of early Israelite prophets or, for that matter, in other religious literature of antiquity. Earlier prophets had been reticent about baring their personal conflicts. Even Hosea, who spoke out of the personal suffering of a broken marriage, receded as a person behind the message he was called to proclaim. And Amos, who expostulated with God about the heavy judgment that was about to fall upon Israel (Amos 7:1–6), did not explicitly identify with the sufferings of the people. With Jeremiah, however, it is different. Not only does he proclaim "the word of Yahweh" but, like the people to whom it is addressed, he struggles against it. He complains about his lot, cries out for vindication, and even hurls defiance at God. He undergoes the trials of faith—faith that is shadowed by doubt, rebellion, self-pity, and despair. Indeed, he has "the courage to doubt."[15]

The application of the term "confessions" to these personal prayers may lead to misunderstanding. The term may suggest a purely psychological view: the private confessions of a person's interior life with an honest-to-God frankness. Jeremiah's confessions, however, are expostulations with God that arise out of, and are essentially related to, his prophetic *office*. These prayers have been influenced by the genre of the "individual lament" found in the book of Psalms (see Chapter 16), in which a suppliant cries out of distress, expresses confidence in God, and pleads for vindication. Using language that was familiar in temple worship, Jeremiah prays to Yahweh out of the depths of the distress he experienced in the exercise of his prophetic role.

Dispersed through chapters 11–20 of the book of Jeremiah are the following laments:

1. 11:18–12:6 "Like a gentle lamb led to the slaughter"
2. 15:10–21 "Wilt thou be to me like a deceitful brook?"
3. 17:14–18 "Heal me, O Yahweh!"
4. 18:18–23 "They have dug a pit for my life"
5. 20:7–13 "A burning fire shut up in my bones"
6. 20:15–18 "Cursed be the day on which I was born"

[15] See Robert Davidson, *The Courage to Doubt* [134], chap. 7.

A Man of Strife and Contention

A key to understanding these poignant laments is given in the account of the prophet's call (Jer. 1:1–10), a passage that reverberates with overtones of the story of Moses' call (Exod. 3). The first literary unit (verses 4–8) discloses the tension between Jeremiah, the man, and his prophetic office. Shy and sensitive by nature, he recoiled from the tremendous task to which he was predestined even before birth: to be "a prophet to the nations." The second literary unit (verses 9–10) also places Jeremiah squarely in the tradition of "the prophet like Moses" to whom it is said, "I [Yahweh] will put my words in his mouth" (Deut. 18:18; cf. Jer. 1:9). The ensuing visions and their interpretation (Jer. 1:11–19) indicate the ominous message that Jeremiah was to proclaim—a message that was sure to arouse the hostility of the people. He was to set himself *against* everyone, because God's judgment was against the whole land of Judah—its kings, princes, priests, and people. "They will fight against you," the prophet was warned. Yet he was to find a deeper resource than human approval: "They shall not prevail against you, for I am with you, says Yahweh, to deliver you" (1:19, see 1:8).

Yahweh's commission went against Jeremiah's natural inclinations and sensitivities. More than anyone else, he seemed to need the affection and acceptance of his family and friends, and he probably would have been quite content to live peacefully on his ancestral estate in Anathoth. But his lot was to be that of a rejected man, "a man of strife and contention to the whole land" (Jer. 15:10), constantly surrounded by enemies, and "sitting alone" because Yahweh's hand had been laid upon him. Even marriage and children were denied him, for, according to an ominous passage in 16:1–13, Yahweh forbade him to take a wife and to have children, or even to take part in social gatherings. The prophet's isolation was to be a sign of the impending catastrophe that would disrupt all family ties and silence the voice of mirth. The anguish of loneliness lay heavily upon his heart. Throughout his career he was torn on the one hand by his natural longing for peace and companionship, and on the other by the prophetic task that catapulted him into the arena of conflict. It is the Confessions, above all, that bear witness to the sufferings involved in being a prophet of Yahweh and the prophet's passionate plea for vindication. The prayer for vindication is not a plea for personal triumph but for the triumph of the cause that the prophet represents.

Jeremiah's Vindication

The first confession apparently harks back to Jeremiah's early career. The passage may belong to the time of the Deuteronomic Reformation and may reflect the fierce animosity of the people of his home town, Anathoth, who were aroused, perhaps, by his advocacy of a reform program that threatened to put local priests out of their jobs (see p. 385). The men of Anathoth plotted against his life, warning him not to prophesy in the name of Yahweh lest he die by their hand (11:21). Even the members of Jeremiah's immediate family joined in the conspiracy (12:6). This treachery evoked from the prophet a prayer for vengeance upon his persecutors and a passionate confession of his own innocence and integrity. To him it seemed inconceivable that Yahweh, who knows people's motives and judges their actions, would allow the wicked to prosper and even to get away with murder! Just as Habakkuk received an answer to his complaint (see above, pp. 388–390), so in this case Yahweh responded to Jeremiah's lament. He was promised that vindication would come in Yahweh's good time, but in the meantime he should realize that far greater ordeals lay ahead:

> If you race with foot-runners and they exhaust you,
> How then can you compete with horses?
> If you are secure only in a tranquil land,
> How will you fare in the jungle of the Jordan?
> —JEREMIAH 12:5 (TNK)

It was during the reign of Jehoiakim, as we have seen, that the plots against Jeremiah's life mounted in fury. After his Temple Sermon he narrowly escaped with his life, and his later message in the Temple court prompted Pashhur to put him in jail for the night. Finally, Jeremiah was forced to hide from Jehoiakim's wrath. The fourth confession specifically refers to plots against his life that were occasioned by his alleged subversive activity against all the religious leaders—priests, prophets, and sages (Jer. 18:18). Incensed that they should treat him thus when he had interceded on their behalf before Yahweh, Jeremiah uttered a merciless prayer that Yahweh not forgive them and that they be destroyed in divine anger.

These are the fierce outbursts of a deeply wounded heart. In another confession (Jer. 15:20), the prophet protests violently against his destiny, like Hamlet bemoaning his fate that the times were out of joint and that he was born to set them right (Jer. 15:20). Jeremiah's faith had brought him to the very brink of despair, to serious doubt about Yahweh's righteous government of the world. In the wild tumult of his spirit he cries out that Yahweh has deceived him, like a deceitful Palestinian wadi (brook) that overflows with water during the heavy spring rains and then quickly dries up (15:18). He accuses Yahweh of having overpowered him, making him a laughingstock all day long and filling him with an inward fire that would not allow him to be silent (20:7–9). Finally, in the deepest midnight of his being, he curses the day of his birth (20:14–18) and castigates his mother for having borne him as ''a man of strife and contention to the whole land'' (15:10).

Few individuals have suffered so deeply, and we must be careful not to criticize too easily the passionate queries and protests that Jeremiah hurled at God. Yet his prayers—like so many human utterances—express the self-pity and even the self-righteousness that often arise when a person's faith is put to the severest test. His question, ''Why does this happen to *me?*'' suggests that he had been badly treated after all the sacrifices he had made for Yahweh's sake. He had not sat in the company of merrymakers, nor had he committed any injustice in borrowing or lending. He was innocent, "like a gentle lamb led to the slaughter." And self-pity is only the other side of self-righteousness. Hence Jeremiah pleads his case to the avenging God, hoping that his own righteousness would be vindicated and that the unrighteousness of his persecutors would be punished (11:20; 12:1–3; 17:17–18; 18:19–23; 20:11–12).

The second confession, like the first, contains Yahweh's answer to Jeremiah's complaint. Yahweh rebuked the prophet, for his bitter lament was based on a self-centered attitude—the very attitude he had criticized in other people! The prophet who had summoned the people to repent (or to "return" to Yahweh) himself stood in need of inward purification:

> At that Yahweh answered me as follows:
>   "If you repent, I'll restore you
>   to serve me once more.
>   If you mix not the cheap and the precious,
>   as my mouth you shall be.
>   Let *them* come over to you;
>   Don't *you* go over to them.
>   Then before this people I'll make you
>   An impregnable wall of bronze.
>   Attack you they will—
>   Overcome you they can't;
>   For with you am I
>   to help you and save you—Yahweh's word.
>   From the grasp of the wicked I'll snatch you,
>   From the clutch of the ruthless release you."
>   —JEREMIAH 15:19–21[16]

It is noteworthy that after these first two confessions, no other answers from Yahweh come. The third confession ends with a plea for divine vengeance upon Jeremiah's persecutors, the fourth concludes by asking God not to forgive the enemies, and the fifth, after a similar prayer for vindication, seems to end with a song of thanksgiving for deliverance (Jer. 20:13). The final poem, if this is included in the sequence, ends dismally with Jeremiah, like Job, cursing the day of his birth. What are we to make of these confessions as a whole?

One way to deal with this question is to regard the confessions by themselves—as a collection of prophetic prayers that once circulated independently. In the view of one interpreter, when these laments are read in succession, they seem to trace a *via dolorosa*—"a road which leads step by step into ever greater despair" and which "threatens to end in some kind of metaphysical abyss."[17] Jeremiah's cross, so to speak, is eclipsed with darkness—the unanswered ques-

---

[16] Translation by John Bright, *Jeremiah* [375], p. 107.

[17] Gerhard von Rad, *Theology*, II [142], 204. See the entire discussion of the Confessions, pp. 201–206.

tion of his own prophetic suffering and the suffering of the people with whom he is identified. The final poem, in which he curses the day of his birth, has the effect of a cry of dereliction: "My God, why have you forsaken me?" (Ps. 22:1, echoed by Jesus on the cross, Mark 15:34).

Another interpretation swings to the opposite pole: "As a collection of poems, the confessions move toward greater praise of Yahweh and certainty about the triumph of the prophetic word."[18] This view is especially appealing when the confessions are read in the context given by the redactor of the Jeremiah traditions. During his career Jeremiah often must have wondered whether he really was a true prophet of Yahweh—especially when the popular prophets had the ear of the people. On one occasion, as we shall see presently, he was publicly humiliated by a prophet from Gibeon, a certain Hananiah, who made just the opposite prophecy regarding the return of the Davidic king and the temple treasures from Babylon (Jer. 28). However, the redactor, who compiled the Jeremiah traditions during the exilic period, knew that Jeremiah's word of doom against Jerusalem had been fulfilled and hence viewed the confessions as testimony to the vindication of Yahweh's word and of Yahweh's prophet (cf. II Chron. 36:20–21).

At whatever level of tradition the Confessions functioned, however, they brought the suffering of a prophet into the center of the prophetic message. As we have said, these poems were not private prayers or soliloquys. Rather, they served as a public witness to the prophet's commission as one who, in a special way, was called to walk through "the valley of deep darkness" (Ps. 23:4) with the divine assurance "I am with you" and in the confidence that vindication lay ahead. Indeed, Yahweh was personally involved in the suffering of the people that was typified by Jeremiah's anguished experience. As a distinguished Jewish philosopher has said, "the fundamental experience of the prophets is a fellowship with the feelings of God, a sympathy with the divine pathos."[19] In a profound sense Jeremiah's suffering was a participation in God's suffering, so much so that God's concern became his concern and God's pathos, whether anger or love, flowed through his whole life and thought.

IN THE REIGN OF ZEDEKIAH

Jehoiakim could afford to display contempt for Jeremiah's scroll, because there seemed to be no immediate threat to the security of his throne. The Babylonian king, Nabopolassar, had died shortly after the battle of Carchemish, and Nebuchadrezzar, the crown prince who had led the army to victory, returned to Babylon to assume the throne. About the year 601 B.C.E. his army swept through

---

[18] Kathleen O'Connor, *The Confessions* [381], chap. 9, part ii. This view requires excluding the final poem, Jeremiah's curse of his birth, from the original collection.

[19] Abraham J. Heschel, *The Prophets* [315], p. 26. The theme of the divine pathos is treated at various points in this important book.

Palestine to the border of Egypt—an invasion that evoked some of Jeremiah's poems on the foe from the north. In the battle against Egypt, heavy casualties were suffered by both sides, and Nebuchadrezzar's crippled army had to return to Babylonia. The defeat of Babylonia and the weakness of Egypt gave Jehoiakim the opportunity he had been waiting for. In the year 600, he made a reckless bid for independence by withholding tribute to Babylonia. This rebellion was an invitation to Nebuchadrezzar to strike (II Kings 24:1-7).[20] (See Chronological Chart 8, p. 412.)

The Good and Bad Figs

Because Nebuchadrezzar was unable to attend to Judah immediately, he first incited raiders from neighboring peoples to devastate the land. During these disturbances Jehoiakim died, leaving his eighteen-year-old son, Jehoiachin, to pay the penalty for his father's political folly.[21] The Deuteronomistic historian, in typical fashion, charges Jehoiachin with doing evil as his father had done, despite the fact that his short reign hardly gave him a chance to do much of anything. In 598-597 B.C.E., Nebuchadrezzar mobilized his army for a full-scale invasion of Judah; and Jehoiachin, after only three months on the throne, was forced to capitulate. The Temple and royal treasuries were emptied, and the young king and his queen mother were taken prisoners to Babylonia. Into exile with the king went the leading figures of Judah, including, as we shall see, a prophet named Ezekiel. Thus began the first chapter in the Babylonian Exile (II Kings 24:10-17).

Nebuchadrezzar now placed Josiah's youngest son, Mattaniah, on the throne of Judah, changing his name to Zedekiah. Under this king, the last member of the Davidic dynasty to rule in Judah, Jeremiah spent the rest of his prophetic career in Jerusalem. A good deal of the material in chapters 1-25, especially chapters 21-24, reflects Zedekiah's reign (c. 597-587), as does most of the material in Baruch's Memoirs found in chapters 26-45.

In contrast to the despotic Jehoiakim, Zedekiah was mild and benevolent. However, he was a weak and vacillating ruler, easily swayed by the advice of those around him. Although this new situation gave the princes a chance to control public policy in their own selfish interests, it also presented Jeremiah with a golden opportunity. Now that the tyrant was dead and a more benevolent regime had been inaugurated, the prophet could appear in public with new prestige, for his prophecies had been confirmed by history. On several occasions, Zedekiah sought the prophet's counsel behind closed doors, and evidently would have liked to follow it had he been more courageous. One can

---

[20] For a discussion of the historical developments during the last days of Judah, see David Noel Freedman, "The Babylonian Chronicle," *Biblical Archaeologist*, XIX (1956), 50-60. Reprinted in *The Biblical Archaeologist Reader*, I [100], 113-27.

[21] Jehoiachin is otherwise referred to as Jeconiah or Coniah. See Jeremiah's oracle in Jer. 22:24-28.

Chronological Chart 8

B.C.E.	Egypt	Palestine		Mesopotamia
		Judah		Babylonia
600		THE BABYLONIAN EMPIRE		
		Jehoiachin (Jeconiah), 3 mos., 598–597		Nebuchadrezzar, 605/4–562
		First Deportation to Babylonia, 597		
	Apries (Hophra),	Zedekiah (Mattaniah), 597–587		
	589–570	FALL OF JERUSALEM		
		SECOND DEPORTATION, 587		
		BABYLONIAN EXILE		
		Ezekiel, c. 593–573		
				Nabonidus, 556–539
				(his son: Belshazzar)
				RISE OF PERSIA
				Cyrus II, 550–530
				Defeat of Media, c. 550
				Invasion of Lydia, c. 546
		(*Second Isaiah*, c. 540)		Conquest of Babylon,
				c. 539
		Edict of Cyrus, 538		FALL OF BABYLON, 539
		THE EMPIRE OF PERSIA		
		THE RESTORATION		
		JUDAH		
	Conquest by	Return of exiles		Cambyses, 530–522
	Persia, 525	Rebuilding of Temple, 520–515		Darius I, 522–486
		(*Haggai*)		
500		(*Zechariah*)		

feel sympathetic toward Zedekiah and wish that he had appeared in a quieter period of Judah's history. Notice that Jeremiah's oracles against the royal house (22:1–23:6) did not include Zedekiah among the kings denounced for oppression and injustice. Rather, by a play on words, Jeremiah may have found in the name of Zedekiah (which in Hebrew means ''Yahweh is my righteousness'') the suggestion that the messianic king of the future would have a similar royal name: ''Yahweh is our righteousness'' (33:16).[22]

Bereft of its first citizens, Judah was only a shadow of its former self. The cream of the leadership—the nobility, the artisans, the highest military ranks—had been shipped off to Babylonia. The nation was crippled—at the very time when the need for resourceful leadership and stable traditions was greatest. Into this vacuum moved a new nobility, ill-equipped for the heavy responsibilities

---

[22] Passages which anticipate a coming Davidic ''messiah,'' such as 23:5–6, 30:9, and 33:14–26, are often regarded as later additions to the book of Jeremiah. It may well be, however, that Jeremiah looked forward to a future ruler, perhaps one of the Davidic line, who would arise from the people (30:21).

Deportation of Prisoners of War, *a scene from the palace of Tiglath-pilesar III (745–727 B.C.E.). As was customary in antiquity, the city was set on a hill and was fortified with double walls and turreted towers. The inscription identifies the city as Astartu, perhaps biblical Ashtaroth (Deut. 1:4). Scenes like this were duplicated by the Babylonians, who perpetuated the dread Assyrian policy of taking conquered people into exile.*

of the hour and even less capable of perceiving the religious meaning of the crisis. Governed by a short-sighted nationalism and swayed by the emotional appeal of prophetic demagogues, these new leaders hastened the downfall of the nation (compare Ezekiel 11). Jeremiah saw no hope in people of such poor grade!

In a vision (chap. 24) he saw two baskets of figs placed before the Temple. One basket, containing good figs, ripe and freshly picked, represented the exiles whom Nebuchadrezzar had carried away. According to Jeremiah, the future lay with them, for they would be restored to the land as Yahweh's covenant people. By contrast, the other basket, containing figs so bad they could not be eaten, represented Zedekiah, his nobles, and the remnant of people left in the land. Yahweh, said the prophet, would drive them out and make them a horror to all the kingdoms of the earth. Later on, Jeremiah sent a letter to the Babylonian exiles (chap. 29) in which he advised them to settle down, build houses, raise families, and even pray for the hostile regime under which they were living.

> Seek the welfare of the city to which I have exiled you, and pray to Yahweh on its behalf, for in its welfare you will find your welfare.
>
> —JEREMIAH 29:7

Contrary to popular prophets who were promising a quick return to the homeland, Jeremiah told the exiles to count on staying in the foreign land for a long time—until "seventy years are completed for Babylon" (29:10; cf. 25:11–12). Jeremiah saw the hope of Israel in these displaced persons, for, as he wrote in the letter, Yahweh had plans for them—"plans for welfare and not for evil, to give you a future and a hope" (29:11).

Plotting for Revolution

Zedekiah was under terrific pressure to break with Babylon. The new nobility was pro-Egyptian, and saw in Necho, or in his successor Psammetichus II, who came to the throne four years after Nebuchadrezzar's invasion (594 B.C.E.), the political potential that might restore a balance of power to the Fertile Crescent and allow Judah and other small nations to regain independence. Throughout this period, Egypt, following its ancient foreign policy, was stirring up discontent among these kingdoms. Moreover, the popular prophets in Judah, like the ancient ecstatics during the time of Micaiah, were beating the drums of nationalism. So it is not surprising that in the fourth year of Zedekiah's reign—the year of the accession of Psammetichus II—Egyptian agents encouraged the formation of an anti-Babylonian coalition consisting of Edom, Moab, Ammon, and Phoenicia. Envoys were sent to Zedekiah to persuade him to throw in his lot with the revolutionary movement (Jer. 27:3).

Speaking with an accent similar to Isaiah's in the Assyrian period (see pp. 343–347), Jeremiah condemned the conspiracy. His word to the envoys was accompanied by a sign. At the command of Yahweh, according to the narrative in chapter 27, he made thongs and yoke bars and put them on his neck, thus dramatizing his prophecy that it was Yahweh's will for the nations to submit to Babylonia. He proclaimed to the conspirators that Yahweh, who created the earth and all that is in it, is sovereign in the affairs of history and therefore can give the earth into the temporary control of a chosen agent. For the time being, Jeremiah declared, Nebuchadrezzar was Yahweh's "servant" (Jer. 27:6–7). Therefore, to revolt against Babylonia was actually to fight against God. His message to Zedekiah and to the leaders of the people was this: "Serve the king of Babylon and live. Why should this city become a desolation?"

In a sense, this was a wiser political policy than the reckless nationalism of the Judean leaders. Jeremiah, however, did not view the situation in terms of ordinary politics. He was not a collaborationist who wanted to see his country under foreign domination, nor was he a pacifist who was opposed to any kind of war on principle. Rather, he saw the crisis as God's sovereign activity in history for the purpose of overthrowing and rebuilding, of judgment and renewal. Therefore the people were not confronted with a choice between two political alternatives—that is, whether to follow a pro-Egyptian or pro-Babylonian policy—but with a decision of faith that called for repentance and utter reliance upon God. Jeremiah's message was either too subtle or too offensive for the people of Judah, however. It made no political sense. Even when he had the ear of Zedekiah, he was misunderstood or repudiated. His advice that Judah should surrender to Babylonia brought him into head-on conflict with the popular prophets, who were saying that Nebuchadrezzar's punitive measure of 597

B.C.E. was only a temporary setback, that the treasures taken from the Temple would soon be brought back, and that life would return to normal (see Jer. 27:12–22). This easy optimism, said Jeremiah, was based on a lie. The popular prophets had not stood in "the Council of Yahweh." They were filling the people with vain hopes and speaking "visions of their own minds, not from the mouth of Yahweh" (see the oracles against the prophets: 23:9–32).

Jeremiah's Clash with the Popular Prophets

Baruch has given us a vivid account of the clash between Jeremiah and the popular prophets, who were evidently attached to the royal court (Jer. 28). In the very year in which the foreign envoys came to talk Zedekiah into joining the anti-Babylonian movement, the prophet Hananiah challenged Jeremiah publicly in the Temple. An advocate of Davidic covenant theology, Hananiah announced that Yahweh would break the yoke of the king of Babylon, and that within two years the Temple treasures and the exiles, including Jehoiachin (Jeconiah), would be brought back. Evidently Hananiah and his prophetic colleagues still believed that the exiled Jehoiachin—instead of his uncle Zedekiah, whom Nebuchadrezzar had elevated to the throne—was the legitimate king of Judah; they pinned their hopes for national revival on his return. Jeremiah's sarcastic response was, in effect: Would that this were true! He reminded Hananiah and the assembled people that one thing had characterized Yahweh's prophets through the years: they all prophesied doom.

> The prophets who preceded you and me from ancient times prophesied war, famine, and pestilence against many countries and great kingdoms.
> —JEREMIAH 28:8 (RSV)

Any prophet who departed from this tradition and prophesied peace must accept the burden of proof. His prophecy must stand the test of historical reality. Incensed, Hananiah dramatically took the yoke bars, which Jeremiah was still wearing on his neck as a prophetic sign, and broke them before the people, repeating that in two years Yahweh would break the yoke of the king of Babylon from the neck of all the nations, and restore the exiled king to his rightful throne. Not to be outdone, Jeremiah proceeded to make a yoke of iron, for, he said, Yahweh had forged "an iron yoke of servitude to Nebuchadrezzar." The yoke could not be broken by human effort because the Babylonian king was the instrument of God's purpose. And it was futile to fight against God! (cf. Acts. 5:39).

The Siege of Jerusalem

For various reasons, including perhaps the influence of Jeremiah, Zedekiah did not join the conspiracy in 594 B.C.E. But the political restlessness continued to

A Reconstruction of Lachish, one of the largest cities of Judah, here shown from its west side. The flat summit of the mound, covering some 18 acres, was surrounded by double walls, the higher one about 20 feet and the lower one about 13 feet thick. The fortified city was conquered and burned by Nebuchadrezzar in 589 B.C.E. The Lachish Letters, written to the commander of Lachish by an officer of a nearby garrison, were found in a guard room near the city's outer gate.

mount, reaching its peak in the year 588, when a new Egyptian monarch, Apries (called Hophra in Jer. 44:30), came to the throne. Hophra's predecessor had confined himself to stirring up intrigue in Palestine, Phoenicia, and Transjordan, but Hophra revived the aggressive policy of Necho and began to organize an expedition into Asia. This turn of events gave new hope to the nations that were chafing under the Babylonian yoke. Revolution broke out anew, and this time the centers of the revolt were Ammon and Judah. Nebuchadrezzar moved swiftly to put down the revolution, and established military headquarters at Riblah, Syria, on the Orontes River. In deciding whether to attack Ammon or Judah first, he resorted to divination, according to a vivid description in Ezekiel (Ezek. 21:18–23). In the year 588 Nebuchadrezzar's army laid siege to Jerusalem.

From this period come the Lachish Letters, found by archaeologists during expeditions between 1932 and 1938.[23] These inscribed fragments contain, among other things, references to military activity, including the sending of fire signals,

[23] See Pritchard, *Ancient Near Eastern Texts* [1], pp. 321–22 for a translation of these letters.

in the vicinity of Lachish and Azekah (see Jer. 34:6–7) and throw light on conditions in the country during the Babylonian invasion. An even more vivid picture of the sufferings experienced during the siege of Jerusalem is given in the lyrical laments of the book of Lamentations, especially chapters 2 and 4.[24]

During the siege, Jeremiah never wavered in his conviction that the only course of action was surrender to Babylonia. This was the counsel that Zedekiah received when he sent a messenger to Jeremiah while the siege was on (chap. 21). The king was hopeful that Yahweh would perform a miracle and make Nebuchadrezzar withdraw, as had happened during Sennacherib's siege in Isaiah's time (701 B.C.E.). But he received no comfort from the prophet. Jeremiah said that Yahweh, the Divine Warrior, would fight against the city "with outstretched hand and strong arm, in anger, and in fury, and in great wrath." Military resistance was futile. He even advised the citizens to desert to the Babylonians if they wanted to escape with their lives:

> Behold, I set before you the way of life and the way of death. Whoever stays in this city shall die by the sword, by famine, and by pestilence; but whoever goes out and surrenders to the Chaldeans who are besieging you shall live and shall have his life as a prize of war.
>
> —JEREMIAH 21:8–9

Zedekiah was desperate. Hoping to gain the favor of Yahweh, he tried to reinstate one feature of Deuteronomic law that had long been ignored: the prohibition against enslaving a fellow-Hebrew (see Deut. 15:12–18). According to Baruch's account in chapter 34, the king made a covenant with the people in Jerusalem to release all slaves, and the covenant was sealed by the ancient ceremony of cutting a calf in two and passing between the two halves (Jer. 34:18–19; cf. Gen. 15:12–18). The upper class was undoubtedly motivated more by economic considerations than by religious conviction, for the emancipation meant that slave-owners would not have to provide slaves with food when rations were short. But when the political situation took a turn for the better, with the advance of Pharaoh Hophra's forces and the temporary lifting of the Babylonian siege (37:5), the slaves were promptly taken back. To Jeremiah this was final proof, if more proof was needed, of the people's violation of the covenant, a violation for which they would suffer the judgment of God.

Jeremiah's Imprisonment

The withdrawal of the Babylonian army to face the troops of Pharaoh Hophra seemed to be a hopeful sign (chap. 37). Again Zedekiah sent a messenger to Jeremiah, this time asking the prophet to pray to Yahweh on behalf of the people. But again, Jeremiah's response was infuriating. The Babylonian army, he

---

[24] See the discussion by Norman K. Gottwald, *Studies in the Book of Lamentations* [389]; also Bertil Albrektson, *Lamentations* [388].

said, would return, and even if the Babylonians were left with only wounded soldiers in their ranks, they would rise up and destroy Jerusalem! This was the last straw. Jeremiah was clearly too dangerous to be left at large. As the princes later said to the king, in words that are used also in one of the Lachish Letters, the prophet was "weakening the hands" of the soldiers and the people by advising capitulation and even desertion to Babylonia (Jer. 38:4–5).[25] So, as Jeremiah was going out to his home town of Anathoth on business, he was arrested, beaten, and thrown into prison (37:11–15). The pretext for the arrest was that Jeremiah was practicing what he preached: he was deserting to the Babylonians.

The scene that follows (Jer. 37:16–21) is filled with pathos. The pitiful king, suspecting that Jeremiah might be right, yet not daring to go against the princes, summoned the prophet from his prison cell and brought him into his presence. Instinctively one feels sorry not for Jeremiah but for Zedekiah, "a king, but much more bound than the prisoner who stands before him."[26] It was the king who was cowardly—a helpless puppet of his princes and a prisoner of circumstances. In the last hours, when darkness was falling upon Judah, he needed the help of the prophet. The meeting took place in secret. "Is there any word from Yahweh?" the king whispered, doubtless knowing that Jeremiah would give the same word he had been proclaiming day in and day out. This time Jeremiah spoke in a mild and friendly tone, tempered with the firm reminder that historical events had not vindicated the popular prophets. Zedekiah seems to have been almost persuaded. Yielding to the prophet's request to be moved to another jail, Zedekiah transferred him to the court of the guard.

Once again the princes intervened. Fearful that Jeremiah's words would ruin the morale of soldiers and people, to say nothing of undermining their own position, they demanded that he be put to death (chap. 38). Lacking the moral courage to be a king, Zedekiah yielded with the pathetic words: "Behold, he is in your hands; for the king can do nothing against you." So the princes let Jeremiah down by ropes into a cistern used to catch water during the rainy season, and there he was left to die in the mire. However, he was rescued by an Ethiopian eunuch who, at the king's orders, drew him out of the pit and restored him to the court of the guard.

Once more Zedekiah sent for Jeremiah (Jer. 38:14–28) and another secret conference took place, but with the same result. So far as we know, this was the last time the prisoner stood before the king. Shortly afterward, the Babylonian army made a breach in the city wall and poured through to destroy the Temple, burn the city, and carry off many of the population into exile, leaving "some of the poorest of the land to be vinedressers and plowmen" (II Kings 25:12). The story of Zedekiah was tragic to the bitter end. Trying to flee from Jerusalem, he was overtaken on the plain of Jericho and taken prisoner to Ne-

[25] See Lachish Ostracon No. VI; above, footnote 23.
[26] The words are those of Bernhard Duhm, quoted by J. P. Hyatt, *Interpreter's Bible*, V [16], 1072.

buchadrezzar's headquarters in Riblah. His sentence was terrible beyond words: his last sight was the execution of his own sons. Then his eyes were put out and he was carried in chains to Babylon. On orders from Nebuchadrezzar, Jeremiah was released from prison (chap. 39).

BEYOND THE DAY OF DOOM

At the time of his call, Jeremiah realized that the word of Yahweh had the double aspect of judgment and renewal, doom and promise. As the determining power in human affairs, the divine word was released through the prophet both "to wreck and to ruin" and "to build and to plant." Much of Jeremiah's preaching, especially in the days when people were seeking the protection of false securities, was devoted to announcing the day of doom. But he never lost sight of the truth that God's purpose was not merely to destroy and overthrow. Jeremiah understood that the ground had to be swept clean of false foundations so that God might build and plant anew (see Jer. 24:6; 42:10; 45:4). So he would have been at odds with his deepest conviction and with the great prophets who preceded him had he not kept his eyes steadily on the vision of the New People and the New Age that lay on the other side of catastrophe. This theme of hope is prominent in a section of the book of Jeremiah that is often called "The Little Book of Comfort" (chapters 30–33).[27]

Jeremiah's Purchase of His Family Estate

One episode stands out clearly as the key to Jeremiah's message. Chapter 32, whose authenticity is beyond question, takes us back to the time when Jeremiah was imprisoned lest his words undercut the war effort. The Babylonian army was pounding at the walls of Jerusalem. Bread was so scarce that the people had resorted to cannibalism (Lam. 4:10). Death stalked the streets and came in at the windows (Jer. 9:21). It was only a matter of hours until the sure doom would fall, "pitiless and dark." Clearly this was no time to think of the future, for most people, in despair, felt that there would be no tomorrow for Judah. Jeremiah did something at this point that must have seemed like sheer madness. Word was brought to him that, as the next of kin, he had an opportunity to buy his cousin's field in the family city of Anathoth, which lay in territory under enemy control. While he was still in prison, he carried out the transaction according to the proper legal form and had the deeds put away in safekeeping. To him, the invitation to acquire the land was a sign from Yahweh that the people Israel would be given a future in the Promised Land, that "houses and fields and vineyards shall be possessed again in the land." This was the same promise

---

[27] Some of the material in this section (for instance the oracles in chapter 33) comes from later Jeremianic tradition.

Jeremiah had given the exiles in his letter, only now he expanded the promise to include others who would undergo a baptism by fire and suffering on the occasion of the destruction of Jerusalem.

The New Community

Jeremiah is often called the prophet of individualism—a dubious tribute, if we have in mind the individualism of our own culture. Often we glorify the "rugged individualist" or the "lone eagle"—the person who acts and lives by private courage and personal faith. In this sense, Jeremiah was certainly not an individualist. True, he knew that in times of tragedy, when the whole social order was shattered, persons may sense with their whole being their utter reliance upon God. This kind of personal faith is magnificently expressed in his Confessions. However, Jeremiah did not advocate an individualism detached from the traditions of a people, separated from the covenant community. Even in his isolation he knew that individuals have access to God and experience "healing" or salvation only within a community. Hence when Jeremiah lifted his eyes to the horizon of God's future, he spoke of a New Community. The deepest cleavage of the history of the people—the tragic separation of the "house of Israel" and the "house of Judah"—would be overcome. As in the Tribal Confederacy of old, though on a higher plane, the people would become one in their one loyalty to the one God who had redeemed them (Jer. 31:27–30).

It is not surprising, then, that some of the oracles now found in chapters 30 and 31 are addressed to Ephraim, the "house of Israel" that had gone into defeat and exile in an earlier period. To the people of the defunct Northern Kingdom is given this promise:

> A people that survived the sword
>   found grace in the wilderness.
> Israel marched to his rest;
>   Yahweh appeared to him from afar.
> I have loved you with an everlasting love,
>   therefore I extend loyalty [ḥésed] to you.
> Once more I will build you, and you will be rebuilt,
>   O Virgin Israel.
>   —JEREMIAH 31:2–4b

Rachel, the ancestress of Northern Israel, is heard weeping bitterly for her children and is asked to stop crying, for "there is hope for your future" (31:15–22):[28]

---

[28] On this intriguing passage, see B. W. Anderson, "'The Lord Has Created Something New': A Stylistic Study of Jer. 31:15–22," *Catholic Biblical Quarterly* 40 (1978), 463–478; reprinted in *A Prophet to the Nations* [382], pp. 367–380. See also the illuminating essay by Phyllis Trible, "The Gift of a Poem: A Rhetorical Study of Jeremiah 31:15–22," *Andover Newton Quarterly* 71 (1977), 271–280.

Isn't Ephraim my precious son,
  a child in whom I delight,
For as often as I speak against him,
  I am still very much concerned for him.
Therefore I yearn for him with my being,
  I am filled with compassion for him,
                the oracle of Yahweh.
                    —JEREMIAH 31:20

These passages echo Hosea's message of Yahweh's love that would not let the people go (Hosea 11:8). And as Hosea spoke near the end of the Northern Kingdom, so Jeremiah stood on the brink of the abyss into which the Southern Kingdom was to plunge, affirming that Yahweh's love, working through the discipline of judgment, would make a new beginning for both Israel and Judah. It was a time of deep distress, Jeremiah said, and yet *out of it* the people would be saved (Jer. 30:7).

The New Covenant

This vision of the restored community of Israel is profoundly expressed in the prophecy of the new covenant (Jer. 31:31–34). This prophecy was stamped more indelibly upon later prophetic tradition than anything else Jeremiah said. Eventually it gave the name to the canon of Christian writings (New Testament means "New Covenant"). Like a finely cut jewel, this prophecy reflects light from several facets. Notice, first of all, that the new covenant, like the old, will rest upon the initiative and authority of God. Israel's faith will be a response to what God does, not a bilateral bargain between equal partners. This is the meaning of the words, "I will make. . . . "

Second, this covenant will not be like the Mosaic covenant, for the history of the people had shown that to be a broken covenant. Even the attempt of the Deuteronomic Reformation to restore the Mosaic covenant had failed—a failure that must have been the background of Jeremiah's prophecy. History as it had been known—the history of the broken covenant—will come to an end and a new kind of history will be inaugurated.

Third—and this is the paradox—the new covenant will be new in the sense that it will fulfill the original intention of the Sinai covenant. The meaning of the original covenant had been eclipsed by religious ceremonies and written laws, as though God intended that the Law should be written on tablets of stone deposited in the Ark. In the new covenant, however, the Torah will be written upon the heart, the inward center of the being. It will find expression in a personal response to the liberating God who says, "Obey my voice."

Fourth, the new covenant will bring into being a new community, Yahweh's *people*. "I will be their God and they shall be my people" (verse 33)—

this, as we have seen repeatedly, is the characteristic formula of the covenant (cf. Jer. 24:7; 32:39–40; etc.). Verse 31 correctly interprets it as embracing "the house of Israel and the house of Judah"—that is, the whole people that Yahweh brought out of Egypt. Individualism is far from Jeremiah's mind, for he stresses that this covenant formula will be true, personally true, for each member of the community from the least to the greatest. Because Yahweh will bring about a change of human nature, by giving a new heart (will), there will be a permanent harmony between Israel's will and Yahweh's will. Indeed, no longer will it be necessary to have religious instruction or covenant-renewal services which appeal for "the knowledge of God," for the whole community will "know" Yahweh, the Suzerain, in the trust and tryst of a loyalty that cannot be broken.[29]

Fifth, the new covenant will rest upon divine forgiveness. In the context of Jeremiah's whole message it is clear that pardon must be preceded by Yahweh's "discipline," which shatters human pride and self-sufficiency and destroys the idols in which people place their trust. When the people of Israel stand humbly before God, shamed by their sordid history and contrite about their betrayal of their covenant commitment, then all things will be made new. "For I will forgive their iniquity, and I will remember their sin no more" (verse 34).

The sixth facet of the prophecy, though it appears first in the passage, has been left until this point in order that it may stand at the climax of our study. We have here a prophecy that pertains to "the last things," the consummation of the divine purpose in history. That is the significance of the opening formula, a characteristic preface to prophecies of the end-time: "Behold, the days are coming. . . . " The coming of the New Age cannot be dated on the calendar. This is the future for which Israel hopes, knowing that the time of its coming is measured by God's activity and purpose. Yet the hope was not for some never-never land, far removed from the concrete realities of Israel's history. As indicated by Jeremiah's symbolic purchase of a field, it was to be realized on the land, to which the exiles would return and where they would once again join in "the dance of the merrymakers" and worship in Zion (Jer. 31:4–6).[30]

As we shall see, the anticipation of the New Age assumed greater and greater significance in the years after the fall of the nation, and eventually—transposed into a new key—it came to assume a central place in the New Testament (I Cor. 11:25; Luke 22:20 and Hebrews 8:8–12).

Since Jeremiah came from a priestly family, it is rather surprising that the Temple had no central place in his pictures of the future restoration. Perhaps this silence resulted from his reaction against the false confidence in the Temple

---

[29] On "the knowledge of God," also a theme in the prophecy of Hosea, see above, pp. 309–311.

[30] See Thomas A. Raitt, *A Theology of Exile* [402], who effectively shows how the crisis of the fall of the nation and the exile of the people brought about a shift from oracles of judgment to oracles of salvation in the prophecies of Jeremiah and Ezekiel.

that had been encouraged by the Deuteronomic policy of centralizing worship in Jerusalem. Perhaps it resulted partly from his being so preoccupied with the crisis of the present that he was not concerned about sketching the details of the future. In any case, his attitude toward Israel's worship contrasts with that of his contemporary, Ezekiel, the prophet-priest, with whom began a new phase of Israel's history.

PART III

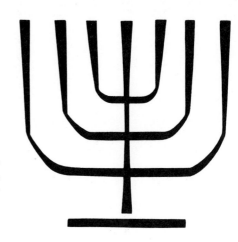

Behold, the days are coming,
says the Lord,
when I will make a new covenant
with the house of Israel.
—JEREMIAH 31:31

THE COVENANT
COMMUNITY
IS RENEWED

CHAPTER 13

By the Waters of Babylon

Although Jeremiah believed that the future lay with the exiles in Babylonia, he decided not to join them when Nebuchadrezzar's commanding officer gave him the chance. His decision to stay on in Jerusalem was clear proof to his accusers that he was not a deserter. The final phase of Jeremiah's career, however, as recorded by Baruch in Jeremiah 40–44, was interwoven with the troubles that beset the remnant left in the ruins of Judah. Gedaliah, whom the Babylonians had appointed governor of Judah, was assassinated by a certain Ishmael, an archpatriot whose Davidic blood was hot with the old nationalism. Ishmael's sword cut down many of Gedaliah's supporters and many of the Babylonian troops stationed at Mizpah. Fearing reprisals from Nebuchadrezzar, the Judean military chiefs, against Jeremiah's advice, fled to Egypt for refuge, taking the unwilling Jeremiah and Baruch with them. We last hear of Jeremiah in Egypt, where he was denouncing the colony of exiles for reverting to the worship of the Queen of Heaven, Ishtar. They justified themselves by recollecting that in the days before the fall of Jerusalem, when they worshiped the mother-goddess in Judah, everything had gone well: they had had plenty of food, had prospered, and had seen no evil. "But since we left off burning incense to the queen of heaven and pouring out libations to her, we have lacked everything and have been consumed by the sword and by famine" (Jer. 44:17–18). The refugees

Biblical readings: In this chapter we shall consider first the message of the priestly prophet, Ezekiel; read Ezekiel 1–24 and 33–39. Then we shall consider the Priestly teaching (P) of the Pentateuch in such passages as Genesis 1:1–2:3; 9:1–17; 17; 23; Exodus 6; 25–31; and 35–40.

seemed to have a strong argument on their side: history showed that people were better off in times when they turned from Yahweh to serve some other god. Nevertheless, Jeremiah insisted to the very last that the "queen-of-heaven theology" was deceptive and that Yahweh's word would be vindicated, despite the ambiguities of historical experience.[1]

THE JEWISH DISPERSION

Egypt came to be one of the major centers of the Jewish Dispersion. About a hundred years after the migration of Jeremiah and his fellow-Jews to Egypt, some of their descendants were settled at the first cataract of the Nile on the island of Elephantine (modern Aswan), as we know from the Elephantine papyri discovered there about the start of the twentieth century.[2] In this Jewish colony there was a temple where Yahweh (or Yahu) apparently was worshiped along with a goddess, Anath. Despite this strange departure from orthodox Mosaic tradition, these Jews recognized their allegiance to the Temple in Jerusalem, which at that time had been rebuilt. Later, important Jewish settlements also sprang up in Alexandria and other Egyptian cities.

But Jeremiah was proven right: the future belonged not to the exiles in Egypt, but to those in Babylonia who preserved the traditions of their past and who eventually returned to Palestine to begin the work of reconstruction. One of the leaders of the Jewish colonies in Babylonia was the prophet Ezekiel. In order to review his career, we must turn back to 597 B.C.E., the year of Nebuchadrezzar's first deportation, and retrace some of the story we have already followed in speaking of Jeremiah (see map, p. 404; Chronological Chart 8, p. 412).

EZEKIEL THE PRIEST

Of priestly descent, Ezekiel, the son of Buzi, was one of the exiles who, along with Jehoiachin and other prominent citizens of Judah, were carried to Babylonia in the first captivity (Ezek. 1:2). The fact that he belonged to the first group of exiles is noteworthy, for Nebuchadrezzar's design was to take away the cream of the population (II Kings 24:14), leaving only the poorest people. We are justified in assuming, then, that Ezekiel belonged to the aristocracy of Jerusalem, and perhaps that he was a member of the powerful priesthood that claimed descent from Zadok, the High Priest installed by Solomon.

With his fellow-exiles he settled by the banks of the river Chebar, a large

---

[1] In this connection, see the perceptive essay by David Noel Freedman, "The Biblical Idea of History," *Interpretation* 21 (1967), 32–49.

[2] See Pritchard, *Ancient Near Eastern Texts* [1], pp. 222–23.

canal that conducted water from the Euphrates through Nippur, a city that lay a short distance southeast of Babylon. In the village of Tel-abib, built on the edge of the canal, he received his call to prophesy five years after the deportation—that is, c. 593 B.C.E. The date given for his last recorded prophecy is c. 571 (Ezek. 29:17). Thus the twenty-year span of his ministry overlapped the periods before and after the fall of Jerusalem in the year 587.

Ezekiel's Babylonian environment undoubtedly exerted a great influence on his thought and imagination. It is likely that he visited the great city of Babylon, whose ancient glory is still dimly visible in the ruins that excavators have uncovered. Guarding the approach to the interior of the city was the magnificent Ishtar Gate—named in honor of Ishtar, mother-goddess and consort of Marduk. Through this gate one entered the processional street and advanced toward the ziggurat that rose above the city like a lofty mountain. Even today the beautiful brickwork, which throws into relief the figures of bulls and dragons, suggests the splendor that must have dazzled Jewish visitors of old (see Color Plate 5).

This external influence, however, cannot account for the strange character of much of the book of Ezekiel. For Ezekiel *himself* was an unusual person whose psychic peculiarities make a fascinating psychological study. We read that his oracles often came to him in ecstasy or trance, when he was seized by "the hand of God" or transported by the Spirit. He was struck dumb, overwhelmed by cataleptic stupor, and seemingly gifted with second sight. It should be emphasized, however, that these psychic abnormalities throw more light on the *form* of his message than upon its *content*. In the final analysis, the truth of what he said cannot be measured by the unusual manner in which his message came to him, any more than a modern writer or artist can be dismissed because he or she happens to be odd. Like many of the ancient prophets, Ezekiel was eccentric. His unusual temperament is evidently reflected in some of the difficulties that are noticeable in the book of Ezekiel itself.

The Problem of Ezekiel

In the book of Jeremiah, we found that the greatest difficulty for the reader is the shapeless, disordered character of the materials collected there. At first glance, the book of Ezekiel presents no such difficulty. The oracles are precisely dated and arranged in relatively good order, as though the prophet had planned and executed the work himself.[3] Careful study of the book in the last generation or so, however, has brought to light many difficulties that lie beneath the surface.

One obvious problem is that in the first twenty-four chapters Ezekiel, though represented as speaking to the exiles in Babylonia, focused his attention

---

[3] As indicated in the *Oxford Annotated Bible* [10], only three dates are out of order: 29:1 (January 7, 587 B.C.E.), 29:17 (April 26, 571—the latest date given in the book) and 32:1 (March 3, 585).

Ancient Babylon *as depicted in a reconstruction (see also Color Plate 5.) A procession is entering the beautiful Ishtar Gate, the entrance through the city's double wall to the palace, which supported on its roof the famous "Hanging Gardens"—one of the seven wonders of the world, according to the Greeks. Beyond the gardens can be seen the ziggurat, Etemenanki, which Nebuchadrezzar rebuilt.*

on Jerusalem and seems to have an intimate knowledge of what was going on there. For instance, in chapter 11 we are told that Ezekiel was "lifted up" by the Spirit and transported to the east gate of the Jerusalem Temple, where he saw twenty-five men plotting iniquity. Ezekiel was commanded by Yahweh to prophesy against them: "and it came to pass, while I was prophesying, that Pelatiah the son of Benaiah died" (verse 13). This seems to mean that Pelatiah, one of the twenty-five men, died at the time Ezekiel was speaking, presumably in Jerusalem. If we take seriously the geographical distance separating Babylonia and Palestine, this passage is baffling. It seems awkward to explain this and similar passages through clairvoyance, or, in Ezekiel's language, to say that God took him by a lock of his hair and spirited him away to Jerusalem (8:1–3). Hence it has been suggested that Ezekiel never did go to Babylonia at all, and that he was really a prophet who lived in Jerusalem during the final years of the kingdom of Judah.[4]

This view, however, is extreme. There is no convincing reason to doubt what is stated at the beginning of the book: that Ezekiel was carried away from Jerusalem in the first deportation, and that his call to prophesy occurred in Babylonia. It may be that some time after this experience he journeyed back to Jerusalem, believing that part of his prophetic commission was to warn Judah of the impending doom. If so, this would explain how he had such good information about Jerusalem during its last days, and why he seems frequently to address his message to people in Palestine rather than Babylonia. On this hypothesis, he later returned to Babylonia and completed his career in the midst of the exiles. This is an attractive solution of the problem, but it raises other difficulties that cannot be dismissed lightly. The most obvious is that Ezekiel was specifically commissioned to preach to the exiles (Ezek. 3:10–11).

At least some of the problems connected with Ezekiel's mission to the exiles are resolved when we consider, first of all, that he had been brought up in Jerusalem and that he knew the city and its environs intimately, especially the Temple. Again, there was undoubtedly fairly frequent communication back and forth between the Jews in Babylonia and the residents of Jerusalem. Ezekiel's oracles against Judah and Jerusalem, if given in Babylonia, could have been sent by letter, as was Jeremiah's message to the exiles (Jer. 29). And chances are that the exiles in Babylonia were kept posted on the latest developments in Jerusalem either by word of mouth or by letters. Of course, Ezekiel's lively religious imagination readily filled in many of the details, and his unusual psychic temperament found expression in his message. In addition, we should keep in mind that the book of Ezekiel, like other prophetic collections, has been edited. It is conceivable that Ezekiel himself, like Jeremiah, revised his oracles during his career, and unquestionably the scroll was further revised and supplemented by later prophetic disciples, although by no means as extensively as some scholars

---

[4] For a brief summary of the various hypotheses that have been proposed for the book of Ezekiel, see H. G. May, *Interpreter's Bible*, VI [16], 41–45. See also the commentaries of Walther Eichrodt [395] and Walther Zimmerli [404].

have insisted.[5] All this adds up to the probability that most of Ezekiel's work was carried on among the Babylonian exiles.

In its present form, the book of Ezekiel is arranged according to a clear outline:

A. Prophecies given before the fall of Jerusalem (593–587 B.C.E.)
    1. Ezekiel's opening vision and commission (chapters 1–3)
    2. Oracles of doom against Judah and Jerusalem (chapters 4–24)
B. Oracles against the neighboring nations (chapters 25–32)
    (The oracles against Tyre and Egypt are clearly from Ezekiel.)
C. Prophecies given after the fall of Jerusalem (587–573 B.C.E.)
    1. Oracles of promise (chapters 33–39)
    2. The New Jerusalem (chapters 40–48)

In the following discussion, our attention will focus chiefly on sections A and C–1 of the above outline.

Ezekiel's Call

Let us turn our attention first to the beginning of Ezekiel's prophetic career. The lot of the exiles, among whom he had been living for several years before his call, was not as bad as might have been feared. Many of the Jews deported in 597 were skilled artisans whose labor was evidently in great demand in Babylonia. Ezekiel, for instance, had a private house (Ezek. 3:24), in which he was visited by the elders of the people from time to time. The Jews must have been given a good bit of freedom to practice their religion, to live together in closely knit communities in the Babylonian cities, and to improve their economic status. Tablets from the reign of Nebuchadrezzar, discovered some years ago by archaeologists in the ruins of ancient Babylon, mention payments of rations in oil, barley, and so forth to foreign captives in exchange for skilled labor. Included in the list were Yaukin [Jehoiachin], king of Judah, five royal princes, and other men from Judah.[6] Evidently it was easy enough for the exiles to accept Jeremiah's advice to build houses and plant gardens, to raise families, and to show interest in the welfare of the city in which they lived (Jer. 29:4–7). Their life was fairly comfortable, even though many yearned to return to their homeland.

Ezekiel's call to be a prophet came as the result of an extraordinary vision in the fifth year of the exile of Jehoiachin. On that day, he says, "the heavens were opened, and I saw visions of God" (Ezek. 1:1). This overpowering experience convinced him that "the hand of Yahweh was upon him there." At

---

[5] In his commentary [396], Moshe Greenberg maintains that nothing in the book of Ezekiel requires a historical setting later than the last date assigned to an oracle, that is, 571 B.C.E (Ezek. 29:17).

[6] Pritchard, *Ancient Near Eastern Texts* [1], p. 308. See also W. F. Albright, "King Joiachin [Jehoiachin] in Exile," *Biblical Archaeologist*, V (1942), 49–55. Reprinted in *The Biblical Archaeologist Reader*, I [101], 106–12.

A Protective Genius—one of a pair which once guarded the gateway to the palace of Ashurnasirpal II (884–860 B.C.E.) at Nimrud. These winged figures, a prominent feature of ancient art, help us to understand the imagery of Ezekiel's vision. The figure has the body of a lion, the wings and feathers of an eagle, and the head of a man.

the time, he was thirty years old, if that is the meaning of the mysterious opening words "in the thirtieth year." The ancient rabbis, who were disturbed by the possiblity that strange doctrines would be based on the account of Ezekiel's vision, are said to have ruled that the opening chapter was not to be read in the synagogue and that persons under thirty years of age were forbidden to read the book privately.

Ezekiel's call, like Isaiah's, came in connection with a vision of Yahweh seated upon a heavenly throne in ineffable glory and transcendent majesty. To understand this vision it is important to remember that, according to Jerusalem theology, Yahweh was enthroned within the Holy of Holies of the Temple, and that the wings of the guardian cherubim stretched out protectively over the throne-seat (the Ark). The imagery of the vision, described in chapter 1, is drawn both from Israel's priestly tradition, with which Ezekiel was familiar through his experience as a priest in the Jerusalem Temple, and the Babylonian religious emblems that had influenced his unconscious mind in exile. According to the narrative, he saw Yahweh's heavenly chariot approaching him from the north in a storm cloud flashing with lightning (cf. Ps. 29). On looking more closely, he saw that the throne-chariot was borne by four strange creatures (cherubim; see also Ezek. 10:18–22), half animal and half human, like the figures familiar in Babylonian art, each moving in perfect coordination with the other because they were all animated by the divine Spirit. Alongside each cherub was a gleaming wheel—or rather, "a wheel within a wheel," as though set at right angles to each other to enable the chariot to move easily in any direction, as the Spirit directed. And above the creatures was something like a crystal platform or firmament (cf. Exod. 24:10), which was carried on the cherubs' wings with a roar like the sound of many waters. Looking still higher, the prophet saw above the firmament the likeness of a sapphire throne, and "seated above the likeness of a throne was a likeness as it were of a human form." In an ecstatic vision the prophet beheld Yahweh seated upon a lofty throne in dazzling radiance, or "glory." The holy God, whom Israel had once worshiped in the Temple at Jerusalem, had come to the people in exile!

Overwhelmed by the infinite distance separating the holy God from a mere mortal, or a "son of man" (for that is the meaning of the latter expression), the prophet fell prostrate. Raised to his feet when the Spirit entered him, he stood to receive his commission. He was to speak to "a nation of rebels," a people "impudent and stubborn" who had been in revolt against Yahweh's sovereignty from the very first. Like a sentry posted on the city wall, it was his duty as a "watchman" to give them Yahweh's warning of approaching catastrophe, although there was little chance that a people with "a hard forehead and a stubborn heart" would respond (see also 33:1–9). But whether they heard or refused to hear, at least they would know that a prophet had been among them. In the prophet's vision a hand was stretched out to him, holding a scroll—the message which the messenger was to deliver to the people. Strangely, Yahweh offered him the scroll to eat and digest. When he did so, he found that it was "sweet as honey" (2:9–10; 3:1–3), indicating that he not only appropriated the message but was in agreement with it, even though he would have to "sit upon scorpions."[7] This vivid account of the prophet's commissioning, related in chapters 2 and 3, recalls Isaiah's unpromising vocation (Isa. 6:9–13) and Jeremiah's unhappy lot of being set like a fortified city against the whole people (Jer. 1:17–19). Awestruck at the vision of Yahweh's unearthly glory, and appalled by the fearsome task set before him, Ezekiel sat overwhelmed among the exiles for seven days.

[7] Von Rad, *Theology,* II [142], 223–24, interprets the symbolism to mean that, unlike Jeremiah, there was agreement between the prophet and his message. Certainly the passage should not be construed to mean that Ezekiel found a sadistic satisfaction in pronouncing judgment against Israel.

DEFINITION: "JEWS, JUDAISM"

In the previous paragraphs the word "Jew" has been used from time to time to refer to the people whose life-story in biblical times we have been exploring. The ancestry of the term can be traced back through Latin *judaeus* and Greek *'ioudaios* to the Old Testament word *Yehudi*, which once referred to citizens of the southern kingdom of Judah who survived the fall of the northern state of Israel, Ephraim, in 722 B.C.E. The term gained currency, however, after the fall of Jerusalem in the year 587, during the period of the Exile and the period after the return. During the post-exilic period the term was used to refer to subjects of the Persian province of Judah (Neh. 1:2) and later to the state established by the Maccabean leaders (I Mac. 8:20). It was not geographically limited, however, for although Jews were "dispersed" or scattered in countries outside Judah, such as Babylonia or Egypt, they continued to cherish their Judean background and ties. Those who did not share this "Jewish" identity were regarded as belonging to "the nations" (Acts 14:2), that is, the gentiles.

Nationality is not the decisive factor in being a Jew, as is evident from the fact that many Jews today are not citizens of the state of Israel. In biblical times, the decisive factor was religion, specifically the conviction that God had entered into special relationship with this people and had called them to be "separate" by virtue of their distinctive way of life. The term Judaism is conventionally applied to the religion of the Judeans or "Jews," among whom the covenant faith came to a new expression under the conditions prevailing after the collapse of the nation in 587 B.C.E. This term is not found in the Old Testament; it seems to have been coined in later Hellenistic circles of the Diaspora or "Dispersion" (see Galatians 1:13–14). In any case, the Exile marked the beginning of a completely new chapter in the history of Israel's faith. It is proper to reserve the terms "Jews" and "Judaism" for this new phase of Israel's life-story.

LAMENTATION, MOURNING, AND WOE

In the days before the fall of Jerusalem, Ezekiel's oracles were, like the writing in the scroll he was given to eat, "words of lamentation, mourning, and woe" (Ezek. 2:9–10). Like his great prophetic predecessors, he prophesied doom. While Jeremiah was prophesying in Jerusalem, Ezekiel was speaking about the imminent downfall of the state and the captivity of the people. It is explicitly stated that he was to speak to "the house of Israel." Here "Israel" is used in its original sense of "the people of the covenant," and is applied to Jews, whether living in Judah or in Babylonian exile. At first glance, it would seem that his message would have been more immediately relevant to the people living in Judah. But granting that he spoke, at least during part of his early ministry, to Jews in exile, what relevance did a message of divine judgment have for them? To deal with this question, we must consider the situation of the Jewish captives.

Smoldering Nationalism

We know from modern history that a legitimate ruler, even when living in exile from his or her own country, continues to be a symbol of nationalistic hope. This was true of Jehoiachin, who would have continued to rule in the succession of Josiah and Jehoiakim had it not been for the intervention of the Babylonians in the affairs of Jerusalem. To the exiles of 597 B.C.E., Jehoiachin was the legitimate Davidic king. Moreover, he was called "king of Judah" in Nebuchadrezzar's tablets, implying that even his captors recognized him as the legitimate ruler and Zedekiah as a regent. So long as the exiled king was free to move about, and even given an allowance by the Babylonian government, there was hope for a revival of the Jewish nation. It seems, then, that Jehoiachin was a symbol for repressed nationalism among the exiles. We know that there was a party in Judah, suspicious of the Babylonian appointee Zedekiah, who pinned their hopes on the exiled king, for the prophet Hananiah opposed Jeremiah by predicting that within the space of two years Jehoiachin and the other exiles would return (see p. 415). Apparently the revolutionary intrigue that centered about the legitimate king, both in Judah and in Babylonia, led to his subsequent imprisonment, although after the fall of Jerusalem he was freed from prison by Nebuchadrezzar's successor and given a regular allowance and a special place at the king's table (II Kings 25:27–30).

Ezekiel, then, faced a situation in which nationalism was still alive, even in the Exile. In Babylon there were popular prophets, of the same stripe as Hananiah, who were fanning the hope that the power of Babylonia would soon be shattered and the exiles would be able to return to the homeland. Every rumor from Jerusalem must have been followed with keen interest, especially the news about the intervention of pharaohs Psammetichus and Hophra. Jeremiah, as we have seen, even found it necessary to write a letter to the exiles, rebuking them for being deceived by the lies of their prophets and advising them to plan on settling in Babylonia for a considerable time (Jer. 29). Two of these fanatical prophets were seized by Babylonian agents and burned alive (Jer. 29:20–23).

So long as Jerusalem was still standing, Ezekiel's message—like that of Jeremiah—was almost wholly one of doom. It was his firm conviction that the fall of Jerusalem to Nebuchadrezzar was divinely ordained, and that rebellion against Babylonia was treason against God (Ezek. 17:20). In the imminent doom of the city he saw the coming of the Day of Yahweh, the day of judgment. As though the event had already occurred, he announced that the end had come upon the land of Israel:

> The word of Yahweh came to me:
> "You, O mortal man—this is what Lord Yahweh says
>   to the land of Israel.
> An end has come!
> The end has come upon the four corners of the land!
> Now is the end upon you [the land]!
> I am going to unleash my wrath against you.
> I will judge you according to your ways,
>   and requite you according to your detestable practices.
> I will show no mercy to you, nor spare you at all.
> But I will requite you for your ways,
>   and the detestable practices among you.
> Then you will realize that I am Yahweh.
> —EZEKIEL 7:1–4

The Prophetic Signs

Ezekiel's prophetic word was accompanied by signs enacted with dramatic power. He was instructed to draw on a clay brick a diagram of Jerusalem under siege, showing the siege-mounds, camps, and battering rams (Ezek. 4:1–3). He was directed to lie for 390 days on his left side, then for 40 days on his right side, to indicate the number of years that Israel and Judah respectively would be punished (4:4–8). While lying on his side, he was to weigh out small rations of food and water to show the privations of the coming siege (4:9–11). He was told to cut off his hair with a sword and to separate it into three parts to portray the three kinds of fate that would befall the people of Jerusalem (5:1–12). He packed his baggage and at night dug through the wall, suggesting a person trying to flee from the city under cover of darkness (12:1–16). He ate his bread with quaking and drank his water with trembling to symbolize the nervous fear that people would experience during the coming siege (12:17–20). When his wife—the "delight" of his eyes—died, he refrained from mourning as a sign to the exiles that the news of the fall of Jerusalem would fill them with sorrow too deep for tears (24:15–27).

Ezekiel's words and signs stirred up mild interest and curiosity, but they did not evoke repentance or even provoke hostility. His signs were performed before those who had eyes to see but saw not, and ears to hear but heard not (12:2). The people even seemed to "enjoy" his sermons, for to them he was like one who sings with a beautiful voice or plays well on an instrument (33:30–33)! The reaction was quite different from the one Jeremiah received, but it was no less indicative that Israel was a "rebellious house."

The History of Rebellion

According to Ezekiel, God's imminent judgment would be the harvest of a persistent apostasy that reached back to the very beginning of Israel's history. Hosea and Jeremiah, it will be recalled, had portrayed the ancient wilderness as the time of Israel's honeymoon, when the bride was faithful to the Groom (Hosea 2:15; Jer. 2:2). Not so Ezekiel. He advocated what may be called a doctrine of "original sin" in historical terms—that is, he insisted that there never was a time in Israel's history when the people were sinless. Recapitulating the "sacred history" with a new twist, he traced Israel's unfaithfulness not only to the wilderness wanderings but also to the sojourn in Egypt, for that was the time when its history began:

> Thus says Lord Yahweh:
> "At the time when I chose Israel, I lifted my hand [in oath] to the descendants of the house of Jacob and I made myself known to them in the land of Egypt. With uplifted hand, I said to them: 'I am Yahweh your God.' At that time I swore to them that I would bring them out from the land of Egypt into a land that I had sought for them, a land flowing with milk and honey, the most glorious of all lands."
>
> —EZEKIEL 20:5–6

Israel's history was corrupted at the very beginning, for the people responded to Yahweh's choice and promise by rebelling against their liberating God and turning to the idols of Egypt. Had it not been for Yahweh's restraint "for his name's sake"—that is, for the sake of Yahweh's own honor and reputation—the people would have been blotted out on the spot. For the holiness of God demanded a holy, faithful people, pure from the stain of idolatry. This is a fundamental theme that runs through all of Ezekiel's discourses. His sense of the sublime majesty of God, vividly expressed in his opening vision, made him deeply aware of the infinite distance of sinful, mortal humanity from the holy, righteous God.

Ezekiel's somber summary of the sacred history from the Exodus to the settlement in Canaan is supplemented by allegories of the two chief cities: Jerusalem and Samaria. In two "extended metaphors" (chapters 16 and 23) he portrayed Israel's history in the figure of harlotry, a figure that had been used effectively by Hosea and Jeremiah. Jerusalem's origin, he said, was Canaanite: "Your father was an Amorite, and your mother a Hittite" (16:3; see verse 45). In a broad sense, this statement has some historical accuracy (see pp. 31–41); Israel did come to birth in the welter of the Canaanite culture. But in this context the prophet is talking in theological, rather than archaeological, language. He affirms that Israel's perversity can be traced to the fact that she was the offspring of a lustful union, thus justifying the proverb: "Like mother, like daughter" (verse 44). Yahweh, however, took pity on this illegitimate child whom others rejected, nurtured her to the beauty of maidenhood, and plighted to her his troth. The covenant, then, was based on Yahweh's grace and initiative. But the maiden "trusted in her beauty," forgetting that she owed her life and beauty to God. Wantonly she lavished her harlotries on any passerby, for her lust was a wild power within her, like that of her passionate Hittite mother. Normally, said the prophet, men pay to go to a harlot; but this passionate "lovesick" wife (16:30) was different—she actually bribed her lovers to come to her. Jerusalem had acted far worse than Samaria (the Northern Kingdom)—a point that is accented in the allegory of the twin harlots Oholah (northern Israel) and Oholibah (Judah) in chapter 23—and had even out-sinned Sodom, whose corruption was proverbial! Therefore, the harlot must bear the disgrace of judgment and must become an object of reproach among the nations. Her history, the history of a broken covenant, must come to an end in order that Yahweh, remembering the covenant made "in the days of her youth," might establish an "everlasting covenant" (see 16:59–63). Here we see that Ezekiel's thought moves beyond the conditional Mosaic covenant to a covenant of grace, something like the Davidic covenant, which would last in perpetuity.

Knowledge of God

However, before Israel could know Yahweh's forgiveness and enter into a new relationship in an "everlasting covenant," the people had to experience divine judgment in their history. Ezekiel's oracles of doom are punctuated with the refrain: "Then they will know [realize] that I am Yahweh." The sovereignty of Yahweh would be demonstrated in acts of judgment against a rebellious people, as had happened with their ancestors in the land of Egypt (Ezek. 20:33–38). On the basis of these historical demonstrations, Israel would come to "know," that is, acknowledge or recognize, Yahweh as the One who is God to them. Here it is important to recall our earlier consideration of the meaning of "knowledge of God" in the context of the covenant (see pp. 98–101, 309–311).

Ezekiel's sense of divine holiness was accompanied by the realization that nothing unholy or profane could stand in God's presence. In the view of this priestly prophet, cultic and ethical sins were on the same level. In an extraordinary vision, described in chapters 8–11, he was carried from Babylonia to the Jerusalem Temple, where he saw the abominations being practiced there: the women weeping for Tammuz (the Babylonian name for the dying-rising god of fertility), men worshiping the sun with their faces toward the east, the secret chamber filled with murals depicting beasts and idols, and the princes—the very men who had persecuted Jeremiah—making their evil plans. Then the prophet saw the Glory of Yahweh—the divine presence that was believed to "tabernacle" in the Holy of Holies—depart from the defiled Temple, borne on the very throne-chariot that the prophet had seen in his vision by the River Chebar (10:18–22). So great was the idolatry of the people, said Ezekiel, that even if three proverbially righteous men, Noah, Daniel, and Job, were to be found in the city, it would not escape destruction (14:12–20). The popular prophets came in for special censure, for they had misled the people by saying "peace" when there was no peace and had tried to whitewash the crumbling walls (chap. 13). In the important chapter 22, the indictment is made in terms of specific sins, including not only cultic abuses like the profanation of the sabbath but also ethical crimes: bloodshed, adultery, extortion, dishonor of parents, and the violation of the rights of the orphan, widow, and sojourner. Princes and prophets were linked in a conspiracy that had corrupted the whole people. No one was righteous.

> I sought for someone among them who should build up the wall and stand in the breach before me for the land, that I should not destroy it; but I did not find anyone.
>
> —EZEKIEL 22:30

The Destiny of the Individual

Ezekiel's message, like the preaching of the prophets who preceded him, was addressed to the people as a whole—to the covenant community known as "the house of Israel." He declared that the community, from the beginning of its history down to his day, was so contaminated with evil that it could not endure. Within the political event of national ruin he discerned the judgment of God. But Ezekiel had to face the meaning of national calamity at another level. For the community, even though it deserved to suffer divine judgment, was made up of persons who were caught in the coils of the tragedy. What, then, about the destiny of the individual?

It must not be supposed that Israel's faith up to this time had stressed only the collective responsibility of Israel, without regard to the individual members of the community. Israel's faith was not totalitarian, if by this we mean that the individual was expendable in the interests of the whole. On the contrary, the covenant relationship, while binding the people together in communal solidarity, brought a sense of God's concern for each person. Within the community individuals had personal fellowship with God, and within the community their rights were legally protected. In the biblical view, one is truly a person only when standing in a community—in relationship to God and to the neighbor. When isolated from the community, like Cain in his banishment, a person suffers the greatest loneliness and misery.

Nevertheless, in a time of great suffering, when the community was temporarily dissolved and the people were uprooted from their homeland, the question of the destiny of the individual had to be faced more seriously than ever before. The question was not entirely new. According to a story in Genesis 18:22–33, Abraham's plea on behalf of Sodom was so moving that Yahweh vowed not to destroy the city if ten righteous persons could be found in it. And according to a story in II Samuel 24, David acknowledged his own guilt, but protested against Yahweh's smiting innocent people too with a plague: "Lo, I have sinned, and I have done wickedly; but these sheep, what have they done?" (verse 17). In the time of Jeremiah and Ezekiel, however, when individuals were torn from the old social context that had given meaning and support to their lives, the suffering of the innocent came to be a burning issue. The popular complaint was expressed in the proverb: "The parents have eaten sour grapes, and the children's teeth are set on edge" (Jer. 31:29; Ezek. 18:1–4). In other words, the people were saying cynically that they were victims of a situation inherited from their parents. Insisting that they were not to blame for the evil that evoked God's judgment, they took the easy way out and shifted the blame to earlier generations. Ezekiel, then, was challenged to defend God's justice to those who were saying, "The way of Yahweh is not fair" (Ezek. 18:25, 29; see also 33:17–20).[8]

It cannot be denied that in the course of human history the "sins of the parents" actually are visited upon the children—say, the "children" who suffered or were killed in World War II for the mistakes and follies of the past. These children were apt to cry out bitterly, protesting against the misfortune that they should have been born when the times were out of joint. It was this mood of fatalism that Ezekiel sought to correct (Ezek. 18:25–29). His generation was caught in a *fateful* situation, to be sure; but he insisted that individuals should not respond *fatalistically*, saying, "What's the use? God is not fair!" With

---

[8] See the discussion of theodicy by Thomas Raitt, *A Theology of Exile* [402], pp. 83–105.

some oversimplification, he argued that the acts of the past generations do not determine the response of the present generation, for a good parent can have a bad child and a bad parent can have a good child. He emphasized that in each case persons are responsible for their own destiny—they are not the puppets of heredity, environment, or historical causation. Each individual must answer personally to God alone, and for no one else.

Had he been dealing with a case in a law court, Ezekiel would have denied the principle of "guilt by association" according to which, in ancient times, Achan's whole family was put to death with him for his sin (Joshua 7). This practice, rooted in ancient religious taboos, had been abandoned by Ezekiel's time. King Amaziah had refused to liquidate the children of the murderers who assassinated his father (II Kings 14:6), and the Deuteronomic code had made it illegal to punish children for the sins of their parents (Deut. 24:16). But Ezekiel had to deal with the question of divine justice, not in a law court, but in the historical arena where the deeds and decisions of one generation do affect later generations, and where the retribution for past errors often falls not upon the parents but upon their children or grandchildren.

Ezekiel did not advocate extreme individualism, any more than did Jeremiah (see pp. 401–423), for—as we have seen—he was deeply aware of the solidarity of the Israelite community, the oneness of the people past, present, and future, in the covenant. How, then, did he try to answer the people's question? He turned the question of God's justice back on the questioners themselves, reminding them that they were not as blameless as they had supposed. They too were entangled in the sins of Israel, and had to accept full responsiblity. Instead of proposing an explanation of the problem of suffering, he insisted that suffering provided an occasion for repentance and faith (cf. Luke 13:1–5). According to Ezekiel, God was puzzled that the imminent danger did not awaken Israel to repentance (see Definition, p. 401).

> Turn, turn from all your offences,
>   and your iniquity will not be your downfall!
> Get rid of all your offences
>   which you have committed against me,
>   and acquire a new heart and a new spirit!
> Why would you die, O house of Israel?
> For I take no pleasure in the death of anyone—
>   the oracle of Lord Yahweh—
> So, turn and live!
> —EZEKIEL 18:31–32 (*cf.* 33:10–20)

Ezekiel's attempt to defend God's justice may strike one as unsatisfactory. For one thing, bad people do not always suffer and the good do not always prosper. Primarily, however, the prophet urged the Israelites to hear in the crisis God's call to repentance and to cast themselves in dependence upon divine mercy. But his message only touched the edge of the mystery. In the centuries afterward, the problem of suffering was raised even more intensely as attempts were made to understand God's ways in history.[9]

THE PROMISE OF A NEW BEGINNING

Ezekiel's appeal was in vain, for the people were too much enslaved by their false loyalties to be moved even by the threat of catastrophe. Hence, the day of doom finally arrived. The prophet's oracles reflect the swift movement of events with which we have become familiar in the study of Jeremiah's career. In an allegory (chap. 17) Ezekiel tells of Zedekiah's revolt against the "great eagle" (Nebuchadrezzar) and his attempt to find refuge with "another great eagle" (Egypt). He sees a great sword, polished and sharpened for slaughter (Ezek. 21:1–18), and portrays Nebuchadrezzar at the parting of the ways, waiting for the oracle's verdict on which rebel state he should attack first, Ammon or Judah (21:18–32). As long as Jerusalem was still standing, however, the exiles refused to believe that the nation would fall. They chose to believe that Ezekiel was talking about the far distant future, not about their own times. "The vision that he sees is for many days hence, and he prophesies of times far off" (12:27; see verse 22).

Israel's Resurrection

Then one day Ezekiel announced that Jerusalem was under siege (24:1–14). In the year 585 B.C.E., after an unexplained delay, a fugitive came with the news that the city had fallen (33:21). From then on, the dominant tone of the prophet's message became one of hope. Earlier, when nationalistic feelings ran high, his task had been to shatter illusions with hard-hitting words of doom; now, in the new situation, when the people were reduced to utter despair and remorse (33:1–11), his message was one of assurance. Apparently he believed that the sovereignty of God demands speaking against any form of human confidence, whether that confidence is expressed positively in faith in the future, or negatively in despair about human possibilities. So after disaster had struck, Ezekiel's recurring refrain, "You shall know that I am Yahweh," took on new meaning. The demonstrations that Yahweh is God to this people were to be found, not just in those acts of judgment that expose human failure and sin, but also in the divine action which initiates a new beginning in history.[10]

This historical miracle is vividly portrayed in the famous vision of the valley of dry bones (chap. 37). Placed in the valley of death's shadow, Ezekiel was

[9] See the essays in J. L. Crenshaw, *Theodicy* [132].

[10] The "demonstration" of Yahweh's deity is treated in Walther Zimmerli's essay, "The Knowledge of God according to the Book of Ezekiel," in his collected essays, *Gottes Offenbarung* (München: Kaiser Verlag, 1963), 41–119. See also the companion essay on the *Erweiswort* (Demonstrative Word), 120–32.

asked: "Can these bones live?" Then at Yahweh's command he prophesied to the bones, and suddenly they became living beings, clothed with sinews and animated by the divine Spirit. In the interpretation that follows, we are told that the bones symbolize Israel in despair. Israel as a community was dead, a historical nonentity. The cry was raised: "Our bones are dried up, and our hope is lost." Israel's extremity was God's opportunity, however. The prophet announced that Yahweh promised to resurrect the people from the grave (that is, from exile), restore them to their homeland, and create new life by breathing the divine Spirit into their lifeless bodies. A divine miracle would occur: life out of death! Yahweh would make Israel one people, embracing both Israel (Ephraim) and Judah, and would anoint one "prince" to rule over them. Then the unity of the people would be a historical fulfillment of the ancient covenant formula: "I will be their God, and they shall be my people."

The Good Shepherd

The restoration is also portrayed in the image of the shepherd and his flock, an image that has an important place in both the Old Testament (Ps. 23; 100:3; Isa. 40:11) and the New (Luke 15:3–7; John 10:1–18). In contrast to the false shepherds who feed themselves instead of their sheep, Yahweh is the Good Shepherd who goes out to seek for sheep that are lost, crippled, or strayed, in order

The Area of En-gedi—an oasis located on the western bank of the Dead Sea some thirty-five miles from Jerusalem. The climate in the depression of the Dead Sea—the lowest place on the earth's surface—is semitropical, and the terrain is ruggedly desolate. En-gedi, fed by a strong spring, was famous for its fertility (see Song of Solomon 1:14). Ezekiel's vision pictures the fertilization of the whole region and the transformation of the Dead Sea into a fresh-water lake (Ezek. 47:1–12).

to restore them to their home pasture (chap. 34). The initiative, according to Ezekiel, lies with Yahweh:

> Now I myself will ask after my sheep and go in search of them. As a shepherd goes in search of his sheep when his flock is dispersed all around him, so I will go in search of my sheep and rescue them, no matter where they were scattered in dark and cloudy days. I will bring them out from every nation, gather them from other lands, and lead them home to their own soil. I will graze them on the mountains of Israel, by her streams and in all her green fields.
>
> —EZEKIEL 34:11–13 (NEB)

After Yahweh has led the people back to their land, they will be given a good shepherd, a Davidic leader:

> Then I will set over them one shepherd, my servant David, and he shall lead them; he shall lead them, and he shall become their shepherd. And I, Yahweh, will be their God, and my servant David shall be a prince [*nasî'*] among them. I, Yahweh, have spoken.
>
> —EZEKIEL 34:23–24 (see 37:24–25)

Notice that the prophet does not refer to a coming Davidic "king," but rather to a prince (*nasî'*), a term once used for a leader of the old Tribal Confederacy. Ezekiel seems to idealize the days before Israel became a nation—when Yahweh ruled as shepherd-king through a designated agent.

It was not because of Israel's goodness that Yahweh was about to act, Ezekiel insisted, but only because other nations had inferred from Israel's tragedy that their God was powerless to save. This erroneous interpretation of Israel's defeat profaned God's honor, God's holy name. Therefore, Yahweh resolved to restore a helpless and hopeless people so that the nations might know who Yahweh is: the holy God who cannot be mocked. As in the case of Jeremiah, however, Ezekiel insisted that Yahweh would have to effect a radical change in human nature if the people were to be a covenant people. Israel's "heart" (mind, will) must be transformed, a change in the people's inner disposition must occur, so that a new lifestyle would be possible:

> A new heart I will give you, and a new spirit I will put within you. I will remove the heart of stone from your flesh and I will give you instead a heart of flesh. My spirit I will put within you, and I will cause you to walk in my statutes and faithfully observe my ordinances. You shall dwell in the land which I gave to your ancestors, and you shall be my people, and I will be your God.
>
> —EZEKIEL 36:26–28 (see 11:19–20)

Then Israel would have the will to obey God's voice, and the relationship between God and people would be that of an "everlasting covenant" (37:26). The affinities between Ezekiel 36 and Jeremiah's prophecy of the "new covenant" (Jer. 31:31–34) are so close that some scholars think that Ezekiel must have seen or heard Jeremiah's oracle.

So, Ezekiel proclaimed the gracious action of the holy God in restoring a holy people to a holy land. In the time of the New Covenant, God would be in their midst, laving the land with ''showers of blessing'' (Ezek. 34:26) and multiplying the people in peace and security. One feature of the restoration was especially prominent in the vision of Ezekiel, the priest: Yahweh would ''tabernacle'' in the midst of the people:

> I will make a covenant of peace with them; it shall be an everlasting covenant with them; and I will bless them and multiply them, and will set my sanctuary in the midst of them forevermore. My dwelling place shall be with them; and I will be their God, and they shall be my people.
>
> —EZEKIEL 37:26–27 (RSV)

The Temple would stand at the center of everything. This theme is elaborated in the concluding chapters of the book (40–48). In elaborate detail, Ezekiel portrays a new Temple in a new Jerusalem. In a vision that recalls the one he had seen at the beginning of his career by the river Chebar, he beheld the ''glory'' of Yahweh returning to tabernacle in the sanctuary.[11] According to the prophet's lively imagination, the restoration of worship would have a transforming effect upon the land itself; for from the temple mount a life-giving river, whose source is the fresh-water Deep beneath the earth, will flow eastward in the wilderness and empty into the Salt Sea. Along its banks will grow trees that bear fresh fruit every month, and in the region of En-gedi fishermen will angle for fish, for the Dead Sea will become a fresh-water lake (47:1–12)! Ezekiel's vision of the New Jerusalem has had a profound effect upon later portrayals of the end-time, such as the vision of ''the holy city Jerusalem coming down out of heaven from God'' described in the last book of the New Testament (Rev. 21).

In Ezekiel's sketch of the new community, the relations between ''church and state'' are carefully regulated. The priests of the line of Zadok, assisted by the Levites, are to have jurisdiction in all religious matters. The responsibility of the civil leader, the prince (*nasî'*), is to support the religious community by providing sacrifices and by upholding law and order (Ezek. 45:7–46:13). The land will be reapportioned among the twelve tribes, and they will find their unity in the service of the central sanctuary in Jerusalem, which will receive a new name: ''Yahweh is there'' (48:35). Thus Israel will become a worshiping community, modeled on the pattern of the ancient Tribal Confederacy. We shall see what a deep influence Ezekiel's priestly view had upon the Judaism that emerged out of the Exile.[12]

---

[11] For a discussion of the theology of Yahweh's *kabôd* (''glory''), see Tryggve N. D. Mettinger [400], chap. 3, especially 97–103.

[12] Discussions of Ezekiel's vision of restoration are found in Jon D. Levenson, *Theology of the Program of Restoration of Ezekiel 40–48*, Harvard Semitic Monograph Series, No. 10 (Missoula: Scholars Press, 1976); also Moshe Greenberg, ''The Design and Themes of Ezekiel's Program of Restoration,'' *Interpretation* 38 (1984), 181–208.

LIFE UNDER CAPTIVITY

Although Ezekiel had envisioned a reunion of the two houses of Israel—the tribes of the north and the south—this dream did not materialize. The remnant of the Northern Kingdom (later known as Samaritans) and the descendants of the state of Judah were eventually divided by such deep rivalry that in New Testament times it could be said that "Jews have no dealings with Samaritans" (John 4:9). Jews claimed that they were the true "Israel"—using Israel not in a political sense but in its ancient religious meaning of "the people of the covenant."

As we have seen, the Exile marked the beginning of a new movement in the unfolding drama of the people Israel, that of Judaism (see Definition, p. 435). True to Jeremiah's prophecy, the future of the covenant people did not lie with the remnant left in Jerusalem. As a result of Nebuchadrezzar's blows, the city was so disorganized and crippled that religious vitality must have been at a very low ebb. Even after the deportations of 597 and 587 B.C.E., Nebuchadrezzar had to intervene again in the year 582, probably because of disturbances in the wake of Gedaliah's assassination. At that time, another group of Jews was rounded up for exile to Babylonia. There is some confusion about the total number of people taken into captivity.[13] It is clear, however, that the Exile did not involve a wholesale movement of the Jewish population to Babylonia, nor did the Babylonians follow the Assyrian policy of repopulating the land with foreign colonists, as in the case of the conquest of the Northern Kingdom in the year 722. Only the cream of Jewish leadership was taken, and the poorer elements of the population were left behind to harvest the crops (see Jer. 29:10; II Kings 25:12). By paralyzing the country in this manner, Nebuchadrezzar effectively removed the threat of national revival. The land was left in such a wreck that even under favorable conditions it would have taken years to recover. The major fortified towns lay in ruins during the Exile, as archaeological discoveries have shown. The former state of Judah was partitioned, part going to the Babylonian province of Samaria and the rest absorbed by the Edomites (the later Idumeans), who had moved out of their homeland southeast of the Dead Sea into the area around Hebron. Many Jews, finding the economic and political conditions intolerable, migrated in a steadily increasing stream to Egypt to start life anew. Only a handful of Jews were left in the immediate environs of the ruins of Jerusalem.

Adjustment to the Babylonian Environment

Things were not going too badly for the exiles in Babylonia. As we have already noted in speaking of Ezekiel, the Jews were given a good bit of social freedom and economic opportunity. They proved to be so enterprising that a century

---

[13] Jeremiah 52:28–30, which is probably fairly accurate, mentions three deportations and gives the total for all three as 4,600, though this may refer only to the males. II Kings 24:14 (compare verse 16) states that 8,000 to 10,000 were taken away in the first deportation of 597 B.C.E. No count is given for the deportation of 587 B.C.E. and the third deportation is not mentioned.

later they held the controlling interest in the business concern of Murashu and Sons in the city of Nippur.[14] Certainly their lot in Babylonia was a great deal better than that of modern Jews who have been crowded into dingy ghettos or herded into concentration camps. In fact, "anti-Semitism" was quite unknown at that time. Babylonian Jews were permitted to move about freely, to live in their communities within or near the great cities, and to carry on their way of life.

The most serious adjustment that the Jews of Babylonia had to make was a religious one. Their faith had been oriented to the land of Palestine, the inheritance Yahweh had given them, and to the Temple of Jerusalem, the place where Yahweh "tabernacled" in the midst of the worshiping people, according to Priestly theology. The greatest danger was that in time the Jewish faith, torn from these historical moorings, would be drowned in the sea of Babylonian culture. For in every respect Babylonian culture was superior to the modest way of life the Jews had known in the land of Judah. Like modern visitors to the United States from some less developed countries, they must have been dazzled by what they saw on every hand. In contrast to the farming and grazing land of Judah, the rich land of Babylonia was a scene of thriving agriculture and teeming industry. The proud Temple of Jerusalem, gutted by Babylonian soldiers, paled into insignificance before the marvelous temples of Babylonia. Many Jews must have wondered whether the high level of Babylonian culture might not be due to the superiority of Babylonian religion over their traditional faith.

The problem faced by the Jews in Babylonia was fundamentally the same as the one faced by early Israelites in their transition from the wilderness to the new land of Canaan. They believed that the sovereignty of Yahweh had been manifested in Palestine, particularly in the Jerusalem Temple. But could Yahweh be worshiped in a strange land where other gods seemed to be in control? Even the most devout Jews, who remembered the joy that they had once shared with worshipers in the Temple of Jerusalem, raised this bewildering question. This mood is reflected in Psalm 137, which concludes (verses 7–9) with a terrible imprecation against the Babylonians who devastated Jerusalem and against the Edomites who gloated over its destruction:

> By the streams of Babylon
> we sat and wept
> at the memory of Zion,
> leaving our harps
> hanging on the poplars there.
>
> For we had been asked
> to sing to our captors,
> to entertain those who had carried us off:
> "Sing," they said,
> "some hymns of Zion."

[14] A tax receipt (Late Babylonian) of Murashu and Sons is found in Pritchard, *Ancient Near Eastern Texts* [1], pp. 221–22.

Excavations at Nippur *in modern Iraq reveal the two principal structures within the Sacred Enclosure: the Temple of Enlil in the foreground and the ziggurat in the background. These were constructed by Urnammu, the first king of the Third Dynasty of Ur, about 2100* B.C.E. *Though rebuilt several times, they were in continual use throughout Neo-Babylonian times.*

> How could we sing
> one of Yahweh's hymns
> in a pagan country?
> Jerusalem, if I forget you,
> may my right hand wither!
>
> May I never speak again,
> if I forget you!
> If I do not count Jerusalem
> the greatest of my joys!
> —PSALM 137:1–6 (JB)

Worship without a Temple

It is a tribute to Israel's tenacity and vitality that the Mosaic faith not only survived this transition but was immeasurably deepened and enriched thereby. In Babylonia, many Jews must have capitulated to the pressures of culture and were soon absorbed into the general population. But others were bound more closely to their Jewish tradition and to the Jewish community. Indeed, it is phenomenal that the faith of Israel was preserved with great purity and zeal in the Babylonian exile, in contrast to the Egyptian exile, where the religious heritage was corroded with alien ideas and practices, as can be seen from the Elephantine papyri.

The great prophets had paved the way for the new expression of Israel's faith by proclaiming that Yahweh was not bound to the Temple of Jerusalem. In Jeremiah's letter to the exiles, he insisted that even in a faraway land where there was no Yahweh temple, the people could have access to God through prayer (Jer. 29:12-14). Ezekiel beheld a vision of Yahweh's "glory" going to the people in exile, just as the ancient ark had moved from place to place during the wanderings of Israel. And in a passage in Deuteronomy, written either in exile or shortly before, we read:

> Yahweh will disperse you among the peoples, and you will be left few in number among the nations to which Yahweh will lead you. . . . But from there you will seek Yahweh your God, and, if you search with all your heart and with all your being, you will find him.
>
> —DEUTERONOMY 4:27, 29

In the Exile, then, the people realized that they could worship anywhere with the confidence that God would hear their prayers and would be their sanctuary in a foreign land (see Ezek. 11:16). Undoubtedly a number of the prayers now found in the book of Psalms were composed during the Exile by unknown individuals who, like Jeremiah in his Confessions, cried to Yahweh "out of the depths" (Ps. 130:1). Moreover, during this period Jews undoubtedly came together in small groups, after the manner of the elders who consulted Ezekiel in his house, to be instructed in their scriptural tradition and to worship informally. It has often been suggested that the synagogue, the "gathering together" (as the Greek word *synagōgē* means) for worship and teaching, may have originated during the exile. There is no evidence, however, that there were any organized local assemblies. All that can safely be said is that the later synagogues, which came to be scattered throughout the countries of the Dispersion, arose in response to a need that was first experienced during the Exile, when Jews were separated from their land and their Temple.

PRESERVATION OF THE TRADITION

Surprisingly, the sense of belonging to the covenant community was intensified, rather than weakened, by the life under captivity. Even though the people were no longer held together by national allegiance, they had a common history and they had received a tradition. Like Isaiah in his time of discouragement (see Isa. 8:16-18), they devoted themselves to preserving the Torah until Yahweh's "face" (presence) would no longer be hidden from Israel. They studied and searched the tradition intensively for its meaning and carefully preserved their sacred lore in writing for future generations. Of course, not all the exiles were trained for this special task. But some of them, like Ezekiel, were priests who either knew the tradition by heart, as was common in the ancient Near East, or who had brought along with them from Jerusalem some of the sacred writings as the most precious part of their light baggage. The people were accustomed to look to the priests for exposition of Israel's faith. They relied especially on a class of priests known as Levites, the descendants of Moses' tribe of Levi.[15] Before the Exile, these Levites had not always been priestly celebrants at the altar. Many of them, as we have seen (above, p. 365), were "teaching priests" (II Chron. 15:3; 17:9; 35:3). Their task was to give the people torah, or teaching, about the ways in which God was to be worshiped and served. Although the Levites lost some prestige as a result of Josiah's reform, which gave great power to the clergy of the Jerusalem Temple, it is safe to assume that priestly instruction was continued in the Temple and later was resumed during the Exile.

Interpreters of the Tradition

The Exile, then, was a time of religious activity, a time of concentrated and consecrated attention to Israel's religious heritage. Some of the "editing" of the prophetic and historical literature was done in this period by redactors, the anonymous interpreters of the tradition who have too often been ignored or underrated in modern biblical study. These editors were not just tampering with the tradition or touching it up for publication. They were interpreters who believed that the sacred heritage was relevant to their time. To them the tradition was not just a museum-piece out of the past, but a living tradition through which God spoke to their contemporary situation. (On redaction criticism, see Definition, p. 394.)

An illustration of the updating of prophecy is found at the end of the book of Amos.[16] In Amos 9:11–12, the reference to the rebuilding of "the fallen booth of David" points to a time when the Davidic dynasty had come to an end; and the prophecy that Israel would possess "the remnant of Edom" reflects the resentment over Edom's grabbing a huge slice of Judah after the fall of Jerusalem. So the prophetic literature was read and interpreted in the light of what happened during the Exile. Increasingly it was realized that the prophetic message had been confirmed by historical events and that it provided a basis for future hope.

As we saw in an earlier chapter, it was during the Exile that the Deuteronomistic History was brought into final shape. Most of the work had been com-

---

[15] The book of Leviticus is named after these Levites in the Septuagint, from which the title has come to us in our English Bibles.

[16] Today there is a tendency to defend Amos' authorship of some or all of the units found in the so-called appendix to the book of Amos (9:9–10, 11–12, 13–15). However, the passage 9:11–12 clearly comes from the exilic or early post-exilic period; and it is difficult to square the other two units with the messages of Amos.

pleted in the years before the fall of Jerusalem, perhaps around 600 B.C.E., slightly before the first captivity of the year 597. It is possible, however, that the first edition appeared around the year 610—that is, just before the death of Josiah at Megiddo—and that it stopped at about II Kings 23:25. Since the reforming king, measured by Deuteronomic standards, was a paragon of virtue, it is hard to believe that the Deuteronomistic historians would have dealt with the king's untimely death and thereby presented evidence to refute their central thesis that Yahweh rewards obedience. In any event, the first edition of the Deuteronomistic History could not have concluded with the last verses of the present book of Kings, which refer to the elevation of the exiled King Jehoiachin in 561 B.C.E. This means that the final chapters of II Kings were added during the Exile, perhaps around the year 550.[17]

The Deuteronomistic History had been addressed to the nation. The writer had taken for granted that the covenant community would be organized politically as a *kingdom,* ideally united under a Davidic king and centered in the Temple of Jerusalem. During the first years of the Exile, however, Ezekiel, a Jerusalem priest, had advocated a modified view of the covenant community. Although Ezekiel's picture of the future left room for a "prince" (Ezek. 44:3), he believed that fundamentally Israel would be a "kingdom of priests" (cf. Exod. 19:6), an ecclesiastical community presided over by the priestly hierarchy of the "sons of Zadok"—that is, the Jerusalem clergy who had been in charge of the Temple ever since the time of Solomon and who claimed direct descent from Aaron (Ezek. 44:13–15). This view was further developed by other members of the Zadok order who were carried into exile, especially in the second deportation of 587 B.C.E. when the Temple was destroyed and its treasures looted.

The Priestly Tradition

The Priestly view of Israel's history is set forth in a large block of material found in the books of Genesis, Exodus, Leviticus, and Numbers. After we take from the Pentateuch the Old Epic tradition (J and E), and after Deuteronomy is subtracted, the residue belongs to the Priestly tradition that is usually designated by the letter P. Although we have referred to the Priestly Writing from time to time, it is now appropriate to deal with it directly.

There was a time when it was believed that the Priestly material was the oldest part of the Pentateuch, and that all other literary sources were built on it. But this view has been abandoned, for it is evident that in style and theological outlook this work reflects the worship and theology of the Jerusalem temple.[18] And yet the first impression of scholars was partially right. In the first

---

[17] See Definition, p. 359, and the essay by Frank M. Cross [363], pp. 285–89.

[18] A major challenge to this scholarly consensus has come from the Jewish scholar Yehezkel Kaufmann. In his important book, *The Religion of Israel* [116], he maintains that the whole Pentateuch is pre-exilic and specifically that P came before D. A more plausible view is that of M. Haran, *Temples and Temple Services* [397], who maintains that the Priestly Work was composed in and around the period of King Hezekiah (c. 715–687) and provided "the ideological conception" of Hezekiah's Reform; later on this work, preserved by priests, was promulgated as the basis of Ezra's Reform.

place, the Priestly Work does preserve many ancient traditions. This does not mean that everything in it is as old as the Mosaic period, for clearly one of the motives of this writing was to authorize the views and practices of Jerusalem priests by showing that they had their origins at Sinai. Still, a good deal of the old tradition, which developed out of the cultic practice of the time of Moses and the Tribal Confederacy, has been preserved in the Priestly Work by the Jerusalem priesthood. Remember that the date of literary composition does not necessarily provide an index to the age of the material itself. No longer do we think of the Pentateuch as being made up of "sources" that followed one another in chronological succession—J about 950, E around 750 or earlier, D after 700, and finally P in the period of the Exile. Rather, these are *parallel* traditions stemming from ancient times, as can be seen by examining the chart on the opposite page.

In writing down the Priestly tradition, the writers drew upon collections of priestly lore that had been preserved in Temple circles. An illustration is the Holiness Code of Leviticus 17–26, so designated because the exhortation to Israel to be a holy people even as Yahweh is holy, is the recurring theme of these ritual and ethical laws (Lev. 20:26). This block of priestly teaching is really an exposition of Israel's faith. It is best known for the high ethical fervor of chapter 19, and especially for the law that is cited in the New Testament as the second great commandment (Mark 12:31):

> You must not exact vengeance or bear a grudge against the children of your people; but you must love your neighbor as yourself. I am Yahweh.
>
> —LEVITICUS 19:18

The date of the Holiness Code is uncertain. The theme of holiness suggests the influence of Ezekiel, and the style at times resembles the exhortation of Deuteronomy (see 19:33–37). The Code may have been written in Jerusalem shortly before the fall of the nation, although it preserves older tradition as well.

So the Priestly tradition did not originate in a single generation. Like the services of the Anglican Prayer Book, this material is the end product of many generations of temple usage. A study of the large mass of priestly instruction concentrated in the latter part of the book of Exodus (chapters 25–31 and 35–40), all of the book of Leviticus, and part of the book of Numbers would show the traces of a long history. This Priestly tradition was available to the exiled priests of the Temple of Jerusalem, some of it in oral and some in written form, some of it early and some recent in origin.

The Formation of the Pentateuch

How, then, did the Priestly Writers unify the religious traditions? To begin with, they did not have to create unity out of a mass of diverse materials. Already a fundamental unity was manifest in the Old Epic tradition that had been received

Northern and Southern Traditions*

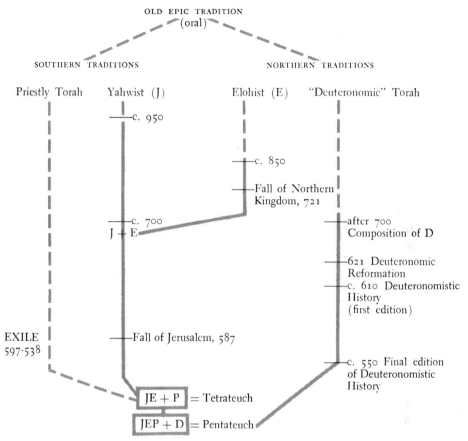

OLD EPIC TRADITION
(oral)

SOUTHERN TRADITIONS   NORTHERN TRADITIONS

Priestly Torah   Yahwist (J)   Elohist (E)   "Deuteronomic" Torah

c. 950

c. 850

Fall of Northern
Kingdom, 721

c. 700   after 700
J + E   Composition of D

621 Deuteronomic
Reformation
c. 610 Deuteronomistic
History
(first edition)

EXILE   Fall of Jerusalem, 587
597-538
c. 550 Final edition
of Deuteronomistic
History

JE + P = Tetrateuch

JEP + D = Pentateuch

*In the above chart the broken lines signify oral tradition, and solid lines signify the transmission of the tradition
in written form. Notice that all the traditions are parallel developments out of the ancient period, although each
was subject to a special development in the circle that preserved it. Like several streams flowing into one river,
these traditions were joined and unified in a Priestly edition, thus forming the Pentateuch.

in expanded form. For after the fall of the Northern Kingdom, the northern (E)
and southern (J) versions of this Epic were fused together (JE). The Priestly Writers used the Old Epic material to enrich and supplement their own presentation,
in the conviction that they were building upon and interpreting the received
tradition. So, for instance, the Priestly creation story (Gen. 1:1–2:3) was supplemented with narratives from the Old Epic about Paradise Lost (Gen. 2–3);
the Priestly version of the Flood was enriched with materials from the Old Epic
account (Gen. 6–9); and the Priestly version of the covenant with Abraham (Gen.
17) was prefaced with Old Epic narratives about the call and covenant with
Abram (Gen. 15). Thus the story of Israel was presented in its final Priestly form
as a comprehensive unity, moving from creation to the constitution of Israel as

a worshiping community at Sinai—in other words, the presentation which we now find in the books of Genesis through Numbers, the so-called Tetrateuch. Later on, the book of Deuteronomy, the preface to the Deuteronomistic History, was added to the Priestly Work, because it too dealt with the classical period that ended with Moses' death. The result was the Pentateuch as we have received it.

DEFINITION: "TETRATEUCH, PENTATEUCH, HEXATEUCH"

Tetrateuch, Pentateuch, and Hexateuch are terms that have been bandied around in recent discussions about the first four, five, or six books of the Bible. Two opposing views have been represented.

According to one, the book of Joshua, which deals with the inheritance of the land, constitutes the climax and the conclusion to the story found in the Pentateuch. Thus we are dealing with a Hexateuch, as Gerhard von Rad maintains, in which the traditions run continuously from Genesis through Joshua (see his seminal essay on "The Form-critical Problem of the Hexateuch" [166]).

According to the other view, the old account of the occupation of the land has been lost, except for the fragmentary report of settlement in Transjordan (Numbers 32), and we are dealing essentially with a Tetrateuch that is separate from Deuteronomy and the Deuteronomistic History (Joshua through Kings). Advocates of this view argue that Deuteronomistic influence is scarcely evident in the first four books of the Old Testament, while the Deuteronomistic style and viewpoint become dominant thereafter. (This view is championed by Martin Noth in *The Deuteronomistic History* [246].)

The importance of the argument for the present discussion is that the Priestly Work is essentially a Tetrateuch which extends from Genesis through Numbers, plus a passage at the end of Deuteronomy about Moses' death (Deut. 34) which resumes the story from the end of Numbers. Apparently the Priestly Writers felt that the climax of the story was the revelation at Sinai, not the story of the contest for the land of Canaan.

THE PRIESTLY POINT OF VIEW

With this background, we turn now to the scope and focus of the Priestly Writing in the Pentateuch. The first thing to notice is that the atmosphere of worship pervades the whole work. To enter sympathetically into this part of the Pentateuch is like standing in an ancient cathedral, whose symmetrical design and religious symbolism, hallowed by centuries of worship, produce a solemn sense of the holiness and majesty of God. To be sure, the modern reader may not get this impression at first when plowing through the prescriptions for various kinds of sacrifice, the elaborate specifications for the tabernacle and the altar, and the minute directions to priests and people. The book of Leviticus, to take one large example of Priestly teaching, seems far removed from modern forms of worship. Nevertheless, all the details bear witness to a long history of worship and to a vital experience of the "tabernacling presence" of God in the sanctuary. Indeed, the purpose of the Priestly Writing is to show that the whole thrust of history, from the time of creation, was the selection of Israel for the "service" of worship. Israel is conceived as a "congregation" (*'edah*) or religious community which not only bears witness to Yahweh's redemptive act of the Exodus but also articulates the creation's praise of the Creator, as in many of the Psalms. Israel's whole life was to be a "liturgy," a service of God. Even today the solemnity of the priestly blessing, entrusted to Aaron and his sons (the Zadokite Jerusalem clergy), brings a reverent hush over a worshiping congregation:

> Yahweh bless you and keep you:
> Yahweh make his face to shine upon you,
>   and be gracious to you:
> Yahweh look with favor upon you,
>   and give you peace.
>   NUMBERS 6:24–26

The Divine Plan in History

The Priestly Writers, then, stand within the worshiping community of Israel, which had been called into being by Yahweh's marvellous deeds in the time of the Exodus; from this standpoint, they look backward to the very beginning, to the Creation. In this perspective, the divine purpose follows a prearranged, systematic plan that unfolds in three successive periods, each marked by an "everlasting covenant" (*berîth 'ôlam*), in which God makes an unconditional commitment. In the Priestly view, the succession of divine covenants represents a history of God's dealings with the world on the basis of pure grace (*sola gratia*), unconditioned by human performance. The first period reached a climax in God's unconditional covenant with Noah (and through him with all creatures, human and nonhuman; Gen. 9:1–17); the high point of the second period was God's unconditional covenant with Abra[ha]m (and through him with all the descendants of Israel's ancestors; Gen. 17:1–14); and the third period culminated in the covenant of Sinai, which in priestly perspective is regarded as an "everlasting covenant" (Exod. 31:12–17), although at the same time a reaffirmation and ratification of the covenant with the ancestors (Exod. 2:24). The Priestly Writers use the Old Epic tradition (JE) to enrich and fill out this "periodized history" of God's covenants, which extends from Genesis through Numbers (Tetrateuch). Let us see how the history unfolds in the final, Priestly version of the Torah.

1. FROM CREATION TO THE FLOOD.   The first period began with the Creation and extended into the time of Noah. The Priestly Writers set forth their understanding of the meaning of this era in the Priestly creation story (Gen. 1:1–2:3), which they supplement with the Old Epic (J) story of Paradise.[19] In majesty of

---

[19] For an exposition of the Priestly story see Gerhard von Rad's commentary [271] and his "Notes on the Priestly Account of Creation," pp. 63–67. Von Rad rightly stresses that the two accounts supplement each other in order to provide a fuller picture.

style and sublimity of thought the Priestly account is excelled by few passages in the Bible. Its stately rhythms and sonorous refrains seem to reflect years of usage in the Temple, where it was solemnly recited and gradually assumed its present form of liturgical prose. In other words, although the story now appears in the Priestly Torah, which was given its final shape in the period of the Exile or even later, it reflects a long history of liturgical usage and bears the marks of intense theological reflection over a period of many generations.[20] Even today the majestic cadences of Priestly prose, which verge on poetry, evoke a sense of wonder before the mystery and marvel of the creation. It was perhaps appropriate that the Space Age was introduced when, during the first human voyage around the moon, Frank A. Borman, commander of Apollo 8, read by radio (Christmas Eve, 1968) the first ten verses of Genesis 1 to millions of listeners on earth.

Anyone who is looking for a scientific account of the origin of the world can find plenty of discrepancies in the Priestly story. To the scientific mind it is odd to hear that the earth was created before the sun, or that light was created before the heavenly lights—the sun, moon, and stars. It is fruitless to try to harmonize this account with modern science by saying, for instance, that the six creative days correspond to geological periods, or that the creation of living things followed a pattern of evolution.[21] The cosmology, or picture of the universe, presupposed in the story was inherited from Israel's cultural environment. Unlike the modern scientific cosmology, the universe was pictured as a three-storied structure: "heaven above, the earth beneath, and the water under the earth," as an editorial expansion of the Ten Commandments puts it (Deut. 5:8). The earth was conceived as having been formed by dividing "the waters from the waters," by raising up a solid substance, or firmament, to hold the primeval ocean back (Gen. 1:6). Thus the habitable world was surrounded on every hand by the chaotic waters which, unless checked by God's creative power, would destroy the earth (see the story of the Flood; Job 38:8–11; Ps. 104:5–9). In this respect, the story has affinities with the mythopoeic view of the universe presented in the Babylonian myth of *Enuma elish*, although in the latter the creation of the universe resulted from a fierce struggle between the god Marduk and Tiamat, the dragon of watery chaos.[22]

But the Priestly account is not a treatise on scientific origins. Here the poetry of faith speaks of something that lies behind or beyond human experience and scientific inquiry: the origination and ordering of all that exists by the sov-

---

[20] See B. W. Anderson, "A Stylistic Study of the Priestly Creation Story," *Canon and Authority* [156], 148–162.

[21] See the various essays in *Is God a Creationist? The Religious Case Against Creation-Science*, ed. by Roland M. Frye (Scribners, 1983).

[22] The Babylonian myth is given in Pritchard, *Ancient Near Eastern Texts* [1], pp. 60–72. See "The Influence of Babylonian Mythology upon the Biblical Creation Story" by Hermann Gunkel, in *Creation in the Old Testament* [129], 25–52, and the essay by the editor, B. W. Anderson, "Mythopoeic and Theological Dimensions of Biblical Creation Faith," 1–24.

The Ancient Pictorial View of the Universe: *(1) The waters above and below the earth; (2, 3, 4) Chambers of hail, rain, snow; (5) The firmament with its "sluices"; (6) The surface of the earth; (7) The navel of the earth: "fountain of the Great Deep"; (8) The mountain-pillars supporting the firmament; (9) Sweet waters (rivers, lakes, seas) on which the earth floats; (10) Sheol, the realm of Death (the "Pit").*

ereign, initiating will of the Creator (see Job 38:4–7). Unlike ancient polytheistic myths, which depicted the birth of the gods out of the intermingling waters of chaos, this liturgy affirms the holy transcendence of the Creator, who originated the cosmos in the beginning and upon whose sovereign will all creatures, terrestrial and celestial, are dependent for their being. The heavens declare God's glory (Ps. 19:1), but the Creator is not a part or a process of the creation. Nothing is independent, self-created, self-sustaining. Indeed, if it were not for the Creator's power, which is the source and vitality of all that exists, the world would revert to primeval, meaningless chaos.

The Babylonian Creation Epic is inscribed in part upon these seven tablets found in the ruins of the library of Ashurbanapal, the Assyrian king of the seventh century B.C.E. The epic, called "Enuma elish" after its two opening words ("when above"), dates back at least to the period of Hammurabi, who was probably a contemporary of Abraham (eighteenth century B.C.E.).

The theme of God's sovereignty over all aspects of the creation reaches climactic expression in the account of the creation of humanity (*'adam*). By placing this act last, the Priestly account indicates that human beings are the crown of God's creation and, as such, are commissioned to have a special role in God's creation. This high calling is emphasized by a solemn decision, announced in the Heavenly Council (see the "us" and "our" of Gen. 1:26), to create *'adam*, consisting co-equally of "male and female," in the "image of God." Just as the image of a king, set up in various provinces of an empire, was a visible token of the king's dominion, so human beings are to be living representatives of God's rule on earth.[23] Contrary to modern views of dominion, human beings are not given a license to exercise power wantonly, raping nature and polluting the earth; rather, they are to be God's image or representative on earth, ad-

[23] The figure of speech comes from Gerhard von Rad, *Genesis* [271], pp. 57–61, who points out that the "image" should not be restricted to the "spiritual" nature, but applies to the whole being, including the human body, which is truly a work of divine art. Elsewhere the Hebrew word for "image" refers to very concrete, visible things, like an idol (Num. 33:52) or a picture (Ezek. 23:14).

ministering God's earthly estate wisely and benevolently. The thought that human beings, so tiny and ephemeral in the vast cosmos, have been given a special role in God's creation excites the wonder of a poet, whose hymnic language has close affinities to the Genesis creation story:

> When I survey your heavens, your fingerworks,
>   the moon and the stars that you have established,
> what are human beings that you consider them,
>   human persons that you seek them out?
> Yet you have placed them slightly below heavenly beings,
>   and with honor and majesty have crowned them.
> You have given them dominion over your handiwork,
>   everything you have put in subjection to them:
>   sheep and oxen altogether, wild beasts also,
>   birds of the air and fish of the sea,
>   everything that courses through the waterways.
>   —PSALM 8:3–8

According to the Priestly scheme, the first period was inaugurated with *'Elohim's* (God's) blessing which empowered man and woman to "be fruitful and multiply, and fill the earth and subdue it" (verse 28). This blessing was accompanied by a divine restriction: human beings were to be vegetarians rather than carnivores. Thus initially humans and animals were to live in a "peaceable kingdom."

The account reaches a conclusion with the "sabbath rest," for after six days God "rested" (*shabath*) from all the work of creation (Gen. 2:2–3; cf. Exod. 20:11; 31:17). Here we see that the story, although dealing with humanity (*'adam*), concerns Israel in a special way; for the Priestly Writers anticipate the institution of the day of rest in the Mosaic period (Exod. 16). In this way they tie the beginning of the narrative to the climactic stage. In so doing, they suggest that the days of the week are not an empty cycle of "tomorrow and tomorrow and tomorrow" but times which are embraced within God's purpose, not only for Israel but also for all humankind. God claims this one segment of time as holy, and thereby endows all times with ultimate meaning.

2. FROM NOAH TO ABRAHAM.   According to the Priestly view, the Flood marked the end of the first period and the beginning of a new era. This great catastrophe, during which the world almost reverted to pre-creation chaos,[24] was motivated by the universal spread of "violence" (Gen. 6:11). The Priestly Writers illustrate "violence" by incorporating episodes from the Old Epic tradition: the rebellion of the first human beings in the Garden (Gen. 3:1–24), mur-

---

[24]In the Flood Story (Gen. 6–9), the Priestly and Old Epic narratives are closely blended (see outline of the Primeval History, p. 159. In the Old Epic tradition the Flood came as the result of a heavy rain (Gen. 7:4, 12). According to the Priestly version, "the fountains of the great deep (*tehom*)" and "the windows of heaven" were opened (Gen. 7:11)—that is, the waters above and the waters below threatened a return to chaos.

der in the first family (Gen. 4:1–16), Lamech's measureless blood-revenge (4:17–26), and the strange story of the heavenly beings ("sons of God") who seized beautiful human maidens and had intercourse with them (6:1–4). At the end of the Flood, however, God made an "everlasting covenant" (berîth 'ôlam)—that is, an unconditional covenant, with Noah and all living creatures, promising never again to threaten the earth with a return to primeval chaos.

This unconditional commitment is prefaced by a renewal of the blessing given at the time of creation to be fertile, multiply, and exercise dominion over the earth (Gen. 9:1–3). The Noachic covenant introduced a new privilege: animal meat might be eaten provided that it was properly slaughtered, for the blood, believed to contain the potency of life, was sacred to God. This principle of "reverence of life" was accompanied by a stringent prohibition: there shall be no wanton shedding of the blood of any creatures, especially the blood of a human being, for humankind ('adam) is made "in the image of God" (9:4–6). Again human beings are summoned to be God's representatives, exercising dominion within the sovereignty of God. Since the Noachic covenant was a universal covenant with human and nonhuman creatures (including the birds, beasts, and cattle) and even with the earth itself, it was signified by a sign visible to all creatures on earth—namely, the rainbow. Every rainbow after a storm would be a token of 'Elohim's (God's) gracious sovereignty over the whole creation (9:8–17). It should be noted that in Jewish tradition the privileges and restrictions of the Noachic covenant are regarded as applicable to all peoples, for the covenant was made not merely with Israel, but with Noah, the father of Shem (Semites), Ham, and Japheth (see Acts 15:20; 21:25). According to the Priestly genealogy, all peoples sprang from these three sons (10:32).

3. FROM ABRAHAM TO MOSES. The third period began with Abraham who, like Noah, was considered to be "blameless" in his generation (Gen. 17). Once again, a divine blessing is given, this time by 'El Shaddai ("God Almighty"), an ancient ancestral epithet for the deity, who promises that the patriarch will have a great posterity. At that time the older name Abram (meaning, "may the [divine] Father be exalted") was changed to Abraham (interpreted as "father of a multitude") to signify the new relationship.

The covenant with Abraham, like that with Noah, is also an "everlasting covenant," unconditional in character. 'El Shaddai promises to give the land as an "everlasting possession" and to "be God" to Abraham and his descendants—an anticipation of the revelation at Sinai when God's personal name was given to the people (Exod. 6:2–9). Here circumcision is not a condition of this covenant but is a physical *sign* of membership in the covenant community. The Priestly Writers state plainly that any male who has not kept his "covenant in the flesh" is to be excluded from the Israelite community. Such a man breaks the covenant and has no claim upon the divine promises. The covenant relationship itself, however, is based solely on divine grace and initiative and cannot be annulled (cf. Gal. 3:16–18). The Priestly Writers prefaced this account with the Old Epic tradition of the Abrahamic covenant (Gen. 15:7–21), which also states that the covenant was based upon the deity's oath, not upon human performance (see p. 44).

God's promise to Abraham is further emphasized in another Priestly narrative found in Genesis 23, the story of Abraham's purchase of a cave at Hebron for a burial place. The burial of Abraham and Sarah in this place was to be an "earnest" or foretaste of the fulfillment of God's promise that Israel would some day inherit the land. Even though Abraham did not live to see that day, he entered into it through his death and burial in the promised land. The Cave of Machpelah, as the traditional site of Abraham and Sarah's interment is known, also supposedly houses the remains of Isaac and Rebekah, and Jacob and Leah. (The traditional grave of Rachel is near Bethlehem.) Today a mosque, situated in the modern city of Hebron, rests upon what is claimed to be this cave; visitors may view the hallowed chamber through a small hole in the floor of the Islamic religious center. The mosque of Hebron is called the Haram el-Khalil, or "the sacred precinct of the friend" [of the Merciful One—i.e., God], in recollection of Abraham's standing as "the friend of God" (II Chron. 20:7; cf. Isa. 41:8).

All these passages lead up step by step to the supreme revelation in the Mosaic period, when the Abrahamic covenant was ratified. The Priestly cov-

The Mosque of Hebron, *called Haram el-Khalil, the traditional burial place of the ancestors of Israel.*

enantal history, as we have seen, begins with a canvas as wide as the whole creation. The scope of vision is ecumenical; for the creation story, which anticipates the covenant with Noah, embraces the entire human and nonhuman realm. But from this wide scope the Priestly vision narrows down until it concentrates on Abraham and Sarah, to whom are given covenant promises that anticipate the revelation at Sinai.

It is striking that the Priestly Writing, in contrast to the Old Epic (JE) tradition, has no independent account of the covenant at Sinai. The reason for this seems to be that the Mosaic covenant, in Priestly perspective, is regarded as an extension and ratification of the Abrahamic covenant (Exod. 2:24; 6:4–5). On this assumption, the Priestly Writers include the Old Epic tradition about the conditional Sinai covenant (Exod. 19–24, 32–34). However, when the ancient covenant tradition was incorporated into the Priestly context, the Sinai covenant received a new theological interpretation.

Let us see how this works out. The Abrahamic covenant, as we have seen, was an "everlasting covenant" which gave the assurance that *'El Shaddai* would be Israel's God in a close relationship and would give Abraham's descendants the land of Canaan as an "everlasting possession." In the Priestly view, the Mosaic covenant is a covenant of the same type, namely a covenant in perpetuity (*berîth 'ôlam*, Exod. 31:16), the sign of which is the institution of the Sabbath (Exod. 31:12–17; cf. 16:22–36). The key Priestly passage in Exodus 6:1–9 affirms that now a special relationship between God and people, symbolized by the giving of the sacred name Yahweh, is in effect. And this new relationship, which constitutes Israel as a worshiping community, fulfills and ratifies the pledge made to Abraham and his descendants, "I will be your God" (Gen. 17:7–8).[25]

In this context of interpretation we can begin to understand why the Tabernacle (*mishkan*) is the central Priestly institution and is located in the center of the Israelite camp (Num. 2). The Priestly Writers build on the ancient tradition of the Tent of Meeting (see p. 116); but they interpret the old shrine to mean that Yahweh has chosen to "tent" or tabernacle in the midst of the people.

> I will tabernacle in the midst of the Israelites, and I will be their God. And so they will know that I am Yahweh their God, who brought them out of the land of Egypt to tabernacle in their midst. I am Yahweh their God.
>
> —EXODUS 29:45–46

The tabernacling presence is "the supreme benefit of the Sinai covenant," as a historian of Israel's religion observes, for "Yahweh would not only become their god, he would become god in their midst."[26] According to another Priestly pas-

---

[25]See further B. W. Anderson, "Creation and the Noachic Covenant," in *Cry of the Environment* [cited under 391], 45–61.

[26] Frank M. Cross, "The Priestly Work" [112], 298–300. He points out that the Priestly Writer, in speaking of the "covenant presence" of Yahweh in his shrine, employed the archaizing technical term škn (*shaken, mishkan*) which in Canaanite meant "to tent" or "to lead the roving life of the tent dweller," and studiously avoided the verb yšb (*yashab*), "to dwell," thereby repudiating the notion that the sanctuary is literally God's dwelling place.

sage which strikes the same note (Lev. 26:11–13), the holy God "walks about among them." Yahweh's sacramental presence in the center of the community requires that no ethical or ritual impurity be permitted to defile the people. The congregation (*'edah*) must be healthy and holy. Just as a doctor gives a patient a prescription to restore health, so the Priestly Writers believed that God had revealed laws and institutions so that Israel could be a holy people. It is important to realize that in the Priestly view there was nothing burdensome in the Torah. Rather, it was a "means of grace" that God had offered the people. Consequently, knowing that the benevolence of God was behind all that was given, the Priestly Writers move through the various periods toward the climax of the Mosaic revelation as one would hasten to receive a great gift. Thus, in connection with the Sinai sojourn as reported in the Old Epic tradition, they introduce a large body of material dealing with the tabernacle and its furnishings, the Ark of the Testimony ("covenant"), various kinds of sacrifice, laws relating to "kosher" or permitted foods, the regulations for the sacred calendar, and so on—everything found between the Old Epic story of the making of the covenant (Exod. 24) and the departure from Sinai (Num. 10:11ff.).

In this Priestly block of material there is a heavy stress upon the system of sacrifices. In Priestly tradition, sacrifice was not understood as a means of appeasing divine wrath or of cajoling God to show favors. Rather, the sacrifices described in Leviticus 1–7 are means of atonement, that is, of healing the breach of the covenant relationship and reuniting the people in communion with God. It was believed that sacrifice was efficacious in restoring a broken relationship, not because there was something magical in the power of blood which contains the potency of life, but because God had provided the means of grace by which guilt was pardoned and the people could live in the presence of the holy God (see the key text in Lev. 17:11). Largely because of prophetic preaching concerning divine judgment as well as the crisis of the Exile which prompted a profound sense of remorse and failure, Priestly tradition was deeply sensitive to the persistence of sin which contaminated the health of the community. One of the great holy days on the sacred calendar, the Day of Atonement (Lev. 16), which has been called "the Good Friday of the Old Testament," provided an occasion for releasing the people from a sense of corporate guilt. And lest sacrifice should become just an end in itself, the Priestly tradition emphasized that no sacrificial rite is effective in the case of deliberate sin—sin "with a high hand"—which represents a downright revolt against God and the revealed law (Num. 15:30). Sacrifice, said the priests, is effective only in the case of "hidden sins"—sins that are inadvertently committed (see Ps. 19:12–13). Even then sacrifice must be accompanied by confession and repentance.

According to the Priestly view, the successive periods of revelation were marked by a sequence of names for the deity. In the first era, when all humankind was in the range of the Priestly writers' vision, the deity was known as *'Elohim* (translated "God" in the Revised Standard Version). In the second period, the deity was known to Abraham by the special name *'El Shaddai* (often translated "God Almighty"). Not until the third period, the Mosaic period, was

The Priestly Periodization of History

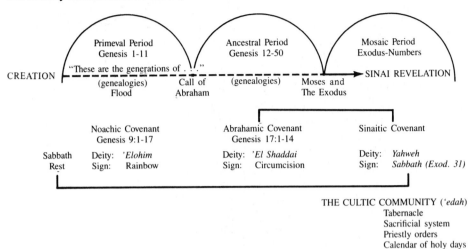

the name Yahweh introduced (Exod. 6:2–3), a name so holy that it must not be taken in vain, and so ineffable that no layperson could pronounce the sacred syllables. Thus the Priestly writers show how the disclosure of the sacred name, at the very climax of God's historical design, inaugurated a new and special relationship between God and Israel. Above all, in this view the goal toward which everything moves is the constitution of Israel as a cultic community (*'edah*)—a community called to serve God by following the laws that order life and worship. In short, Israel is a holy people living in the presence of the holy God. The Priestly view of the historical movement from creation through a succession of covenants to the realization of the divine purpose is illustrated in the accompanying diagram: "The Priestly Periodization of History."

The Priestly View of History

It is sometimes said that the Priestly view is an "interpretation" that does not give us a realistic view of Israel's past. Admittedly, these writers view Israel's past through the tinted glasses of priestly bias and give a somewhat artificial picture of the Mosaic period. But can there be *any* history without interpretation? Standing in the crisis of the Exile, the Priestly Writers attempted to understand why Israel had failed; and, by providing a reconstruction of the Mosaic period, presented a program which the people should follow when they returned to the land to claim their "everlasting possession." Therefore they retell the story in a different way than was appropriate, for instance, at the time of Elijah or Jeremiah.[27] For our word "history," they would probably use the word "geneal-

---

[27] See Walter Brueggemann, "The Kerygma of the Priestly Writers," *The Vitality of Old Testament Traditions* [63], pp. 101–130.

(Above) A reconstructed temple stands back of the ruins of the famous Ishtar Gate at the site of ancient Babylon. (Below) The processional street of Babylon which led through the Ishtar Gate to the great "Tower of Babel" ziggurat was adorned with sacred dragons and bulls of Hadad.

PLATE 6

(Above) The eastern portal of the Gate of Xerxes at Persepolis, the main Persian capital, was guarded by colossal human-headed "bulls." An inscription on the gate reads: "King Xerxes says: By the grace of Ahura Mazda, I constructed this gateway called All-Countries." This splendid piece of architecture was a casualty of Alexander's conquest. (Below) A relief carved on the Behistun Rock commemorated Darius I's victory over rebels who seized the Persian throne.

PLATE 7

The Rose City of Petra. (Top right) The only access to the Nabatean capital was through the Siq, a narrow ravine nearly a mile long running between sheer walls of rock over 260 feet high in some places. (Lower left) The Treasury (Khazneh), meaning "the Rock" in Greek), one of the many buildings carved out of the rose-red sandstone by the ancient Nabateans. (Lower right) The hills surrounding Petra, the "rose-red city" that was the capital of the Nabateans and probably the former city of the Edomites, Sela (II Kings 14:7). In the background is the facade of a tomb cut into a cliff.

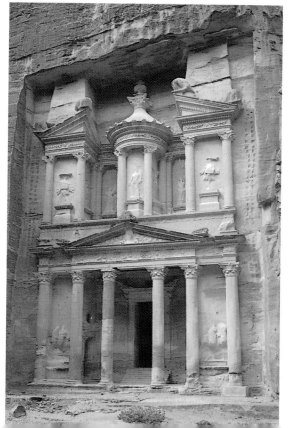

This famous mosaic map from the sixth century A.D., inlaid on the floor of a church of Madaba (biblical Medeba) near Mount Nebo, depicts the ford of the Jordan near Jericho (the area marked by date palms). A church incorporating twelve stones (Josh. 4:8, 20) stands at Gilgal. Fish swim past the ford, here spanned by a small bridge, but turn back in terror when they taste salty Dead Sea water.

ogy," as in Genesis 37:2, which the Revised Standard Version renders: "This is the history of the family Jacob." Indeed, the Priestly writers punctuate the Primeval History (Gen. 2–11) and the Ancestral History (Gen. 12–50), which they received from Old Epic tradition, with the recurring formula: "These are the generations [that is, the genealogy] of . . . " (Gen. 2:4a; 5:1; 6:9; 10:1; 11:10; 11:27; etc.). In this way they set forth the history of God's covenants.

Like some of Israel's prophets, the Priestly writers combined belief in God's universal sway with belief in God's special revelation to Israel. They affirmed that God, the Creator of all that is and the Sovereign of the nations, chose Israel out of all the peoples and separated Israel for a special blessing by giving them the Torah. We can see this increasing narrowing of attention in the genealogies or "family trees" that make up the skeleton of the Priestly Writing in the book of Genesis. With the exception of Jacob and Esau, the line is traced through the firstborn son, and other offspring are left aside, as the following chart shows.

Thus, even in these dry genealogical tables (the "begats" of the King James Version of the Bible) we can see that the Priestly Writing is governed by a theological purpose. Just as—looking forward—the Creation sets the stage for the historical scheme that reaches its climax with the giving of the Torah to Moses, so—looking backward—Israel's line can be traced back through the generations to the first man, Adam (Gen. 5:1). In other words, the Creator has singled out Israel for special service in response to special revelation. The Priestly writers did not believe that Israel's special place in God's plan was based solely on birth,

Israel's Family Descent

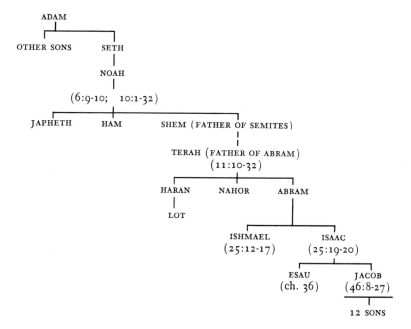

for Esau as the firstborn should have been the rightful heir, rather than Jacob. By departing in this instance from tracing the line through the firstborn son, they recognize that Israel's election rests solely upon the grace of God who chooses freely. Nevertheless, later on, when the Jews returned from the Exile, it was considered very important to be born in a Jewish family that could trace its ancestry back through the generations. Eventually, John the Baptist was to attack the false confidence in birth and genealogy, saying that God could raise up children for Abraham out of stones (Matt. 3:9)—a vivid way of saying that one's position in the chosen community is dependent on divine grace rather than on family ties or national allegiance.

A Priestly Theocracy

In this chapter we have covered a good deal of ground. During the Exile, as we have seen, the people sought a new understanding of the community that still bound them together despite national disaster. As they searched their scriptural tradition, they were reminded that the covenant community originated at a time when Israel was not a nation and had no king, except Yahweh. To this ancient theocracy the priests sought to return. Ezekiel, a member of the Zadokite clergy of the Temple, was influential in establishing the view that Israel was fundamentally a worshiping community—a holy people, living in a holy city, and worshiping in a holy Temple. Judaism had its major roots in the Exile. As we shall see later (Chapter 15), Ezra brought with him from Babylonia the Torah that priests had compiled in Babylonia and made it the basis of the post-exilic community. But before we consider further these developments, we must turn to another figure of the Exile, one in whom Israel's prophetic movement reached its highest and deepest expression.

CHAPTER **14**

The Dawn
of a New Age

According to the historian Charles A. Beard, one of the lessons of history can be summarized in the proverb: "The bee fertilizes the flower it robs." This is particularly true of the history of Israel during the Exile. Although the experience seemed bitter to many at the time, they came to realize that in it God was working for good. As prophets like Hosea prophesied, Yahweh led the people of Israel into the wilderness—not just the desert but the "wasteland" of despair—in order to speak to their heart. Had it been possible to bypass this journey—this new pilgrimage "round about by way of the wilderness"—Israel's political situation might have been better at the time, but its faith would have been immeasurably impoverished. For although the nation had been robbed and plundered by conquerors, Israel's experience of historical tragedy fertilized and deepened religious understanding.

NEW WORLD HORIZONS

We know from our own experiences in the twentieth century that worldshaking events often have a double—and seemingly contradictory—effect on people's lives. They bring about both a renewal of national loyalties and a wider vision

Biblical readings: The essential reading for this chapter is Isaiah 40–55. This may be supplemented with the closely related chapters 56–66, and with the "enthronement psalms," Psalms 47 and 93, 96–99.

of "one world." This twofold attitude came to expression during Israel's exile. The collapse of the nation brought about an intense awareness of the uniqueness of Israel's calling, a point of view that was championed, as we have seen, by Ezekiel and by the Jerusalem priests who produced the Priestly edition of the Pentateuch. The surrounding culture was regarded as a threat to Israel's faith, as it had proved to be throughout Israelite history. Israel was called, therefore, to be a worshiping community and to build its whole life upon God's Torah. Israel was to be a holy people separated from the rest of the nations by the purity of its life and its complete submission to God's rule. But the Exile also awakened a new world-consciousness. Israel's faith was enlarged by the vision of new horizons that had never been seen so clearly before, not even in the cosmopolitan age of Solomon. Israelites realized that they must look beyond their own circumscribed community to the whole civilized world if they would behold the glory and majesty of Yahweh's purpose in history. The time was ripe for a deeper understanding of the conviction, expressed narratively in the all-Israelite Epic, that Yahweh's purpose spans the ages from the beginning of history, and that Israel was called to be Yahweh's agent in bringing blessing to "all the families of the earth" (Gen. 12:1–3; see above, pp. 167–177).

The Second Isaiah

The new understanding of Israel's special place in world history was magnificently expressed by an unknown prophetic interpreter—presumably a disciple of the eighth century prophet Isaiah of Jerusalem (see Chap. X)—whose writings are found in the latter part of the book of Isaiah, beginning with chapter 40. In contrast to Jeremiah, with whom this prophet had close affinities, or even to Ezekiel, whose message also influenced him, we know absolutely nothing about his life or the events of his personal career. He is known to us only through the impact of his words, which, in the last analysis, are the best approach to the interior life of any person. For want of a better title, this poet is usually called Second Isaiah (or Deutero-Isaiah), because his writings are bound up in the scroll of Isaiah of Jerusalem. In spite of his anonymity, many have acclaimed him as one of the greatest, if not the greatest, prophet of the Old Testament.

Troubles in Babylonia

Before turning to the poems of so-called Second Isaiah, let us look for a moment at the sweeping historical changes that took place about the middle of the sixth century B.C.E. To appreciate these changes, we must remember that for centuries the center of world civilization had been the Fertile Crescent. This area had been under the domination of Semitic empires ever since the time of Hammurabi in the eighteenth century, with the exception of the interval of Hittite and Egyptian ascendancy in the middle of that millennium. The old Babylonian empire, which held sway about the time of Abraham, was succeeded eventually by the Assyrian empire, which rose to power in the time of Amos and Hosea. After more than a century of Semitic rule under the Assyrians, the Fertile Crescent next came under the sway of the Neo-Babylonian (or "Chaldean") empire. But this empire lasted not much longer than its first and greatest emperor, Nebuchadrezzar (605/4–562). His death set off a reaction of murder and intrigue, and the throne changed three times in the space of seven years. One cause of the unrest was an attempt by the Babylonian priesthood, whom Nebuchadrezzar had sought to keep under the control of the crown, to regain power. Rumors of these troubles spread throughout the vast empire, and to many it must have seemed that the end of Babylonian tyranny was near.

In spite of the tolerable conditions in exile, the Jews' hope for a return to Jerusalem (Zion) burned intensely. The Deuteronomistic History, which was completed after the fall of Jerusalem in 587 B.C.E., was dominated by the conviction that even the fall of the Temple and the exile of the people would not eclipse Yahweh's promise to David, and so it concludes with the news that one of David's descendants, Jehoiachin, was still alive in exile. According to this historian, the successor of Nebuchadrezzar, Amel-Marduk (called Evil-merodach in the Hebrew Bible), did something that must have kindled "Zionist" hopes. Jehoiachin, the legitimate claimant to the Davidic throne, was released from prison in the year 561 and was given a position of prestige in the Babylonian court (II Kings 25:27–30). The name of the exiled Jewish king probably stood as a symbol to the nationalists who still dreamed of a restored Jewish state in Palestine under Davidic rule. Sheshbazzar, the man who later negotiated permission for the Jews to return to their homeland, was one of the sons of Jehoiachin.[1]

The favorable moment for Jewish "Zionism" came very soon. After the seven years of instability referred to above, Nabonidus came to the throne of Babylon (556–539). He was an unpopular king, especially with the priests of Marduk, who hated him for constructing a rival sanctuary to the moon god Sin. Nabonidus went off on a distant expedition to Tema in Arabia, and, after conquering the city, established it as his royal residence. The rule of his empire was shared with his son, Belshazzar, about whom we shall hear more when we come to study the book of Daniel. Political troubles started in the plateau of Iran (Airyana), the home of Aryan-speaking people. In the middle of the sixth century B.C.E., the Iranian highland was divided into three areas: Media, Persia, and Elam, although Elam was actually under the control of Persia. Thus the two peoples of the region were the Medes and the Persians, and the Medes enjoyed political ascendancy. Earlier the Medes had joined with the Babylonians to give the death-blow to the Assyrians, and the two allies had divided the spoils of the Assyrian empire between them (see p. 387).

---

[1] According to W. F. Albright, Sheshbazzar appears as a son of Jehoiachin under the name Shenazzar in the genealogy in I Chronicles 3:18. See *The Biblical Period* [90], pp. 48–49.

The Rise of Cyrus of Persia

Belshazzar must have seen the handwriting on the wall as he considered with envy and apprehension the growing Median kingdom which stretched from central Asia Minor into the territory now known as Iran. When Cyrus, a Persian king from the Elamite city of Anshan, challenged the power of his Median overlord in the year 553 B.C.E., he was probably encouraged by Babylonia. After all, it was to Babylonia's advantage to cut down the power of its former ally. In the unpredictable game of politics, however, events took an unexpected turn. Within three years Cyrus had defeated the Median king, Astyages (550 B.C.E.). On the crest of this victory, he pressed on to further triumphs beyond the Median borders in Asia Minor. In the year 546, he conquered the kingdom of Lydia (now the western part of Turkey), ruled by Croesus, whose great wealth is still proverbial. As a result of these smashing victories, Cyrus controlled a vast empire, extending from the Persian Gulf to the Aegean Sea. Finally, Nabonidus, realizing the gravity of the situation, returned to Babylon to celebrate the New Year's festival. But it was too late to check the internal disorder within his empire and to halt the momentum of the Persian advance. In the year 539, the Persians and the Babylonians fought a great battle at Opis on the Tigris River. The Persians won, and serious Babylonian resistance came to an end. A few weeks later, the city of Babylon capitulated to Cyrus without a struggle (see Chronological Chart 8, p. 412).

Cyrus' account of his Babylonian triumph is recorded on the famous Cyrus Cylinder—an inscription written on a clay barrel.[2] The account begins with a condemnation of Nabonidus for ignoring the temple of Marduk and for subjecting the Babylonian people to slave labor. It was for this reason, we are told, that "the lord of the gods [Marduk] became terribly angry" and, accompanied by his retinue of gods, withdrew from Babylon. Seeing the terrible ruin of the country, however, Marduk abated his anger and showed mercy on Babylonia.

> He scanned and looked (through) all the countries, searching for a righteous ruler willing to lead him [Marduk] (in the annual procession on New Year's Day). (Then) he pronounced the name of Cyrus, king of Anshan, declared him the ruler of all the world.

The Persian account goes on to say that Marduk ordained Cyrus to march against Babylon, "going at his side like a real friend," for Marduk was pleased with the conqueror's kind treatment of his subjects. Hence, it is reported, Cyrus was allowed to enter Babylon "without any battle," and the whole population of Marduk's city "greeted him as a master through whose help they had come

---

[2] See Pritchard, *Ancient Near Eastern Texts* [1], pp. 315–16.

The Famous Cyrus Cylinder tells of Cyrus' conquest of Babylon "without any battle" and of his policy of allowing captives to return to their homelands and rebuild their temples. Although Second Isaiah claims that Cyrus was Yahweh's agent, this inscription affirms that Marduk, the god of Babylon, selected Cyrus to become "the ruler of the world" and then went by his side "like a real friend."

(again) to life from death.'' Cyrus boasts of his efforts to obtain peace in Babylonia. He claims to have abolished forced labor, improved housing conditions, and enjoyed the affection of the people. The account concludes by referring to the renown of his name throughout the world, owing to his power and benevolence. Explicitly, it is stated that he returned the sacred images to the peoples from whom they had been taken and rebuilt their sanctuaries, that he gathered together foreign exiles and returned them to their former homes, and that he restored the idols of Sumer and Akkad that Nabonidus had displaced from their own chapels.

This, of course, is the victor's story, and it undoubtedly contains a good bit of propaganda. Nevertheless, in contrast to other ancient Near Eastern conquerors, especially the Assyrians and the Babylonians, Cyrus was extraordinarily benevolent and humane. Instead of executing Astyages of Media and Croesus of Lydia, he permitted each of them to retain a royal retinue. He protected the treasures of Babylon, and respected traditional forms of religion. He abrogated the Assyro-Babylonian policy of deporting captive populations to a foreign land, and even permitted exiles to return to their homelands. He has rightly been called one of the most enlightened rulers in human history.

So began the great Persian empire, an empire that was destined to last for two hundred years, until the rise of Alexander the Great. It is against the background of these momentous international developments, which sent a wave of expectancy throughout the ancient world and which widened horizons of thought as never before, that we should understand the prophecy of Second Isaiah.

THE POEMS OF SECOND ISAIAH

For many years it was held that the latter part of the book of Isaiah (chapters 40–66) was written in the Assyrian period by Isaiah of Jerusalem. But today there is wide-spread agreement among biblical critics that "First Isaiah" did not write this section.

First Isaiah and Second Isaiah

The most obvious reason for this judgment is the different historical circumstances that are presupposed in the two main sections of the book of Isaiah. In the writings of Isaiah of Jerusalem (found in Isa. 1–39), the people are still living in Judah under Davidic kings, Jerusalem is regarded as the holy City which Yahweh will not allow to fall, and the Temple—the scene of Isaiah's inaugural vision—is still standing. But when we turn to the section beginning with Isaiah 40, a complete change in the historical situation is apparent: the cities of Judah are desolate, the Temple lies in ruins, and the people are in Babylonian exile. Clearly the Israelite monarchy is a thing of the past. These historical circumstances are not predicted for some time in the future, but are assumed to be existing in the *present* (see, for instance, Isa. 44:26; 49:19; 51:3). Moreover, the Assyrians, whose advance across the Fertile Crescent Isaiah mentions specifically, are ignored. Instead, Babylonia is the ruler of the world (chap. 47), although the end of its rule is at hand (48:14, 20; 52:11–12). Cyrus of Persia is mentioned twice (44:28; 45:1). He is hailed as Yahweh's "shepherd" who will soon decree the rebuilding of Jerusalem and the Temple, and he is called Yahweh's "messiah"—that is, the one who is anointed to fulfill the divine purpose.[3]

The study of vocabulary, poetic structure, and meter gives further support for the view that the poems in Isaiah 40–66 were not written in the eighth century by Isaiah of Jerusalem. Literary style is always an important criterion of authorship. Even in the English translation the literary difference between the two main sections of the book of Isaiah is noticeable. The oracles of Isaiah of Jerusalem are expressed in a balanced, stately, poetic form that was appropriate to the seriousness of his warnings of the impending day of disaster. In the last section of the book, however, we encounter poetry of great beauty and power. Commanding a Hebrew vocabulary that depends somewhat on First Isaiah but that is really a new poetic idiom, the poet breaks forth into lyrical strains of triumphant song. Prophecy and poetry are merged in such a matchless synthesis that we are justified in calling Second Isaiah one of the greatest poets of all time.

Accompanying this rhapsodic language is a new theological emphasis that gives the poems an entirely different tone from that found in the message of

---

[3] At that time "messiah" was not a technical term for the future messianic king. See Definition, p. 233).

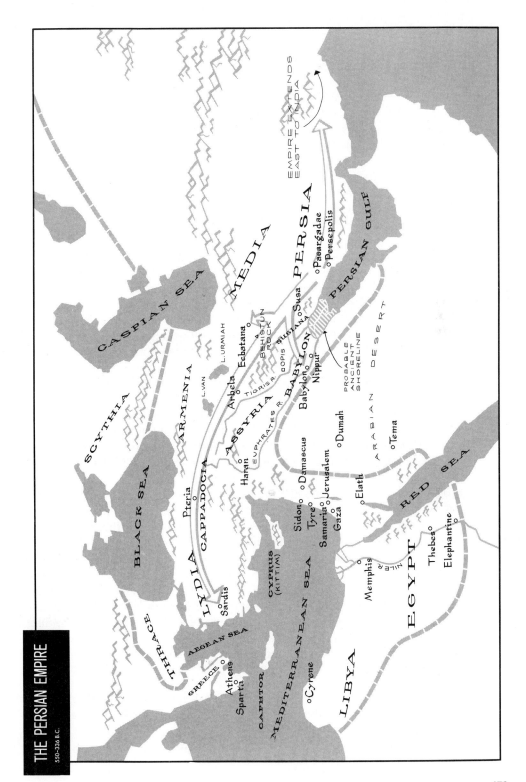

THE PERSIAN EMPIRE

550–336 B.C.

EMPIRE EXTENDS EAST TO INDIA

PERSIA

Pasargadae

Persepolis

PERSIAN GULF

MEDIA

CASPIAN SEA

Ecbatana

L. URMIAH

BEHISTUN ROCK

Susa

SUSIANA

Arbela

L. VAN

TIGRIS R.

OPIS

EUPHRATES R.

BABYLON

Babylon

Nippur

PROBABLE ANCIENT SHORELINE

ARABIAN DESERT

ARMENIA

ASSYRIA

Haran

Dumah

Tema

SCYTHIA

CAPPADOCIA

Pteria

Damascus

Sidon

Tyre

Samaria

Jerusalem

Gaza

Elath

RED SEA

BLACK SEA

LYDIA

Sardis

CYPRUS (KITTIM)

MEDITERRANEAN SEA

Memphis

NILE R.

EGYPT

Thebes

Elephantine

THRACE

AEGEAN SEA

GREECE

Athens

Sparta

CAPHTOR

Cyrene

LIBYA

First Isaiah. While Jerusalem was still standing and the nation of Judah was involved in the political storm of the time, it was appropriate for Isaiah to speak in the language of warning and rebuke. To him the Day of Judgment was at hand, and he appealed to the people to repent while there was still time. But Second Isaiah strikes a different note. According to him, the divine judgment had already taken place; Jerusalem had received from Yahweh's hand "double for all its sins" (Isa. 40:2). Second Isaiah's commission was to "speak tenderly" to Jerusalem, proclaiming to a despairing people that Yahweh was coming not to judge but to release Israel from bondage and to restore the shattered foundations of the homeland. Pardon, deliverance, restoration, and grace are the characteristic notes of his message of comfort and hope.

These three lines of argument—historical setting, literary style, and theological perspective—lead to the conclusion that the author of much of the material found in Isaiah 40–66 was a prophet of the Exile who lived some 200 years after Isaiah of Jerusalem. His writings presuppose that Cyrus was already a prominent political figure, perhaps as a result of his victory over Croesus, king of Lydia, in the year 546, or of his early triumphs in northern Babylonia shortly thereafter. In fact, Cyrus' victorious campaign is actually described (see Isa. 41:2–3, 25). Since the fall of Babylon (539 B.C.E.) had not yet taken place, although it was expected at any moment, it is plausible to date the beginning of Second Isaiah's prophetic career at approximately the year 540.

It is important—as we shall see presently—to return to reading the book of Isaiah as a whole and to realize that "the whole is greater than the sum of its parts," to quote a cliché of canonical criticism. The message of Second Isaiah, however, becomes much more meaningful when we *begin* to read it in the context of the stirring events that were happening in the mid-sixth century B.C.E. The word of the prophets, as we have seen again and again, was addressed to immediate, concrete historical circumstances. The prophets were not clairvoyants who, as it were, gazed into a crystal ball and predicted the shape of a political situation far in the future. Their predictions about the future were oriented to the present situation of Israel. It is noteworthy that nowhere in Isaiah 40–66 is it claimed that Isaiah was the author of the poems, nor is his name mentioned even once. To be sure, the New Testament attributes quotations from this section to "the prophet Isaiah" (Matt. 3:3; Luke 3:4; 4:17), but this can hardly be used as evidence of authorship. In a day when scripture was not yet divided into chapter and verse, this was simply a convenient way of indicating where the passage was to be found. Above all, the New Testament writers were not concerned with the critical question of authorship, but with the theological meaning and fulfillment of the prophecy.

In the Tradition of Isaiah

It is doubtful, however, whether *all* these chapters belong to Second Isaiah. Chapters 56–66 apparently presuppose a different historical setting from that of chapters 40–55. Whereas Second Isaiah addressed himself to exiles in Babylonia, chapters 56–66 presuppose that the people had returned to Jerusalem and that they were facing some of the difficulties of the Restoration. True, these chapters are much more closely related to Isaiah 40–55 than the latter are to the oracles of Isaiah of Jerusalem. The prevailing view, however, is that chapters 56–66— often called "Third Isaiah" or "Trito-Isaiah"—were written by disciples of Second Isaiah shortly after the return from Babylonia.

It seems strange to us, who inevitably think in terms of modern conceptions of authorship, that the prophet could write poems of such great literary charm and theological depth without giving any inkling of personal identity. But we must remember what has been said before about these prophetic collections. By and large, the major prophetic scrolls are the end-result of a tradition that received its impetus from a great prophetic leader. This is particularly true of the book of Isaiah. Indeed, there is good reason to believe that there was a school of Isaiah that extended over several generations. Remember that at one point in his career Isaiah had gathered his disciples around him in order to "bind up" and "seal" the teaching for a future time when Yahweh's "face" would no longer be hidden from Israel (Isa. 8:16). It has even been suggested that Second Isaiah believed himself to be one of Isaiah's later "apprentices" whose task was to give a fresh exposition of his master's teachings in a time when Yahweh was doing "a new thing" (Isa. 43:19) in the people's history. This would help to explain why Second Isaiah's oracles are not represented as being spoken directly to him, as were those of First Isaiah, and why the prophet's personality recedes into the background. Moreover, it would explain why the poems of Second Isaiah are attached to Isaiah's teachings as an interpretive supplement. For it was Second Isaiah who broke the seal of Isaiah's prophecy and gave the contemporary sense of his master's words, which had been preserved in the tradition and hearts of the disciples.[4]

If all this is so, we have here a classic example of the student surpassing the teacher. But Second Isaiah did not limit himself to a re-interpretation of Isaiah of Jerusalem. He was also the heir of a larger prophetic tradition, including especially Jeremiah and Ezekiel. And he was not just an expositor of ancient prophecy; he was fresh and original in his prophetic insight. In him, prophecy reached a new height of poetic elevation, and plumbed a profounder depth of historical understanding than ever before.

A HERALD OF GOOD TIDINGS

From beginning to end, the prophecy of Second Isaiah is an exultant proclamation of good news. The people who dwell in darkness hear that a new day is dawning. Captives are told that deliverance is on the way. The broken-hearted

---

[4] This is the view of Martin Buber, *The Prophetic Faith* [311], pp. 202–5.

are comforted. Every poem is filled with the excitement and expectancy of great events about to come to pass. When we enter this arena of faith, "it is as if the hell and the horror had been left behind, and one is moving up a high, sun-drenched summit to the very doors of the Kingdom of God."[5] No wonder the message of Second Isaiah was appropriated in the New Testament to proclaim the "good news" that "the Kingdom of God is at hand!" (Mk. 1:15).

In the Heavenly Council

The setting of the opening poem (Isa. 40:1–11) is apparently placed in heaven, where Yahweh's Council is assembled. Several times before, we have noticed that prophetic authority rested upon a direct commission given to the prophet standing in this Council (see Jer. 23:18), as, for instance, in the case of Isaiah's vision in the Temple (see above, pp. 325–327).[6] The prophecy of Second Isaiah also begins with good news heard in the Heavenly Council. Then the poetry moves from heaven to earth. Since the first poem serves as a prologue to the whole poetic cycle, we shall give it special attention.[7]

In the ancient view, the decisions affecting human destiny were made in the Heavenly Council. According to the Babylonian creation myth, *Enuma elish* (see p. 456), which was recited in the temple of Babylon during the New Year's Festival, the council of the gods invested Marduk with supreme authority and acclaimed him with the shout: "Marduk has become king!" His victory over the chaos monster Tiamat and her allies gave assurance that for the coming year the world would be subject to the high god's sovereign decrees. Perhaps Second Isaiah, who must have been familiar with Babylonian myth and ritual, was in-fluenced by this religious background as he portrayed Yahweh's kingship over the world. His deepest debt, however, was to the prophets who preceded him, and to the great convictions that were celebrated in Israel's worship in the con-text of the "Zion theology."[8] He was heavily dependent upon the hymns and liturgy of the pre-exilic worship services of the Jerusalem Temple, especially the services of the Fall festival when a number of psalms (47, 93, 96–99) were used to extol Yahweh as King of the nations and of the whole universe (see Chapter 16, pp. 565–566). So Second Isaiah was speaking primarily out of Israel's tra-ditions in his portrayal of Yahweh, the King *par excellence*. Thus the first poem begins with two imperatives, "comfort, comfort." In the Hebrew text these im-

---

[5] John Bright, *The Kingdom of God* (New York: Abingdon, 1953), p. 137.

[6] See Frank M. Cross, "The Council of Yahweh in Second Isaiah," *Journal of Near Eastern Studies*, XII (1953), 274–277. Roy Melugin, in *The Formation of Isaiah 40–55* [410], pp. 83–86, also argues that the text reflects the view of a prophetic commission in the Heavenly Council, on the analogy of the call of Isaiah of Jerusalem (Isa. 6), although he restricts the opening literary unit to Isa. 40:1–8.

[7] See the excellent discussion by James Muilenburg, *Interpreter's Bible*, V [16], 422ff.

[8] On Zion theology, see above, pp. 230–233, 349–352; see further Bennie C. Ollenburger, *Zion* [352].

peratives are in the plural, because God is speaking to the members of the Heavenly Council, announcing the destiny of Israel and the nations.

The Coming of God's Kingdom

The opening words are arresting. When the first Isaiah envisioned himself standing in the Heavenly Council, he was commissioned to proclaim a message of judgment upon an unresponsive people (Isa. 6:9-13). But according to Isaiah 40:1-2, the declaration that Yahweh now makes to the Council is a message of consolation to weary and despairing exiles. The note of divine judgment is scarcely more than an echo from the past, for it is announced that Israel's "time of service" in exile—like a military "draft"—is completed. The people have suffered heavily under the hand of Yahweh's punishment (42:24-25; 48:17-19). But all that is past. Now the time has come of which Hosea spoke when he said that in the wilderness Yahweh would "speak to the heart" of Israel. So Yahweh commissions the heavenly messengers to speak tenderly to (literally, "speak to the heart of") "my people" in the desolation of their bondage. Israel, moreover, will be released from a heavier thralldom than that of foreign captivity: the people will be released from the bondage of guilt. Yahweh's message is one of pardon and grace. Israel's past has been forgiven, not because sin and punishment have been balanced on the divine books, but only because the free gift of God's forgiveness makes a wholly new beginning (43:23; cf. Jer. 31:34). Israel stands on the threshold of the new age. The decisive moment has come. The time is fulfilled and the kingdom of God is drawing near.

In First Isaiah's temple vision, the seraphs had antiphonally "called out" or "proclaimed" that Yahweh's glory fills the whole earth. And in this poem too an unidentified speaker—evidently one of the Heavenly Council—responds to the divine decree announced in verses 1-2. From the New Testament (Mk. 1:3) many readers are accustomed to the translation (which is derived from the Septuagint) that makes this a "voice crying in the wilderness." But the perfect poetic parallelism of the Hebrew has been restored in the Revised Standard Version (and other recent translations):

> A voice cries:
>> "In the wilderness prepare the way of [Yahweh],
>> make straight in the desert a highway for our God."
>>> —ISAIAH 40:3

The first main strophe, then, portrays Yahweh coming, like a conquering king, to lead the uprooted people from exile to their homeland. All obstacles are to be removed from the path. Along "the highway of God" the people will be led through the wilderness, in a manner reminiscent of Yahweh's deliverance of Israel from Egyptian bondage. The "new exodus," says the speaker, will be a disclosure of "the glory of Yahweh" unto "all flesh" (humanity). Ezekiel had said that the glory that had departed from the Temple would return to a New Jerusalem. Now it is announced that Yahweh's glory will be visible to all in the marvelous event that opens the new age.

The Word of God Stands Forever

In the next strophe (verses 6–8), a second speaker, presumably another member of the Heavenly Council, resumes the proclamation. But suddenly another voice breaks in, indicated by the words "and I said" (verse 6b).[9] Probably the "I" is none other than the prophet himself. If so, the passage suggests that the prophet is standing within the Heavenly Council, where he receives his "call" from the King (compare Isaiah 6). In response to his commission he asks, "What shall I proclaim?" The earlier announcement that "all flesh" would see Yahweh's glory awakens the melancholy thought that "all flesh" is transient. The span of human life is like the grass of the field or the wayside flower—green and lovely in its season, but withered when the hot desert wind blows over it. Taken by itself, this is a cry of despair, based on the gloomy but realistic view that human beings are finite, their achievements evanescent, their existence merely temporal. But the prophet's despondent observation is the preface to a supreme affirmation of faith:

> The grass withers, the flower fades;
> but the word of our God will stand forever.
> —ISAIAH 40:8 (RSV)

Here we have an exposition of what it means for "all flesh" to behold the display of Yahweh's glorious power in the restoration of a captive people to their homeland. Although involved in the human world, Yahweh is transcendent, above history. Therefore Yahweh's "word" (expressed plan and intention) is not subject to the change and decay that can be seen all about but is the dynamic power within human history (see Isa. 55:8–11). Second Isaiah understands profoundly one of the crucial tenets of Israelite and Christian faith: the revelation of the eternal God in time.

Good News

In exultant language, which has been set to music in Handel's *Messiah*, the poem sweeps toward its climax and conclusion (verses 9–11). The poet's thought moves from heaven to earth as he contemplates Yahweh's purpose in history. He sees that purpose concentrated in a particular City, which represents the

---

[9] The received Hebrew text of Isa. 40:6 reads "and he said" (see the King James Version). Most modern translations (e.g. RSV, NAB, NIV, JB) render "and I said" on the basis of the Septuagint, the Vulgate, and a manuscript of the book of Isaiah found among the Dead Sea Scrolls (photo p. 8).

people of Israel. This concrete language is significant, for according to Davidic theology Yahweh had elected the mountain of Zion as the divine dwelling-place in the midst of the people. So Jerusalem, although in ruins, is summoned to be a herald of "good news."[10] Ascending to a high mountain, she is to announce loudly and clearly to the stricken cities of Judah that Yahweh, the liberating God, is coming in might. Once again Yahweh will display the "mighty hand and outstretched arm" which, according to Israel's ancient confession of faith, delivered the people from Egyptian bondage. With consummate skill the prophet fuses the two major theological traditions of Israel—the liberation of Israel in the Exodus and the election of Zion (and David)—to announce the gospel of the Kingdom.[11]

To the ordinary observer, the imminent collapse of Babylonia and the rise of Persia was a political event with a political result: the release of exiles to return to their homeland. But this event, like the Exodus, is seen in a deeper dimension by Second Isaiah. The theological horizon of the event, he affirms, is the advent of Yahweh, the conquering King, who intends to make Zion the center of a kingdom of righteousness and peace that includes not only Israel but also the whole world. The poem ends (verse 11) on the same comforting note with which it began. Blending the figure of the conquering Warrior-King with that of the Good Shepherd, the poet proclaims that Yahweh will gather and feed the "flock" (i.e. the community of Israel) with tender care. The range of Second Isaiah's thought spans the whole of heaven and earth, but the central focus on the restoration of Israel is never lost.

THE CREATOR AND REDEEMER

As a Bach fugue introduces a major theme and subjects it to complex contrapuntal development, so the poems of Second Isaiah are an elaboration of the theme announced in the prologue: Yahweh's imminent coming to inaugurate the Kingdom of God on earth. In the remaining poems, this central theme is artistically blended and enriched with other motifs as the work dramatically unfolds. There is no substitute for reading the literature itself, and we can only call attention to a few of the major movements in the poet's composition.

Of all the titles that Second Isaiah ascribes to God, two of the most significant are Creator and Redeemer. Creation and redemption are the two manifestations of Yahweh's kingship over Israel and the nations. Of course, the connection between the Creation and Israel's sacred history was not original with this prophet. We have found it already in the Israelite Epic, in which the

[10] The meaning of the New Testament word for "gospel," *evangel*, is undoubtedly derived through the Septuagint from the verb used by Second Isaiah.

[11] See the author's essay, "Exodus and Covenant in Second Isaiah and Prophetic Tradition" in *Magnalia Dei* [157], where the prophet's synthesis of Mosaic and Davidic covenantal perspectives is discussed.

call of Abraham is seen against the spacious background of "the first things" (Genesis 2–11); and we have seen it in the Priestly Writing, in which Creation provides the foundation for Yahweh's special revelation to Israel. Second Isaiah was influenced profoundly by Israel's epic tradition, and the creation story of Genesis 1 was undoubtedly familiar to him. But he grasped the connection between God's activity in the Creation and God's redeeming work in history more profoundly than anyone before or after him in the Old Testament.

Like the Priestly Writer of Genesis 1, Second Isaiah affirms that the heavens and the earth originated through Yahweh's creative act "in the beginning."[12] In fact, the prophet emphasizes the special verb of the Genesis creation account (*bara'*) which refers to effortless creation, a theme later understood as "creation out of nothing" (*ex nihilo*; see 2 Macc. 7:28). Yahweh created the heavenly host (Isa. 40:26), "the ends of the earth" (40:28), and humanity (45:12). Hence Yahweh alone is the sovereign of history, who shares the power and glory of Creator with no other deity. This truth is announced in the magnificent poem (40:12–21) which follows the prologue—a poem that bears marks of the rhetoric of wisdom teachers. In contrast to the God who has measured the waters "in the hollow of his hand" and has marked off the limits of the heavens with a handbreadth, the nations are "like a drop from a bucket." Their proud claim to control the affairs of history is absurd when contrasted with the sovereignty of the God whose hand holds the whole world in its grasp. Having seen idols made in Babylonia, the prophet pokes fun at the notion that these frail products of human craftsmanship have any influence over human destiny. Enthroned above the vault of the heavens (verse 22), Yahweh is incomparable in power and majesty. No image or likeness can be made of Israel's God, as the Mosaic commandment had affirmed from ancient times. Yahweh, who is "God and not a human being" (Hosea 11:9) is "the Holy One of Israel"—an expression of First Isaiah to which Second Isaiah gave great emphasis.

Creation as the Foundation of History

The purpose of this appeal to Yahweh's power as Creator was to comfort Israel, who in the desolation of the Babylonian exile believed that Yahweh did not see or care about what happened to this people. Many Jews, observing the spectacular procession of the idols in the great Babylonian festivals, must have all but conceded that Babylonian victory was historical proof that Marduk was the divine Warrior-King. Against this mood of despair the prophet raised his voice:

> Haven't you known? Haven't you heard?
> Yahweh is the everlasting God,
>   Creator of the farthest reaches of the earth.

---

[12] See Walther Eichrodt, "In the Beginning," in *Israel's Prophetic Heritage* [152], 1–10; also in *Creation in the Old Testament* [129], pp. 65–73. In the latter see the introductory essay, especially pp. 14–18 ("Creation as Origination").

He does not grow weary and get tired;
   His understanding is unfathomable.
To the weary he gives strength,
   and for the powerless he increases vitality.
Young people may weary and tire,
   youths may stumble and fall,
But those who wait for Yahweh will regain strength,
   they will soar on wings like eagles,
   they will run and not get weary,
   they will walk and never tire.
                —ISAIAH 40:28–31

Second Isaiah's argument rests upon the conviction that the God of Israel is Creator and Sovereign; therefore, the weary exiles should "wait for God," as though standing on tiptoe and eagerly straining toward the future when Yahweh comes to liberate them from bondage and to inaugurate a new age. Although caught in the grip of massive international forces, the people should hope in the God whose purpose overarches history from beginning to end, from creation to consummation.

We see, then, that belief in Yahweh's wisdom and power as Creator undergirds the proclamation of Second Isaiah's good news of redemption. The prophet's thought reaches beyond Israel's sacred history, which had proved to be a history of failure, and grounds hope for the future in the sovereignty of God who is "the first" and "the last", the Alpha and the Omega (Isa. 41:4; 44:6; 48:12). Viewed in the ultimate horizons of beginning and end, human affairs are not governed by historical processes, human ambition, fate, or chance: they are controlled by "the everlasting God" who as Creator is Redeemer. The human drama presses toward the goal of the Creator's purpose, and in this drama Israel has a significant role.

It is in this wide perspective that Second Isaiah understands the events of his time. Vividly he describes the advance of "one from the east whom victory meets at every step of the way"—a reference to the far-flung victories of Cyrus in Media and as far west as the Aegean (Isa. 41:2–4, 25–29; 46:11). In a remarkable disputation that uses the language of a court trial (chap. 41), the prophet challenges the nations to show evidence that their gods had been able to anticipate and bring about the rise of Cyrus, an event that aroused new hope for peoples living under the Babylonian yoke. Emphatically he affirms that it was Yahweh who summoned the victor from the east. The event did not catch Yahweh by surprise, so to speak, but was part of a prearranged divine plan. Yahweh, the liberating God, had been directing the course of history and working purposely for the day of release from bondage. Thus the trial between Yahweh and the nations demonstrates that Yahweh alone is God.[13]

From the perspective of Second Isaiah, this international event has a spe-

---

[13] See Roy Melugin, *The Formation of Isaiah 40–55* [410], chap. IV on "Trial Speeches" in Second Isaiah, especially pp. 53–63.

cial meaning for Israel. Israel may be pitifully weak and insignificant in the eyes of the powerful nations. But this "worm" is the object of Yahweh's love and concern (Isa. 41:14). More than that, Yahweh had chosen to become involved with this "family" and would act as Israel's "redeemer" to secure their "justice" (40:27), that is, their rightful place in the larger assembly of the nations.

DEFINITION: "REDEEMER"

The special word for Redeemer (*Go'el*), which has many nuances in the Old Testament and the New, came originally out of the realm of family law. It was the duty of the next of kin, the *go'el*, to vindicate a family member whose "justice" was threatened or violated. If the family member was forced to sell property for some reason, then the "redeemer" was obligated to buy it and keep it in the family, if at all possible. A good illustration is Jeremiah's purchase of the ancestral estate in Anathoth during the Babylonian siege (Jer. 32:6–12; see above, p. 419). The story of Ruth presents another example of how property redemption worked out in practice (Ruth 4:4–6). In the case of murder, it was the obligation of the "redeemer" to obtain justice for the deceased family member by taking revenge; he was to be the *go'el haddam*, the blood avenger (cf. Num. 35:19). The practice of blood revenge was abandoned early in Israelite history, but the belief survived that, at a higher level, Yahweh is the Champion, the Redeemer, who vindicates the justice of the people. This belief, however, led into the larger question of "theodicy," that is, the question of whether God actually acts to vindicate the rights of the weak and oppressed. It was Job, above all, who appealed to God to be his *go'el* and to vindicate his justice (see Chapter 17).

Convinced that Yahweh is Israel's Redeemer, Second Isaiah predicts the restoration of the people. Yahweh, he says, will gather the children of Israel from the north and the south (Isa. 43:6–7), breaking the bars of their captivity and restoring them to their homeland (43:14–15; see 48:14, 20). After subjecting this theme to rich variation, the prophet mentions Cyrus by name (44:28–45:6). In a previous time Isaiah of Jerusalem had said that the Assyrian conqueror was to be "the rod of Yahweh's anger." Second Isaiah, however, affirms that Cyrus, though unbeknownst to him, is the historical agent by whom Yahweh will redeem the people Israel.

There are striking affinities between the language of the Cyrus Cylinder and Isaiah 45:1–6 (also verse 13), so much so that some scholars have conjectured that Second Isaiah must have been acquainted with the Persian document. The cylinder says, for instance, that Marduk searched the countries for a righteous ruler, that he accompanied Cyrus as a friend, and that he called him by name. Second Isaiah, for whom Marduk is a powerless idol, ascribes these actions to Yahweh, who "anointed" the Persian to be the agent for liberating Israel.

A Gate Relief from Cyrus' palace at Pasargadae, the city he established as his royal residence. This is the one detail that has survived from the monumental gateway into the palace area. The relief of the four-winged figure on whose head is the triple crown seems to reflect cultural influences from as far away as Egypt. The door-jamb once carried the superscription: "I, Cyrus, the King, the Achaemenian." The winged figure may have been intended as a guardian genius or as an unusual representation of Cyrus himself.

The New Exodus

One of the central motifs in Second Isaiah's message is that of the New Exodus.[14] In his thinking the Exodus was the decisive event of Israel's past. It was the time of Israel's creation, even as it was the time of its redemption. Hence, he portrays Israel's imminent liberation from the bondage and despair of exile in imagery drawn from the Exodus and wilderness traditions: the flight from Egypt, the deliverance at the Reed Sea, the march through the wilderness, the triumphant journey toward the Promised Land.

[14] For discussions of this motif, see B. W. Anderson, "Exodus Typology in Second Isaiah," *Israel's Prophetic Heritage*, [152], 177–195; Walther Zimmerli, "Der 'neue Exodus' in der Verkündigung der beiden grossen Exilspropheten," *Gottes Offenbarung* (Munich: Chr. Kaiser Verlag, 1963), 192–204; C. Stuhlmueller, *Creative Redemption* (Rome: Biblical Institute Press), 59–98, 272.

Moreover, Second Isaiah blends with this historical tradition imagery drawn from the old creation myth, according to which creation was the outcome of a fierce conflict between the Creator-god and the monster of chaos, Tiamat. As we have noticed before, this myth, called *Enuma elish*, figured prominently in Babylonian religion and was transmitted to Israel through the Canaanites.[15] In Israel's faith the myth is transformed by being blended with the remembrance of Yahweh's deeds *in history*. According to Second Isaiah's poetic imagination, the waters of the Reed Sea, through which Israel crossed long ago, were the waters of chaos, hostile to Yahweh's creative and redemptive act. And just as the arm of the Divine Warrior was victorious in that conflict, so in the present historical crisis Yahweh comes to achieve victory on behalf of a people suffering under the powers of historical chaos. Yahweh commands the Deep, ''Be dry,'' and prepares a way for the people to pass through the waters (Isa. 44:27). The poetry rises to a pitch of exultation as the prophet, contemplating the New Exodus, addresses the ''arm'' of the Divine Warrior:

> Awake, awake! Clothe yourself with strength,
> O Arm of Yahweh!
> Awake as in days of old,
> in ancient times.
> Was it not you [i.e., the Arm] that hacked Rahab in pieces,
> that pierced the Dragon through?
> Was it not you that dried up Sea,
> the waters of the great Abyss,
> and made the sea depths a roadbed
> for the redeemed to pass over?
> So those whom Yahweh has liberated will come back,
> they will enter Zion with singing.
> They will be crowned with unending rejoicing;
> joy and gladness will come upon them,
> sorrow and sighing will vanish.
> —ISAIAH 51:9–11

So the approaching redemption is viewed as a new beginning, a New Creation. According to Second Isaiah, the Creation was not just an event of the past. In the new age, which the prophet heralds, God will make all things new. In God's creative work there is no boundary between ''nature'' and ''history,'' for both human life and the natural setting will be marvelously transformed (Isa. 41:17–20). The wilderness, which the prophet identifies with the waste places of Judah, will be converted into a garden like Eden (51:3; see also 41:17–20; 43:19–21). Above all, there will be a New Israel, bound to Yahweh in a new relationship (54:4–10), and singing a ''new song'' (42:10–12).

[15] See the seminal essay by Hermann Gunkel, ''The Influence of Babylonian Mythology Upon the Biblical Creation Story,'' in *Creation in the Old Testament* [129], 25–52; also B. W. Anderson, *Creation versus Chaos* [128], chap. 4.

DEFINITION: "RAHAB, SEA"

In the previous paragraphs we have referred to the chaos monster or "dragon" which was slain by the Divine Warrior at the time of creation. The Babylonian creation myth *Enuma elish* portrays the conflict between the young warrior-god, Marduk, and the powers of chaos, headed by the monster Tiamat. Marduk's victory, for which he was acclaimed King in the Heavenly Council, resulted in the separation of the upper and lower parts of her body and thus the limitation of the spheres of heaven and earth. The mythical victory was not decisive, however, for each year, in the rotation of the seasons, the powers of chaos seem to get the upper hand as the fertility of springtime is overtaken by the barrenness of winter. Hence the "myth of the eternal return"[16] was celebrated each New Year, when the Divine Warrior again won a victory over the powers of chaos.

This myth was known in various forms in the ancient world. The Western Semitic name for the monster of chaos (as in the passage from Second Isaiah cited above) is Rahab (see also Job 9:13; 26:12; Ps. 89:19) or Leviathan (Ps. 74:14; 104:26; Isa. 27:1). Sometimes the powers of chaos are described merely as Sea (Hebrew: *Yam*), or Abyss (Hebrew: *Tehom*), "mighty waters," or "floods." Language of this kind is found in ancient Canaanite (Ugaritic) mythology, where the sky-god Baal enters into conflict with *Yamm* (Sea) or subdues L-t-n (Leviathan) who is described as a fleeing, twisting serpent (cf. Isa. 27:1).

The myth portrayed the divine maintenance of the ordered cosmos against the powers of disorder. As the representative of the god, the king was empowered to maintain order in the mundane realm, and to put down enemies that threatened the social order with chaos. This ancient myth has been used in various ways to express Israel's faith in the supreme King, Yahweh, who is Creator and Liberator.

A LIGHT TO THE NATIONS

We have seen that Second Isaiah's perspective is as wide as the Creation and as long as the whole sweep of history. These spacious horizons reflect the immense vistas opened to the Jewish people, who had been thrust out of the narrow corridor of Palestine into a larger world. Cyrus' conquests had carried him to the Aegean shores. Second Isaiah's frequent references to the "coastlands" or the "isles" (that is, the shores of the Mediterranean area) show that people were thinking of the world in wider terms than the Fertile Crescent. There is a broad universality in Second Isaiah's message, and yet never does this prophet surrender the conviction that Israel occupies a special place in Yahweh's historical plan. The prologue begins by referring to Israel as "my people," and by announcing that Yahweh is Israel's God ("your God," Isa. 40:1). The ancient motif of the covenant faith, "I am your God and you are my people," runs through all the poems. So the great poem about redemption found in Isa. 51:1–16 concludes with Yahweh's assurance:

---

[16] See Mircea Eliade, *Cosmos and History: The Myth of the Eternal Return* [120].

> I have put my words in your mouth,
> and hid you in the shadow of my hand,
> stretching out the heavens
> and laying the foundations of the earth,
> and saying to Zion, "You are my people."
> —ISAIAH 51:16 (RSV)

In Second Isaiah's message, the liberation of Israel involved the redemption of all peoples. This theme had already been enunciated in the Israelite epic where the call of Abraham (that is, Israel), viewed in the perspective of universal history, is to yield future blessing for all the families of the earth (Gen. 12:1-3). Second Isaiah appropriated this theme, which is echoed elsewhere (e.g. Jer. 4:1-3), and gave it a new theological emphasis. In this view, God's choice of Israel was a commission to perform a special task in the Creator's far-reaching and world-embracing plan. It was Yahweh's intention that Israel should be "a light to the nations." Given as "a covenant to the nations," Israel was to demonstrate that the Gentiles—that is, the non-Jewish peoples—are also included within the divine promise (Isa. 42:5-9). Eventually every knee will bow before Yahweh, every tongue swear by the sacred name (45:23).

The Critique of Idolatry

There was a time when scholars tried to trace an ascending evolution from the presumed polytheism of the early period of Israel's history to the lofty heights of reflective monotheism in Second Isaiah. But it is being recognized more and more that this reconstruction, which reflects the perspective of Western rationalism, does not do justice to Israel's religious development. Israel's approach to the theological question—that is, the question of God—was not "reflective." In the Bible the primary concern is not with the question of God's existence, but with the question of who God is and what God demands. From the very first the Decalogue had stipulated that Israel was to worship one God—the "sole Power" manifest in the "saving experience" of the Exodus and the "commanding experience" of Sinai, in short, the story in which God was identified by the personal name, Yahweh. Later on, prophets contended with the problem of polytheism in practical terms. They perceived that Israel was tempted to "forget" Yahweh (and hence the story in which the identity and purpose of Yahweh are known) and to yield to the seductive allurements of other gods and their stories (myths). Prophets like Hosea and Jeremiah condemned the worship of the gods of Canaan and the Fertile Crescent, not because these religions were intellectually indefensible, but because following "strange gods" was a fundamental breach of the covenant, a rebellion against the one God whose power and purpose sustained Israel's history.

Second Isaiah expands and deepens this prophetic teaching—found classically in Israel's Epic tradition, Amos, Isaiah, Deuteronomy, Jeremiah, and the Priestly Writing—with the result that it becomes relevant not just for Israel alone but for all the nations. Fundamentally, his critique of the idols is that they are *powerless* in history, and therefore they are nothing. Again and again he challenges the nations to bring proof that their gods have been able to announce a plan in history and carry it through (Isa. 42:5–17; 43:8–13; 44:6–8, 21–23; 44:24–45:13; chap. 48). With some caricature of Babylonian worship, he pokes fun at the idol-making industry (see 40:18–20; 44:9–20), arguing that these artifacts are mere expressions of human cleverness. Being projections of the human mind, they do not have the divine power to control the issues of history, nor can they sustain human life from birth to old age. With sharp satire, he ridicules the Babylonian idols, Bel and Nebo—the very gods whom, according to the Cyrus Cylinder, Cyrus restored to their sacred cities—who have to be loaded on the backs of dumb animals, causing them to strain and stoop under the burden. These pathetic "gods" have to be carried, but—says the prophet—Yahweh carries the people and lifts their burdens. Yahweh alone has the power to accomplish a saving purpose in history (chap. 46).

A Theology of World History

Second Isaiah, then, advocated a historical monotheism—that is, he perceived that the whole course of history is under the control of Yahweh, who alone is Creator and Sovereign. This prophet has been called "the originator of a theology of world history."[17] That statement may seem a bit exaggerated when we consider the universal horizons of Israel's Epic tradition, which portrays the call of Abraham (Gen. 12:1–3) against the background of universal primeval history (Gen. 2–11). The remark is certainly true, however, in the sense that for the first time a vision of history's unity under the purpose of one God is made the basis of an appeal to all humankind. Yahweh is Israel's redeemer, but closely allied with Israel's liberation is the redemption of all peoples. Therefore, although the prophet first speaks a word of comfort to Israel in its despair and bondage, he addresses the same message to other nations who may see in the rise of Cyrus and the imminent return of the Jewish exiles the approach of a new age in which they too may participate. Since Yahweh is the Creator of the ends of the earth, all nations must also know that there is no other Savior. Yahweh's wisdom is the source and ground of the meaning of all history. Yahweh's power emancipates all peoples from their bondage (Isa. 42:7). Hence the prophet extends an invitation, in the name of the liberating God, to the farthest boundaries of the world of that time:

> Turn to me and be saved,
>   all the ends of the earth!
> For I am God, and there is no other.
>   —ISAIAH 45:22 (RSV)

---

[17] Martin Buber, *The Prophetic Faith* [311], 208ff.

This universalism is reminiscent of a poem found in both the book of Isaiah (2:2–4) and Micah (4:1–5), which announces that in the end-time the Temple hill will become the highest mountain, and "all the nations" will stream to it so that they may hear Yahweh's teaching. When the nations recognize the Temple of Zion as the spiritual center of the world, it is said, they will beat their swords into plowshares and their spears into pruning hooks. Second Isaiah's universalism runs even deeper than this, however. The prophet proclaims that Yahweh actively achieves this world salvation through a chosen agent, Israel. In other words, Israel's redemption—which includes the forgiveness of past sins, the release from captivity, the return to Zion, and the beginning of a new age—is not an end in itself. Israel is to be a light to the nations. Its mission is to be the servant of God's world-embracing purpose. Through the witness of its life all the families of the earth will know divine blessing (cf. Gen. 12:2–3). This is the true meaning of Israel's election.

THE SERVANT OF YAHWEH

We come now to the most difficult, and at the same time the most important, problem in the interpretation of Second Isaiah's message. Several times there appears in the poem a mysterious figure designated as "the Servant of Yahweh." In at least four passages, the Servant is described, although not clearly identified:

1.	42:1–4	"He will bring forth justice to the nations."
2.	49:1–6	"Yahweh called me from the womb."[18]
3.	50:4–9	"Morning by morning he wakens my ear."
		(Notice the reference to the Servant in verse 10.)
4.	52:13–53:12	"A man of sorrows, and acquainted with grief."

The last poem is best known in Christian circles because it was appropriated as a portrayal of the Passion of Jesus, the Christ. From the Christian standpoint, this is the deepest meaning and fulfillment of the prophecy. But instead of putting the cart before the horse by committing ourselves in advance to a "messianic" interpretation, let us try to understand the Servant poems within the context of the message of Second Isaiah.

At the outset it should be recognized that some scholars question this procedure, because they believe that the Servant poems had an independent origin. They argue that these poems stand by themselves as originally independent pieces, and that they display a conception of the Servant not to be found elsewhere in the writings of Second Isaiah. Hence, they allege that the poems have

---

[18] The extent of this Servant poem is disputed. It may end with verse 7, verse 9, or verse 13, according to various views.

been introduced into Second Isaiah's writings either by the prophet himself later in his career, or by prophetic editors. These arguments are not conclusive, however. The Servant poems are written in the style that is typical of Second Isaiah's poetry, and they fit well into their context. So we shall approach the question from the premise that the poems belong to Second Isaiah and see where our investigation leads.

The Servant as Israel

One of the Servant poems gives an important clue to the mystery. In Isaiah 49:3, the Servant is explicitly identified with Israel:

> And [Yahweh] said to me, "You are my servant,
>   Israel in whom I will be glorified."

To be sure, the mystery does not vanish, for in the same poem it is stated, at least according to the usual interpretation of the Hebrew, that the Servant has a mission to Israel (verses 5–6). Nevertheless, this poem provides a bridge to another series of poems in which Israel is addressed as Yahweh's servant. In these cases the role of the Servant is associated with Israel's task as Yahweh's chosen people, as is clear from the recurring parallelism: "Israel, my servant—Jacob, whom I have chosen" (Isa. 41:8–10; 43:8–13; 44:1–2; 44:21; 45:4; cf. 48:12). All these passages give the impression that in some sense Israel's task is that of the Servant.[19]

The figure of the Servant first appears in a disputation sometimes called "the trial of the nations" (Isa. 41:1–42:4).[20] The nations are arraigned before Yahweh, the Creator and Sovereign of history, and are asked to interpret the meaning of the rise of Cyrus (verses 1–4). When they can give no answer, save to encourage one another in their pitiful idol-making (verses 5–7), Yahweh turns to Israel:

> But you, Israel, my servant,
>   Jacob, whom I have chosen,
>   the offspring of Abraham, my friend;
> you whom I took from the ends of the earth,
>   and called from its farthest corners,

---

[19] See Tryggve N. D. Mittinger's discussion of the Servant Songs [411]. He argues that these poems are of one piece with the rest of Second Isaiah's poetry and that the Servant is Israel or "at least the exiled minority."

[20] James Muilenburg, *Interpreter's Bible* V [16], 406–414, 447–466, maintains that the Servant poem in Isa. 42:1–4 is the climax of the last strophes of—and indeed the whole poem—41:1–42:4, a passage which he treats as "The Trial of the Nations." However, Roy F. Melugin, in *The Formation of Isaiah 40–55* [410], pp. 8–10 and 53–63, questions whether the passage in its entirety actually reflects the language of a "court trial" and prefers to regard it as a disputation, the purpose being "to convince doubters that Yahweh is God."

> saying to you, "You are my servant,
>   I have chosen you and not cast you off";
> fear not, for I am with you,
>   be not dismayed, for I am your God;
> I will strengthen you, I will help you,
>   I will uphold you with my victorious right hand.
> —ISAIAH 41:8–10 (RSV)

Here the prophet uses a traditional literary form, with its characteristic command "fear not" (cf. Jer. 1:8), in order to encourage Israel to perform its God-given task.[21] Interestingly, the prophet traces Israel's election or calling back from the time of the Exodus to the period of Israel's ancestors. It was then, at the beginning of Israel's history, when the future people were still in Sarah's womb (Isa. 51:1–2), that Israel was called to be Yahweh's Servant.

In a later section of the poem, the nations are summoned once again to present their case before Yahweh, and in particular to give evidence that their gods have been able to foretell the new age initiated by Cyrus' victories. Again there is no answer (verses 21–29); so Yahweh turns a second time to the Servant. This time the Servant is not explicitly identified with Israel, but in the context of the whole poem (Isa. 41:1–42:4) this view seems to be presupposed:

> Behold my servant, whom I uphold,
>   my chosen, in whom my soul delights;
> I have put my spirit upon him,
>   he will bring forth justice to the nations.
> He will not cry or lift up his voice,
>   or make it heard in the street;
> a bruised reed he will not break,
>   and a dimly burning wick he will not quench;
>   he will faithfully bring forth justice.
> He will not fail or be discouraged
>   till he has established justice in the earth;
>   and the coastlands wait for his law [torah].
> —ISAIAH 42:1–4 (RSV)

Here something is added to the portrait of the Servant in the previous poem. Not only does Yahweh "uphold" or "hold" the Servant (41:10 and 42:1); the Servant is also Yahweh's agent, endowed with divine charisma, who in a quiet way will bring justice to the nations. Israel's election is for responsibility. Like Cyrus, the Servant too is the agent of Yahweh's historical purpose, but the Ser-

---

[21] Edgar W. Conrad, in "The 'Fear Not' Oracles in Second Isaiah" [407], maintains that the "fear not" oracles in Isa. 41:8–13 and 41:14–16 are not really "oracles of salvation"; rather, they have a function similar to ancient war oracles that encouraged a person to perform a task in battle (cf. Josh. 8:1–2; 10:8; 11:6). In this case, however, Israel's warfare is ended (cf. 40:2) and the task of the Servant is to announce the victory of Yahweh, the Divine Warrior. See further his book, *Fear Not, Warrior* [238].

vant's achievement of victory, as described in this poem, contrasts sharply with the methods of a military conqueror, even one as benevolent as Cyrus.

So far, it would seem that Second Isaiah identifies the Servant with the covenant community of Israel. Plumbing the meaning of the intense suffering occasioned by the fall of the nation, he affirms that in "the furnace of affliction" (Isa. 48:11) Yahweh has refined the people for greater service. In one sense, the national catastrophe came as God's judgment upon Israel's foolishness and disobedience, just as prophets of the past had prophesied (see 42:18–25). But, according to this prophet, Israel has paid the penalty for the past, and is now accepted and renewed by Yahweh's freely offered forgiveness (40:1–2; 43:22–44:5). As iron is tempered by fire and shaped on the anvil, so Yahweh re-creates the people through sufferings so that they may be a more effective instrument of the divine purpose in history.

The Servant as an Individual

There are, however, difficulties in this interpretation. The poems also suggest that the Servant is an individual. The second poem (Isa. 49:1–6) is crucial. Although in this passage it is emphatically said that the Servant is Israel (verse 3), it is also said that he has a mission *to* Israel, implying a distinction from the covenant community. The Servant affirms that Yahweh has called him from the womb (cf. Jer. 1:5) to gather Israel to Yahweh. And, lest this task should appear "too light," he is also given the mission of being a light unto the nations in order that Yahweh's salvation may reach to the ends of the earth (verses 5–6). In this poem (see verses 1–4) one is struck by the similarity of the Servant's testimony to the Confessions of Jeremiah. The "I" who speaks appears to be an individual, and this impression is strengthened by the concrete, personal description of "the man of sorrows" in Isaiah 53. So we are confronted with a singular problem: On the one hand, in many cases the similarities between Israel and the Servant are so close as to indicate that they are the same; and, on the other, the differences seem to be so sharp as to indicate that Israel is not the Servant. Some of these likenesses and differences are summarized in the table on p. 492.

Some interpreters believe that the differences outweigh the similarities. If the Servant is interpreted in a corporate sense, they say, either as the covenant community of Israel or as a faithful remnant, this does not account for the fact that the Servant has a role to perform on behalf of Israel, as well as on behalf of the nations. Nor does it do justice to the concrete detail of the Servant's portrait, which is modeled after that of an individual, especially in Isaiah 53. Hence a long list of candidates for the Servant has been proposed, beginning with Moses and coming down to Second Isaiah himself. Others, believing that no historic person of ancient Israel fits the picture, propose that the figure is one who appears on the horizon of God's future—that is, the Messiah. Still

The Servant of the Lord

THE SERVANT ISRAEL	THE ANONYMOUS SERVANT
Likenesses:	
1. Chosen by Yahweh 41:8–9; 45:4; 43:10; 44:1; 49:7	1. Chosen by Yahweh 42:1
2. Formed by Yahweh in the womb 44:2; 44:21, 24	2. Formed by Yahweh in the womb 49:1, 5
3. Upheld and comforted by Yahweh 41:10; cf. 42:6	3. Upheld and comforted by Yahweh 42:1
4. Hid in the shadow of Yahweh's hand 51:16	4. Hid in the shadow of Yahweh's hand 49:2
5. Endowed with Yahweh's spirit 44:3	5. Spirit-endowed 42:1
6. Honored by Yahweh 43:4	6. Honored by Yahweh 49:5
7. A light to the nations 42:6; cf. 51:4	7. A light to the nations 49:6
8. Gives torah and justice to the nations 51:4–8; cf. 42:21, 24	8. Gives torah to the nations, establishes justice 42:4
9. Yahweh glorified in Israel 44:23	9. Yahweh glorified in the Servant 53:10c; cf. 49:3
Differences:	
1. Israel despairs 40:27; 41:8–10; 49:14, etc.	1. The Servant is undiscouraged 42:4; 50:7–9 (*But see 49:4*)
2. Israel is rebellious, sinful 48:4; cf. 43:27	2. The Servant is not rebellious but faithful 50:5; 53:4–6, 12
3. Israel is blind and deaf 42:18–25	3. The Servant is attentive, responsive 50:4–5
4. Israel suffers unwillingly, seeks 51:21–23, etc.	4. The Servant suffers patiently, willingly 50:6; 53:4–9 (*Notice 50:7–9*)
5. Israel suffers for her own sins 42:24–25; 43:22–28; 47:6; 50:1	5. The Servant innocently suffers for the sins of others chap. 53
6. Israel is to be redeemed 43:1–7, etc.	6. The Servant's mission is to redeem Israel 49:5

others, impressed with the Babylonian background of Second Isaiah's thought, believe that the portrait of the Servant is influenced by the role of the king who acted as the representative of the people in the Tammuz cult (the Babylonian fertility religion), suffering ritual humiliation for them and taking upon himself their sins.[22]

[22] For a review of the various theories on the identity of the Servant, see C. R. North, *The Suffering Servant* [413]; H. H. Rowley, *The Servant of the Lord* [414], pp. 3–60; John L. McKenzie, *Second Isaiah* [409], xxxviii-lv.

The One and the Many

Two questions emerge out of our discussion: Did Second Isaiah understand the Servant in a corporate or in an individual sense? Did the prophet understand that the work of the Servant was to take place in his time or in the messianic future (the "last days")? A sympathetic study of Isaiah 40–55 will disclose that these sharp alternatives have no real basis in the prophet's message.

A great deal of light is thrown on the first question by considering how the relationship between the individual and the community is understood in the scriptures of Israel. Again and again we have seen that an individual may incarnate the whole community of Israel or, vice versa, the community may be addressed as an individual who stands in direct, personal relation to God. According to our way of thinking, the alternative is either collectivism or individualism, but in Israel's covenant faith the issue is not an either-or. Take the case of the ancestors of Israel—Abraham and Sarah, and the others. They were certainly individuals. But the various stories told about them also portray the life of the whole community that they represent. The individual and the community are fused inseparably in psychic unity.[23] So when Yahweh speaks to Abraham, for instance, Israel in every age is involved in the call and the promises. In the individual ancestor, Israel sees its whole life mirrored and condensed, for the parent lives on in the child. The "one" includes the "many" in a spiritual unity that binds all generations together. Therefore Second Isaiah exhorts Israel to turn to its ancestors, in whom the contemporary meaning of its history is represented:

> Look to the rock from which you were cut,
>   to the quarry from which you were mined,
> Look to Abraham your father
>   and to Sarah who gave birth to you.
> For when he was but one I called him,
>   I blessed him and made him many.
> —ISAIAH 51:1–2

Looking at the same matter from the other side, the community of Israel is often personalized or regarded as a "corporate personality."[24] Yahweh does not deal with a collection of individuals but with a *people*, bound so closely together by a common history and single covenant obligation that Israel is addressed in the dialogue of "I and Thou." The covenant tradition, as we have seen, is cast in the form of personal address. Moreover, the most personalized images are applied to the relation between Yahweh and Israel: a mother carrying

---

[23] J. Pedersen, *Israel*, I–II [117], 476. See especially the discussion of the Israelite sense of community, pp. 52–60, 263–79. See also J. Muilenburg, *Interpreter's Bible*, V [16], 410–12.

[24] See H. Wheeler Robinson, "The Hebrew Conception of Corporate Personality," in *Corporate Personality in Ancient Israel* (Philadelphia: Fortress Press, 1964), 1–20.

a child in her womb (Isa. 46:3), a widow restored to her husband (Isa. 54:4–8), children who are returned to a parent (49:19–21). In other words, the community is considered as an individual. This throws light on something that is confusing to the modern mind—the fluctuating use of singular and plural verbs and pronouns. For instance, in Hosea 11 Yahweh begins by addressing Israel in the singular: "I loved him . . . I called my son." But in the very next line (verse 2) the language suddenly shifts to the plural: "The more I called them, the more they went from me."

So it is unnecessary to choose between an individual and a corporate interpretation of the Servant of Yahweh, for both are true to the Israelite sense of community. The conception oscillates between the servant Israel and the personal servant who would perfectly fulfill Israel's mission. The portrait of the Servant is painted with colors drawn from many sources in Israel's history. Some scholars have emphasized that the prototype of the Servant is Moses, who, especially in Deuteronomistic tradition, was portrayed as the true prophet: the covenant mediator who interceded for his people and who finally died vicariously for their sins (Deut. 3:23–27; 4:23, etc.). Thus Second Isaiah, whose message is dominated by the "new exodus," envisions the rise of a prophet *like Moses* to lead Israel into the new age.[25] Doubtless this was a major influence upon Second Isaiah's thought, but he also drew upon other traditions, especially the Confessions of Jeremiah, in shaping the portrait of the Servant. In his prophecy, the Servant is a person, although no single person, past or contemporary, corresponds completely to the type. For the person also includes and represents Israel, the community that is explicitly designated as Yahweh's servant.

The Servant Who Is to Come

The second question—whether the Servant's work was thought of as present or future—must be considered from the standpoint of Second Isaiah's proclamation that the new age was beginning. The prophet was not looking ahead into the distant future, envisaging the coming of a Servant who was not yet visible on the horizon. His prophetic task was to interpret the contemporary political situation occasioned by the rise of Cyrus and the imminent collapse of the Babylonian empire. In the political ferment of the time he saw the sign of Yahweh's coming to liberate captive people and to inaugurate the kingdom of God. With the advent of Yahweh, according to the prophet, the Servant would appear upon the world stage, born out of the travail of Israel's history, to be Yahweh's agent for bringing salvation to the ends of the earth. In the past, Yahweh had called the Servant, had tested and refined his life by suffering, and had hidden him like an arrow in his quiver. But now the time was fulfilled. The

---

[25] This view is presented by von Rad, *Theology*, II [142], 260–62, 273–77. He calls attention to the expectation of a prophet like Moses in Deut. 18:15–19, and to the "suffering prophet" tradition which developed especially in the time of Jeremiah and Ezekiel.

work of the Servant was about to begin. Yahweh's victory through the Servant was coming near.

In a sense, the Servant was a future figure, but he was also a figure of the present age. He stood in the dawn—when the darkness of the old order was lingering and the light of the new day was breaking on the horizon. This seems paradoxical to us, for we insist on measuring time as a chronological progression from present to future. Hence, we say, the work of the Servant must be *either* present or future, *either* today or tomorrow. But in prophetic literature historical time is not measured by the calendar, but by God's activity, God's purpose. From this perspective, the future can enter the present, the power of the coming Kingdom can be felt in the old order. The task of the Servant, then, must be considered in relation to Second Isaiah's gospel concerning the "last things" or the consummation of history. Within this theological perspective, the prophet perceived the meaning of Israel's suffering and the role of the "suffering Servant" depicted in the Servant poems.

VICTORY THROUGH SUFFERING

Throughout the poems of Second Isaiah runs the theme of Israel's exaltation. With this exultant note the message of the prophet begins in chapter 40 and ends in chapter 55. Israel's *mishpaṭ*—its "justice" (Isa. 40:27)—was not disregarded by God. Rather, the people of God were invited to walk along a royal highway leading from bondage into the glorious freedom of a new life. Had Second Isaiah's message been stated *only* in the language of deliverance from captivity, it would have been no more than a lofty nationalism inspired in the heart of a poet by the stirring international developments of his time. But the prophet proclaimed that through the witness of Israel the good news of the Kingdom of Yahweh would reach to the ends of the earth. Israel's nobility was to be that of a servant who performs a task in the service of God. The people had to learn what their famous son was to say later, that the least are the greatest in the Kingdom of God, and that those who lose their life for the sake of the gospel will find life (Mark 8:3).

Second Isaiah affirmed that Israel would be highly exalted through suffering. This was the deepest mystery of its calling. The mystery is illumined by the figure of the Servant who, unlike Cyrus or any great nation, would tread a path leading through defeat to victory.

The four Servant poems depict the unusual character of the Servant's task. His method is extraordinary: a bruised reed he will not break, and a dimly burning wick he will not quench, but quietly, gently, he will persist until he has established *mishpaṭ* ("justice") in all the earth (Isa. 42:1–4). Despite his discouragement he believes that Yahweh has hidden him like an arrow in a quiver until the appointed time when he will be sent forth victoriously to accomplish his mission, a mission that will have an effect far beyond the confines of Israel

(49:1–6). Like a disciple schooled in suffering, his close fellowship with God enables him to bear affliction submissively: the lash of the smiters, the disgrace of the plucking of the beard and of being spat upon (50:4–9). In all his suffering he knows that Yahweh has chosen him to walk this *via dolorosa*, at the end of which will be vindication and exaltation. *It is through the suffering of the Servant that Yahweh inaugurates the kingdom of God.* The nations will share with Israel the good news of the herald: ''Your God reigns''—that is, Yahweh is King (see 52:7).

The Man of Sorrows

The theme of the exaltation of the Servant rises to a great climax in the fourth Servant poem, which portrays ''the man of sorrows (Isa. 52:13–53:12). In view of the dramatic power of the poem, as well as its far-reaching influence upon Israelite and Christian thought, it deserves special attention, strophe by strophe. It is divided into five poetic units. At the beginning and end of the poem Yahweh is the speaker. When Yahweh speaks, the nations hear the verdict that the Servant will be exalted through suffering.

In the first strophe (Isa. 52:13–15), Yahweh introduces the Servant and announces his triumph and elevation. Although the promise is spoken primarily to Israel, for whom the prophet's words are meant most immediately, the attention centers on the nations. The Servant has an international role, as is indicated in two other Servant poems where it is said that ''the coastlands wait for his torah'' (42:4) and where the Servant addresses himself to the peoples from afar (49:1). The mystery of the Servant's suffering, it is said, will finally be understood by the peoples. His garb of humiliation will be removed, and they will come to know who he really is. The contrast between his ultimate triumph and his present form—''marred beyond human semblance''—will be so overwhelming that the nations will be astonished, kings will bow in reverent silence before him. Thus the strophe deals with a motif that runs through the entire message of Second Isaiah: the reversal of Israel's position of distress and humiliation and the recognition of its *mishpat*, its proper and just place in Yahweh's world order.

The new understanding of the nations is elaborated in the following three strophes, in which the rulers of the nations are represented as speaking for their peoples. In the second strophe (Isa. 53:1–3), the kings express their astonishment at what they finally see and hear. To them the whole thing is fantastic and unbelievable. The Servant had grown up before Yahweh (or perhaps, ''before us''—that is, the nations) like a young sapling, like a root in dry, unpromising ground. Some interpreters find here an allusion to the Messiah, who elsewhere is called a ''branch'' or a root from the stock of Jesse (see 11:1, 10; Jer. 23:5), but it is more likely that the kings are describing Israel's unpromising career. Possibly with the figure of leprosy in mind, the poet portrays the Servant's ''form'' (52:14) as so marred that people hide their faces from him (cf. Lev. 13:45). The kings are utterly amazed that such an unlovely, despised, revolting figure is actually the one to whom "the arm of Yahweh"—that is, the victorious power of the Divine Warrior—has been revealed. For the Servant had appeared among them *incognito*—unrecognized in his humiliation.

The world's rulers continue to speak in the next strophe (verses 4–6). Although they formerly had no esteem for the Servant, their eyes are suddenly opened to perceive the true meaning of his suffering. In their previous understanding, the Servant was stricken, smitten, and afflicted by God for his own sins. Actually, he had been suffering in their stead—taking upon himself the consequences of their transgressions and restoring them to "wholeness" (*shalom*, which means "peace" or "well-being"). Astonishingly, the one who seemed to be diseased was the source of their health and healing! It was not Israel's sins that the Servant was bearing, for according to the initial proclamation of the prophet Israel had suffered more than enough for its sin. The "overplus" of Israel's suffering was vicarious—for the nations. The nations confess that the Servant's sacrifice was Yahweh's redemptive act for their welfare, their salvation:

> All of us like sheep have gone astray,
>   we have each turned to our own way,
> and Yahweh has imposed on him
>   the guilt of us all.
> —ISAIAH 53:6

Here is a profound insight into the meaning of suffering, for which there is no parallel elsewhere in the Old Testament.

In the fourth strophe (verses 7–9), the nations are still speaking. This passage emphasizes the way the Servant endured his suffering (cf. 42:1–4; 50:4–9). Unlike most sufferers—even Jeremiah, according to his Confessions—he did not cry out in bitterness or self-pity when affliction fell upon him. He bore his burden silently, without any complaint or vindictiveness, "like a lamb that is led to the slaughter, and like a sheep that before its shearers is dumb" (see Jer. 11:19, where the same figure appears with a slightly different nuance of meaning). The speaker goes on to describe the character of the Servant's affliction, although the details are not too clear. Evidently the meaning is that the Servant was imprisoned, brought to trial, and led away to death (verse 8a). He died in complete loneliness, for no one gave a thought to his "generation"—that is, the posterity in whom his life would continue.[26] He was "cut off from the land of the living" for the sake of other peoples (each king is represented as speaking of his nation as "my people," verse 8d). And to add insult to injury he was even buried in a criminal's grave. The strophe ends by repeating the theme of the sacrificial lamb: he was meek and innocent through the whole ordeal.

---

[26] The translation "generation" is advocated by a number of scholars. Others translate the Hebrew word (*dor*) as "fate"—that is, "who gave a thought to his fate. . . . " (New English Bible), or "who would have thought any more of his destiny?" (New American Bible).

But the Servant typifies the meek who will inherit the earth. In the concluding strophe (verses 10–12), as in the opening one, Yahweh is the speaker. The tones of all the preceding strophes are blended together in this great climax in which the glorification of the Servant is announced. Here it is apparent that the Servant was not just a martyr who bore "the slings and arrows of outrageous fortune." His stroke of affliction was not a fate that accident or circumstance imposed upon him. It was a divine event. It was enfolded in Yahweh's purpose. That is the meaning of the words of verse 10, which sound harsh to modern ears: "Yahweh was pleased to crush him with suffering" (JB). Here the thought is not that Yahweh was punishing the Servant or releasing on him the anger that should have been displayed toward others who deserved it. Rather, the intention is to say that God was identified with, involved in, the Servant's voluntary sacrifice (compare Hosea 11). The Servant's sacrifice was an activity within the activity of God. Thus the poet stresses that the Servant is, in one sense, the subject of the action: "He makes himself an offering for sin" or "his life shall make an offering for sin."

Vicarious Sacrifice

The conception of the Servant's sacrifice set forth here has exerted a profound influence on Christian theology. Christians cannot read this poetry without thinking of many passages in the New Testament—for instance, the important saying of Jesus found in Mark 10:45: "For the Son of man also came not to be served but to serve, and to give his life as a ransom for many." In Isaiah 53:10 it is said that the Servant offers himself as a "guilt offering"[27] and that his offering will bring acquittal or justification to "many" (verse 11). This conception of vicarious sacrifice—a sacrifice on behalf of others—was widely prevalent in the ancient world, and the belief underwent a special development within Israel's cultic tradition. One thinks, for instance, of the famous Israelite ceremony of the scapegoat that was driven into the wilderness after the sins of the community had been put upon it (Lev. 16:8–26). The belief was widespread that animal sacrifice was a means of sustaining life and overcoming a broken relationship with the deity. As we have indicated earlier, some of the language of the Servant poems suggests the ritual drama of the Babylonian Tammuz cult, in which the king, on behalf of his people, subjected himself to humiliation and pain.

Undoubtedly Israel appropriated a great deal of its sacrificial practice and liturgical language from others. But a profound transformation took place in the process of borrowing. In other religions of the ancient world, sacrifice was a powerful technique for controlling the will of the gods. When correctly performed, sacrifice was effective, for it was filled with magical power. As devel-

---

[27] In Isaiah 53:10 the Hebrew word translated "offering for sin" (*'asham*) is a priestly term for the "guilt offering" (Lev. 5:14–6:7), one of the sacrifices that effects atonement (that is, restores communion with God) through the efficacy of sacrificial blood.

oped in the Priestly Writing of the Pentateuch, however, sacrifice was based on an entirely different conception. In this view, it was God who graciously approached the people and who provided the means for overcoming guilt and living in the divine presence. Sacrifice was an avenue which carried "a two-way traffic," as one interpreter has put it; that is, it was the channel of God's approach to humanity in grace and of the human approach to God in responsive faith.[28] At its best—although it seldom reached this level, according to prophetic critics—sacrifice was a "sacrament," a visible means of grace.

In Second Isaiah's portrait of the suffering Servant the theology of sacrifice attained its highest expression in the Old Testament. The Servant is led like a lamb to the sacrificial slaughter, but this sacrifice has a far greater power than any animal sacrifice. It is a willing self-sacrifice, made for others. The sacrifice moves the nations to confess that power is made available for their healing. Through it they are made whole, pronounced righteous (or "justified"), transformed into new persons. This is because the Servant's sacrifice, in the conviction of the prophet, represents God's gracious approach to Israel and all peoples with healing power. The Servant is not a mere scapegoat upon whom people can cast their sins and lightly dismiss the burden of responsibility for their actions. On the contrary, the Servant poem shows that the sacrifice is powerful only when it moves the nations to confess that, like sheep, they have followed their own self-centered way and that the Servant suffered on their behalf. Above all, the poem stresses the central point that back of and within the Servant's suffering is the initiative and pathos of God. The Servant is the agent through whom God overcomes broken relations and effects reconciliation.

The Exaltation of the Servant

Let us return to the concluding strophe of the poem. Here the speaker, Yahweh, announces that the outcome of the Servant's mission will be victory and exaltation. According to Second Isaiah, this follows from the fact that the power of God is manifest in the Servant's sacrifice. The Servant is not a victim, but a victor. For Yahweh will reverse the Servant's position of humiliation and disgrace and will establish his "justice" before the whole world. In Yahweh's determination the Servant will have a posterity and a long life (verse 10)—both of which, to the Israelite mind, were signs of God's favor. The purpose of God will prosper in the career of the Servant, and the Servant himself will look with satisfaction upon the successful result of his travail.

At first glance, it would seem that the prophet had in mind an individual Servant, whose resurrection from the grave is implied in this passage. But this is by no means certain. The doctrine of the resurrection of the individual appeared later in Israelite tradition, as we shall see in a subsequent chapter. A

---

[28] H. H. Rowley, *The Unity of the Bible* (Philadelphia: Westminster, 1953), p. 56. The whole chapter (pp. 30–61) deserves attention. See also R. de Vaux, *Studies in Old Testament Sacrifice* [425].

doctrine as revolutionary as that of individual resurrection surely would have been introduced here in less veiled language, if that were the meaning intended. The only instance of resurrection that we have found so far is Ezekiel's vision in the valley of dry bones, and Ezekiel was speaking of the resurrection of Israel from the grave of exile (Ezek. 37). Probably this is the meaning in Isaiah 53. The prophet portrays the victorious destiny of Israel in language that oscillates between the conception of the Servant as an individual and the conception of the Servant as the community.

The poem ends by referring back to the beginning. Just as it was said in the opening that great kings and many nations would be astonished at the Servant, so it is announced in the conclusion that Yahweh will make him great. His greatness is described in the concrete terms characteristic of Israelite tradition. The Servant will receive a portion with the great and will divide the spoil of conquest, for he is the true conqueror who advances along the royal road of God's kingdom.

THE SERVANT AND THE MESSIAH

To summarize, we have seen that the belief in Israel's election is a basic conviction of Second Isaiah. Understanding this belief more profoundly than any of his predecessors, Second Isaiah expounds its universal implications for the whole of human history. But he never wavers from his central premise that Yahweh has chosen Israel for a special task in a world-embracing plan. Second Isaiah's message begins with the "good news" of Yahweh's comfort and grace to Israel, and after many variations on this theme the poems reach a mighty climax on the same note (chapters 54 and 55):

> For a brief instant I forsook you,
>   but with tremendous compassion I will gather you.
> In bursting wrath for a moment
>   I had my face from you,
> but with everlasting loyalty I'll have compassion on you,
>   says Yahweh, your Redeemer.
>   —ISAIAH 54:7–8

It is striking that nowhere does Second Isaiah include the Davidic king in his portrayals of the coming Kingdom of God. This is particularly surprising when one considers the resurgence of messianic hope among Jews who returned from exile to Jerusalem, as we shall see in the next chapter. His thinking is so dominated by the sacred history which centered in the Exodus that he seems to have found it necessary to modify the royal theology, based as it was on the twin pillars of Yahweh's election of Zion and covenant with David. Although he frequently refers to the Holy City, he mentions the Davidic covenant only once, in connection with Yahweh's invitation to an eschatological banquet

(Isa. 55:1–5). In this instance, however, the "everlasting covenant" (*berîth 'ôlam*) is not made with the Davidic king but with all Israelites who respond to the call:[29]

> Give ear and come to me,
>   listen, that you may have life to the full!
> I will make an enduring covenant with you,
>   the reliable manifestations of my loyalty [*ḥésed*] to David.
> Even as I made him a witness to the peoples,
>   a leader and commander of the peoples,
> so you shall call a nation you do not know,
>   nations unknown to you shall hasten to you,
> on account of Yahweh your God,
>   because of the Holy One of Israel who has honored you.
>   —ISAIAH 55:3–5

Thus Second Isaiah affirms that Yahweh's promises of grace (*ḥésed*) to David do not guarantee the continuance of a dynasty but rather support Israel, whose suffering will bring divine blessing to the world.

Jewish thought did not usually identify the Messiah with the suffering Servant. This revolutionary identification was carried out mainly in Christianity, although the way had been prepared in some Jewish circles, like the Essene community which occupied the site of Qumran on the northwestern shore of the Dead Sea at the beginning of the Common Era (see p. 636). However, in the message of Second Isaiah the ground was prepared for a messianic interpretation, as we have seen in our discussion of the prophet's gospel of the new age. A distinguished Jewish interpreter affirms that "in the essential point" the messianic interpretation "approximates closely" the intention of Second Isaiah.[30] For the Servant represents true Israel. Whenever the humble worshiper lives in such close fellowship with God that his or her suffering is borne willingly, thereby becoming God's power for restoring and renewing humanity, then Israel is fulfilling its task. Then, this Jewish authority continues, "God's purpose for Israel has put on skin and flesh." The Kingdom makes its beginning.

In the Acts of the Apostles (8:26–39) there is a story about an Ethiopian eunuch who, while riding alone in his chariot, was reading from the book of Isaiah, specifically the description of the suffering Servant in Isaiah 53. Perplexed about the meaning of the passage, he asked Philip, the Christian apostle,

---

[29] This point is discussed by Otto Eissfeldt in "The Promises of Grace to David in Isaiah 55:1–5," in *Israel's Prophetic Heritage* [152], 196–207. In this essay Eissfeldt contrasts the motif of the Davidic covenant in Psalm 89 with the use of the same motif by Second Isaiah.

[30] Martin Buber, *The Prophetic Faith* [311], p. 218; see also, p. 232. See also Abraham Heschel's treatment of God's "pathos" and prophetic "sympathy" with the divine pathos (*The Prophets* [315], chaps. 12 and 18)—a theme which is taken up into Christian theology by Jürgen Moltmann, "The Crucified God," *Theology Today*, XXXI (1974), 6–18.

a question that we have been raising in this discussion: ''About whom, pray, does the prophet say this, about himself or about someone else?'' The story goes on to say that Philip, ''beginning with this passage'' (Isa. 53), told him ''the good news of Jesus.'' In the New Testament, and throughout the history of the church, Christians understand the mission of Jesus in the light of the Servant poems of Second Isaiah.[31] Christians are convinced that the vocation of the Servant is realized in Jesus. He is the true Israelite—''Israel reduced to one.'' Through his vicarious sacrifice, a new Israel is gathered around him, and the doors of the Kingdom are thrown open to all nations. The whole of Israel's history comes to focus and fulfillment in him. According to Christian tradition, Jesus opened his ministry in Nazareth by reading a passage from the scroll of Isaiah and announcing that ''today this scripture has been fulfilled in your hearing'' (Luke 4:16ff.). The passage was the opening of Isaiah 61—a passage that some scholars believe was written by Second Isaiah and that was probably understood as a Servant poem in Jesus' day:

> The spirit of Lord Yahweh is upon me,
>   because Yahweh has anointed me,
> to bring good news to the afflicted he has sent me,
>   to build up those who are brokenhearted,
> to proclaim liberation to captives,
>   release for those imprisoned,
> to proclaim the year of Yahweh's favor,
>   the day of vindication for our God,
> to comfort all who mourn . . .
>   —ISAIAH 61:1–2

THE CONTINUING ISAIAH TRADITION

The previous discussion has been based on the widely held view that chapters 40–55 of the book of Isaiah constitute a separate body of literature that was composed by an inspired poet—a disciple of the eighth century Isaiah of Jerusalem. The unity of this collection is evident in its very structure: it begins with the keynote of the New Exodus (Isa. 40:3–5), and it ends by resounding the same theme (Isa. 55:12–13). Here we find a carefully wrought literary whole which reflects the situation of the Babylonian exile and which announces a message of consolation to a captive people.

The Disciples of Second Isaiah

As noted earlier, the remaining chapters of the book of Isaiah (chaps. 56–66), often put under the rubric of ''Third Isaiah,'' seem to reflect the early post-exilic period (to be considered in the next chapter) when disciples of Second Isaiah handed on and reinterpreted their master's message in a new situation, namely,

---

[31] See *The Servant of God* [420] by Walther Zimmerli and J. Jeremias.

the time of the building of the second temple (c. 520–515 B.C.E.).[32] When one reads these chapters with this struggling Palestinian community in mind, the shift of emphasis from the message of Second Isaiah becomes clear. Second Isaiah's poetry pulses with the excitement of an imminent return to Jerusalem— a New Exodus and a new entry into the Promised Land; the poems found in Isaiah 56–66, on the other hand, reflect a mood of bitter disillusionment and acrimonious controversy in the Palestinian community. Second Isaiah had announced that Israel's vocation was to be the Servant of Yahweh, who mediates through suffering the blessing of God to all peoples; the poems found in Isaiah 56–66 speak of the faithful remnant as "servants" (Isa. 65:8–12, 13–16) who are oppressed by elements within the Jewish community. On the whole these poems lack the lyrical quality and theological depth of Isaiah 40–55. Yet there are clear echoes of the poetry of Second Isaiah, both in form and content, especially in chapters 60–62, the context from which Jesus' scripture reading in the Nazareth synagogue, mentioned above, was taken (see Luke 4:16–30). Reverberations of Second Isaiah's poetry are also heard in a passage (Isa. 57:14–21) which recapitulates the motif of preparing a "way" for the people into the future (57:14; compare 40:1–4). Here Israel's consolation is based on the grace of the holy God, who is both transcendent in celestial majesty and redemptively present in human history.

> Thus says the high and exalted One,
>   who inhabits eternity, whose name is Holy:
> "I dwell in a lofty and holy place,
>   but also with the crushed and humble in spirit,
> to give the humble in spirit new life,
>   and to revive the heart of the crushed."
>   —ISAIAH 57:15

Moreover, no finer interpretation of the demands of the covenant can be found anywhere in the scriptures of Israel than this passage, which interprets the meaning of the cultic rite of fasting (58:1–12).

> Is not this the sort of fast that pleases me
>   —it is the Lord Yahweh who speaks—
> to break unjust fetters
>   and undo the thongs of the yoke,
>   to let the oppressed go free,
>   and break every yoke,
>   to share your bread with the hungry,
>   and shelter the homeless poor,
>   to clothe the man you see to be naked
>   and not turn from your own kin?

---

[32] James Smart, in *History and Theology in Second Isaiah* [415], and a few others attempt to defend the thesis that Second Isaiah wrote all of chapters 40 through 66, but this view has not won a wide following.

> Then will your light shine like the dawn
>   and your wound be quickly healed over.
> Your integrity will go before you,
>   and the glory of Yahweh behind you.
>   —ISAIAH 58:6–8 (JB)

In this poetic collection, however, the message of Second Isaiah has been transposed into a new key. Whereas Second Isaiah portrayed the saving activity of Yahweh within the context of the political realities attending the rise of Cyrus and the beginning of the Persian empire, the poetry of his disciples tends to move away from the plane of history into a transhistorical realm of religious imagination. Here the Divine Warrior is portrayed as coming to conquer the powers of evil and chaos that corrupt the world and to introduce a new age, one that is discontinuous with all previous history. We hear about a New Jerusalem, indeed a cosmic "new creation."

> For behold, I create new heavens
>   and a new earth,
> and the former things shall not be remembered,
>   or come into mind.
> But be glad and rejoice for ever
>   in that which I create;
> For behold, I create Jerusalem a rejoicing,
>   and her people a joy.
> I will rejoice in Jerusalem,
>   and be glad in my people;
> No more shall be heard in it the sound of weeping,
>   and the cry of distress.
>   —ISAIAH 65:17–19 (RSV)

Poems like these bring us into "the dawn of apocalyptic" and thus to the new theological horizons of the post-exilic community to be considered later.[33]

THE BOOK OF ISAIAH AS A WHOLE

In this chapter and a previous one (Chapter 10), we have seen that the large scroll of Isaiah, sixty-six chapters in all, actually falls into three major parts: chapters 1–39, which reflect the Assyrian period when Isaiah of Jerusalem was active (c. 740–700 B.C.E.); chapters 40–55, which reflect the transition from the Babylonian to the Persian periods when Second Isaiah flourished (c. 538); and chapters 56–66, which reflect the conditions of the early post-exilic period under Persian rule (c. 520–500). We have found no less than three "Isaiahs." Before the rise of modern biblical criticism, however, the whole book was regarded as a literary unity, and as such it entered the canon of the Bible. The question that

[33] See Paul D. Hanson, *The Dawn of Apocalyptic* [427], chap. II, an important work that has influenced this discussion.

we now face is whether, without sacrificing our gains in historical understanding, it is possible to move from analysis to synthesis. Can this Humpty-Dumpty, which lies broken in several pieces, be put back together again?

At this stage of study it is possible to make only a beginning in this difficult task.[34] Notice, first of all, that the sections that have been labeled Second Isaiah and Third Isaiah were never intended to stand by themselves. This is evident from the fact that, unlike other prophetic collections (including First Isaiah), there is no superscription that associates the materials with a particular prophet or a particular historical time (e.g., Isa. 1:1; Jer. 1:1–3; Hag. 1:1; Zech. 1:1). Apparently, so-called Second Isaiah and Third Isaiah were meant to be subsumed under the seminal work of the eighth century prophet, Isaiah of Jerusalem.

Moreover, both of these blocks of material seem to serve as supplements to, and even commentaries on, previous prophetic tradition. Second Isaiah is a theological supplement to the message of First Isaiah, composed in a later time for the purpose of contemporizing the original message. The disciple elaborated on the message of his predecessor who proclaimed that Yahweh, the exalted King of the cosmos, is "the Holy One of Israel," whose earthly rule is manifest through the Davidic king and the Temple of Zion. But the student also enriched, and even went beyond, the thought of his teacher. Whereas Isaiah of Jerusalem had ignored the Exodus tradition, II Isaiah drew deeply upon the Israelite epic: the promises to the ancestors, the deliverance from Egypt, the wanderings in the wilderness, the entrance into the land. As we have seen, he combined the Exodus and Zion traditions in the exuberant proclamation that Yahweh, the cosmic Creator and King, was leading an uprooted people in a New Exodus through the wilderness to Zion, Yahweh's holy hill (cf. Exod. 15:1–18). Moreover, he "democratized" the unconditional promises of grace to David by loosing them from the fallen Davidic dynasty and applying them to the people (Isa. 55:3–5).

Similarly, the collection known as Third Isaiah is actually a supplement to Second Isaiah, as evident by the reworking of the received poetic forms and theological motifs. In these chapters, as one scholar observes, "we are dealing with a living, ongoing tradition, restlessly seeking new applications as the situation changes."[35]

However, something more needs to be said about the book as a whole. In the last analysis, we are not just dealing with a series of supplements to an original Isaianic prophecy but with a new work, in which "the whole is greater than the sum of its parts." The question of the unity of Isaiah may lead to a consideration of the "canonical shape" of the book as it was used scripturally

---

[34] The question of the unity of the book of Isaiah has been opened in a new way by Brevard Childs' canonical approach in *Introduction* [37], pp. 325–338. For further discussion see the articles in *Interpretation* 36 (1982), especially Ronald C. Clements, "The Unity of the Book of Isaiah," 117–129; Walter Brueggemann, "Unity and Dynamic in the Isaiah Tradition," *Journal for the Study of the Old Testament* 29 (1984), 89–107; R. C. Clements, "Beyond Tradition-History: Deutero-Isaianic Development of First Isaiah's Themes." *JSOT* 31. 1985. pp. 95–113.

[35] Paul Hanson, *Dawn of Apocalyptic* [427], p. 45.

in the synagogue.[36] At the very least the question leads to "redaction criticism"—that is, an examination of how the final redactors organized and interpreted the various levels of the Isaiah tradition so that as a whole, it spoke to the situation of their time.[37]

In an earlier chapter (Chapter 12) we noticed that redactors, probably members of the Deuteronomistic school, were responsible for shaping the materials of the book of Jeremiah so that the message of the prophet would speak to people in exile. Can anything be said about the redaction of the book of Isaiah? In attempting to answer this question we grope in mists of uncertainty. One important clue, however, seems to be found in the latter chapters of the book where prophecy moves into the idiom of apocalyptic. This transition entailed "a growing indifference to the concrete events of plain history" and "a flight into the timeless repose of myth."[38] Accordingly, Second Isaiah's message was detached from its historical moorings in the political realities of the mid-sixth century B.C.E. and was lifted into the symbolic world-view of apocalyptic. No longer is the scene restricted to Israel's history. Rather, it enlarges into a universal drama, in which the Kingdom of God is in opposition to the powers of evil that afflict and crush people.

It is not enough, however, to see what has happened in the transition from Second Isaiah to the disciples designated as Third Isaiah. The apocalyptic interpreters of Isaiah have not only called for a new reading of Second Isaiah, but also for a new reading of the whole Isaiah tradition. This helps to explain the presence of the so-called "Little Apocalypse of Isaiah" (Isa. 24–27), usually regarded as having no relation to its context. This also helps us to understand why the book of Isaiah is punctuated at other points with passages that are akin to the apocalyptic idiom (e.g., chaps. 34 and 35). Viewed in this total context, the thread that binds all the Isaianic traditions together is the City of Zion, regarded as the earthly locus of the Kingdom of God and, in apocalyptic thinking, the symbol of the new age introduced through Yahweh's decisive triumph over the powers of chaos.[39] Thus we read in an apocalyptic passage, found in the very heart of the book of Isaiah, about the ultimate victory of the Divine Warrior:

> In that day Yahweh will punish with his heavy, great, and mighty sword Leviathan the fleeing serpent, Leviathan the twisting serpent, and he will slay the Dragon that is in the Sea.
>
> —ISAIAH 27:1

Much more could be said on this subject. Already, however, we have anticipated developments that lie ahead.

---

[36] Brevard Childs, *Introduction* [37]. See Definition, p. 638 for a further discussion of this canonical approach.

[37] See the Definition of Redaction Criticism above, p. 394.

[38] See Paul Hanson's illuminating discussion of myth and history, *The Dawn of Apocalyptic* [427], pp. 126–134.

[39] The mythical dimensions of Zion theology are explored in Bennie C. Ollenburger, *Zion* [352].

CHAPTER 15

A Kingdom
of Priests

In modern political experience, we have had many vivid illustrations of people who have gone wild with joy at the approach of an army of liberation. The Cyrus Cylinder (see pp. 470–471) is a first-hand historical witness to the jubilation evoked by the advance of the Persian army in the middle of the sixth century B.C.E. Cyrus' benevolent policy was a welcome relief from Babylonian tyranny, both to the Babylonians themselves, who in high anticipation opened the doors of their cities and their hearts to him, and to the many captive peoples under his rule. Apparently Cyrus understood the futility of trying to lash people of diverse backgrounds and national traditions into subservience—a policy that had been the foundation of the empires whose lands he inherited. To be sure, he did not relax his political power. The Persian army had proved to be a powerful fighting force, and the Persian government soon developed a swift system of communications—a forerunner of the American "pony express." This system made it possible to supervise the far-flung empire, which was efficiently divided into satrapies or provinces. However, Cyrus seems to have understood the limitations of power, or perhaps he realized that the emperor who enjoys honor and loyalty from his people also enjoys an increase of power.

Biblical readings: The period of the return from Babylonian captivity is dealt with in the books of Ezra and Nehemiah. For further understanding of the period, read the small prophetic collections of Haggai, Zechariah 1–8, Malachi, Obadiah, and Joel. The meaning of the Torah for Judaism is expressed in Psalms 1; 19:7–14; 119.

DEFINITION: "ARAMAIC"

A word about the Aramaic language, which gradually became the common tongue of the Jewish people during the post-exilic period. Although Aramaic became particularly popular at this time, actually it is at least as old as Hebrew, and both belong to a common family of Semitic languages. The differences and resemblances between them are like those between such modern Romance languages as Spanish and Italian. The close relations that existed between the Aramean (Syrian) and Hebrew people, as recorded in the ancestral stories of Jacob and Laban, existed between the two languages as well. Like Jacob and Laban, Aramaic and Hebrew are relatives. In the ancient Mediterranean world, Aramaic commanded great international prestige, for like English today it was used as a *lingua franca*. Remember that when the Rabshakeh came to demand the surrender of Jerusalem in Isaiah's day (Isa. 36:11; II Kings 18:26), he was asked to speak in Aramaic rather than in the native tongue of the Judeans. During and after the Exile, the Persian authorities' use of Aramaic as an international language in speaking to their satrapies enhanced its importance. Gradually, the Jews came to think of Hebrew as a literary or classical language, and in Palestine and throughout the Dispersion (for instance, at Elephantine) their spoken language was Aramaic. Well before the Christian era, Hebrew scripture had to be accompanied by a "targum," a free translation into Aramaic, to enable ordinary Jews to understand it. Moreover, the Babylonian Talmud, a voluminous collection of writings that set forth Jewish religious and civil law, was written in an eastern branch of the Aramaic language. And it was in Palestinian Aramaic, the western branch, that Jesus proclaimed the gospel of the Kingdom of God.

CYRUS' EDICT OF LIBERATION

In one passage of the Cylinder, where Cyrus is speaking of various regions that he has conquered, he says: "I returned to (these) sacred cities on the other side of the Tigris, the sanctuaries of which have been in ruins for a long time, the images which (used) to live therein and established for them permanent sanctuaries. I (also) gathered all their (former) inhabitants and returned (to them) their habitations."[1] Clearly, Cyrus chose to abandon the "scorched-earth" tactics of the Assyrians and Babylonians, who had destroyed cities and temples, looted sacred treasuries, and transported idols and people into captivity. With a political right-about-face, he permitted the subject peoples to carry on their customs, to worship their gods, and to settle in their homelands (see Chronological Chart 8, p. 412).

It is against this background that we should read the account of the edict of liberation that Cyrus proclaimed to the Jewish exiles in the first year after Babylon's fall (538 B.C.E.). This edict is preserved in two versions: one is written in Hebrew, the traditional language of Israel (Ezra 1:2–4), and the other is written in Aramaic (6:3–5).

The very fact that Cyrus' edict is preserved in two versions speaks in favor of its authenticity. Although some scholars believe that the Aramaic version is

---

[1] Pritchard, *Ancient Near Eastern Texts* [1], p. 316.

the original account, there are no fundamental discrepancies between the two.[2] According to the Hebrew version, Cyrus claimed that "Yahweh, the God of heaven" had given him all the kingdoms of the earth and had charged him to build Yahweh a temple in Jerusalem. This claim reminds us of Second Isaiah, who regarded Cyrus as Yahweh's agent by whom Jerusalem would be rebuilt (Isa. 44:28; 45:1–3, 13). Undoubtedly the Jewish historian has touched up the edict theologically, for in his Cylinder, Cyrus had claimed that it was Marduk who gave him world dominion. Still, the Hebrew report is not inconsistent with Cyrus' policy, for he regarded himself as the patron of the gods of conquered peoples, restored sacred images to their sanctuaries, and supported the rebuilding of their temples. Both versions of the edict say that he permitted the Jews to return to their homeland, ordered the Temple of Jerusalem to be rebuilt with support from the Persian treasury (Ezra 6:4), and commanded that the vessels taken by Nebuchadrezzar from the Temple be returned (Ezra 1:7–11).

The Return under a Davidic Prince

To head up the first return of Jews from exile, Cyrus appointed "a prince of Judah" who carried a Babylonian name Sin-ab-uṣur (Sheshbazzar). He may have been of Davidic lineage; if so, his appointment would accord with the Persian practice of turning now and then to a member of a royal house for leadership of a local state.[3] Not much is known about his term as governor, although it is reported that he was responsible for laying the foundations of the temple (Ezra 5:16). He was succeeded by a better known figure who also bore a Babylonian name: Zer-babili (Zerubbabel), a descendant of Jehoiachin (I Chron. 3:19), the exiled king whom many had regarded as the legitimate king of Judah. Clearly the Persian administration was following a conciliatory policy, for not only was the observance of Jewish customs encouraged but also, to a limited degree, a national revival was permitted. These developments must have stirred the hearts and kindled the hopes of many Jews. It must have appeared that the new age, in the dawn of which Second Isaiah stood, was about to break into the full light of day.

But Second Isaiah's picture of the new age was so elevated in grandeur, so transfigured in the light of eternity, that no ordinary historical era, least of all the post-exilic period of Judaism, could measure up to his vision. He spoke, not of a Davidic king, but of the Servant exalted through suffering. He pictured

---

[2] It has been argued that the "ornamented" Hebrew version rests on the oral proclamation of a herald, and the Aramaic version represents the official document. See R. A. Bowman, *Interpreter's Bible*, III [16], 571–73.

[3] See Frank M. Cross, "A Reconstruction of the Judean Restoration," [424], pp. 198–199. Some have suggested that Sheshbazzar was a Davidite on the basis of I Chron. 3:18, where the Davidic line after Jehoiachin includes a certain Shenazzar; so W. F. Albright, *The Biblical Period* [90], p. 86 and John Bright, *History* [91], pp. 361–362. The identification of Shenazzar with Sheshbazzar, however, has been challenged on linguistic grounds; see Peter Ackroyd, "Israel in the Exilic and Post-Exilic Periods," *Tradition and Interpretation* [153], 331, and n. 35.

no ordinary Jerusalem, but a New Jerusalem which would be a sign to all nations that Yahweh is King. He described a marvelous transformation that would begin in people's hearts and that would be mirrored in the whole drama of history and the vast scenery of nature. His message had to do with "last things," the consummation of all history in the redemptive purpose of God. But the exiles who chose to return to Jerusalem under the protection of Cyrus experienced not the poetry of Second Isaiah but the prose of a grim and bitter struggle.

To tell the story of the return as briefly as possible, we shall concentrate on three figures and three events: first, Zerubbabel and the rebuilding of the Temple; second, Ezra and the renewal of the covenant; and third, Nehemiah and the rebuilding of the walls of Jerusalem. We shall also look briefly at prophets like Haggai and Zechariah, Joel and Malachi, and try to understand the character of the Judaism that emerged with Ezra.

THE WORK OF THE CHRONICLER

Before turning to the period of post-exilic Judaism, let us consider the major historical source for our knowledge of Jewish life in Palestine during the Persian period—that is, from the rise of Cyrus to the coming of Alexander the Great (333 B.C.E.). The only biblical history of the Persian period is found in two seldom-read books, Ezra and Nehemiah, and even this history covers no more than half the period. Admittedly, after the stirring poems of Second Isaiah these two books may seem anticlimactic. Yet this period of Judaism is an important chapter in Israel's life-story, far more important than is often realized. Without it we would not have received the spiritual heritage that has profoundly influenced Western civilization.

The Books of Ezra and Nehemiah

The books of Ezra and Nehemiah tell the story of Israel's history from the first return to Jerusalem to the end of Nehemiah's second term as governor of Judah (538 to shortly before 400 B.C.E.). Apparently the material was first split up into two books by Jerome, who about the last of the fourth century C.E. produced the Latin translation known as the Vulgate, which came to be the authoritative translation of the Roman Catholic Church. Before that time, the account was treated as one book in the earliest Hebrew and Greek manuscripts.[4] During the early centuries of the Christian era, the standard text (called the *Masora*, or "tradition") was meticulously preserved by Jewish scholars known as Masoretes, who counted all the words in order to be sure that no one would ever add or take away a single one. On the basis of their count, they indicated that the exact

---

[4] In the Greek translation of the Old Testament (Septuagint), the single work is known as "Ezra" (Esdras B); see Chart, p. 642. There is also an apocryphal work called I Esdras, which contains II Chron. 35-36, Ezra, and Neh. 8:1-12 plus other material.

The Tomb of Cyrus at Pasargadae, his royal residence. According to Plutarch, a Roman writer of the early Christian era, it bore this inscription: "O man, whosoever thou art and whencesoever thou comest, for I know that thou wilt come, I am Cyrus, and I won for the Persians their empire. Do not, therefore, begrudge me this little earth which covers my body." Alexander visited Cyrus' tomb on his return from India and, Plutarch reports, was deeply moved by the inscription.

middle of the account of Ezra and Nehemiah was at what we would designate as Nehemiah 3:32. This, of course, is not the middle of our present book of Nehemiah, but of the single book Ezra-Nehemiah, which was one scroll when the rabbis did their counting. Since we are dealing with a single book, we can understand why the story of Ezra is found partly in our book of Ezra and partly in Nehemiah (Neh. 7:73b–10:39).

In the original Hebrew, the scroll of Ezra-Nehemiah was part of a large historical work, the first part of which was I and II Chronicles. The whole work displays such an overall unity that it undoubtedly belongs to the work of ''the Chronicler,'' a term that is applied to a school of historical interpreters active in the post-exilic period. The nucleus of this work is I and II Chronicles (one book in the Hebrew Bible), which may have been composed in the early post-exilic period around the time of the building of the Second Temple (520–515 B.C.E.),[5] and enlarged in various stages until it was given its final form—I–II Chronicles, Ezra and Nehemiah—sometime after the year 400 B.C.E.[6] Some, including the philosopher Spinoza, have surmised that Ezra was the final editor.

---

[5] This is the position of David Noel Freedman, ''The Chronicler's Purpose,'' *Catholic Biblical Quarterly* 23 (1961), 436–42.

[6] See the discussion of ''The Chronistic Historical Work'' by J. R. Porter in *Tradition and Interpretation* [153], 152–162.

Curiously, in the Hebrew Bible the book called *Dibre Hayyim*, or "Events of [Past] Times" (our I and II Chronicles), is found—at least in most manuscripts—at the very end of the third part, the Writings, and immediately after Ezra-Nehemiah. This puts the cart before the horse, however, for clearly the proper chronological order is just the reverse. The concluding verses of II Chronicles, which deal with the rise of Cyrus, are identical with the opening verses of Ezra, which is the ancient scribe's way of connecting the narratives in their proper sequence.

Thus we add one more major historical work to those that we have already investigated in earlier chapters. Leaving out the Old Epic tradition (J and E), which belongs in the category of historical epic, the list includes:

1. The Deuteronomistic History (Joshua through II Kings with Deuteronomy as introduction).
2. The Priestly Writing (Genesis through Numbers).
3. The Chronicler's Work (I and II Chronicles, Ezra-Nehemiah).

The list probably should be reduced by one, for, as we have found, the Priestly Writing is actually an expanded version of the ancient Israelite Epic. We are left, then, with two major works that recount the history of Israel. The Deuteronomistic History begins with the last days of Moses and in its final form concludes with the fall of the nation and the exile of the people. The Chronicler's Work begins essentially with the rise of David and carries the story into the postexilic period to about 400 B.C.E.

The Chronicler's Priestly Perspective

It would be interesting to compare in parallel columns the Deuteronomistic History and I and II Chronicles. (The remainder of the Chronicler's history—Ezra, Nehemiah—is not paralleled at all in the Deuteronomistic History, which concludes with the Exile.) A comparison of the David story, for instance, as given both in I Samuel 15 to I Kings 2 and in I Chronicles 10–29, would reveal how the past is reviewed in the Chronicler's work. Sometimes these historians excerpted passages from Samuel-Kings word for word—another indication that our conceptions of authorship (or plagiarism!) did not apply in antiquity. At other times they ignored or changed the tradition according to their interests. This seems a cavalier way of writing history. But in defense of these historians it must be said that they were primarily *interpreters* of the past, who selected the materials that would emphasize aspects of the tradition that were relevant to their own time. Of course, when any historians deal with a sweep of 600 years— a much longer span than the whole of American history—they cannot avoid selecting and weighting their materials. Obviously they cannot include everything, especially in a work of about 100 pages, the extent of the Chronicler's Work. We can see their theological bias clearly when we observe how, in dealing with the tradition of Samuel-Kings, they select, omit, add, and modify. This is propaganda, not in the derogatory sense that the word has acquired in our time, but in its primary meaning of an effort to spread particular doctrines.[7]

It is erroneous, however, to suppose that this work, just because it was written in a late period and from a priestly point of view, is pure fiction. The Chronicler's Work relied not only on Samuel-Kings, but also on source material that either was not included in the Deuteronomistic History or was not available at the time it was written. An excellent example of the Chronicler's use of good historical sources is found in Ezra-Nehemiah, where the historians excerpt almost verbatim the autobiographical Memoirs of Nehemiah—one of the most trustworthy historical sources for Jewish history in the Persian period. The autobiographical Memoirs of Ezra, although more open to question, are also a very important historical witness. These two sources are found in the following places:

1. Nehemiah's Memoirs: Nehemiah 1:1–7:73a; 11:1–2; 12:27–43; 13:4–31.
2. Ezra's Memoirs: 7:27–9:15.[8]

The Chronicler's Work is fundamentally a revision—or reinterpretation—of Israel's history. So it is important to understand the overall purpose of this history, for the story of Ezra-Nehemiah is the final phase of the unfolding history that begins with David. The writers were dominated by one central conviction: Israel was called to be a "church," a worshiping community. In a broad sense, Israel was to be "a kingdom of priests and a holy nation"—that is (as the phrase means in Exod. 19:6), a people whose whole life was to be a "liturgy" or divine service. But in a special sense the community was to have its center in the Temple, where priests and especially Levites had an indispensable place in the conduct of worship. This liturgical interest is one of the major motifs of the Chronicler's Work. In fact, the Chronicler's Work is essentially a history of Israel's worship centering in Zion, the Holy City.[9]

---

[7] It needs to be added, however, that not all of the deviations can be explained on the basis of the Chronicler's tendentious interests. Werner E. Lemke shows that in many instances the differences arise from the fact that the Chronicler was using a different version of the original text (*Vorlage*) than that presupposed in the received Masoretic text. This *Vorlage*, he argues, lies back of the Greek translation known as the Septuagint and is presupposed in some manuscripts from Qumran. See his article, "The Synoptic Problem in the Chronicler's History," in *Harvard Theological Review*, LVIII (1965), 349–63.

[8] It is difficult to determine how much of the Ezra narrative, (Ezra 7:11–10:24; Neh. 7:73b–9:5) belongs to the Ezra Memoirs. One of the problems is that sometimes Ezra speaks in the first person and sometimes he is spoken of in the third person.

[9] See Jacob M. Myers' commentary, I [429], especially "The Intention of the Chronicler," xviii–xl, where he deals with the continuity of true worship in Jerusalem.

David as a Churchman

In Samuel-Kings, David is presented as a political leader, a man with strengths and weaknesses that endeared him to his people as the first and greatest king of all Israel. But the authors of the Chronicler's Work were not particularly interested in David's *political* genius, for by the time they wrote, Israel had ceased to be a nation. To be sure, they gloried in David's military accomplishments and the splendor of his kingdom. Furthermore, they emphasized the covenant with David (I Chron. 17; compare II Sam. 7) that guaranteed the continuation of the Davidic house. In fact, there is something "messianic" in their depiction of David, for he is the ideal king, the prototype of "the messiah" (Anointed One). For these historians, however, David was primarily the one who organized Israel as a worshiping community. It was David who had made Jerusalem, the Holy City, his religious capital; who had conceived the building of the Temple according to a plan alleged to have come directly from Yahweh (see I Chron. 29:19); who had organized the music of the Temple and had assigned the Levites their duties. The ecclesiastical robes with which the authors of the Chronicler's Work invested David tend to cover up David the man.

The Chronicler's Work ignores aspects of the tradition that might detract from David's "messianic" stature, such as the story of David's earlier career as an outlaw, his adultery with Bathsheba, Absalom's rebellion, and much of the material in the Court History. Most striking of all, it glorifies David's last words. Suppressing David's death-bed instructions to liquidate Joab and Shimei (I Kings 2:5-9), it affirmed that David's mind was engrossed to the very last with the dream of the future Temple (I Chron. 28-29), and placed on his lips one of the finest prayers to be found in the Old Testament (I Chron. 29:10-19). No one tried more earnestly than the authors of the Chronicler's Work to encircle David's head with a halo.

And yet the authors did not make all this up out of whole cloth, for there is considerable basis in the tradition for David's "churchly" interest. After all, David had brought the Ark to Jerusalem, had purchased Araunah's threshing-floor to build an altar (II Sam. 24), and had set in motion plans for building a temple. Moreover, David's interest in temple music was well established in Israelite tradition. He was "a skillful player on the lyre" (I Sam. 16:14-23; cf. Amos 6:5) and was noted as a composer of songs and laments, like the exquisite lament over Saul and Jonathan (II Sam. 1:17-27). Surely it is wrong to regard David as the author of the whole book of Psalms, which contains hymns, laments, and supplications from many times and poets.[10] But in view of David's reputation as a poet-musician, we can understand how later generations attributed the Psalter to him. Probably there is a strong element of truth in the Chronicler's claim that David instituted changes in Israel's worship service, especially

[10] Less than half of the psalms are attributed to David in the headings. The Davidic Psalter is discussed further in Chapter 16.

in instrumental music (I Chron. 23–27). But after all this has been said, it is still true that the Chronicler's ecclesiastical portrait of David was colored by the interests of post-exilic, priestly Judaism.

Israel's Ecclesiastical History

From the account of the origin of the worshiping community under David, the authors of the Chronicler's Work proceed to tell the history of Israel in ecclesiastical terms. Agreeing with the author of II Samuel 7, they affirm that Yahweh's blessing rested upon the Davidic dynasty. (Since there was only one legitimate kingship, they even pass over the tradition about the anointing of Saul!) The Northern Kingdom fell because, owing to the sins of Jeroboam I, it had separated itself from the true community of worship. The Southern Kingdom, too, eventually proved to be so corrupt that Yahweh brought severe judgment upon it. Thus the Holy City fell, the Temple—which David planned to be "exceedingly magnificent, of fame and glory throughout all lands" (I Chron. 22:5)—was destroyed, and the priests and people were taken into exile.

At this point the Chronicler begins the story found in Ezra-Nehemiah. The historian tells how the edict of Cyrus enabled faithful Jews to return to Jerusalem, where they immediately built an altar on which to offer burnt offerings to the God of Israel, and some years afterward rebuilt the Temple. However, the Jewish community was threatened by the paganism that had precipitated the destruction of the first Temple. So next—according to the Chronicler's scheme—Ezra the priest came from Babylonia with the Torah of Moses in his hand, and initiated a great religious reform aimed at maintaining the identity of the community. Shortly thereafter, if we follow the present order of the narratives, Nehemiah came from Babylonia to Jerusalem. Vested with the authority of governor of the Persian district of Judah, he supervised the rebuilding of the walls of Jerusalem and instituted various social and religious reforms.

Israel came back from exile, not as a nation, but as a religious community. This account is in keeping with the historical situation of the post-exilic period, as we shall see. The Chronicler's intention, however, is to show that this profound change in Israel's life was not just a response to the political vicissitudes of the period. Rather, it was a return to the charter of Judaism handed down from David.

ZERUBBABEL, THE BRANCH

Now that we have seen the place of the books of Ezra and Nehemiah in the Chronicler's history, let us turn to the pioneers who responded to Cyrus' edict and set their faces toward the homeland. We must not suppose that there was a mass exodus from Babylonia. The list given in Ezra 2 (cf. Neh. 7) puts the number at about 50,000; but this is undoubtedly an expanded census list from the time of Nehemiah several generations later. For in Nehemiah 7:5 it is explicitly stated that Nehemiah published the list.[11] The number of those "whose spirit God had stirred to go up to rebuild the house of Yahweh in Jerusalem" (Ezra 1:5) was unquestionably much smaller, and the immigration took place over a period of several generations. Many of the Jews were comfortably settled and were doing well in business; so Josephus (37 to after 100 C.E.), the famous Jewish historian, was correct in saying that many were loath to leave their possessions.[12] To many Jews it must have seemed sheer recklessness to start out on a long, hazardous, and costly journey that could end only in uncertainty and insecurity in the impoverished environs of Jerusalem.

Tensions within the Palestinian Community

Some time later, however, we do find a small community of people in Jerusalem under the leadership of the High Priest Jeshua (or Joshua) and Zerubbabel, the latter having succeeded Sheshbazzar as the recognized civil authority. Among the first acts of this community, according to the Chronicler's account in Ezra 3, were the building of an altar, the installation of the Levites, and the laying of the foundation of a new temple. The worship was carried out "according to the directions of David king of Israel" (Ezra 3:10), which, of course, shows the Chronicler's interest in the Davidic charter for Judaism.

During the remaining years of Cyrus' reign, however, the work of restoration was hampered by controversies and conflicts within the Palestinian community. For one thing, "the people of the land," that is, those who did not take part in the Babylonian *golah* (captivity) but stayed in Palestine, caused trouble. The Chronicler's Work is based on the assumption that the true "Israel" was represented by the exiles—the "good figs" of Jeremiah's vision (Jer. 24)—and that they had the God-given authority to rebuild the foundations of the Jewish community. We may be sure, however, that the people who had been living in the land for several generations did not welcome wholeheartedly the influx of thousands of refugees, nor did they accept unquestioningly the view that leadership belonged to the newcomers. Indeed, the literature of the period, when studied carefully, seems to betray evidence of bitter controversy between the priestly establishment in Jerusalem (the priests in the line of Zadok who returned from exile) and others who felt themselves to be oppressed by their claims of power and authority.[13]

Trouble was also stirred up by the neighboring people to the north who lived in the province of Samaria. Here we see the first sign of the tension between Samaritans and Jews that eventually led to outright hostility and the

---

[11] See W. F. Albright, *The Biblical Period* [90], p. 49, and note 122.

[12] *Antiquities of the Jews*, xi, I, 3.

[13] This interpretation is set forth persuasively by Paul Hanson, *The Dawn of Apocalyptic* [427], in connection with his study of "Third Isaiah" and other prophetic literature of the time.

building of a rival Samaritan temple on Mount Gerizim overlooking Shechem. From the Jewish standpoint, the Samaritans had been corrupted by mixing with the foreign people whom the Assyrians had settled in that area (see Ezra 4:2). But the Samaritans themselves felt that they were faithful adherents to the Mosaic tradition and shared the Jewish interest in rebuilding the Temple at Jerusalem. Besides, as inhabitants of the area of the former Assyrian province of Samaria, they looked with apprehension and resentment upon the possible revival of a Jewish state on their very doorstep.

The Samaritans offered to cooperate with the Jews in rebuilding the Temple, but their offer was spurned by Zerubbabel. So the hand extended in friendship curled into a fist. Samaritan hostility was not prompted by the Jewish rebuff alone, however, for there was undoubtedly economic and political rivalry between the two peoples. In any case, the Samaritans did everything in their power to stop the building of the Temple, which they regarded as a symbol of revived Jewish nationalism. These were the political troubles that led to the suspension of the work during the remainder of the reign of Cyrus (he died in 530 B.C.E.), during the reign of his successor, Cambyses II (c. 530–522), and on into the reign of Darius I, the Great (Ezra 4:4–5:24;[14] see Chronological Chart 8, p. 412).

The Time of Haggai and Zechariah

Then, after a lapse of about eighteen years, in the year 520, the second year of the reign of Darius I (522–486 B.C.E.),[15] the work of rebuilding the Temple was resumed. We must understand Zerubbabel's leadership at that time in the context of the events that shook the Persian empire to its foundation. Darius' predecessor, Cambyses, under whose military leadership Egypt was conquered and incorporated into the Persian empire, finally went insane and committed suicide. His death was followed by murder and intrigue within the court and by nationalistic uprisings in the Persian provinces.

After a time, Darius managed to quell the far-flung revolution and celebrated his triumph by carving a huge relief and trilingual inscription high on the Behistun Rock. The relief, whose inaccessibility challenged the acrobatic ability of earlier archaeologists before a platform and stairs were installed, is pictured in Color Plate 6. It portrays Darius, followed by two attendants, putting his foot on the prostrate rebel chief and pointing to the winged disc, symbol of the Zoroastrian god, Ahura Mazda. Before him stand nine rebel leaders, their necks tied together by a rope and their hands manacled behind their backs. The accompanying cuneiform inscription—written in three languages: Old Persian,

---

[14] Ezra 4:6–23 obviously is out of place, for the passage deals with the reigns of Xerxes (Ahasuerus) and Artaxerxes I, kings who succeeded Darius. For historical details, see A. T. Olmstead, *History of the Persian Empire* (University of Chicago Press, 1948); R. Ghirshman, *Iran: From the Earliest Times to the Islamic Conquest* (Harmondsworth, Middlesex: Penguin Books, 1954).

[15] The Chronicler has mistakenly dated the laying of the foundation of the Temple in the second year of Cyrus (Ezra 3:6–13) rather than the second year of Darius (Haggai 1:1–6).

Elamite, and Akkadian—opened up new vistas of knowledge, for by decipher-
ing the Old Persian, scholars were able to translate the other two languages.

Then in the second year of his reign revolt broke out in Babylonia under
the leadership of Nebuchadrezzar, a namesake of the ruler we have met previously in our study of Jeremiah. Scarcely a month after the Babylonian uprising, the Jews started to rebuild the Temple under the Davidic leadership of
Zerubbabel and the High Priest Joshua.

According to Ezra 5:1, the work was inspired by two prophets, Haggai and
Zechariah, whose brief writings are preserved in the Old Testament.[16] Encouraged by the apparent success of the Babylonian revolution in 520 B.C.E., Haggai
preached with the fire of nationalism in his words. He proclaimed to the people
that economic conditions in the land were precarious because they had left Yahweh's house lying in ruins while they lived in fine, paneled houses. His very
first oracle aroused the Jews to action. Hoping that Yahweh would favor them
if they put first things first, the people fell in behind the leadership of Joshua
the priest, and Zerubbabel the governor (Haggai 1). A month later, when the
people became downcast over the contrast between their inferior structure and
the splendor of Solomon's Temple, Haggai fired their imaginations with the
dream of an edifice whose glory would outshine that of the former Temple. He
announced that divine intervention would soon come, and prophesied that Yahweh would shake the heavens and the earth, as well as all nations (2:1-9), so
that the treasures of the nations would be brought into the new Temple. Evidently, Haggai was looking forward to the downfall of the Persian empire. His
final oracle, which struck the same nationalistic note, was addressed to Zerubbabel, and announced in veiled language that the Jewish governor—a descendant of Jehoiachin—was Yahweh's Anointed One, the Davidic messiah (2:20-
23).

The prophecy of Zechariah, dated slightly later, expresses the same hope
for a restoration of the Jewish state under the co-leadership of the High Priest
and the Davidic prince. The oracles are cast in a bizarre apocalyptic form that
was popular in Judaism in the late post-exilic period. Like the prophecy of Second Isaiah, this new type of prophecy deals with the end-time, the consummation of history in Yahweh's sovereign purpose; but unlike the earlier
prophecy, it is couched in cryptic language, abounds with marvelous visions of
the future, and foresees the coming of a dramatic finale when the foes of Yahweh will be shattered and the kingdom of God will be established.[17] In the conviction that the might of the nations will be broken by Yahweh in a miraculous
fashion (see Zech. 4:6-10), the prophet Zechariah names Zerubbabel as the Dav-

---

[16] The authentic prophecies of Zechariah are found in chapters 1-8; the rest of the chapters
come from a circle of later disciples.

[17] This type of prophecy is known as an "apocalypse," a Greek term meaning "revelation"—
that is, revelation of the shape of things to come. Since the book of Daniel is the best Old Testament
example of apocalyptic literature, discussion of this kind of thinking will be postponed until the
final chapter of this book.

idic messiah. Speaking to the High Priest Joshua, who was given charge over the Temple, Yahweh says through the prophet: "Behold, I will bring my servant the Branch" (3:8). The word "messiah" (anointed one) is not used here, for it was only in the later period of Judaism that the term took on the special meaning of *the* Anointed One, the Messiah (Greek: *Christos*). In the earlier tradition of messianic prophecy, the future Davidic king is referred to as "a shoot from the stump of Jesse," "the branch" that will "grow out of his roots" (Isa. 11:1). With Zechariah, the word "branch" is a term for the messianic king, the descendant of David's line. According to the prophet, the sign of Zerubbabel's messianic authority is that he will complete the building of the Temple:

> Thus says Yahweh of Hosts:
> "Behold, a man whose name is The Branch. He will sprout up [lit. "branch out"] where he is, and will build the temple of Yahweh. It is he who will build the temple of Yahweh, and he will bear royal majesty. He will sit upon his throne and rule, and a priest will be at his right hand [Septuagint translation], and between both of them there will be peaceful agreement."
> —ZECHARIAH 6:12–13; cf. 4:6–10

Possibly the name Zerubbabel once stood in the passage from which this quotation is taken (verses 9–15), but for some unknown reason it was deleted. In any case, the prophecy of Zechariah leaves no doubt that the symbol of the Branch referred to Zerubbabel. It may well be that the first part of the Chronicler's Work (I and II Chronicles) was composed to lend support to this messianic movement.[18]

The Second Temple

In spite of attempts by Tattenai, the satrap of Syria, and the leaders of Samaria to obstruct the project, the Temple was finished in the year 515 B.C.E. When the project is viewed in light of the troubles of the Persian empire in the first years of Darius' reign, it is apparent that the Jews were motivated by hope for the revival of the Jewish state. Zerubbabel mysteriously vanished from the scene at this point. What happened to him we do not know. It has been conjectured that the Persians spirited him away, fearing that the messianic movement centering in him was a symptom of revolution. More likely, his appointment, like that of other governors, was limited and was not extended owing to political circumstances in the Persian administration that elude our knowledge.[19] In any event, we hear no more of attempts to revive the Davidic state during the Persian period. The leadership of the community was now vested in the High Priest, Joshua, and his successors. Henceforth Israel was to be a temple-centered community, a kingdom of priests, patterned after the instructions which, according to the Chronicler, were given by David.

---

[18] See the essay by David Noel Freedman on "The Chronicler's Purpose" [426].

[19] So argues Peter Ackroyd, "Israel in the Exilic and Post-Exilic Periods," *Tradition and Interpretation* [153], 338.

It was, however, "a day of small things" (Zech. 4:10). The second Temple did not compare in splendor to the Temple of Solomon, which had been a product of the artistry of Phoenician architects. We are told that when the old men who remembered the former Temple saw the foundations of the second Temple laid, they wept with a loud voice (Ezra 3:12–13). And yet the modest new Temple served as the center and bulwark of Israel's life in the post-exilic period. What was lacking in architectural beauty was covered over by the great devotion that the people lavished upon it, and above all, by the conviction that it was the place where Yahweh tabernacled in the midst of Israel.

As we have seen, the Chronicler was right in emphasizing the importance of music and praise in the history of Israel. To be sure, the writing of these historians reflects the interests of the post-exilic Temple, but fundamentally they were correct in believing that the continuity of worship extended back to David. In a profound sense, the foundation of the second Temple was the religious devotion of the people. As a worshiping community Israel was a singing people, and instrumental and choral music had an important place in their life. Both in the Chronicler's Work and in the headings of the Psalms we hear of leaders of musical guilds—choristers like Heman, Asaph, and Ethan or Jeduthun—who had a special role in the worship service. According to the Chronicler, the main function of the Levites was to lead the worshiping congregation in praise and prayer.

Israel's life and thought were nourished in the Temple until its final destruction in the Roman period (70 C.E.). Because it was not always possible for Jews living outside Jerusalem to attend the Temple services, however, synagogues began to dot the Palestinian countryside during the post-exilic period and eventually were found throughout the Dispersion, as, for instance, during Paul's missionary travels. The synagogue made a deep impression upon Israel's life and thought, and in the long run outlived the Temple. During the post-exilic period, however, there was no real substitute for the Temple. Devout Jews made pilgrimages to Jerusalem to participate in the drama of priestly sacrifice and congregational praise. In the services of worship, as we can sense from the book of Psalms—sometimes called "the hymnbook of the second Temple"—they found comfort in their sorrow, forgiveness in their guilt, and hope in time of trouble. A day in Yahweh's courts, said a psalmist, was better than a thousand spent elsewhere.

> How lovely is your tabernacle,[20]
> O Yahweh of hosts!
> My whole being longs and yearns
> for Yahweh's [Temple] courts.
> My heart and my flesh sing for joy
> to the living God.
> —PSALM 84:1–2

[20] The word translated "tabernacle" (*mishkanôth*, the Hebrew word is in the plural) reflects the ancient view that Yahweh "tents" or "goes about" among the people. The temple is Yahweh's dwelling-place, not in the sense that Yahweh resides there but in the sense that it is the place of divine visitation from time to time. See above, pp. 482–483).

RECONSTRUCTION AND REFORM

From the completion of the Temple (515 B.C.E.) to the appearance of Nehemiah in Jerusalem (445 B.C.E.) there is a span of about three generations. In this period, Persian culture reached its greatest height, as evidenced by the impressive ruins standing at Persepolis, the main capital of the Persian empire (see color Plate 6). Both Darius I and Xerxes, builders of this magnificent capital, waged campaigns against Greece, only to be defeated at the famous battles of Marathon (490), Thermopylae, and Salamis (480).

Since the Chronicler leaps over this period in order to come as quickly as possible to the great cultic reform of Ezra, we must turn to other sources for the meager information about Jewish affairs that is available. The Elephantine pa-

Remains of the Apadana or Audience Hall, at Persepolis, the place to which Darius I moved the main Persian capital from Pasargadae. The structure was begun by Darius and completed by Xerxes. Thirteen of the 72 columns that once supported the wooden roof of the spacious room (about 195 feet square) still stand. The monumental stairways leading to the royal terrace were adorned with exquisite reliefs. This capital, which represented the height of Persian art and architecture, was destroyed by Alexander the Great in 331 B.C.E. (See also Color Plate 6.)

pyri, to which we have alluded before (p. 428), come from the fifth century, but they are chiefly important for an understanding of Judaism in the Egyptian Dispersion. There are, however, several minor prophecies that throw some light on conditions in Palestine during this period, in addition to the writings of so-called "Third Isaiah" (Isa. 56–66) considered previously (see pp. 502–504).

Obadiah's Denunciation of Edom

The prophecy of Obadiah is a bitter outcry against Edom, the nation which—it will be remembered—had seized part of the territory of Judah after the fall of Jerusalem (see Mal. 1:2–5). Obadiah denounced the pride and treachery of Edom, which was traditionally related to Israel according to the story of the twin brothers, Jacob and Esau. Yahweh, said the prophet, was about to summon the nations to destroy Edom for the violence done to "Jacob." The date of Obadiah's prophecy cannot be determined exactly. The reference to Edom's malicious actions on the day of Judah's ruin (verses 11–14) dates it after the fall of Jerusalem in 587 B.C.E. Yet because the destruction of Edom is presented as a future threat, not a description of what was happening (verses 1–10), it must have been written before the fifth century when Arab tribes began pressing into Edomite territory from the Arabian Desert. By the fourth century these invaders, known as Nabateans, had claimed the Edomite mountain acropolis of Sela (cf. Obad. 3) and in time carved into the red limestone cliffs their splendid capital, the "rose city" of Petra, which today is one of the archaeological attractions on the eastern side of the Jordan (see Color Plate 7).

Malachi's Plea for Sincere Worship

Other evidence on conditions in the Jewish community is provided by the book of Malachi, which was probably written a generation or so before Nehemiah's arrival in Jerusalem. At this time the Jewish community was ruled by a Persian governor (see Mal. 1:8). The second Temple had been completed, but the people's heart was no longer in their worship. Echoing Obadiah's outcry against Edom, this prophet began by giving a bitter twist to the ancestral story of the twin brothers: "I have loved Jacob, but I have hated Esau"—in this way stressing Yahweh's favor for Israel (1:2–5). This divine favor, said the prophet, only throws into sharp relief the people's faithless and ungrateful actions. He accused them of dishonoring Yahweh by placing polluted food on the altar and by offering sacrifices—blind, lame, sickly animals—that would not even be accepted by their governor. The people were going through the motions of ritual, but clearly they found the whole thing boring and wearisome (1:13). It would be better, said the prophet, to close the doors of the Temple than to go on like that, for Yahweh deserved nothing but the best gifts and the most sincere worship. With a note of universalism, he pointed out that even the Gentiles magnified Yahweh's name (1:11; see 2:10), whereas Israel was profaning it by

Darius on his Throne *holds a scepter in one hand and a lotus blossom in the other. Behind him stands the crown prince, Xerxes—the Ahasuerus mentioned in Ezra 4:6 and in the book of Esther. The king is receiving a foreign dignitary, whose hand is raised to his mouth in a gesture of respect. This belief was found at Persepolis.*

inadequate and insincere worship. The priests were not guarding the true torah, men were divorcing their Jewish wives to marry foreign women, and social injustices abounded. To make matters worse, the people were complaining that serving God did not "pay off," for it was evident to them that it was the evildoers who came out on top. "Where is the God of justice?" they asked (2:17). Why serve God if religion yields no tangible benefits (3:13–15)?

Despite the vigor of Malachi's critique, the prophet himself does not measure up to the stature of his predecessors. He suggested that if the people would only present a tenth (tithe) of their income, and stop "robbing God" of what was due, then Yahweh would pour upon them a great blessing, and Israel would be great among the nations (Mal. 3:6–12). In a vivid passage—later interpreted by Christians to refer to John the Baptist, the forerunner of the Christ—he announced that the Messenger[21] would appear to prepare the way for the coming of Yahweh. Suddenly, he said, Yahweh would come to the holy Temple, and on "the day of his coming" people would shrink back in fear, "for he is like a refiner's fire." Yahweh's purpose, first of all, is to refine the priests, purifying them until they present "right offerings" to Yahweh. Then, divine judgment will fall upon sorcerers, adulterers, false witnesses, and those who oppress the poor and defenseless (3:1–5). Even now, said the prophet, the segregation of the righteous from the wicked is beginning, for the names of those who fear Yahweh are recorded in a "book of remembrance," and they will be spared on the day of judgment (3:16–18). The writing ends with the prophecy that Yahweh

---

[21]The expression "my messenger" in 3:1 is *mal'aki* in Hebrew—that is, the name of the prophet as given in Mal. 1:1. Probably this is the source of the name attributed to the prophet. Actually, we know nothing about the author of the book.

will send Elijah, the prophet *par excellence,* to summon Israel to repentance and to prepare the people for "the great and terrible day of Yahweh" (4:5).

Joel and the Army of Locusts

The prophecy of Joel may come from this same period, although it is difficult to assign any precise date to it. It is generally believed that Joel lived sometime in the period from 500 to 350 B.C.E. Whatever the date, the occasion of his preaching was a plague of locusts, that had devastated the country, not an uncommon scourge in ancient Palestine. Moreover, the land had suffered a great famine. To Joel, the "army" of invading locusts, whose attack he described with extraordinary vividness, was the sign of the impending Day of Yahweh.[22] Urgently the prophet summoned the people to a great fast, perhaps in connection with the festival of the New Year in the autumn, for repentance and lament.

> "But now, now—it is Yahweh who speaks—
>   come back to me with all your heart,
>   fasting, weeping, mourning."
> Let your hearts be broken,
>   not your garments torn,
> turn to Yahweh your God again,
> for he is all tenderness and compassion,
>   slow to anger, rich in graciousness,
>   and ready to relent.
>   —JOEL 2:12–13 (JB)

Then, with a sudden shift from warning to promise, he announced that beyond the judgment was the day when Yahweh would restore "the years which the swarming locust has eaten" (2:25) and would pour out the divine spirit upon young and old (2:28–29; cf. Acts 2). Joel's prophecy is reminiscent of pre-exilic preaching concerning the Day of Yahweh, but it also contains descriptions of cosmic upheavals like those found in post-exilic apocalyptic literature (2:30–32).

Thus the books of Obadiah, Malachi, and Joel present a picture of a struggling Jewish community, threatened from the outside by neighboring peoples and the pressures of foreign culture, and weakened from within by poverty, discontentment, and religious apathy. This was the situation when Ezra and Nehemiah appeared on the scene.

The Sequence of Events

Before proceeding further, we must consider briefly one of the major conundrums in biblical studies. Who came to Jerusalem first—Ezra or Nehemiah? There

---

[22] Some scholars believe that the locust army is a veiled description of an invading foreign power. See the discussion by Arvid S. Kapelrud, *Joel Studies* [435], pp. 14–17.

is no doubt about the date of Nehemiah's arrival. The beginning of his first term as governor is definitely fixed as the twentieth year of the reign of Artaxerxes (Neh. 1:1; 2:1); and, by general agreement, this is a date during the reign of Artaxerxes I Longimanus, not one of the later Artaxerxes (see Chronological Chart 9, p. 532). Therefore we can peg the date of Nehemiah's arrival as 445 B.C.E. Beyond this point, however, the historical picture becomes blurred.

THE DATE OF NEHEMIAH'S MISSION

Archaeological evidence enables us to fix the date of Nehemiah's mission as 445 B.C.E. One of the Elephantine letters, dating from the year 407 B.C.E., mentions "the sons of Sanballat, the governor of Samaria" (Pritchard, *Ancient Near Eastern Texts* [1], "Petition for Authorization to Rebuild the Temple of Yaho," p. 491). Governor Sanballat was a contemporary of Nehemiah, a fact which precludes dating Nehemiah under a later Persian king bearing the name Artaxerxes.

This date is further confirmed by archaeological evidence from a cave in the Wadi Dalyeh, located in cliffs overlooking the Jordan Valley about nine miles north of Jericho. Administrative documents found there enable archaeologists to establish the sequence of governors in Samaria, beginning with Nehemiah's contemporary, Sanballat the Horonite. (See further Frank M. Cross, "A Reconstruction of the Judean Restoration" [424], especially p. 190.)

The authors of the Chronicler's Work believed that Ezra came first and dated his appearance in Jerusalem in the seventh year of Artaxerxes I—that is, 458 B.C.E. (Ezra 7:7–8). Hence, in the Chronicler's scheme the next event after the completion of the temple in the year 515 (Ezra 6) is the account of Ezra's return with a band of Zionists in the mid-fifth century—a leap of more than a half a century (Ezra 7–8). Some time after his arrival, he gathered the people before the Water Gate for the reading of the book of the Torah of Moses (Neh. 8–10). Before and after this event the Chronicler placed the memoirs of Nehemiah (Neh. 1–7 and 11–13) on the assumption that the careers of the two men overlapped.

Problems arise when one reads the Chronicler's account in its final form. For one thing, the insertion of Nehemiah's Memoirs has had the effect of postponing Ezra's reading of the Torah from the seventh year of Artaxerxes (the year of his arrival) to the twentieth year (Neh. 2:1). According to this editorial arrangement, thirteen years elapsed before Ezra initiated the reform based on the Mosaic Torah. It seems a bit strange that he waited so long to carry out the task for which he was commissioned by the Persian king. Moreover, if Ezra's reform was carried out first, as the present text indicates, he must have failed, for Nehemiah had to redo much of the work during his second term as governor (Neh. 13). Finally, if the two leaders collaborated, Nehemiah implementing the reform of Ezra, it is curious that Nehemiah's Memoirs do not refer to Ezra ex-

Tombs of Persian Kings *were hewn into the solid rock of this cliff face near Persepolis. At right is the tomb of Darius I, who authorized the rebuilding of the Temple (Ezra 3:5–6); the center tomb is that of Artaxerxes I, possibly the king who appointed Nehemiah as his cup-bearer; the one at the left is that of Darius II.*

cept, possibly, in one place (Neh. 12:36) where Ezra heads a procession at a dedication ceremony. Ezra's Memoirs do not pay much attention to Nehemiah, either.[23]

Given these, and other problems, it is understandable that historians do not see eye to eye on this complicated question.[24] There are three possibilities for the date of Ezra's arrival in Jerusalem.

1. 458 B.C.E. The date given by the Chronicler. This traditional view is defended by some scholars, "liberals" as well as "conservatives."[25]

2. 428 B.C.E. This hypothesis requires changing the chronological notation in Ezra 7:7 from the seventh to the thirty-seventh year of Artaxerxes on the assumption that, by a common kind of scribal error, the word "thirty" was omitted.[26]

3. 398 B.C.E. This is based on the view that the Persian ruler referred to in Ezra 7:7 is not Artaxerxes I (c. 465–414) but Artaxerxes II (c. 404–358).[27]

[23] The reference to Ezra's presence at the dedication of the wall of Jerusalem in Nehemiah's Memoirs (Neh. 12:36) may be a harmonizing addition. In the first-person sections of the Ezra Memoirs, Nehemiah is not mentioned at all. In the third person sections he is referred to twice: at the ceremony of the reading of the law (Neh. 8:9) and as one of the signers of the covenant document (Neh. 10:1).

[24] A thorough discussion of the whole question is given by John Bright, *History* [91], Excursus II on "The Date of Ezra's Mission to Jerusalem," 391–402.

[25] See especially Frank M. Cross, "A Reconstruction of the Judean Restoration" [424].

[26] A major champion of this view is John Bright, *History* [91], 379ff.

[27] In "The History of Israel in the Exilic and Post-Exilic Periods," *Tradition and Interpretation* [153], Peter Ackroyd states: "The late date of 398 B.C.E. (Artaxerxes II) remains possible, even probable, but unproven" (p. 334).

In part, this problem arises because the book of Chronicles underwent a long history of redaction before receiving its final form. According to one attractive view, three stages can be traced in the Chronicler's work: a first edition, consisting essentially of I–II Chronicles, composed in the time of the rebuilding of the temple 520–515 B.C.E.; a second edition, including the Ezra story, composed around the year 450; and a third edition to be dated around 400, in which the final redactor added the Nehemiah memoirs and otherwise edited the completed work to give it overall unity.[28] In the final edition, the Chronicler was interested primarily in giving priority to the reform of Ezra, not in harmonizing previous accounts for the sake of keeping the historical record straight.

Although this question may never be settled, the testimony of the final Chronicler, who probably wrote within a reasonably short time after the Judean restoration, deserves the benefit of doubt. In this view, Ezra preceded Nehemiah, although the two men worked contemporaneously, at least during part of their careers. It seems that Ezra's reform was not highly successful at first, for he needed the administrative power and organizational ability of Nehemiah to institute changes and make them stick.[29] After all, we must remember that the great "Deuteronomic" Reform, even when authorized and supported by the power of King Josiah, proved to be short-lived (see above, p. 388). For the sake of this discussion we shall assume that the Ezra-Nehemiah sequence is the proper one, although leaving the whole question open for further investigation.

EZRA, THE ARCHITECT OF JUDAISM

In the year 458 B.C.E., if our chronology is correct, Ezra conducted a second caravan of exiles from Babylonia to Palestine. Unlike Nehemiah who was to follow later, Ezra was not sent to Palestine by the Persian king as a political authority; rather, with Persian authorization he went to investigate and regulate religious matters in Jerusalem and Judah, which belonged to the fifth Persian satrapy (the province "Beyond the River"). He was entitled to institute judicial arrangements that were in accord with "the law of your God and the law of the [Persian] king" (Ezra 7:26), and specifically to instruct the people in their own religious laws. He is pictured as "a scribe skilled in the law of Moses, which Yahweh, the God of Israel, had given" (Ezra 7:6). Elsewhere, he is referred to as "Ezra the priest, the scribe of the law of the God of heaven" (7:12, 21).

On arriving in Jerusalem, Ezra's first task was to insure the strength of the family, an institution which has always been fundamentally important for maintaining a sense of Jewish identity and for preserving the traditions of Israel. Accordingly, he took stern measures against intermarriage with foreigners, especially mixed marriages involving non-Jewish women. His authority for exe-

---

[28] See Frank M. Cross, "A Sketch of the Era of the Restoration," in [424], 198–201.

[29] So argues Sigfried Hermann, *History* [94], 315. See the whole discussion, pp. 307–19.

cuting this unpopular policy was derived from two sources. First, he had the backing of the Persian government in the appointment of judges and magistrates who enforced the decree; second, and more fundamentally, he appealed to tradition going back to Moses and specifically to Israel's obligations as a people of the covenant.

A Ceremony of Covenant Renewal

One of the important items in the baggage that Ezra brought from Babylonia was a copy of "the book of the Torah of Moses" (Neh. 8:1). In the month of the autumn harvest festival, which was known as the Feast of Tabernacles,[30] the people gathered "as one person" into the square before the "Water Gate" of Jerusalem to hear what was in Ezra's book of the Torah (Neh. 8:1-8). Ezra climbed up to a specially constructed wooden pulpit and, while the people stood in rapt attention, read to them from early morning until noon. Levites stood at his side to give "the sense" in order that the people could "understand the reading." The next day the people began the celebration of the Feast of Tabernacles according to the directions of the Torah (see Lev. 23:42-43): they cut branches and built booths ("tabernacles") to live in during the seven-day festival, and during this whole time the readings from the Torah continued (Neh. 8:13-18). The climax of the ceremonies came in a solemn act of covenant renewal (Neh. 9) when the people confessed their sins and Ezra, as a covenant mediator, offered a prayer on behalf of the people, ending with the words of covenant renewal (Neh. 9:38). The covenant document was officially signed by the representatives of the people, and all the rest of the people joined with them and took an oath under penalty of a curse "to walk in God's Torah which was given by Moses the servant of God" (Neh. 10). According to the present text of the Chronicler, "Nehemiah the governor" was a signatory to the covenant (Neh. 10:1).

This procedure is strikingly similar to the covenant ceremony of Josiah's time as related in II Kings 23:1-3. The same features are present: the public reading of the Torah, the confession of sin, the cultic and social reform, and the solemn covenant to follow the divine commandments under penalty of a curse. The covenant ceremony under Ezra, as well as that under Josiah, was based on an ancient tradition of periodic covenant renewal at the sanctuary. At such times it was the function of the Levites to act as interpreters of the Torah when it was read in the public assemblies, for the Torah was not just special direction to the priests but teaching for the whole community. Thus the distinction arose between the "priest" and the "Levite," as we find it, for instance, in the parable of the Good Samaritan (Luke 10:30-37). The priests who claimed descent from

---

[30] For a discussion of this festival which was celebrated at the beginning of the year, see R. de Vaux, *Ancient Israel* [113], pp. 495-502. He explains the building of booths (*sukkoth*) by referring to the ancient custom, which survives to the present in Palestine, of erecting huts made out of branches in the orchards and vineyards during the fruit and grape harvest.

Dor
DOR
GILEAD
Samaria
MT. GERIZIM ° Shechem
Joppa
SAMARIA
Bethel
JUDAH
Jericho
Rabbath-Ammon
AMMON
Ashdod°
ASHDOD
Jerusalem
Beth-zur
SALT SEA
Lachish
Hebron
MOAB
IDUMAEA
Beer-sheba
MEDITERRANEAN SEA
JORDAN R.

JUDAH
IN NEHEMIAH'S TIME

▬ ▬ ▬ BOUNDARIES
OF THE FIFTH
PERSIAN SATRAPY

Aaron were in charge of the sacrifice at the altar; the Levites who claimed Moses as an ancestor (Exod. 2:1) had the task of giving an exposition of the meaning of Israel's faith (II Chron. 15:3; 17:8-9; 30:22; 35:3), just as they are described as doing when Ezra read the Torah.[31]

Ezra's Book of the Law

What was "the book of the Torah" that Ezra read to the people? A variety of suggestions has been made, including the Holiness Code, the Priestly Code, Ezekiel's plan of restoration (Ezek. 40-48), Deuteronomy, and the Pentateuch. The problem could be solved, some think, by figuring out how long it took Ezra to finish his reading. But this is a difficult task, since the Levites used up some unknown amount of time in giving their interpretations. And it is not explicitly stated that Ezra read the whole "book of the Torah" from beginning to end. Perhaps he selected certain key passages as a prelude to the covenant-renewal ceremony. The Deuteronomic Torah is a good possibility, especially in view of the place given to the Levites in Deuteronomic tradition, but Ezra's reform seems to presuppose instruction in matters of a more priestly character. Some suggest

[31] See Gerhard von Rad, *Studies in Deuteronomy* [cited under 367], pp. 13-14, and G. Ernest Wright, *Interpreter's Bible*, II [16], pp. 315-16.

the Priestly "source" of the Pentateuch, but this view assumes that the Priestly Writing at this time had an independent existence, which is dubious (see pp. 451–455). So we come to the view that was evidently held by the Chronicler, namely, that the "book of the Torah" that Ezra read was the Pentateuch itself, that is, the Priestly Writing (Tetrateuch) plus Deuteronomy.[32]

If this is true, Ezra's greatest contribution was to establish the Pentateuch as the authoritative canon for Jewish faith and practice. The word "canon," which is Sumerian in origin, refers in its primary sense to any measurement or yardstick—a carpenter's rule, for example. In a metaphorical sense, the Greeks referred to their classics as *kanones*—that is, standards of excellence. But as applied to the Old Testament the word does not refer to the literary excellence of "classics," even though parts of the Old Testament do rate high according to literary standards. Rather, the claim is made that this literature is *sacred* scripture and as such constitutes the community's rule for faith and conduct. In the time of Ezra and later, the authority of the Pentateuch was underscored by the dogma that this was none other than the "book of the Torah of Moses" that had been delivered by God to Moses on Mount Sinai. Ezra probably introduced the Pentateuch as the officially recognized Mosaic tradition and, by his cultic reforms, brought Israel's life into conformity with this norm. He is truly "the architect of Judaism," for under his influence the life and religion of the Jews were molded by the sacred Torah.

The Samaritan Pentateuch

The Jews had no monopoly on the Pentateuch, however. It was also the scripture of the Samaritan community, who followed Mosaic tradition too. The tension that developed between Jew and Samaritan was not over the authority of the Torah (Pentateuch), but over the interpretation of its meaning, and particularly over the issue of who the true people of the Torah were. Occasioned originally by political and economic factors in the early post-exilic period, the split between the Jews and the Samaritans gradually widened until eventually, perhaps in the middle of the fourth century, the Samaritans built their own temple on Mount Gerizim (see photo, p. 260).[33] According to a New Testament story, when Jesus paused at Jacob's well while passing through Samaria, a Samaritan woman reminded him that the Jews had no dealings with the Samaritans, for they worshiped God in separate places (John 4:4–29). Even today a colony of Samaritans lives near Mount Gerizim. Their priests proudly display

---

[32] That Ezra's "book of the Torah" was essentially the Pentateuch in its penultimate form has been argued persuasively by Sigmund Mowinckel, *Studien zu dem Buche Ezra-Nehemian*, III (Oslo: Universitetsforlaget, 1965), 124–41.

[33] The Gerizim temple was destroyed by the Jewish leader John Hyrcanus in 128 B.C.E., 200 years after it was built, according to Josephus (*Antiquities*, xiii, 9, 1; *Jewish Wars*, i, 2, 6). If Josephus' reckoning is correct, it must have been built about the middle of the fourth century B.C.E.

to visitors their scrolls of the Pentateuch, which is the sole scriptural basis of their religion.

NEHEMIAH'S TERMS AS GOVERNOR

We turn, now, to the leadership of Nehemiah who, according to the Chronicler's picture of the times, was Ezra's contemporary. With the exception of chapters 8–10—the materials dealing with Ezra—the book of Nehemiah is based largely on the Memoirs of Nehemiah, which were written by his own hand.[34] This is the only example of the continuous story of a person's career, written in the style of autobiography, that we have in the Old Testament. It is a historical record of the greatest importance; and as a narrative it is written in a fresh and interesting manner. Here we can only summarize what the reader should pursue in detail independently. The story tells how Nehemiah, a cup-bearer to Artaxerxes I in the court at Susa, the Persian winter capital (see picture, p. 000), heard of the dismal conditions within Jerusalem; how he prevailed upon the king to send him there with the authority of a governor; how, after an inspection tour of the walls at night, he roused the people to undertake the rebuilding of the city's defenses; how the project was completed in fifty-two days, even though some of the workers had to carry a tool in one hand and a weapon in the other because of the hostility of neighboring peoples; and how at last, amid scenes of singing and thanksgiving, the walls were dedicated.

Nehemiah's Reforms

Throughout his first term as governor, as well as during the second term, which began in 432 B.C.E. (Neh. 13:6–7), Nehemiah introduced various reforms to bind the Jews into a closely knit community. When we remember the powerful pressures that threatened to erase Israel's identity, it is clear that this policy was necessary, even though today we might look at it askance. During the days when the walls were being rebuilt, Sanballat, the governor of Samaria, and his allies did everything in their power to frustrate the project. Sanballat laid claim to the Jewish territory, for it had been assigned to the province of Samaria by the Babylonians after the destruction of Jerusalem. Moreover, the Ammonites of Transjordan and the Edomites to the south of Jerusalem looked with a jealous eye upon the Jews' activities. First these enemies accused the Jews of plotting a revolution against Persia; then they ridiculed the feeble strength of the walls; and finally they threatened to attack. Clearly their design was to break the morale of the workers. And some of the Jews themselves, especially members of the wealthier class, took an easy-going attitude toward their neighbors, even to

---

[34] The Memoirs, found in the passages listed on p. 513, have been supplemented by lists and other material added by the Chronicler.

Chronological Chart 9

B.C.E.	Egypt	Palestine	Mesopotamia
		Judah	*Persia*
			Persia
500	Egypt under Persian rule, 525–401	(*Malachi*, c. 500–450)	Xerxes I (Ahasuerus), 486–465
		Ezra's mission, 458(?)	Artaxerxes I (Longimanus), 465–424
		Nehemiah arrives, 445	
		Ezra's mission, c. 428(?)	Xerxes II, 423
400			Darius II, 423–404
		Ezra's mission, c. 398(?)	Artaxerxes II (Mnemon), 404–358

the point of mingling and intermarrying with them. To meet these circumstances, Nehemiah enforced a stiff policy of exclusivism, thereby sharpening the division between Jew and Gentile, and between Jew and Samaritan.

Membership in the Jewish community, according to Nehemiah, was determined by two standards. The first was birth. We are told that when the walls were built God put it into Nehemiah's head to enroll all the citizens according to genealogy (Neh. 7:5–69; see also Ezra 2). In the context of the rest of Nehemiah's work, this can mean only one thing: it was important to be born into the right family and to be able to trace one's ancestry to a Jewish parent, grandparent, and so on. During his second term, Nehemiah strictly prohibited intermarriage, on the basis of the Deuteronomic legislation (Neh. 13; see Deut. 23:3ff.), and even banished a priest from office when it was discovered that he was married to a daughter of Sanballat, the Samaritan governor. Nehemiah was especially angered by the fact that children of mixed marriages could not even speak the Hebrew tongue. Ezra had carried these reform measures even further. Not only did he denounce mixed marriages, but also he forcibly broke up any that had already been made (Ezra 10:2–5).

The Crisis of Identity

Another qualification for being a Jew, according to Nehemiah's policy, was that of loyalty to the Torah and faithful support of the Temple. The purity of the people demanded strict observance of the sabbath. When he found that work and commercial activity were being carried on during the holy day, he threatened that divine wrath would fall upon the people if the abuse were not stopped. He organized a regular service of worship in the Temple and demanded that the people support the Temple staff with their tithes. Thus a strong wall was built around the Jewish community—not just the wall of Jerusalem but the wall of an exclusiveness based on birth and religious loyalty.

What was the real motive behind these severe measures? Political factors were present, to be sure. But more was involved than just a question of Jewish survival or of restoring prestige to Jerusalem. The desire to maintain Jewish purity was fundamentally a struggle to preserve the identity of the people Israel and the distinctiveness of Israel's faith in the face of the tremendous cultural pressures of the Persian period. With some justification, Nehemiah reminded the people of the folly of Solomon's cosmopolitanism, especially the influence of his foreign wives. The sympathetic student will agree that the work of Ezra and Nehemiah did not rest on nationalism or racialism, but upon a passionate loyalty to Israel's religious heritage, for "they feared that the faintly burning flame of Judaism might be quenched altogether."[35]

We have seen that the problem of syncretism had haunted Israel ever since the time of the occupation of Canaan. During the Exile, when the people lived an uprooted existence, the problem was intensified. And in the post-exilic period the threat of cultural assimilation persisted, especially with the conscious effort after the rise of Alexander the Great to absorb all religious and cultural differences into the synthesis known as Hellenism. The mystery is that Israel resisted assimilation, and creatively transformed what was borrowed from others into a vehicle for expressing its own faith. Israel's calling was not to be "like the nations," eventually to be swallowed up in whatever empire ruled the earth, but to be a "peculiar" people, set apart from the nations. It is easy to criticize the narrow theological focus of Judaism under Nehemiah and Ezra. There was an all too intense concentration upon membership in the holy community through family descent and obedience to the stipulations of the Torah. But it was this circumscribed community that preserved the spiritual heritage which eventually burst with transforming power upon nations and cultures and turned the course of Western civilization into a new channel.

THE LAW AND THE PROPHETS

The developments that we have considered gave great impetus to the rise of "legalism"—the strict conformity to Torah stipulations that came to be one of the major characteristics of post-exilic Judaism. In Christian circles, legalism is a loaded word, largely because of the Christian protest against the view that one's relation to God, one's "justification" or rightness with God, is based on righteous deeds in obedience to the Law (see the parable of the Publican and the Pharisee in Luke 18:9–14, and Paul's discussions of justification by faith, Gal. 2:16; 3:11). In time, a sharp antithesis grew up between grace and Law, and in some Christian circles it was believed that the whole Old Testament was under the dominion of Law. Although we cannot go into the issue as presented

[35] H. H. Rowley, *The Rediscovery of the Old Testament* (Philadelphia: Westminster, 1946), p. 164.

in the New Testament, in fairness to post-exilic Judaism we must correct certain one-sided views about the place of Torah in Jewish faith.

To begin with, Ezra did not invent the emphasis on Torah obedience. As we have seen time and again in earlier chapters, the giving of the commandments had an important and indispensable place in Israel's covenant faith from the very first. A person's relation to God, according to the Israelite faith, imposes obligations in the area of worship and social relations within the covenant community. The Ten Commandments, which probably go back to the Mosaic period, are the ancient witness to the divine demand. And, as we have seen, the legal tradition was expanded and refined as Israel faced in new historical situations the question: "What does Yahweh require of you?" The detailed prescriptions found in the Pentateuch are the end result of a legal development that had its source in the ancient covenant of Sinai.

Grace and Law

Second, there is no basis for the notion that the Torah sets forth a law code to be obeyed as dutifully as the laws of a city or a state. Back of the specific laws stands the Law-giver, who is none other than the God who graciously redeemed the people and guided them in their historical pilgrimage. The preface to the Ten Commandments, "I am Yahweh your God who brought you out of the land of Egypt, out of the house of bondage," is the introduction to all the laws of Israel. As we have seen repeatedly, prior divine grace, manifest in deeds of benevolence, stirred the people to responding service with heart, being, and strength. The book of Deuteronomy, which was the basis for a great social reform, is one of the most eloquent expressions of Israel's understanding that grace has priority over law. In Israel's faith, the good news of what God has done precedes the exposition of what the people must do.

The relationship between gospel and law is clearly expressed in the covenant-renewal ceremony of Ezra's time. According to Nehemiah 9, the making of the covenant was preceded by a long prayer, which is essentially a confession of Israel's faith. The public prayer is unique in that it is a recital of the whole history of Israel—or, better, the history of Yahweh's dealings with the people. It articulates the community's remembrance of its shared history, its unique life-story. Here is an outline of the salient aspects of the prayer:

1. Yahweh, the sole God, is creator and sustainer of all that is (verse 6).
2. Having called Abraham out of Ur of Babylonia, Yahweh promised to give his descendants an inheritance in Canaan (verses 7-8).
3. When Israel was oppressed in Egypt, Yahweh kept that promise. Yahweh's gracious presence in the midst of the people was demonstrated by various signs and wonders, and by giving the commandments to Moses on Mount Sinai (verses 9-15).
4. In spite of Israel's incapacity for faith, Yahweh proved to be "a God ready to forgive, gracious and merciful, slow to anger and abounding in faithfulness [ḥésed]." Rebellious Israel was sustained in the wilderness by divine grace (verses 16-21).
5. Yahweh gave Israel kingdoms and peoples, and brought them victoriously into Canaan. Thus the people prospered and increased (verses 22-25).
6. Nevertheless, Israel continued to be rebellious. So Yahweh disciplined the people, raising up prophets to warn them and giving the people into the hand of enemies when they refused to listen. However, Yahweh graciously spared a remnant (verses 26-31).
7. Especially since the time of the kings of Assyria, the hardships have been grievous. Yet Yahweh has been just in all these events. Indeed it is Yahweh who has been faithful; the people have been unfaithful (verses 32-34).
8. Because of their sins the people are now slaves (i.e., vassals of Persia) in the very land that Yahweh gave them, and its rich yield is taken away by heavy taxation (verses 35-37).

This prayer is a stirring recital of past events in which, according to the confession of faith, Yahweh had been active in Israel's history. It resounds with the note of Yahweh's gracious initiative and redemptive activity. On the basis of this declaration the people renewed the covenant and dedicated themselves to serve Yahweh according to "the Torah which was given by Moses." Among other things, this pledge required the refusal to engage in marriage with foreigners, as stipulated in Deuteronomy 7:1-4.

Rejoicing in the Torah

Third, we must not get the idea that the Torah, conceived of as a gift from God, was regarded as burdensome. Later on, it is true, the canonical laws were hedged about by so many casuistic rules—for instance, on the subject of what constitutes work on the sabbath—that the common people found difficulty in keeping it. According to rabbinical count, there were 613 laws in the Torah that had to be followed. However, in the Old Testament period, and even more so in the rabbinic period that followed, the Jewish attitude was that of "rejoicing in the Torah" (*simḥath hat-torah*). To obey the Torah was, to use a biblical expression, to take upon one's self "the yoke of the Kingdom"—that is, to surrender to the sovereignty of God. But, according to testimonies found in the Psalms, the yoke was easy and the burden was light. The devout Jew took great delight in the study of the Torah, for it was the source of life and blessing (see Ps. 1). Its precepts, "rejoicing the heart," were "more to be desired . . . than gold" (Ps. 19:7–14). The longest psalm in the Psalter is devoted to a praise of the Torah (Ps. 119).

Finally, we must not suppose that there was a sharp antithesis between the Torah and the prophetic tradition. To be sure, the corpus called the Prophets—the second division of the present Hebrew Bible (see Chart, p. 642) was not canonized until considerably later. But it was preserved, read, and interpreted during the post-exilic period. Indeed, instead of opposing prophecy, the post-exilic priests wanted to take the prophetic demands seriously, as can be seen by a careful study of Ezra's prayer. They realized that the prophetic message of divine judgment had been confirmed by the events of history. The remnant, whom Yahweh had spared from national destruction and exile, took to heart the lessons of history as interpreted by prophets. Far from repudiating the ethical demands of the prophets, the priests of Judaism attempted to "put teeth" into prophetic teaching. "It is very doubtful," says one scholar, "if Ezra thought of this religion [Judaism] as in any way the antithesis of prophetic religion. He doubtless thought he was serving the ideals of the prophets, and embodying them in the Law, that they might achieve more than the preaching of the prophets had hitherto achieved."[36]

Prophet and Priest

This is a good opportunity to review the relationship between prophet and priest in Israel's tradition. Many modern religious people have tended to "play down" the priestly emphasis of Judaism, even to the point of affirming that prophetic religion was fundamentally opposed to priestly religion. There can be no doubt that prophets like Amos, Hosea, and Jeremiah were radical in their criticism of

---

[36] H. H. Rowley, *Rediscovery of the Old Testament* (Philadelphia: Westminster, 1964), p. 166, and the whole discussion, pp. 161–86. See further Peter Ackroyd, *Exile and Restoration* [421], pp. 254–56.

the rituals of worship. But every religion must have a cultus—that is, forms in which faith and worship can find expression. A noncultic religion is a contradiction in terms. Cultic forms were particularly important in Israel's faith, which, by its very nature, required participation in the community that had been called to serve Yahweh, both by proper worship and by social responsibility. Indeed, the Mosaic tradition was transmitted as a living faith through the services of worship. At the great festivals the people engaged in rites that recalled their past; the Torah was read and expounded; the priests performed the sacrifices that displayed Israel's grateful obligation to God; and worshipers acknowledged what God had done for them by acts of praise. The little "confession of faith," found in Deuteronomy 26:5–9 ("A wandering Aramean . . . "), which gives the basic story of Israel's life, was made in connection with a "cultic act" at the sanctuary: the presentation of the first fruits of the harvest (see pp. 11–13). And as the context of the confession makes clear (Deut. 26:1–11), this solemn recital was an act of worship.

Israel's prophetic movement emerged out of the cultus. Many of the early prophets were "cultic prophets," intimately associated with the sanctuary. Indeed, it is no exaggeration to say that all the great prophets were dependent upon the cultus, even those who criticized it most radically.[37] Isaiah and Ezekiel were especially indebted to the Temple, although both criticized the kind of worship that was an abomination to Yahweh. We must, of course, be aware of the difference in emphasis between prophet and priest, but it is no more necessary to regard the two as fundamentally incompatible than to say that a "liturgical" and "prophetic" ministry are mutually exclusive in modern synagogues and churches.

What the prophets and the priests had in common was, above all, a sense of Israel's failure as a covenant people. In the period before the fall of the nation in 587 B.C.E., the prophets, speaking with various accents, interpreted Israel's suffering under the world powers as the consequence of covenant failure. Something had gone wrong, radically wrong. Indeed a prophet like Ezekiel could say that Israel's history, right from the very beginning, was a history of failure. The crisis of the Exile only deepened the sense of remorse and prompted the somber sense of sin and failure that is reflected in the Priestly theology which now governs the Pentateuch, the "book of the Torah" which Ezra brought with him from Babylonia. The purpose of this Priestly presentation of Israel's sacred history was to portray the age of Moses, when the Torah was given and the cult was established, as the ideal and the norm to which the people must return if they were to have a future in the Promised Land from which they were exiled. Inspired by this Priestly vision, Ezra the reformer came to Jerusalem. He sought to restore and reshape the community of Israel so that Yahweh, the holy God, could tabernacle in their midst and give them a future on the land.

It is true, as we have noticed in this chapter, that the spacious horizon of

---

[37] See R. E. Clements, *Prophecy and Covenant* [312], especially chap. 1.

Second Isaiah was obscured during the post-exilic period of biblical Judaism. But had the people of Israel been absorbed by the surrounding culture, the Servant's vocation could not have been performed. So the leaders of Judaism turned to the laws, rituals, and cultic acts of priestly religion, believing that the foundation of Israel's life was the pure worship of God, for this too was Israel's "service." In doing so, they were restoring what was most basic in Israel's life from the very first. For before Israel became a nation, before prophets were raised up to proclaim Yahweh's word, before the world was confronted with the mystery of the Servant, Israel was a worshiping community.

The Weaknesses of Judaism

Judaism also had its weaknesses, and they became increasingly apparent through the years. The rituals of the Temple too often became—as they had in Malachi's day—empty forms, devoid of the deep contrition, sincerity, and joy of worship. Devotion to the Torah easily lapsed into legalism, the fruit of which was a complaining bitterness about one's lot or a proud self-righteousness—notes that sometimes are heard in the Psalms. The Torah could become so overladen with minutiae or so twisted by clever legal interpretation that it could be used as a means of escaping from God's demand—an accusation that Jesus made against the scribes and Pharisees of his day (Matt. 15:1-9). Moreover, the exclusive policy of Nehemiah and Ezra later developed into a narrow and rigid outlook and even into a snobbish attitude toward "the lesser breeds without the law." It was too easy to assume that human beings—rather than God—could determine the boundaries of the chosen community on the basis of a genealogical list or the scrupulous observance of circumcision, sabbath, and the many details of the Torah. We have only to read the New Testament to become aware of this weakness in Judaism. It should be added that the rabbis of the post-biblical period at times were just as severe in their criticism of the dangers and corruptions to which the Jewish faith was exposed.

Moreover, it is noteworthy that prophecy at this time almost ceased. There were, to be sure, a few prophets—persons like "Third Isaiah," Haggai, Zechariah, Obadiah, Malachi, and Joel—but they were mostly second-rate in comparison with the great prophets who had gone before. Preoccupation with the Torah seemed to stifle the spirit of prophecy. This is understandable, for if the basis of the holy community was the Torah, regarded as directly revealed to Moses and written in a book, the greatest need was for scribes (like Ezra) who could study it, expound its meaning, and preserve it carefully. In the Chronicler's history the prophets are, for the most part, good churchmen. Instead of viewing their role as interpreters of the events of the time, as was true of all the major prophets we have studied, the Chronicler insisted that the prophets' chief function was in the worship service. They were definitely "cultic prophets," like many of the professional prophets of the pre-exilic period. They "prophesied" by leading the congregation in music (I Chron. 25:1). In addition, they may have taken part in the liturgical recitation of some of the psalms. After Ezra's time the belief emerged that the age of charismatic prophecy was over until the coming of the messianic age.

Yet in one sense prophecy did continue within Judaism. The writings of the prophets were preserved and eventually canonized, which shows the great importance that the exponents of Judaism attached to the prophetic message. The Pentateuch, the charter of Judaism, contains many "prophetic" elements, as we have seen in our study of the history of this work, from the Old Epic tradition of the oral period down to its final literary formulation in the time of the Exile. Although Judaism regarded cultic and ethical offenses as equally serious, insisting that the most trivial offenses were as blameworthy as important ones, there was not the slightest intention of disregarding the great exhortation that Yahweh requires the people to do justice, to practice steadfast love, and to walk humbly with God (Micah 6:8). The two great commandments, singled out by rabbis as the quintessence of covenant obligations (Mk. 12:28–34), are from the Torah.

In the post-exilic period prophecy found a new form of expression in the literature known as "apocalyptic," to which we have alluded from time to time. Although this type of literature was anticipated by Ezekiel, Third Isaiah, and Zechariah, it flourished in the later years of Judaism, beginning with the Maccabean period. The chief example in the Old Testament is the book of Daniel. Before we turn to this new expression of prophecy, however, we must pause to give special attention to two matters that have been slighted up to this point: Israel's worship as reflected in the book of Psalms (Chapter 16), and the reflections of the sages of Israel (Chapter 17).

CHAPTER **16**

The Praises of Israel

As we look back over the ground we have traveled so far, one thing stands out clearly: Israel understood its history to be a life of "co-existence with God," as the Jewish philosopher Abraham Heschel has put it—that is, a "partnership with God" in a historical drama.[1] In the time of the Exodus Yahweh created a people out of nothing and entered into a covenant relationship with them. Hence "existence in faith" was a response to God's being with and going with the people, through the wilderness and on toward the Promised Land. In the course of time Yahweh initiated a new phase of the drama by raising up David to be king and by opening up to Israel wider horizons than the people had ever seen. Prophetic interpreters declared that Yahweh was active in the secular sphere of politics, punctuating Israel's life-story with historical events which manifested God's active presence in the midst of the people. Even the most catastrophic event—the end of Israel as a nation—was interpreted as Yahweh's coming to

---

Biblical readings: Read at least selected hymns laments, and thanksgivings such as the following: Hymns (psalms of praise): 8, 19:1-6, 33, 93, 95-100, 103, 105, 135, 136, 145-150. Laments (psalms of supplication): 3, 7, 10, 22, 25, 27:7-14, 31, 38, 44, 51, 77, 88, 130, 137, 143. Songs of thanksgiving: 92, 116, 118, 138; Jonah chap. 2.

[1] See further "Coexistence with God: Heschel's Exposition of Biblical Theology," by B. W. Anderson, in *Abraham Joshua Heschel: Exploring His Life and Thought* (New York: Macmillan, 1985).

judge and to renew the people and to mediate, through Israel's suffering, blessing for all nations. This view of history as the dramatic narrative of God's deeds was a new breakthrough in the field of the religions of the world. "It may be said with truth," writes an authority on comparative religions, "that the Hebrews were the first to discover the meaning of history as the epiphany of God."[2]

Israel, however, was called to be a partner with God in this historical drama, and to respond to the divine presence and activity. Although it is appropriate for the accent to fall primarily on Yahweh's actions, the Old Testament shows that—to quote a leading Old Testament theologian—when these "mighty acts" of Yahweh occurred, "Israel did not keep silent." Not only did the people recall these "acts of Yahweh" in various historical writings from time to time, but they "also addressed Yahweh in a wholly personal way." The people, he goes on to say, raised hymns of praise, boldly asked questions, and complained in the depths of distress; for Israel was chosen "for converse with Yahweh"— not to be "a mere dumb object" of the divine will.[3]

THE BOOK OF PSALMS

The finest examples of Israel's "converse" with Yahweh are found in the book of Psalms, often called the Psalter. In previous chapters we have found it necessary to refer to the book of Psalms frequently in discussing the various phases of Israel's history. Just as the hymnbooks of church or synagogue unite the voices of many generations, so the Psalter is a condensed account of the whole drama of Israel's history with God from the time of David down to the late period of the Old Testament. The trouble is, however, that it is practically impossible to deal with the Psalms in their proper historical periods or life-situations. Unlike modern hymnbooks, no reliable indication of the date or occasion of a particular psalm is provided at the beginning or end.[4] Moreover, with the exception of Psalm 137, which clearly presupposes a situation in the Babylonian exile (see above, pp. 447–448), the content of particular psalms tells us very little about the time and circumstance of their composition. So even though the book of Psalms reflects a long history of worship, it is appropriate to begin our study of it within the context of the period of Judaism when the hymns and prayers of many generations were compiled for use in the second Temple, which was completed in 515 B.C.E.

---

[2] Mircea Eliade, *Cosmos and History* [120], p. 104.

[3] A paraphrase of Gerhard von Rad, *Theology*, I [142], 354. His discussion of the Psalter is placed under the rubric, "Israel Before Yahweh (Israel's Answer)."

[4] It is generally recognized that the few superscriptions or headings which associate psalms with particular events in David's career were added later. Such superscriptions are found at the head of thirteen psalms: 3, 7, 18, 34, 51, 52, 54, 56, 57, 59, 60, 63, 142.

DEFINITION: "PSALMS, PSALTER"

The title "book of Psalms" actually comes from the New Testament (Luke 20:42; Acts 1:20). The early Christian community read the Scriptures of Israel (their "Old Testament") in the Greek translation (Septuagint), where the prevailing title was *psalmoi*, referring to songs sung to the accompaniment of stringed instruments. Another title, found in one codex of the Greek Bible, is *psalterion*, referring primarily to a zither-like instrument, and secondarily to songs sung to stringed accompaniment. From this title comes the often used term, Psalter.

While these Greek titles emphasize the musical dimension of the psalms, the title in the Hebrew Bible, *Tehillim* ("praises") stresses their content. In whatever mood or mode, these songs are praises to God.

Although there is some variation in the numbering of psalms, the traditional total of the collection is 150. The Greek Bible, however, contains an additional psalm, Ps. 151, associated with the incident of David's single-handed combat with Goliath, although the superscription explicitly states that it is "outside the number." Interestingly, archaeologists discovered at the site of the ancient monastery of Qumran a scroll containing other psalms not found in the Hebrew Bible, and this provides further evidence of the flexibility in the number.[5]

Enthroned on the Praises of Israel

The title found in the Hebrew Bible, *Tehillim* or "praises," is most appropriate for these songs of adoration and thanksgiving, confession and supplication, with which Israel responded to Yahweh's active presence in its history. Whether the mood was elation or sorrow, bewilderment or confidence, these songs were intended as anthems to the glory of God. They usher us into the sanctuary where, as one psalmist put it, Yahweh was "enthroned on the praises of Israel" (Ps. 22:3, RSV). The faith of the Psalms has rightly been described as "theocentric piety."[6]

From the outset, Israel was a covenant *community* whose primary bond of unity was the worship of Yahweh. The twelve-tribe Confederacy, instituted by Joshua, had its focal point in the central sanctuary to which the people gathered for the great festivals, especially the festival of covenant renewal. During the time of David, Jerusalem became the worship center of the new nation, and Solomon contributed further to the centrality of Zion by building a great temple. So strongly did the people feel the pull to go to Jerusalem to worship Yahweh that, after the disruption of the monarchy, Jeroboam I found it necessary to establish pilgrimage shrines in his own territory, especially at Bethel. When the exiles returned from Babylon after the destruction of Jerusalem, their first thought was to rebuild the Temple. The history of Israel shows, then, that the

---

[5] See J. A. Sanders, *The Dead Sea Psalms Scroll* (Ithaca, N.Y.: Cornell University Press, 1967), pp. 93–117.

[6] See Helmer Ringgren, *The Faith of the Psalmists* [454], chap. 3.

The Blind Harper of Leiden is one of a group of musicians portrayed on a tomb in a temple of Hatshepsut at Karnak, dating from the Amarna period (c. 1400–1350 B.C.E.). In Israel the "harp" and "lyre" were used to accompany religious songs (Pss. 92:3; 150:3), but we have to turn to the art of Egypt to visualize what these stringed instruments were like.

fundamental reality, through all social changes and historical vicissitudes, was *Israel as a worshiping community*. For this reason the book of Psalms lies at the very heart of the Old Testament.

More and more we are coming to realize that the religion of the Psalms is "cultic"—that is, it is the faith of this community at worship, especially on the occasions of temple festivals. It is quite true that many of these hymns, laments and thanksgivings were composed by individuals who spoke out of their concrete life-situations. Even so, it is not necessary to suppose that in every case these individual psalms were composed as private meditations; some may have been intended for use in connection with a liturgical act or for recitation at a temple festival. In any case, the treasury of Psalms was appropriated by the worshiping community, precisely as songs of various origins are incorporated into modern hymnbooks. Thus when the pronouns "I" and "my" are used, as in the well-known Shepherd's Psalm (Ps. 23), we must think of the whole community joining to express its faith.

One of the great difficulties that stands in the way of understanding the Psalter is the modern individualism which assumes that worship is a private affair between an individual and God, and that God is accessible apart from the established means of public worship. Starting from this premise, the first step would be to divide the psalms into those that reflect public worship and those that reflect personal piety. But this contrast between the individual and the community is completely alien to Israel's covenant faith, according to which the individual is related to God as a member of a community. God is free to meet a person at any time or place (invariably to the surprise of the one who receives the theophany); but to have access to God one should come to the designated rendevous and seek God at the appointed times. Only as a member of the community does the individual share in the promises and blessings of the covenant. To be a solitary individual, cut off from the established means of grace and therefore, as fugitive David said, having "no heritage of Yahweh" (I Sam. 26:19), was the greatest calamity imaginable. According to Israel's faith, Yahweh is present—enthroned on the praises of the people—when the congregation worships together at the sanctuary on the occasion of holy days or festivals.[7] The individual praises God *with* the worshiping community:

> O magnify Yahweh with me,
> and let us exalt his name together!
> —PSALM 34:3

The Hymnbook of the Second Temple

The book of Psalms in its present form is the product of the post-exilic community of Israel. Insofar as the Psalter reflects the liturgical practice of this period, it is proper to speak of it as "the hymnbook of the second Temple." The staff of this Temple undertook the task of arranging the hymns and supplications of the ages in suitable form, and provided them with musical and liturgical notes which survive to puzzle the modern reader. Although their notations clearly suggest that the psalms were to be sung in public worship, we cannot be sure of the details. For example, the term *selah*, which occurs repeatedly in some psalms (e.g., Ps. 46), apparently was the signal for a musical interlude and the singing of a refrain. In other instances, a note at the beginning indicates the kind of musical accompaniment, whether stringed instruments or flutes (e.g., Ps. 5); and it may be that some of the superscriptions indicate the tune to which

---

[7] On the cultic character of Israel's worship, see for instance R. E. Clements, *Prophecy and Covenant* [312], pp. 86–102; also H. Ringgren [454], pp. 1–19. Claus Westermann, in *The Praise of God in the Psalms* [457], is critical of an excessive emphasis upon the cultic character of the psalms of Israel, though he is equally critical of reading into them individualistic piety. He prefers to speak of the "forensic character of the praise of God" (p. 10), by which he means that praise occurs "in public" and makes the individual conscious of being "a member of a congregation." See especially pp. 15–25.

the psalm is to be sung.[8] A clearer picture of the place of the psalms in post-exilic worship is provided by the Chronicler, whose work was treated in the preceding chapter. For instance, the bringing of the Ark to Jerusalem reaches a climax in a worship service which is rather post-exilic in style (I Chron. 16:7–36): the Temple choir chants certain psalms (portions of Psalms 105, 96, and 106), and the people respond at the appropriate point with "Amen."

The Psalter, however, did not receive its final form in a single edition. The process of completion took place in several stages, extending from about the fifth to the second centuries B.C.E. The Psalter is composed of five collections of "books," each of which concludes with a doxology (which is not a part of the psalm with which it is connected). Psalm 1, which extols the Torah, now serves as an introduction to the entire Psalter, and Psalm 150 is the concluding doxology for the whole compilation. The organization is as follows:

Book I: Psalms 1–41
          (Concluding doxology: Ps. 41:13)
Book II: Psalms 42–72
          (Concluding doxology: Ps. 72:18–19)
Book III: Psalms 73–89
          (Concluding doxology: Ps. 89:52)
Book IV: Psalms 90–106
          (Concluding doxology: Ps. 106:48)
Book V: Psalms 107–150
          (Concluding doxology for the whole Psalter: Ps. 150)

This fivefold arrangement seems to be patterned after the five books of the To-rah.

An important clue to the origin of the Psalter is found in the postscript which follows Book II: "The prayers of David, the son of Jesse, are ended" (Ps. 72:20). This means that at one stage in the formation of the Psalter it was felt that the "Davidic" collection ended here. It is interesting that in this first book almost all of the psalms are prefixed with the words *leDawid*, which means "to David" or "belonging to David." This collection is undoubtedly the oldest, and probably goes back to the liturgical usage of the pre-exilic Temple in Jerusalem. To this old nucleus other collections gravitated, until eventually the fivefold arrangement of the Psalter came into being. Yet these successive editions were all issued under the aegis of David. Despite the fact that only 73 out of the 150 psalms are attributed explicitly to David, while others are assigned to Moses (Ps. 90), Solomon (Psalms 72, 127), and others, the view was popularly held that David was the author of the entire Psalter. This view undoubtedly reflects

---

[8] For instance, "according to The Hind of the Dawn" (Ps. 22:1) may refer to a well-known tune. Perhaps the Israelite community appropriated secular tunes for its hymonody, just as modern churches and synagogues have sometimes done.

the community's conviction, highlighted in I–II Chronicles (see Chap. 15), that David was the "messiah" (Anointed One)—the ideal king with whom the people identified as they came before God in worship,[9] and the prototype of the coming King who would fulfill the hopes of Israel. Yet the ascription of the Psalms to David is not a complete fiction for, as we have previously observed, David gave leadership in music and worship, and he undoubtedly composed psalms. Thus the relation of David to the Psalter is analogous to the relation of Moses to the Pentateuch.

The Worship of Pre-Exilic Israel

It is one thing to speak of the creation of the present book of Psalms as the hymnbook of the second Temple; it is quite another thing, however, to deal with the origin and use of individual psalms contained in this compilation. A generation or so ago it was stylish to date most of the psalms in the post-exilic period or even in the Maccabean period near the dawn of the Common Era. However, our increasing knowledge of the worship of Israel during the period of the monarchy, as well as our wider understanding of the psalmody of the ancient Near East, has led us to believe that a great number of psalms were composed and used liturgically during the pre-exilic period.[10] In fact, there is now a disposition to say that, although the Psalter received its final shape at the hands of the staff of the second Temple, most of the psalms reflect the official, pre-exilic worship of Israel.

The origin and earliest use of many of the psalms are beyond recovery, just as the authorship of many of the hymns in modern hymnbooks is unknown. However, through the application of the method of study known as "form criticism" it is possible to gain a deeper understanding of the pre-exilic worship of Israel as reflected in the Psalms.

When analyzed in terms of literary form and liturgical function many psalms fall into three major categories. The first genre is the *hymn*, in which the worshiping community celebrates the majesty and faithfulness of God. The second genre is the *lament* (or petition), which presupposes a problematic situation in which God's sovereignty is temporarily eclipsed. The third is the *thanksgiving* which expresses praise for divine deliverance from trouble, although this form

---

[9] Christoph Barth, *Introduction to the Psalms* [447], points out that David was a "typical" or representative figure for the Israelite people; therefore, in worship they remembered "the king, pursued and abandoned in innocence and guilt, but always delivered and restored to power by the faithfulness of God, in whom their own existence as the People of God had found an expression that was valid for all time" (pp. 64–65).

[10] For the Babylonian hymns, see Pritchard, *Ancient Near Eastern Texts* [1], pp. 383–92; for Egyptian literature, pp. 365–81. See also the works by Charles Cumming [438] and George Widengren [445].

DEFINITION: FORM CRITICISM

Three things are involved in the literary approach known as form criticism. First, one determines the bounds of a particular literary unit or *pericope*, a Greek term ("a cutting all around") which suggests that a passage, when cut out of its context, has its own integrity: a definite beginning and end, internal structure and dynamic, and a self-contained meaning. A parable would be a good example. Second, one attempts to understand the function of the literary unit in its setting in social life (*Sitz im Leben*), perhaps in everyday affairs (e.g. a wedding song or a funeral dirge) or, as in the case of the Psalms, in the worship of the community. Finally, one asumes that these literary units, which reflect general human experiences, display formulaic patterns and literary conventions evident elsewhere, either within the Bible or in other literature of the ancient Near East. Therefore, a study of analogous literary forms, biblical and extra-biblical, may be illuminating.

The pioneer in form-critical study of the Psalms was Hermann Gunkel; see *The Psalms: A Form-Critical Introduction* [450]. His work was advanced by Sigmund Mowinckel; see *The Psalms in Israel's Worship, I–II* [453]. Whereas Gunkel stressed the classification of psalms according to literary type (e.g. hymn, lament, thanksgiving), Mowinckel concentrated on the function of the psalms in the setting of the temple festivals, especially the New Year's festival.

Closely related to form criticism is the method known as rhetorical criticism, which concentrates on the stylistic features and literary patterns of a text rather than on social setting or historical context. See James Muilenburg, "Form Criticism and Beyond" [75].

admittedly is closely related to the lament and overlaps with the hymn.[11] In this discussion we shall consider these literary types briefly, and then turn our attention to the Temple festivals in which various psalms were used liturgically.[12]

ISRAEL AT WORSHIP

A people's worship is inevitably the expression of its conviction about who God is and how God is related to the world. If the gods are part of nature's cycle of decay and renewal, as in archaic societies, then worshipers leave the profane sphere of everyday life and enter a sacred realm where they experience the divine renewal of the world.[13] If God is beyond the phenomena of the human world and is the numinous, ineffable Reality, as in mystical religions, then the

[11] Artur Weiser in his commentary on the Psalms [456], pp. 52–91, follows the usual major distinctions: hymns, laments, and thanksgivings. Claus Westermann, however, in his *The Praise of God in the Psalms* [457], insists that "thanksgiving" should be subsumed under "praise" and therefore there are only two major types: hymns and supplications. See also H. Ringgren [454], pp. 76–91, who maintains that "thanksgiving is simply one way of praising God."

[12] For further discussion of the psalms according to their literary type or genre, see the author's introduction, *Out of the Depths* [446].

[13] On this archaic view see especially M. Eliade, *The Sacred and the Profane* [121].

worshiper takes the path of withdrawal from the realm of change and illusion in order to enter into ineffable communion or union with ''It.'' According to Israel's faith, however, the holy God is the One who enters the human world, who acts to make history, who intervenes to deliver the oppressed and to humble the proud and mighty. Therefore the beginning of praise is meditation upon what God has done, is doing, and will do:

> One generation shall laud thy works to another,
> and shall declare thy mighty acts.
> On the glorious splendor of thy majesty,
> and on thy wondrous works, I will meditate.
> —PSALM 145:4–5 (RSV)

These ''mighty acts'' which evoke praise undoubtedly include things that the psalmist had experienced personally. But the psalmist mainly refers to the great events of the past, right back to the creation of the world, in which the greatness and goodness of Yahweh were displayed. Indeed, one of the characteristic features of Israel's worship is the remembrance of the tradition. This remembrance, however, is not just the recollection of what happened once upon a time. Rather, it is a ''cultic remembrance'' in the presence of Yahweh which makes the past present, so that worshipers become contemporary with the historic events that are crucial for the community of faith. As observed earlier (p. 9), even today believing Jews regard themselves as being contemporary with the event of the Exodus.

It must not be supposed that ancient Israel had a corner on the view of divine activity in history. In the religions of other peoples, such as the Babylonians, the gods were believed to be active in historical affairs.[14] One of the distinctive traits of Israel, however, was that in the cult the people turned primarily to their own historical experiences to confess faith in God.

> Yahweh achieves vindication
> and justice for all the oppressed.
> He manifested his ways to Moses,
> his actions to the Israelites.
> —PSALM 103:6–7

Hymns of Praise

The hymn is a song which extols God's greatness and goodness manifest in deeds of history and creation. Psalms of this type generally begin with an im-

---

[14] See Bertil Albrektson, *History and the Gods* [194]. At the end of his study, Albrektson notes the peculiar way that Yahweh's acts in history were remembered and celebrated in the Israelite cult.

perative call to worship; then comes a section which gives the ground for praise, often introduced by "for" (*kî*); and sometimes they conclude with a renewed summons to praise, thus echoing the note sounded at the first. The structure of the hymn can be seen plainly in Psalm 117, the shortest psalm of the Psalter:

A.   Introduction: *Invocation to worship*
        Praise Yahweh, all nations!
          Extol him, all peoples!
B.   Main section: *Motive for praise*
        For (*kî*) great is his steadfast love (*ḥésed*) toward us,
          and the faithfulness of Yahweh endures for ever.
C.   Conclusion: *Recapitulation*
        Praise Yahweh!

This structure is found with various modifications in a number of hymns contained in the Psalter, such as Psalms 33, 95, 100, 145, 148, 149, and 150.

In previous chapters we have seen that Israel characteristically confessed its faith by telling the story of how Yahweh acted with liberating power. The poetic couplet composed by Miriam to celebrate the crossing of the Reed Sea (Exod. 15:21) is a terse example of a hymnic cry of praise to Yahweh: the first line is a summons to praise, and the second grounds praise in Yahweh's deed at the Sea. In line with this ancient tradition, a number of psalms extol Yahweh by reciting and elaborating the major themes of the story: the Exodus, the deliverance at the Reed Sea, the wandering through the wilderness, and the occupation of the land. In these story-telling psalms, or psalms of sacred history (e.g., Ps. 78, 105, 106, 135, 136), the psalmists re-present Israel's history as the story of Yahweh's actions which centered in the deliverance from Egypt.

Psalm 136 is an excellent illustration of how Israel's praise (or thanksgiving)[15] is evoked by the recitation of what Yahweh has done. The invocation, which appears in the same form at the beginning and end, strikes the keynote:

    Sentence: O give thanks to Yahweh, for he is good,
    Response: for [*kî*] his faithfulness [*ḥésed*] endures for ever.

This pattern of call to praise followed by liturgical response runs through the whole psalm, sentence by sentence. The first three sentences (verses 1, 2, 3) represent the summons to worship, with which hymns characteristically begin. The concluding sentence (vs. 26) rounds off the whole by recapitulating the theme struck at the beginning. The remaining portion of the psalm gives the

---

[15] Although this psalm seems to begin with a call to thanksgiving, it is actually a hymn, as Weiser correctly recognizes, [456], p. 53. Here we have further evidence that there is no sharp difference between praising God and thanking God.

ground for this praise by reciting the marvelous acts of Yahweh. In Hebrew, each of these "ascriptions" usually begins with a participle. For instance:

> to the One who smote the first-born of Egypt,
> *response*
> and brought Israel out from among them,
> *response*
> with a strong hand and an outstretched arm,
> *response*
> to the One who divided the Reed Sea in two,
> *response*
> and made Israel pass through the midst of it,
> *response*
>   etc.
>
> —PSALM 136:10–14

In this section of the psalm (verses 10–22), the psalmist is elaborating the ancient Israelite story.

DEFINITION: "ASCRIPTION"

An "ascription" (referred to above) is a grammatical form in which a narrative clause follows, or even takes the place of, the divine Name for the purpose of identifying who God is as known through divine actions. In the Bible, ascriptions are usually formulated grammatically either by using the relative pronoun ("who") or a participle referring to the actor (or action), as in the psalm cited above ("the One who"). Other examples are found in Psalm 103:3–5 and in hymnic passages of Second Isaiah (e.g. Isa. 44:24–28). Ascriptions often belong to hymnic style because the hymn praises God by telling what God has done, is doing, or will do. The story that identifies who God is may be reduced to a single sentence, as in the prologue to the Decalogue: "I am Yahweh your God, who brought you out of the land of Egypt." See further James T. Clemons,"God, Ascriptions to" in *International Standard Bible Encyclopedia* II, rev. ed., G. W. Bromily, ed. (Grand Rapids, MI: Eerdmans, 1979), pp. 503–504.

It is striking, however, that in this recitation of Yahweh's mighty acts the psalmist begins with Creation:

> to the One who alone does great wonders,
> *response*
> to the One who by understanding made the heavens,
> *response*
> to the One who spread out the earth upon the waters,
> *response*
> to the One who made the great lights,
> *response*

the sun to rule over the day,
> *response*

the moon and stars to rule over the night,
> *response*

> —PSALM 136:4–9

Here Creation is not an independent article of faith but is the *beginning* of *history*—that is, the first of the series of divine acts which unfold into the story of God's dealings with Israel. Looking at it another way, Israel expanded its own sacred history by tracing Yahweh's actions back to the very beginning. Thus the worshiping community confessed that Yahweh's "faithfulness" (*ḥésed*), revealed in Israel's history, underlies all historical times and embraces all humankind, a theme also found in Israel's Old Epic tradition (see Chapter 5, pp. 170–177).

In other psalms, however, the praise of God the Creator is not linked directly with the sweep of sacred history which has its center in the Exodus, but is prompted by the marvelous order of the cosmos and the dependence of the world upon the God who originated and ordered the heavens and the earth (see the Zion theology discussed on pp. 230–233). An excellent example is Psalm 104, which was influenced by the Egyptian "Hymn to the Aton," the deity symbolized by the sun disc whom the reforming Pharaoh Akhnaton worshiped in the fourteenth century B.C.E.[16] In its present form the hymn follows the general order of the Priestly creation story in Genesis 1, emphasizing that all creatures, human and animal, are radically dependent upon the Creator at every moment for existence. In fact, if the Creator's upholding power ("spirit") were to be withdrawn, everything would collapse. The Hebrew verbs, translated in the present tense, indicate God's *continuing* creative activity:

> All of them [animals and humans] look to you
>> to give them their food in its season.
> When you give to them, they gather up,
>> when you open your hand, they are satisfied to the full.
> When you hide your face, they are disturbed,
>> when you take away their breath, they expire
>> and return to their dust.
> When you send forth your spirit, they are [re]created,
>> and you renew the surface of the soil.
>> —PSALM 104:27–30

Laments in Distress

The remembrance of Yahweh's deeds can also have the effect of plunging an individual or the whole Israelite community into bewilderment about the pres-

---

[16] The text of this magnificent Egyptian hymn is found in Pritchard, *Ancient Near Eastern Texts* [1], pp. 369–71. See further the author's *Creation versus Chaos* [128], chap. 2.

ent situation of suffering and distress. Although "theoretical atheism" was unknown in the Old Testament period, Israel was afflicted from time to time with the feeling that Yahweh had abandoned the people. These were times of "the eclipse of God," to cite the title of a book by Martin Buber. When one considers that Israel, situated in a storm-center of world politics, so often suffered deeply, it is not surprising that fully one third of the Psalter consists of laments in which a suppliant cries to God "out of the depths" (Ps. 130:1). The surprising thing is that psalms of this type display so little whining self-pity or vindictive bitterness and that the praise of Yahweh reverberates through human sorrows. Indeed, "lament" may not be the best description of this literary form. There is a difference between a lamentation and a lament, according to form critics. A lamentation (dirge) is suitable in a situation that cannot be changed (a person's death), whereas a lament presupposes that a situation of distress can be changed if and when Yahweh intervenes with a display of "amazing grace."

The lament has a characteristic literary form, although it displays some variation in the details.[17]

A. *Invocation*: Address to God, which may be a brief cry or may be expanded into an ascription of praise to the God who is addressed.

B. *Complaint*. In community laments the distress may be some great crisis such as enemy attack, famine, or plague. Individual laments may be occasioned by such problems as sickness, persecution, or acute awareness of guilt.

C. *Confession of Trust*. In spite of the problematic situation, the suppliant relies on God's faithfulness.

D. *Petition*. The suppliant appeals to God to intervene and change the situation.

E. *Vow of Thanksgiving*. In the confidence that God hears and answers prayer, the suppliant vows to testify before the community about what God has done. (This element is usually lacking in community laments.)

A good example of a community lament is Psalm 44: (A) In the *Invocation* the community, in a time of crisis, recalls the faith of ancestors who had told about the marvelous acts that Yahweh performed in the past (verses 1–8). (B) The community raises its *Complaint* as it contrasts former days with the present, when Yahweh has "cast us off" and "made us like sheep for slaughter" (verses 9–16). (C) Then comes the community's *Confession* of its steadfast trust in Yahweh in poignant language. (Abraham Heschel quoted part of this psalm in the dedication of his great work on *The Prophets* "to the martyrs of 1940–45," the victims of the Nazi holocaust in which six million Jews were consumed in a "burnt offering."[18])

> All this has come upon us,
>   though we have not forgotten thee,

---

[17] See especially the work by Claus Westermann [457], 52–81; also the author's *Out of the Depths* [446], chap. 3.

[18] Abraham J. Heschel, *The Prophets* [315].

or been false to thy covenant.
Our heart has not turned back,
   nor have our steps departed from thy way,
that thou shouldst have broken us in the place of jackals,
   and covered us with deep darkness.
                    —PSALM 44:17–19 (RSV)

(D) The lament concludes with the community's fervent *petition* to Yahweh to act once again and to bring to an end the time of the eclipse of God's presence (verses 13–16). Other examples of community laments are found in Psalms 10, 74, 79, 106, and 137.

Many of the laments are the cries of individuals in distress. In these cases the supplicant's suffering is veiled in traditional imagery, so that it is next to impossible to determine the concrete situation out of which the lament is raised. The heart of the complaint is that the supplicant feels abandoned by God and about to be overwhelmed by the powers of death (often described as Sheol or the subterranean waters surrounding it). As an example of an individual lament, we may take the moving Psalm 22, whose opening words, according to Christian tradition, became Jesus' cry of dereliction from the Cross (Mark 15:34). The supplicant begins with a poignant cry:

My God, my God, why have you forsaken me?
   and are distant from my cry for help,
      my groaning words?
O my God, I call out by day, and you don't answer,
   by night and find no repose.
                    —VERSES 1–2

As a member of the worshiping community, the supplicant falls back on the faith of the fathers and mothers which lives on in spite of fire and sword.

But you are holy,
   enthroned on the praises of Israel.
In you our ancestors trusted,
   they trusted and you rescued them.
To you they cried, and they were delivered,
   in you they trusted and were not disconcerted.
                  —VERSES 3–5 (also 9–10)

However, the recollection of the past, when Yahweh's mighty acts were made known to the ancestors, is only "an island of comfort in the midst of the ocean" of suffering (Artur Weiser). In ever-shifting figures of speech, the supplicant complains to God:

Many bulls surround me,
   mighty bulls of Bashan encircle me.
Open-mouthed to swallow me
   are ravenous and roaring lions.

> I am drained away like water,
>   and all my bones are out of joint.
> My heart has become like wax,
>   it melts inside me.
> My palate is dry like earthenware,
>   and my tongue sticks to the roof of my mouth.
> You have brought me to the point of death.
> —VERSES 14–15

In the ensuing verses the crisis is described in different imagery: the supplicant is being attacked by a pack of dogs, or by brigands who take away everything, including garments, and divide the spoil (verses 16–18). The supplicant's complaint reaches a climax in a cry for help out of the depths of distress:

> But you, O Yahweh, do not be distant!
>   O my Strength, hurry to my aid!
> Rescue my life from the sword,
>   my solitary self from the power of the dog!
> Save me from the mouth of the lion,
>   from the horns of the wild ox!
> —VERSES 19–21

Then, if we follow the Hebrew text, the supplicant breaks out into an exclamation, "You have answered me!" (verse 21c),[19] and the whole mood in the following verses modulates from the minor mode of lament to strains of praise in a major key (verses 23–31). The supplicant's prayer has been heard; no longer is Yahweh's "face" (presence) hidden (verse 24). The psalm ends with a jubilant testimony before the congregation to Yahweh's demonstration of grace which opens up a new possibility of life.

How can one account for this abrupt shift from a minor to a major key, here and elsewhere in laments (e.g. Ps. 28:6)? Many scholars believe that in the interval between the final parts of the psalm a minister of the temple, perhaps a priest or a temple prophet, uttered "words of assurance" (an "oracle of salvation") to the effect that God had heard the supplicant's prayer and promised deliverance.[20] Perhaps one of these "oracles of salvation," spoken in the name of the liberating God, is preserved in Psalm 12:5. The response to this liturgical act was a vow of praise before the worshiping community (Ps. 22:22–28):

> You are the source of my praise in the great community;
>   I will fulfill my vows before those who fear Yahweh.
> Let humble ones eat and be satisfied!
> Let those who seek Yahweh praise him,
>   their hearts ever full of vitality.
> —VERSES 25–26

[19] Most translations usually change the Hebrew text here. In the above literal translation of the Hebrew, we are following the interpretation of H. J. Kraus in his commentary on the Psalms [452].

[20] For an exposition of this view see the above-mentioned works by Weiser [456], pp. 219–26; Westermann [457], pp. 64–81.

Suppliants Appealing to a royal servant are depicted on a tomb relief of Hor-em-heb at Memphis (c. 1349– 1319 B.C.E). Such gestures of prostration were also appropriate to express humble and fearful adoration of God (see Psalm 95:6).

This interpretation helps us to understand more clearly the place of individual psalms of lament within the Israelite cult. It also shows how lament does not stand by itself but, like the second movement of a symphony, moves through the minor strain to the major key of the final movement, from petition out of distress to joyful praise of God. Other individual laments—to mention a few— are found in Psalms 3, 13, 31, 54, 56, and 102.

In a number of the laments suppliants cry out to God for vindication and even pray for divine vengeance against enemies: unidentified persons or powers that threaten people's welfare and security. Several psalms are usually called "imprecatory psalms" (Pss. 35, 59, 69, 70, 109, 137, 140), because the psalmist's passion for vindication finds expression in imprecations or curses against hostile powers. A conspicuous example is Psalm 137 (referred to above, pp. 447–448), a folk song that cries out for vengeance against the Babylonians who destroyed Jerusalem in 587 B.C.E. and the Edomites who assisted in the destruction (cf. Obadiah 10–14). These human passions are understandable, although not nec- essarily commendable, in instances when the weak suffer under oppressors or are victimized by a powerful establishment. These psalms, like the rest of the laments, presuppose the view that God has entered into covenant relationship with the people Israel and therefore can be appealed to as the Judge who de- fends the weak and upholds justice. "Vengeance," that is, vindication, is the prerogative of God, not the right of those who take justice into their own hands (Deut. 32:35; cf. Rom. 12:19).

At the opposite extreme to the imprecatory psalms are a number of psalms which have been called "penitential psalms" (Pss. 6, 32, 38, 51, 102, 130, 143). In these cries *de profundis* (see Ps. 130:1), the human problem is not located "out there," in the powers and structures of society, but within, in the heart. Conscious of human fallibility and failure, suppliants cast themselves upon the mercy and forgiveness of Yahweh. Psalm 51, composed in the typical pattern of the lament, is an exquisite illustration. The suppliant begins with an appeal to God:

> Have mercy upon me, O God, according to thy steadfast love [*ḥésed*],
>   according to thy abundant mercy blot out my transgressions.
> Wash me thoroughly from my iniquity,
>   and cleanse me from my sin!
>   —VERSES 1–2 (RSV)

Then comes the expression of distress: an inner sense of being in the wrong (verses 3–5):

> Against thee, thee only, have I sinned,
>   and done that which is evil in thy sight.
>   —VERSE 4

The suppliant petitions for purification, forgiveness, and inner renewal (verses 6–12):

> Create in me a clean heart, O God,
>   and put a new and right spirit within me.
> Cast me not away from thy presence,
>   and take not thy holy Spirit from me.
>   —VERSES 10–11

Finally the suppliant vows to help other troubled people to know God's grace and to offer the sacrifice which is acceptable to God: "a broken and contrite heart" (verses 13–17). It is generally recognized that verses 18–19 were added in the early post-exilic period by editors who believed that when the Temple was rebuilt, Yahweh would delight in animal sacrifices too.

Songs of Thanksgiving

The third literary type, which contains elements of the hymn and the lament, is the song of thanksgiving. The main characteristic of the individual song of thanksgiving is its retrospective character: it looks back to the time when a suppliant, in a situation of lament, cried to Yahweh for help. That former situation, however, no longer exists. The interim of the eclipse of God has ended. In response to a cry out of the depths, Yahweh has heard and has acted with liberating grace, with the result that the suppliant now sings ''a new song.''

> I waited and waited for Yahweh
>   and he turned to me,
>   and heard my cry.
> He raised me out of the pit of despair,
>   out of the miry clay,
> and he set my feet on a rock,
>   securing my steps.
> He has put on my lips a new song,
>   praise to our God.
> Many will observe and fear,
>   and will put their trust in Yahweh.
>   —PSALM 40:1–3

The individual song of thanksgiving also has a distinctive literary form which is subject to poetic variation. An excellent illustration is Psalm 116.

A. *Introduction* (Ps. 116:1–2)
   The individual begins by offering praise to Yahweh and, as in the case of hymns, gives the motive (*kî*) for praise.
B. *Main Section*: Narration of the Psalmist's experience in the past (Ps. 116:3–9).
   1. Portrayal of the distress that the psalmist once experienced when the power of death almost prevailed (verse 3).
   2. Recollection of the cry for help (verse 4).
   3. Yahweh's response to the prayer:

> For you have delivered my life from death,
>   my eyes from tears,
>   my feet from stumbling.
> I walk before Yahweh in the land of the living.
>   —PSALM 116:8–9

C. *Conclusion*: Praise to Yahweh for deliverance (Ps. 116:10–19).
   In gratitude for Yahweh's gracious deliverance, the suppliant testifies to the divine grace that supports all the people.

> What shall I give back to Yahweh
>   for all his bounty to me?
> The cup of salvation I'll lift,
>   and call on the name of Yahweh.
> My vows to Yahweh I will complete
>   here in the presence of all his people.
>   —PSALM 116:12–14

Other individual psalms of thanksgiving are Psalms 92, 118, 138 and the psalm found in the book of Jonah (Jonah 2:1–9).

Fewer in number are the community songs of thanksgiving (e.g. Pss. 107, 124), which were used at the major festivals in the temple.

ISRAEL'S PILGRIMAGE FESTIVALS

From the time when Israel was organized as a Tribal Confederacy it was customary to make pilgrimages to the central sanctuary (see I Sam. 1:3ff.). Three times a year, according to the covenant law, representatives of the people were to "appear before Yahweh, God of Israel" (Exod. 23:14; 34:23). These three pilgrimage feasts, adopted from the old Canaanite calendar, were the feasts of Unleavened Bread, of Weeks, and of Tabernacles.[21] In the course of time these agricultural feasts were historicized—reinterpreted in terms of Israel's sacred history. The spring feast of Unleavened Bread, held at the beginning of the barley harvest, was connected with the Passover, and both became commemorations of the Exodus. The feast of Weeks, held seven weeks later at the time of wheat harvest, may have been observed in a special way at Gilgal, the threshold of the Promised Land, where it commemorated Yahweh's gift of the land to Israel.[22] The fall festival, known as the feast of Ingathering or Tabernacles, and held at the turn of the year (New Year), came to be a time for the renewal of the covenant with Yahweh. The ancient custom of making pilgrimages to the central sanctuary was perpetuated throughout the period of the monarchy and was revived after the completion of the second Temple. The little collection of psalms comprising Psalms 120–134, each of which is titled "a song of ascents," appears to have been a handbook used by pilgrims who went up to Jerusalem for the great festivals. One of these songs expresses the joy of going to Jerusalem, the city which was decreed as the pilgrimage shrine for the tribes of Israel:

> How I rejoiced when they said to me,
> 'Let us go to the house of Yahweh!'
> And now our feet are standing
> in your gateways, Jerusalem.
> —PSALM 122:1–2 (JB)

Do the Psalms tell us anything, directly or indirectly, about worship during these great festivals?

Covenant Renewal Festivals

Although our knowledge of the history of Israelite worship is very limited, there is good reason to suppose that the ancient covenant renewal festival, first held at Shechem during the period of the Tribal Confederacy, was revived in the Northern Kingdom. We are told that Jeroboam I, the first king of North Israel,

---

[21] For a discussion of the festivals, see R. de Vaux, *Ancient Israel* [113], pp. 484–506; also see the author's *Out of the Depths* [446], chap. 6.

[22] This theory, first advanced by Gerhard von Rad, has been developed by H. J. Kraus, *Worship in Israel* [443], pp. 152–61.

instituted a Fall festival in his domain "like the feast that was in Jerusalem" (I Kings 12:32–33), in order to counteract the custom of making pilgrimages to the Jerusalem Temple. Apparently the Jerusalem festival had acquired important features of Davidic theology, as we shall see presently; the northern festival, however, must have been quite like the old covenant renewal festival that had been popular during the days of the Tribal Confederacy. In both cases the festival in question is the great annual festival (the Feast of Tabernacles) that was held in the fall at the turn of the year.

Form-critical studies of the Psalter have led scholars to classify various psalms as belonging to this festival.[23] But of all of those proposed, Psalm 81 is one of the best candidates. It has close affinites with the classic account of covenant renewal found in Joshua 24, which tells of the gathering of the tribes to Shechem, the recitation of Yahweh's saving acts, the challenge to give undivided allegiance to Yahweh, and the promulgation of the covenant law in connection with the covenant pledge (see above, pp. 147–149). In this psalm the initial verses (verses 1–5) present a summons to worship "the God of Jacob" at the sanctuary "on our feast day." The next section (verses 6–10) is a recitation of the deeds of benevolence performed by Yahweh, the God who brought the people up out of the land of Egypt. It is noteworthy that the announcement "I am Yahweh" is associated with the first commandment, precisely as in the Decalogue. The psalm reaches a climax with an appeal to the community to hear Yahweh's voice and receive divine blessings (verses 11–16). It has been suggested that cultic prophets may have taken part in the service, particularly at the point where the challenge to renew loyalty to the God of the covenant was presented.

It is quite possible that the psalm we have just discussed is a psalm from the northern covenant renewal festival. Doubtless there are a number of northern psalms, once used in the sanctuary at Bethel, which after the fall of the northern kingdom found their way into the south, where they were adapted for use in Zion festivals. Psalm 50 is another good illustration of a covenant psalm, though in this case the old Sinai theophany has become a theophany on Mount Zion (verse 2). This psalm presupposes the form of the "covenant lawsuit" which we have discussed from time to time (see, for instance, pp. 339–340). In the first part (verses 1–6) Yahweh is described as coming to judge the people in the presence of heaven and earth as witnesses. The main part of the psalm (verses 7–21) contains the charge: Israel's failure to live up to the requirements of the covenant in daily life invalidates ritual and sacrifices ("I will accept no bull from your house," as the RSV translates!)—a note which the prophets had struck. The conclusion (verses 22–23) is a reminder to those who "forget God" that God shows salvation only to those who order their way aright.

---

[23] In his commentary on the Psalms [456], pp. 35–52, Weiser classifies a great number of psalms in this category. Walter Harrelson, in *Interpreting the Old Testament* [42], pp. 421–24, more conservatively lists as covenant renewal psalms: 50, 76, 78, 81, 82, 89, 105, 111, 114.

The Festival at Jerusalem

As we have already indicated, the covenant festival celebrated in the south was unique in some respects, owing to the profound changes brought about by the Davidic monarchy. Remember that David, in order to support his regime with the religious sanctions of the Tribal Confederacy, brought the Ark to his capital and planned to install it in a temple. David's plan, which was realized by Solomon, called for a reinterpretation of Yahweh's covenant with Israel. The royal court of Jerusalem advanced a new theology of king and temple,[24] the substance of which was that Yahweh had elected the Davidic king to be "the son of God" and had chosen Zion as the central sanctuary, the place of Yahweh's sacramental presence (see pp. 230–232). The effect of this new theology, especially under Solomon's influence, was to modify Israel's worship. The covenant renewal festivals of the former Confederacy were transformed into fall New Year celebrations of the foundation of the Temple and the election of the Davidic house. It was not until the great reformation of Josiah that the Mosaic convenant tradition was "rediscovered."

In view of this southern theology, which is reflected in the prophet Isaiah of Jerusalem, it would be natural for the Jerusalem fall festival to take on a character of its own. From various psalms we glean fragmentary references to cultic activities. In an "entrance liturgy" (Ps. 24) we read about the command to the gates of Jerusalem to lift up their arches so that Yahweh, the King of Glory (presumably enthroned invisibly on the Ark), may come in. We read about festal processions into the sanctuary, led by singers and musicians (Psalms 68:24–25; 118:27), about dancing and making melody to Yahweh (Ps. 149:3), about the blowing of trumpets and the raising of "the festal shout" (Ps. 89:15). Even when these details are read in the light of extrabiblical sources, such as texts dealing with the New Year celebrations of other peoples in the ancient Near East, there is much that remains obscure[25] But doubtless a major aspect of the festival was the processional bearing of the Ark into the Jerusalem Temple, where Yahweh was acclaimed as King of the universe and where Yahweh's covenant with the house of David was reaffirmed.

Psalm 78, which undoubtedly reflects pre-exilic worship in Jerusalem, is an interesting example of how the Exodus-Sinai tradition and the Davidic-Zion tradition were related in the south. Most of the psalm (verses 1–66) is a long summary of Yahweh's historical acts, beginning with the Exodus. The purpose of this recitation is to show how Yahweh's people, especially the north Israelites, did not keep the covenant. Then the psalmist shifts to the Davidic covenant tradition:

[24] See Frank M. Cross, "Ideologies of Kingship" [112], 238f. See also H. J. Kraus, *Worship in Israel* [443], pp. 179–236.

[25] Sigmund Mowinckel has pioneered in the study of the bearing of Bablonian and other Near Eastern cultic ceremonies upon the Israelite cult. See his *The Psalms in Israel's Worship*, I–II [453].

[Yahweh] rejected the tent of Joseph,
  He did not choose the tribe of Ephraim;
but he chose the tribe of Judah,
  Mount Zion, which he loves.
He built his sanctuary like the high heavens,
  like the earth, which he has founded for ever.
He chose David his servant,
  and took him from the sheepfolds,
from tending the ewes that had young he brought him
  to be the shepherd of Jacob his people,
  of Israel his inheritance.
With upright heart he tended them,
  and guided them with skilful hand.
                      —PSALM 78:67–72 (RSV)

Here the psalmist affirms that the old sacred history which centered in the Exodus and the inheritance of the land has reached its dramatic climax in events that occurred in Judah: the founding of Zion and the establishment of the Davidic dynasty. Owing to Yahweh's rejection of Ephraim, in this slanted view, Judah is from now on the bearer of the sacred tradition.[26]

The festival of Zion is clearly reflected in the liturgical hymn, Psalm 132, which refers to the processional of the Ark to Zion (II Sam. 6) and the promises of grace to David (II Sam. 7; 23:1–7). The first part of the psalm tells of David's oath to provide a shrine for Yahweh (verses 1–5) and of the discovery of the Ark in Kiriath-jearim (verses 6–7; see I Sam. 7:1–2). In words that recall the ancient Song to the Ark (Num. 10:35–36), Yahweh—enthroned invisibly on the Ark—is summoned to go triumphantly to a new abode.

Arise, O Yahweh, and go to your resting place,
  you and the ark of your power!
Let your priests be vested in righteousness,
  and let your devotees sing for joy.
                      —VERSES 8–9

The second part of the psalm (verses 11–18) recalls Nathan's oracle to David:

Yahweh swore to David
an oath faithful and irrevocable:

"One of your own offspring
I will put on your throne.

---

[26] Some scholars have interpreted this psalm to mean that the old sacred history centering in the Exodus and Conquest had been superseded, for Yahweh made a new beginning by raising up David and selecting Mount Zion as the central sanctuary. Kathe Pfisterer Darr holds, however, that it is Ephraim's participation in the sacred history that has come to an end, not the sacred history of Exodus and Conquest—events that Judah celebrates in the context of the climactic events of the Davidic period.

> If your descendants keep my covenant,
>   and my testimonies that I teach them,
> then their descendants too in perpetuity
>   will sit upon your throne.''
>
> For Yahweh has chosen Zion,
>   coveted it for his dwelling-place:
>
> ''This is my resting-place for all time,
>   Here I will dwell for that is what I desire.''
>   —PSALM 132:11–14;
>   see II Sam. 7:11–15

A similar view is expressed in Psalm 89.[27] The first part of this psalm is a hymn (verses 1–37) to Yahweh, who showed covenant faithfulness (*ḥésed*) to David by choosing the dynasty of David. The second part (verses 38–52) is a lament in which the psalmist complains that Yahweh's oath has been violated by the defeat of the Davidic king. The suppliant appeals to Yahweh to remove the national distress and thereby to reaffirm the promises of grace once made to David.[28]

Temple and King

The twofold emphasis upon the election of Zion and the election of the Davidic king helps us to understand the theological significance of two other groups of psalms in the Psalter.

One group is the so-called Zion psalms (Psalms 46, 48, 76, 84, 87, 122). These psalms are based on the conviction that Zion, the city which enshrines the Temple, is the place of Yahweh's presence in the midst of the people. One of the best known Zion psalms is Psalm 46, the psalm which provided the keynote for Martin Luther's hymn, ''A Mighty Fortress is our God.'' In three strophes, each of which concludes with a choral refrain on the theme of Immanuel (''God is with us''),[29] the psalm announces that human confidence is grounded in the transcendent sovereignty of the cosmic Creator and King whose rule on earth is made known and celebrated in Zion. The liturgy reaches a resounding climax in the proclamation of the ''word of Yahweh'':

---

[27] Note that in Ps. 132:12 and Ps. 89:30–32 a conditional ''if'' is introduced, which qualifies Yahweh's *berîth 'ôlam* with David, without cancelling the unconditional promises of grace. Apparently the Davidic covenant was influenced by the conditional Mosaic covenant at some stage in the history of the tradition.

[28] Otto Eissfeldt has a good discussion of Psalm 89 in his essay on ''The Promises of Grace to David,'' *Israel's Prophetic Heritage* [152], 196–207.

[29] The Immanuel theme (cf. Isa. 7:14) is heard in verses 7 and 11 and probably should resound at the end of verse 3 at the point marked by *Selah* (perhaps referring to a musical interlude), as in some modern translations (e.g. JB and NAB).

> Yield, and acknowledge that I am God!
> I am exalted among the nations,
>   exalted in the earth!
>   —PSALM 46:10

The Hebrew imperative, often translated ''Be still. . . . ,'' is not a call to quiet meditation. Rather it is a stentorian command (''Be quiet!'') to the nations to cease and desist from their wars and military buildup and to recognize the deity of Yahweh, whose will is for *shalom* (peace, welfare, wholeness).

The other group, often called royal psalms, consists of prayers on behalf of the reigning king, Yahweh's ''anointed one'' or ''messiah'' (Psalms 2, 20, 21, 45, 72, 110). Israel shared with other peoples the view that the task of the king was to mediate the order and righteousness of the cosmic order to human society and thus to be the agent of God in bringing blessing to the nation. However, unlike other nations who absolutized monarchy or deified kings (e.g. Egypt), Israel affirmed that the reigning king was only the *chosen* agent or the *adopted* ''son of God'' (Ps. 2:7). The monarch does not have autonomous power but rules in the judgment and grace of Yahweh.[30]

> For the king trusts in Yahweh,
>   and through the faithfulness [*ḥésed*] of the Most High
>   will never be made to totter:
>   —PSALM 21:7

The Cosmic King

It can be seen, then, that the worshipers in the Jerusalem temple were aware of both the transcendence and imminence, the distance and the presence of God. The God whose glory fills the Holy of Holies in the temple is—to recall Isaiah's vision—enthroned ''high and lifted up'' as cosmic king and creator (see pp. 323–324). A number of psalms belong together because they celebrate this theme of the ''kingdom'' or ''reign'' of Yahweh on earth (Psalms 47, 93, 96, 97, 98, 99). One of the intriguing issues in the study of the history of Israelite worship is the place of these hymns in the pre-exilic cult.

For a number of years scholars, influenced by the creative work of Sigmund Mowinckel, have described these hymns as ''enthronement psalms.''[31] Under the assumption that a common pattern of ''myth and ritual'' prevailed in the ancient Near East, it has been argued that the enthronement psalms belonged in the cultic setting of a ''throne-ascension festival,'' held every New

---

[30] On this point see especially Martin Noth's essay on ''God, King, and People'' in his volume of collected essays [165].

[31] Sigmund Mowinckel, *Psalms* [453]. See further J. H. Eaton, *Kingship and the Psalms* [440].

Year, when Yahweh's kingship over Israel, the nations, and the cosmos was celebrated in song, ritual, and pageant. Every New Year, when the cycle of the seasons returned to its beginning, the worshipers reexperienced and reactualized the victory of the powers of life over the powers of death. The creation myth of *Enuma elish* depicted the victory of the god Marduk over the dragon of chaos, Tiamat.[32] Not only was the myth recited, but the battle was reenacted during the festival. At the climax of the celebration worshipers joined in the acclamation, ''Marduk has become king!'' This is interpreted to mean that the deity had reascended his throne for another year.

At first glance, it is tempting to understand the biblical psalms in the light of this mythological drama, and to suppose that at the New Year festival in Jerusalem, Israelites celebrated with hymn singing Yahweh's victory over hostile powers and Yahweh's throne-ascension. Psalm 93, for instance, begins with the festal shout: *Yahweh malak*, which some propose to translate ''Yahweh has become king! Or one could translate:

> Yahweh is King!
>   He is robed in majesty.
> Yahweh is robed!
>   He is girded with strength.
> Indeed, you have established the world,
>   it will never be moved.
> Your throne is from primordial time,
>   you are from everlasting.
> —PSALM 93:1–2

Admittedly, it is grammatically possible to translate the opening cultic exclamation as either ''Yahweh has become king'' or ''Yahweh is king [reigns].'' But it is very doubtful whether, even in the cosmopolitan atmosphere of Jerusalem, Israelite poets adopted wholesale the mythical views of the ancient world. The notion that Yahweh is caught up in the cycles of the seasons and must fight anew to win kingship over the powers of chaos cannot be squared with the faith of Israel. These psalms explicitly say that Yahweh's throne is established ''from of old,'' that Yahweh's kingship is ''from everlasting.'' Yahweh does not have to reclaim the heavenly throne at every turn of the New Year. It is proper, then, that modern versions render ''Yahweh reigns'' or ''Yahweh is king.''

Nevertheless, scholars have been right in suspecting that the mythical view has influenced Israel's hymns of worship. In the realm of worship, as in other areas, Israel borrowed from the cultural environment. What was borrowed, however, was transmuted in the alchemy of Israel's covenant faith so that it enriched the praise of Yahweh as King. The ancient myth of a divine victory over the ''floods'' or the ''sea'' (that is, the rebellious ''waters of chaos'' which threaten the security of the world) was employed to express the faith that Yah-

---

[32] See Pritchard, *Ancient Near Eastern Texts* [1], pp. 60–72.

weh is triumphant over all powers, especially historical enemies which threaten to convert the world into dark and meaningless chaos.[33]

> The floods lift up, Yahweh,
>> the floods lift up their sound,
>> the floods lift up their pounding,
> More majestic than the thunders of many waters,
>> more majestic than the breakers of the sea,
>> on high Yahweh is majestic!
>> —PSALM 93:3–4

It is not surprising that Jerusalem, which came to be a metropolitan center under David and especially Solomon, was hospitable to cultural influences of this sort. Indeed, the theologians who developed the royal covenant theology seem to have capitalized on the doctrine of creation to buttress the stability of Yahweh's sanctuary in Zion (Ps. 78:69) and the permanence of the Davidic dynasty (Ps. 89:36–37). Psalm 89 is completely consistent with Davidic theology when, to emphasize the firmness of the covenant with David, the poet praises Yahweh's power as Creator and even portrays Yahweh's victory over the primeval powers of chaos, Rahab and her allies. (Ps. 89:5–14).

All of this seems to indicate that the hymns to Yahweh as King belong to the New Year's festival celebrated in Jerusalem during the pre-exilic period.[34] Impressive testimony to the ancient cultic celebration is found in Psalm 24, which in all probability goes back to the time of David when the ceremonial bringing of the Ark into Jerusalem was reenacted in the cult. The psalm opens with an ascription of praise to the Creator:

> To Yahweh belongs the earth and everything in it,
>> the world and those who inhabit it.
> For he has founded it upon seas,
>> and established it upon floods.
>> —PSALM 24:1

The remainder of the psalm reflects a temple liturgy. It reaches a climax as the procession, with priests bearing the ark, reaches the gates of the Zion, where voices sing responsively:

> Lift up your arches, you gates,
>> lift yourselves up, you venerable doors,
> so that the King of glory may enter.

---

[33] Recall that in Isa. 51:9–10 the victory over the chaos-dragon Rahab is reinterpreted as a historical event: Yahweh's victory at the Reed Sea. See the author's *Creation versus Chaos* [128], chap. 3.

[34] This view is opposed by H. J. Kraus, in *Worship* [443], pp. 205–8, who maintains that the so-called enthronement psalms come from the post-exilic period and show dependence on Second Isaiah (e.g., Isa. 52:7–8). Claus Westermann's form-critical studies [457], pp. 145–51 have led him to the same conclusion. The view taken in the above discussion is also held by J. H. Eaton, "The Psalms and Israelite Worship," in *Tradition and Interpretation* [153], 238–273.

> Who is this King of glory?
>
> Yahweh strong and mighty,
>   Yahweh mighty in battle!
>
> —PSALM 24:7–8

Enthroned beyond and above the earthly king is the King *par excellence*—Creator of the universe and Ruler of history (Isa. 6:1). The Davidic king, however, is the chosen agent of Yahweh, the one through whom the divine rule on earth is manifest. The cosmic King, whose palace is a bulwark against threatening foes (Ps. 8:2), has promised to maintain the Davidic throne in the face of all foes arrayed against the Anointed One (Ps. 2:4–6). Hence the Zion festival was a time not only when Israel acclaimed Yahweh as the "King of glory" but also when the people heard anew Yahweh's promises of grace to David.

MEDITATING ON THE TORAH

Up to this point we have considered the Psalter as a collection of hymns, laments and thanksgivings for use in temple worship, mainly in connection with the great festivals. Of course, the faithful Israelite expressed reverence and gratitude at other times and places, especially in the family circle, but there was no substitute for the temple. It was believed that Yahweh was present there in the "beauty of holiness."

> One thing I ask of Yahweh,
>   that I seek:
> To dwell in the house of Yahweh
>   all the days of my life,
> to contemplate the favor of Yahweh,
>   and to inquire in his temple
>
> —PSALM 27:4

Moreover, as indicated in this psalm (verse 6) and numerous other psalms (see especially Ps. 66:13–15), the service of worship at the Temple included animal sacrifices. Some psalmists were critical of burnt offerings and other sacrifices, particularly when they were performed without true covenant obedience (e.g., Ps. 40:6–8); but there was no thought of abandoning the "means of grace," which provided for communion and reconciliation with God, in favor of a spiritual, noncultic religion.[35]

There are some psalms, however, which do not presuppose the worship of Yahweh in the Temple and in this sense may be called noncultic. Illustrative of psalms of this sort is a group whose central theme is that of meditating upon and delighting in the Torah (Psalms 1; 19:7–14; 119). One of these psalms (Ps.

---

[35] See the discussion of sacrifice, pp. 498–499. In addition, consult R. de Vaux, *Studies in Old Testament Sacrifice* [425], especially chaps. 2 and 4; also his *Ancient Israel* [113], pp. 415–56.

119), the longest in the Psalter, is organized according to a very schematic pattern. It is an "acrostic," or alphabetical study, consisting of as many eight-line stanzas as there are letters in the Hebrew alphabet. Each of the eight lines begins with the same Hebrew letter, according to the position of the stanza in the alphabetical sequence. Here it is plain that the Torah has become an object of study and devotion. Psalms of this kind (especially Psalms 1 and 119) probably have their setting in the post-exilic period when another institution, the synagogue, came to have increasing influence. The synagogue did not, of course, replace the Temple—at least not until the Temple was finally destroyed by the Romans in 70 C.E. But it began to develop a distinctive pattern of worship in which the reading and study of the Torah had a central place.

One of the striking things about the Torah psalms is the theme that the study of the Torah makes one wise and happy ("blessed"). This idea is expressed above all, in Psalm 1, the psalm which now introduces the whole Psalter. Just as Jesus told a story about a wise man who built his house on a rock and a foolish man who built on sand (Matt. 7:24–27), so this psalmist, though with a different intention, divided people into two types, as was customary in the wisdom schools. The righteous individual, who meditates on God's law day and night, is likened to a tree planted by running water, which yields fruit in season and is ever green. The wicked, on the other hand, are likened to chaff blown away by the wind, for their success is evanescent and their doom sure.[36]

> Fortunate are those who
>> do not follow the counsel of the wicked
>> do not stand in the way [lifestyle] of sinners,
>> and do not sit in the company of the insolent.
>
> Rather, in the Torah of Yahweh they delight,
>> and on his Torah they ponder day and night.
>
> They are like a tree planted by a fresh stream,
>> that yields its fruit at the proper time,
>> and whose foliage never fades.
>> Whatever they do comes to fruition!
>
> Not so are the wicked, not so.
>> Rather, they are like chaff the wind scatters.
>
>> Hence, in the divine judgment the wicked will not stand,
>>> nor sinners [stand] in the community of the righteous.
>
> For Yahweh recognizes the way of the righteous,
>> but the way of the wicked leads to naught.
>
> —PSALM 1:1–6

In the Torah psalms the sharp contrast between the righteous and the wicked, the wise and the foolish, is too neat and simple. As we shall discover in the next chapter, Israel's wisdom movement had to probe to a much deeper level of understanding to deal adequately with the problem of life's imbalances.

---

[36] For the following translation, and further discussion of Torah psalms, see "Meditations on the Good Life," in the author's *Out of the Depths* [446], 215–233.

CHAPTER 17

The Beginning of Wisdom

Philosophy literally means "the love of wisdom," as can be seen from the elements making up the word (*philo-sophia*). Among the ancient Greeks, from whom we have received our philosophical tradition, the search for wisdom reached its greatest maturity and refinement, especially in the age of Pericles (460–429 B.C.E.) with Socrates, and in succeeding generations with Plato and Aristotle. But the Greeks knew that the love of wisdom is not bounded by culture, nation, or race. Wisdom is a fundamentally human concern: Greek or Jew, Babylonian or Egyptian, male or female, monarch or slave. The quest for wisdom is the quest for the meaning of life. And this quest is the basic interest of every human being.

THE WISDOM OF THE EAST

Long before the meeting of East and West in the Hellenistic empire founded by Alexander the Great (333 B.C.E.), the search for wisdom was carried on in the Fertile Crescent, especially in Egypt and Babylonia.[1] Since wisdom writings cir-

Biblical readings: To read all the wisdom literature would be a big assignment. Read at least Proverbs 1–9, Ecclesiastes, and Job (omitting chapters 32–37). Also, Psalms 1, 32, 34, 37, 49, 112, and 128 belong to this type of literature. If one were to go beyond the limits of the Hebrew Bible, the Wisdom of Ben Sira (or Ecclesiasticus) and the Wisdom of Solomon would deserve first attention.

[1] See Pritchard, *Ancient Near Eastern Texts* [1], pp. 405–40 for Egyptian and Babylonian literature. A brief introduction to "International Wisdom and its Literature" is found in R. B. Y. Scott's commentary on Proverbs and Ecclesiastes [471], pp. xl–lii. See further James L. Crenshaw, *Old Testament Wisdom* [459], pp. 212–35.

culated far beyond the country of their origin, and Israel was situated at the cultural crossroads of the ancient world, the wisdom of the East early influenced its thought. Although wisdom writings date back to the Egyptian Pyramid Age (c. 2600–2175) and to the Sumerian era in Mesopotamia, wisdom had a timeless quality. The sages seemed to transcend the limitations of their time and culture. To be sure, they reflected on problems of society as they knew them, but these were human problems found in varying forms in all societies. Thus the wisdom movement was in essence international.

The Sage's Individualism

Another trait of wisdom literature is its focus on the individual. The sages were interested in the human person—more concerned, it appears, with human being ('*adam*), as in the epic narrative of Genesis 2–3, than with *peoples* identified by particular histories and societies. This is hardly a fair comparison, however, for the Old Epic tradition portrays the human problem in terms of a historical drama that moves from the beginning toward the fulfillment of the divine purpose. Wisdom literature, however, did not have this kind of historical perspective. The sages brought history to a standstill, so to speak, in order to analyze in depth the problem of human existence. They were not concerned with the unrepeatable events and the dynamic movement of a people's unique history, but with the recurring experiences and the fixed moral order in which every individual participates.

Wisdom literature falls into two classes. The first consists of practical advice to the young on how they may attain a successful and good life. This "prudential literature" is illustrated by the Egyptian *Teaching of Amen-em-opet*, the Babylonian *Counsels of Wisdom*, and the maxims found in the biblical book of Proverbs. The second consists of reflective probing into the depth of human anguish about the meaning of life, often in a skeptical mood. This "reflective literature" is well illustrated by the Egyptian *Dispute over Suicide*, the Babylonian composition entitled *I will Praise the Lord of Wisdom*, and the biblical books of Ecclesiastes and Job. Both types of wisdom literature isolate the human problem from the particularities of history, and in this respect they stand in contrast to most of the literature of the Bible.

Most of us are more at home in the wisdom literature than in the historical literature of the Bible. For although the Hebrew-Christian faith has given Western civilization a dynamic sense of history, as shown in the doctrines of Progress or the Marxist view of history, modern people are profoundly indebted to the "love of wisdom" inherited from Greeks, Egyptians, Babylonians, and others. It is more natural for us to think of a human being as a "citizen of the world" than in the context of a particular history, especially the history that begins with Abraham and Sarah. Modern sages insist that the way to solve the problem of world unity is to concentrate on the human person, whose needs and aspirations are fundamentally the same in all situations, and to discount the memories, loyalties, and cultural peculiarities that make for human diversity and conflict.

ISRAEL'S WISDOM LITERATURE

A certain amount of wisdom literature is included in the Hebrew Bible, and with it comes the tension that exists between these two ways of viewing humankind—in a particular historical context or simply as a human being. The three wisdom writings in the Hebrew Bible are Proverbs, Ecclesiastes, and Job.[2] In addition, there are a number of poems, now included in the Psalter or the prophetic collections, which apparently came from the circle of Israel's sages.

The wisdom literature of the Old Testament seems to stand apart from the rest of the books. All the literature we have considered so far is marked by Israel's awareness of having a unique history. This historical sense, as we have seen, is the very heart of Israel's faith, and is summed up in the confession that Yahweh is the God of Israel, and Israel the people of Yahweh. To be sure, within the covenant community there were different ways of viewing this history, but there was general agreement that of all the peoples of the earth Yahweh had "known" Israel in a unique way (Amos 3:2). When we turn to Israel's wisdom literature, however, we find that the distinctive features of Israel's faith are lacking. The prophetic themes that dominate the Pentateuch and the prophetic writings—Israel's election, the Day of Yahweh, the covenant and the Law, the priesthood and the Temple, prophecy and the messianic hope—are dealt with hardly at all.

Although much of the wisdom literature was produced in the post-exilic period, when Israel was deeply conscious of being a worshiping community, there are strikingly few references to acts of worship, and what few there are say little of the centrality of worship (Prov. 3:9–10; Eccles. 5:4–5; Job 12:19; cf. 1:5; 42:8–9). Also, the personal name Yahweh is not used in Ecclesiastes or (with a couple of exceptions) in the poem of Job, for the writers of these books prefer to use a general name for deity. Even when the name is used, as in Proverbs, nothing is made of the special relationship between Yahweh and Israel. Yahweh is not identified as the One who brought Israel out of Egypt or who acted repeatedly in the long history of the people. Indeed, there are no explicit allusions to Israelite history or to outstanding Israelite personalities, with the single exception of Solomon who ruled in Jerusalem (Eccles. 1:1, 13–14). The form of address, "my son" (as in Prov. 1–7), follows the ancient tradition of the wisdom schools in which sages counseled their pupils in this fashion.

Israel's wisdom literature, then, stands by itself—so much so that some

---

[2] Outside of the Hebrew Bible, but included in the Roman Catholic and Orthodox canons, are the important wisdom books called Ecclesiasticus or the Wisdom of Ben Sira (dating from the early second century B.C.E.) and the Wisdom of Solomon (from the first century B.C.E.). Both books are included in the Protestant Apocrypha. (see Chart, pp. 4–5).

An Egyptian Scribe from the Fifth Dynasty (c. 2500–2350 B.C.E.) holding on his lap a partly opened papyrus roll. After the invention of writing in the early third millennium B.C.E., the scribe came to be regarded as a person having special skill and intellectual power, and often held an influential post at a royal court. From the Pyramid Age come several wisdom writings, such as the Instruction of Ptah-hotep *(c. 2250 B.C.E.), principal minister of a king of the Fifth Dynasty.*

theologians have great difficulty in understanding how it relates to the mainstream of Israel's faith. Yet it is hard to believe that these books were forced into the Hebrew canon as one drags a story into a speech by its heels. More and more we are coming to realize that from a very early period Israel had its own wisdom movement and that this movement exerted a pervasive influence upon all phases of Israelite literature: historical, prophetic, and poetic.[3] Eventually Israel's wisdom literature was fully baptized into Israel's historical faith as evidenced by the identification of Torah and Wisdom.[4] This identification took place in Deuteronomistic tradition, for instance, in one of Moses' sermons where he exhorts Israel to live by the statutes and ordinances of the covenant.

> For that will be your wisdom and your understanding in the sight of the peoples who, on hearing all these statutes, will say: "Surely this great nation is a wise and discerning people."
>
> —DEUTERONOMY 4:6

Moreover, the book of Psalms contains psalms which celebrate the wisdom of meditating upon the Torah (see pp. 566–567) as well as a group of "wisdom

[3] See J. A. Emerton, "Wisdom," in *Tradition and Interpretation* [153], especially 221–227 and the literature cited there. A helpful discussion of the criteria for determining the presence of "wisdom" is given by J. L. Crenshaw, "Method in Determining Wisdom Influence upon 'Historical' Literature," *Journal of Biblical Literature* 88 (1969), 129–142.

[4] J. C. Rylaarsdam, *Revelation in Jewish Wisdom Literature* [467].

psalms,'' including Psalms 32, 34, 37, 49, 112, 128.[5] Finally, in the apocalypse of Daniel, to be considered in the next chapter, Daniel's wisdom, which exceeded that of the Babylonian sages, was based on fidelity to the Torah.

It was in the period of the early monarchy, however, beginning especially with the age of Solomon, that we find the beginnings of an indigenous wisdom movement which in time culminated in the full assimilation of wisdom literature into Israel's sacred heritage. Although Israel took over wisdom materials from the cultural environment, borrowed materials were stamped with Israel's distinctive faith and experience.

What was the place of the sage in Israel's life? And how did the wisdom literature of the Bible, which drew deeply on the wisdom of the East, ultimately come under the sway of Israel's distinctive religious tradition?

The Counsel of the Wise

One confession of Jeremiah refers obliquely to the three important classes of religious leaders in Israelite society. The conspiracy against Jeremiah, we are told, sprang from the conviction that ''the torah shall not perish from the priest, nor counsel from the wise, nor the word from the prophet'' (Jer. 18:18; see also 8:8–9; Ezek. 7:26). This passage clearly implies that all three leaders spoke with authority derived from Yahweh—an authority that Jeremiah allegedly was trying to subvert. But the passage also indicates that each leader had a different spiritual gift. The prophet, who claimed to have stood in the Heavenly Council, spoke the ''word of Yahweh'' for concrete situations. The priest gave the people torah or instruction, based on the Mosaic tradition. The sage, however, gave counsel, with the insight derived from keen observation of life, from years of experience, and from wide acquaintance with the fund of ancient wisdom.

It is sometimes said that the sage's counsel was based on ''rational'' or ''empirical'' observation, in distinction from the priest and the prophet who relied on ''supernatural'' sources of insight. But this distinction between ''reason'' and ''faith'' was not made in ancient Israel. Wisdom was regarded as a divine gift, not just a human ability based on superior intelligence, serious study, or long years of experience. This charismatic gift was bestowed on the elders who sat at the gate (cf. Prov. 1:21), the skilled artisans (Exod. 31:1–5), counselors, and above all the ruler of the people. According to Israelite tradition, the gift of wisdom was bestowed in greatest measure upon Solomon, who was such a wise ruler that his fame for wisdom spread far beyond the boundaries of his empire.

The prophets were from time to time critical of ''wisdom'' (see Isa. 29:14, Jer. 8:9), an indication that the wisdom movement was strong enough to war-

---

[5] The question as to whether it is proper to speak of ''wisdom psalms'' as a distinctive literary form is considered by Roland E. Murphy, ''A Consideration of the Classification, 'Wisdom Psalms' '' in Supplements to *Vetus Testamentum*, Congress Volume IX (Leiden: Brill, 1963), 156–67.

rant their attack.[6] In fact, in Israel the wisdom tradition preceded and outlasted the prophetic movement, and reached its peak of development only after prophecy had declined. The origin of Israel's wisdom movement is lost in the haze of the early oral tradition. Probably there was a vigorous wisdom movement among the Canaanites, from whom it was carried over into Israel in the period before the monarchy. The various affinities between the book of Proverbs and the Ras Shamra literature suggest that Israel assimilated wisdom material from the Canaanite environment. Balaam, the Babylonian diviner (Num. 22–24), was related in some sense to Israel's early wisdom movement. Moreover, it is from the earliest period of Israel's oral tradition that we have the proverb, the riddle (see Judg. 14:14), and the fable (Judg. 9:8–15)—ancient types of Near Eastern wisdom that were gradually integrated into Israel's heritage. Also, Egyptian wisdom motifs have been detected in the Joseph novella.

In any event, by the time of the early monarchy the sage was a well-known and respected leader in Israelite society. We are told that the counsel of Ahithophel, one of David's court advisers, was ''as if one consulted the word of God'' (II Sam. 16:23)—that is, it was virtually filled with prophetic power. During Absalom's rebellion a wise woman from Tekoa, the home town of Amos, was summoned to use her influence on David (II Sam. 14:1–21), and later during the same crisis another wise woman negotiated with Joab (II Sam. 20:14–22). The remark that the wise woman went to the people ''in her wisdom'' indicates that she was a recognized leader with professional standing, perhaps like the ''wise women'' who were found in the Canaanite court, according to the Song of Deborah (Judg. 5:29). Certainly women were found among Israel's sages, just as they were sometimes found among the prophets (Judg. 4:4; II Kings 22:14).

Solomon, Israel's Patron Sage

Israel regarded Solomon as the fountainhead of its wisdom. Just as the Pentateuch was ascribed to Moses, and the Psalms to David, so it was believed that a great deal of the wisdom literature stemmed from Solomon. To him are ascribed the books of Proverbs, Ecclesiastes, the Song of Songs, and Psalms 72 and 127; and, outside the Hebrew Bible, the Wisdom of Solomon, the Psalms of Solomon, and the Odes of Solomon are attributed to him. Although this is an extravagant claim, it is nevertheless true that Solomon had a lively interest in wisdom and doubtless sponsored education that was related to the royal court (see Chap. 7).

The historian reports that Solomon uttered three thousand proverbs and one thousand and five songs (I Kings 4:32). The last part of that statement supported the later tradition that the ''sweetest'' of Solomon's songs, about twenty-five of them, are found in the Song of Songs. The two lovers mentioned in these songs are the glorious King Solomon himself and apparently the famed Shu-

---

[6] See William McKane, *Prophets and Wise Men* [462].

lammite or Shunammite beauty who, according to I Kings 1:1–4, was brought to David to minister to him and to keep him warm during his declining days. There is no clear evidence that Solomon took Abishag as his wife (cf. I Kings 2:13–25), and there is still less basis for the claim that Solomon composed these sensuous love lyrics. Nevertheless, their association with Solomon and their popularity at wedding festivities established them so firmly in Israelite life that eventually they were admitted to the rank of sacred scripture, on the ground that the songs present an allegory of the covenant love between Yahweh and Israel. Quite apart from this rather strained interpretation, the songs accent truths that are basic to Israel's faith: that a human being should live before God as a total personality; that man and woman should find fulfillment in their union with each other, and that sexual love should partake of the goodness of God's creation. Hellenistic notions of a dualism of "body" and "soul" find no support in the Old Testament, certainly not in the Song of Songs![7]

The other part of the historian's statement, which refers to Solomon's proverbs, became the basis for the claim that Solomon was the author of the book of Proverbs. In English the word "proverb" refers to a maxim or aphorism, like "A word to the wise is sufficient." The Hebrew word *mashal* may have this meaning, but it can also refer to a longer unit like the "parable" of the New Testament. Solomon may have spoken some of the proverbs found in the oldest sections of the book of Proverbs (chaps. 10–29), but we cannot be sure of what comes from him. Probably most of the treasury of Solomonic wisdom has passed imperceptibly into the reservoir of Israel's wisdom tradition.

It was appropriate for Israel's sages to ascribe the whole fund of Israelite wisdom to Solomon, for his cosmopolitan interests admirably qualified him to be the patron of wisdom. When the Queen of Sheba came on a visit from far-off Arabia, Solomon displayed his wisdom by propounding and solving riddles (I Kings 10:1–10). And it is said that God gave Solomon "largeness of mind like the sand of the sea-shore" (I Kings 4:29). This claim is confirmed by the historical record, which shows that Solomon was extremely hospitable to the cultural influences of the Fertile Crescent, and established close relations with Phoenicia and Egypt. As we have seen previously (Chap. 7), it was in the age of Solomon that Israel broke out of the confines of the former Tribal Confederacy, with its limiting religious institutions and perspectives, and enlarged its horizons of faith beyond the boundaries of the Mosaic covenant heritage. The spirit of the time was one of "secularization" (although this word must be used cautiously), in the sense that, in some circles, there was a disposition to concentrate upon the *human* element in social experience. This trend can be seen in one way in the Court History of David (II Sam. 9–20; I Kings 1–2), which portrays the chain-reaction of action and consequence in the royal court with a surprising lack of divine intervention. And it can be seen also in the wisdom

---

[7] See Jack M. Sasson, "Unlocking the Poetry of Love in the Song of Songs," *Bible Review*, I (1985), 11–19.

tradition found in the oldest section of the Book of Proverbs, which discerns a seemingly self-operating law of cause and effect in human experience and cherishes the worldly benefits of long life, honor, family welfare, and possessions.[8]

Egyptian wisdom made a deep impression on Israel's thought from at least the time of Solomon, who established diplomatic ties with Egypt. The close parallels between the *Instruction of Amen-em-opet* and Proverbs 22:17-24:22 indicate that the Israelite collection depended heavily on the Egyptian writing (dated during the period 1000-600 B.C.E.).[9] There are only a few verses of this section of Proverbs that have no counterpart in the Egyptian source. The subject matter, the form of presentation, and even the telescoping of the thirty chapters of the Egyptian work into thirty sayings in the book of Proverbs (cf. Prov. 22:20) provide eloquent proof of Israel's contact with the wisdom of Egypt.[10]

AN ANTHOLOGY OF PROVERBS

The history of Israel's wisdom movement is condensed in the pages of the book of Proverbs. It is generally agreed that this book, in its final form, comes from the period of Judaism, probably after the time of Ezra, when the wisdom schools were flourishing. But like the Pentateuch, the book of Proverbs represents the final stage of a tradition that goes back at least to the time of Solomon, who may have composed or collected the original nucleus. As the following headings indicate, several wisdom collections are contained in this one book:

1. Chaps. 1-9 "The proverbs of Solomon"
2. 10:1-22:16: "The proverbs of Solomon"
3. 22:17-24:22: "The words of the Wise"
   24:23-34: "These also are sayings of the Wise"
4. Chaps. 25-29: "The proverbs of Solomon collected by the men of king Hezekiah"
5. Chap. 30: "The words of Agur the son of Jakeh"
6. 31:1-9: "The words of Lemuel king of Massa"
7. 31:10-31: An alphabetic poem on the good housewife

A glance at this material is enough to show the diversity of the book. Notice that, in general, numbers 1-4 belong to the tradition of Solomon, while the remainder of the book is of foreign origin. And within these four, many scholars regard the second collection as the oldest portion of the book of Proverbs. The first collection is often regarded as the latest, but in view of the Canaanite elements in this section some believe that at least part of it belongs to the pre-exilic

[8] See Gerhard von Rad, *Wisdom in Israel* [465], pp. 57-65. He maintains that in the Solomonic age the "experience of reality" took a completely new form.

[9] See Pritchard, *Ancient Near Eastern Texts* [1], pp. 421-24.

[10] On the interrelation between the two wisdom movements, see Glendon E. Bryce, *A Legacy of Wisdom* [458].

tradition. All we can say for sure is that the book of Proverbs represents a complex tradition, extending throughout almost the whole of the Old Testmant period.

Common-sense Proverbs

The wisdom sayings of this anthology are often short, crisp, two-line sentences dealing with some aspect of experience. In some instances, the second line of the proverb runs parallel to the thought of the first. An example of this "synonymous parallelism" is found in Proverbs 22:1 (RSV):

> A good name is to be chosen rather than great riches,
>   and favor is better than silver and gold.

Often the lines are a balanced pair of opposites. This type of "antithetic parallelism" is illustrated by Proverbs 10:1:

> A wise son makes a glad father,
>   but a foolish son is a sorrow to his mother.

And sometimes the second line of the pair completes the thought of the first, in a kind of "ascending parallelism," as in 4:18:

> The path of the righteous is like the light of dawn,
>   which shines brighter and brighter until full day.

In addition to the short "two-liners," there are also a number of proverbs which expatiate on a theme for the purpose of instruction. These units, which apparently belong to an "instruction genre," are in the imperative, rather than the indicative, and adduce reasons for following the advice that is enjoined.[11] In one passage the industry of the ant provides a lesson in planning for the future:

> Go to the ant, O sluggard,
>   consider her ways, and be wise.
> Without having any chief,
>   officer or ruler,
> she prepares her food in summer,
>   and gathers her sustenance in harvest.
> A little sleep, a little slumber,
>   a little folding of the hands to rest,
> and poverty will come upon you like a vagabond,
>   and want like an armed man.
> —PROVERBS 6:6–11 (RSV)

[11] See W. McKane, *Proverbs* [470].

Another characteristic rhetorical device is the numerical saying, based on the scheme x + 1, as in the collection found in Proverbs 30 and 31:10–31.

> Three things are too wonderful for me;
>   four I do not understand:
> the way of an eagle in the sky,
>   the way of a serpent on a rock,
> the way of a ship on the high seas,
>   and the way of a man with a maiden.
>   —PROVERBS 30:18–19 (RSV)

Many of the proverbs give the impression of being rather "secular," although this term may be too modern to do full justice to them. It is true that the oldest proverbs show a positive, healthy view toward worldly affairs. Reflecting on various courses of human conduct, the sages suggest that the good life can be won through diligence, sobriety, and prudence, and that the marks of the good life are success, well-being, and a long and fruitful life. In this respect, the proverbs are quite similar to the prudential advice given by sages in Babylonia, Egypt, and elsewhere. Many of the biblical proverbs deal with ordinary problems that hinder one from attaining fullness of life: laziness (Prov. 6:6–11; 24:30–34), drunkenness (23:20–21, 29–35), relations with harlots (5:9–10), unwise business dealings (6:1–5), and so on.

This seemingly "secular" advice, however, is infused with a religious spirit. The book of Deuteronomy, it will be recalled, bases the theme of rewards and punishments upon the Mosaic covenant with its curses and blessings. Yahweh had taken the initiative to establish a relationship with the people, and obedience to the covenant law insured prosperity and success, whereas disobedience brought hardship and disaster. The sages of Israel held a similar view, although they began from a different starting-point. They believed that written into the very nature of things is a divine order which can be found through human search and reflection. To live in harmony with this order brings the good life; to go against it results in personal disaster. The convergence of these two points of view, which rested upon divine initiative and human initiative respectively, eventually prompted the identification of Torah and Wisdom in Israel's history of traditions.

The Fear of the Lord

The characteristic teaching of Israel's sages is summed up in a poetic couplet:

> The fear of Yahweh is the beginning of wisdom,
>   and the knowledge of the Holy One is insight.
>   —PROVERBS 9:10

This formulation, which occurs several times in the Old Testament with some variation, is also found at the beginning of the first collection (Prov. 1:7) and at the conclusion of the second (15:33; see also Job 28:28 and Ps. 111:10). True wisdom, according to Israel's sages, comes only to the person who acknowledges the sovereignty of Yahweh, who "fears," or lives in reverence before, the Holy One (see Prov. 1:29; 2:5). Faith in Yahweh is the "beginning," that is, the foundation or starting-point from which one seeks understanding.

> Trust in Yahweh with your whole heart,
>   and do not rely on your own perception;
> In all your ways recognize him,
>   and he will make your paths smooth.
> Do not be wise in your own eyes,
>   fear Yahweh and turn from evil.
> It will be health for your body,
>   and refreshment for your bones.
>   —PROVERBS 3:5–8

On the other hand, "fools" grope in confusion and "evil persons" lack an understanding of justice (28:5) precisely because they fail at the starting-point. Here we can see that reason is not regarded as an obstacle to faith, as many people suppose today; rather, faith is the precondition for understanding.[12]

In this theme, which was unique to Israel's wisdom tradition, we can discern a direct contact between wisdom teachers on the one hand, and Israel's exposition of the covenant traditions on the other. You will remember that the same theme was emphasized by Israel's prophets. Hosea insisted that Israel's lack of "the knowledge of God" (see pp. 309–311) was the fundamental flaw in its history. Similarly, Jeremiah contrasted true wisdom with folly:

> Thus says Yahweh:
> Let not the wise boast in their wisdom,
>   let not the strong boast in their strength,
>   let not the rich boast in their riches;
> rather, let those who boast boast in this,
>   that they understand and know me,
> For I am Yahweh who practices faithfulness [ḥésed],
>   justice, and righteousness in the earth.
>   for in these things I delight,
>   says Yahweh.
>   —JEREMIAH 9:23–24

Moreover, the motif of "the fear of Yahweh," which is central to the wisdom literature of the Bible, was deeply ingrained in Israel's religious traditions from early times (see Gen. 22:12). Of course, the profound differences between the wisdom perspective and Israel's traditional covenant faith should not be mini-

---

[12] This point is made by Gerhard von Rad, *Wisdom in Israel* [465], pp. 65–73. He observes that this wisdom formulation contains in a nutshell "Israel's entire theory of knowledge," or epistemology.

mized. It is clear, however, that wisdom teachers developed in their own way theological interests that also belonged to Israel's covenant traditions.

One theme that was basic to the covenant perspective was divine retribution, that is, the notion that Yahweh brings upon people the fruit of their own deeds. We have seen how the notion of reward and punishment (blessing and curse) was inherent in the Mosaic covenant and how prophets, Jeremiah, for instance, preached on this theological platform. In the wisdom of the ancient Near East, the pattern of action and consequence was perceived to be written into the creation itself.[13] One cannot violate the moral order of the universe, any more than one can defy the force of gravity by driving horses up cliffs or plowing the sea with oxen (cf. Amos 6:12). Israel's sages agreed with this teaching, but apparently they did not go so far as to say that the moral order operates independently of Yahweh's control or that Yahweh is bound by the fixed order of creation. As the holy and transcendent God, Yahweh retains the initiative (Exod. 33:19: "I will be gracious unto whom I will be gracious"), and thus "the scheme is sometimes shattered by the free (and, it must be said, somewhat irrational) grace of God."[14]

> No wisdom, no understanding, no counsel
>   can prevail against Yahweh.
> A horse is made ready for the day of battle,
>   but to Yahweh belongs the victory.
> —PROVERBS 21:30, 31

Theological Wisdom

Thus under the influence of Israel's faith in Yahweh, a change took place in the traditional conception of wisdom. It is difficult to chart the history of the wisdom tradition in Israel. Some scholars maintain that Israel's wisdom tradition underwent a development from robust "secularity" toward theological sophistication and maturity. At first, the sage, while recognizing wisdom to be a divine gift, was not particularly interested in reflecting upon its divine Source. Rather than attempting to explore divine mysteries, wisdom helped people to harmonize their conduct with the order of things and thus to achieve happiness and practical benefits. Only later, according to this view, did wisdom become theologically conscious, as evident in the late section of the book of Proverbs (chaps. 1-9).[15] Wisdom is not just the key to proper ethical behavior (Prov. 4:10-19); it seeks to grasp the secret of the divine plan behind the whole creation.

[13] See H. H. Schmid, "Creation, Righteousness, and Salvation" in *Creation in the Old Testament* [129], 102-117. He maintains, somewhat extremely, that wisdom's creation theology is the "broad horizon" of biblical theology.

[14] J. A. Emerton, "Wisdom," in *Tradition and Interpretation* [153], 288; see his whole discussion of divine retribution, 215-221.

[15] This view of the increasing theological maturity of the wisdom movement is advocated by Gerhard von Rad, *Wisdom* [465], pp. 53-73.

> By wisdom Yahweh founded the earth,
>   by understanding established the heavens;
> by his knowledge the deeps broke forth,
>   and the clouds rain down dew.
> —PROVERBS 3:19–20

This view of a straight line development from the secular to the theological may oversimplify the matter however. For one thing, we cannot be absolutely sure that all of the materials in Proverbs 1–9 come from the post-exilic period. Moreover, in the period of the monarchy, as we have seen, the royal theologians of the Jerusalem court resorted to a high conception of wisdom to justify the foundation of the Davidic throne upon the cosmic order.[16] Even in Israel's early wisdom tradition the line between the worldly and the sacred was not sharply drawn; and wisdom reflection, at least in some circles, probably ventured beyond mundane concerns to the cosmic realm. Clearly, there was a great interest in theological wisdom in the period of Judaism, but the later sages built upon and elaborated the religious dimensions of wisdom that were present from the first. Thus the affirmation that the fear of Yahweh is the beginning of wisdom came to have, on the basis of theological reflection, a wider and deeper meaning than ever before. Israel's sages were overwhelmed with the mystery of God's creation, and their reflections, reaching the very limits of human thought, erupted into praise of the Creator.

> Lo, these are but the outskirts of [God's] ways;
>   and how small a whisper do we hear of him!
> But the thunder of his power who can understand?
> —JOB 26:14 (RSV)

Dame Wisdom

One development in the wisdom tradition deserves special attention. In the maturing view of Israel's sages, wisdom is not just a human capacity: wisdom is personified as the agent of God. In an exquisite poem, the sage portrays wisdom as a woman who stands in the market-place, like a prophetess, summoning people to follow her ways (Prov. 1:20–33).[17] She calls for turning from foolish ways, reprimands for ignoring her counsel, and announces judgment in the form of actions having their consequences.

> Because they hated knowledge,
>   and did not choose the fear of Yahweh,
> because they have not accepted my counsel,

---

[16] The author's view, set forth in *Creation versus Chaos* [128], pp. 60–74; *Creation in the Old Testament* [129], pp. 7–11.

[17] See the illuminating essay by Phyllis Trible, "Wisdom Builds a Poem: The Architecture of Proverbs 1:20–33," *Journal of Biblical Literature* 94 (1975), 509–518.

and have spurned all my warnings,
they shall eat the fruit of their ways,
and be surfeited with their devices.
—PROVERBS 1:29–31

In contrast to Dame Wisdom is Dame Folly, portrayed as a harlot who sits at the door of her house and calls seductively to passers-by (Prov. 9:13–18).

In another passage wisdom is portrayed as the agent of God's creation. In language that seems to parallel the prologue to the Gospel of John (John 1:1–18) it is said that she was a child of God, present with God in the beginning and rejoicing in the works of creation (Prov. 8:22–31).[18]

Then I was at his side each day,
  his darling and delight,
playing in his presence continually,
  playing on the earth, when he had finished it,
while my delight was in mankind.
—PROVERBS 8:30–31 (NEB)

Some scholars have found a resemblance between this personification of wisdom and the Egyptian figure of *Maat* ("order, truth, righteousness"), regarded both as the cosmic principle of order and a goddess, the daughter of the creator-god Atum.[19]

The Wise and the Foolish

Despite this refinement of the conception of wisdom, the book of Proverbs sets forth a doctrine of rewards and punishments which sounds too neat. To be sure, in some circles, there was an awareness that human knowledge is limited by the wonderful mystery of God, who has hidden the meaning and order of Creation from the wise. As we read in a striking proverb, "It is the glory of God to conceal things" (Prov. 25:2). Nevertheless, the search for wisdom, according to the sages, divides people into two classes: the wise and the foolish, the righteous and the wicked. This classification, admittedly, is the result of a decision made in freedom; it has nothing to do with native intelligence, social position, or right doctrine. The "fool" is not deficient in intelligence; rather, this person has decided against the course of wisdom, owing to pride and passion, and must accept the consequences of that decision.[20] Nevertheless, the sages be-

---

[18] In the following NEB translation, the Hebrew word *'āmôn*, whose meaning is much debated, is read *'āmûn*, "darling." Another possible translation, which has the support of the principal ancient versions, is "master workman" or "craftsman" (so RSV, JB, NAB).

[19] This view is set forth by C. Kayatz, *Studien zu Proverbien* 1–9, WMANT 22 (1966). Her study is summarized by Emerton [153], pp. 232–33.

[20] Several terms are used to describe the fool: "the evil one," "the self-confident one," "the empty person," and "the thick-headed one." Regardless of how much one knows or how skilled one is, a person is a fool if he or she ignores the starting-point of wisdom: the fear of Yahweh.

lieved that there are two types of people: one who follows the way of life and the other who pursues the way of death.

> In the path of righteousness is life,
> but the way of error leads to death.
> —PROVERBS 12:28 (RSV)

The Deuteronomic portrayal of the Two Ways (Deut. 11:26–28; 30:15–20) was a forceful and urgent appeal for covenant renewal in a time of national crisis; but when this teaching was applied to the experience of individuals in society it could easily be misconstrued. Psalm 1, which has affinities with wisdom thinking, also points to the Two Ways (see p. 567). The happy person, who does not mingle with "sinners" and "babblers," is like a tree planted by streams of water; the "wicked" person is like chaff driven away by the wind. The inadequacy of this doctrine, whether expressed in terms of wisdom or torah, became apparent to other sages who wrestled profoundly with the riddle of life's meaning.

THE SKEPTICISM OF ECCLESIASTES

As we have seen, the distinctive teaching of Israel's sages was that wisdom is a gift of Yahweh, not a human achievement.

> To human beings belong the plans of the mind,
> but from Yahweh comes the answer of the tongue.
> —PROVERBS 16:1

This, however, was a positive emphasis. Even though the sages were aware of the limits of the human quest, they firmly believed that wisdom, when based upon the fear of Yahweh, could not only show the right course of action but could lead to some understanding of the divine secret underlying the Creation. Instruction in "the words of the wise" was given "that your trust may be in Yahweh" (Prov. 22:19).

This confidence was challenged by the author of the book of Ecclesiastes. Unlike the book of Proverbs, which is a "collection of collections" covering a long history of wisdom tradition, Ecclesiastes is fundamentally the work of one sage who wrote during the late post-exilic period, perhaps between 250 and 200 B.C.E. Ecclesiastes' bold challenge to Judaism, with its simple "Deuteronomic" doctrine of rewards and punishments, offended the religious sensibilities of the more orthodox. Consequently, the book was touched up here and there to make it more palatable.[21] Two conclusions were added. One disciple, who wrote the appendix in 12:9–11, praised the sage for the genius displayed in weighing,

[21] Among the passages that are held to come from orthodox editors are 2:26, 7:18b, 26b; 8:5–12b; 11:9b; 12:7b.

studying, and arranging proverbs. But another editor, who wrote 12:12–14, cautioned the reader to take the teaching with a grain of salt, for "of making many books there is no end, and much study is a weariness of the flesh." According to this editor, the fundamental tenet of Judaism still stands unscathed in spite of the book's teaching: fear God and keep God's commandments.

Had it not been for these pious revisions, and the tradition that Solomon had written the book, it is doubtful whether it would have found its way into the Hebrew canon. In fact, Ecclesiastes was one of the three books whose right to be included in the Bible was seriously questioned by the rabbis during the Tannaitic period (first century B.C.E. to third century C.E.).[22] Today Jews read Ecclesiastes on the third day of the Feast of Tabernacles, in order to add a serious note to the festivity by reminding the congregation that the joys of life are transient and that we should number our days in the hope of acquiring wisdom (see Ps. 90:12).

The Melancholy Preacher

The word "Ecclesiastes" comes to us from the Greek Old Testament (Septuagint) by way of Jerome's translation, the Latin Vulgate. The Greek translator used the word *ekklesiastes* to render the Hebrew *qohéleth*, a participle related to the noun meaning "assembly, congregation" (Hebrew: *qahal*; Greek: *ekklesia*). Apparently the Hebrew word refers to "one who speaks to an assembly"—that is, a speaker or preacher. Thus Qoheleth is not a proper name, but a description of a function. It was believed that this function was performed by Solomon, who "assembled" the leaders of Israel in Jerusalem (cf. I Kings 8:1) and showed himself to be the preacher *par excellence* (see Eccles. 1:1). Having been "king over Israel in Jerusalem," Solomon is represented as saying that all through his career he has tried to search out by wisdom the meaning of human experience (1:12–13; cf. 2:4–11).

The word "preacher" may be misleading, however, for the book is not a sermon in the usual sense, but rather a rambling lecture on the meaning of life given by a professional wisdom teacher. The book as a whole is not arranged according to any pattern or scheme of development. Indeed, the reader gets the impression that the main point of the discourse has been made by the end of the second chapter. The thesis of the lecture, announced at the beginning and again at the end, is that all human activity is vanity and a striving after the wind:

> Vanity of vanities, says the Preacher,
>   vanity of vanities! All is vanity.
>   —ECCLESIASTES 1:2; 12:8

Writing in the melancholy vein of Omar Khayyám's *Rubáiyát*, the sage announces that human wisdom cannot "grasp the sorry scheme entire." Wisdom,

---

[22] The other two questionable books were Esther and the Song of Songs.

admits the Preacher, does have some value, for it enables one to walk circumspectly, aware of the limitations of mortal life. "The sage has his eyes in his head, but the fool walks in darkness" (2:14). Indeed, wisdom is the source of strength greater than ten rulers (7:19). But the advantage won through practical wisdom is doubtful (2:12–23; 7:7–8), for with wisdom comes increase of sorrow (1:18), and in the end death comes alike to the sage and the fool (2:14–17). Ecclesiastes advises his pupils to make the best of life while they are alive, enjoying the present and not trying to probe into the future (2:24–25; 3:12–15; 7:14). For the grim truth is that, despite its practical value, wisdom cannot penetrate the mystery of life and deal with the ultimate questions; yet it is on the answers to these questions that the very existence of a person hangs. Unable to gain access to the divine wisdom that underlies the Creation, the sage is thrown back upon personal insight and experience to define the meaning of life. As a result, the sage feels despair over the emptiness of life, or even develops a hatred of life (2:17) that reminds one of the "nausea" expressed by some modern existentialists.

God's Hidden Purpose

Some scholars believe that the author of Ecclesiastes, or Qoheleth, living in the Hellenistic period inaugurated by Alexander the Great, was influenced by Greek philosophy and by the sense of fate (*moira*) that obsessed Greek culture. There is at least a superficial resemblance to the philosophy of Epicureanism, for the sage advises "seizing the day" (*carpe diem*) and enjoying momentary pleasures while they last (8:15–9:9; cf. I Cor. 15:32). Moreover, there is a kind of determinism in the outlook of Ecclesiastes—a realization that whatever happens has been foreordained long ago. The sage knows how to accept the joys and sufferings of life with an inner serenity, undisturbed by the ebb and flow of fortune (6:10–11; 9:1). It is often pointed out that this teaching is reminiscent of the philosophy of Stoicism, and some have suggested that several of the words used by Qoheleth are taken from a Greek context. For instance, the word translated "chance, accident" (2:14; 3:19; 9:2–3) is said to be the philosophical equivalent of Greek *tyche* ("chance").

It seems clear that Ecclesiastes was influenced in some degree by the spirit of Greek culture. This was the atmosphere that he breathed, and he could no more escape the Hellenistic spirit than a modern writer can avoid the influence of the scientific spirit of the twentieth century. But it is doubtful that Greek concepts influenced Qoheleth in any fundamental way. In spite of his "tragic sense of life," he never surrenders the conviction that God is sovereign over human affairs. The tragedy of life is not that the inexorable power of fate governs both human beings and the gods, as in Greek culture, but rather that divine wisdom is so inscrutable that, from the human angle of vision, life has no rhyme or reason. Since human beings cannot know the ways of God, everything seems to happen by chance. Indeed, says Qoheleth, "there is nothing new under the sun,'' for to all appearances the weary course of life turns back in a circle to the beginning (1:4–11). Nevertheless, he emphatically affirms that everything is ''in the hand of God'' (9:1). The trouble is that God's sovereignty is so completely hidden to human view that a person is left in the dark about the divine plan. Therefore, to human wisdom events are matters of caprice. The days turn in a circle, rather than moving toward the fulfillment of purpose.

The Times of Our Lives

This outlook of Qoheleth is disclosed in a very important discussion of the nature of time (chapter 3). We might compare his sense of time with that reflected in a hymn often sung today:

> Time, like an ever-rolling stream,
>   Bears all its sons away;
> They fly forgotten, as a dream
>   Fades at the break of day.

Like the hymn-writer, Qoheleth was poignantly aware of the transience of life. But to this sage life's tragedy is not that people are caught in an inexorable process of time that mechanically grinds out the days and years. Rather than speaking of time abstractly, Qoheleth writes of concrete ''times''—that is, times that have a specific content or purpose. ''For everything there is a season and a time for every matter under heaven'' (Eccles. 3:1). To take a few examples, there is

> a time to be born, and a time to die;
> a time to plant, and a time to pluck up
>   what is planted;
> a time to weep, and a time to laugh;
> a time to embrace, and a time to refrain
>   from embracing;
> a time to keep silence, and a time to speak;
> a time for war, and a time for peace.
>   (See ECCLESIASTES 3:2–9)

[handwritten margin notes: 3 tragedies — 1. Don't know what time it is — 2. Know #1 but do nothing about it — 3. Try to do too much!]

A time is an opportunity that invites a particular action, just as we say ''now the time is ripe'' or describe an action as ''timely.'' Qoheleth speaks of times in the plural—the times of human life. Moreover, according to this sage somehow our times are in God's hand (cf. Ps. 31:13). Each time is a heaven-sent opportunity, for God ''has appointed a time for every matter, and for every work'' (Eccles. 3:17).[23]

---

[23] The Hebrew word is equivalent in meaning to the New Testament word *kairos*, as found, for instance, in Mark 1:15.

The trouble is that human beings, with their limited wisdom, cannot discern any overall purpose running consistently through life's varied experiences. Consequently, the times just come one after another, and everything seems to turn in a circle of futility. Qoheleth acknowledges that God, with transhuman wisdom, can see the whole drama from beginning to end or, to change to a musical figure, can hear the successive notes as a melody. We are human beings, however, not God. Humans are like the animals in that they must die; but they are more miserable than animals for—to use a phrase from Matthew Arnold—they long to "see life steadily and see it whole." Qoheleth testifies that God has given humans "a sense of time past and future, but no comprehension of God's work from beginning to end" (3:11, NEB).[24] Mortals cannot peer beyond the veil that hides the purpose of God from human understanding. Consequently, they are overwhelmed with the meaninglessness of human experiences. For if one cannot discern the thread that binds the times together purposefully, the verdict of futility must be pronounced on all human thought and activity.

The Problem of Death

For Qoheleth the tragedy of life is heightened by the intense realization that the problem of existence must be answered within the brief span between birth and death (see Eccles. 8:6–8). The problem of death—the most universally human experience—casts a dark shadow over the whole book. The death of the individual had not loomed as a serious problem in the early period of Israel, for then it was believed that the individual's life was given meaning through participation in the covenant community. The parent lived on in the child, and all generations were bound together in the psychic solidarity of Israel. Unlike the Egyptians, who developed elaborate preparations for the afterlife, Israel was not preoccupied with death. The doctrine of the resurrection of the self (body) emerged very late in the period of Judaism, as we shall see in the next chapter. Qoheleth, however, is governed by the individualistic spirit of the Hellenistic age, rather than by the covenant thinking of the priests and prophets of Israel.[25] Separated from a historical community that bears life's meaning, the destiny of the individual becomes an acute problem. Qoheleth does not evade the problem by affirming the survival of the individual beyond death, for he knows too well the limitations of human nature. Human beings are mortal. There is nothing in them that is immortal or "deathless." In this respect, humans are no better than the animals (3:18–22), for at death "all go to one place" (3:20). Only in this life

---

[24] The Hebrew word ('ôlam), which the Revised Standard Version translates as "eternity" and the New American Bible as "the timeless," is difficult to understand here. The translation of the New English Bible, "a sense of time past and future," seems appropriate to the context. In any case, 'ôlam does not refer to eternity in a philosophical sense.

[25] The word "Israel" appears only once (Eccles. 1:12), and refers to the people over whom Solomon ruled.

is there hope, for "a living dog is better than a dead lion" (see 9:5-6). Because Qoheleth takes death seriously, he takes life seriously.

This sage, then, looks upon the world with a pessimistic eye. Unable to see in nature the handiwork of God, he complains that the sun, wind, and sea follow an aimless course, for "all things are full of weariness" (1:5-8). According to him, the doctrine of the Two Ways does not ring true to experience, for the righteous are rewarded with suffering and the wicked are chastened with success. Ironically, a person who has toiled with wisdom has to leave everything to someone who did not work for what was received (2:18-23). The dead, says the sage, are more fortunate than the living, but better than both is not to be born at all (4:1-3; see 6:3-6). He advises discreet reverence in the house of God, "for God is in heaven, and you upon earth; therefore let your words be few" (5:1-7). He recommends moderation in both wisdom and folly, for too much of either may lead to disaster (7:15-18). He counsels enjoying marital bliss and finding satisfaction in work, for all too soon one must go to Sheol, the land of the dead, where there is "no work or thought or knowledge or wisdom" (9:9-10). He broods over the accidents of life that make it absurd to plan for the future:

> Again I saw that under the sun the race is not to the swift, nor the battle to the strong, nor bread to the wise, nor riches to the intelligent, nor favor to the men of skill; but time and chance happen to them all.
>
> —ECCLESIASTES 9:11 (RSV)

A person does not know his or her "time"—that is, the time of one's death; for, like a bird caught in a snare, the evil time suddenly "falls upon" one. Ecclesiastes concludes with the exhortation to enjoy life while one is young, before the infirmities of age, or the bludgeonings of death, take their toll (11:9-12:8).

The Shadow of Despair

This skepticism, however, is fundamentally religious. To be sure, Qoheleth does not pretend to give divine teaching, after the manner of prophets or priests, but rather to set forth the lessons derived from experience and reflection (see Eccles. 1:13; 7:23; 9:1). Yet his conception of God is fundamental to his world outlook, even though he uses the general name Elohim instead of the special Israelite name, Yahweh. The basic tenet of his theology is that God is hidden. There is a precedent for this theme in Israel's religious heritage, for from ancient times it had been affirmed that the God revealed is also the God concealed. Yahweh entered into personal relationship with the people, symbolized by the giving of the divine name; but Yahweh was the Holy One who eluded human sight or conceptual grasp. Yahweh gave "signs" of being present in the midst of the people, but never provided proofs that eliminated the possibility of doubt. In the Confessions of Jeremiah, to take one major example, we are given a picture of the trials that accompany faith like a shadow. Ecclesiastes writes within the shadow of despair. For him God is transcendent, completely other, separated from the human world by an infinite gulf (see 5:2). No other writer puts more emphasis on divine sovereignty. God orders and controls all events, but God's sovereignty is completely hidden to human understanding (8:17; 11:5). Even though human wisdom cannot probe the divine mystery, however, one has no ground for questioning God, for "who can make straight what God has made crooked?" (7:13). A human being "is not able to dispute with one stronger than he" (6:10). Yet Qoheleth makes these statements from the standpoint of "the fear of the Lord," that is, in faith.

> I know that whatever God does lasts for ever; nothing can be added to it, nor anything taken from it; God has made it so, in order that people should fear before him.
>
> —ECCLESIASTES 3:14

The book of Ecclesiastes is a vigorous repudiation of the claim that traditional wisdom can discern the purpose of God. The sages of the book of Proverbs had claimed confidently that wisdom, beginning with "the fear of Yahweh," could chart the Two Ways and even identify the travelers along each road. But Qoheleth insisted that wisdom can do none of this, for the human mind cannot fathom the wisdom of God:

> When I applied my mind to know wisdom and to discern the business that is done on earth, I perceived that a person is unable to discover all God's work that is done under the sun, even though one's eyes find no sleep day or night. However much one struggles in seeking, one will not find it out. Even if a sage claims to know, he is unable to find it out.
>
> —ECCLESIASTES 8:16–17

Since religious people are prone to settle down comfortably in their faith, supposing that they possess the answer to life's questions under their hats, it is fortunate that the rabbis finally decided to include the book of Ecclesiastes in the canon. For, as one of the editors of Ecclesiastes wrote, "the sayings of the wise are like goads" (12:11). Like the prophets, they awaken people from complacent orthodoxy and stimulate the struggle for faith that can stand all the tests of doubt and despair.[26]

THE BOOK OF JOB

We turn now to the greatest monument of wisdom literature in the Old Testament, the book of Job. Through the centuries, this book has received the highest praise. Luther extravagantly said that Job is "magnificent and sublime as no

---

[26] See the excellent treatment of Ecclesiastes in Robert Davidson, *The Courage to Doubt* [134], chap. 10.

other book of Scripture." Tennyson called it "the greatest poem of ancient and modern times," and Carlyle declared that "there is nothing written, I think, in the Bible or out of it of equal merit." Philosophers, supposing that the book is concerned with the problem of evil or theodicy, have manifested great interest in it. In our day the writer has been acclaimed as "the Shakespeare of the Old Testament." Archibald MacLeish has attempted to interpret the meaning of the biblical book for our time in his play, *J.B.*[27]

The Impatience of Job

The strange thing is that many who celebrate Job have only a faint understanding of what the book is about. This ignorance is clearest among those who refer to the "proverbial patience" of Job (see James 5:11). In the popular mind, Job is a model of piety—a man who patiently and serenely suffered "the slings and arrows of outrageous fortune" without losing his faith. But this portrait holds true only in the prologue (1:1–2:13) and the epilogue (42:7–17), both of which are written in prose. The main part of the book is in poetic form, and here Job is anything but a paragon of patience. He begins by cursing the day of his birth, and his spirit gathers the fury of a tempest as he hurls his protests to God. Only at the very end, after Yahweh has rebuked him, does he repent of his wild and impatient charges, lapsing into something like the lull that follows a storm.

Before we go into the relation between the prose and poetic sections of this book, let us summarize the contents of the prologue and epilogue. The narrative tells the story of Job, a man renowned for his piety and blessed with the divine favor that accompanied his righteousness. However, Job's sincerity was suspect to one of the members of the Heavenly Council—"the satan." Notice that the definite article is used with *satan*, a Hebrew word which literally means "adversary." In the prologue, the satan is not represented as the arch-enemy of God, as in later Jewish and Christian thought (where "Satan" becomes a proper name), but rather is an angel in good standing in the Heavenly Council (see Zech. 3:1ff.) whose special function is to investigate affairs on earth.

When Yahweh boasted to the Council about "my servant Job," the prosecuting angel, suspecting that Job's service was motivated by self-interest, cynically asked: "Does Job fear God for nought?" Thereupon he made a wager with Yahweh that if Job's prosperity and family were taken away his faith would be destroyed. These losses did not shake Job's faith, however, for in his sorrow he patiently murmured: "Yahweh gave, and Yahweh has taken away; blessed be the name of Yahweh." So the satan proposed a more severe test. Job was stricken with loathsome sores from head to foot, making it necessary for him to sit alone in the city refuse ground. Ignoring his wife's advice, he still refused to "sin with his lips" by cursing God. Then his three friends—Eliphaz, Bildad,

---

[27] Archibald MacLeish, *J.B.: A Play in Verse* (Cambridge, Mass.: Riverside Press, Sentry Edition, 1961).

and Zophar—came to comfort him in his plight. In the end, according to the epilogue, Yahweh accepted Job's prayer and restored to him twice as much as he had before. And, as in all good folktales, Job lived happily ever after.

The Relation between the Prose and Poetry

It is generally agreed that the author of the poetic sections did not compose the story that appears in the prologue and epilogue. Not only is there the difference between prose and poetry, but the portrait of Job himself differs, as we have noticed. Moreover, the author of the narrative uses the name Yahweh, whereas the author of the poems uses general terms for deity, such as *'Eloah* (God) or *Shaddai* (The Almighty).[28] And finally, the narrative is written in the charming manner of a folktale, whereas the poetic sections resemble the wisdom literature in Proverbs and Ecclesiastes. It follows, then, that if we are to understand the viewpoint of the author of Job we must rely primarily on the poems rather than on the prologue and epilogue.

This does not mean, however, that the prose narrative is unrelated to the poetic meditations. In fact, the effectiveness of the poems is due largely to their being framed within the context of the folk story. Since the story is located in Edom, the area southeast of the Dead Sea on the border of the Arabian desert, it is possible that the Job legend originated in Edomitic territory around Teman (Job 1:1; 2:11; cf. Hab. 3:3). In any case, the author of the poems appropriated the old story as a literary framework within which to place the poetry. The story provides the life-situation that occasions the poetic meditations. Intending to speak to the deepest problem of every human being, the poet wisely bases this meditation upon the experience of one man whose legendary righteousness was well known in antiquity. As we noticed in an earlier chapter, Ezekiel mentions Job together with Daniel as legendary wise and righteous men (Ezek. 14:14, 20). Daniel (or Dan'el) was celebrated in Canaanite legend now known to us in the Ras Shamra literature. Similarly, the story of Job must have circulated orally for many years before it was written down as we now have it. In short, the author took a well-known story and inserted the poetic meditation between the first part and the conclusion—and specifically substituted the poetic dialogue for the conversation between Job and his three friends. As a result, the prose and poetic sections constitute *a unified literary whole* that elaborates a single theme.

It is worth repeating that the author's distinctive theological viewpoint is found within the poetic section of the book (Job 3:1–42:6). The uniting of the prose story with the poetic cycle has created both harmony and dissonance, demanding that one reread the old story critically. Clearly the author must not be held accountable for some theological problems in the narrative, such as the satan's gamble with Yahweh over a man's life. On the other hand, some of the

---

[28] Outside the prologue, the name Yahweh occurs only in the headings in chapters 38–42. It also occurs in 28:28, which many scholars regard as a later addition, and in 12:9 where the text is not certain.

narrative elements, such as the restoration in the end, may be understood more deeply when seen through the courageous sufferings of Job.[29]

The Poetic Pattern

Let us glance briefly at the material found in the poetic sections. Unlike other wisdom literature, such as Proverbs and Ecclesiastes, the poetry is devoted to a single theme, which is developed in the exchange between Job and his friends. Job speaks first, uttering a terrible lament over the day of his birth (Job 3). Then Eliphaz responds (chaps. 4–5), and Job gives his rebuttal (chaps. 6–7). Next, Bildad joins the discussion (chap. 8), and Job replies (chaps. 9–10). The third friend, Zophar, adds his advice (chap. 11), to which Job again responds (chaps. 12–14). Here we have a complete cycle, during which Job has answered each of his friends. The discussion then goes back and forth in the same manner until three full rounds are completed. After a final monologue by Job (chaps. 29–31), Yahweh answers him out of the whirlwind, and Job repents (38:1–42:6).

It is clear that what we have here is a carefully planned literary scheme. The third cycle (chaps. 22–27), however, has been thrown out of order by revisers who tried to tone down Job's heretical utterances. Furthermore the poem on wisdom (chap. 28) has been inserted into its present context by later editors. Another irregularity is the presence of a long poetic rebuke of Job by Elihu (chaps. 32–37), which is definitely an intrusion into the literary scheme. Elihu is not mentioned as one of Job's friends in either the prologue or epilogue. He has nothing to say during the three rounds of discussion, and his advice comes as an afterthought, following the statement that "the words of Job are ended" (31:40). It is generally held that the Elihu speech was added by a later Jewish writer who sought to uphold orthodox Judaism even more vigorously than the three friends.

To summarize, the book of Job falls naturally into the following outline:

1. The prose prologue (1:1–2:13)
2. Three cycles of discussion
   a. Job's lament (chap. 3)
   b. First cycle:
      Eliphaz (chaps. 4–5)
         Job's answer (chaps. 6–7)
      Bildad (chap. 8)
         Job's answer (chaps. 9–10)
      Zophar (chap. 11)
         Job's answer (chaps. 12–14)
   c. Second cycle:
      Eliphaz (chap. 15)
         Job's answer (chaps. 16–17)

---

[29] In his commentary on Job [478], Normal Habel defends the unity of the book of Job on structural grounds.

> Bildad (chap. 18)
> > Job's answer (chap. 19)
> Zophar (chap. 20)
> > Job's answer (chap. 21)
> d. Third cycle:[30]
> > Eliphaz (chap. 22)
> > > Job's answer (23:1–24:17, 25)
> > Bildad (25:1–6; 26:5–14)
> > > Job's answer (26:1–4; 27:1–12)
> > Zophar (24:18–24?; 27:13–23?)
> > > Job's answer is displaced by the chapter on wisdom (28)
> e. Job's final defense (chaps. 29–31)
> 3. Yahweh's answer from the whirlwind
> > a. The first speech (chaps. 38–39), followed by Job's submission (40:1–5)
> > b. The second speech (40:6–41:34), followed by Job's repentance (42:1–6)[31]
> 4. The prose epilogue (42:7–17)

The Author of Job

The date and authorship of the poem of Job are exceedingly difficult to determine, for the writer gives us no hint about circumstances of the time of composition. Like Ecclesiastes, the author displays no interest in the traditional motifs of Israel's faith, such as Yahweh's activity in history or the election of Israel. The hero of the book is not an Israelite, but an Edomite sheik from the land of Uz, which was evidently in the southeastern part of Palestine around Edom (cf. Gen. 31:2; Jer. 25:19–24; Lam. 4:21), the area from which Job's friends came (Job 2:11). The locale of the book is not the city of Jerusalem, but the edge of the desert. All these facts, together with certain peculiarities of language, have led to the conjecture that the author was not an Israelite at all. According to one theory, the author was an Edomite.[32] But the hypothesis that the author of Job was a foreigner has yet to be proved. It is plausible to assume that the author was an Israelite sage who lived perhaps on the outskirts of Palestine.

The fact that the Edomites are pictured in a favorable light seems to indicate that the oral version of the Job folktale arose in the pre-exilic period, for beginning with the sixth century B.C.E., when the Edomites encroached upon Judean territory, the Jews viewed their southern neighbors with bitter hatred (cf. Obad. 10–14). It is hard to believe that the old story would have circulated

---

[30] Various reconstructions of the third cycle have been attempted. In the above outline, the proposal of Samuel Terrien, *Interpreter's Bible*, III [16], 888, is followed. Notice that according to the confused state of the received text the speech of Zophar is missing, that of Bildad is curiously short, and Job inconsistently seems to endorse the view of his friends (see 24:18–24; 26:5–14; 27:13–23). Evidently, editors have tried to correct Job's statements by rearranging the text.

[31] The Yahweh speeches apparently have been expanded, perhaps by the addition of the poem on the ostrich (39:13–18) and some of the description of Leviathan (41:12–34). Some scholars regard the descriptions of Behemoth (hippopotamus) and the Leviathan passage (40:15–41:34) as later additions.

[32] The view of Robert H. Pfeiffer, *Introduction to the Old Testament*, rev. ed. (New York: Harper & Row, 1949), pp. 678–83.

during this period of animosity. As to the poetic section of Job, however, there is no general agreement on whether it should be assigned to the period of the Exile or to some time in the post-exilic period. A possible clue is the relationship of the poems of Job to Second Isaiah, for between the two writings there are numerous parallels of thought and language. Did Second Isaiah depend upon Job or vice versa? If the author of Job knew the poems of Second Isaiah, it is strange that when exploring all the possible answers to the mystery of suffering, no allusion is made to Second Isaiah's treatment of suffering as a sacrificial witness for others. On the other hand, it is possible that the suffering of Job influenced Second Isaiah's portrayal of the Suffering Servant. These considerations lead some scholars to the conclusion that Job preceded Second Isaiah, and that the book was written between the time of Jeremiah and Second Isaiah, speaking in general terms.[33]

The date of Job is not decisive for the interpretation of the poem, however, for, like the wisdom literature in general, it deals with a human situation that cannot be confined to any particular time. Even the Edomite locale of the story is incidental, for the writer deals with human existence as such, whether the person in question be an Edomite, Israelite, Egyptian, or of some other nationality. Not that the author is unconcerned with historical existence, however. The concrete portrayal of the hero Job is evidence enough that the poetry deals with the stuff of daily experience—with human life as it is lived in history. And yet the author raises the historical question in such a way that it has universal relevance, regardless of one's social background, historical milieu, or religious tradition. In the last analysis, the historical question is the religious question raised with infinite concern: What is the meaning of *my* life—this solitary person who thinks and loves, remembers and hopes, lives and dies? The poet looked intensively into the depths of one person's existence, and in so doing exposed the *human* question. This intensive concentration gives to the book of Job a dramatic quality—not in the sense that it was intended for stage performance like a Greek drama, but in the sense that, like any great drama, the reader knows that the hero is undergoing one's own interior struggles. Job is the existing one, hence everyone.

Job and Other Wisdom Literature

Behind the writing of the book of Job was the wisdom literature of many generations, not only that of Israel but also of the whole Near East. The author may have been acquainted with a Babylonian writing often referred to as the "Babylonian *Job*."[34] According to this story, a man who was originally rich and in-

---

[33] See Marvin H. Pope, *Job* [480], xxx–xxxvii, who judiciously discusses the problem and inclines to a date in the late pre-exilic period: the seventh century B.C.E. Pfeiffer (*Intoduction,* 677) dates Job about 600. Terrien (*Interpreter's Bible,* III [16], 888–90) proposes a date between 580 and 540. Other scholars favor a later date in the fifth or fourth century B.C.E.

[34] It is entitled *I Will Praise the Lord of Wisdom,* after its opening words. See Pritchard, *Ancient Near Eastern Texts* [1], 434–37.

fluential was suddenly stricken with great illness and trouble. Bitterly he complained that his prayers and sacrifices had been in vain. Like Job, he protested his innocence, and insisted that the will of the god was beyond human understanding:

> Oh that I only knew that these things are well pleasing to a god!
> What is good in one's sight is evil for a god.
> What is bad in one's own mind is good for his god.
> Who can understand the counsel of the gods in the midst of heaven?
> The plan of a god is deep waters, who can comprehend it?
> Where has befuddled mankind ever learned what a god's conduct is?
> —LINES 33–38; *cf.* JOB 9:1–12

Finally, when the hero was on the verge of death, the god Marduk suddenly rewarded him for his virtue and restored him to health.

Even more interesting is the Babylonian *Dialogue about Human Misery*[35] between a skeptic who, having known nothing but suffering, questions the justice of the gods, and a pious friend who advocates humble surrender to the divine will and faithful performance of religious obligations. As in the book of Job, the coversants speak in turn. The skeptic begins, the pious man responds, and so on. This dialogue resembles the book of Job so strikingly, both in form and content, that it is tempting to believe that the author of Job was influenced by it.

From Egypt come other examples of the literary form used in the book of Job. For instance, in the *Protests of the Eloquent Peasant*, the poetic discussion is framed between a prose prologue and epilogue. Also, Egyptian pessimism is illustrated by the *Dispute with His Soul of One Who Is Tired of Life*, otherwise known as the *Dispute over Suicide*.[36]

It is impossible, of course, to prove that the author of the book of Job was directly dependent on these and other writings of antiquity. Clearly the poet was a person of broad vision and education, who was influenced by currents of thought from Mesopotamia, Egypt, Arabia, Edom, and elsewhere. But this writer was no mere eclectic, who borrowed indiscriminately from a variety of sources. What was borrowed was stamped with the impression of a highly original mind and a creative poetic genius. Moreover, the poet's interpretation of human existence was undoubtedly influenced by the Israelite heritage, even though no special interest was taken in the traditional themes of Israel's faith.

FROM DESPAIR TO FAITH

Many people assume that the purpose of the book of Job is to discuss the problem of suffering (evil), or to raise the philosophical question of how absolute goodness and absolute power are reconciled in the nature of God (theodicy).

---

[35] See Pritchard, *Ancient Near Eastern Texts* [1], pp. 438–40.

[36] Ibid., pp. 407–10 for reference to the former (*Protests*), and pp. 405–7 in the case of the latter (*Dispute*).

But the reader who approaches the book expecting to find an answer to these questions will be disappointed. Indeed, it is doubtful whether the author had any intention of trying to answer them. To be sure, the poet wrestles with an inescapable problem of human life: the suffering of the innocent. But the problem of suffering—and its counterpart, the question of divine justice—provides the occasion for probing a much deeper question, namely, *the character of a person's relationship to God*. This issue is first introduced in the prologue, where the satan insinuates that Job's relation to God is not one of unqualified trust "for better or for worse," but a fair-weather service in order to obtain the blessings of health, reputation, family, and long life. In the poetic sections, the nature of Job's faith is explored at a much deeper level. Finally, after the discussion has ranged through the whole realm of experience, Yahweh gives an answer out of the whirlwind. Job then submits in silence and *repents*, whereupon his life is put on a new axis. In order to understand the book of Job, we must view the poetic meditations in the light of the whole composition, which reaches its climax when Yahweh speaks and Job humbly repents.

The Dialogue between Job and His Friends

Let us consider briefly the dialogue between Job and his friends. Underlying the friends' argument is the doctrine of rewards and punishments that was widespread in the wisdom literature of antiquity. According to this view, virtue was rewarded with prosperity, health, and long life; and, conversely, sins were punished by poverty, sickness, and untimely death. This doctrine, as we have seen, was applied to Israel's national history by the Deuteronomistic historian and was applied to the individual in the book of Proverbs and, later on, in the Wisdom of Ben Sira. The three friends claim to understand the meaning of life in terms of this doctrine of retribution.

The dialogue is introduced by Job's lament, one of the most poignant passages in the Bible. Akin to one of Jeremiah's confessions (Jer. 20:14–18), it expresses the aching misery of existence in language of rare imaginative power. Notice that Job's death wish springs from his sense of the emptiness of life when he is estranged from a meaningful relation to God. He does not question God's sovereignty; rather, he laments that divine sovereignty is so completely eclipsed that life has no meaning (Job 9:11; 13:24). Job's outcry is an expression of the anxiety that afflicts the most sensitive sufferer: the anxiety of meaninglessness. Such suffering, more terrible than the torment of physical pain, can be assuaged only by death, "the king of terrors" (18:14), or, better, by not coming through birth to consciousness. With a fine poetic touch, Job wishes that the light had never dawned upon his natal day, and that the night of his conception had never seen "the eyelids of the morning." (3:9–10).

Eliphaz tries to give comfort by suggesting that the flaw lies in Job himself. At first, Eliphaz is courteous in offering his advice. All human beings have sinned, he points out; therefore Job should humbly confess his sin rather than hurl his protest at God. Since the fault really lies within Job, as the friends agree, the remedy also is within his power (see Job 11:14 ff.; 22:21). As Job stubbornly insists on his innocence, the friends become vehement in their accusation. Attempting to defend the majesty of God, they use every argument available to demonstrate the justice of God's ways according to the orthodox formula of rewards and punishments. They accuse Job of pride, charging that he does not accept the finite limitations of humankind. They say that if he were really honest he would have to admit that God had punished him more lightly than he actually deserved. Again and again they entreat him to surrender his haughty defense of his righteousness and to make supplication to the Almighty.

The poet portrays the three friends in such a manner that they are more to be pitied than Job, the sufferer. Although they are sincere in their stand, and at times speak of the meaning of faith in eloquent language, they cling desperately to their orthodoxy, and sense in Job's dangerous words a threat to their own security. Orthodoxy has invariably feared the heretic, as the history of Western civilization amply shows. In a truly prophetic spirit, the author of Job championed the creative power of heresy, for faith is often most vigorous when it dares to break with theological dogmas—yes, even with "religion"—and to enter into uncharted areas. The three friends were too smug in their orthodoxy, too sure of the answers to life's enigmas, too confident that God was bound by their logic. In the face of opposition, they could answer only with clichés. Eventually their rigidity prevented them from having any real sympathy for Job. They supposed that they had grasped the wisdom of God. "It is not God they defend," writes a modern interpreter, "but rather their own security. Indeed, it is their pride which they uphold when they condemn Job, and it is their sin which they reveal when they pay tribute to divine sovereignty."[37]

Job's Promethean Defiance

Job retorts that the friends speak only "windy words" that bring poor comfort to him in his search for the meaning of life. Despite their claim that they have diagnosed his malady, they are "worthless physicians." Annoyed by their pious taunts, he maintains his innocence and integrity with increasing passion. He admits that he may have sinned, as all people do, but insists that he is comparatively righteous and, in any case, that the punishment does not fit the crime (14:1–6). At first he contented himself with cursing his miserable existence, or wishing that God would crush him instantly instead of prolonging his torture (6:8–9). But soon his words break beyond all restraint. The flaw, he cries, is not in himself but in God, who is responsible for his misery. He accuses God of appearing as a sinister enemy. Instead of caring for a mortal creature, God is like a capricious tyrant (9:18–19), a savage beast (16:7, 9), a treacherous assailant

---

[37] The quotation comes form Samuel Terrien [481], p. 900, whose insights have influenced this whole discussion.

(16:12–14). In a display of wild imagination, he likens himself to the mythical sea-monster (Tiamat or Rahab), the arch-enemy of God, over whom God has set a watch (7:11–12). In utter misery, he wishes that God would let him alone, even long enough for him to swallow his saliva, for if he could only escape God his spiritual agony would end. Job's question reflects a mood opposite to that of a psalmist who raised the same query (Ps. 8:4):

> What is man, that You make much of him,
> That You fix Your attention upon him?
> You inspect him every morning,
> Examine him every minute.
> Will You not look away from me for a while,
> Let me be, till I swallow my spittle?
> —JOB 7:17–19 (TNK)

In the prologue, as we have seen, Job is a very submissive man who, despite the enormity of his misfortune, does not "sin with his lips." But in the poems Job is a different person altogether. His accusations are so wildly defiant that they must have appeared heretical to any orthodox Jew, which undoubtedly accounts for the fact that the third cycle of poems was rearranged and the Elihu speeches added. Jeremiah in his Confessions had hurled bold questions to God; but Job goes even further in challenging the Almighty. Clinging adamantly to his own integrity (Job 27:6; 31:36), he virtually sets himself up as the judge of God. In one mood he wishes that he could escape God's clutches, and in another he wishes that he could meet God in a fair debate, even as an equal, in order that his integrity could be vindicated (Job 31:37). Like Prometheus, Job is a titanic figure who doubts, rebels, and shouts defiance at God.

Job's Plea for Vindication

Throughout his spiritual struggle, Job is tortured by the remoteness and hiddenness of God—the God who "hides his face" (Job 13:24). If there were only some point of contact, some common meeting ground, then Job could present his case to God and receive a fair hearing.

> Oh, that I knew where I might find him,
>   that I might come even to his [judgment] seat!
> I would lay my case before him
>   and fill my mouth with arguments.
> I would learn what he would answer me,
>   and understand what he would say to me.
> Would he contend with me in the greatness of his power?
>   No; he would give heed to me.
> There an upright man could reason with him,
>   and I should be acquitted for ever by my judge.
> —JOB 23:3–7 (RSV)

With increasing clarity, however, he sees that a great gulf is fixed between the Creator and the creature, and that one is foolish to try to span the chasm (Job 9:32–33). The wisdom of God completely surpasses the reach of human wisdom; for God is the wholly Other, the transcendent One, the absolutely Sovereign. By contrast a human being is an earthbound creature, held under the power of sin which taints human nature (4:17–21; 14:4; 15:14–16; 25:4–6) and subject to the dominion of death (4:19; 7:6).

Although Job finds no access to God from the human side, he dares to hope that some day, somehow, a reconciliation will take place. Then the impassable gulf will be bridged, and the contradiction between divine goodness and divine power will be overcome. Now and then he speaks of a mediator—an "umpire" between him and God (Job 9:33–35) or a "heavenly witness" who would speak for him even after his death (16:18–21). Apparently this is the meaning of the well-known passage, set to music in Handel's *Messiah*, in which Job affirms that his Vindicator (*Go'el*) will defend his case and restore him to wholesome relationship with God.[38]

> I know that my redeemer [Vindicator] lives,
>   and at last he will stand upon the earth;
> and after my skin has been thus destroyed,
>   then without my flesh I shall see God,
> whom I shall see on my side,
>   and my eyes shall behold, and not another.
> My heart faints within me!
>   —JOB 19:25–27 (RSV)

Unfortunately the Hebrew text is so uncertain, especially in verse 26, that no reliable translation can be given. For instance, the meaning of the phrase translated "without my flesh" is very obscure. Does the phrase refer to a vindication before death or after? If after death, this passage may be the earliest reference in the Hebrew Bible to the resurrection of the body. But even assuming that the thought of life beyond the grave occurred to Job, it is clear that he rejected a post-mortem solution to his problem. To him, death was a tormenting issue precisely because it appeared to be the end, beyond which there could be no satisfactory answer to the enigma of life (14:7–15). And whatever may lie beyond that final barrier, the existential problem is whether a person can find, in the midst of the brief interim of existence, an ultimate meaning which sanctifies birth and glorifies death.

Job's search for the meaning of life has carried him to the very limits of thought, where momentarily his vision is enlarged. However, his stance is not changed. Still he is concerned primarily with his own self-vindication. Still, his questions betray his stubborn self-sufficiency, his determination to find the meaning of life on his own terms. To the very end he asserts his integrity. In

---

[38] For the meaning of the word *go'el*, see Definition, p. 482. Marvin Pope [480], pp. 134–35, compares this mediator or arbiter, who will prove Job's innocence, to the personal god in Sumerian tradition who acts as a defender in the Council of the gods.

answer to his friends' accusations, he reviews his life with the conviction that the record is unblemished:

> Far be it from me to say that you are right;
>   till I die I will not put away my integrity from me.
> I will hold fast my righteousness, and will not let it go;
>   my heart does not reproach me for any of my days.
>   —JOB 27:5–6 (RSV)

Job's concluding defense is a long declaration of the high ethical standards by which he has lived, and a vivid portrayal of a righteous person (chap. 29 and 31). His final word is a ringing challenge: "Let the Almighty answer me!" (31:35).

The Voice from the Whirlwind

Then Yahweh—notice the shift to the personal divine name—answers Job out of the whirlwind. But what a response! One wonders whether God even heard Job. As Martin Buber remarks, "What God says does not answer the charge; it does not even touch upon it."[39] Indeed, Job is told that he is not the one to raise questions but is the one to be questioned by God.

> Who is this that obscures divine plans
>   with words of ignorance?
> Gird up your loins, now, like a man;
>   I will question you, and you tell me the answers!
>   —JOB 38:2–3 (NAB)

Then follows a series of ironical questions intended to make Job's questions irrelevant. The effect of the questioning is to overwhelm Job with the realization that he is a creature whose finite standards are completely ineffective for judging the Creator.

In the two divine discourses (Job 38:1–40:5 and 40:6–41:34) Yahweh's response to Job is essentially twofold. First, God is the Creator who originated the whole cosmos in the beginning, when no human being was present. It is presumptuous, then, for a creature like Job to challenge God.

> Where were you when I founded the earth?
>   Tell me, if you have understanding.
> Who determined its size; do you know?
>   Who stretched out the measuring line for it?
> Into what were its pedestals sunk,
>   and who laid the cornerstone,
> While the morning stars sang in chorus,
>   and all the sons of God shouted for joy?
>   —JOB 38:4–7 (NAB)

---

[39] Martin Buber, *At the Turning: Three Addresses on Judaism* (New York: Farrar, Straus, & Young, 1952), p. 61.

And secondly, God the Creator upholds the cosmos with uncontested divine power. Here, in contrast to other Israelite traditions, for example the poetry of Second Isaiah, there is no attempt to demonstrate Yahweh's sole power by appealing to a discernible plan or purpose in history. Rather, the argumentation, strictly cosmological, is intended to show that the cosmos would return to chaos if it were not for God's upholding power.

Job had been talking as if he could advise God on how to run the world. His sense of integrity had been the basis of his presumptuous claim that God should have treated *him* better. Outraged that he could not square his innocence with his fate, Job had dared to challenge and judge his Creator. His religious quest had been motivated by a Promethean defiance. Therefore, Yahweh's answer came in the form of a rebuke—an overwhelming reminder that the first religious obligation of the creature is to acknowledge and glorify the Creator.

Job's Repentance

Yahweh's speeches raised questions that Job could not answer. He had presumed to know too much, to be more than he was. Silenced, he admits that he has no ground for arguing with God (Job 40:1–3). As his final word, he retracts his rash charges and casts himself humbly and repentantly before God:

> Therefore I have uttered what I did not understand,
>   things too wonderful for me, which I did not know. . . .
> I had heard of thee by the hearing of the ear,
>   but now my eye sees thee;
> therefore I despise myself,
>   and repent in dust and ashes.
>
> —JOB 42:3, 5–6 (RSV)

Along with Job's confession of his sin of self-sufficiency went a new consciousness of relationship with God—not the God of traditional religion, but "the Living God." This in itself was a form of "vindication," but not the kind that Job had asked for. Although not the composer of the Job folktale, the poet appropriately placed the prose epilogue just after Job's words of repentance, with the implication of Job's restoration to a new and meaningful relationship to God. Indeed, the epilogue now functions to endorse Job's honest-to-God struggles to have a faith that seeks understanding. Yahweh's final verdict is that Job was to intercede for his three friends, for they "have not spoken of me what is right, as my servant Job has" (42:8).

To some readers it is disconcerting that the book of Job does not end with a resolution of the problem of suffering. However, that is expecting too much of a work that grapples with the problem of evil so radically and courageously. It is clear that the poet has made some major contributions to Israel's theological understanding. For one thing, the book of Job is a powerful challenge to any notion that calamity is to be understood as deserved punishment for human sin. That doctrine, whether stated in terms of Israel's covenant faith or in terms of wisdom's perception of the unbreakable connection between action and consequence, is inadequate in the face of the enormous suffering that too often falls, like rain, upon both the just and the unjust.

Moreover, the book of Job is a challenge to any attempt to provide a rational theodicy, that is, to give a philosophical explanation of the ways of God. The mystery of suffering is left rationally unanswered, as it is finally unanswered in the Bible as a whole. For the crux of the human problem, in the perspective of Israelite faith, is not the fact of suffering: Israel was born in suffering and was bred in affliction. Rather, the basic issue is a relationship with God which is initiated by a decision of faith in response to divine grace. Outside the I-thou relationship, for which human beings were created, suffering may drive people to despair, or to the easy solutions of popular religion. Within the relationship of faith—the relationship that finally defined Job's existence—suffering may be faced in the confidence that the times of a person's life "are in God's hand" (Ps. 31:15) and that "in everything God works for good with those who love him, who are called according to his purpose" (Rom. 8:28). Thus the climax of the Job poetry occurs at the very end, when a false relationship based on a conception of God received from tradition ("I had heard of thee by the hearing of the ear") is converted into a relationship of personal trust and surrender ("but now my eye sees thee").

DEFINITION: "THEODICY"

Theodicy is an important issue in literature which deals with the problem of suffering and evil. Coined by the German philosopher Leibniz (1646–1716), the term is composed of two Greek words, *theos* (God) and *dike* ("justice, righteousness"), and refers to attempts to give a rational explanation of the justice of God in allowing evil to exist in a world under divine control.

Beginning with ancient Greek philosophy, the attempt to "justify" or vindicate the ways of God arises from the demand and the potentiality of human reason. If God is, in terms of Aristotle's philosophy, the summit of being (imagine a triangle representing "being," with God at the apex), then reason, which human beings share with the divine, should be able to achieve a rationally intelligible and comprehensive view of the whole. Standing in this philosophical tradition and attempting to show the limitations of reason, the philosopher Immanuel Kant (1724–1804), in his monograph *On the Failure of All Philosophical Attempts in Theodicy*, devoted considerable space to interpreting the book of Job.

The book of Job presents a challenge to rational theodicy from the perspective of Israelite wisdom. God is neither the summit of being nor a process or entity within the phenomenal world, but rather is the Creator who transcends the whole creation—the One who originated all being (the "triangle" referred to above) and sustains all being. In this perspective, mystery is not a perplexity capable of rational explanation but a fundamental datum of faith which responds in amazement and wonder to the holiness of God.

LATER REFLECTIONS ON WISDOM

Before concluding this chapter, a further word must be said about the cosmic significance of the wisdom of God that lies beyond human grasp. We have noticed passages in the book of Proverbs that portray wisdom as a distinct personality, a prophetess, and the "child" who was present with Yahweh from the foundation of the earth. In these cases, something more is involved than the mere description of abstract concepts in the concrete terms of Hebraic thought. Wisdom is, or is moving toward becoming, a "hypostasis"—that is, a distinct entity or "person" (to use the language of later Christian metaphysical discussions of the Godhead).

This lofty conception of wisdom was not original with Israel, but the conception was subjected to a special development in the Israelite tradition. In the magnificent hymn to wisdom found in Job 28, it is affirmed that wisdom, the plan of the universe, is hidden from human beings.[40] Search as one will, wisdom cannot be found in the sky, the earth, or the Deep. God alone knows the path to wisdom, for God established it at the time of the Creation:

> God understands the way of it,
>   and he knows its place.
> For he looks to the ends of the earth,
>   and sees everything under the heavens.
> When he gave to the wind its weight,
>   and meted out the waters by measure;
> When he made a decree for the rain,
>   and a way for the lightning of the thunder;
> Then he saw it and declared it;
>   he established it, and searched it out.
>   —JOB 28:23-27 (RSV)

Beyond the boundaries of the Hebrew Bible the cosmic significance of wisdom received even greater attention. In the book known as the Wisdom of Ben Sira (or Ecclesiasticus), written in the early second century B.C.E., wisdom is compared to the breath issuing from the mouth of God—an emanation that penetrates all things:

> I came forth from the mouth of the Highest,
>   and like vapor I have covered the earth;
> I have made my abode in the heights,
>   and my throne on a pillar of cloud.
>   —ECCLESIASTICUS 24:3-4 (RSV)

Here, too, it is said that wisdom was created before all things and poured out upon all that God made (Ecclesiasticus 1:1-20). However, wisdom is said to have

---

[40] Clearly out of place in Job's mouth before Yahweh's speech reminded him of the limitations of human understanding, the poem has obviously been inserted into its present context. It may have been written by the author of Job and placed here by later editors.

found rest only in Israel, where she was associated with the Temple of Jerusalem and the Law of Moses (Ecclesiasticus 24).

In another writing, the Wisdom of Solomon (c. 50 B.C.E.), wisdom is clearly a hypostasis, almost identified with God. In a portion of the relevant passage (Wisd. Sol. 7:22–8:1) it is written:

> For Wisdom is more mobile than any motion,
>   and she penetrates and permeates everything
>   because she is so pure;
> for she is the breath of the power of God,
>   and a pure emanation of his almighty glory;
> therefore nothing defiled can enter into her,
>   for she is a reflection of the everlasting light,
> and a spotless mirror of the activity of God,
>   and a likeness of his goodness.
> Though she is one, she can do all things,
>   and while remaining in herself, she makes everything new.
>   —WISDOM OF SOLOMON 7:27 ff. (RSV)

Thus wisdom came to be regarded as a semi-independent power—the agent of God's creation and the intermediary between God and the world. Israel's sages had become aware of the chasm between the world and God, between human wisdom and the wisdom of God. But their reflection also led them toward the understanding that the gulf is spanned from God's side through the agency of the divine wisdom that dwells in the world of human experience.

We have noticed that the wisdom literature of the Old Testament displays no interest in the revelation of God in Israel's history. The sage was interested in human beings as such, rather than in the unique historical drama in which God was known to a particular people, Israel. In the late period of biblical Judaism, however, wisdom was understood in relation to Israel's sacred history. An excellent witness of this development is the Wisdom of Ben Sira. Here a Jewish sage, by identifying wisdom and Torah, brought the wisdom literature into the central stream of the Mosaic tradition. Wisdom was "nationalized," that is, related positively to the redemptive activity of God in Israel's history. In order to gain wisdom, said Ben Sira, one must keep the commandments of the Torah (Ecclesiasticus 1:26).

For the Christian church, the wisdom movement came to its fulfillment in Jesus Christ. Paul identified wisdom with Christ, through whom redemption came to all humankind (I Cor. 1:24, 30). Moreover, it is probable that the prologue to the Fourth Gospel, which begins with the words, "In the beginning was the Logos [Word], and the Logos was with God, and the Logos was God," should be understood in the light of the wisdom of the East, especially that of Israel's sages. Thus the Christian church received from Israel a conception of cosmic, preexistent wisdom in terms of which the significance of God's revelation in Jesus Christ could be expressed.

CHAPTER **18**

The Unfulfilled Drama

Looking back over a nation's past, it seems that there are times when the river of history flows quietly, smoothly, like the wide waters of the St. Lawrence, and at other times cascades with a thunderous roar, like the falls of the Niagara. This figure of speech may be applied to Israel's history in the new period inaugurated by Cyrus' edict releasing Jews from exile in Babylonia. Despite the troubles faced by the struggling Jewish community during the Reconstruction, there is considerable reason for believing that throughout most of the Persian period the Jews of Palestine enjoyed great security. To be sure, this inference is drawn from silence. The story of the Jewish community, which breaks off with the Chronicler's account of reconstruction under Ezra and Nehemiah, is not resumed until I Maccabees, a book (outside the Hebrew Bible) which covers events of the second century B.C.E. (175–132). Much of the interim, especially the fourth century, is obscure or totally blank. This historical silence may mean that Judah was relatively secure for a century or more after Ezra and Nehemiah. But the times were destined to change. Before the Old Testament closes, we see the stream of Israel's history plunging and swirling along a turbulent course.

Biblical readings: After brief consideration of the books of Jonah and Esther, our attention will focus on the book of Daniel, whose historical background is presented in the book of I Maccabees. The ''little apocalypse,'' found in Isaiah 24–27, and so-called Second Zechariah (Zech. 9–14), belong to the same type of literature as Daniel.

TENSIONS WITHIN JUDAISM

So long as the remarkable stability of the Persian empire persisted (539–333 B.C.E.), the Jewish community in Palestine was not molested by external political threats. At the height of its power, this empire included the whole Fertile Crescent and extended beyond to the Aegean on the west, the Indus Valley on the east, the steppes beyond the Caspian Sea on the north, and Egypt on the south (see map, p. 473). Long before the rise of Alexander the Great, the Persians had created a far-flung political regime that encouraged citizens to widen their horizons, to lengthen their trade arteries, and to jostle with people and ideas from other lands. Even though there was no attempt to superimpose Persian religion upon the whole empire, we may be sure that the influence of Zoroastrianism was felt in Judah.

Thus Judah's problem was no longer that of being caught in the rip tide of rivalry between the two power centers of the Fertile Crescent, Mesopotamia and Egypt. The problems were more local. We have already referred to the increasing tension between Jews and Samaritans (pp. 516–517), which led to the building of the rival Samaritan temple on Mount Gerizim, probably in the middle of the fourth century. In the future, we may expect more light from archaeology on these local affairs of the post-exilic community.

There were also tensions within Judaism itself. We must not think of Judaism as a monolithic structure, fashioned by the great reforms of Ezra and Nehemiah. True, the reconstruction along the lines of an exclusive community, with the Temple as its center and the Torah as its constitution, was carried out with great vigor, for Nehemiah's position as a Persian governor gave great prestige to his leadership, and Ezra too enjoyed the blessing of the Persian government. But there were also other currents within Judaism, currents that are reflected in the book of Psalms and other anonymous literature composed in this period. At the very time when Jewish exclusivism was developing, wisdom teachers were reflecting on the meaning of life in an atmosphere of thought that was more international than Israelite.

The Story of Jonah

A prophetic universalism, reminiscent of Second Isaiah, finds expression in the book of Jonah, which stands in the collection of the Twelve (see Chart on p. 123). As in the case of so much of the literature of the post-exilic period, the name of the author is not given. Rather, the message of the author is presented in the form of a story concerning a prophet who lived in the classical period of Israelite prophecy—back in the days of Jeroboam II (see II Kings 14:25). This is not a biographical account of what actually happened in the experience of the prophet—Jonah, son of Amittai—but a short story told to drive home a prophetic message to the writer's generation. In the judgment of many scholars, it was written in the post-exilic period, no earlier than the fifth century B.C.E. and perhaps toward the end of the Persian period in the fourth century.

Many people think of Jonah as a "fish story"—perhaps the biggest one ever told. Modern literalists ingeniously search the seven seas for a "whale" whose belly is big enough to accommodate a man, and they try to produce documentary evidence that there have been other instances of persons who have come out alive after a sojourn in a whale's stomach. Once we recognize that this is a short story, however, all this speculation is beside the point.

The story tells how Jonah was commissioned by Yahweh to go to Nineveh, the Assyrian capital, and preach that the city would be destroyed if it did not repent. No task could have been more distasteful, for the Assyrians, who had oppressed Israel cruelly, were bitterly detested (see Nahum). So Jonah ran as fast as he could go in the opposite direction. From Joppa, the fugitive took a ship bound for Tarshish, somewhere in the western Mediterranean, whereupon Yahweh hurled a great wind upon the sea. The panic-stricken sailors cried out to their gods to discover the cause of the divine anger that was on the verge of destroying the ship. The lot fell on Jonah, who was sleeping peacefully in the hold, and he was arraigned before the captain. After some discussion, it was agreed to throw Jonah overboard—and suddenly the sea became calm. Yahweh, however, prepared a great fish (the narrative says nothing about a whale) to swallow Jonah and after three days and nights in the fish's belly, he was vomited forth upon the land.[1]

Once again the commission was given to preach to Nineveh—a city so expansive, according to the writer's exaggerated description, that it took three days to walk through it. This time Jonah began to preach in the wicked city, only to be shocked that his preaching was successful. The whole city was converted and Yahweh "repented" of the evil planned against Nineveh. Like Elijah, but for just the opposite reason, Jonah was so discouraged and angry about this turn of events that he wished to die. On the outskirts of the city he made a booth for himself, and sat down beneath its protective shade to observe what would happen. Yahweh then commanded a gourd to grow up as an umbrella over Jonah's head; but the next day Yahweh sent a worm to wilt it, thus exposing Jonah to the merciless heat of the sun. When Jonah expressed pity for the gourd, Yahweh rebuked the prophet for not being able to understand that Yahweh would show at least as much pity toward the city of Nineveh, with its 120,000 infants and many cattle.

Many readers have recognized that the story is designed to tickle one's sense of humor. Surely the author did not have a straight face when telling how a big fish belched Jonah back in the direction from which he had come, that the

---

[1] It is generally agreed that the psalm Jonah 2:2–9, which Jonah is represented as reciting in the fish's belly, has been inserted into the Jonah story by an editor. For a discussion of the function of the psalm in the final redaction, see George M. Landis, "The Kerygma of the Book of Jonah," *Interpretation* 21 (1967), 3–31.

Assyrian king immediately believed Jonah's preaching and commanded every-one—including livestock—to put on sackcloth, and that no sooner had Jonah settled down comfortably in the shade of a plant than Yahweh, the jokester, needled him further by sending a worm to eat the plant and a withering desert wind (sirroco) to boot.

The story-teller's humor and satire, however, only make the theological truth of the story more pointed.[2] Jonah was troubled by a Mosaic teaching that is echoed in various parts of Israel's tradition, namely, the announcement that Yahweh is the God who is "gracious and merciful, slow to anger and abounding in faithfulness [ḥésed]" (Jonah 4:2; see Exod. 34:6–7). Jonah's preaching was based on the conviction that God's word of doom upon Assyria was inexorable and that God would not go back on the threat. However, there is a wideness to God's compassion and a freedom in divine mercy which is irrational, in the sense that it goes beyond the bounds of what people expect or deserve. Abraham Heschel has put the matter incisively:[3]

> God's answer to Jonah, stressing the supremacy of compassion, upsets the possibility of looking for a rational coherence of God's ways with the world. History would be more intelligible if God's word were the last word, final and unambiguous like a dogma or an unconditional decree. It would be easier if God's anger became effective automatically: once wickedness had reached its full measure, punishment would destroy it. Yet beyond justice and anger lies the mystery of compassion.

At the very time when the policies of Ezra and Nehemiah were fostering a narrow nationalism and a doctrinaire exclusivism, the unknown prophetic writer of the book of Jonah proclaimed "the mystery of [God's] compassion." Yahweh's grace cannot be programmed theologically or circumscribed by exclusive boundaries, for Yahweh is free to "be gracious unto whom I will be gracious" and "to show mercy upon whom I will show mercy" (Exod. 33:19).

The Book of Esther

At the opposite extreme from the book of Jonah is another story—a novella—the book of Esther. Found in the third section of the Hebrew Bible (the Writings; see Chart, p. 642), Esther is one of five festal scrolls that are still read on important festivals of the Jewish calendar. Despite the fact that it does not contain a single explicit reference to God or the religious practices of Judaism, the scroll of Esther came to be regarded as the scroll *par excellence*, and in later Jewish

---

[2] See E. M. Good, *Irony in the Old Testament* (Philadelphia: Westminster, 1965). Millar Burrows gives a judicious discussion of the various scholarly views on the book of Jonah and a perceptive interpretation in "The Literary Category of the Book of Jonah," in *Translating and Understanding the Old Testament* [159], 80–107.

[3] Abraham J. Heschel, *The Prophets* [315], pp. 486–487.

tradition it was given a place second only to the Torah.[4] Because of its seemingly nonreligious character, and because its nationalistic spirit might be misunderstood, various rabbis of the Tannaitic period (first century B.C.E. to third century C.E.) expressed uncertainties about its right to be included in the canon. But owing to the popularity of the Feast of Purim, with which the book was associated, these doubts eventually proved too weak to have any lasting effect and faded away.

The story is placed during the reign of Ahasuerus—that is, Xerxes I (486–465 B.C.E.). The scene opens in Xerxes' winter palace at Susa, whose remains, once comparable with the beautiful architecture of Persepolis (see picture, p. 521 and Color Plate 6), have been excavated. When Vashti the queen refused to show off her beauty at the king's lavish wine banquet, she was deposed and a search was made throughout the empire for the most beautiful young women from whose number the king might select a new queen. Esther (or Hadassah—her Jewish name) took part in the beauty contest. Her loveliness was so natural that, without having to go through the year of beauty treatments required by the other maidens, she captured the king's affections. Her position as queen of Persia enabled her to avert a plot to liquidate her Jewish people.

The writer has subtly constructed the story around the ancient hostility between Israel and the Amalekites, which began in the time of Moses (Exod. 17:16; cf. Num. 24:20; Deut. 25:17–19) and which blazed up in Saul's day when the Israelite king was commanded to subject king Agag and his Amalekite tribesmen to the sacrificial ban or ḥérem (Definition, p. 142). This hostility is embodied in two of the principal figures of the story: Mordecai the Jew, who is regarded as a Benjaminite descendant of Kish, the father of Saul (I Sam. 9:1); and Haman, described as the son of Hammedatha, "the Agagite"—a descendant of the Amalekite king conquered by Saul. Because Mordecai refused to pay him the proper courtesies, Haman the grand vizier planned to liquidate the Jews scattered throughout the empire. When Haman pointed out to Xerxes that the Jews refused to be assimilated, choosing instead to live by their own laws (Esther 3:8), Xerxes granted him permission to issue an edict for a wholesale massacre of Jews on the thirteenth day of the month Adar (February-March).

Mordecai, however, persuaded Esther, his cousin, to risk her life on behalf of her people by going to the king, even though an unsummoned visit was punishable by death. Favored by a remarkable series of coincidences, the tables were now turned on the enemies of the Jews. The ḥérem was executed on Haman, who, ironically, was hanged on the towering gallows (83 feet high) that he had constructed for Mordecai. Haman's ten sons were also executed—thus bringing the last of the "Amalekites" to an end. Moreover, by royal decree the thirteenth of Adar became a day on which the Jews of Susa were permitted to

---

[4] The Greek Old Testament (Septuagint) contains several extra passages which give the story a more religious tone. The translator of the Vulgate, Jerome, placed these additions to the Hebrew scroll at the very end of the story (after Esther 10:3). They are included in the Protestant Apocrypha under the title: "The Additions to the Book of Esther."

The Mound of Ancient Susa as seen from the air. Once the capital of ancient Elam, Susa was inhabited as early as the fourth millennium B.C.E. Under Cyrus, the city was one of several capitals of the Persian empire (see Neh. 1:1; Esth. 1:2); it later served as a winter residence for Persian kings. The mound is situated on roads leading to the sites of other former Persian capitals: Ecbatana (a summer capital), and Persepolis (the main capital). The chateau visible in the center of the picture was built by archaeologists whose work in the nineteenth century uncovered the Code of Hammurabi and the Stele of Naram-Sin (pp. 32, 35). The cone-like building to the left is a mosque which, according to Moslem tradition, covers the tomb of Daniel.

slaughter their persecutors throughout the empire, and on another day—the fourteenth of Adar—the Jews in Susa got extra time to continue the bloodshed. At the end of the *ḥérem* a festival of rejoicing was held, which came to be known as Purim in remembrance of the lot (*pur*) that Haman had cast to determine the day of vengeance. The story not only purports to explain the origin of this popular festival but also to account for its celebration on two days.

There are, of course, numerous elements of fiction in the story—like the irrevocable royal decree that a husband should be boss in his own house (1:21-22), and the fabulous bribe that Haman promised to raise (the equivalent of $18,000,000 before inflation began; see 3:9). The story of how Haman was duped into proposing the way Mordecai should be honored by the king (chapter 6), and how he was trapped in an absurd situation that resulted in his death on the very gibbet he had prepared (chapter 7), was unquestionably designed to tickle Jewish humor. It is quite possible, however, that the story rests on the historical memory of a real threat to Jews of the Dispersion. If this is true, Esther is a historical novel that dates from the latter part of the Persian period, when the memories of Xerxes' reign were dim, and when Jews were subject to persecution owing to their refusal to be assimilated.[5] In any event, the story of the origin of Purim came to be very popular during the Maccabean period, when the separation of Jews from Gentiles occasioned violent persecution. And throughout the tumultuous Jewish history since then, Haman has been the symbol of a number of wicked leaders (like Adolf Hitler) who have carried out vicious programs of anti-Semitism.

Esther is unique among the books of the Jewish Bible in that it studiously avoids religious matters. The author seems to make a point of avoiding direct mention of God, as for instance in Esther 4:14 where the reference to deliverance coming "from another place" is often regarded as a veiled allusion to help from God. This theological reticence was probably motivated by the fear that the Name of God might be profaned in connection with the carefree festival of Purim when, as we learn from the Talmud (*Megillah* 7b), it was permissible to drink wine freely, until the difference between "Blessed be Mordecai" and "Cursed be Haman" became blurred! However, beneath the heady worldliness of the book of Esther—as the Septuagint version rightly interprets—is the conviction that God has called this people to be separate from the world (see 3:8) and to demonstrate an exclusive covenant loyalty.

The book of Esther lacks the wide vistas of Second Isaiah or Jonah; its provincial and vindictive spirit is much closer to the prophecy of Nahum. But in a time of foreign domination and aggressive cultural influence, when the vitality of Israel's tradition was threatened, it seemed that the only course of action was a narrowing of loyalty. In its own way the book of Esther intended to say with Elijah: "I have been very jealous for Yahweh God of hosts" (I Kings 19:10). This jealousy, or "zealousy," became religiously articulate in another writing composed under foreign domination: the book of Daniel. Before turning to Daniel, however, we must sketch the political changes brought about by the rise of Alexander the Great.

THE HELLENISTIC ERA

The westward expansion of the Persian empire had resulted in a series of clashes between Greeks and Persians in such famous battles as Marathon, Thermopylae, and Salamis. The courageous Greeks fought hard to keep the Persians from their soil. Then, in the latter part of the fourth century, the political tide turned

---

[5] A number of scholars, however, believe that the book of Esther reflects the persecution of Jews during the Maccabean period. For a discussion of the question, see Bernhard W. Anderson, *Interpreter's Bible*, III [16], pp. 825–28. For a literary study, see Sandra B. Berg, *The Book of Esther* [510].

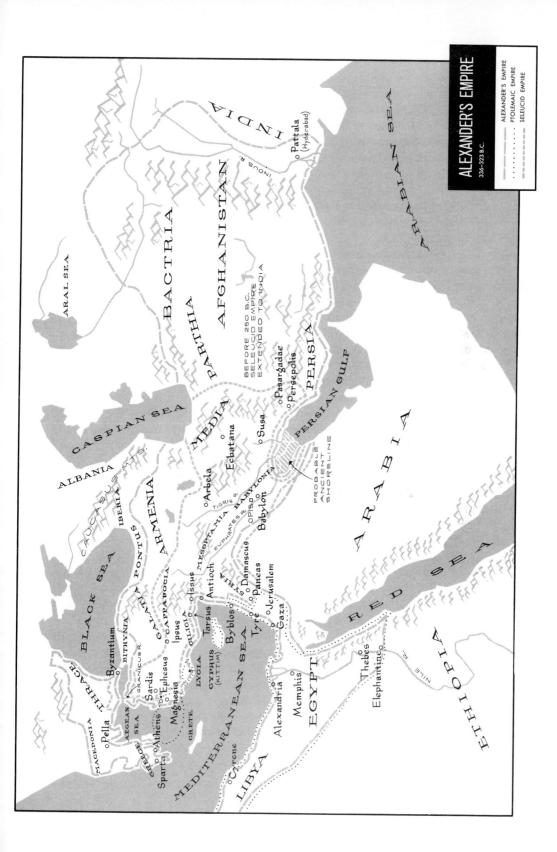

ALEXANDER'S EMPIRE
336–323 B.C.

ALEXANDER'S EMPIRE
PTOLEMAIC EMPIRE
SELEUCID EMPIRE

INDIA

Pattala
(Hyderabad)

ARABIAN SEA

BACTRIA

AFGHANISTAN

PARTHIA

BEFORE 250 B.C.
SELEUCID EMPIRE
EXTENDED TO INDIA

ARAL SEA

Pasargadae
Persepolis

PERSIA

MEDIA

Ecbatana

Susa

PERSIAN GULF

CASPIAN SEA

Arbela

PROBABLE
ANCIENT
SHORELINE

ALBANIA

ARMENIA

TIGRIS R.

MESOPOTAMIA

BABYLONIA

A R A B I A

CAUCASUS MTS.

IBERIA

EUPHRATES R.

OPIS

Babylon

PONTUS

Issus

Antioch

SYRIA

Damascus

Paneas

RED SEA

BLACK SEA

GALATIA

CAPPADOCIA

CILICIA

Tarsus

Ipsus

Byblos

Tyre

Jerusalem

Gaza

Byzantium

THRACE

BITHYNIA

GRANICUS R.

Sardis

LYCIA

CYPRUS
(KITTIM)

Thebes

Elephantine

NILE R.

MACEDONIA

Pella

AEGEAN SEA

Ephesus

Magnesia

GREECE

Athens

CRETE

MEDITERRANEAN SEA

Alexandria

Memphis

EGYPT

ETHIOPIA

Sparta

Cyrene

LIBYA

with the rise to power of one of the greatest military leaders in the history of civilization, Alexander of Macedon (336–323 B.C.E.). Twenty years of age when his father, Philip of Macedon, was assassinated, he set out on a dramatic military career in which victory followed victory—at the Granicus in Asia Minor (334), at Issus in upper Syria (333), at Tyre and Gaza (332), and at Arbela in Mesopotamia (331). From these triumphs his armies swept on through Persia and Afghanistan, and by 326 had reached the Indus River in present-day Pakistan. Never before had a military leader been crowned with such dazzling victories. According to legend, Alexander stood weeping on the banks of the Indus River because there were no more worlds to conquer (See Chronological Chart 10, p. 624).

Having studied under the Greek philosopher Aristotle, Alexander was interested not only in military conquest, but also in spreading the best fruits of Greek culture. The city of Alexandria, Egypt, which was named after him, came to be a monument to the Greek way of life in all its aspects: intellectual, athletic, artistic. Alexander dreamed of ''one world''—a world bound together by Greek culture. Believing that Greek learning was superior to all other, he considered it to be his divine mission—for he was honored as a god—to leaven ancient civilization with Greek scholarship, art, and manners.

Alexander did not live to see his dream fulfilled, for he died in the year 323 B.C.E. before he reached his thirty-third birthday. His vast empire was partitioned among his generals, two of whom inherited the eastern domains. Mesopotamia and Syria eventually went to Seleucus, and Egypt came under the sway of Ptolemy. Once again, Palestine was caught in a struggle between the powers of the Fertile Crescent, this time with the capitals located at Antioch (Seleucid) and Alexandria (Ptolemaic). Alexander's policy of spreading Greek culture through the world was continued by the leaders of these two sections of his empire, despite the political rivalry between them.

The Struggle for Cultural Unity

The term ''Hellenism'' is applied to the Greek-like culture that was fostered by Alexander's successors. Derived from Hellas, the ancient name for Greece, it refers to the perpetuation of the Greek spirit within the countries of the Alexandrian empire. Just as the American visitor to the Middle East today can see signs of the spread of western civilization—for instance, advertisements for cola drinks, American fashions, or Hollywood movies—so in the Hellenistic period a visitor to the same area would have found gymnasiums, theaters, stadiums, and so on. Greek dress became fashionable, especially among the more well-to-do. And an obvious sign of the spread of Hellenism was the widespread use of the Hellenistic vernacular known as *koine* Greek—that is, the spoken language of international business and political affairs as distinct from the classical Greek of the age of Pericles. Like English today, Greek was the *lingua franca*. Hellenism, then, represents a synthesis of the Occident and the Orient.

The rivalry between Seleucids and Ptolemies was not just military: both Antioch and Alexandria vied to become cultural capitals as great as Athens had been in the past. The "school of Antioch," however, was surpassed by Alexandria. The Ptolemies, patrons of the arts and sciences, built up a famous museum at Alexandria, with a huge library that would compare favorably with the best libraries of today. Under their sponsorship, research was carried on by a band of notable scholars, including the mathematician Euclid and the physicist Archimedes. The cultural ascendancy of Alexandria was enhanced by the city's strategic commercial relations with the Mediterranean world on the one hand, and with Arabia and the Fertile Crescent on the other.

At first, the Jews apparently did not regard Hellenism as a serious threat to their faith. No problem was felt in Alexandria, for ever since the days of the founding of the Elephantine colony (see p. 428), Egyptian Jews had been receptive to foreign influences. In this part of the Dispersion, Aramaic was superseded by *koine* Greek, and under the aegis of Ptolemy II (285–246 B.C.E.) scholars began the task of translating Jewish scripture into Greek. Thus, over a period of years, the Septuagint was produced, the translation to which we have referred from time to time. Since language inevitably conditions one's manner of thinking about the world, it is not surprising that Greek-speaking Jews produced a number of books, like the Wisdom of Solomon, which were influenced by a Hellenistic world view.[6]

Shortly after the partition of Alexander's empire, Palestine came within the orbit of the Ptolemies. These Egyptian rulers, rather easy-going in contrast to the aggressive Seleucids, made no attempt to coerce Jews into cultural conformity. It is said that Ptolemy III (246–221 B.C.E.), on a visit to Jerusalem, deferred to Jewish custom and presented a thank-offering at the Temple. Under the mild patronizing rule of the Ptolemies, undoubtedly many modernistic Jews welcomed Hellenism, seeing no contradiction between the new cultural fashion and their traditional faith. Many of these modernists were found in the upper classes, whose education and commercial interests exposed them to the attractions of Hellenism.

The Resistance Movement

The spread of Hellenism, then, posed anew the problem with which Israel had had to wrestle ever since the entrance into Canaan: the relation between faith and culture. Again and again, when Israel's faith was on the verge of being sold out in the world's markets, individuals arose who rigorously protested in the name of the jealous God of the covenant. Like Elijah, these champions were zealots—individuals who were zealous to uphold the covenant faith and to bring about its renewal in times of degeneration. As we have seen repeatedly, this protest against the seductiveness of foreign culture was often accompanied by

[6] On the Wisdom of Solomon, see the remark in Chapter 17, footnote 2.

Alexander the Great *presents an offering to the Egyptian god Amon in this relief on a wall of the Temple of Karnak. Although Alexander himself (left, holding tray of objects) never visited Thebes, he had no difficulty appropriating the ancient Egyptian belief that a king is the son of a god. The blending of occidental and oriental culture in Hellenism is also symbolized by the Greek inscription underneath the Egyptian hieroglyphic.*

the revival of Israelite nationalism, as in the case of the Deuteronomic Reform. In the Hellenistic era, the stage was prepared for another revival, kindled by both conservative religious loyalty and by the nationalistic hope for the re-establishment of a Davidic state. The revival caught fire in the circle of a sect known as the Hasidim (the "loyal, or pious ones"), the forerunners of the later Pharisees. Although the Hellenizers tended to be found among the Jewish upper classes, the Hasidim in many (but certainly not all) instances came from a rural background, where they were more or less isolated from the allurements of the Hellenistic world. Filled with great zeal for the Torah, they frowned upon the modernism of fellow Jews who were welcoming Hellenistic styles of thought and behavior, and they clung conservatively to the faith of their ancestors. Although this resistance movement must have started very early in the Hellenistic period, it did not appear on the scene of history until there occurred a dramatic turn in political affairs, which ended the rule of the Ptolemies in Palestine.[7]

The Outbreak of Jewish Persecution

Although the Seleucids of Syria had repeatedly tried to gain control of the Mediterranean coastland, which they claimed belonged to them by right, Palestine remained under the control of Egypt during the third century. Then, in 223 B.C.E., Antiochus III (the Great) came to the Syrian throne in Antioch. After more than two decades of war with Egypt, in 198 the Syrian king won a decisive victory over Ptolemy V at Panias (or Paneas), near the source of the Jordan River, thereby bringing Palestine into his political orbit.

Antiochus the Great was a vigorous apostle of Hellenism. His policies were fanatically upheld by one of his successors, Antiochus IV (175–163), known as Antiochus Epiphanes because he claimed to be god (Zeus) manifest (*theos epiphanes*). The coins that bore his image were inscribed with *theos* (god). His pretensions to divinity, although in line with the claims of Alexander and others, prompted him to rule with absolute authority, and to stop at nothing in imposing Hellenistic culture upon his realm. He did not object to people having other gods and following local religious customs. But the test of political loyalty was the worship of Zeus, and this meant submission to the absolute authority of the king—"god manifest." No policy could have been better calculated to stir up trouble in Palestine. For the cardinal tenet of Israel's faith from the very first was the jealousy of Yahweh, who absolutely refused to have a place beside any other god and who was fiercely intolerant of idolatry in any form.

Antiochus' enthusiasm for Hellenism, however, was not the only, or even the initial, reason for his intervention in Jewish affairs. He needed money badly, for the protracted wars with the Ptolemies and the staggering expense of keeping the sprawling Seleucid kingdom under control had drained his treasury. Jewish resentment against Antiochus was first felt at the economic level—in stepped-up taxation. But it rose to a pitch of rioting when the most sacred office, that of the High Priest, was auctioned off to the highest bidder. This scandal involved two Jewish "Hellenizers," Jason and Menelaus, both of whom bore Greek names. Jason handsomely bribed Antiochus to depose his brother, Onias

---

[7] Ancient sources for the history of the Maccabean period are I–II Maccabees—works found outside the Hebrew Bible. They are included in the Roman Catholic canon and found in the Protestant Apocrypha (see Chart, pp. 4–5). In addition, there are the important works by the first-century C.E. Jewish historian, Josephus.

Antiochus IV in profile according to a coin bearing his image. The reverse side carries the Greek words: Basileos Antiochou, Theou Epiphanous, Nikephorou—"(coinage) of King Antiochus, God Manifest, Bearer of Victory." The king represents himself as Zeus, seated on a throne, holding in his left hand a royal staff and in his right the figure of the goddess of victory, Nike, who holds in her hand the laurel wreath, symbol of victory.

III, and to give him the high priesthood, and in addition he offered to build a Greek-type gymnasium in Jerusalem in honor of Antiochus (I Macc. 1:11–15). While Jason was attending the Greek games held at Tyre in honor of Heracles, however, Menelaus out-bid his rival and was given the office. In the ensuing riots, Jason returned and banished Menelaus, who, naturally enough, appealed to Antiochus for help. So Antiochus came to Jerusalem with his army, reinstated Menelaus, and punished the populace by plundering the Temple and shedding Jewish blood (II Macc. 4–5).

This action only made matters worse. Infuriated over the Jews' stubborn defiance of his will, and smarting under a defeat that his army had received in an Egyptian campaign, Antiochus determined to ''get tough'' with the rebels. He issued orders for the outlawing of Jewish religion and the complete Hellenization of Jewish life. According to the edict, mothers who circumcised their children were to be put to death, copies of the Torah were to be burned, and observance of the Sabbath and possession of a copy of the Torah were made capital offenses. To carry out his plan to exterminate Judaism, in 168 B.C.E. he marched his troops into Jerusalem. The Temple was desecrated by the erection of ''an abomination of desolation''—the Jewish description of an altar to Zeus—over the altar for burnt offerings in the Temple court; and it was further defiled by sacrificing swine upon it—the most unclean animal of all, according to Jewish law (I Macc. 1:54; see Dan. 9:27; 11:31; 12:11; Mk. 13:14). Pagan altars were built in the land; Jews were forced to make sacrifices to Zeus and to eat swine's flesh. And Antiochus' troops policed the country to see that the royal edict was obeyed.

The Maccabean Revolt

During this reign of terror, many Jews—not only the Hellenizers but the weak-hearted as well—yielded to the king's decree. Others, refusing to surrender their faith at any cost, went to their death or fled into hiding. The tinder for revolution was ready, needing only a spark to ignite it.

The spark was struck one day in Modein, a little town in the hill country a few miles northwest of Jerusalem. When a Syrian officer demanded that local

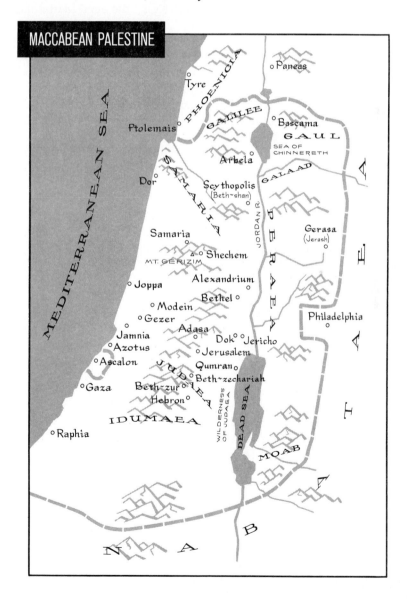

MACCABEAN PALESTINE

citizens comply with his order to make a pagan sacrifice, Mattathias, a village priest, flatly refused. Filled with rage at the sight of a Jew who had come forward to make a sacrifice, Mattathias killed both the Jew and the Syrian officer who had issued the order. He and his five sons fled to the hills, where they gathered around themselves a band of loyal Jews. What they lacked in numbers and weapons, they hoped to make up for by guerrilla tactics, and, above all, by their zeal. Their battle cry was the shout of Mattathias: "Let everybody who is zealous for the Torah and stands by the covenant come out after me" (I Macc. 2:27).

On his death-bed in 166 B.C.E., the aged Mattathias commissioned his oldest son, Judas, to carry on. So vigorous a fighter was Judas that he was given the title "Maccabeus," a word that is sometimes interpreted to mean "hammer," in reference to his hard-hitting blows against the enemy, both Jewish assimilationists and Syrians. Despite overwhelming odds, Judas and his band of recruits soon won a surprising victory over Antiochus' general and demanded a peace treaty. On the twenty-fifth day of the month of Kislev (December), 165 B.C.E., he rebuilt the altar of the Temple and restored the service of Jewish worship, thereby inaugurating the Hanukkah (Rededication) feast, or the Feast of Lights, which Jews still celebrate around Christmas time.

Thus began the Maccabean wars, carried on successively by the brothers Judas, Jonathan, and Simon. What began as a resistance movement eventually flared up into a full-scale war. Favored by international developments, especially Rome's increasing intervention in eastern affairs, the energetic, zealous Jews were able to achieve a century of independence that lasted until the coming of the Roman ruler, Pompey, to Jerusalem in 63 B.C.E.

THE APOCALYPSE OF DANIEL

Shortly after the outbreak of the Maccabean wars, an unknown writer composed the book of Daniel. Undoubtedly this person was one of the Hasidim, who felt a revulsion for the ways of Hellenism and the tyranny by which it was imposed upon the Jews. The purpose of the writing was to rekindle the faith of Israel, at that time in danger of being extinguished by the aggressive and severe policies of the Seleucids, and to summon the Jewish people to unyielding loyalty even in the face of persecution. Affirming that the course of history was completely under Yahweh's sovereignty, the author summoned the Jewish people to courageous faith. For when the people believe that the issues are in the hand of God, rather than in human control, they can act without fear of the consequences. The book of Daniel, then, sets forth the theology of the Maccabean revolution. It has been rightly called "the Manifesto of the Hasidim."

Some people have been misled by the author's portrayal of incidents and visions experienced by Daniel during the Babylonian Exile. Supposing that the book of Daniel was written during the Exile, they have regarded it as a prophetic preview of several centuries of future history and, indeed, of the divine program for a future that still lies ahead. Thus the book has become a happy hunting ground for those who are fascinated by "biblical prophecy" and who look for some mysterious blueprint of the future hidden in its pages. We have already questioned this view of prophecy (see pp. 247–249), pointing out that although the prophets looked to the future, they were concerned primarily with the meaning of the present. This observation holds true for the book of Daniel, even though, properly speaking, it is not classed with the Prophets in the Hebrew Bible but in the catalogue of the Sacred Writings, or Hagiographa (see Chart, p. 642). The author of Daniel spoke to people of the day in the guise of a writing that was predated in the Babylonian period, as though one were looking forward into the future rather than backward from the present. In the late postexilic period, when prophecy was believed to have ceased, it was common to release writings under the name of some figure of ancient Jewish tradition.[8] In this case, the author chose the name of Daniel—a traditional, pious Israelite, according to Ezekiel (14:14, 20; 28:3), and a legendary hero of the Ras Shamra literature.

Prophecy and Apocalyptic

The book of Daniel belongs to a special class of literature known as apocalyptic (from the Greek word *apokalyptein,* "to uncover, reveal"), of which there are many examples in the late post-exilic and early Common Era.[9] To take one outstanding illustration, the last book of the New Testament—called the Revelation, or the Apocalypse of John—is written in an idiom that is strikingly similar to, and even dependent upon the book of Daniel. Apocalyptic literature abounds with bizarre visions, strange symbolism, and supernatural happenings. Written in times of persecution, it employs a kind of spiritual code that makes it a "sealed book" (Dan. 12:4) to those outside the circle of faith.

The central theme of apocalyptic literature is God's revelation concerning the end-time, the coming of the kingdom of God. Even though this literature arose in a time when prophecy supposedly had ceased, it continues and gives new expression to the prophetic message. From the very first, Israel's faith had been oriented toward the future. Yahweh's work in history, according to Israel's faith, was *purposeful,* and events were pressing toward the realization of the divine goal for Israel and the nations. History was not spinning in circles, like the cycle of the seasons; nor was it governed by blind fate or chance. Israel perceived that its history was part of a great drama which, under the direction of God, was moving toward a final consummation.

---

[8] A collection of late writings called the Pseudepigrapha (spurious writings) contains works issued under the names of various biblical characters, such as the Assumption of Moses, the Testament of the Twelve Patriarchs, and so on. Writings of this type are found in R. H. Charles, *Apocrypha and Pseudepigrapha of the Old Testament* [6] and James H. Charlesworth, *The Old Testament Pseudepigrapha* [7].

[9] See D. S. Russell, *The Method and Message of Jewish Apocalyptic* [493], for a full discussion of this type of literature.

In the pre-exilic period, this hope found expression in the popular doctrine about the coming "Day of Yahweh"—the Day when Yahweh would vindicate Israel by humbling its foes and raising the nation to a position of prestige and blessing in the world. This is what the people derived from the confessional affirmation that Yahweh had chosen Israel out of all the nations, and that "God is with us" (Immanuel). The great prophets, as we have seen, challenged this popular view. They too believed that Yahweh had chosen Israel and was with the people, tabernacling in their midst and guiding them in their historical pilgrimage. But with one voice they insisted that God's presence gave no justification for pride or complacency; on the contrary, God's activity in history was for the purpose of shocking the people into an awareness of their unfaithfulness to the covenant and bringing about a "return" or repentance. Therefore, the prophets stood up in the market place, in the Temple, or in the presence of kings and rebuked the people for their failure. Speaking to the present situation, they interpreted the meaning of political events—such as the rise of Assyria or the destruction of Jerusalem—in the light of God's judgment and mercy. Convinced that Yahweh was about to act in the historical arena, using some historical agency, they preached to the people with great urgency to mend their ways while there was still time.

These prophets, then, were also concerned about the end-time, the divine consummation of history. Beyond the darkness of the Day of Judgment they saw the dawn of a new era which Yahweh, in divine mercy, would introduce. They proclaimed that the kingdom of God was near at hand, for the King was coming both to judge and renew the people. Sometimes they portrayed the New Age in glorious colors. In the last day, they said, the political schism of the Israelite monarchy would be healed, the blessings of fertility would be poured out abundantly, nations would beat their swords into plowshares, and the wilderness would blossom like a rose. But in general the great prophets did not speculate on the diagram of the New Age, for their concern was with the future as it impinged upon the present.

Prophecy in a New Idiom

Beginning with the Exile, however, a shift in prophetic emphasis gradually took place. We can see this change in the prophet Ezekiel, who stood on the boundary between the old national era and emerging Judaism. Although he spoke in accents of doom and hope like his prophetic predecessors, his message was cast in a new style of bizarre visions and weird symbolism. Looking beyond the Day of Judgment, he produced a diagram of the New Age, drawn according to the pattern of a priestly utopia. If the oracles found in chapters 38–39 came from Ezekiel himself, he believed that this New Age would be preceded by a final assault on Jerusalem by Gog from the land of Magog. In that day, Yahweh would intervene decisively, shaking nature itself with cataclysmic power, and destroying the mysterious hosts of Gog with a great slaughter. Thus the earlier prophets' vision of the coming of a foe from the north (as, for instance, in Jeremiah) was transformed into the prophecy of the final battle of history that would usher in the Kingdom of God.

The overthrow of Gog, a symbolic foe, is a good illustration of how apocalyptic literature tends to shift the burden of responsibility from Israel's covenant failure to the uncanny sway of mysterious powers of evil (the mythical powers of chaos) that must be overthrown in the final battle of history. We have seen that prophets tried to account for the sufferings of the present age in the context of a covenant with Yahweh and had called Israel to repent. But apocalyptic writers knew that the sufferings of Israel—or other peoples—cannot be explained on the basis of sin—that is, a failure in human responsibility. Israel is the victim of a monstrous power of evil that sweeps like an avalanche over the righteous and the wicked, as the prophet Habakkuk perceived (Hab. 1:6–11). Too often in history the punishment is out of all proportion to the crime, as we know from the holocausts of Hiroshima and Auschwitz. Therefore apocalyptic writers, grappling with the mystery of evil, are profoundly pessimistic about the present sorry scheme. "The present age," to use their language, is separated from "the age to come" by a deep qualitative gulf. The present age is under the dominion of sinister evil powers, symbolized by Satan, the archenemy of God. The age to come will be a time of freedom from moral corruption, evil oppression, and death. Between these two ages there is no continuity; humanly speaking, nothing can be done to change things as they are. God must intervene to destroy the whole present system cataclysmically and, as in the Apocalypse of the New Testament, overthrow the kingdom of Satan. In the apocalyptic vision, history is moving with inexorable momentum and predetermined divine plan toward the final showdown and the final victory of God's Kingdom.

Outside the book of Daniel, a number of passages in the Old Testament are written in the apocalyptic idiom. One example is found in the last part of the book of Zechariah, particularly chapters 12–14.[10] Here an unknown apocalyptist portrays the last great conflict, when all nations will gather to Jerusalem for battle (cf. Joel 3:9–21), and when Yahweh will overthrow resisting forces and become Ruler over all the earth. Perhaps from about the same time comes a section of the book of Isaiah often called "the little apocalypse" (Isa. 24–27). The writer portrays the Last Judgment, when Yahweh will judge all the nations by bringing about a cosmic catastrophe. The earth will be turned upside down and will reel to and fro like a drunkard, the sun and the moon will be eclipsed, and universal chaos will reign. But in the midst of this catastrophe, Israel—"the righteous nation that keeps the truth" (26:2)—will remain secure, with its mind stayed on Yahweh. The righteous of earlier generations will be raised from the dead in order that they too may participate in the consummation of history

---

[10] Zech. 9–14, often called Deutero-Zechariah, consists of prophecies that are usually assigned to a period much later than that of the prophet Zechariah, perhaps in the last of the third century B.C.E.

(26:19). Apparently here we have the first reference in the Old Testament to the resurrection of the individual. Ezekiel had spoken of the resurrection of Israel (Ezek. 37), but the doctrine was extended to that of a general resurrection at the end-time, in order that the wicked might not escape the final judgment and that the righteous might receive the reward of their faithfulness.[11]

The apocalyptic literature, then, is prophecy in a new idiom.[12] Although it represents a shift in emphasis, it expresses the prophetic convictions that Yahweh is King, that the Kingdom of God is near at hand, and that individuals are called to be faithful under all circumstances. It is not surprising that in our time, when many people have been subjected to the cruelest suffering, and when it often seems that history is controlled by powerful political or social forces, the message of an apocalyptic writing like Daniel has spoken with new relevance.

THE KINGDOM THAT IS GOD'S

The book of Daniel falls into two sections: chapters 1-6, which relate stories about Daniel and his companions; and chapters 7-12, which contain Daniel's visions.[13] Part of the book is written in Aramaic rather than Hebrew, but, oddly enough, the Aramaic portion overlaps the two main sections (2:4b-7:28). Probably, the author has drawn upon earlier materials, adapting them for his purpose. In any case, the book in its present form is fundamentally a unity, issued during Antiochus Epiphanes' persecution—probably about 165 B.C.E.

By placing the narratives in the time of the Babylonian exile, the author has made several blunders on historical details. The book begins with a glaring historical error, for Nebuchadnezzar did not take Jerusalem in the third year of King Jehoiakim (606 B.C.E.),[14] and it was Jehoiakim's son—Jehoiachin—who was borne away to captivity (see II Kings 24). The author did not have the history of the Persian empire straight, as is shown by confusion about the sequence of kings (see Dan. 5:31; 9:1) and the telescoping of historical periods (11:2). These and other errors indicate that the writer was looking back over four centuries of history from a time when memories were blurred or distorted by popular

---

[11] Notice that in the Bible the hope for the future life of the individual beyond the grave is expressed in terms of the resurrection of the body—that is, the self. The doctrine of the immortality or deathlessness of the "soul"—a deathless substance imprisoned within the body—rests upon an extrabiblical view of human nature.

[12] Among others Paul Hanson, in *The Dawn of Apocalyptic* [427], has argued that apocalyptic belongs in the prophetic tradition, against Gerhard von Rad who maintains that apocalyptic is primarily related to Wisdom (*Theology,* II [142], 301-315, Wisdom [465], 263-283. A helpful summary of recent discussions is provided by E. W. Nicholson, "Apocalyptic," in *Tradition and Interpretation* [153], 189-213.

[13] The Greek (Septuagint) version of the book of Daniel is longer than the Hebrew-Aramaic text. It contains at the beginning "The Story of Susanna" and at the end "The Story of Bel and the Dragon," as well as "The Song of the Three Children" (see footnote 15). This surplus material is included in the Roman Catholic canon, and is found in the Protestant Apocrypha as Additions to Daniel.

[14] In the book of Daniel the Babylonian king's name is spelled as Nebuchadnezzar. On the spelling, see p. 388, footnote 30.

views. After all, his purpose was not to give a correct history, after the manner of Thucydides or Herodotus, but to proclaim a religious message to embattled fellow Jews. Writing in a cryptic code that the enemy could not understand, the author cleverly disguised references to contemporary historical events and personalities in narratives and visions that allegedly originated at a time long past.

Loyalty to the Torah

The author of Daniel belonged to the Hasidim, whose religious faith demanded loyalty to the Torah at any cost. As we read the stories in chapters 1-6, we should keep in mind that this apocalyptic tract was released at a time when even the possession of a copy of the Torah was a capital offense. We do not have to do much reading between the lines to guess who was in mind in the description of the tyrants of the past—rulers who did everything in their power to destroy the faith of Daniel and his friends.

The book opens by relating how Daniel and his friends were brought to Nebuchadnezzar's court in Babylon and trained for royal service (chap. 1). Even in foreign surroundings, where they were under great pressure to eat the king's sumptuous fare, they were faithful to the dietary regulations of the Jewish Torah. Even though they ate nothing more than vegetables and water, they proved stronger than anyone else in the training program. Moreover, God gave them wisdom that put to shame all the magicians and enchanters of the empire. Here we see that in the period of Judaism "wisdom" was identified with understanding and obeying the Torah (see pp. 566-567).

Daniel proved that his wisdom far surpassed that of all the sages of Babylonia by performing an impossible task set by the king: not merely to interpret his dream, but to guess what it was (chap. 2). Nebuchadnezzar was so impressed by this feat that he confessed faith in Daniel's God, "a revealer of mysteries" of the future (here we see the meaning of "apocalypse"; Dan. 2:47), and elevated Daniel to the position of governor of the province of Babylon and leader of all the Babylonian sages.

There follows a series of familiar stories on the theme of faithfulness to Yahweh under the most severe ordeals. When Nebuchadnezzar commanded that all his subjects must either bow down and worship a huge golden idol or else be thrown into a fiery furnace (a veiled reference to the forced worship of Zeus), everyone complied except Daniel's three friends (chap. 3). Their courageous faith reflects the spirit of the Hasidim of the Maccabean Revolution:

> If it be so, our God whom we serve is able to deliver us from the burning fiery furnace; and he will deliver us out of your hand, O king. But if not, be it known to you, O king, that we will not serve your gods or worship the golden image you have set up.
>
> —DANIEL 3:17-18 (RSV)

In a fit of rage, Nebuchadnezzar (Maccabean readers would inevitably think of Antiochus Epiphanes) ordered that the furnace be heated seven times hotter

Chronological Chart 10

B.C.E.	Egypt	Palestine	Mesopotamia Persia
			Artaxerxes III, 358–338
			Arses, 338–336
			Darius III, 336–331
400 to 300		EMPIRE OF ALEXANDER THE GREAT, 336–323	
	Ptolemaic Kingdom		*Seleucid Kingdom*
		Egyptian Control	(Mesopotamia and Syria)
	Ptolemy I, 323–285		Seleucus I, 312/11–280
	Ptolemy II, 285–246		Antiochus I, 280–261
300 to 200	Ptolemy III, 246–221		Antiochus II, 261–246
		Egyptian Control	Seleucus II, 246–226
			Seleucus III, 226–223
	Ptolemy IV, 221–203		Antiochus III, 223–187
	Ptolemy V, 203–181	Syrian Conquest, 200–198	
	Ptolemy VI, 181–146		Seleucus IV, 187–175
			Antiochus IV (Epiphanes), 175–163
		MACCABEAN REVOLT, 168 (167)	Antiochus V, 163–162
200 to 100			Demetrius I, 162–150
		Judas, 166–160	Alexander Balas, 150–145
	Ptolemy VII, 146–116	Jonathan, 160–143	Demetrius II, 145–138
		Simon, 143–134	Antiochus VI, 145–141
		John Hyrcanus, 134–104	Antiochus VII, 138–129
		Conquest of Shechem, 128	
100 to C.E.	Roman Conquest, 30	Pompey captures Jerusalem, 63	Roman occupation of Syria, 63
		THE EMPIRE OF ROME	

than usual. Once again, the astonished king was moved to have faith in the God of Israel when he saw the three men, joined by an angel, walking around in the furnace unsinged by the roaring fire.[15] The outcome was that the king promoted the three Jews to a higher rank.

[15] In the Septuagint, after Dan. 3:23, there is an account of how one of the friends, named Azariah (Abednego), prays to God for deliverance from the fiery furnace; when deliverance comes, the three friends sing a song of praise. This addition to the Hebrew Bible (''The Song of the Three Children'' and the accompanying prayer of Azariah) was incorporated into the Vulgate. It is included in the Protestant Apocrypha under Additions to Daniel.

Another story (chap. 4) tells how one day Nebuchadnezzar bragged about his imperial glory as he surveyed from his palace roof the new Babylon, which, as archaeology has confirmed (see Color Plate 5), was his very own creation. But just as Daniel had predicted in his interpretation of the king's dream, in which an angel chopped down a huge tree (verses 4–27), the proud king had a great fall. A voice from heaven spoke, reminding Nebuchadnezzar who really controls history; at this point, the king went insane and lived a beastly existence, eating grass like an ox. After seven years of this humiliation, he was restored to sanity. In a hymn of praise, he confessed that the kingdom, power, and glory belong to the God of Israel alone.

We are told that Belshazzar, supposedly Nebuchadnezzar's successor to the Babylonian throne, held a great banquet for a thousand nobles of his kingdom (chap. 5).[16] While they were carousing, they decided to drink wine out of the sacred vessels that Nebuchadnezzar had taken from the Temple of Jerusalem. But a great hush fell on the scene of merriment when "the fingers of a human hand appeared and wrote on the plaster of the wall of the king's palace." When the king saw the ghostly hand write MENE, MENE, TEKEL, and PARSIN, he was overcome with great fright, and summoned the wise men of the realm to interpret the mysterious message. When they failed, Daniel was called. He interpreted the words as a message of doom upon Belshazzar's kingdom: the king had been "weighed in the balances and found wanting." Daniel was given the highest honors for his success in decoding the message, but that very night Belshazzar was slain and the kingdom passed to "Darius the Mede." (Notice that Cyrus and Cambyses actually followed after Nabonidus/Belshazzar.)[17]

Darius was so pleased with Daniel that he made him one of three presidents over the 120 satraps of his empire (chap. 6). Fearing that Daniel would soon become the chief administrative officer of the realm, the jealous presidents and satraps persuaded the king to sign an irrevocable decree that anyone, except the king himself, who made a petition to a god or human being during a thirty-day period would be thrown to the lions. When Daniel was found praying to his God in his upper chamber, the king reluctantly commanded that he be cast into the den of lions, although he expressed the hope that Daniel's God would

---

[16] Actually Belshazzar never reigned as king of Babylon, and the statement that he was the son of Nebuchadnezzar (5:2, 11) is a glaring error. It is true, however, that when Belshazzar's father, Nabonidus, went off into Arabia to spend his final years at Teman, the empire was left temporarily in Belshazzar's control. See the brief discussion above, p. 469 and Chronological Chart 8, p. 412. It is interesting to note, however, that in a fragmentary document from Qumran, designated as "The Prayer of Nabonidus," a story similar to that of Daniel 4 is told of Nabonidus, rather than Nebuchadnezzar. This seems to suggest an older tradition in which Nabonidus was regarded as the father of Belshazzar (see Dan. 5:2). "The change of names," writes Frank M. Cross, "as well as the development of the elaborate details of Nebuchadnezzar's theriomania, is best attributed to the refracting tendencies of oral transmission, in this case the shift of a legend from a lesser to a greater name." *The Ancient Library of Qumran* [513], pp. 166–68.

[17] Strictly speaking, the idea of a Median kingdom *between* the Babylonian and Persian regimes is a historical inaccuracy. It is true that in the Babylonian period the Medes were a formidable power; indeed, they joined with Babylonia to overthrow Assyria (see above, pp. 386–387). But they never established themselves as imperial successors to the Babylonians. Rather, their leader, Astyages, was vanquished by Cyrus, who established the Persian empire as the successor to Babylonia.

deliver him because of his faithful obedience to the Torah. To the king's great joy, Daniel was found unharmed the next morning, and his accusers were then thrown to the lions. Orders were issued for everyone in the empire to reverence the God of Daniel. Daniel prospered during the reign of Darius' presumed successor, Cyrus the Persian. (See Chronological Chart 8, p. 412.)

In all these stories, the faith of the Hasidim during the trials of the Maccabean period finds magnificent expression. Individuals must be loyal to the Torah at all costs, for God is able to deliver the faithful. God's kingdom is an everlasting kingdom, in contrast to the kingdoms of the world, which are symbolized in a dream (Dan. 2:31–36) by a colossal statue with a head of gold (the Babylonian kingdom), chest and arms of silver (Median kingdom), abdomen of brass (Persian kingdom), legs of iron (Alexander's kingdom), and feet of iron mixed with potsherds (the Hellenistic kingdoms of Syria and Egypt). Though tyrants strut and boast, their days are numbered; their power is nothing when measured against the Ruler of history. Like "the stone cut without hands" which shattered the statue and became a great mountain, God's kingdom—with its center in the holy community of Judaism—will vanquish all earthly kingdoms and endure forever.

Visions of the End-Time

The second part of the book of Daniel (chapters 7–12) consists of four visions that portray the dramatic movement of historical events toward the final consummation when God will overthrow the tyrannical rule of the world powers and establish the kingdom of God on earth, as in heaven. Four successive empires are pictured—the Babylonian, Median, Persian, and Greek, each surpassing the preceding one in evil and brutality. In this view, the accumulated evil of history was finally concentrated in one kingdom (the Seleucid) and in one depraved king (Antiochus Epiphanes). To the writer, this increase in evil meant that history was hastening toward the final showdown.

In the first vision (chap. 7), Daniel saw four beasts arising out of the "great sea"—that is, the watery chaos, the mythical source of powers hostile to God's creation. The last of these beasts was the worst: it was "terrible and dreadful and exceeding strong," and it had ten horns. An "interpretive angel" explained that these beasts were four successive empires (verses 15–17): the Babylonian (a lion with eagle's wings), the Median (a bear with three ribs in it mouth), the Persian (a leopard with four wings and four heads), and the Hellenistic or Seleucid (the ten horns refer to Seleucid kings, and the little horn "speaking great things" is Antiochus Epiphanes).[18] "The Ancient of Days," presiding over the Heavenly Council at the Last Judgment, sentenced the fourth kingdom to de-

---

[18] In a passage from the Sibylline Oracles (3:381–400), written about 140 B.C.E., the expression "ten horns" refers to the ten kings who preceded Antiochus Epiphanes. As a matter of historical fact, Antiochus was the seventh in the series of Seleucid kings after Alexander's death.

struction, and the other three, whose rule had not been so monstrously evil, were deprived of their dominion and permitted to survive for a time. Then, with the clouds of heaven, in contrast to the beasts' origin from the depths of the sea, came "one like a human being"—that is, a figure with a human rather than a beastly countenance. The angel interpreted this heavenly figure to symbolize the holy community of Israel—"the saints of the Most High." Instead of a transient kingdom, they would be given everlasting and universal dominion which was to be inaugurated after "a time, two times, and a half a time" of the little horn—a cryptic reference to the three and a half years when Antiochus Epiphanes persecuted the Jews (168–165 B.C.E.).

DEFINITION: "SON OF MAN"

The vision of Daniel 7 introduces a motif that became increasingly important in apocalyptic literature: in Aramaic, *bar 'anash,* literally "a son of man."

Elsewhere in the Old Testament a comparable expression is sometimes used to refer to "a human being," for instance, in Psalm 8:4 which was translated in the King James Version:

> What is man, that thou art mindful of him?
> and the son of man, that thou visitest him?

In the Hebrew the expression translated "son of man" (*ben 'adam*) really means a mortal person (cf. the NEB translation), for "son" is an idiomatic way of referring to a member of a class. Examples of this idiomatic usage are "sons of the prophets" (*benê han-nebe'îm*), i.e. a prophetic company, and "sons of God" (*benê ha-'elohîm*), namely, the angels in Yahweh's Heavenly Council (Job 1:6). The same expression is used frequently in the book of Ezekiel, as we have seen, with a special emphasis: to highlight the mortal weakness and finite humanity of the prophet in contrast to the holy, majestic deity of Yahweh.

In the apocalypse of Daniel, however, the expression has a special linguistic function in the context of Daniel's vision. Notice, first, that we are dealing with a similitude: "one like" a human being, in contrast to the oppressive empires that are like beasts. And, second, this human-like figure is a heavenly being, one who comes transcendently "with the clouds of heaven" in contrast to the beasts who emerge from the sea, the locus of the powers of chaos. It would be erroneous to literalize the symbolism and think of the offspring ("son") of a man or even a "human one."

In an apocalyptic writing known as the book of Enoch, which is based on a tradition reaching back into a time before the Common Era (first century B.C.E.), there are references to a figure of the end-time, "the Son of Man," who comes to establish God's kingdom (Enoch 46:1; 48:2–10). In the Jewish apocalypse called II Esdras found in the Apocrypha (Fourth Ezra/Fourth Esdras according to another designation), from the close of the first century B.C.E., a vision is described in which Ezra sees emerging out of the sea "as it were the likeness of a man [human being]" who flies on the clouds of heaven (chap. 13). This figure is understood to be the heavenly agent of God's judgment in the last days. In this messianic sense "Son of Man" or "The Heavenly Being" is often used in the gospels of the New Testament (e.g. Mark 8:31). For the Enoch literature, see editions of the *Apocrypha and Pseudepigrapha* by R. H. Charles [6] and James Charlesworth [7].

The same theme is developed in the second vision (chap. 8), whose interpretation was given by Gabriel, the patron angel of the Jewish people (cf. Dan. 12:1). A two-horned ram (the Medo-Persian empire) was charging to the west, north, and south. He held undisputed sway until a he-goat (the Greek empire), with a conspicuous horn between his eyes (Alexander the Great), came to engage him in battle and decisively defeated him. But when the he-goat was strong, the "great horn" was broken (the death of Alexander), and in its place came up four horns (the partition of Alexander's empire into four kingdoms). Out of one of these horns (the Seleucid kingdom) sprouted "a little horn" (Antiochus Epiphanes), whose power extended southward and eastward. In his pride, this horn exalted himself against the heavenly host, and challenged the authority of the Prince of the host (God) by defiling the Temple, casting down truth to the ground, and interrupting the daily sacrifice. The celestial being announced that the power of the boastful tyrant would be broken, although "by no human hand." The daily sacrifice would be resumed after 2,300 evenings and mornings—that is, the three years and two months from Antiochus' proscription of Jewish worship in 168 B.C.E. to Judas' rededication of the Temple in 165 B.C.E. Daniel was reminded that "the vision was for the time of the end," for it would be fulfilled "many days hence."

In the third vision, however, Daniel came to see that the "many days" were not too far away, for according to the divine timetable, the Kingdom of God was near at hand (chap. 9). Daniel was puzzled by Jeremiah's prophecy that seventy years must pass before the desolation of Jerusalem would be ended (Jer. 25:11–12; 29:10), and he prayed to God for light on this mystery. His prayer, like that of Ezra (Neh. 9), gratefully acknowledged Yahweh's great deeds of mercy, beginning with the deliverance from Egypt, and humbly confessed Israel's persistent covenant disloyalty for which great calamity had fallen on the people. His petition for speedy relief was not based on Israel's faithfulness to the covenant, but solely on Yahweh's steadfast and gracious goodness:

> For we do not present our supplications before thee on the ground of our righteousness, but on the ground of thy great mercy. O Lord, hear; O Lord, forgive; O Lord, give heed and act. . . .
>
> —DANIEL 9:18–19 (RSV)

It is worth noting that Judaism, even when it concentrated on obedience to the Law, affirmed that in the last analysis Israel had no ground for boasting—except the incalculable mercy of God. The parable that portrays the Pharisee boasting before God that he is better than other persons (Luke 8:11) is a caricature of Judaism, although devotion to the Law often did lead to self-righteousness.

While Daniel was praying, confessing his sin and the sin of his people Israel, the angel Gabriel came to interpret the seventy years (Dan. 9:20–27). In the prophecy of Jeremiah the figure seventy apparently referred to the full span of a human life; but here it comes to mean "seventy weeks of years" (490 years), at the end of which the Jews will have atoned for their sins and the desolation of Jerusalem will have ended. This period falls into three periods: seven weeks, sixty-two weeks, and one week. The first seven weeks (49 years) apparently extend from King Zedekiah to Joshua the High Priest (587–538 B.C.E.), who was in office in the days of Cyrus; the sixty-two weeks (435 years) extend from the return from Exile to the assassination of the High Priest Onias III (538–171); and the last week covers the reign of Antiochus Epiphanes. During the first half of this week (171–168), Antiochus showed some lenience toward the Jews; but during the last half (168–164), in which the author of Daniel was living, Antiochus attempted to abolish Jewish religion and desecrated the Temple by installing an altar to Zeus of Olympus. In Hebrew, this altar was ascribed to the ''Lord of heaven'' (*Baal shamáyim*), which came to be, by a malicious pun, ''the abomination of desolation'' (*shiqqutz shomem*; see 11:31; 12:11).

According to this view, history follows a prearranged timetable in which the length of each period is set by divine decree. Once we realize that the author was not really looking forward from the time of the Babylonian Exile, but looking backward over the ages from the Maccabean period, this mathematical calculation, even though too mechanical, has religious meaning. The writer believed that people were living in the ''last days,'' in the final moments of the second half of the last week of years. The days of Antiochus were numbered, for he had insulted God. The clock was beginning to strike midnight. The time was near when God, through a mighty act, would win the decisive victory, would end Israel's long years of desolation, and would introduce the messianic age. Unfortunately, this chronological calculation has led to many attempts, ancient and modern, to predict the date of the coming of God's Kingdom (but see Acts 1:7).

The author's backward glance from the Maccabean period also explains why historical knowledge about the period before the rise of Alexander is blurred, and why historical information becomes more exact and detailed as one comes closer to the time of writing. This point is illustrated in the final vision (chapters 10–12). Although it is dated in the third year of Cyrus of Persia (10:1), the Persian period is sketched in only one verse (11:2)—enough space, however, to make a major historical blunder, for ten Persian kings (not three) succeeded Cyrus. The author knows of Alexander's triumph over Persia (11:3; cf. 8:6–8, 21; 10:20), and the fact that, because he had no heir, his empire was divided (11:4; cf. 8:8, 22). From this point on, the author's historical memory improves, as the following explanatory summary of the biblical text (11:5–20) shows.

Ptolemy I (323–285), the king of the south, will establish a strong kingdom, but even stronger will be that of Seleucus I (312/11–280), the king of the north, whose kingdom will include Syria and Mesopotamia (11:5). Ptolemy II (285–246) will make an alliance with the Seleucid kingdom by marrying his daughter, Bernice, to Antiochus II (247 B.C.E.). This will anger Laodice, Antiochus' former wife, and she will conspire to have the couple and their son murdered (11:6). To avenge his sister Bernice, Ptolemy III (246–221) will march triumphantly against Seleucus II (246–226), the son of Laodice, but after a few years the latter will counterattack and a truce will be declared (11:7–9).

The seer's vision then focuses on the shift in the balance of power under two sons of Seleucus II—Seleucus III (226–223) and especially Antiochus III, the Great (223–187). The latter will be successful at first in a war against Egypt (11:10), but the king of the south, Ptolemy IV (221–203), will successfully counterattack at Raphia in 217 (11:11–12). Then, in the see-saw struggle, Antiochus will overrun Palestine by defeating the Egyptians at Gaza in 201 (11:13–15) and Panias in 198 (11:16). Hoping to secure his grip on Egypt, Antiochus will marry his daughter Cleopatra (not the same woman whose charms proved irresistible to Julius Caesar and Mark Antony) to Ptolemy V, but this move will not work to his political advantage (11:17). When he attempts to conquer "the coastlands" (Asia Minor and Greece), he will be defeated by a Roman general at Magnesia in 190, and on his return to his own country will die as a result of his plunder of a temple (11:18–19). Seleucus IV (187–175) will be assassinated by the very tax-collector he had appointed to raise money for the reparations owed to the Romans after the battle of Magnesia (11:20).

The rest of chapter 11 deals with prophecies concerning "a contemptible person," Antiochus IV Epiphanes. Pushing aside his brother, who legally had title to the throne (11:21), he will plot the assassination of "the prince of the covenant," the High Priest Onias III, in 171 B.C.E. (Dan. 11:22), and will plunder the riches of the provinces (11:23–24). After his first campaign against Egypt in the year 170, he will return in triumph to Palestine and set his heart against "the holy covenant," thus initiating his anti-Jewish program (11:25–28). His second campaign against Egypt (in the year 168), however, will be frustrated by the interference of "ships of Kittim" (the Romans) and, on his return, he will vent his spleen on the Jews, sparing only those who desert their faith (11:29–30). He will station his troops in the Temple area, abolish the daily sacrifices prescribed by the Torah, and set up "the abomination of desolation" on the altar (11:31). At this time, the lines will be drawn between the Jews who betray the covenant, and the Hasidim who stand firm under persecution, receiving "a little help" through the brave leadership of Judas Maccabeus (11:32–35). Antiochus will magnify himself above every god by taking the title Epiphanes, and will honor the Olympian Zeus, a Greek deity strange even to his own Syrian countrymen (11:36–39). Finally, "at the time of the end," Antiochus will attack the king of Egypt and win a great victory (11:40–43), but on his way home will die "by no human hand" (cf. 8:25) while encamped in Palestine between Jerusalem and the Mediterranean Sea (11:44–45).

Although Daniel's historical summary is cast in the form of a vision of events to come which are written down in God's "book of truth" (Dan. 10:21), actually very little of it is prediction in the proper sense of the word. Rather, it is primarily a resumé of past events. The only example of pure prediction is the prophecy concerning the death of Antiochus (Dan. 11:40–45), an event that had not yet transpired in the author's time. And this prediction lacks the accuracy of the author's treatment of past events of the Maccabean period, for Antiochus did not die near Jerusalem (the setting of the final apocalyptic battle), but in Persia in 163 B.C.E. (I Macc. 6:1–16; Josephus, *Antiquities*, xii, 9, 1). The author's haziness about this event supports the view that the book of Daniel was written before the death of Antiochus in the East, yet after the outbreak of the Maccabean revolution—in other words, between 168 and 164 B.C.E.

Thus the story of the past is told so that persecuted Jews may see their sufferings in the perspective of God's purpose in history. The author insists that none of these events happened by accident. Like a master chess player, God knew in advance every play that would be made and let the game run its course. Even the tyranny of Antiochus was part of God's preordained plan. "He shall prosper till the indignation is accomplished; for what is determined shall be done" (11:36). This extreme emphasis on God's absolute sway in human affairs was not intended to encourage complacency, any more than the Marxist vision of the inevitable movement of history toward the classless utopia is meant to discourage revolutionary activity. On the contrary, the confidence that history moves inevitably and by prearranged plan toward the Kingdom of God fired the zeal of a small band of Jews, and enabled them to act and hope when everything seemed against them. "The people who know God shall stand firm and take action" (11:32). If God was for them, what did it matter how many battalions were against them? And who cared how many battles were lost, so long as the saints were fighting on the winning side, which God would soon crown with victory? Here is expressed the dynamic faith of a courageous group who lived and died to the glory of God, confident that their martyrdom would "cleanse" and "refine" the community and somehow prepare for the coming of God's Kingdom (11:35).[19]

The Messianic Hope

In the book of Daniel there is no mention of the Anointed One (Messiah) who, in the last days, would appear as God's agent, either to execute judgment on Israel's oppressors or to rule over God's people in righteousness. To be sure, the expression "one like a human being [son of man]" was soon interpreted to mean a heavenly ruler whom God would send to shatter the powers of evil and to inaugurate the kingdom.[20] In Daniel 7, however, the heavenly figure symbolizes the covenant community—"the saints of the Most High"—as the interpretation of Daniel's dream makes clear. Yet in a broad sense this is a messianic passage, for the Hasidim are the standard-bearers for the Kingdom of God. In

---

[19] This view of martyrdom, which came to have great importance in Jewish circles and in later Christian history, is stressed in II Maccabees (chaps. 6–7), a book later than I Maccabees, probably dating from about the dawn of the Common Era.

[20] See the previous reference to Enoch and IV Ezra in the foregoing Definition, p. 627. For further discussion, see Sigmund Mowinckel, *He That Cometh*, trans. by. G. W. Anderson (New York: Abingdon, 1956), chap. 10.

their faithful martyrdom they bear witness to the Kingdom that God will in-augurate with power and glory at the end of the times. They live and die in anticipation of the messianic age, which, the writer believed, would soon dawn—indeed, according to one passage, in three and a half years (12:7), the time of the cessation of the regular sacrifices in the Temple (9:27; cf. 7:25).[21]

According to one strand of tradition, found in the Old Testament and later literature, the Messiah would be of David's lineage and would come to restore David's kingdom (see Isa. 9:1-7; 11:1-9). This political messianism, which filled the air in Jesus' day, is illustrated in a psalm from the late Maccabean period:[22]

> Behold, O Lord, and raise up unto them their king, the son of David,
> At the time in which thou seest, O God, that he may reign over Israel, thy servant.
> And gird him with strength, that he may shatter unrighteous rulers,
> And that he may purge Jerusalem from nations that trample her down to destruc-tion.
> —PSALMS OF SOLOMON 15:21-25 (RSV)

In the book of Daniel, however, the coming Kingdom is not portrayed in terms of political realities such as inspired the messianic movement in Zerubbabel's time (see pp. 515-519). Rather, the consummation is to be a divine victory, tran-scending and transfiguring the ordinary realities of history. So Daniel's last vi-sion finally leaves the sphere of politics, where the Seleucids and the Ptolemies vie for power, and moves on to a higher plane (chapter 12). The goal of history is *God's* Kingdom—not a human kingdom of any description or a utopia of any social planning. It will come solely by God's miraculous power and in God's good time. According to Daniel, the Kingdom will be preceded by "a time of trouble"—the birth pangs of the messianic age (Dan. 12:1). The faithful whose names are written in "the book" will be rescued from the trouble. Moreover, many who have already died will be raised up in order that they too may share in the grand fulfillment of the historical drama:

> And many of those who sleep in the dust of the earth shall awake, some to everlasting life, and some to shame and everlasting contempt. And those who are wise [the Hasidim] shall shine like the brightness of the firmament; and those who turn many to righteousness, like the stars for ever and ever.
> —DANIEL 12:2-3 (RSV)

This doctrine of the future life, one of the great contributions of apocalyptic literature, was late in coming. Unlike the Greek doctrine of the immortality of the soul, it is infused with the Israelite sense of history. According to Israel's way of thinking about the future, the individual cannot experience the fullness of life without participating in the redeemed community, the Kingdom of God.

---

[21] Later editors extended this time to 1,290 days (Dan. 12:11) and to 1,335 days (12:12).

[22] The Psalms of Solomon, found in a body of literature known as the Pseudepigrapha, date from about 50 B.C.E.

Therefore, the resurrection of the body (that is, the self) is portrayed as occurring in the end-time, at the very consummation of the historical drama, when God's victory over the powers of evil is complete. In one sense, the apocalyptic literature is other-worldly, for it proclaims that the historical drama points beyond the tragic strife of this world to God's ultimate kingdom. But in another equally important sense, it is profoundly this-worldly, for the sufferings of this world are to be fulfilled in history's grand finale. Unlike some forms of Eastern mysticism, it does not encourage a repudiation of this world, but appeals to the faithful to face present suffering in the confidence that the whole historical drama, from the beginning to end, is embraced within the sovereign plan of God.

BEYOND THE OLD TESTAMENT

With the book of Daniel the Old Testament period comes to a close—if we limit our attention to the books included within the Hebrew Bible.[23] Israel's life-story, as recorded in the pages of the Old Testament, ends on a note of intense expectation that soon the time would come of which the prophets had spoken: the dawning of God's Kingdom. But the apocalyptic vision of the speedy arrival of the messianic age—a vision that stirred faithful Jews to resist the tyranny of Antiochus Epiphanes—did not become a historical reality in the years that followed. Contrary to Daniel's dating of the time of the Kingdom, history moved on in its usual course. To be sure, the Maccabean revolution was successful for a time. But the successors of the Maccabees lost the religious zeal that had initially inspired the revolution, and turned to the old political game of intrigue and deceit, in which the reward for the successful schemer was the office of the high priesthood. Finally, after about a century of Jewish independence, the Jews were subjected to an empire that had not been envisioned in Daniel's scheme— the empire of Rome. This phase of the story of Israel lies beyond our purview.

Party Movements within Judaism

In the period between the outbreak of the Maccabean revolution and the dawn of the Common Era, the religious struggle continued. There were, to be sure, external sources of conflict, such as the rivalry with the Samaritans that exploded in 128 B.C.E. when one of the Maccabees, John Hyrcanus, conquered Shechem. And throughout the period the shadow of Rome was lengthening across the world. The struggle also went on, however, in the very heart of Judaism. All devout Jews subscribed to what is central in the book of Daniel: the authority of the Torah, the sacrificial services of the Temple, and the promise

---

[23] Other books found in the Greek Old Testament (Septuagint), such as I–II Maccabees and the Wisdom of Solomon, actually date from a slightly later period. In the arrangement of the Hebrew Bible, Daniel is found before the works of the Chronicler with which the list ends (see Chart, p. 642).

that God's Kingdom would have its center in the Holy Land. Party differences arose, however, over how the devout Jew should interpret these tenets of faith in the daily world.

One group, known as the Sadducees, advocated a policy of tolerance and compromise—an understandable attitude, since they came from families of priestly prestige and political influence. They claimed to be strict devotees of the Torah (the Pentateuch)—so strict that they would not accept the body of oral law that gathered around it. They rejected the doctrine of the resurrection because they found no support for it in the Torah (see Mk. 12:18), and for the same reason they opposed other aspects of apocalyptic thought, such as the belief in angels and demons, and predictions about the end-time. Their view of history was essentially that of the Priestly version of the Pentateuch (pp. 454–466), according to which the divine plan was realized in the establishment of a theocratic community, designed according to the pattern revealed to Moses. Instead of looking to the future, they sought to maintain this existing holy community by strict fidelity to the Torah, especially the regulations dealing with sacrifice and priestly prerogative. Since they were interested in the priestly *status quo*, they advocated a policy of collaboration with foreign rulers and even a certain degree of compromise with Hellenism, provided the Temple services were permitted to continue.

On the other side were various religious groups who stood in the tradition of the Hasidim, those whose zeal for the Torah brought them into conflict with Hellenistic culture and with all Jews who wanted to collaborate with foreign rulers. Like the author of the book of Daniel, they believed that the present age was under the dominion of wicked powers, and they anticipated the time when God would intervene and establish the Kingdom of God on earth, thus restoring the Holy Land to the Jewish people. Out of the circles of the Hasidim there eventually arose a party known as the Pharisees. Like Daniel and his friends, they practiced strict devotion to the customs that separated Jews from Gentiles: dietary rules, circumcision, fasting, prayer. Although in one sense they were stricter than the Sadducees, in another sense they were more liberal, for, unlike the latter, they accepted the teachings found in books outside the Torah, such as the Prophets. In addition, they believed that Moses had not only promulgated the written Torah but also a body of oral law that interpreted the meaning of what was written. This oral law, called "the tradition of the elders," was eventually codified in the Mishnah (c. 200 C.E.) and finally came out in an expanded edition known as the Talmud.[24]

The Pharisees, then, were able to adapt the rules and teachings of the written Torah to the changing conditions of life, and even to accept doctrines not found therein, like, the resurrection of the body and the apocalyptic Kingdom. Most Pharisees opposed fanatical revolt against foreign rulers. They preferred

---

[24] See H. Danby, *The Mishnah,* translated from the Hebrew with introduction and brief explanatory notes (Oxford: Clarendon Press, 1954). The Talmud is a large library. See Jacob Neusner, *Invitation to the Talmud* [490].

to maintain the strictest separation from the contaminations of the world, waiting for the time when God would establish the Kingdom. But closely related to the Pharisees was another group, known as the Zealots, whose views on political action were more in line with the Maccabean revolutionaries.

In 1947 C.E. and subsequent years public attention was aroused by the discovery of the Dead Sea Scrolls and the excavation of the ancient community headquarters of Essenes (or a closely related sect) located toward the northwest end of the Dead Sea near the mouth of the Wadi Qumran. The fascinating story of this community—its history, practices, and religious beliefs—would carry us far afield. Suffice it to say that this group, regarding itself as the community of ''the new covenant,'' separated itself from the world in order to practice a monastic devotion to the Torah and to await the end of the historical drama, when God would overthrow the powers of evil and inaugurate the divine Kingdom. In many respects these covenanters resembled the Hasidim of the early Maccabean period. Their zeal for the Torah and their hope for the apocalyptic Kingdom led them to revive the ancient conception of holy war (*ḥérem*), by which

Cave Number Four is located in a cliff overlooking the Wadi Qumran. In this cave were found many fragments of manuscripts that belonged to the library of the monastic community of the ancient Essenes. Some eleven caves in the area have yielded materials, including the famous Isaiah Scroll pictured on p. 8.

the land would be purified of the contaminations of pagan culture in "the war of the sons of light against the sons of darkness," and would be converted into the Holy Land. There are close affinities, and at the same time significant differences, between the eschatological beliefs of this Jewish sect and those of the early Christian community.[25]

It can be seen, then, that many currents were moving through Judaism in the two centuries preceding the Common Era. The book of Daniel is only one sample of the great amount of religious literature produced in this creative period. Some of this literature has been known for years, such as the writings found in the Apocrypha and the Pseudepigrapha. The manuscripts of Qumran include not only portions of the Hebrew Bible and manuals for the sect, but also a whole library whose fragmentary remains were found in caves near the community center.[26]

But of all the types of literature coming from this period—wisdom literature, history, short stories, psalms, interpretation of Torah—the most popular was the apocalypse. In troubled times, when faith was put to the severest tests, devout Jews hoped for the coming Kingdom. And since it came to be believed that "the exact succession of the prophets" ended in the time of Ezra (Josephus, *Against Apion*, i, 8) and even that prophecy had ceased altogether (see I Macc. 9:27), anonymous writers couched their prophecy in the form of a revelation (that is, apocalypse) given to a figure of ancient times, like Adam, Enoch, Noah, or Moses, or to a figure who lived in the centuries just before the cessation of prophecy, like Jeremiah, Baruch, Daniel, or Ezra. The apocalyptic hope for the Kingdom was one of the major influences upon the early Christian community.

The Canon of Israel's Scriptures

Clearly, devotion to the Torah was the unifying force of Judaism. Within this cohesive community there was great richness and diversity, however, as evidenced by the literature of the period and by the sectarian movements. The new horizons opened up by the study of the Qumran community show that "the tree whose trunk was the Old Testament had then many branches which later were lopped off or withered away."[27] This "lopping off" and "withering away" occurred during the terrible ordeals of Judaism in the Roman period, especially the smashing blow struck against Jewish nationalism by the war of 66–70 C.E., when the Temple was destroyed, never to stand again, and when Jews were

---

[25] See Frank M. Cross, Jr., *The Ancient Library of Qumran* [513], pp. 216–30; also "The Early History of the Apocalyptic Community at Qumran" [112], 326–42.

[26] Thanks to this archaeological discovery, we now have extensive manuscripts of the Hebrew Bible, such as the famous Isaiah Scroll (see p. 8). Before this discovery, with the exception of the small Nash Papyrus (first century C.E.) which contains a few verses of Exodus 20 and Deuteronomy 5–6, the oldest manuscripts of the Hebrew Bible came from the ninth century C.E. and later. Every book of the Hebrew Bible, except Esther, is represented, at least in fragmentary form, in the Qumran library.

[27] Millar Burrows, *The Dead Sea Scrolls* (New York: Viking Press, 1955), 345.

scattered or reduced to an insignificant remnant in Palestine. The Sadducees, whose religion was inseparably bound to the Temple, were shorn of their *raison d'être* by this catastrophe. Many of the covenanters of Qumran perished in the conflict, and their headquarters was destroyed, as we know from archaeological excavation. Only the Pharisees survived with strength. Their flexible interpretation of the written Torah, and their support of synagogue worship, enabled them to meet this crisis and to place the stamp of Pharisaic thought upon subsequent Judaism.

The crisis of Judaism resulting from the fall of Jerusalem and the destruction of the second Temple raised in a new way the question of the identity of the people known as Israel. In our study we have seen that this question had persisted ever since the formation of the community out of the historical oblivion of slavery in Egypt. In times of social change, as in the transition from tribal confederacy to monarchy, the question became inescapable; indeed, much of

Jewish Catacombs at Beth She'arim (Sheikh Ibreiq), located not far from modern Haifa. After the fall of Jerusalem in c.e. 70, and especially from the second to the fourth centuries, a loyal group of Jews lived here. Tombs were cut into the solid rock and arranged in stories. Of all the symbols carved in the interior, the menorah, or seven-branched candlestick, was the most important and apparently had a significance to Jews comparable to the cross in Christian catacombs.

the prophetic message should be understood as response in various theological accents to new situations. In times of political catastrophe, especially the first fall of Jerusalem in 587 B.C.E. and the uprooting of many of the people from their homeland, the "identity crisis" was met by priests who demonstrated the deep-lying continuity of the divine purpose, by prophets who announced the *Novum*—the "new thing" (Isa. 43:19)—that Yahweh was about to perform, and by sages who perceived the congruity between Wisdom and Torah.

It has also become clear in our study that these crises, which called into question both the identity and vocation of Israel and the identity and faithfulness of Yahweh, were not faced in a vacuum. The present was understood by appealing to, and reinterpreting, the heritage received from the past. God spoke to the people "in many and various ways" (Heb. 1:1) as inspired spokespersons kept alive and contemporized the sacred tradition, whether it existed in oral or written form, or both.

The new crisis that came upon Judaism in the centuries just before and after the dawn of the Common Era provided great impetus for the "stabilization" and "fixation" of the whole tradition. The loss of Judaism's vital center—the Temple in the Holy Land—posed the threat that the tradition would be distorted or weakened by various cultural influences and that Jews, scattered from the vital center, would lose their sense of identity and vocation. The result was an increasing concern for "scripture" (i.e., what is written) and "canon" (the writings that are normative for faith and practice).

DEFINITION: "CANONICAL CRITICISM"

Previously, in connection with the discussion of Ezra as the architect of Judaism (Chapter 15), we touched briefly on the question of canon. It was noted that the word, which literally means "a measuring line" or "rule," usually refers to sacred writings that conform to the "rule" of the community's faith and practice.

This is a narrow definition, however, which hardly does justice to the biblical canon, and especially to recent discussions about "canonical criticism." Two main views have emerged.

The first, championed by Brevard Childs (see especially his *Introduction to the Old Testament as Scripture* [37]), places the emphasis on the final form of a biblical book or canonical unit (e.g. the Pentateuch). By final form Childs does not mean the form given to a writing by redactors who revised given materials for a new situation in the life of the people. That kind of study, or other modes of historical criticism (source, form, stylistic [rhetorical] criticism) may have value in helping us to understand the prehistory of the final text. Childs, however, does not want his approach to be regarded as "canonical criticism," if that means another mode of criticism which is added to and crowns historical-critical methods. The various modes of historical criticism, he contends, attempt to go behind the text and reconstruct a prior text or prior historical situations in the life of the people of God. But to read a book in "canonical context" is to read it as it was shaped by the community of faith through use in worship and teaching, that is, as "scripture" in which the word of God is mediated through the *given* written form. The Pentateuch (Torah), for instance, is to be read "holistically" as a work in which the parts are related to one another, and hence as a work in which the whole is greater than the sum of the parts. The same applies to each book within the whole, e.g. Genesis, which in its final, canonical shape "serves the community of faith and practice as a truthful witness to God's activity on its behalf in creation and blessing, judgment and forgiveness, redemption and promise" (*Introduction*, p. 158).

The other view, advocated by James A. Sanders (see his *Torah and Canon* and *Canon and Community* [85 and 86]), places the emphasis upon "the canonical process." By this is meant the whole sweep of Israel's history of traditions in which the word of God comes to the community of faith as their heritage is reappropriated and contemporized in ever-new situations in history. "The Bible," he says, "is a veritable textbook in contemporization of tradition" (*Canon and Community*, p. 27). To be sure, "canonical criticism is very interested in what a believing community had in mind at that passing moment when the final form was achieved," but it does not concentrate on that "moment," for once the text was "frozen into final form" the community found ways "to break it down to reapply to their purposes and needs" (Ibid, p. 25). There were "periods of intense canonical process," such as the period after the first fall of Jerusalem in the sixth century B.C.E. and especially the period around the second fall of Jerusalem in the first century C.E., but *tradition*, even when fixed in scripture, always proved to be "adaptable for life" and hence was able to answer for the believing community "the two essential and existential questions of *identity* and *lifestyle*" (Ibid, pp. 28ff.).

The reader will notice that the story/history approach of this book leans more toward so-called "canonical process" than to the hermeneutical stance which seems to place excessive weight upon the final "scriptural" or "canonical" shape given the traditions in the late period of biblical Judaism.

At one time, a great deal of emphasis was placed on the rabbinical discussions held in an academy established at Jabneh, or Jamnia (the name used in Christian circles), on the coast of Palestine. The school was founded by a certain Rabbi Johannan ben Zakkai, who had escaped from Jerusalem during the bitter siege of the city. By attracting to it some of the ablest and most learned Jewish leaders, Jamnia came to be an important center of Pharisaic Judaism. Scholars formally referred to the "Council of Jamnia" held about 90 C.E.

It is now increasingly recognized, however, that the question of "canonicity" was not decided in conciliar debate in a fashion analogous to early Christian councils that dealt with theological and christological matters (e.g. Nicea). One Jewish scholar warns against the notion that Jamnia was a kind of modern convention during which rabbis debated an agenda and reached binding decisions by vote. "Canon," he says, "was a matter of the evolution of opinions which converged over a period of decades, 90 being a likely terminal date, but far from a definite one."[28]

Undoubtedly rabbinical discussions at Jamnia were very influential, but they were not decisive. Long before this, the main contours of the scriptural "canon" were in the process of being determined. The Torah (Pentateuch), as we have seen in an earlier chapter, was promulgated by Ezra as the authoritative basis of the post-exilic covenant community, and from that day on it had a unique place in Jewish life. Moreover, shortly after 200 B.C.E. the collection known as the Prophets (Former and Latter) was regarded as sacred scripture—for in-

---

[28] Samuel Sandmel, *The Hebrew Scriptures* [45], p. 14, footnote 6. See also Jack P. Lewis, "What Do We Mean by Jabneh?" in *Journal of Bible and Religion*, 32 (1964), 125–32.

stance, in the prologue to Ecclesiasticus (c. 130 B.C.E.). By the time of the New Testament, "the Law and the Prophets" was a standing expression for Jewish Scripture (Matt. 22:40; Luke 24:27). In addition, a third collection of miscellaneous literature, called the Writings (Hagiographa), was gradually taking shape. One of these books, the Psalms, gained a place of scriptural importance owing to the use of the psalms in worship (see Luke 24:44). Thus well before Jamnia, the community of faith had been registering its verdict on the authority of certain books by making them central in its life and worship.

It has become increasingly clear, however, that there was considerable fluidity in the boundaries of Jewish scripture, especially beyond the authoritative nucleus of the Torah. Striking evidence of this fluidity has come from Palestine itself—from the monastary of Qumran, referred to earlier. The library of the Essene community, founded during the life of the Maccabean brothers, contained—as we would expect—"biblical" books such as the famous Isaiah manuscript, and numerous commentaries on biblical books such as Psalms, Hosea, Habakkuk, and Nahum. But in addition the library contained a rich variety of apocryphal and pseudepigraphical writings, some of which were scarcely known before.[29] All of this prompts one scholar to observe: "Pluralism is a part of responsible perception of the concept of canon."[30]

Further evidence of the fluidity in the understanding of "scripture" is found in the Greek version of the Old Testament (Septuagint) which was produced by Hellenistic Jews in Alexandria. At the basic level, the student is confronted with the problem of trying to establish the scriptural text itself (so-called text criticism). The many differences between the received Hebrew text and the Greek version have been explained in various ways. According to one hypothesis, there were several textual traditions in the period of biblical Judaism: a) an Egyptian text which was the basis of the Septuagint; b) a Palestinian text that included the Samaritan version of the Pentateuch; and c) a Babylonian text that eventually was adopted as the standard (Masoretic) text, the one that students of biblical Hebrew study today. According to another view, there was a "central stream" of textual tradition, with variant rivulets running alongside of it.[31]

Furthermore, the Greek translation indicates that there was flexibility in regard to the number of books regarded as scripture. As the accompanying chart shows, the Egyptian Jews translated a larger number of books than we find in the received Hebrew Bible. The differing scriptural usage of Jews in Palestine and Jews in Alexandria seems to point to an uncertainty about the extent of the sacred writings. It is not surprising, then, that the theologians of the early Christian church were not clear about the extent of the Old Testament. Jerome (c. 342–419 C.E.), the great scholar who translated the Latin Vulgate, was inclined

---

[29] See Frank M. Cross, Jr., *The Ancient Library of Qumran* [513], 30–47.

[30] J. A. Sanders, *Canon and Community* [521], p. 15.

[31] For futher discussion, see J. A. Sanders, "Text and Canon: Concepts and Method," *Journal of Biblical Literature* 98 (1979), 5–29.

to follow the "Babylonian" tradition and to relegate the "extra" writings found in the Septuagint to a secondary place. But his contemporary, Augustine (354–430 C.E.), insisted that the catalog of Old Testament books also included books found in the Septuagint scriptural tradition which had been established in the usage of the Christian church. For a long time uncertainty about the extent of the so-called "Old Testament" continued in the Christian community.[32]

In the Jewish community, however, the canonical issue was more or less settled by around 100 C.E., with the academy of Jamnia providing great leadership in rabbinical discussions. To be sure, the rabbinical opinions expressed were "unofficial," that is, not "conciliar"; but in the light of further discussion and the needs of the Jewish community, they were accepted as valid.[33] The major uncertainty was over which books belonged to the Writings; there was no question about the authority of the Torah, and by this time there was general agreement on the number of books that belonged in the category of Prophets. It stands to reason that in this discussion a major criterion was harmony with the scriptural Torah. The book of Esther, for instance, posed difficulties, for besides its seemingly secular character, it deals with a festival (Purim) for which there is no explicit provision in the Torah. Even the book of Ezekiel was questioned by some rabbis, for at some points it seems to conflict with prescriptions of the Torah (compare, for instance, Ezek. 46:6 with Num. 28:11). According to the Talmud, one rabbi filled three hundred jars of oil and, as modern students would say, "burned the midnight oil" until he solved the problem. The Pharisaic freedom of interpretation, based on the oral law, meant that the principle of harmony with the scriptural Torah could be applied flexibly.

Another principle applied by the rabbis was a doctrine of prophetic inspiration that assumed that prophecy ceased in the post-exilic period, just after the time of Ezra. According to this view, Haggai, Zechariah, and Malachi were the last of the prophets, for—as the rabbis said—with their death "the Holy Spirit departed from Israel." Therefore, only writings coming from the period before the cessation of prophetic inspiration were regarded as having religious authority. This criterion may have been adopted because the rabbis believed that the more recent prophetic (apocalyptic) movement, closely associated with the Maccabean revolt and the war of 66–70 C.E., had finally been proved false by historic tragedy in Palestine. In any case, this principle automatically excluded books that were known to have arisen in the Hellenistic period, like the Wisdom of Ben Sira or I and II Maccabees. The rabbis had serious questions about the

---

[32] The issue came to the fore in the sixteenth century. The Protestant Reformers, insisting upon a return to the Bible, called for the elimination of the extra books not found in the Hebrew Bible. The disputed writings were put in a separate section, entitled "Apocrypha," either at the end of the Old Testament or of the entire Bible, with the note that they deserve to be read but are not equal with canonical books. The Roman Catholic Church at the Council of Trent (1545–1563 C.E.) officially adopted a larger canon, which included both protocanonical and deuterocanonical books (see above, p. 5, footnote 3 and chart, pp. 4–5). The acceptance of deuterocanonical books was based on long use of these books in Christian liturgy.

[33] See Alfred C. Sundberg, Jr. [522], chap. 8, on "The Jewish Canon."

The Old Testament Canon*

The Hebrew Bible or Masoretic Text	The Septuagint or Greek Version
I. THE TORAH The five books of Moses, each designated according to opening words.	*PENTATEUCH* Genesis Exodus Leviticus Numbers Deuteronomy

II. NEBI'IM (Prophets)
Former Prophets:
  Joshua
  Judges
  I-II Samuel
  I-II Kings
Latter Prophets:
  Isaiah
  Jeremiah
  Ezekiel
  The Twelve:
    Hosea, Joel, Amos, Obadiah, Jonah, Micah,
    Nahum, Habakkuk, Zephaniah, Haggai,
    Zechariah, Malachi
	HISTORICAL BOOKS
	Joshua
	Judges
	Ruth
	I-II Kingdoms (I-II Sam.)
	III-IV Kingdoms (I-II Kings)
	I-II Paralipomenon (I-II Chron.)
	*Esdras A*ᵃ
	Esdras B (Ezra-Nehemiah)
	Esther (plus *Additions to Esther*)
	Judith
	Tobit
	I-II Maccabees
	*III-IV Maccabees*ᵇ

III. KETHUBIM (Writings) Tehillim (Songs of Praise) Job Proverbs The Festal Scrolls: Ruth, Song of Songs, Ecclesiastes, Lamentations, Esther Daniel Ezra-Nehemiah I-II Chronicles	*POETRY AND WISDOM* Psalms Odes of Solomon including the *Prayer of Manasseh*ᶜ Proverbs Ecclesiastes Song of Solomon (Song of Songs) Job *Wisdom of Solomon* *Ecclesiasticus* (Wisdom of Ben Sira) *Psalms of Solomon* *PROPHETIC WRITINGS* The Twelve: Hosea, Amos, Micah, Joel, Obadiah, Jonah, Nahum, Habakkuk, Zephaniah, Haggai, Zechariah, Malachi Isaiah Jeremiah *Baruch* Lamentations *Letter of Jeremiah*ᵈ Ezekiel Daniel, plus additions: *The Story of Susanna* *The Song of the Three Children* *The Story of Bel and the Dragon*

*Items found in the Protestant Apocrypha are italicized. Compare this list with the one found on pp. 4–5, where deuterocanonical books of the Catholic canon are indicated.

Song of Songs and Ecclesiastes, but these books were admitted on the supposition that Solomon had written them. Finally, the rabbis rejected books written in Greek, since that language was not employed in the period of prophetic inspiration. On this basis, writings like the Wisdom of Solomon were rejected, even though they had been published under the name of great figures of Israel's tradition.

These criteria may strike us as rather arbitrary. It would certainly not have detracted from Jewish scripture if, for instance, some reason had been found to include the Wisdom of Ben Sira or some of the psalms from the Qumran community. We must remember, however, that the question of the authority of most of the writings now found in the Hebrew Bible had been answered before the closure of the canon, especially in the worship practice of the community. Those writings were preserved and used devotionally which spoke authoritatively to the community of faith.

ISRAEL'S PILGRIMAGE

Pausing for a concluding moment to survey the ground covered in this book, one point stands out clearly: the Old Testament represents the memories and interpretations of the historical experiences of Israel, from the formation of the community to the time of its great test of faith in the Maccabean period. It is Israel's life-story—a story that cannot be told adequately apart from the conviction that God had called this people in grace, separated them from the nations for a special responsibility, and commissioned them with the task of being servants of, and witnesses to, the One who is Creator of the universe and Ruler of human history. Remembering its sacred past and preserving its traditions, the "pilgrim people" were able to live in the present with their face set toward the future—the time of the new covenant, the new creation, the Kingdom of God. The scriptures of Israel end like an incomplete drama. According to Pharisaic Judaism, Israel's pilgrimage leads through the Hebrew Bible to the Talmud and to a continued life of messianic expectancy. According to the early Christian community, the pilgrimage of the people of God leads through the Old Testament to Jesus, the Christ, who came not to destroy, but to fulfill the Torah and the Prophets.

---

[a]Esdras A is I Esdras in the Protestant Apocrypha and III Esdras in the Vulgate tradition. The Protestant Apocrypha also includes an apocalyptic book called II Esdras from the close of the first century C.E. Since the Council of Trent, these works have been printed in the Roman Catholic Vulgate as appendices to the New Testament, where they are called III and IV Esdras. The Greek text of the main part of II (IV) Esdras (chaps. 3–14) has been lost.

[b]Though popular in parts of the ancient church, these never gained canonical recognition.

[c]This beautiful prayer, based on a late tradition in II Chron. 33:11–13, is found as a separate entry in the Protestant Apocrypha. It is not part of the Roman Catholic canon but, since the Council of Trent, has been included as an appendix to the Vulgate.

[d]This letter, supposedly the one Jeremiah sent to Jewish exiles in 597 B.C.E., is often attached to the book of Baruch. It is included as a separate entry in the RSV of the Apocrypha.

Comprehensive
Chronological Chart

B.C.E.	Egypt	Palestine and Syria	Mesopotamia (and Asia Minor)
2000 to 1900 *(Middle Bronze Age)*	XII Dynasty	Egyptian Control	Third Dynasty of Ur (c. 2060–1950) Hurrian Movement Amorite Invasion
1900 to 1800	XII Dynasty		First Babylonian Dynasty (c. 1830–1530)
1800 to 1700	Hyksos Invasion (c. 1720)	Abraham	The Mari Age Hammurabi (c. 1728–1686)
1700 to 1600	Hyksos Rule (XV to XVI Dynasties) XVII (Theban Dynasty)	Hyksos Control Descent of Jacob family into Egypt	Decline of Babylonia
1600 to 1500 *(Late Bronze Age)*	XVIII Dynasty Ahmose (c. 1552–1527) Expulsion of Hyksos	Egyptian Control	Old Hittite Empire (c. 1600–1500)
1500 to 1400	Thutmose III (c. 1490–1436)		Kingdom of Mitanni (c. 1500–1370)
1400 to 1300	Amenhotep III (c. 1403–1364) Amenhotep IV or Akhnaton (c. 1364–1347)	Amarna Age (c. 1400–1350) Egyptian Weakness	New Hittite Empire (c. 1375–1200) Rise of Assyria (c. 1356–1197)
1300 to 1200	XIX Dynasty: Seti I (c. 1305–1290) Rameses II (c. 1290–1224) Merneptah (c. 1224–1211)	Egyptian Revival (The Exodus, c. 1280) Israelite Conquest (c. 1250–1200) Merneptah's Victory (c. 1220)	Assyrian Dominance
1200 to 1100 *(Iron Age)*	XX Dynasty (c. 1185–1069) Sea Peoples defeated by Rameses III (c. 1175) Egyptian decline	Period of the Judges (c. 1200–1020) Philistines settle in Canaan Battle of Megiddo (c. 1125)	Collapse of Hittite Empire Assyrian decline
1100 to 1000	XXI Dynasty (c. 1069–935) Egyptian decline	Philistine ascendancy Fall of Shiloh (c. 1050) Samuel and Saul (c. 1020–1000)	Brief Assyrian revival Tiglath-pileser I (c. 1116–1078)

B.C.E.	*Egypt*	*Palestine*		*Phoenicia*	*Mesopotamia*
(Iron Age)	Decline XXII Dynasty Shishak I (c. 935–914)	THE UNITED KINGDOM David, c. 1000–961 Solomon, c. 961–922 Division of the kingdom at death of Solomon, c. 922		Hiram I, c. 969–936	Assyrian Decline
1000 to 900	Shishak invades Judah c. 918	THE DIVIDED KINGDOM JUDAH DAVIDIC DYNASTY: Rehoboam, c. 922–915 Abijah (Abijam), c. 915–913 Asa, c. 913–873	ISRAEL Jeroboam I, c. 922–901 Nadab, c. 901–900		Assyrian Revival
900 to 850	Egyptian Weakness	Jehoshaphat, c. 873–849 Jehoram, c. 849–843 Ahaziah, c. 843/2	Baasha, c. 900–877 Elah, c. 877–876 Zimri, c. 876 (7 days) *Omri Dynasty:* Omri, c. 876–869 Ahab, c. 869–850 (*Elijah*, c. 850) Ahaziah, c. 850–849 Jehoram, c. 849–843/2	SYRIA Ben-hadad I, c. 885–870 Ben-hadad II, c. 870–842	Adad-nirari II, c. 912–892 Ashur-nasir-apal II, c. 884–860 Shalmaneser III, c. 859–825 Battle of Qarqar, 853
850 to 750	Decline	Athaliah, c. 842–837 Joash, c. 837–800 Amaziah, c. 800–783 Uzziah (Azariah), c. 783–742	*Jehu Dynasty:* Jehu, c. 843/2–815 Joahaz, c. 815–801 J(eh)oash, c. 802–786 Jeroboam II, c. 786–746 (*Amos,* c. 750) (*Hosea,* c. 745) Zechariah (6 mos.), c. 746–745	Hazael, c. 842–806	(Jehu pays tribute, 841) Shamshi-Adad V, c. 824–812 Adad-nirari III, c. 811–784 Decline

B.C.E.	Egypt	Palestine — DIVIDED KINGDOM		SYRIA	Mesopotamia — ASSYRIA
		JUDAH	ISRAEL		
750 to 700	Decline	Jotham (regent), c. 750–742 Jotham (king), c. 742–735 (Isaiah, c. 742–700) Jehoahaz (Ahaz), c. 735–715 Invasion by Syro-Israelite Alliance, 735 (Micah: before 722 to c. 701)	Shallum (1 mo.), c. 745 Menahem, c. 745–737 Pekahiah, c. 737–736 Pekah, c. 736–732 SYRO-ISRAELITE ALLIANCE Hoshea, c. 732–724 FALL OF SAMARIA 722–721	Rezin, c. 740–732 FALL OF SYRIA, 732	Tiglath-pileser III, c. 745–727 EXPANSION OF ASSYRIAN EMPIRE Siege of Damascus, 732 Shalmaneser V, 726–722 Siege of Samaria, 722/721 Sargon II, 721–705 Siege of Ashdod, 712 Sennacherib, 704–681 Invasion of Palestine, 701
	XXV Dynasty (Ethiopian) c. 716/15–663	JUDAH Hezekiah, c. 715–687/6			

Date	Egypt	Judah	Assyria / Babylonia
700 to 600	Tirhakah, c. 685/4–664 Invasion by Assyria, 671 Sack of Thebes, 663, by Ashurbanapal XXVI Dynasty, c. 664–525 Psammetichus I c. 664–610 Necho II, 610–593	Manasseh, 687/6–642 Amon, 642–640 Josiah, 640–609 First show of Judean independence, 629 (Zephaniah, c. 628–622) (Jeremiah, c. 626–587) Josiah's "Deuteronomic Reform," 621 Death of Josiah at Megiddo, 609 Jehoahaz II (Shallum), 609 (3 mos.) Jehoiakim (Eliakim), 609–598/7 (Habakkuk, c. 605)	Esarhaddon, 680–669 Invasion of Egypt, 671 Ashurbanapal, 668–627 RISE OF BABYLONIA Nabopolassar, 626–605 Fall of Ashur to Medes, 614 Fall of Nineveh to Medes and Babylonians, 612 Babylonian defeat of Assyrians and Egyptians at Haran, 609 Battle of Carchemish, 605 FALL OF ASSYRIA

B.C.E.	Egypt	Palestine	Mesopotamia
			BABYLONIA
600 to 500	Apries (Hophra), 589–570	THE BABYLONIAN EMPIRE Jehoiachin (Jeconiah), 3 mos., 598–597 First Deportation to Babylonia, 597 Zedekiah (Mattaniah), 597–587 FALL OF JERUSALEM SECOND DEPORTATION, 587 BABYLONIAN EXILE *Ezekiel*, c. 593–573 (*Second Isaiah*, c. 540) Edict of Cyrus, 538 THE EMPIRE OF PERSIA THE RESTORATION JUDAH Return of exiles Rebuilding of Temple, 520–515 (*Haggai*) (*Zechariah*)	Nebuchadrezzar, 605/4–562 Nabonidus, 556–539 (his son: Belshazzar) RISE OF PERSIA Cyrus II, 550–530 Defeat of Media, c. 550 Invasion of Lydia, c. 546 FALL OF BABYLON, 539 Cambyses, 530–522 Darius I, 522–486
500 to 400	Conquest by Persia, 525 Egypt under Persian rule, 525–401	(*Malachi*, c. 500–450) Ezra's mission, 458 (?) Nehemiah arrives, 445 Ezra's mission, c. 428 (?)	PERSIA Xerxes I (Ahasuerus), 486–465 Artaxerxes I (Longimanus), 465–424 Xerxes II, 423 Darius II, 423–404
		Ezra's mission, c. 398 (?)	Artaxerxes II (Memnon), 404–358 Artaxerxes III, 358–338 Arses, 338–336 Darius III, 336–331

B.C.E.	Egypt	Palestine	Mesopotamia
		EMPIRE OF ALEXANDER THE GREAT, 336–323	
400 to 300	*Ptolemaic Kingdom* Ptolemy I, 323–285	Egyptian Control	*Seleucid Kingdom* (Mesopotamia and Syria) Seleucus I, 312/11–280
300 to 200	Ptolemy II, 285–246 Ptolemy III, 246–221 Ptolemy IV, 221–203	Egyptian Control	Antiochus I, 280–261 Antiochus II, 261–246 Seleucus II, 246–226 Seleucus III, 226–223 Antiochus III, 223–187
200 to 100	Ptolemy V, 203–181 Ptolemy VI, 181–146 Ptolemy VII, 146–116	Seleucid (Syrian) Conquest, 200–198 MACCABEAN REVOLT, 168 (167) Judas, 166–160 Jonathan, 160–143 Simon, 143–134 John Hyrcanus, 134–104 Conquest of Shechem, 128	Seleucus IV, 187–175 Antiochus IV (Epiphanes), 175–163 Antiochus V, 163–162 Demetrius I, 162–150 Alexander Balas, 150–145 Demetrius II, 145–138 Antiochus VI, 145–141 Antiochus VII, 138–129
100 to C.E.	Roman Conquest, 30	Pompey captures Jerusalem, 63 THE EMPIRE OF ROME	Roman occupation of Syria, 63

Selected
Bibliography

No attempt has been made to mention all important books on Old Testament subjects or even to include everything referred to in footnotes. Rather, the list includes selected basic works which will be valuable to the student who for the most part is confined to what is available in English. To facilitate footnote references, the various items are listed by number.

TOOLS FOR BIBLE STUDY

TRANSLATIONS: When a student is unable to read the Old Testament in the original language, it is important to consult more than one recent translation. Among the best are:

The Revised Standard Version (Division of Christian Education, 1973). This translation, endorsed by Protestant, Roman Catholic, and Eastern Orthodox representatives, has been issued as the *Common Bible* (New York: Collins, 1973).

The New American Bible (New York: P. J. Kenedy & Sons, 1970). A translation by members of the Catholic Biblical Association of America.

The New English Bible (New York: Oxford University Press, 1970). A vivid, idiomatic translation by British scholars.

The Jerusalem Bible (Garden City, N.Y.: Doubleday, 1966). Another translation by Roman Catholic scholars.

The New International Version (Grand Rapids, Mich.: Zondervan, 1978). A fresh translation by a team of "evangelical" scholars.

The Torah, The Prophets, The Writings. A new translation of the Holy Scriptures according to the Masoretic text (Philadelphia: Jewish Publication Society of America, 1962-1967). A translation by Jewish scholars, soon to be available in a one-volume edition.

Extra-biblical Sources

1. *Ancient Near Eastern Texts Relating to the Old Testament*, 3rd ed. with supplement, ed. by J. B. Pritchard (Princeton: Princeton University Press, 1969). A basic tool for the study of the Old Testament period.

2. *The Ancient Near East in Pictures Relating to the Old Testament*, 2nd ed. by J. B. Pritchard (Princeton: Princeton University Press, 1969).

3. *The Ancient Near East: An Anthology of Texts and Pictures*, ed. by J. B. Pritchard (Princeton: Princeton University Press, 1965). Contains selections from Nos. 1 and 2.

4. *Documents from Old Testament Times*, ed. by D. Winton Thomas (New York: Nelson, 1958). Contains a smaller collection of texts than Pritchard's work [1].

5. *Near Eastern Texts Relating to the Old Testament*, ed. by W. Beyerlin, Old Testament Library (Philadelphia: Westminster, 1978).

6. *Apocrypha and Pseudepigrapha of the Old Testament*, 2 vols., ed. by R. H. Charles (Oxford: Clarendon, 1912).

7. *The Old Testament Pseudepigrapha*, ed. by James H. Charlesworth (Garden City, N.Y.: Doubleday). vol. I: Apocalyptic Literature and Testaments (1983); vol. II dealing with ''expansions of the 'Old Testament' '' a..d other literature is scheduled for 1985.

Single Volume Commentaries

8. *The Interpreter's One Volume Commentary on the Bible*, ed. by Charles M. Laymon (New York: Abingdon, 1971).

9. *Jerome Biblical Commentary*, 2 vols. bound together, ed. by Raymond E. Brown, J. A. Fitzmeyer, and Roland E. Murphy (Englewood Cliffs, N.J.: Prentice-Hall, 1969). An excellent commentary by Roman Catholic scholars; revised edition forthcoming.

10. *The New Oxford Annotated Bible with Apocrypha*, ed. by Herbert G. May and Bruce M. Metzger (New York: Oxford University Press, 1973). Based on the Revised Standard Version and provided with brief articles, notes, maps, and other aids.

11. *The New English Bible with the Apocrypha*: Oxford Study Edition, ed. by Samuel Sandmel (New York: Oxford University Press, 1976). Provided with introductions, annotations, maps, and other aids.

Commentary Sets

12. *The Anchor Bible*, ed. by W. F. Albright and D. N. Freedman (Garden City, N.Y.: Doubleday). Still in process, this series contains fresh translations and commentary.

13. *The Cambridge Bible Commentary on the New English Bible*, ed. by P. R. Ackroyd et al. (Cambridge: Cambridge University Press). A series of brief commentaries begun in 1972.

14. *Hermeneia: A Critical and Historical Commentary*, ed. by Frank M. Cross et al. (Philadelphia: Fortress). Volumes of this important series appear from time to time.

15. *Interpretation: A Bible Commentary for Teaching and Preaching*, ed. James L. Mayes, Patrick D. Miller, and Paul J. Achtemeier. (Atlanta, Ga.: John Knox Press). A promising series begun in 1980.

16. *The Interpreter's Bible*, ed. by G. A. Buttrick (New York: Abingdon, 1952–57). Some of the commentaries, by a previous generation of scholars, still deserve attention.

17. *The New Century Bible Commentary*, ed. by Ronald E. Clements and Matthew Black (Grand Rapids, Mich.: Eerdmans). A series based on the Revised Standard Version.

18. *The Old Testament Library*, ed. by Peter Ackroyd, Bernhard W. Anderson, James L. Mays. (Philadelphia: Westminster). An outstanding series.

19. *Torch Bible Commentaries*, ed. by John Marsh et al. (London: SCM, 1952 and onwards).

Bible Dictionaries and Reference Works

20. *The Books of the Bible*, ed. by Bernhard W. Anderson. Basic treatments of the books of the Old Testament, New Testament, and Apocrypha (New York: Scribner's, forthcoming).

21. *Dictionary of the Bible*, ed. by James Hastings, rev. by F. C. Grant and H. H. Rowley (New York: Scribner's, 1963).

22. *Encyclopedic Dictionary of the Bible*, ed. and trans. by Louis F. Hartman (New York: McGraw-Hill, 1963). A comprehensive work by Roman Catholic scholars.

23. *Harper's Bible Dictionary*, ed. by Paul J. Achtemeier (San Francisco: Harper & Row, Pubs., 1985). A basic reference work.

24. *International Standard Bible Encyclopedia*, rev. ed., 4 vols., ed. by B. W. Bromiley et al. (Grand Rapids, Mich.: Eerdmans, 1979 and on). A work by a team of ''evangelical'' scholars.

25. *The Interpreter's Dictionary of the Bible*, 4 vols., ed. by G. A. Buttrick et al. (New York: Abingdon, 1962). A standard work.

26. *The Interpreter's Dictionary of the Bible*, Supplementary Volume, ed. by Keith Crim et al. (New York: Abingdon, 1976). Updating of some of the entries in the work listed above.

27. *Theological Dictionary of the Old Testament*, in several volumes, ed. by G. J. Botterweck and Helmer Ringgren, trans. by J. T. Willis et al. (Grand Rapids, Mich.: Eerdmans, 1974 and on).

Bible Atlases and Geography

28. Aharoni, Y., *The Land of the Bible*, trans. by A. F. Rainey (Philadelphia: Westminster, 1967).
29. Grollenberg, L. H., *Atlas of the Bible*, trans. and ed. by J. Reid and H. H. Rowley (New York: Nelson, 1956). An unusually impressive work.
30. Baly, Denis, *The Geography of the Bible*, 2nd ed. (New York: Harper & Row, Pub., 1974). See also his collaborative work with Douglas Tushingham, *The Atlas of the Biblical World* (New York: World Publishing Co., 1971).
31. Aharoni, Y. and M. Avi-Yonah, *The Macmillan Bible Atlas* (London and New York: Macmillan, 1968).
32. May, Herbert G., *Oxford Bible Atlas*, 3rd ed., revised by John Day (New York: Oxford University Press, 1984).
33. Smith, G. A., *Historical Geography of the Holy Land*, 25th ed. (New York: A. C. Armstrong & Son, 1931). A classic.
34. *The Westminster Historical Atlas to the Bible*, rev. ed., edited by G. Ernest Wright and Floyd V. Filson (Philadelphia: Westminster, 1956).

Journals

The best way to keep abreast of biblical research is to read the journals. A good nontechnical journal is *Interpretation*, published quarterly (Richmond, Va.); also *The Expository Times*, published monthly (Edinburgh). Other important quarterly journals, to mention a few, are

The Catholic Biblical Quarterly
The Journal of Biblical Literature
Journal for the Study of the Old Testament
Vetus Testamentum

In the field of archaeology, there are two nontechnical journals: *The Biblical Archaeologist*, and *The Biblical Archaeology Review*.

A new journal, *Bible Review*, entered the field in 1985 and promises to do interesting things in the field of biblical interpretation.

Introductions to the Old Testament

In recent years many general introductions have appeared, many of them based on a book by book approach to the Old Testament. For the most part the following selected list is limited to more technical works.

35. Anderson, G. W., *A Critical Introduction to the Old Testament* (London: Duckworth, 1959). See also his nontechnical survey *The History and Religion of Israel* (London: Oxford University Press, 1966).
36. Bentzen, Aage, *Introduction to the Old Testament*, I–II, 2nd ed. (Copenhagen: G. E. C. Gad, 1952). A balanced presentation by a Scandinavian scholar, stressing the importance of oral tradition.
37. Childs, Brevard S., *Introduction to the Old Testament as Scripture* (Philadelphia: Fortress Press, 1979). Not an "introduction" in the technical sense, so much as a foundation for a canonical approach. Note the excellent bibliographies.
38. Driver, S. R., *Introduction to the Literature of the Old Testament*, rev. ed. (New York: Scribner's, 1913; Meridian, 1956). A classic work, helpful for understanding the literary criticism of an older generation.
39. Eissfeldt, Otto, *The Old Testament: An Introduction*, trans. from the 3rd German edition by P. R. Ackroyd (New York: Harper & Row, Pub., 1965). Preeminent among works of this kind.
40. Fohrer, Georg, *Introduction to the Old Testament*, trans. by David E. Green (Nashville: Abingdon, 1968). A thorough revision of Ernst Sellin's *Introduction* (1910), stressing a form-critical approach.
41. Gottwald, Norman K., *The Hebrew Bible: A Socio-Literary Introduction* (Philadelphia: Fortress, 1985). A comprehensive approach based on the sociological premises of his previous work, *The Tribes of Yahweh* [240].
42. Harrelson, Walter, *Interpreting the Old Testament* (New York: Holt, Rinehart & Winston, 1964). A one-volume commentary based on the structure of the Hebrew canon.

43. Kaiser, Otto, *Introduction to the Old Testament: A Presentation of Its Results and Problems*, trans. by John Sturdy (Minneapolis: Augsburg, 1974).

44. La Sor, W. S., D. A. Hubbard, and F. W. Bush, *Old Testament Survey: The Message, Form, and Background of the Old Testament* (Grand Rapids, Mich.: Eerdmans, 1982). An "evangelical" approach, based on "verbal inspiration," although open to critical biblical scholarship.

45. Sandmel, Samuel, *The Hebrew Scriptures: An Introduction to their Literature and Religious Ideas* (New York: Knopf, 1963). A presentation by an eminent Jewish scholar.

46. Soggin, J. A., *Introduction to the Old Testament*, Old Testament Library [18], 1976.

47. Weiser, Artur, *The Old Testament: Its Formation and Development*, trans. from the 4th German ed. by Dorothea M. Barton (New York: Association Press, 1960).

BIBLICAL CRITICISM

History of Biblical Criticism

48. *The Cambridge History of the Bible*, vol. I, From the Beginnings to Jerome, ed. by P. R. Ackroyd and C. F. Evans; vol. II, The West from the Fathers to the Reformation, ed. by G. W. H. Lampe; vol. III, The West from the Reformation to the Present Day, ed. by S. L. Greenslade (London: Cambridge University Press, 1970).

49. Clements, R. E., *One Hundred Years of Old Testament Interpretation* (Philadelphia: Westminster, 1976).

50. Fishbane, Michael, "Jewish Biblical Exegesis: Presuppositions and Principles," *Scripture in the Jewish and Christian Traditions: Authority, Interpretation, Relevance*, ed. by Frederick E. Greenspahn (Nashville: Abingdon, 1982), 91–110.

51. Frei, Hans, *The Eclipse of Biblical Narrative* (New Haven: Yale University Press, 1974). A penetrating discussion of biblical interpretation since the Enlightenment.

52. Froehlich, Karlfried, *Biblical Interpretation in the Early Church* (Philadelphia: Fortress, 1984). A valuable translation and introduction to major sources for understanding biblical interpretation in the "patristic" period. Notice the bibliography.

53. Grant, R. M., *A Short History of the Interpretation of the Bible*, a revised and updated version of *The Bible in the Church* (Philadelphia: Fortress Press, 1983). With a special word from David Tracy on the modern use of the Bible.

54. Hahn, H. F., *The Old Testament in Modern Research*, 3rd ed. with bibliographical survey by Horace D. Hummel (Philadelphia: Fortress, 1966).

55. Knight, Douglas A. and Gene M. Tucker, *The Hebrew Bible and Its Modern Interpreters* (Philadelphia: Fortress, 1985). Deals with the history of biblical interpretation in the period after World War II.

56. Kraeling, Emil G., *The Old Testament Since the Reformation* (New York: Harper & Row, Pub., 1955; Schocken Books, 1969). A helpful survey of the history of historical criticism.

57. Smalley, B., *The Study of the Bible in the Middle Ages*, 2nd ed. (Oxford: Basil Blackwell, 1952).

Methods of Biblical Criticism

Depending on the nature of the material under study, biblical texts may be approached from various angles.

58. Amerding, Carl E., *The Old Testament and Criticism* (Grand Rapids, Mich.: Eerdmans, 1983). A general introduction to methods of biblical criticism, written particularly for "evangelicals."

59. Barton, John, *Reading the Old Testament: Method in Biblical Study* (Philadelphia, Pa.: Westminster Press, 1984). A judicious discussion of various approaches to the Bible, including the "canonical" approach advocated by Brevard Childs [37].

1. Source Criticism (see p. 22)

Note: This method is advocated in older Introductions, e.g., S. R. Driver [38]; see the summary by Walter Harrelson [42], pp. 28–40, and his source analysis of the Pentateuch, pp. 28–40, and further, the appendix to Martin Noth's *Pentateuchal Traditions* [70].

60. Cassuto, U., *The Documentary Hypothesis and the Composition of the Pentateuch*, trans. by Israel Abrahams (Jerusalem: Magnes, 1961). A criticism of the source hypothesis by a Jewish scholar.

61. Clements, R. E., "Pentateuchal Problems," in *Tradition and Interpretation* [153], 96–124. A judicious discussion which upholds, in general, the results of literary criticism, although welcoming subsequent developments in scholarly research.

62. Habel, Norman C., *Literary Criticism of the Old Testament* (Philadelphia: Fortress, 1971).

63. Wolff, H. W. and Walter Brueggemann, *The Vitality of Old Testament Traditions*, 2nd ed. (Atlanta: John Knox Press, 1982). Essays on the "kerygma" or message of various literary traditions: the Yahwist (J), the Elohist (E), the Deuteronomistic Historian, the Priestly Writer (P).

2. Form Criticism (see Definition, p. 547)

64. Hayes, John, ed., *Old Testament Form Criticism* (San Antonio: Trinity University Press, 1974). Essays dealing with various types of Old Testament literature.

65. Koch, Klaus, *The Growth of the Biblical Tradition: the Form-critical Method*, trans. by S. M. Cupitt (New York: Scribner's, 1969). A basic work.

66. Tucker, Gene M., *Form Criticism of the Old Testament* (Philadelphia: Fortress, 1971). A helpful, brief introduction.

See also the projected series, under the editorship of Rolf Knierim and Gene M. Tucker, which "eventually will present a form-critical analysis of every book and each unit of the Old Testament," as evidenced, for instance, in George W. Coats' study on Genesis [268]. A special issue of *Interpretation* (Vol. 27, No. 4, 1973), is devoted to this method of biblical interpretation.

3. History of Traditions

This method, based on a form-critical analysis of the genres of oral tradition, studies the history of the transmission of the tradition through various stages of composition until the end result of canonical scripture.

67. Coats, G. W., "Tradition Criticism, O. T." in Supplement to *The Interpreter's Dictionary of the Bible* [26], 912–914.

68. Jeppensen, Knud and Benedikt Otzen, eds., *Tradition History in Old Testament Scholarship* (Decatur, GA: Almond Press, forthcoming).

69. Knight, Douglas, *Rediscovering the Traditions of Israel* (Missoula: Scholars Press, 1975). See the review of *Tradition and Theology in the Old Testament* by B. W. Anderson, *Religious Studies Review*, vol. 6, no. 2 (1980), 104–110, where this method is evaluated.

70. Noth, Martin, *A History of Pentateuchal Traditions*, trans. with introduction by Bernhard W. Anderson (Chico, CA: Scholars Press, 1981; original German edition, 1948). A fundamental work in the field of traditio-historical investigation.

71. Rast, Walter E., *Tradition History and the Old Testament* (Philadelphia: Fortress, 1972).

The so-called Scandinavian School rejects source criticism and emphasizes the oral history of traditions. See:

72. Anderson, G. W., "Some Aspects of the Uppsala School of Old Testament Study," in *Harvard Theological Review*, XLIII (1950), 239–56.

73. Engnell, Ivan, *A Rigid Scrutiny: Critical Essays on the Old Testament*, trans. and ed. by John T. Willis (Nashville: Vanderbilt University Press, 1969). One of the leaders of the Uppsala School.

74. Nielsen, Eduard, *Oral Tradition*, Studies in Biblical Theology, No. 11 (Naperville: Alec R. Allenson, 1954).

4. Rhetorical (Stylistic) Criticism

This method attempts to move "beyond form criticism" into a study of the literary and structural features in a particular text of scripture.

75. Muilenburg, James, "Form Criticism and Beyond," *Journal of Biblical Literature* 88 (1969), 1–18.

76. Jackson, Jared J. and Martin Kessler, eds., *Rhetorical Criticism* [162]. See the introductory essay by B. W. Anderson, "The New Frontier of Rhetorical Criticism."

Excellent studies in rhetorical criticism are found in Phyllis Trible, *God and the Rhetoric of Sexuality* [145], chap. 4, "A Love Story Gone Awry." See also B. W. Anderson, " 'The Lord Has Created Something New': A Stylistic Study of Jer. 31:15-22," *Catholic Biblical Quarterly* 40 (1978), 463-478; reprinted in Perdue and Kovacs, eds., *A Prophet to the Nations* [382], 367-380.

5. Redaction Criticism
(see Definition, p. 394)

77. Anderson, Bernhard W., "From Analysis to Synthesis: the Interpretation of Genesis 1-11," *Journal of Biblical Literature* 97 (1978), 23-39.
78. Perrin, Norman C., *What is Redaction Criticism?* (Philadelphia: Fortress, 1969). Although this book deals with the New Testament, the method is also pertinent to the Old Testament.

The essay by Hans Walter Wolff, "The Kerygma of the Deuteronomic Historical Work," in *The Vitality of Old Testament Traditions* [63], is essentially a study in redaction criticism.

6. Narrative Criticism
and Structuralism

79. Alter, Robert, *The Art of Biblical Narrative* (Philadelphia: Fortress, 1976). This essay, in the field of rhetorical criticism, picks up on contributions from "the new literary criticism."
80. Crenshaw, James L., *Samson: A Secret Betrayed, A Vow Ignored* (Atlanta: John Knox, 1978). The author describes his approach as "aesthetic criticism."
81. Culley, R. C., *Studies in the Structure of Hebrew Narrative* (New York: Basic Books, 1981).
82. Fishbane, Michael, *Text and Texture: Close Readings of Selected Biblical Texts* (New York: Schocken Books, 1979).
83. Patte, Daniel, *What is Structural Exegesis?* (Philadelphia: Fortress, 1976). Deals with the New Testament, but is relevant to biblical studies in general. Notice the bibliography.
84. Polzin, Robert M., *Biblical Structuralism: Method and Subjectivity in the Study of Ancient Texts* (Philadelphia: Fortress, 1977).

7. Canonical Criticism

This is a method which is related to tradition-history and redaction criticism.

85. Sanders, J. A., *Torah and Canon* (Philadelphia: Fortress, 1972). See also his essay "Adaptable for Life: The Nature and Function of Canon," in *Magnalia Dei* [157], 531-560.
86. Sanders, J. A., *Canon and Community: A Guide to Canonical Criticism* (Philadelphia: Fortress, 1984).

See also the canonical approach advocated by Brevard Childs in his *Introduction* [37]. For critical responses, see James Barr, *Holy Scripture: Canon, Authority, Criticism* [see 130], and John Barton, *Reading the Old Testament* [59].

8. Sociological Approach

87. Gottwald, Norman, "Sociological Method in the Study of Ancient Israel," in *Encounter with the Text* [155], 69-82. This approach is spelled out in his *Tribes of Yahweh* [240] and *Introduction* [41].
88. Wilson, Robert R., *Sociological Approaches to the Old Testament* (Philadelphia: Fortress, 1984). A new, and yet not so new (cf. Max Weber), horizon in biblical studies.

HISTORY OF ISRAEL

89. *Cambridge Ancient History* see especially Vol. I, 1, 3rd ed. (London: Cambridge University Press, 1975). This important work is constantly being updated.
90. Albright, W. F., *The Biblical Period from Abraham to Ezra* (Pittsburgh: Biblical Colloquium, 1950; New York: Harper & Row, 1963). A concise history of Old Testament times.
91. Bright, John, *A History of Israel*, 3rd ed. (Philadelphia: Westminster, 1981). Highly recommended.
92. De Vaux, Roland, *The Early History of Israel*, trans. by David Smith (Philadelphia: Westminster, 1978). An important work, left incomplete at the time of the author's death. The discussion extends from Israel's origins to the settlement in Canaan.

93. Hayes, John H. and J. Maxwell Miller, eds., *Israelite and Judaean History* (Philadelphia: Westminster, 1977). The various essays include thorough bibliographies.

94. Hermann, Siegfried, *A History of Israel in Old Testament Times*, trans. by John Bowden (Philadelphia: Fortress, 1975). Excellent brief history.

95. Jagersma, H., *A History of Israel in the Old Testament Period*, trans. by John Bowden (Philadelphia: Fortress, 1983).

96. Kitchen, K. A., *The Bible in Its World: Archaeology and the Bible Today* (Exeter: Paternoster Press, 1977).

97. Meek, T. J., *Hebrew Origins*, rev. ed. (New York: Harper & Row, Pub., 1950; Harper Torchbook, 1960).

98. Noth, Martin, *The History of Israel*, 2nd ed., trans. by Stanley Godman from 2nd German edition and revised by P. R. Ackroyd (London: Adam and Charles Black, 1960). One of the major works in the field, by a leader of the German school of tradition-history.

99. Ramsey, George W., *The Quest for the Historical Israel* (Atlanta: John Knox Press, 1981). A valuable discussion which updates the student to the present situation in scholarship.

100. Soggin, J. Alberto, *A History of Ancient Israel: From the Beginnings to the Bar Kochba Revolt, A. D. 135,* trans. by John Bowden (Philadelphia: Westminster Press, 1985).

ARCHAEOLOGY

A good way to keep up with current archaeology is to read the quarterly issues of *The Biblical Archaeologist* (BA), published by the American School of Oriental Research, or *The Biblical Archaeology Review* (BAR).

101. *The Biblical Archaeologist Reader*, I (1961), II (1964), III (1970), IV (1983), ed. by G. E. Wright, E. F. Campbell, and D. N. Freedman. (New York: Doubleday Anchor). Selected articles from past issues.

102. Albright, W. F., *The Archaeology of Palestine.* (New York: Pelican, 1961). A fully revised publication by a distinguished American archaeologist. See also his *Archaeology and the Religion of Israel* [111].

103. Avi-Yonah, M. and Ephraim Stern, eds., *Encylopaedia of Archaeological Excavations in the Holy Land,* 2 vols. (London: Oxford University Press, 1975–1978). Important essays on sites excavated.

104. Freedman, David N. and Jonas C. Greenfield, eds., *New Directions in Biblical Archaeology* (Garden City, N.Y.: Doubleday, 1969).

105. Kenyon, Kathleen, *Archaeology in the Holy Land* (New York: Praeger, 1960). A basic work by a distinguished archaeologist.

106. Kitchen, K. A., *The Ancient Orient and the Old Testament* (Leicester: Intervarsity Press, 1966). See also *The Bible in Its World* [96].

107. Lapp, Paul W., *Biblical Archaeology and History* (New York: World, 1969).

108. Sanders, J. A., ed., *Near Eastern Archaeology in the Twentieth Century: Essays in Honor of Nelson Glueck* (Garden City, N.Y.: Doubleday, 1970).

109. Thomas, D. Winton, ed., *Archaeology and Old Testament Study* (Oxford: Clarendon, 1967). Jubilee volume of the British Society for Old Testament Study. See further J. Gray, "Recent Archaeological Discoveries and Their Bearing on the Old Testament," in *Tradition and Interpretation* [153], 65–95.

110. Wright, G. Ernest, *Biblical Archaeology*, 2nd ed. (Philadelphia: Westminster, 1962). A valuable book by an eminent authority.

RELIGION OF ISRAEL

111. Albright, W. F., *From the Stone Age to Christianity* (Baltimore: Johns Hopkins, 1940). Rev. ed. (New York: Doubleday Anchor, 1957). A classic in modern scholarship. See also his *Archaeology and the Religion of Israel*, 2nd ed. (Baltimore: Johns Hopkins, 1946; Doubleday, 1969).

112. Cross, Frank M., *Canaanite Myth and Hebrew Epic: Essays in the History of the Religion of Israel* (Cambridge, Mass.: Harvard University Press, 1973). Creative essays covering the whole Old Testament period.

113. De Vaux, Roland, *Ancient Israel: Its Life and Institutions*, trans. by John McHugh (London: Barton, Longman and Todd, 1961). A monumental study by the one-time director of the Dominican Ecole Biblique in Jerusalem.

114. Fohrer, Georg, *History of Israelite Religion*, trans. by David E. Green (Nashville: Abingdon, 1972).

115. Harrelson, Walter, "The Religion of Ancient Israel," *Listening: Journal of Religion and Culture,* 19 (1984), 19–29.

116. Kaufmann, Yehezkel, *The Religion of Israel*, trans. and abridged by Moshe Greenberg (Chicago: University of Chicago Press, 1960; Schocken, 1972). A provocative study by a highly original Jewish scholar who departs from many of the accepted tenets of historical criticism.

117. Pedersen, Johannes, *Israel: Its Life and Culture* I–II, 1926; III–IV, 1940 (New York: Oxford). A major study of the socio-psychological characteristics of ancient Israel.

118. Ringgren, Helmer, *The Religion of Israel* (Philadelphia: Fortress, 1966). One of the best works in this field.

119. Vriezen, Th. C. *The Religion of Ancient Israel*, trans. by Hubert Hoskins (Philadelphia: Westminster, 1967).

ANCIENT RELIGION IN GENERAL

120. Eliade, Mircea, *Cosmos and History: The Myth of the Eternal Return* (New York: Harper Torchbook, 1954). This work, and the one listed next, are indispensable studies of the religious mentality of the so-called archaic societies.

121. Eliade, Mircea, *The Sacred and the Profane: The Nature of Religion.* (New York: Harper Torchbook, 1961).

122. Frankfurt, H. and H. A., et al., *The Intellectual Adventure of Ancient Man* (Chicago: University of Chicago Press, 1946). Reprinted as *Before Philosophy* (New York: Penguin, 1949). See especially the chapters on Egypt and Babylonia.

123. Gaster, T. H., *Thespis: Ritual, Myth and Drama in the Ancient Near East* (New York: Henry Schuman, 1950; New York: Doubleday Anchor, 2nd ed., 1961). See also his compendium, *Myth, Legend, and Custom in the Old Testament* (New York: Harper & Row, Pub., 1969).

124. Kramer, S. N., ed., *Mythologies of the Ancient World* (Chicago: Quadrangle Books, 1961; New York: Doubleday Anchor, 1961).

125. Otto, Rudolf, *The Idea of the Holy*, 2nd ed., trans. by John W. Harvey (London: Oxford University Press, 1950). See also *Rudolf Otto: An Introduction to his Philosophical Theology*, by Philip C. Almond (Chapel Hill, N.C.: University of North Carolina Press, 1984).

126. Ringgren, Helmer, *Religions of the Ancient Near East*, trans. by John Sturdy (Philadelphia: Westminster, 1973).

127. Van der Leeuw, G., *Religion in Essence and Manifestation*, trans, by J. E. Turner (London: Allen & Unwin, 1938; New York: Harper Torchbook, incorporating the additions of the 2nd German edition by Hans H. Penner, ed. 1963).

OLD TESTAMENT THEOLOGY AND HERMENEUTICS

128. Anderson, Bernhard W., *Creation versus Chaos: The Reinterpretation of Mythical Symbolism in the Bible* (New York: Association Press, 1967).

129. Anderson, Bernhard W., ed., *Creation in the Old Testament* (Philadelphia: Fortress, 1984). The collection of essays includes an excerpt from Hermann Gunkel's classic, *Schöpfung und Chaos* (Creation and Chaos).

130. Barr, James, *The Bible in the Modern World* (New York: Harper & Row, Pub., 1973). A stimulating treatment of the authority and relevance of the Bible. See also his previous book, *Old and New in Interpretation* (New York: Harper & Row, Pub., 1966), and his *Holy Scripture: Canon, Authority, Criticism* (Philadelphia: Westminster, 1983).

131. Childs, Brevard, *Biblical Theology in Crisis* (Philadelphia: Westminster, 1970). Evaluates the "Biblical Theology Movement" in America since 1940 and proposes a new canonical approach.

132. Crenshaw, James L., ed., *Theodicy in the Old Testament* (Philadelphia: Fortress, 1983).

133. Clements, R. E., *Old Testament Theology: A Fresh Approach* (Atlanta: John Knox Press, 1978).

134. Davidson, Robert, *The Courage to Doubt: Exploring an Old Testament Theme* (London: SCM Press, 1983). An invigorating study of the faith that boldly seeks understanding.

135. Eichrodt, Walther, *Theology of the Old Testament*, vol. I, trans. by J. A. Baker from the 6th German ed. (Philadelphia: Westminster, 1961); vol. II (1967). One of the best theological works of our time, to be compared with the work by Gerhard von Rad listed below [142].

136. Hasel, Gerhard, *Old Testament Theology: Basic Issues in the Current Debate* (Grand Rapids, Mich.: Eerdmans, 1972).

137. Hayes, John H. and Frederick Prussner, *Old Testament Theology: Its History and Development* (Atlanta: John Knox Press, 1985).

138. Knight, Douglas A., ed., *Tradition and Theology in the Old Testament* (Philadelphia: Fortress, 1977). Theological essays based on a traditio-historical approach; see the review essay by B.

W. Anderson, *Religious Studies Review*, vol. 6, No. 2 (1980), pp. 104–110.

139. Laurin, Robert B., *Contemporary Old Testament Theologians* (Valley Forge, Pa.: Judson, 1970).

140. Levenson, Jon D., *Sinai and Zion: An Entry into the Jewish Bible* (Minneapolis: Winston-Seabury Press, 1985). A Jewish perspective on the relationship between two major theological trajectories in Hebrew scripture.

141. McKenzie, John, *A Theology of the Old Testament* (Garden City, N.Y.: Doubleday, 1974).

142. Rad, Gerhard von, *Old Testament Theology*, vol. I: The Theology of Israel's Historical Traditions, trans. by D. M. G. Stalker (New York: Harper & Row, Pub., 1962); vol. II: The Theology of Israel's Prophetic Traditions (1965). A major work based on the history of Israel's traditions; compare the work by Eichrodt listed above [135].

143. Sakenfeld, Katherine D., *Faithfulness in Action: Loyalty in Biblical Perspective* (Philadelphia: Fortress Press, 1985). See further her doctoral dissertation, *The Meaning of Ḥésed in the Hebrew Bible*, Harvard Semitic Monographs 17 (Missoula, Mont.: Scholars Press, 1973).

144. Terrien, Samuel, *The Elusive Presence: Toward a New Biblical Theology* (New York: Harper & Row, Pub., 1978).

145. Trible, Phyllis, *God and the Rhetoric of Sexuality* (Philadelphia: Fortress, 1978). A brilliant example of how rhetorical criticism (see above under "methods of biblical criticism, No. 4") illuminates biblical interpretation. See further her studies of troublesome Old Testament stories: *Texts of Terror: Literary-Feminist Readings of Biblical Narratives*, Overtures to Biblical Theology (Philadelphia: Fortress, 1984).

146. Voegelin, Eric, *Israel and Revelation* (Baton Rouge: Louisiana State University Press, 1956). A monumental work by a political philosopher. See the review essay by B. W. Anderson, "Politics and the Transcendent," in *Eric Voegelin's Search for Order in History*, ed. by Stephen A. McKnight (Baton Rouge: Louisiana State University Press, 1978), 62–100.

147. Vriezen, Th. C., *An Outline of Old Testament Theology*, trans. by S. Neuijen (Oxford: Blackwell, 1958).

148. Westermann, Claus, *Elements of Old Testament Theology*, tr. by Douglas W. Stott (Atlanta: John Knox, 1982). A central aspect of his theological exposition is developed in *Blessing in the Bible and in the Life of the Church*, Overtures to Biblical Theology, trans. by Keith Crim (Philadelphia: Fortress, 1978).

149. Wright, G. Ernest, *The Old Testament and Theology* (New York: Harper & Row, Pub., 1969). A vigorous theological discussion by an exponent of "theology of recitation" (see No. 174).

150. Zimmerli, Walther, *Old Testament Theology in Outline*, trans. by D. E. Green (Atlanta: John Knox Press, 1978).

Collected Essays (not listed in another category)

151. Alt, Albrecht, *Essays on Old Testament History and Religion*, trans. by R. A. Wilson (Garden City, N.Y.: Doubleday, 1967). Important essays by a leading German scholar of a former generation.

152. Anderson, Bernhard W., and Walter Harrelson, eds., *Israel's Prophetic Heritage; Essays in Honor of James Muilenburg* (New York: Harper & Row, Pub., 1962).

153. Anderson, G. W., ed., *Tradition and Interpretation* (Oxford: Clarendon, 1979). Essays on major aspects of Old Testament studies by members of the British Society for Old Testament Study.

154. Butler, James, Edgar Conrad and Bennie Ollenburger, eds., *Understanding the Word, Essays in Honor of Bernhard W. Anderson* (Sheffield: JSOT Press, 1985).

155. Buss, Martin, ed., *Encounter with the Text: Form and History in the Hebrew Bible* (Philadelphia: Fortress, 1979). A consideration of the central principles of interpretation, using various methods of approach.

156. Coats, George and Burke O. Long, eds., *Canon and Authority* (Philadelphia: Fortress, 1977). Essays dedicated to Walther Zimmerli.

157. Cross, Frank M., Werner E. Lemke, and Patrick D. Miller, eds., *Magnalia Dei: The Mighty Acts of God* (Garden City, N.Y.: Doubleday, 1976). Essays in memory of G. Ernest Wright.

158. Durham, John I., and J. R. Porter, eds., *Proclamation and Presence* (Richmond: John Knox Press, 1970). Essays in honor of G. H. Davies.

159a. Frank, H. T. and W. L. Reed, eds., *Translating and Understanding the Old Testament* (New York: Abingdon, 1970). A collection of essays in honor of Herbert G. May.

159b. Halpern, Baruch and Jon D. Levenson, eds., *Traditions in Transformation: Turning Points in Biblical Faith* (Winona Lake, IN: Eisenbrauns, 1984). Essays in honor of Frank M. Cross.

160. Huffmon, H. B., et al., *The Quest for the Kingdom of God, Studies in Honor of George E. Mendenhall* (Winona Lake, IN: Eisenbrauns, 1984).

161. Hyatt, J. Phillip, ed., *The Bible in Modern Scholarship* (New York: Abingdon, 1963).

162. Jackson, Jared J., and Martin Kessler, eds. *Rhetorical Criticism, Essays in Honor of James Muilenburg* (Pittsburgh, Pa.: Pickwick Press, 1974).

163. Mendenhall, George E., *The Tenth Generation: The Origins of the Biblical Tradition* (Baltimore: Johns Hopkins University Press, 1973). Creative essays on the period of Israel's origins, supplementing his seminal study on "The Hebrew Conquest of Palestine" [244].

164. Meyers, Carol L. and M. O'Connor, eds., *The Word of the Lord Shall Go Forth, Essays in Honor of David Noel Freedman* (Winona Lake, IN: Eisenbrauns, 1983).

165. Noth, Martin, *The Laws in the Pentateuch and Other Studies* (Philadelphia: Fortress, 1967).

166. Rad, Gerhard von, *The Problem of the Hexateuch and Other Essays* (New York: McGraw-Hill, 1966). The lead essay is especially important for understanding form criticism and the traditio-historical method.

167. Rowley, H. H., *From Moses to Qumran: Studies in the Old Testament* (London: Lutterworth Press, 1963).

168. Westermann, Claus, ed., *Essays on Old Testament Hermeneutics*, trans. and ed. by J. L. Mays (Richmond, Va.: John Knox Press, 1971).

169. Zimmerli, Walther, *The Law and the Prophets*, trans. by R. E. Clements (Oxford, Eng.: Blackwell, 1965).

READINGS CHAPTER BY CHAPTER

INTRODUCTION:
THE OLD TESTAMENT
AS THE STORY
OF A PEOPLE

170. Brueggemann, Walter, *The Creative Word: Canon as a Model for Biblical Education* (Philadelphia: Fortress, 1982).

171. Gese, Hartmut, "The Idea of History in the Ancient Near East and the Old Testament," *Journal for Theology and Church*, vol. 1 (1965), 49–64.

172. Herberg, Will, "Biblical faith as *Heilsgeschichte*: The Meaning of Redemptive History in Human Existence," in *Faith Enacted as History: Essays in Biblical Theology*, ed. by Bernhard W. Anderson (Philadelphia: Westminster, 1976), 32–42. In the same volume see the essay on "Five Meanings of the Word 'Historical,' " 132–137.

173. Niebuhr, H. Richard, *The Meaning of Revelation* (New York: Macmillan, 1941). Chap. 2, on "The Story of Our Life," is especially valuable in this connection.

174. Wright, G. Ernest, *God Who Acts*, Studies in Biblical Theology, No. 8 (Naperville, Ill.: Alec R. Allenson, 1952). An exposition of Israel's historically oriented faith. For a challenge to this understanding of biblical theology, see Brevard Childs, *Biblical Theology* [131].

CHAPTER 1:
CREATION OF A PEOPLE

The Nature of the Tradition

Today it is recognized that the refined analysis of putative literary "sources," as found, for instance, in S. R. Driver's *Introduction* [38], is inadequate. Attention has turned to a study of the oral formation and transmission of the traditions (form criticism, history of traditions, canonical criticism) or the formulation of the traditions in final, written form (rhetorical criticism, redaction criticism, structuralism) [See No. 64–86]. Also, attention has turned to the narrative character of Israel's history and the limitations of historical method.

175. Barr, James, "Story and History in Biblical Theology," *Journal of Religion* 56 (1976), 1–17.

176. Bright, John, *Early Israel in Recent History Writing*, Studies in Biblical Theology, 19 (London: SCM, 1965). A vigorous criticism of the historical approach of Martin Noth [98].

177. De Vaux, Roland, "Method in the Study of Early Hebrew History," in *The Bible in Modern Scholarship* [161], 15–29. See also the responses to this article by George E. Mendenhall and Moshe Greenberg in the same volume.

178. Harvey, Van A., *The Historian and the Believer* (New York: Macmillan, 1966). An important study of the relation between religious faith and a "scientific" approach to history. See further the book by George Ramsey, *The Quest* [99], chap. 1, "The Historian's Craft."

179. Miller, J. M., *The Old Testament and the Historian* (Philadelphia: Fortress, 1976). Guides to biblical scholarship.

180. Noth, Martin, "Analysis of the Elements of the Traditions," in *Pentateuchal Traditions* [69], 52ff. See also the translator's introductory essay on Noth's "traditio-historical approach."

181. Rad, Gerhard von, "The Form-critical Problem of the Hexateuch," in his volume of essays [166], 1–78. His position is summarized in his commentary on Genesis [271], pp. 1–23.

Historical and Religious Background— Period of Israel's Ancestors

182. Alt, Albrecht, "The God of the Fathers," in *Essays* [151], 1–100. A fundamental essay on "patriarchal" religion; compare Cross's essay listed next.

183. Cross, Frank M., "The Religion of Canaan and the God of Israel," [112], 1–75. An important and illuminating discussion based on his earlier essay, "Yahweh and the God of the Patriarchs," *Harvard Theological Review*, LV (1962), 225–259.

184. De Vaux, Roland, "The Hebrew Patriarchs and History," in *The Bible and the Ancient Near East, Essays in Honor of W. F. Albright*, ed. by G. Ernest Wright (Garden City: Doubleday, 1965), 111–121.

185. Greenberg, Moshe, *The Hab/piru* (New Haven: American Oriental Society, 1955). A basic work on the subject.

186. Holt, John, *The Patriarchs of Israel* (Nashville: Vanderbilt University Press, 1964). Emphasizes a core of historicity in patriarchal traditions; compare this view with the chapter on "The Patriarchal Period" in George W. Ramsey, *The Quest* [99], chap. 2.

187. Luke, J. T., "Abraham and the Iron Age: Reflections on the New Patriarchal Studies," *Journal for the Study of the Old Testament*, 4 (1977), 35–47. See other essays in this journal.

188. Mazar, B., "The Historical Background of the Book of Genesis," *Journal of Near Eastern Studies*, 28 (1969), 78–83.

189. McKane, W., *Studies in the Patriarchal Narratives* (Edinburgh: Handsel Press, 1979).

190. Rowley, H. H., *From Joseph to Joshua* (London: Oxford University Press, 1950). A valuable historical discussion, which needs to be updated in the light of subsequent archaeological research.

191. Thompson, T. L., *The Historicity of the Patriarchal Narratives, Beiheft zur Zeitschrift für die alttestamentliche Wissenschaft* 133 (1974). This monograph, and the book by Van Seters listed next, are at the center of current controversy.

192. Van Seters, J., *Abraham in History and Tradition* (New Haven: Yale University Press, 1975). Argues that Israel's Epic traditions date from the post-exilic period. Summarized in "Patriarchs," Supplement to *Interpreter's Dictionary of the Bible* [26], 645–648.

193. Wright, G. E., "History and the Patriarchs," in *Expository Times*, LXXI (1960), 292–96. See also the response by Gerhard von Rad, "History and the Patriarchs," in *Expository Times*, LXXII (1961), 213–216.

Neighboring Peoples

194. Albrektson, Bertil, *History and the Gods: An Essay on the Idea of Historical Events as Divine Manifestations in the Ancient Near East and in Israel* (Lund, Sweden: C. W. K. Gleerup, 1967). A challenge to the notion that the theme of divine acts in history was unique with Israel. See the review of this important book by W. G. Lambert, *Orientalia* 39 (1970), 170–77.

195. Dever, W. G., "The Peoples of Palestine in the Middle Bronze I Period," *Harvard Theological Review* 64 (1971), 197–226.

196. Gurney, O. R., *The Hittites*, 2nd ed. (New York: Pelican, 1954). An authoritative discussion.

197. Kramer, S. N., *The Sumerians: Their History, Culture, and Character* (Chicago: University of Chicago Press, 1963). One of the definitive works in this field.

198. Lichtheim, M., *Ancient Egyptian Literature*, I–II (Berkeley, Calif.: University of California Press, 1973–76).

199. Morenz, Siegfried, *Egyptian Religion*, trans. by Ann E. Keep (Ithaca, N.Y.: Cornell University Press, 1973).

200. Moscati, Sabatino, *The World of the Phoenicians*, trans. by Alastair Hamilton (New York: F. A. Praeger, 1968).

201. Oppenheim, A. Leo, *Ancient Mesopotamia: Por-*

trait of a Dead Civilization (Chicago: University of Chicago Press, 1964). Emphasizes the complexity and variety of Mesopotamian religion.

202. Pitard, Wayne T., Ancient Damascus: A Historical Study of the Syrian City-State from Earliest Times Until Its Fall to the Assyrians in 732 B.C.E. (Winona Lake, IN: Eisenbrauns, forthcoming).

203. Saggs, H. W. F., The Greatness that Was Babylon (New York: Hawthorne Books, 1962).

204. Steindorff, George, and Keith C. Seele, When Egypt Ruled the East, 2nd ed. (Chicago: University of Chicago Press, 1957; Phoenix, 1963). Reliable, interestingly written, beautifully illustrated.

205. Wilson, John A., The Burden of Egypt (Chicago: University of Chicago Press, 1951). The Culture of Ancient Egypt (1963). An illuminating exposition of Egyptian history and culture. See especially chaps. 7–10.

CHAPTER 2: LIBERATION FROM BONDAGE

206. Beegle, Dewey M., Moses, Servant of Yahweh (Grand Rapids, Mich.: Eerdmans, 1972). Advocates the essential historicity of the Moses story on the basis of literary criticism and archaeology.

207. Buber, Martin, Moses (London: East & West Library, 1946; Harper Torchbook, 1968). Selections from this study by the great Jewish philosopher appear in The Writings of Martin Buber, part II, ed. by Will Herberg (New York: Meridian, 1956).

208. Campbell, Edward F., "Moses and the Foundations of Israel," Interpretation, 29 (1975), 141–154.

209. Cassuto, U., A Commentary on the Book of Exodus, trans. by Israel Abrahams (Jerusalem: Magnes, 1967). An important work by a Jewish scholar who rejects the conclusions of source criticism.

210. Childs, Brevard S., The Book of Exodus, The Old Testament Library [18], 1974. A fresh study which stresses the place of the book of Exodus in the biblical canon.

211. Clements, Ronald E., Exodus, Cambridge Commentary on the New English Bible [13], 1972.

212. Croatto, J. Severino, Exodus: A Hermeneutics of Freedom, trans. by Salvator Attanasio (Maryknoll, N.Y.: Orbis Books, 1981). A superb example of Latin American "liberation theology." See also the works of Gustavo Gutierrez, e.g.

A Theology of Liberation (Maryknoll, N.Y.: Orbis Books, 1973) and The Power of the Poor in History (Maryknoll, N.Y.: Orbis Books, 1983).

213. Fackenheim, Emil L., God's Presence in History: Jewish Affirmations and Philosophical Reflections (New York: Harper & Row, Pub., 1970). A profound philosophical discussion of Exodus and Sinai in Jewish tradition.

214. Greenberg, Moshe, Understanding Exodus (New York: Melton Research Center of the Jewish Theological Seminary of America, 1969). A very helpful commentary.

215. Miller, Patrick D., The Divine Warrior in Early Israel (Cambridge, Mass.: Harvard University Press, 1973).

216. Nicholson, E. W., Exodus and Sinai in History and Tradition (Richmond: John Knox, 1973).

217. Noth, Martin, Exodus, trans. by J. S. Bowden, The Old Testament Library (Philadelphia: Westminster, 1962). This commentary is too brief to do justice to Noth's work.

218. Rad, Gerhard von, Moses, World Christian Books (London: Lutterworth, 1960). A profound little book, simply written.

219. Widengren, G. "What Do We Know About Moses?" in Proclamation and Presence [158], 21–47.

CHAPTER 3: COVENANT IN THE WILDERNESS

220. Alt, Albrecht, "The Origins of Israelite Law," in Essays [151], 101–71. A basic form-critical study of types of law in the Pentateuch.

221. Baltzer, Klaus, The Covenant Formulary in the Old Testament, Jewish and Early Christian Writings, trans. by David E. Green (Philadelphia: Fortress, 1971). One of the basic studies of the treaty or covenant form.

222. Beyerlin, Walter, Origins and History of the Oldest Sinaitic Traditions, trans. by Stanley Rudman (Oxford: Blackwell, 1965). Argues that Exodus and Sinai traditions have a common origin. See also E. W. Nicholson [216].

223. Coats, George W., Rebellion in the Wilderness (New York: Abingdon, 1968).

224. Harrelson, Walter, The Ten Commandments and Human Rights, Overtures to Biblical Theology (Philadelphia: Fortress, 1980).

225. Hillers, Delbert R., Covenant: The History of a Biblical Idea (Baltimore: Johns Hopkins, 1969). Clearly written, illuminating discussion of covenant language and motifs in the Old Testa-

ment. See further the work of Mendenhall listed below [229].

226. Huffmon, Herbert B., "The Exodus, Sinai and the Credo," in *Catholic Biblical Quarterly*, XXVII (1965), 101–13.

227. McCarthy, Dennis J., *Treaty and Covenant, A Study in Form in the Ancient Oriental Documents and in the Old Testament* (Analecta Biblica 21; Rome: Pontifical Biblical Institute, 1963). Another important investigation of the relation between Israel's covenant form and the treaty form of Hittite (also pre-Hittite and non-Hittite) documents.

228. McCarthy, Dennis J., *Old Testament Covenant* (Richmond: John Knox Press, 1972). A summary of discussions on the subject.

229. Mendenhall, George E., *Law and Covenant in Israel and the Ancient Near East* (Pittsburgh: Biblical Colloquium, 1955), reprinted from *The Biblical Archaeologist*, XVII, 2 (May 1954), 26–46; and no. 3 (Sept. 1954), 49–76. A seminal discussion of Israel's covenant tradition, seen in the light of Hittite parallels. See also his later article, "Covenant," *The Interpreter's Dictionary* [25], and his book, *The Tenth Generation* [163].

230. Muilenburg, James, "The Form and Structure of the Covenantal Formulations," *Vetus Testamentum*, IX (1959), 347–65.

231. Newman, Murray Lee, *The People of the Covenant: A Study of Israel from Moses to the Monarchy* (New York: Abingdon, 1962). An analysis of two major covenant traditions, showing their bearing upon Israel's history.

232. Nielsen, Eduard, *The Ten Commandments in New Perspective*, trans. by David J. Bourke, Studies in Biblical Theology, 2nd series, No. 7 (Naperville, Ill.: Alec R. Allenson, 1968).

233. Noth, Martin, "The Laws in the Pentateuch: Their Assumptions and Meaning," in *Essays* [165], 1–107.

234. Stamm, J. J. and M. E. Andrew, *The Ten Commandments in Recent Research*, Studies in Biblical Theology, 2nd series, No. 2 (Naperville, Ill.: Alec R. Allenson, 1967). See also the discussion of the Decalogue in Brevard Childs' commentary [210], pp. 385–439.

CHAPTER 4: THE PROMISED LAND

On the geography of Canaan see especially Nos. 28–34.

235. Alt, Albrecht, "The Settlement of the Israelites in Palestine," *Essays* [151], 133–169.

236. Bright, John, "Introduction and Exegesis to the Book of Joshua," in *Interpreter's Bible*, II [16]. See further his *History* [91], chap. 3.

237. Brueggemann, Walter, *The Land, Overtures to Biblical Theology* (Philadelphia: Fortress, 1977).

238. Conrad, Edgar W., *Fear Not Warrior: A Study of 'al tîra' Pericopes in the Hebrew Scriptures*, Brown Judaic Studies (Chico, CA: Scholars Press, 1985).

239. Freedman, D. N. and D. F. Graf, *Palestine in Transition: The Emergence of Ancient Israel* (Sheffield, England: The Almond Press, 1983). Important essays dealing with the origins of Israel, especially in the light of the sociological approach advocated by Gottwald [240].

240. Gottwald, Norman, *The Tribes of Yahweh: A Sociology of the Religion of Liberated Israel, 1250–1050 B.C.E.* (Maryknoll, N.Y.: Orbis Books, 1979). A monumental study which builds on Mendenhall's thesis of a "peasant revolt" [244], and uses a sociological method for interpreting Israel's early history.

241. Kenyon, Kathleen, *Digging Up Jericho* (New York: Praeger, 1957). By the distinguished archaeologist who excavated the ancient city.

242. Lapp, Paul, "The Conquest of Palestine in the Light of Archaeology," *Concordia Theological Monthly*, 38 (1967), 283–300.

243a. Lind, Millard C., *Yahweh is a Warrior: The Theology of Warfare in Ancient Israel* (Scottdale, PA: Herald Press, 1980). A fresh and illuminating treatment of the subject.

243b. Mayes, A. D. H., *The Story of Israel between Settlement and Exile: A Redactional Study of the Deuteronomistic History* (London: SCM Press, 1983).

244. Mendenhall, George E., "The Hebrew Conquest of Canaan," *The Biblical Archaeologist*, XXV (1962), 66–87; reprinted in *Biblical Archaeological Reader*, III [100], 100–120. See further *The Tenth Generation* [163]. A seminal and influential theory that the conquest was a revolution within Canaan.

245. Miller, J. M., and G. M. Tucker, *The Book of Joshua*, Cambridge Bible Commentary [13], 1974.

246. Noth, Martin, *The Deuteronomistic History*, Supplement to *Journal for the Study of the Old Testament*, 15 (Sheffield: JSOT Press, 1981). A fundamental work on the Deuteronomistic History; the section on the Chronicler's Work is not translated.

247. Rad, Gerhard von, *Holy War in Ancient Israel*, trans. by E. W. Conrad and M. Lattke, with an introduction by E. W. Conrad (Sheffield: JSOT Press). Forthcoming.

248. Soggin, J. A., *Joshua*, trans by R. A. Wilson, Old Testament Library [18], 1972. Advocates essentially the view of Noth.

249. Weippert, Manfred, *The Settlement of the Israelite Tribes in Palestine*, Studies in Biblical Theology, 2nd series, No. 21 (Naperville, Ill.: Alec R. Allenson, 1971). An important study which advocates the "peaceful entry" hypothesis.

250. Wright, G. Ernest, "The Literary and Historical Problems of Joshua 10 and Judges 1," *Journal of Near Eastern Studies* 5 (1946), 105–114. Argues that the two accounts reflect different phases of Israel's incursion into Canaan.

251. Wright, G. Ernest, *Shechem: The Biography of a Biblical City* (New York: McGraw-Hill, 1965). A vivid account of the results of excavation at the former center of the Tribal Confederacy.

252. Yadin, Yigael, *Hazor: The Rediscovery of a Great Citadel of the Bible* (London: Weidenfeld & Nicolson, 1975).

See also the works cited under "History" and "Archaeology."

CHAPTER 5: THE FORMATION OF AN ALL-ISRAELITE EPIC

On Myth and Legend

253. Anderson, Bernhard W., "Mythopoeic and Theological Dimensions of Biblical Creation Faith," in *Creation in the Old Testament* [129], 1–24.

254. Brandon, S. G. F., *Creation Legends of the Ancient Near East* (London: Hodder & Stoughton, 1963).

255. Buber, Martin, "Saga and History," in *The Writings of Martin Buber*, Will Herberg, ed. (New York: Meridian Books, 1956), 149–56. A valuable aid to understanding the character of biblical narratives.

256. Gunkel, Hermann, "The Influence of Babylonian Mythology Upon the Biblical Creation Story," in *Creation in the Old Testament* [129], 25–52. Excerpted from his seminal work, *Schöpfung und Chaos in Urzeit und Endzeit* (1895).

257. Gunkel, Hermann, *The Legends of Genesis: The Biblical Saga and History* (New York: Schocken, 1964). This little book, which carries a preface by W. F. Albright, is a reprint of the introduction to Gunkel's monumental commentary on Genesis, dating to the year 1901, which pro-

vided the foundation for modern form-critical studies. See also the translation of his work, *The Folktale in the Old Testament*, Historic Texts & Interpreters 4 (Decatur, GA: Almond Press, forthcoming).

258. Heidel, Alexander, *The Babylonian Genesis*, 2nd ed. (Chicago: University of Chicago Press, 1951; Phoenix Books, 1963). Also *The Gilgamesh Epic and Old Testament Parallels* (Chicago: University of Chicago Press, 1946; Phoenix Books, 1963).

259. Hooke, S. H., *Middle Eastern Mythology* (Baltimore: Penguin Books, 1963).

260. Lord, Albert, *The Singer of Tales* (Cambridge, Mass.: Harvard University Press, 1964; Atheneum, 1973). A treatment of the transmission of Homeric poetry which may throw light on the history of Israelite storytelling.

261. Otzen, Benedikt, et al., *Myths in the Old Testament* trans. by Frederick Cryer (London: SCM Press, 1980). This book, which is impressively introduced by a word from the Harvard Professor Thorkild Jacobsen, carries on the important Scandinavian contribution to biblical studies. See above, Nos. 72–74.

262. Rogerson, J. W., *Myth in Old Testament Interpretation*, BZAW 134 (Berlin and New York: W. de Gruyter, 1974).

On mythology, see also Nos. 120–127.

On the Israelite Epic Tradition

See above all the essays by Gerhard von Rad on the formation of the Israelite epic [166].

263. Clements, R. E., "Pentateuchal Problems" in *Tradition and Interpretation* [153], 66–124. A valuable discussion of trends in the understanding of the Torah.

264. Clines, David J. A., *The Theme of the Pentateuch*, Supplement to *Journal for the Study of the Old Testament* 10 (Sheffield, England: JSOT Press, 1978). A study of the overall thematic unity of the Pentateuch in its final form, which does not ignore the history of traditions.

265. Ellis, Peter, *The Yahwist: The Bible's First Theologian* (Notre Dame, Indiana: Fides Publishers, 1968).

See also works by J. A. Sanders, especially *Torah and Canon* [85], which stress the dynamic character of the "Torah Story."

On the Book of Genesis

266. Brueggemann, Walter, *Genesis*, in the Interpretation series (Atlanta: John Knox Press, 1982). A fresh and illuminating commentary.

267. Cassuto, U., *A Commentary on the Book of Genesis*, 2 vols., trans. by Israel Abrahams (Jerusalem: Magnes, 1961, 1964). A valuable commentary by a conservative Jewish scholar. It extends only to Gen. 13:5, for it was cut short by the author's death.

268. Coats, George W., *Genesis*, with an Introduction to Narrative Literature, Vol. I, The Forms of the Old Testament Literature (Grand Rapids, Mich.: Eerdmans, 1983). The first in a form-critical series designed to cover the whole Old Testament.

269. Davidson, Robert, *Genesis*, 2 vols., Cambridge Bible Commentary [13], 1973, 1979.

270. Jacob, B., *The First Book of the Bible: Genesis*, trans. and ed. by Ernest I. Jacob and Walter Jacob (New York: KTAV, 1974). A condensation of a major work in German.

271. Rad, Gerhard von, *Genesis*, trans. by John Marks, rev. ed., Old Testament Library [18], 1972. A masterful, perceptive interpretation in the light of form-critical studies.

272. Sarna, Nahum M., *Understanding Genesis*; The Heritage of Biblical Israel (New York: McGraw Hill, 1966; Schocken, 1970). An excellent study by a Jewish scholar.

273. Speiser, E. A., *Genesis*, Anchor Bible (New York: Doubleday, 1964). A fresh translation with helpful notes, many of which deal with alleged Near Eastern parallels.

274. Vawter, Bruce, *On Genesis: A New Reading* (Garden City, N.Y.: Doubleday, 1977). A valuable work by a leading Roman Catholic scholar.

275. Westermann, Claus, *Genesis*, 3 vols., Biblischer Kommentar (Neukirchener Verlag, 1970–1982). Genesis 1–11, trans. by John J. Scullion (Minneapolis, MN: Augsburg Publishing House, 1984). A monumental work based on a form-critical approach.

See also the study of the legends of Genesis by Gunkel [257] and some of the studies listed under "Methods of Biblical Criticism" [58–84].

CHAPTER 6: THE STRUGGLE BETWEEN FAITH AND CULTURE

276. Albright, W. F., *Yahweh and the Gods of Canaan* (Garden City, N.Y.: Doubleday Anchor Books, 1969). Israel's faith is compared and contrasted with surrounding Canaanite culture. See also his *Archaeology and the Religion of Israel* [111], chap. 4.

277. Anderson, G. W., "Israel: Amphictyony: '*Am; Kāhāl; 'Edah*," in *Translating and Understanding the Old Testament* [159], 135–151.

278. Boling, Robert G., *Judges*, Anchor Bible [12], 1975.

279. Buber, Martin, *The Prophetic Faith* [311], especially the discussion of the Song of Deborah and the clash between Israel's faith and Canaanite religion, pp. 8–12 and 70–80.

280. Cross, Frank M., "The Cultus of the Israelite League," in *Canaanite Myth and Hebrew Epic* [112], chaps. 4, 5, 6.

281. Dothan, Trude, *The Philistines and Their Material Culture* (New Haven: Yale University Press, 1982).

282. Driver, G. R., *Canaanite Myths and Legends* (Edinburgh: T. & T. Clark, 1956).

283. Gray, John, *The Legacy of Canaan*, 2nd ed. (Leiden: Brill, 1965). A study of the Ras Shamra texts and their bearing on the Old Testament. A popular study by the same author as *The Canaanites* (London: Thames Hudson, 1964).

284. Gray, John, *Judges*, New Century Bible [17], 1967.

285. Martin, J. D., *The Book of Judges*, Cambridge Bible Commentary [13], 1975.

286. Morton, James D., *Judges*, Cambridge Bible Commentary [13], 1975.

287. Noth, Martin, *Das System der Zwölf Stämme Israels* (1930; reprinted, Darmstadt: Wissenschaftliche Buchgeschellschaft, 1966). A seminal essay arguing that Israel was constituted as a twelve-tribe amphictyony. For one critical response, see the essay by G. W. Anderson listed above [277].

288. Smend, R., *Yahweh, War and Tribal Confederation*, trans. by Max G. Rogers (Nashville: Abingdon, 1970).

289. Wright, G. Ernest, *The Old Testament Against Its Environment*, Studies in Biblical Theology, No. 2 (Naperville, Ill.: Alec R. Allenson, 1950).

See also works on the Religion of Israel, Nos. 111–119; and works dealing with the History of Israel, 89–100.

CHAPTER 7: THE THRONE OF DAVID

290. Ackroyd, P. R., *The First Book of Samuel* (1971), *The Second Book of Samuel* (1977), Cambridge Bible Commentary [13].

291. Alt, Albrecht, "The Formation of the Israelite State in Palestine," in *Essays* [151], 223–309.

292. Birch, Bruce C., *The Rise of the Israelite Monarchy: The Growth and Development of I Samuel 7–15* (Missoula: Scholars Press, 1976). See also his essay on "The Development of the Tradition on the Anointing of Saul in I Sam 9:1–10:16," *Journal of Biblical Literature* 90 (1971), 55–68.

293. Clements, R. E., *Abraham and David*, Studies in Biblical Theology, 2nd series, No. 5 (Naperville, Ill.: Alec R. Allenson, 1967).

294. Cross, Frank M., "The Ideologies of Kingship in the Era of the Empire: Conditional Covenant and Eternal Decree," in *Canaanite Myth and Hebrew Epic* [112], chap. 9.

295. Gray, John, *I and II Kings*, 2nd ed., Old Testament Library [18], 1970.

296. Hertzberg, H. W., *The Books of Samuel*, trans. by J. S. Bowden, Old Testament Library [18], 1964.

297. Long, Burke, *I Kings*, with an Introduction to Historical Literature. The Forms of the Old Testament Literature, IX (Grand Rapids, Mich.: Eerdmans, 1984). Another work in the form-critical series.

298. McCarter, P. K., *I–II Samuel*, Anchor Bible [12], 1980.

299. Mendenhall, G. E., "The Monarchy," *Interpretation*, 29 (1975), 155–170. Suggests that Israelite society was corrupted by alien political and social models.

300. Mettinger, Tryggve N. D., *King and Messiah: The Civil and Sacral Legitimation of the Israelite Kings* (Lund, Sweden: Gleerup, 1976). A study that brings one to the frontier of research in this area.

301. Porter, J. R., "Old Testament Historiography," in *Tradition and Interpretation* [153], 125–162. Discussion of recent research on the Deuteronomistic History (as well as the Chronicler's Work).

302. Roberts, J. J. M., "The Davidic Origins of the Zion Tradition," *Journal of Biblical Literature* 92 (1973), 329–344.

303. Robinson, J., *I Kings* (1972), *II Kings* (1976), Cambridge Bible Commentary [13].

304. Rylaarsdam, J. C., "Jewish-Christian Relationship: The Two Covenants and the Dilemmas of Christology," *Journal of Ecumenical Studies* 9 (1972), 249–270. Reprinted in *Grace Upon Grace,* *Essays in Honor of L. J. Kuyper* (Grand Rapids, Mich.: Eerdmans, 1975), 70–84. This essay contains a clear and illuminating comparison of the Mosaic and Davidic covenant traditions. See also the work by Jon D. Levenson [140].

Literature of the Period

305. Campbell, E. C., *Ruth*, Anchor Bible [12], 1975. Persuasively places this short story in the context of the literature of the early monarchy.

306. Gunn, David, *The Story of David, Genre and Interpretation*, Supplement to *Journal for the Study of the Old Testament*, 6 (Sheffield, England: JSOT Press, 1978).

307. Miller, P. D. and J. J. M. Roberts, *The Hand of the Lord* (Baltimore: Johns Hopkins Press, 1977). A study of the ark narratives in I Sam.

308. Rost, Leonard, *The Succession to the Throne of David*, trans. by M. D. Ritter and D. M. Gunn. Supplement to *Journal for the Study of the Old Testament* (Sheffield: Almond Press, 1982). A basic study of the Court History.

309. Whybray, R. N., *The Succession Narrative: A Study of II Samuel 9–20; I Kings 1 and 2*, Studies in Biblical Theology, 2nd series, No. 9 (Naperville, Ill.: Alec R. Allenson, 1968). Contrary to Rost [308], he questions the historical reliability of this narrative.

On the Yahwist, see Peter Ellis [265], Wolff and Brueggemann [63].

CHAPTER 8: PROPHETIC TROUBLERS OF ISRAEL

General Works on Prophecy in Israel

310. Blenkinsopp, Joseph, *A History of Prophecy in Israel* (Philadelphia: Westminster, 1983).

311. Buber, Martin, *The Prophetic Faith*, trans. by C. Witton-Davies (New York: Macmillan, 1949; Harper Torchbook, 1960). A subtle, sensitive interpretation of the prophetic tradition.

312. Clements, R. E., *Prophecy and Covenant*, Studies in Biblical Theology, No. 43 (Naperville, Ill.: Alec R. Allenson, 1965).

313. Crenshaw, James, *Prophetic Conflict: Its Effect upon Israelite Religion*, Beiheft zur Zeitschrift für die alttestamentliche Wissenschaft, 124 (Berlin: Walter de Gruyter, 1971).

314. DeVries, Simon, *Prophet Against Prophet* (Grand Rapids, Mich.: Eerdmans, 1978). A discussion of the role of the Micaiah Narrative (I Kings 22) in early prophetic tradition.

315. Heschel, Abraham J., *The Prophets* (New York: Harper & Row, Pub., 1963). A discerning work by a Jewish philosopher; one of the best books on prophecy.

316. Johnson, Aubrey R., *The Cultic Prophet in Ancient Israel*, 2nd ed. (Cardiff: University of Wales Press, 1962). This valuable study traces the connection of many early prophets with the cult.

317. Lindblom, Johannes, *Prophecy in Ancient Israel* (Philadelphia: Muhlenberg, 1963). A fundamental work by a Swedish scholar.

318. McKane, William, *Prophets and Wise Men*, Studies in Biblical Theology, No. 44 (Naperville, Ill.: Alec R. Allenson, 1965).

319. Mowinckel, Sigmund, *Prophecy and Tradition*, Avhandlinger utgitt av Det Norske Videnskaps-Akademi (Oslo, Norway: Jacob Dybwad, 1946). A traditio-historical approach to the study of Israelite prophecy.

320. Newsome, James D., Jr., *The Hebrew Prophets* (Atlanta: John Knox Press, 1984).

321. Noth, Martin, "History and Word of God in the Old Testament," in his *Essays* [165], 179–93. Prophecy at Mari compared with Israelite prophecy.

322. Parker, S. B., "Jezebel's Reception of Jehu," *Maarav I* (1978–79), 67–78. A reconsideration of Jezebel's motives in the story found in II Kings 9:30–37.

323. Rad, Gerhard von, *The Prophetic Message*, trans. by D. M. G. Stalker (London: SCM, 1968). Based on his *Old Testament Theology*, II [142].

324. Ross, James, "Prophecy in Hamath, Israel, and Mari," *Harvard Theological Review*, LXIII (1970), 1–28. See also his essay, "The Prophet as Yahweh's Messenger," in *Israel's Prophetic Heritage* [152], 98–107.

325. Rowley, H. H., "Elijah on Mount Carmel," in *Bulletin of the John Rylands Library*, XLIII (1960–61), 190–210.

326. Scott, R. B. Y., *The Relevance of the Prophets*, rev. ed. (New York: Macmillan, 1968). This book continues to have great value.

327. Westermann, Claus, *Basic Forms of Prophetic Speech*, trans. by Hugh K. White (Philadelphia: Westminster, 1967). A form-critical study of the genres used in prophetic speech.

328. Wilson, Robert R., *Prophecy and Society in Ancient Israel* (Philadelphia: Fortress, 1980). An important sociological approach to the types of prophecy in ancient Israel.

See also the essays on Israelite prophecy in the issue of *Interpretation* 32, 1 (1978).

CHAPTER 9: FALLEN IS THE VIRGIN ISRAEL

See the general books listed in the preceding chapter. For an introduction to eighth century prophecy, see the following:

329. Anderson, Bernhard W., *The Eighth Century Prophets* (Philadelphia: Fortress, 1978).

330. Koch, Klaus, *The Prophets*, Vol. I: The Assyrian Period, trans. by Margaret Kohl (Philadelphia: Fortress, 1983).

On Amos

331. Barton, J., *Amos' Oracles Against the Nations* (London and New York: Cambridge University Press, 1980).

332. Coote, R. B., *Amos Among the Prophets: Composition and Theology* (Philadelphia: Fortress, 1981).

333. Kapelrud, Arvid S., *Central Ideas in Amos* (Oslo, Norway: Oslo University Press, 1961; first printed 1956). See also "New Ideas in Amos," Supplements to *Vetus Testamentum*, XV (1965), 193–206.

334. Mays, James L., *Amos*, The Old Testament Library [18], 1969. Highly recommended.

335. Smith, George Adam, *The Book of the Twelve Prophets*, I, rev. ed. (New York: Harper & Row, Pub., 1940). This is a great classic. Smith's treatments of Amos and Hosea deserve special attention.

336. Ward, James M., *Amos and Isaiah: Prophets of the Word of God* (New York: Abingdon, 1969).

337. Wolff, H. W., *Amos, the Prophet: The Man and His Background*, trans by Foster R. McCurley, ed. by John Reumann (Philadelphia: Fortress, 1973). Argues that Amos' native environment was that of clan wisdom.

338. Wolff, H. W., *Joel and Amos*, Hermeneia Series, trans. by W. Janzen et al. [14], 1977.

On Hosea

339. Anderson, F. I. and D. N. Freedman, *Hosea*, Anchor Bible (Garden City, N.Y.: Doubleday, 1980).

340. Brueggemann, Walter, *Tradition for Crisis: A Study in Hosea* (Richmond: John Knox, 1968).

341. Mays, James L., Hosea, Old Testament Library [18]. Highly recommended.

342. Robinson, H. Wheeler, The *Cross of Hosea* (Philadelphia: Westminster, 1949). Still valuable.

343. Rowley, H. H., ''The Marriage of Hosea,'' in *Bulletin of the John Rylands Library, XXXIX (1956)*, 203-233. A good survey of a major problem in the book of Hosea.

344. Snaith, Norman H., *Mercy and Sacrifice: A Study of the Book of Hosea* (London: SCM Press, 1953).

345. Ward, James M., *Hosea: A Theological Commentary* (New York: Harper & Row, Pub., 1966).

346. Wolff, H. W., *Hosea*, Hermeneia Series (Philadelphia: Westminster, 1977). One of the best commentaries.

CHAPTER 10: JUDAH'S COVENANT WITH DEATH

On Isaiah of Jerusalem

347. Childs, Brevard, *Isaiah and the Assyrian Crisis*, Studies in Biblical Theology, 2nd series, No. 3 (Naperville, Ill.: Alec R. Allenson, 1967).

348. Clements, R. E., *Isaiah 1-39*, New Century Bible [17], 1981. See also *Isaiah and the Deliverance of Jerusalem: A Study of the Interpretation of Prophecy in the Old Testament* (Sheffield, England: JSOT Press, 1980).

349. Jensen, Joseph, *Isaiah 1-39*, Old Testament Message 8 (Wilmington, Del.: Michael Glazier, 1984). A compact, illuminating commentary by a leading Roman Catholic scholar.

350. Kaiser, Otto, *Isaiah 1-12*, Old Testament Library; also 13-39, Old Testament Library, trans. by R. A. Wilson [18], 1972, 1974.

351. Kissane, Edward J., *The Book of Isaish*, 2nd ed., 2 vols. (Dublin: Browne & Nolan, 1960).

352. Ollenburger, Bennie C., *Zion, The City of the Great King: A Theological Investigation of Zion Symbolism in the Tradition of the Jerusalem Cult.*

Diss., Princeton Theological Seminary (Ann Arbor: University Microfilms International, 1983). Excellent introduction to Zion theology.

353. Roberts, J. J. M., *Isaish 1-39*, Interpretation Series (Atlanta: John Knox Press, forthcoming).

354. Scott, R. B. Y., ''Introduction and Exegesis to Isaiah 1-39,'' in *Interpreter's Bible*, V [16], 1956.

355. Smith, George Adam, *The Book of Isaiah*, rev. ed. (London: Hodder & Stoughton, 1927). Old, but still worth reading.

356. Vriezen, Th. C., ''Essentials of the Theology of Isaiah,'' in *Israel's Prophetic Heritage* [152], 128-46.

See also J. M. Ward [336].

On Micah

357. Hillers, Delbert, *Micah*, Hermeneia Series [14], 11.

358. Mays, James L., *Micah*, Old Testament Library [18], 1976. An important commentary, concerned with redaction criticism.

359. Wolff, H. W., *Micah the Prophet*, trans. R. D. Gehrke (Philadelphia: Fortress, 1981).

CHAPTER 11: THE REDISCOVERY OF MOSAIC TORAH

360. Bright, John, ''The Date of the Prose Sermons of Jeremiah,'' in *Journal of Biblical Literature*, LXX (1951), 15-35. Opposes the view, maintained, for instance, by Hyatt [379], that the book of Jeremiah has been radically reworked by Deuteronomistic editors. Reprinted in *Prophet to the Nations* [382], 193-212.

361. Clements, R. E., *God's Chosen People: A Theological Interpretation of the Book of Deuteronomy* (London: SCM, 1968).

362. Craige, P. C., *The Book of Deuteronomy*, New International Commentary on the Old Testament (Grand Rapids: Eerdmans, 1976). Represents a conservative position on date and unity.

363. Cross, Frank M., ''The Themes of the Book of Kings and the Structure of the Deuteronomistic History,'' in *Canaanite Myth and Hebrew Epic* [112], chap. 10.

364. Nicholson, E. W., *Deuteronomy and Tradition* (Philadelphia: Fortress, 1967).

365. Nicholson, E. W., *Preaching to the Exiles: A Study of the Prose Tradition in the Book of Jeremiah* (Oxford: Blackwell, 1970). Holds that the "Deuteronomic" prose sermons of the book of Jeremiah were addressed to the situation of the Exile.

366. Philips, Anthony, *Deuteronomy*, Cambridge Bible Commentary [13], 1973.

367. Rad, Gerhard von, *Deuteronomy*, trans. by Dorothea Barton, Old Testament Library [18], 1966. See also his *Studies in Deuteronomy*, Studies in Biblical Theology, No. 9 (London: SCM Press, 1953).

368. Rowley, H. H., "The Prophet Jeremiah and the Book of Deuteronomy," in the book edited by the same author, *Studies in Old Testament Prophecy* (Edinburgh: T. & T. Clark, 1950), 157–74. Also in Rowley's *From Moses to Qumran* (London: Lutterworth, 1963), 187–208.

369. Weinfeld, M., *Deuteronomy and the Deuteronomic School* (Oxford: Clarendon, 1972). Shows the affinity of Deuteronomic theology to Wisdom.

370. Welch, A. C., *The Code of Deuteronomy* (London: J. Clarke & Co., 1924) and *Deuteronomy: The Framework to the Code* (London: Oxford University Press, 1932). Old works that are still important.

371. Wright, G. Ernest, "Introduction and Exegesis to Deuteronomy," in *Interpreter's Bible*, II [16], 1953. An excellent treatment.

See also essays on Jeremiah's call, his relation to the Deuteronomic Reform, and the Foe from the North in Perdue and Kovacs, eds., *A Prophet to the Nations* [382]. Works on the Deuteronomistic History are listed above under Chapter 4.

CHAPTER 12: THE DOOM OF THE NATION

372. Anderson, Bernhard W., "The New Covenant and the Old," in *The Old Testament and Christian Faith* (New York: Herder and Herder, 1969), 225–242. A discussion of a crucial passage in Jer. 31:31–34.

373. Berridge, John M., *Prophet, People, and the Word of Yahweh: An Examination of Form and Content in the Proclamation of the Prophet Jeremiah* (Zurich: EVZ Verlag, 1970).

374. Blank, Sheldon, *Jeremiah: Man and Prophet* (Cincinatti: Hebrew Union College Press, 1961).

375. Bright, John, *Jeremiah*, Anchor Bible 9 [12], 1965.

A fresh translation with helpful interpretation. See also his essay listed above [360].

376. Carroll, R. P., *From Chaos to Covenant: Prophecy in the Book of Jeremiah* (New York: Crossroad, 1981). A revolutionary work which maintains that Jeremiah is known only through the community that produced the book of Jeremiah. See also his essay, "Prophecy, Dissonance, and Jer. 26," in Perdue and Kovacs, eds., *A Prophet to the Nations* [382], 381–391.

377. Habel, Norman, *Jeremiah, Lamentations*, Concordia Commentary (St. Louis: Concordia Publishing House, 1968).

378. Holladay, William A., *The Architecture of Jeremiah 1–20* (Lewisburg, PA: Bucknell University Press, 1975). See also his brief introduction, *Jeremiah, Spokesman Out of Time* (Philadelphia: Fortress, 1974).

379. Hyatt, J. P., *Jeremiah, Prophet of Courage and Hope* (New York: Abingdon, 1958). See also his "Introduction and Exegesis to Jeremiah" in *Interpreter's Bible*, VI [16], 1956.

380. Lundbom, Jack R., *Jeremiah: A Study in Ancient Hebrew Rhetoric*, SBL Dissertation Series 18 (Missoula, Montana: Scholars Press, 1975).

381. O'Connor, Kathleen, *The Confessions of Jeremiah*, SBL Dissertation Series (Chico, CA: Scholars Press, 1985).

382. Perdue, Leo G. and Brian Kovacs, eds., *A Prophet to the Nations: Essays in Jeremiah Studies* (Winona Lake, IN: Eisenbrauns, 1984). Notice Perdue's introductory essay, "Jeremiah in Modern Research: Approaches and Issues."

383. Rowley, H. H., "The Early Prophecies of Jeremiah in their Setting," in *Bulletin of the John Rylands Library*, XLV (1962), 198–234. Reprinted in Perdue and Kovacs, eds., *A Prophet to the Nations* [382], 33–61.

384. Skinner, John, *Prophecy and Religion* (New York: Cambridge, 1922). This has long been a standard book on Jeremiah.

On Zephaniah

385. Kapelrud, A. S., *The Message of the Prophet Zephaniah* (Oslo, Norway: Universitetsforlaget, 1975).

On Habakkuk

386. Albright, W. F., "The Psalm of Habakkuk," in *Studies in Old Testament Prophecy: Essays in Honor of T. H. Robinson*, ed. by H. H. Rowley (New York: Scribners, 1950), pp. 1–18.

387. Gowan, D. E., *The Triumph of Faith in Habakkuk* (Atlanta: John Knox Press, 1976).

On Lamentations

388. Albrektson, Bertil, *Studies in the Text and Theology of the Book of Lamentations* (Lund, Sweden: Gleerup, 1963).

389. Gottwald, Norman K., *Studies in the Book of Lamentations*, Studies in Biblical Theology, No. 14 (Naperville, Ill.: Alec R. Allenson, 1954).

390. Hillers, Delbert R., *Lamentations*, Anchor Bible [12], 1972.

CHAPTER 13: BY THE WATERS OF BABYLON

391. Anderson, Bernhard W., "A Stylistic Study of the Priestly Creation Story," in Coats and Long, eds., *Canon and Authority* [156], 148–162. Another study relevant to the Priestly Work is "Creation and the Noachic Covenant," in *Cry of the Environment: Rebuilding the Christian Creation Tradition*, ed. by P. N. Joranson and Ken Butigan (Santa Fe, N.M.: Bear Press, 1984), 45–61.

392. Brueggemann, Walter, "The Kerygma of the Priestly Writers," in *The Vitality of Israel's Traditions* [63], chap. 6.

393. Carley, Keith, *Ezekiel Among the Prophets*, Studies in Biblical Theology, 2nd series (London: SCM Press, 1971).

394. Cross, Frank M., "The Priestly Work," in *Canaanite Myth and Hebrew Epic* [112], 293–325. Fundamental for understanding the Priestly edition of the Pentateuch (or Tetrateuch).

395. Eichrodt, Walther, *Ezekiel*, trans. by Cosslett Quin, Old Testament Library [18], 1970.

396. Greenberg, Moshe, *Ezekiel 1–20*, Anchor Bible [12], 1983. A creative work that moves in a new direction.

397. Haran, M., *Temples and Temple Service in Ancient Israel: An Inquiry into the Character of Cult Phenomena and the Historical Setting of the Priestly School* (London: Oxford University Press, 1978). A new slant on the Priestly tradition.

398. Klein, R. W., *Israel in Exile: A Theological Interpretation*, Overtures to Biblical Theology 6 (Philadelphia: Fortress, 1979).

399. McEvenue, Sean E., *The Narrative Style of the Priestly Writer*, Analecta Biblica 50 (Rome: Biblical Institute, 1971). Emphasizes the rhetorical and dramatic qualities of the Priestly Writing.

400. Mettinger, Tryggve N. D., *The Dethronement of Sabaoth: Studies in the Shem and Kabod Theologies* trans. by Frederick H. Cryer (Lund Sweden: CWK Gleerup, 1982). See especially chap. 3 on "Kabod Theology."

401. Noth, Martin, *Leviticus*, trans. by J. E. Anderson, Old Testament Library [18], 1965.

402. Raitt, Thomas A., *A Theology of Exile* (Philadelphia: Fortress Press, 1977).

403. Wevers, J. W., *Ezekiel*, Cambridge Bible Commentary [13], 1982.

404. Zimmerli, Walther, *Ezekiel*, 2 vols., Hermeneia [14], 1979. A monumental work. See also his essay, "The Message of the Prophet Ezekiel," in *Interpretation* 23 (1969), 131–157.

CHAPTER 14: THE DAWN OF A NEW AGE

405. Anderson, Bernhard W., "Exodus Typology in Second Isaiah," in *Israel's Prophetic Heritage* [152], 177–195; also "Exodus and Covenant in Second Isaiah and Prophetic Tradition," in *Magnalia Dei* [157], 339–360.

406. Clines, David J. A., *I, He, We, and They: A Literary Approach to Isaiah 53*, Supplement to *Journal for the Study of the Old Testament*, 1 (Sheffield, England: JSOT Press, 1976).

407. Conrad, Edgar W., "Second Isaiah and the Priestly Oracle of Salvation," *Zeitschrift für die Alttestamentliche Wissenschaft* 93 (1981), 234–246; "The 'Fear Not' Oracles in Second Isaiah," *Vetus Testamentum* 34 (1984), 129–152. See his book, *Fear Not Warrior: A Study of 'al tira' Pericopes in the Hebrew Scriptures*, Brown Judaic Studies, 75 (Chico, CA: Scholars Press, 1985).

408. Knight, George A. F., *Deutero-Isaiah: A Theological Commentary on Isaiah 40–55* (New York: Abingdon, 1965).

409. McKenzie, John L., *Second Isaiah*, Anchor Bible [12], 1968.

410. Melugin, Roy F., *The Formation of Isaiah 40–55*, Beiheft zur Zeitschrift für die Alttestamentliche Wissenschaft 141 (Berlin: Walter de Gruyter, 1976). An illuminating literary study.

411. Mettinger, Tryggve N. D., *A Farewell to the Servant Songs: A Critical Examination of an Exegetical Axiom* (Lund, Sweden: Gleerup, 1983).

412. Muilenburg, James, "Introduction and Exegesis to Isaiah 40–66," in *Interpreter's Bible*, V [16], 1956. One of the best commentaries on

Second Isaiah, emphasizing rhetorical criticism.

413. North, Christopher R., *Isaiah 40–55* (New York: Macmillan, 1964). Also his book, *The Suffering Servant in Deutero-Isaiah*, 2nd ed. (New York: Oxford, 1956) gives a good discussion of the various interpretations of the Servant.

414. Rowley, H. H., *The Servant of the Lord and Other Essays on the Old Testament*, 2nd ed. (Oxford: Blackwell, 1965), 3–60. A good review of various interpretations.

415. Smart, James D., *History and Theology in Second Isaiah: A Commentary on Isaiah 35, 40–66* (Philadelphia: Westminster, 1965). Places Second Isaiah in Judah, not Babylonia.

416. Stuhlmueller, Carroll, *Creative Redemption in Deutero-Isaiah*, Analecta Biblica, No. 43 (Rome: Biblical Institute, 1970).

417. Waldow, H. E. von, "The Message of Deutero-Isaiah," *Interpretation* 21 (1968), 259–287.

418. Westermann, Claus, *Isaiah 40–60*, trans. by D. M. G. Stalker; Old Testament Library [18], 1969. A major work, using a form-critical approach.

419. Whybray, R. N., *Isaiah 40–66*, New Century Bible Commentary [17], 1975. The same author has produced a brief, valuable introduction: *The Second Isaiah*, Old Testament Guides (Sheffield, England: JSOT Press, 1983).

420. Zimmerli, Walther, and J. Jeremias, *The Servant of God*, Studies in Biblical Theology, No. 20 (Naperville, Ill.: Alec R. Allenson, 1957). Zimmerli's study on this subject now appears in Kittel's *Theological Dictionary of the New Testament*, V (Grand Rapids, Mich.: Eerdmans, 1968), 655–677.

On new attempts to understand the unity of the whole book of Isaiah, see Brevard Childs, *Introduction* [37], chap. 17. The whole issue of *Interpretation*, Vol. 36 (1982), is devoted to the book of Isaiah; see especially the article by R. E. Clements, pp. 117–129. See the illuminating essay by Walter Brueggemann, "Unity and Dynamic in the Isaiah Tradition," *Journal for the Study of the Old Testament* 29 (1984), 89–107; also in the same journal, issue 31, pp. 95–113, R. C. Clements, "Beyond Tradition-History: Deutero-Isaianic Development of First Isaiah's Themes."

CHAPTER 15: A KINGDOM OF PRIESTS

421. Ackroyd, Peter, *Exile and Restoration: A Study of Hebrew Thought of the Sixth Century B.C.* (Philadelphia: Westminster, 1968); also *Israel under Babylon and Persia* (London: Oxford, 1970). Important works by an authority in this field. See also his essays, "The Chronicler as Exegete," *Journal for the Study of the Old Testament* 2 (1977), 2–32, and "History and Theology in the Writings of the Chronicler," *Concordia Theological Monthly* 38 (1967), 501–515.

422. Clines, David J. A., *Ezra, Nehemiah, Esther*, New Century Bible Commentary [17], 1984.

423. Coggins, R. J., *First and Second Books of Chronicles*, Cambridge Bible Commentary [13], 1976.

424. Cross, Frank M., "A Reconstruction of the Judean Restoration," *Journal of Biblical Literature* 94 (1975), 4–18.

425. De Vaux, Roland, *Studies in Old Testament Sacrifice* (Cardiff: University of Wales Press, 1964). A perceptive discussion of how sacrificial worship was transformed in Israel's faith.

426. Freedman, D. N., "The Chronicler's Purpose," *Catholic Biblical Quarterly* XXIII (1961), 436–42. An illuminating essay.

427. Hanson, Paul, *The Dawn of Apocalyptic* (Philadelphia: Fortress Press, 1975). Discussion of the historical and sociological roots of apocalyptic, concentrating on so-called Third Isaiah and related literature.

428. Kidner, D., *Ezra and Nehemiah: An Introduction and Commentary*, Tyndale Old Testament Commentaries (London: Inter-Varsity Press, 1979). Conservative; sensitive to critical issues.

429. Myers, Jacob M., *I and II Chronicles*, 2 vols., Anchor Bible [12], 1965. See also his Anchor volume on Ezra-Nehemiah (1965).

430. Rowley, H. H., "Nehemiah's Mission and Its Background," in *Bulletin of the John Rylands Library*, XXXVII (1955), 528–61.

431. Rowley, H. H., *The Rediscovery of the Old Testament* (Philadelphia: Westminster, 1964). Chapter 7 gives an appreciative treatment of the ethos of Judaism.

On Haggai and Zechariah

432. Ackroyd, P. R., "The Book of Haggai and Zechariah 1–8," *Journal of Jewish Studies* 3 (1952), 151–56; and "Studies in the Book of Haggai," in the same journal, 163–176.

433. Peterson, David L., *Haggai and Zechariah 1–8*, Old Testament Library [18], 1984. An up-to-date and helpful study.

On Joel

434. Prinsloo, Willem S., *The Theology of the Book Joel*, Beiheft zur Zeitschrift für die Alttestamentliche Wissenschaft (1985).
435. Kapelrud, A. S., *Joel Studies* (Uppsala: Almquist & Wiksell, 1948).
436. Wolff, H. W., *Joel and Amos*, Hermeneia [14], 1977. An excellent work.

CHAPTER 16: THE PRAISES OF ISRAEL

See the Akkadian and Egyptian hymns and prayers, translated in J. B. Pritchard, ed., *Ancient Near Eastern Texts* [1], pp. 365–392. On worship in ancient Israel, see the following:

437. Clements, R. E., *God and Temple* (Philadelphia: Fortress, 1965). A study of the Jerusalem Temple as the center of Yahweh's presence in ancient Israel.
438. Cumming, Charles G., *The Assyrian and Hebrew Hymns of Praise* (New York: Columbia University Press, 1934). Treats formal parallels to Israel's hymnody.
439. De Vaux, Roland, *Ancient Israel* [113], especially Part IV which deals with Israel's sacral institutions.
440. Eaton, J. H., *Kingship and the Psalms*, Studies in Biblical Theology, 2nd series, 32 (London: SCM Press, 1976).
441. Harrelson, Walter, *From Fertility Cult to Worship* (Garden City, N.Y.: Doubleday, 1970).
442. Johnson, Aubrey R., *Sacral Kingship in Ancient Israel*, 2nd ed. (Cardiff: University of Wales Press, 1967).
443. Kraus, H. J., *Worship in Israel*, trans. by Geoffrey Buswell (Richmond: John Knox Press, 1965). Especially helpful for understanding the Zion cult.
444. Rowley, H. H., *Worship in Ancient Israel: Its Forms and Meaning* (Philadelphia: Fortress Press, 1967).

445. Widengren, George, *The Accadian and Hebrew Songs of Lamentation* (Uppsala: Almquist & Wiksell, 1936). Helpful for understanding the genre of the laments.

On the Book of Psalms

446. Anderson, Bernhard W., *Out of the Depths: The Psalms Speak for Us Today*, rev. ed. (Philadelphia: Westminster, 1983). An introduction that uses a form-critical approach.
447. Barth, Christoph, *Introduction to the Psalms*, trans. by R. A. Wilson (New York: Scribner's, 1966). An excellent introduction, especially illuminating on theological issues.
448. Eaton, J. H., *Psalms: Introduction and Commentary*, Torch Commentary Series [19], 1967.
449. Gerstenberger, E., "Psalms," in *Old Testament Form Criticism* [64], 179–224.
450. Gunkel, Hermann, *The Psalms: A Form-critical Introduction*, trans. by Thomas M. Horner, with an introduction by James Muilenburg (Philadelphia: Fortress, 1967). A basic introduction to the genres of the Psalter, by the great pioneer of form criticism and author (with Joachim Begrich) of *Einleitung in die Psalmen* (1933).
451. Guthrie, Harvey H., *Israel's Sacred Songs* (New York: Seabury, 1966).
452. Kraus, H. J., *Psalmen*, Biblischer Kommentar, 2nd ed. (Neukirchen: Neukirchener Verlag, 1961). A major work on the Psalms.
453. Mowinckel, Sigmund, *The Psalms in Israel's Worship*, I–II, trans. by D. R. Ap-Thomas (New York: Abingdon, 1962). See also his earlier *Psalmenstudien* I–VI (Amsterdam: Verlag P. Schnippers, 1921–1924). The works of Mowinckel and Gunkel are fundamental to all modern study of the Psalter.
454. Ringgren, Helmer, *The Faith of the Psalmists* (London: SCM Press, 1963).
455. Terrien, Samuel, *The Psalms and Their Meaning for Today* (Indianapolis: Bobbs-Merrill, 1952).
456. Weiser, Artur, *The Psalms*, Old Testament Library, trans. by Herbert Hartwell [18], 1962). An important work which, however, overstresses the place of many psalms in covenant-renewal festivals.
457. Westermann, Claus, *The Praise of God in the Psalms*, trans. by Keith R. Crim (Richmond: John Knox Press, 1965). An important form-critical study which suggests a new way of classifying the types of psalms. See also *Praise and Lament in The Psalms*, trans. by Keith R. Crim

and Richard N. Soulen (Atlanta: John Knox Press, 1981).

CHAPTER 17: THE BEGINNING OF WISDOM

458. Bryce, Glendon E., *A Legacy of Wisdom: The Egyptian Contribution to the Wisdom of Israel* (Lewisburg, Pa.: Bucknell University Press, 1979). By an Old Testament scholar who was also an Egyptologist.

459. Crenshaw, James L., *Old Testament Wisdom: An Introduction* (Atlanta: John Knox Press, 1981). A valuable introduction by one of the authorities in this field.

460. Emerton, J. A., "Wisdom," in *Tradition and Interpretation* [153], 214–237. A discriminating survey of discussions of the subject.

461. Gammie, J. G. et al., eds., *Israelite Wisdom, Theological and Literary Essays in Honor of Samuel Terrien* (Missoula, Montana: Scholars Press, 1978). Valuable contributions; the essay by Hans-Jürgen Hermisson on wisdom and creation theology is reproduced in *Creation in the Old Testament* [129], pp. 118–134.

462. McKane, William, *Prophets and Wise Men*, Studies in Biblical Theology, No. 44 (Naperville, Ill.: Alec R. Allenson, 1965).

463. Murphy, Roland, *Wisdom Literature*, Forms of Old Testament Literature 13 (Grand Rapids: Eerdmans, 1981). Another volume in the series on form criticism. See also his valuable brief introduction, *Wisdom Literature & Psalms*, Interpreting Biblical Texts (Nashville: Abingdon, 1983) and the literature cited there.

464. Noth, Martin, and D. Winton Thomas, eds., *Wisdom in Israel and in the Near East*, Supplement to *Vetus Testamentum*, III (Leiden: Brill, 1955).

465. Rad, Gerhard von, *Wisdom in Israel*, trans. by James D. Martin (New York: Abingdon, 1973). The best theological introduction to the subject.

466. Rankin, O. S., *Israel's Wisdom Literature* (Edinburgh: T. & T. Clark, 1936). Schocken Books, 1969. An older standard work.

467. Rylaarsdam, J. Coert, *Revelation in Jewish Wisdom Literature* (Chicago: University of Chicago Press, 1946). This valuable little book shows how Wisdom and Torah were eventually identified.

468. Scott, R. B. Y., *The Way of Wisdom in the Old Testament* (New York: Macmillan, 1971).

469. Whybray, R. N., *The Intellectual Tradition in the*

Old Testament, Beiheft zur Zeitschrift für die Alttestamentliche Wissenschaft (Berlin: Walter de Gruyter, 1974).

On Proverbs

470. McKane, William, *Proverbs: A New Approach*, Old Testament Library [18], 1970. One of the best commentaries available.

471. Scott, R. B. Y., *Proverbs and Ecclesiastes*, Anchor Bible [12].

472. Whybray, R. N., *The Book of Proverbs*, Cambridge Bible Commentary [13], 1972. See also his earlier book, *Wisdom in Proverbs: The Concept of Wisdom in Proverbs 1–9*, Studies in Biblical Theology, No. 45 (London: SCM, 1965).

On Ecclesiastes

473. Gordis, Robert, *Koheleth, The Man and His World* (New York: Jewish Theological Seminary of America Press, 1951). rev. ed., Schocken Books, 1967. A fresh translation with commentary.

474. Ogden, Graham S., "The 'Better'-Proverb (Tob-Spruch), Rhetorical Criticism, and Qoheleth," *Journal of Biblical Literature* 96 (1977), 489–505. See also his various essays on passages in Ecclesiastes, e.g. *Vetus Testamentum* 30 (1980), 27–37, 309–15.

475. Rankin, O. S., "Introduction and Exegesis to Ecclesiastes," in *Interpreter's Bible*, V [16].

On the Book of Job

476. Dhorme, Édouard Paul, *A Commentary on the Book of Job*, trans. by Harold Knight (London: Nelson, 1967). A classic commentary, first issued in 1926.

477. Gordis, Robert, *The Book of God and Man: A Study of Job* (Chicago: University of Chicago Press, 1965).

478. Habel, Norman C., *The Book of Job*, Old Testament Library [18]. An illuminating, up-to-date commentary.

479. Jantzen, J. Gerald, *Job*, Intepretation Series [15], 1985.

480. Pope, Marvin H., *Job*, Anchor Bible [12]. A fresh translation with notes.

481. Terrien, Samuel, "Introduction and Exegesis to Job," In *Interpreter's Bible*, III [16]. An excellent commentary, with respect to both literary analysis and theological interpretation. See also his

book, *Job: Poet of Existence* (Indianapolis: Bobbs-Merrill, 1958).

482. Westermann, Claus, *The Structure of the Book of Job: A Form-Critical Analysis* (Philadelphia: Fortress Press, 1981).

For a structuralist analysis of the book of Job, see the study by Robert Polzin [84].

On the Song of Songs

483. Gordis, Robert, *The Song of Songs and Lamentations*, revised and augmented (New York: KTAV, 1974).

484. Murphy, Roland E., "Form-Critical Studies in the Song of Songs," *Interpretation*, 27 (1973), 413–22. See also his forthcoming commentary in the Hermeneia series.

485. Pope, Marvin, *The Song of Songs*, Anchor Bible [12], 1977.

486. Rowley, H. H., "The Interpretation of the Song of Songs," in his collected essays, *The Servant* [414], 195–245.

487. Sasson, Jack, "Unlocking the Poetry of Love in the Song of Songs," *Bible Review*, Vol. I (1985), 11–19. An illuminating essay, which provides an excellent brief introduction.

CHAPTER 18:
THE UNFULFILLED DRAMA

See editions of the Apocrypha and Pseudepigrapha listed above [6–7], especially the work edited by James Charlesworth. For a selection of literature bearing on early Judaism, see the following:

488. Nickelsburg, George W. E., and Michael E. Stone, *Faith and Piety in Early Judaism: Texts and Documents* (Philadelphia: Fortress, 1983).

History and Literature of the Period

489. Metzger, Bruce, *An Introduction to the Apocrypha* (New York: Oxford, 1957).

490. Neusner, Jacob, *Invitation to the Talmud*, rev. ed. (San Francisco: Harper & Row, Pub.; 1984); also *Midrash in Context* (Philadelphia: Fortress Press, 1983).

491. Nickelsburg, George W. E., *Jewish Literature Be-tween the Bible and the Mishnah: A Historical and Literary Introduction* (Philadelphia: Fortress, 1981). An indispensable work, by a leading scholar in the field.

492. Pfeiffer, R. H., *History of New Testament Times with an Introduction to the Apocrypha* (New York: Harper & Row, Pub., 1949).

493. Russell, D. S., *The Method and Message of Jewish Apocalyptic*, Old Testament Library [18], 1964. A comprehensive study of apocalyptic from 200 B.C.E. to 100 C.E. See also his paperback, *Apocalyptic: Ancient and Modern* (Philadelphia: Fortress, 1978).

494. Schürer, Emil, *The History of the Jewish People in the Age of Jesus Christ*, vol. 1, rev. ed. by G. Vermes and F. Millar (Edinburgh: T. & T. Clark, 1973).

495. Tcherikover, Victor, *Hellenistic Civilization and the Jews*, trans. by S. Appelbaum (Philadelphia: Jewish Publication Society of America, 1959; New York: Atheneum, 1970).

On Eschatology and Apocalyptic

496. Brown, Raymond E., *The Semitic Background of the Term 'Mystery' in the New Testament*, Facet Books (Philadelphia: Fortress, 1968). Illuminates the motif of "secret" in prophecy and apocalyptic.

497. Frost, S. B., *Old Testament Apocalyptic* (London: Epworth, 1952). See also "Apocalyptic and History" in *The Bible in Modern Scholarship* [161], 98–113.

498. Funk, Robert W., "Apocalypticism," the subject of the *Journal for Theology and the Church*, No. 6 (New York: Herder and Herder, 1969). An important discussion by outstanding scholars.

499. Hanson, Paul, "Jewish Apocalyptic against its Near Eastern Environment," *Revue Biblique* 78 (1971); also "Old Testament Apocalyptic Reexamined," *Interpretation* 25 (1971), 454–79. *Visionaries and Their Apocalypses*, Issues in Religion and Theology No. 2 (Philadelphia: Fortress, 1983) is a collection of important essays edited by him.

See especially *The Dawn of Apocalyptic* cited above [427].

500. Koch, Klaus, *The Rediscovery of Apocalyptic*, trans. by Margaret Kohl (Naperville, Ill.: Alec R. Allenson, 1970).

501. Mowinckel, Sigmund, *He That Cometh*, trans. by G. W. Anderson (New York: Abingdon,

1956). One of the most important works on Israelite eschatology.

502. Nicholson, E. W., "Apocalyptic," in *Tradition and Interpretation* [153], 189–213. A perceptive survey of recent scholarly discussions.

503. Schmithals, Walter, *The Apocalyptic Movement: Introduction and Interpretation,* trans. by John E. Steely (Nashville: Abingdon, 1975).

See also Gerhard von Rad's discussion of apocalyptic in his *Theology*, Vol. II [142]. He maintains that apocalyptic belongs primarily in the circle of wisdom, rather than of prophecy.

On the Book of Daniel

504. Collins, John J., *Daniel*, with an Introduction to Apocalyptic Literature (Grand Rapids, Mich.: Eerdmans, 1985). A book in the form-critical series which discusses genre and structure of the book of Daniel.

505. Hartman, L. F. and A. A. Di Lella, *The Book of Daniel*, Anchor Bible [12], 1978.

506. Lacocque, Andre, *The Book of Daniel*, trans. by David Pellauer (Atlanta: John Knox Press, 1979).

507. Porteous, Norman W., *Daniel*, Old Testament Library [18], 1965.

508. Towner, W. Sibley, *Daniel*, Interpretation Series [15], 1984.

On the Book of Esther

509. Anderson, Bernhard W., "Introduction and Exegesis to the Book of Esther," *Interpreter's Bible*, vol. III [16].

510. Berg, Sandra, *The Book of Esther: Motifs, Themes and Structure*. SBL Dissertation Series, 44 (Missoula: Scholars Press, 1979).

511. Clines, David J. A., *Ezra, Nehemiah, Esther*, New Century Bible Commentary [17], 1984.

512. Clines, David J. A., *The Esther Scroll: The Story of the Story* (Sheffield, England: JSOT Press, 1984). Considers both the final form and the history of redaction.

On the Dead Sea Scrolls

Of the voluminous literature that has appeared, only a few books can be mentioned.

513. Cross, Frank M., *The Ancient Library of Qumran and Modern Biblical Studies* (Garden City, N.Y.: Doubleday, 1961). A comprehensive, perceptive treatment of the scrolls and their significance. See also "The Early History of the Apocalyptic Community at Qumran," in *Canaanite Myth and Hebrew Epic* [112], chap. 12.

514. Driver, G. R., *The Judean Scrolls: The Problem and a Solution*, rev. ed. (New York: Schocken Books, 1965). Discusses the significance of the scrolls for Old Testament study.

515. Dupont-Sommer, A., *The Essene Writings from Qumran*, trans. by G. Vermès (New York: Meridian, 1961). Introduction to and translation of Qumran literature.

516. Gaster, T. H., *The Dead Sea Scriptures*, rev. ed. (Garden City, N.Y.: Doubleday, 1964). Introduction, translation, and notes.

517. Ringgren, Helmer, *The Faith of Qumran*, trans. by Emilie T. Sander (Philadelphia: Fortress, 1961).

518. Vermès, Géza, *The Dead Sea Scrolls in English* (Baltimore: Penguin Books, 1962). Translation and illuminating introduction.

On the Canon

Especially the works of Brevard Childs [37] and James A. Sanders [85, 86] have called for a reconsideration of the canon.

519. Blenkinsopp, Joseph, *Prophecy and Canon: A Contribution to the Study of Jewish Origins* (Notre Dame, Ind.: University of Notre Dame Press, 1977).

520. Neusner, Jacob, *From Politics to Piety: The Emergence of Pharisaic Judaism* (Englewood Cliffs, N.J.: Prentice-Hall, 1973).

521. Sanders, James A., *Canon and Community* [86]. An indispensable treatment of this subject.

522. Sundberg, Albert C., *The Old Testament of the Early Church*, Harvard Theological Studies, XX (Cambridge, Mass.: Harvard University Press, 1964). A seminal reconsideration of the problem of canon.

523. Weingren, J., *From Bible to Mishnah: The Continuity of Tradition* (Manchester, England: Manchester University Press, 1976).

524. Wright, G. Ernest, "The Canon as Theological Problem," in *The Old Testament and Theology* [149], chap. 7.

See also James Barr, *Holy Scripture* [cited under 130].

Index

SUBJECT INDEX